NEWCOMER'S
HANDBOOK®

FOR MOVING TO AND LIVING IN

BOSTON

Including Cambridge,
Brookline, and Somerville

4th Edition

FIRST BOOKS

503-968-6777
www.firstbooks.com

Authors: Jon Gorey and Gina Favata, 4th edition; Heather Gordon, 3rd edition
Editors: Emily Horowitz, Linda Weinerman
Series Editor: Linda Weinerman
Cover design: Annelise Ouimet
Interior design: Erin Johnson Design and Tricia Sgrignoli/Positive Images
Interior layout and composition: Tricia Sgrignoli/Positive Images
Maps provided by Jim Miller/fennana design
Transit maps courtesy of the Massachusetts Bay Transportation Authority. Used with permission.

ISBN-13: 978-0-912301-85-3
ISBN-10: 0-912301-85-6

Printed in the USA on recycled paper.

Published by First Books®, 503-968-6777, www.firstbooks.com.

What readers are saying about Newcomer's Handbooks:

I recently got a copy of your Newcomer's Handbook for Chicago, and wanted to let you know how invaluable it was for my move. I must have consulted it a dozen times a day preparing for my move. It helped me find my way around town, find a place to live, and so many other things. Thanks.

– Mike L.
Chicago, Illinois

Excellent reading (Newcomer's Handbook for San Francisco and the Bay Area) ... balanced and trustworthy. One of the very best guides if you are considering moving/relocation. Way above the usual tourist crap.

– Gunnar E.
Stockholm, Sweden

I was very impressed with the latest edition of the Newcomer's Handbook for Los Angeles. It is well organized, concise and up-to-date. I would recommend this book to anyone considering a move to Los Angeles.

– Jannette L.
Attorney Recruiting Administrator for a large Los Angeles law firm

I recently moved to Atlanta from San Francisco, and LOVE the Newcomer's Handbook for Atlanta. It has been an invaluable resource—it's helped me find everything from a neighborhood in which to live to the local hardware store. I look something up in it everyday, and know I will continue to use it to find things long after I'm no longer a newcomer. And if I ever decide to move again, your book will be the first thing I buy for my next destination.

– Courtney R.
Atlanta, Georgia

In looking to move to the Boston area, a potential employer in that area gave me a copy of the Newcomer's Handbook for Boston. It's a great book that's very comprehensive, outlining good and bad points about each neighborhood in the Boston area. Very helpful in helping me decide where to move.

– no name given (online submit form)

TABLE OF CONTENTS

CONTENTS

I N THE 1850s, OLIVER WENDELL HOLMES REFERRED TO BOSTON
as the "Hub of the Solar System," a title proud Bostonians swiftly
changed to "Hub of the Universe." Since then, Boston has earned many other
nicknames, including "The Athens of America" and "Beantown." Whatever the
moniker, Boston is one of the most desirable, albeit expensive—it consistently
ranks among the costliest cities in the US—places to live in the country. High
cost of living aside, Boston is a nice place to call home. Less intimidating than
New York City, sunnier than Seattle, Boston proper is a small city with good public transportation, easy access to the Atlantic Ocean and three mountain ranges
(White, Green, and Berkshire), dozens of colleges and universities, museums,
professional and college sports teams, music and theater, and an abundance of
historical sites. Live here and you can gorge on fresh fried clams, or sip the finest
Guinness poured this side of the Atlantic. You can rollerblade for miles through
the heart of the city along the Charles River, or ice skate in the Common. In the
summer you can catch top-notch productions of Shakespeare, Boston Pops
concerts, or Friday-night, family-friendly movies, all outdoors and all for free. In
foul weather, you can spend entire days immersed in the bookstores and coffee
shops of Harvard Square, or linger over a gourmet meal at any one of the South
End's trendy bistros. And wherever you go, you will be surrounded by history.

Of course, life in Boston isn't without fault: much of Boston's nightlife and
many of its neighborhoods are geared toward the college crowd; summer
weather brings jams of tourists to some neighborhoods (particularly the North
End, Back Bay, Beacon Hill, and Harvard Square); winters are cold; street patterns
seem designed to take drivers to the brink of madness; and Bostonians are "fast-
paced" (read: impatient), and may not seem very welcoming. Just have patience:
there *are* good places to live and socialize for the post-college crowd; the tourist season *does* subside each winter—which, while cold, is often filled with crisp
sunny days—and once you've settled in, you will certainly make friends. You may

even find that getting around isn't quite as difficult as it initially seemed, and that the city's annoying quirks have become endearing. It just takes time. Getting back to the weather, Boston enjoys all four seasons, and New England's weather is famously fickle. Summers are warm, usually around 80° to 90° Fahrenheit, and often blanketed by the "three H's" (hazy, hot, and humid); occasionally a dramatic thunderstorm will break the heat. Autumn, typically beginning in late September and lasting into November, is crisp and beautiful with legendary foliage. Winter is cold, windy, and often well below freezing, though typically not below zero. Boston receives an average of about 42 inches of snow each year, but this amount fluctuates: sometimes it seems every week brings another Nor'easter (a nasty winter snowstorm; see **Local Lingo**), and other times a whole winter may pass with just a few inches. Spring is often a quick flutter of cool wet weather and blossoming flowers sandwiched between late winter frosts and early summer heat. Fortunately, while it occasionally receives a blizzard or the last breaths of a hurricane, Boston is not especially prone to the natural disasters that plague other regions of the country (knock on wood).

Politically, the Commonwealth of Massachusetts is firmly liberal, though lawmakers on Beacon Hill have managed to retain some odd vestiges of Boston's puritanical past. For example, despite the large population and the substantial number of students who are prone to keeping late hours, the subway stops running around 12:30 a.m. every night, and bars and clubs stay open no later than 2 a.m. In addition, Boston is still subject to many "blue laws," most of which regulate the sale of alcohol—until recently it was impossible to purchase alcohol on Sundays, and for the most part, alcohol sales are restricted to liquor stores only. That generally means that no beer, wine, or spirits are available in grocery stores, gas stations, or convenience stores; there are exceptions, however, as grocery store chains are permitted to sell wine and beer at a limited number of locations statewide.

Ever a hot political topic, the infamous Big Dig is finally completed, after nearly 20 years of construction and billions of dollars in cost overruns—not to mention corruption charges and safety concerns. One of the largest public works projects in history, the massive undertaking replaced the antiquated and traffic-congested eyesore that was the north-south Central Artery (I-93) with a wider, tunneled highway system running beneath downtown Boston. It also gave us the Ted Williams Tunnel, which connects the Mass Pike (I-90) directly to Logan Airport. The final ramp was opened in January of 2006, and development of the Rose F. Kennedy Greenway has commenced where the old highway once loomed in the center of the city.

While the Big Dig has eased downtown traffic somewhat, you're still likely to find driving Boston's streets time-consuming and frustrating. Since much of the city was originally built for 17th- and 18th-century traffic (read: pedestrians and horse-drawn carriages), many streets are winding, indirect, narrow, and only permit one-way traffic. Giving or receiving directions is difficult, and finding parking is expensive and exasperating, as spots are scarce. Depending on where you choose to live, newcomers should consider whether a car is necessary. Boston's efficient public transportation system makes life without a vehicle convenient and hassle-free in much of the city. Alternatively, a car-sharing company, Zipcar, caters to those who don't want the aggravation or responsibility of owning a vehicle; members can rent cars by the hour to run errands or go to the beach. (See **Transportation** for more details).

This book covers much more than just Boston proper. While the City of Boston itself contains about 589,000 people, the greater Boston area as a whole, including the city, exceeds 3.5 million residents. In this Fourth Edition of the *Newcomer's Handbook® for Moving to and Living in Boston* you'll find new profiles of outlying towns, as well as expanded and updated coverage of Boston's own neighborhoods and bordering communities that, as much as the city itself, make up the essence of the Boston area: Cambridge, Brookline, Somerville, Medford, Newton, Quincy, and more. Much has changed in a few short years—the Big Dig is done!—and, accordingly, we've updated and added to important sections like **Getting Settled**, **Transportation**, **Helpful Services**, **Cultural Life**, and **Money Matters**, while streamlining throughout to make this the most readable, useful, and enjoyable edition yet. Don't forget, as a new resident, you'll be able to find answers to many of your questions—from property and excise taxes to fun places to take the kids—at www.cityofboston.gov.

As usual, we welcome reader suggestions and comments on the tear-out page at the back of the book. We hope that the information presented on the following pages will help you establish a Boston residence smoothly and speedily. We also hope that once you select your neighborhood and settle in, the book will help you get on with the fun part: enjoying the city's many treasures, sites, and resources. Welcome to the "Hub of the Universe!"

HISTORY

According to the Massachusetts Office of Travel and Tourism, nearly 27 million visitors come to the state each year, many drawn by the historical wealth of the region. Massachusetts' history includes the Plimoth Plantation, the Salem Witch Trials, and the Boston Tea Party. During its 375-odd years, Boston has been the launch site of influential politicians, authors, musicians, entrepreneurs, and tragedies and triumphs that have shaped the world.

Until the arrival of the first group of Pilgrims on the Mayflower, this region was home to many different Native American tribes. Locally, the most common tribes were the Massachusetts, Wampanoags, Pokanokets, Nausets, Pamets, Narragansetts, Agawams, Pennacooks, and Pawtuckets. Obviously, the state takes its name from the Massachusett tribe, which translates to "people of the great hills," a reference to the Blue Hills south of Boston. Many places in the region were named after English settlers' hometowns, the Native American words for places, or the native tribes that inhabited them.

European explorers, including Captain John Smith in 1614, Giovanni Verrazano in 1524, and John Cabot in 1497, knew of the Massachusetts Bay area well before it was actually colonized. And there is speculation that Leif Eriksson's Viking colony of Vinland was actually situated in Cambridge along the Charles River. Generally, though, it is accepted that the first European settlement in Massachusetts was in 1620, when the Pilgrims settled on a south shore of Massachusetts in a colony they called Plymouth. Today, Plymouth has many exhibits and relics of its Pilgrim past, including a replica of their ship and a living museum of the plantation.

In the decade following 1620, more settlers arrived from England, including those who founded Salem and Charlestown. In 1630, Governor John Winthrop of the Massachusetts Bay Company led a group of between 700 and 800 Puritans who sailed eleven ships over from England. Initially, Winthrop and his Puritans put into port at Salem, but there were already too many people in that settlement to accommodate all of them. Some stayed, but the rest headed south to Charlestown, where again, resources were limited. And so they headed across the Charles River. On the Shawmut Peninsula, at the foot of what is now Beacon Hill, there lived an Anglican pastor-cum-hermit by the name of William Blaxton. This pastor, originally a minister to a group of settlers who had since returned to England, had stayed behind to live a quiet life with his books. Winthrop purchased the peninsula from Blaxton for £30, and he and the remaining 150 Puritans finally started the colony that was to become Boston.

These early Puritan settlers greeted a much different landscape than exists today. The local Native Americans called this peninsula "Mushauwomuk," meaning "where there is a big river." Governor Winthrop first called it "Trimountaine" for the three hills that he could see from his vantage point of Charlestown. The settlers later changed the name to Boston in reference to the town in England from where many of them hailed. Today, the title Trimountaine survives (shortened to Tremont) as a street name. Two of the three hills are gone, the third (Beacon Hill) is dramatically shorter, and the original, thin Shawmut peninsula has been filled in to bear almost no resemblance to its pre-Puritan topography.

Religious beliefs and practices were a pressing concern of the early Puritan colonists in the Massachusetts Bay. Although they fled their home country in search of freedom from religious persecution, they tended to be just as closed-minded as those from whom they fled. Largely they believed that their ways were right, and had little tolerance for non-Puritans, including the Native Americans, Quakers, Presbyterians, Baptists, and Catholics, to name a few. Both Native Americans and non-Puritan, Christian "heretics," were forbidden from Puritan Massachusetts, and many took refuge in nearby Rhode Island. Indeed, within their first century here, this religious-themed exclusivity and paranoia reached a fevered pitch; in 1692, Salem's notorious trials resulted in 19 people being hanged for allegedly practicing witchcraft.

Boston emerged as a key port in the Triangle Trade route during the colonial period. Sugar cane harvested in the West Indies came to Boston where it was turned into rum, which was then shipped to West Africa and traded for slaves, who were sent to the West Indies to harvest sugar cane, and so on. Merchant families grew wealthy, and their financial means began to elevate them to the status of the local aristocracy. Later, they would be christened the "Boston Brahmins" by Oliver Wendell Holmes and immortalized in a John Collins Bossidy poem that pays homage to Boston as "the home of the bean and the cod, where the Lowells talk to Cabots, and the Cabots talk only to God." As Boston's popularity and prosperity rose, so did the taxes levied upon it by Great Britain. American colonists protested this "taxation without representation" in Parliament, and the ensuing clampdown of imperial rule eventually escalated into the Revolutionary War. First came the "Boston Massacre" in 1770, when a mob of rabble-rousing civilians began taunting a redcoat guard posted alone in front of the Customs House by throwing snowballs at him. The conflict grew until a small British squad fired shots into the crowd, killing five colonials. The Boston Massacre became fodder for the patriotic movement, which smoldered along until the "Boston Tea Party," when the British Empire gave the East India Tea Company a monopoly to sell tea in the colonies and then taxed that tea. As an act of protest, sixty Bostonians, some disguised, marched down to Griffin's Wharf, secretly boarded three British ships, and then quietly dumped 342 chests of tea into Boston Harbor.

By 1775, the British Empire was fed up with its rebellious American colonies, especially Massachusetts, and had increased its military presence. The Revolutionary War officially kicked off the night of April 18th, when patriots learned of British plans to attack a suspected munitions store in Concord. "Sons of liberty" Paul Revere and William Dawes were dispatched to warn their brethren in the countryside of the impending attack. (As retold in Henry Wadsworth Longfellow's famous poem, "Paul Revere's Ride," two lanterns were also hung in the Old North Church—then known as Christ Church—to warn Charlestown that the British were approaching from the river.) The colonial militia heard the call to arms, and on the morning of April 19th, nearly 500 colonial "Minutemen"—mostly farmers and working men with little if any formal military training—clashed with the British army in Lexington and Concord. By the end of this crucial day, the British suffered almost 300 dead or wounded, compared with only 100 colonial casualties.

The Battle of Bunker Hill (a bit of a misnomer, it actually transpired on Breed's Hill) was fought two months later on June 17th, 1775. Though dramatically outnumbered and low on ammunition, the ragtag colonial militia managed to hold the line for two of three charges against the better-equipped and trained British forces, and inflicted heavy damages on the world's mightiest military. While the British won the day in the end, it cost them twice as many casualties as the colonial army, and the battle proved a tremendous confidence boost to the revolutionaries. Years later, their brave stand was commemorated with the Bunker Hill Monument, a 221-foot-tall obelisk, which rather resembles the Washington Monument and still stands in Charlestown today. General George Washington took charge of the colonial troops in Boston the following month, and stayed here until he won the city back from England in March of 1776.

Many tourists interested in the sites made famous in colonial and revolutionary Boston walk the Freedom Trail, a 2.5-mile alternately red-painted or brick-lined path that runs through the city. It connects Bunker Hill and the USS *Constitution* in Charlestown with Paul Revere's house, Copp's Hill Burying Ground, and the Old North Church in the North End, and continues on to Faneuil Hall. It then leads into downtown Boston, passing by the Old South Meeting House, the Old State House, and the King's Chapel and Burying Ground, where some of Boston's settlers like John Winthrop and the woman who purportedly served as Nathaniel Hawthorne's inspiration for Hester Prynne in *The Scarlet Letter* are buried. The trail ends up in Beacon Hill at the Boston Common after bringing tourists by the Park Street Church, the (new) State House, and the Granary Burying Ground, which is the final resting place for John Hancock, Samuel Adams, and Paul Revere, as well as Mary Goose (alleged by some sources to be Mother Goose), and the parents of native son Benjamin Franklin.

After the colonies won their independence, Massachusetts began rebuilding itself, as much of the state had been decimated during the war. In this era, merchants again rose to prominence, diversifying their reach into the whaling, shipbuilding, and textile industries. Beginning in the late 1700s, immigrants from all over Europe came to Boston, many to work as laborers in the factories and warehouses. By 1822, Boston's numbers had swelled enough (over 43,000 residents clocked by the census of 1820) to warrant a change from the "Town of Boston" to the "City of Boston." Tiny Shawmut Peninsula, home of the original settlement, could no longer contain its burgeoning population and city leaders were forced to find a solution. First, they leveled the steep hills of Boston and used the soil to extend the shorelines of the Charles River and Boston Harbor, increasing the livable space within the existing peninsula. A steady string of land reclamation projects followed, creating new real estate throughout the city in neighborhoods like the South End, the Back Bay, Chinatown, the Fenway, and South Boston. During the height of construction, trains delivered 3,500 carloads of landfill per day from the Needham gravel pits west of the city. In 1883, noted landscape architect Frederick Law Olmsted set up his office in Brookline, and began to design and construct the beloved Emerald Necklace, an interconnected chain of parks that stretch across seven miles of the city. Then, in 1887, the country's first subway system opened in Boston. Streetcars connected nearby environs with downtown, earning them the moniker "streetcar suburbs" and causing them to experience booms of their own.

Throughout the 19th century, moneyed Bostonians sought to build a refined city, and their focus was to create cultural institutions that would rival those in Europe. Libraries and museums went up, and within the first decade of the 1800s, Boston began attracting and turning out notable literati. Over the century, Massachusetts produced writers whose works play an integral role in the world's literary canon, including Ralph Waldo Emerson, Henry Wadsworth Longfellow, Nathaniel Hawthorne, Edgar Allan Poe, Herman Melville, Louisa May Alcott, Emily Dickinson, and Henry David Thoreau.

One more notable writer reflects a metamorphosis that took place amidst Boston's physical and cultural transitions of the 19th century. During the late 1700s, a slave named Phillis Wheatley became the first African-American on the continent to publish poetry—at the young age of fourteen, having only learned English a few years before. Wheatley was emancipated in 1773, followed by the emancipation of all Boston slaves in 1783. By the 1800s, Boston's prominent African-American community was the largest in the nation. Most of the city's black citizenry lived on the northern slope of Beacon Hill and the West End, where they erected the African Meeting House in 1806 and the Abiel Smith School in 1835. Despite federal laws to the contrary, local authorities generally considered a fugitive slave who'd escaped to Boston to be free. When Congress passed the Fugitive Slave Act in 1850, entitling Federal Marshals to capture and arrest escaped slaves anywhere in the country, black and white Bostonians banded together to prevent them from doing so on their turf. If anything, the law served to catalyze Boston's community into rallying for Abolition. Vocal opponents of slavery such as Frederick Douglass furthered the movement by establishing the New England Anti-Slavery Society, and many locals smuggled runaway slaves in safe houses along the Underground Railroad. Harriet and Lewis Hayden owned and ran one of the most famous of these homes, which still stands at 66 Phillips Street. When the issue of slavery finally came to blows in the Civil War, the white Bostonian Robert Gould Shaw led his all-black 54th Regiment of the Massachusetts Volunteer Infantry, the first African-American regiment in the North, into battle. Sixty-two soldiers of 54th Massachusetts, including Shaw, died during the assault on Fort Wagner in Charleston, South Carolina. Those wanting to learn more can walk the 1.6-mile Black Heritage Trail, which traverses the north slope of Beacon Hill. It includes many of the historic sites mentioned here, including a memorial to Shaw and his men, who were depicted in the Academy Award–winning film *Glory*.

Another particularly influential group in 19th-century Boston was the Irish Catholics, who began migrating here throughout the first third of the 1800s and then in droves between 1845 and 1852, during the Irish Potato Famine. As is often the case, many citizens were prejudiced against the new group of immigrants; but after the Civil War, negative public sentiment against the Irish diminished as their skills and hard work helped rebuild the city. Original Irish enclaves include Charlestown, South Boston, and Dorchester, where many remain today. As the

20th century began, the Irish Catholics created what has been described as a "political machine," attaining a toe-hold on Boston politics that has proven unshakable even into the present. In 1906, the grandfather of JFK, John "Honey Fitz" Fitzgerald, became Boston's first Boston-born, Irish Catholic mayor. Less than 10 years later, the corrupt yet beloved "Boss" James Curley took office. His career in Boston politics spanned until 1949, during which time he held a number of influential offices—including governor of Massachusetts—despite the fact that he spent portions of his terms in prison! The Fitzgerald family returned to public office in 1946 with John Fitzgerald Kennedy's election to the House of Representatives; the Brookline native went on to win a US Senate seat in 1952, and of course, the Presidency in 1960.

During the early- to mid-1900s, Boston experienced a major economic and cultural decline. Businesses and families moved out of the city for the cheaper, cleaner suburbs, and Boston fell into a serious state of disrepair. Many attribute the problems to the inability of the city's two most influential groups—the conservative, wealthy, Protestant old guard lawmakers, and the Irish Catholic politicians—to cooperate. Adding to the decline was 40 years of censorship. In 1904, Boston appointed an official whose function it was to censor or ban all morally indecent art for the good of the public. This city censor oversaw and banned questionable books, plays, and films—anything that might "corrupt" upstanding Bostonians, lending credence and fame to the phrase "Banned in Boston." During this period of "cultural communism," Boston saw its cultural status within the nation suffer as artists mimicked the Quakers' flight to Rhode Island of the 1600s. This time, the more avant-garde headed south to nearby New York.

It was also during the mid-1900s, particularly after WWII, when many of the city's mansions and old Victorian residences were partitioned into apartment buildings or sold off to local colleges. John B. Hynes, who served as interim mayor while Curley was doing a stint in jail, became Boston's official mayor in 1949. Mayor Hynes set about the task of revitalizing the crumbling city, launching the still active Boston Redevelopment Authority (BRA) in 1957. The goal: to form a "New Boston" by targeting the city's problem areas for urban renewal. Although in many ways the much rejuvenated status of modern Boston is attributable to Hynes's vision, one of the first of these projects—the razing of the West End—was, in retrospect, a huge mistake. Although the intentions were good—to reinvigorate the city center by clearing away and rebuilding a foundering area—it didn't work, and Bay Staters were bitter about it. The thriving and integrated immigrant neighborhood was so quickly demolished that many residents were displaced without provisions, and the area was so thoroughly leveled that virtually no vestiges of it survive—today, portions of Beacon Hill and the Mass General Hospital campus stand in the space. In the wake of this project, historic societies cropped up throughout the city specifically to prevent future such bulldozing of other districts. Later projects enjoyed varying success: the razing of Scollay Square's bars, jazz clubs, and adult entertainment venues made way for the mammoth City

Hall Plaza and Government Center, while the BRA's restoration of the Faneuil Hall Marketplace—all but abandoned and slated for demolition in 1968—proved to be a widely imitated success. Now a focal point of local tourism, it is largely credited for bringing life back to the downtown area.

Mid-19th-century Boston's African-American population centered around Roxbury and the South End, which housed the city's jazz scene of the 1950s. It was during this era that Dr. Martin Luther King, Jr., attended theology school at BU and preached on the weekends at Roxbury's Twelfth Baptist Church. As the civil rights movement grew, Boston entered the trying time of school integration. Because the Boston School Committee had made no effort to desegregate its schools, the NAACP filed a lawsuit. In June of 1974, Federal Judge Arthur Garrity, Jr., ordered an immediate integration of Boston's public schools by a system in which black students were bused to public schools in white neighborhoods and vice versa. It is an understatement to say the busing program was not well met by many residents of affected neighborhoods; during its early years it set off a great deal of racial conflict and regrettable violence within the city. Today, in addition to remaining the epicenter of Boston's African-American community, Roxbury is notable as the one-time residence of Malcolm X and childhood home of his contemporary, Louis Farrakhan, the modern leader of the Nation of Islam.

Boston again rose to prominence in the late 20th century; before the dot-com crash of 2000–2002, Massachusetts was considered a "mini–Silicon Valley." High tech professionals moved here *en masse* and many graduating students from area universities stayed to take advantage of the economic opportunity. At the turn of the 21st century, the housing vacancy rate was less than 1%, and the real estate market exploded between 1996 and 2005. While high tech, tourism, and finance jobs suffered after the dot-com bubble burst, some of that ground has been regained; the city's economy was also buoyed somewhat by its mainstays of education, healthcare, and professional services. Boston now serves as an industry hotbed for biotech and medicine. A recent housing slowdown has created a more reasonable residential marketplace, but while vacancy rates shift with the economy, it is never an inexpensive proposition to rent or buy a home in Boston.

Further out of the city, New England offers Bostonians a diverse range of escape opportunities. Cape Cod, Newport, Rhode Island, and New Hampshire's Lakes Region boom during the summer, while the idyllic inns of Vermont fill up during autumn's foliage season. Ski resorts in the Green and White Mountains are flooded with "Massholes" all winter long, while Maine's famous fresh lobster, outlet shopping, and miles of coastline attract tourists year round. Closer to home, the possibilities are seemingly endless. See **Cultural Life** and **Quick Getaways** for a rundown on area events and nearby vacation destinations.

WHAT TO BRING

- **Walking shoes**; this is a walkable city, for the most part. With all the traffic and the expensive taxis, tourists and locals alike often choose to hoof it from place to place. The architecture is varied, and cozy neighborhood squares are inviting and much easier to access without having to park the car.

- **A map**; a good idea anywhere, but essential in Boston! For those used to the ease of a city or town where the streets are laid out in a sensible and easily navigable grid, Boston will be quite a surprise. Boston's somewhat hilly topography, combined with its centuries-old streets that meander or turn into one-ways, makes getting around difficult. If you're driving, get a map that covers the greater Boston area, not just downtown Boston.

- **A CharlieCard**; the local mass transit system, called the MBTA (or simply the "T"), revamped its fare system in late 2006 in an effort to get away from tokens and exact change. Regular commuters and even occasional riders would be smart to obtain a plastic, rechargeable "CharlieCard" (named for the Kingston Trio song "Charlie on the M.T.A.") to avoid the frustrating surcharges associated with disposable paper tickets and cash. The cards can be purchased with stored value online at http://www.mbta.com, at most convenience stores, and at several T stations, including Back Bay, Downtown Crossing, Harvard, North Station, and South Station.

- **Patience and optimism**; there's no doubt about it, Boston is quirky. The street patterns will confuse you at first, and if you drive, be prepared for the honking of impatient residents. Also, many Bostonians have lived here their whole lives and therefore have already defined their social circles, which can then be challenging to break into. Don't be too discouraged when you encounter these obstacles; they will pass. Boston is a vibrant, rich city, and if you give it time, you will find your own rewarding place in it.

LOCAL LINGO

Certainly you've heard about the unmistakable Boston accent. In what can be described as part Puritan, part Kennedy, and part speech impediment, Bostonians routinely drop their "r's" ("Clahk" Kent is "Supahman's" alta ego). Some even recycle them at the ends of other words where they don't belong; if your name is Linda, brace yourself for the occasional "Linder." Stretching out some vowels (aunt is "awnt," not "ant") and squishing others ("room" is more like "rum") is common. You'll figure all this out pretty quickly, but what you may not have heard about are the less obvious Massachusetts slang terms. Compiled here is a small list of essential local lingo and pronunciations. (Many abbreviations listed here will be used throughout the book.)

- **Across the River**: Cambridge, on the other side of the Charles River from Boston.

- **BC:** Boston College
- **Beacon Hill:** although this usually refers to a neighborhood in Boston, sometimes it is extended to mean the local government, as the State House is located here.
- **Blue Laws:** conservative legislation enacted in Puritan New England settlements regarding behavior, so called for the blue paper upon which they were printed. Some of these laws are still on the books, and in Boston the term "blue laws" is most often invoked in reference to the strict rules regarding the sale of alcohol.
- **Book:** a verb meaning to hurry away.
- **Brahmin:** from the earlier centuries of Boston's elite class: White Anglo Saxon Protestant upper-class aristocrat of the families Appleton, Bacon, Boylston, Cabot, Codman, Coolidge, Cunningham, Forbes, Hunnewell, Lodge, Lowell, Parkman, Russell, and Shaw.
- **BU:** Boston University
- **The Cape:** Cape Cod. Not to be confused with Cape Ann, which is on the North Shore.
- **The Central Artery:** previously the main route in and out of Boston, the big, green, double-decked and traffic-clogged eyesore has finally been demolished.
- **The Charles:** the Charles River
- **The Combat Zone:** former red-light district in the Chinatown area. It is mostly phased out now, although a couple of seedy stores and establishments still remain.
- **Comm Ave:** Commonwealth Avenue
- **Concord:** town to the west of Boston that figured prominently in the Revolutionary War, pronounced like "conquered," as in what you've done when you've defeated someone.
- **Dot Ave:** Dorchester Avenue
- **Dedham:** suburb west of Boston, pronounced "DEAD-um."
- **Dunky's, or Dunkin's:** Dunkin Donuts. A local institution born on the South Shore, there are 1,100 of them within 50 miles of Boston; this is the only area of the country where they outnumber Starbucks.
- **Eastie:** East Boston
- **Frappe:** a milkshake with ice cream, pronounced "frap," not "frapp-ie."
- **Mass General:** Massachusetts General Hospital, also referred to as MGH.
- **Gloucester:** town on the north shore, pronounced "GLOSS-ter."
- **Haverhill:** small city on the border of New Hampshire, pronounced "HAY-vrill."
- **Jimmies:** chocolate sprinkles on ice cream.
- **JP:** Jamaica Plain
- **Mass Ave:** Massachusetts Avenue
- **Natick:** town west of Boston, pronounced "NAY-tick."

- **Needham:** suburb west of Boston, pronounced "NEED-um."
- **Nor'easter:** intense winter storm, often responsible for heavy snows or blizzards, formed when a strong area of low pressure moving in from the Atlantic Ocean, accompanied by northeasterly winds, collides with a high-pressure system of Arctic air from Canada.
- **Packie:** package store, i.e., liquor store.
- **Peabody:** a town on the north shore of Boston, pronounced "PEE-b'dee."
- **The Pike:** the Massachusetts Turnpike, which runs east-west across the state.
- **The Pru:** the Prudential Tower
- **P-town:** short for Provincetown, a predominantly gay and artistic town on the tip of Cape Cod.
- **Quincy:** city just south of Boston, pronounced "KWIN-zee."
- **Reading:** town north of Boston, pronounced "RED-ing."
- **Regular:** at Dunkin Donuts (and other local coffee shops), a regular coffee means "with cream and sugar," as in, "I'll have a medium regular, please."
- **Rotary:** traffic circle; not common in other states, there are plenty here.
- **Rozzie:** Roslindale
- **Scrod:** white fish catch of the day, usually cod or haddock, pronounced "skrawd."
- **Southie:** South Boston, not the South End.
- **The T:** The subway, bus, and commuter rail system, short for MBTA.
- **Tonic:** soda pop; soft drinks are also called "soda," but *never* "pop!"
- **Triple-deckers:** three-floor, three-family houses that sprang up in the 1800s to meet the growing housing demands of immigrant workers (also called "three-deckers" or "Irish battleships"). Within the city of Boston, one quarter of the one- to three-family housing stock was listed as a triple-decker in 2000.
- **Triple Eagle:** someone who went to BC High School, BC, and BC Law School.
- **Wicked:** an all-purpose intensifier, as in, "That movie was wicked good," or "Sully's wicked crazy."
- **Woburn:** suburb north of Boston, pronounced "WOO-burn."
- **Worcester:** city about one hour west of Boston, pronounced "WIRS'-ter," or even "WUH-sta," but not "War-ches-ter," "Worsh-stir," or anything else.

NAVIGATING THE STREETS

You *will* get lost in Boston…often. Keep in mind, however, that during those frustrating times spent wandering aimlessly on side streets, one ways, and confusing traffic circles (rotaries), you may happen upon unexpected treats—quaint squares with inviting bookstores and cozy cafés, or lovely tucked-away parks. *Never* feel embarrassed about being lost here; even lifelong Bostonians occasionally have trouble finding their way.

So how is the city organized? Local legend holds that the streets of Boston were carved out of old cow trails, and while, outside of a few streets around

Boston Common, that's not actually true, it certainly feels like it given the illogical street patterns. In truth, the original Shawmut peninsula upon which Boston was settled was so small and hilly that residents walked almost everywhere, thus creating the winding footpaths that circled around salt marshes and tidal flats. It was these ambling foot paths that laid down Boston's original (and nowadays confusing) street patterns in much of downtown, including the Financial District, North End, and Beacon Hill. It wasn't until the 1800s, when Boston began its epic land reclamation efforts, that some rhyme and reason entered urban street planning. Thus, neighborhoods that developed later, such as the Back Bay, the South End, South Boston, and East Boston, were laid out in logical grids and are easier to navigate.

The good news is that while many of the street patterns throughout the city and surrounding areas are convoluted, Boston is so compact you'll quickly learn to recognize major landmarks and roadways. The best advice on getting around Boston is to buy a good map, one that details downtown Boston as well as surrounding communities and outlying areas. (You can go to www.firstbooks. com, publisher of this *Newcomer's Handbook®*, for the best Boston area maps.) When scouting an address, keep in mind that Boston is small and you may inadvertently leave the city limits without realizing it. Furthermore, most Boston area towns and cities have streets with the same names and which aren't necessarily connected, so when looking for an address, make sure you are certain of its city location. Recurring street names in Boston and its surrounds include Broadway, Cambridge, Harvard, and Washington, to name a few. When asking for directions, you should know that when people tell you something is "on massave," what they mean is it's "on Mass Ave," short for Massachusetts Avenue. Similarly, "commave" refers to Commonwealth Avenue. Learning the names and locations of the significant squares in and around the city is a good idea, because directions are often given in relation to the nearest square. (FYI, squares are frequently triangular.) Also become familiar with the old New England traffic institution called the rotary, which you might know as a roundabout or traffic circle. The most important thing to remember about rotaries is that the driver in the rotary has the right of way, *not* the driver entering it.

The following tips should prove useful as you begin your discovery of Boston's labyrinthine streets.

- **Washington Street**, named for George Washington after his visit to Boston in 1789, is unique in that all streets change names upon intersecting with it: Court Street turns into State Street, Winter Street turns into Summer Street, LaGrange Street turns into Beech Street, East Brookline Street turns into West Brookline Street, etc. The exceptions to this rule are Mass Ave, Columbus Avenue, and Melnea Cass Boulevard.
- **Some streets change names at town borders**; other streets change names for no apparent reason, such as the Fenway, which becomes the Riverway, Ja-

maicaway, and Arborway as you head south. Major streets that *keep* the same name as they run from community to community are Mass Ave, Comm Ave, Beacon Street, Boylston Street, Washington Street, and Pleasant Street, although the numbering changes from town to town—good to keep in mind if you are searching for a particular address. Other streets disappear and then reappear—Boylston Street, for example.

Gridded parts of Boston include:

- **The Back Bay**, designed by city planners in the French style to resemble the Champs-Elysees, was laid out in an easy-to-memorize grid. The major boulevards that run in a roughly east/west direction are Beacon Street, Marlborough Avenue, Comm Ave, Newbury Street and Boylston Street. Comm Ave is the only one of these streets with two-way traffic. The smaller cross streets, which run roughly north/south, are named after British royals and run alphabetically in alternating one-way directions: Arlington Street, Berkeley Street, Clarendon Street, Dartmouth Street, Exeter Street, Fairfield Street, Gloucester Street, and Hereford Street. After Hereford, the Back Bay ends at Mass Ave, which has two-way traffic.

- **South Boston's** streets are also laid out in a grid fashion, although they're not as clear-cut as those of the Back Bay, since Southie's landmass is shaped somewhat like the letter "v." In general, streets running north/south are lettered, and run alphabetically (M Street, N Street, O Street), and east/west running streets are numbered, and arranged consecutively. Numbered streets are further modified by either east or west, depending on where they fall in relation to Broadway.

- **East Boston** is also fairly grid-like, although there's no easy mnemonic device to remember how the streets here lie. Some of East Boston's thoroughfares are Saratoga, Bennington, and Meridian.

Main thoroughfares in **Boston**:

- **Beacon Street** begins at Tremont Street downtown and runs in an east/west direction parallel with the Charles River through the Back Bay and Kenmore Square. It continues in a straight line heading southwest through Brookline until Cleveland Circle in Brighton, where it curves around the Chestnut Hill Reservoir and then winds slightly through Newton, terminating at Washington Street/Route 16. **Note**: do not confuse Beacon Street with North Beacon Street, an entirely separate roadway in northern Brighton, between Cambridge Street and the Mass Pike, which then crosses into Watertown, where its name changes to just Beacon Street.

- **Boylston Street** begins downtown at Washington Street and runs east/west through the Back Bay, parallel to the Charles River and ending at the Fens. Boylston picks up again on the other side of the Fens and continues straight through until it ends at Brookline Avenue. Boylston Street begins again further south in Brookline at the border of Olmsted Park, which is where Route 9 (formerly Huntington Avenue) becomes Boylston Street.

- **Columbus Avenue** begins in the Back Bay, picking up Route 28, and heading southwest through the South End, curving south in Roxbury and terminating at the northern border of Franklin Park.

- **Comm Ave** begins at the Public Garden and runs east/west, parallel with the Charles River, through the Back Bay and Kenmore Square, passing BU, until it intersects with Brighton Avenue in Allston-Brighton. Then Comm Ave meanders through Allston-Brighton and continues into Chestnut Hill, Newton, and runs past Boston College (BC).

- **Dorchester Avenue** (**Dot Ave**) begins at Congress Street on the Downtown Waterfront and heads south over Fort Point Channel through the western boundary of South Boston and into Dorchester, terminating at Adams Street just north of the Neponset River.

- **Mass Ave** begins at the intersection with Columbia Road in Dorchester and runs northwest through the South End, the Fenway, and the Back Bay until it crosses over the Charles River into Cambridge. In Cambridge it passes through MIT and Central Square, hooks north in Harvard Square, continues through Porter Square and on into Arlington and then Lexington.

- **The Mass Pike** (**Massachusetts Turnpike**)/**I-90** is a major toll road that runs from Boston to the state's western border. Now that the Big Dig is complete, the Pike extends all the way to Logan Airport in East Boston via the Ted Williams Tunnel.

- **Storrow Drive** is a small, several-lane roadway that runs along the banks of the Charles River. It begins just east of the Museum of Science at the Charles River Dam Bridge, and follows the river past Beacon Hill, the Back Bay, and BU, then continues as Soldiers Field Road through Allston-Brighton. (*Note:* Due to very low clearance under bridges, trucks and oversized vans are not allowed on Storrow Drive.)

- **Summer Street** begins at Downtown Crossing and runs southeast over the Fort Point Channel by the South Boston wharves and then over the Reserved Channel into the rest of Southie, ending at Dorchester Bay.

- **Tremont Street** begins at Government Center and heads southwest past Boston Common and New England Medical Center into the South End and Roxbury, ending at its intersection with Columbus Avenue.

- **Washington Street** begins at Downtown Crossing and runs southwest through Chinatown, the South End, Roxbury, JP, Roslindale, West Roxbury, and into Hyde Park.

Main thoroughfares in Cambridge:

- **Mass Ave** runs southeast to northwest, bisecting Cambridge all the way from Boston to Arlington, passing through MIT, Central Square, Harvard Square, and Porter Square.

- **Memorial Drive**, Cambridge's answer to Storrow Drive, follows the Charles River in Cambridge from the Longfellow Bridge to the Watertown border. Although it is several lanes wide, it is windy and narrow at points, so be careful.
- **Broadway and Cambridge streets** run east/west from East Cambridge, ending at Harvard Square. Cambridge Street goes right through Inman Square.
- **Fresh Pond Parkway/Alewife Brook Parkway** runs north/south on the western edge of Cambridge, past Fresh Pond on the south end and up to Arlington in the north. Also called Routes 2, 3, and 16.
- **Main Street** begins by the Charles River at the end of the Longfellow Bridge and runs through Kendall Square, terminating at its intersection with Mass Ave in Central Square.

Main thoroughfares in **Brookline**:

- **Beacon Street** cuts east/west through the most densely populated section of Brookline, from Kenmore Square to Cleveland Circle, where it heads into Newton.
- **Boylston Street** runs east/west, roughly parallel to Beacon Street, but further south, from the Fenway area of Boston to Newton. It passes by the Brookline Reservoir, Brookline Village, and Brookline Hills. Also called **Route 9**.
- **Harvard Street** heads north/south from Brookline Village at Boylston Street through Coolidge Corner at the intersection of Beacon Street and north into Allston.
- **Washington Street** runs southeast to northwest from Boylston Street through Washington Square at the intersection of Beacon Street to Cambridge Street in Brighton.
- **Hammond Pond Parkway** runs north/south through southwestern Brookline, from Newton past the Putterham Meadows Golf Course, where it meets up with Newton Street.

Main thoroughfares in **Somerville**:

- **Somerville Avenue** runs southeast/northwest through the southern portion of Somerville.
- **Beacon Street** is a southeast/northwest thoroughfare along the border with Cambridge. Turns into Hampshire Street when it crosses the border.
- **Holland Street**, **Elm Street**, **and College Avenue** all intersect in Davis Square.
- **Broadway** runs east/west through the northern portion of Somerville, from the McGrath Highway into Arlington. Passes by Tufts University.

For more information on the local highways (I-93, Route 128/I-95, and the Mass Pike/I-90), see the **Transportation** chapter.

OSTON IS A CITY OF ETHNICALLY, ECONOMICALLY, AND SOCIALLY diverse neighborhoods. While gentrification has blurred the borders of the urban mosaic somewhat, you will still find Italians in the North End, Irish in South Boston, a prominent gay community in the South End, and the city's "upper crust" in Beacon Hill. At first glance, Boston can appear fairly homogeneous; it is a city of distinct neighborhoods, after all, and what you see might depend on where you are. However, it's more diverse than is initially obvious. According to the 2000 Census, half of the city's residents are ethnic minorities. African Americans make up about 25% of the city, and growing Hispanic (14.4%) and Asian (7.5%) populations also call Boston home.

With more than 40 colleges and universities in the metro area, the city's demographics are on the young side; during the school year in particular, Boston is unquestionably a college town. From September to May, students form an influential sub-group within the city, and many of the living, dining, and social options—particularly in Brighton/Allston, the Fenway, and Cambridge—are targeted to those in school or recent graduates. If you're further along in life, fear not, as there's a neighborhood for everything and everyone.

Over the years, Boston has successfully annexed many of its surrounding communities, such as Charlestown and Roslindale. This means a resident may report his address as either 600 South Street, Roslindale, MA, or 600 South Street, Boston, MA…and still receive his mail either way. Complicating matters further are Brookline, Cambridge, and Somerville. While they are, for all intents and purposes, integral neighborhoods of the city, they are not technically part of Boston, and have their own city or town governments and bylaws (in fact, it's illegal for a Boston taxi driver to pick up a fare in Cambridge, or vice versa). So when someone says she lives in Boston or in "the city," she could mean a bordering community like Cambridge, one of the annexed areas like Charlestown, or somewhere in old Boston proper like the North End. Newcomers should keep in mind that non–Boston proper neighborhoods are very much part of the metropolitan

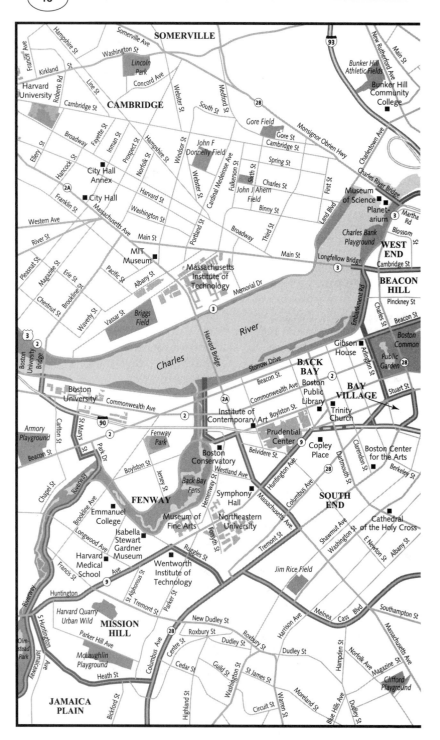

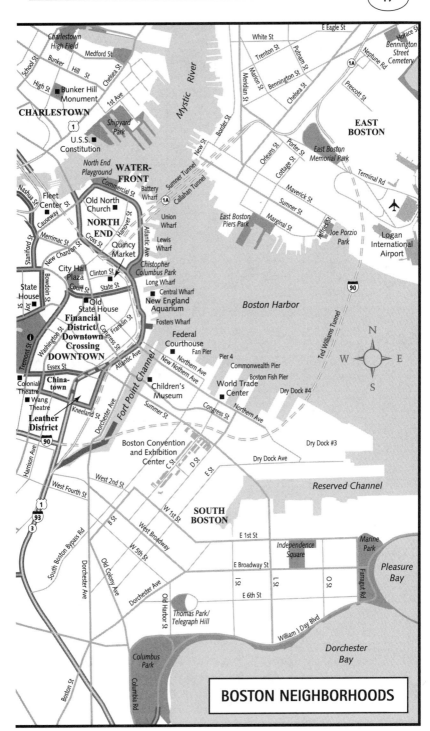

BOSTON NEIGHBORHOODS

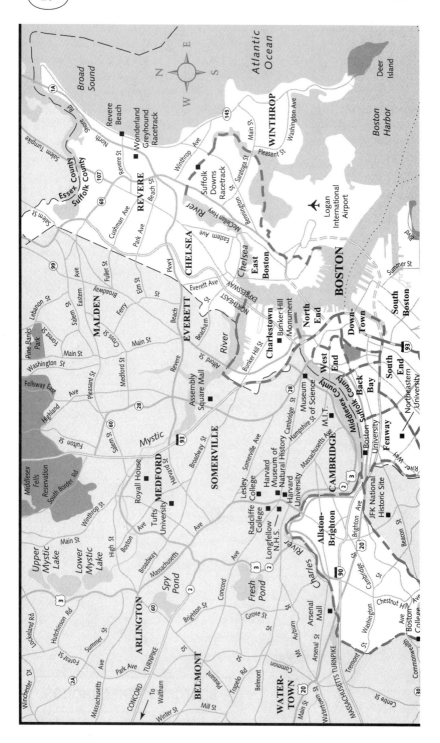

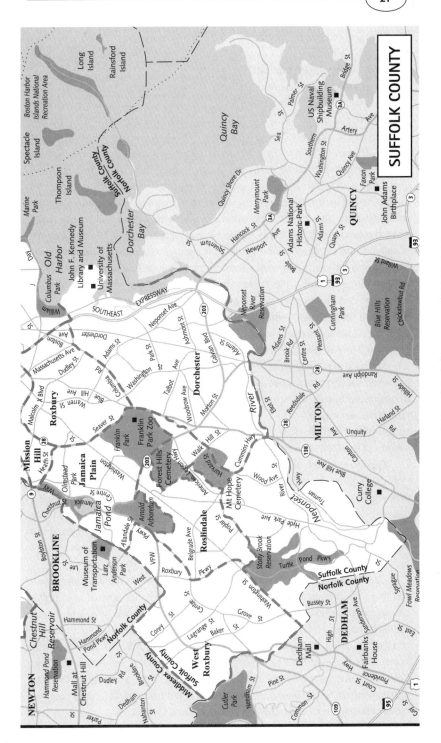

SUFFOLK COUNTY

area—all are linked to public transit—and since these surrounding communities can be more affordable, it's a good idea to consider places like Brookline, Cambridge, or Somerville in your housing search.

As in any other major American city, crime is a fact of life in Boston. After a decade of steadily sinking crime levels prompted envious city leaders from around the country to study the "Boston Miracle"—when murders in the city plunged from a high of 152 in 1990 to 39 in 1999—the murder rate shot back up in 2005. That year's 75 murders represented a ten-year high and a 17% increase over the year before; 2006 didn't fare much better, with 74 murders. Nonfatal shootings doubled in those two years, and reported rapes, vehicle theft, and aggravated assault rates all remain higher than average. While these statistics are discouraging to say the least, the majority of violent crime in Boston tends not to be random, and is largely isolated in poorer areas of the city like Roxbury, Mattapan, and Dorchester. And when combined with adjacent Cambridge—or Newton, the safest city in America according to the 2005 findings of the research group Morgan Quitno—the Boston metropolitan area as a whole feels much safer. (You can view an interactive map of reported crimes at http://www.boston-online.com/crime.) Keep in mind that everyone's comfort level varies, and what is fine for some may not work for others. Those arriving from another big city should feel at ease in most Boston neighborhoods. Newcomers from smaller cities or rural areas will want to pay close attention to how comfortable they are when visiting prospective neighborhoods. The communities profiled in this book should appeal to most newcomers in terms of amenities and safety issues. However, regardless of where you live, you should always be aware of your surroundings and take safety precautions. For more, see the **Crime and Safety** section of the **Getting Settled** chapter.

Parking in Boston and its surrounds is notoriously difficult, and winter's snow only exacerbates the situation. Once someone has shoveled out "his" spot, he will often mark it with a trashcan, milk crate, or chair. If you are circling for parking on a wintry day, no matter how desperate you are—or how unjust the whole thing seems—it's probably best to leave such spaces alone. For more details about street parking, parking permits, and ease of parking, see the neighborhood profiles (below), as well as the **Parking** section in **Getting Settled**.

County demarcations are mostly a thing of the past in the Bay State. If you see them mentioned at all, it is usually in terms of weather advisories or political campaigns. However, for ease of navigating this book, we have split up the region by county and then listed the neighborhoods alphabetically therein. Boston itself (along with Chelsea, Revere, and Winthrop) is in Suffolk County. To the north and west, in Middlesex County, lie the profiled communities of Arlington, Belmont, Cambridge, Everett, Malden, Medford, Newton, Somerville, Waltham, and Watertown. To the west and south, we profiled the Norfolk County communities of Brookline, Dedham, Milton, Needham, and Quincy.

Neighborhood and community profiles include statistical information as well as descriptions of housing, area amenities, and other characteristics. After each profile is a list of resources: post offices, library branches, police stations, parks, etc. Also included are brief summaries of some of the more popular suburbs surrounding Boston, where many people choose to live and then commute into the city to work. These suburbs and satellite cities in the greater Boston area have been arranged by county and then alphabetically. Under the **Greater Boston Area** heading, you will find a few lines describing the character, housing, and contact information for communities on the North and South shores and the metro-west region in Norfolk, Middlesex, Essex, Plymouth, and Bristol counties.

SUFFOLK COUNTY

ALLSTON-BRIGHTON

Boundaries: North: Charles River; **East:** The Fenway; **West:** City of Newton; **South:** Brookline

Allston-Brighton may not be the prettiest place in the city, but what it lacks in aesthetics it makes up in affordability and convenience. Wedged between BC to the west, BU to the East, and Harvard to the north, Allston-Brighton is particularly popular with students and recent graduates, as well as young families and immigrants. It is a big, diverse, and safe neighborhood served by the Green Line's slow, plodding B Train—the little engine that could.

While technically separate neighborhoods, Allston and Brighton evolved together, and share a similar vibe and blurry boundaries; the two are typically mentioned in the same breath, evidenced by resident parking permits issued for "Allston-Brighton." Essentially the 02134 zip code—the northern and eastern section that touches the rest of Boston—is considered Allston, while 02135, the larger, western portion, constitutes Brighton.

Established in 1635 with colonial land grants, Allston-Brighton was originally part of the city of Cambridge. In 1807, the neighborhood (then called Little Cambridge) found itself disconnected from Harvard Square due to a damaged bridge, and when government officials did not move to repair it, Allston-Brighton seceded from Cambridge and became its own entity. Eventually Allston and Brighton were home to stockyards, slaughterhouses, and meatpacking, an industry made possible by the Charles River and the railroad. In 1874, Allston and Brighton were annexed by Boston, and once the Back Bay was filled in and streetcar service extended here, housing sprang up. Many of the Victorians and row houses built during this time are still standing.

Today, Allston-Brighton is part academic, part industrial, and part residential, made up of a diverse populace that includes people of Irish, Italian, Greek, Jewish,

Asian, African-American, Russian, and Hispanic descent. Homes and their sur-rounding grounds vary in size and style, from the tried and true triple-decker, to Victorian bow fronts, to 1960s-style block apartment complexes. Location, gen-eral lack of upkeep—with portions of the BC, BU, and Harvard campuses within its bounds, some sections are heavily devoted to and populated by students—and simple architecture all contribute to keeping housing prices low, particularly when compared to more sought-after parts of town. While living quarters here tend to be much bigger than what is available downtown, and you might even get a parking spot, quaint just isn't a word that comes to mind in Allston-Brigh-ton. On the other hand, this neighborhood has everything you'll need for services: hardware, sporting goods, antique, and furniture stores, as well as a surplus of high-quality and affordable ethnic restaurants and grocers, pubs and taverns, and all the nightlife a young Bostonian could ever want. The prime shopping and dining areas are along Comm Ave, Brighton Avenue, Harvard Avenue, Cam-bridge Street, Beacon Street, and Washington Street. When those options aren't enough for you, hop on the Green Line's B train, which makes frequent stops along Comm Ave all the way from Boston College to downtown. With so many stops on this line, the ride into the city center can be tedious, but it is nonetheless convenient, and apartments close to the Green Line are abundant.

Allston borders the rest of Boston at the western end of BU's campus, where Brighton Avenue splits off from Comm Ave at **Packard's Corner**. BU's presence is evident here in both the official university property and unofficial, student-geared businesses lining Comm Ave, such as used furniture stores and cheap dining options. This area wasn't much developed until around 1910, when street-cars arrived and spurred construction. Much of the housing stock dates from the same period: mostly three- to five-story brick masonry apartments representa-tive of the Georgian, classical, Renaissance, and Federal Revival styles.

About a half mile farther from downtown, where Harvard Avenue connects Comm Ave and Brighton Avenue, is the heart of Allston: the funky, grungy, and bustling **Allston Village**. Here you'll find a dense cluster of commerce and culture, comprising the majority of Allston's shops, bars, restaurants, music venues, and local services. If you don't mind nightlife, then this is the place to be—except for the summer months, the area is reliably thriving. If you want to live somewhere a little quieter, think more seriously about Brighton, or even Lower Allston.

For years, Harvard has been buying land in **Lower Allston**—the area north of Allston Village between the Mass Pike and the river—in preparation for fu-ture expansion. Harvard's Business School is already located here, just across the JFK Bridge from the school's main campus, and, surprisingly, the university owns more land in Allston than it does in Cambridge. In 2007, Harvard unveiled the first stages of a 30-year development plan aimed at revamping the industrial and rather bleak Western Avenue into a "new Harvard Square." For the time be-ing, the area's slightly secluded location lends it a nice neighborhood feel, home to working-class families and students alike. Most of Lower Allston's two- and three-family houses have backyards and driveways, and there is easy access to the Mass Pike and Storrow Drive; however, one must cross either the river or the highway to reach the subway.

Brighton begins within earshot of Allston Village's nightly din, and stretches all the way to the borders of tranquil Newton and Brookline. Home to its share of undergraduates and recent grads, particularly around the BC campus, it is nonetheless peppered with a heavier mix of families and young professionals. **Comm Ave**, accompanied by the B Line, winds westward through Brighton, lined with apartment complexes and the occasional restaurant, bar, or laundromat. Branching off Comm Ave to the south, you'll find more apartment buildings and peaceful, winding streets leading to Brookline; north of Comm Ave is **Aberdeen**, a hilly region of large single- and multi-family homes. To its northwest, where Chestnut Hill Avenue intersects with Washington Street, is recently gentrified **Brighton Center**, home to an established Irish population—and with it, some excellent pubs—and many orthodox Jews. Following Washington Street west (and downhill) will take you to **Oak Square** along the Newton border. This charming, hilly residential area—made up of mostly single- and multi-family homes—is fairly distant from any T lines, but is served by express buses to downtown and boasts a number of conveniences, including a library, fire station, bars, restaurants, easy access to the Mass Pike, and an affordable health club option in what is arguably the nicest YMCA in the city.

South from Brighton Center, where Chestnut Hill Avenue intersects Beacon Street at the Brookline border, is **Cleveland Circle**, home to many a BC student and young professional. Developed mostly between 1870 and 1950, architecture here reflects the Queen Anne, shingle, and classical revival styles for single-family homes, and classical and Georgian revival (as well as your basic 1950s and '60s block buildings) for apartment complexes. Benefits of this sub-neighborhood include its proximity to three Green Line trains (B, C, and D), not to mention the Chestnut Hill Reservoir and surrounding park.

While most of southern Brighton is very T accessible, having a car can be handy in Oak Square and Brighton Center, and borders on necessary farther into North Brighton by Market and North Beacon streets. Be advised: winter parking wars in Brighton are as fierce as anywhere in the city. Resident parking stickers are required in densely populated areas like Aberdeen, Cleveland Circle, and along Comm Ave.

Area Code: 617
Zip Codes: 02134, 02135
Post Offices: 47 Harvard Ave, Allston; 409 Washington St, Brighton
Police: District D-14, 301 Washington St, 617-343-4260; www.cityofboston.gov/police
Emergency Hospitals: St. Elizabeth's Medical Center, 736 Cambridge St, 617-789-3000, www.caritas-semc.org; Franciscan Hospital for Children, 30 Warren St,

617-254-3800, www.franciscanhospital.com; Kindred Hospital Boston, 1515 Comm Ave, 617-254-1100, www.kindredbos.com

Libraries: Allston Branch, 300 N Harvard St, 617-787-6313; Brighton Branch, 40 Academy Hill Rd, 617-782-6032; Faneuil Street Branch, 419 Faneuil St, Brighton, 617-782-6705; www.bpl.org

Parks & Open Space: Charles River Reservation; Chestnut Hill Reservoir; Chandler Pond/St. John's Seminary; Soldiers Field/Harvard Athletic Fields; Ringer Playground; Rogers Park; McKinney Playground; Hobart Park; www.mass.gov/dcr, www.cityofboston.gov/parks

Community Publication: *Allston-Brighton TAB*, 617-254-7530, www.townonline. com/allston/

Community Resources and Web Sites: www.cityofboston.gov; www.allston village.com; www.brightonmainstreets.org; www.oaksquare.com; Allston-Brighton Community Development Corporation, www.allstonbrightoncdc. org; Jackson/Mann Community Center, 500 Cambridge St, 617-635-5153; Community Rowing, 1400 Soldiers Field Rd, 617-782-9091; Allston/Brighton APAC, 143 Harvard Ave, 617-783-1485, www.bostonabcd.org; Allston-Brighton YMCA, www.ymcaboston.org; Brighton Board of Trade, 617-787-9049, www.brightonbot.com; Brighton Allston Historical Society, www.bahistory. org; for area colleges and universities, see the **Childcare and Education** chapter.

Public Schools: Boston Public Schools, 26 Court St, 617-635-9000, www.boston publicschools.org

Public Transportation: *Trains*: Green Line B trolleys run between BC and downtown with many surface stops along Comm Ave; Green Line C trolleys run down Beacon Street through Brookline, from Cleveland Circle to downtown; Green Line D trolleys are accessible in Cleveland Circle from the Reservoir stop and go downtown.

Buses: #57 (Watertown Yard–Kenmore Station via Brighton Center), #66 (Harvard-Dudley Sq via Allston and Brookline), #86 (Cleveland Circle–Sullivan Sq Station via Harvard), Express Bus #501 (Brighton Center–Downtown via Oak Sq), Express Bus #503 (Brighton Center–Copley Sq via Oak Sq); for MBTA route and schedule information contact the MBTA Traveler's Information Center: 617-222-3200, 800-392-6100, or go to www.mbta.com.

BACK BAY

Boundaries: **North**: the Charles River; **East**: Arlington St & the Public Garden; **South**: (roughly) the Mass Pike/Huntington Ave/Columbus Ave; **West**: Mass Ave/Charlesgate East

Sitting on the steps of your $7 million Comm Ave townhouse on a quiet spring morning, gazing at your neighbors' ivy-covered, Beaux-Art brownstones across the lush green mall, it's easy to believe—save for the cars—that this area hasn't changed in 200 years. Boy, how wrong you'd be. Almost two centuries ago, what is now the Back Bay consisted of swampy mudflats, a byproduct of the 1819 damming of the Charles River. So nasty and foul-smelling, this area was declared "nothing less than a cesspool" by the Boston City Council. In 1849, the health department demanded the land be filled, and thus the Back Bay was born—one of Boston's several landfill projects that ultimately reshaped the face of the city. From 1857 to 1882, mostly Irish laborers filled more than 450 acres in the Back Bay basin with earth and gravel shipped in 24 hours a day, 6 days a week, from quarries in Needham. The outcome: yet another splendid neighborhood for Boston's lucky affluent. What a difference 25 years can make.

Architect Arthur Gilman, who laid out the Back Bay's streets according to Baron Haussmann's Parisian boulevard model, designed a carefully planned community of Victorian architecture. However, the Back Bay diverges from (and perhaps improves upon) this tradition, in that his streets hold to a strict grid pattern. No pretty-but-perplexing pathways risen from footpaths here; instead, stick-straight thoroughfares run east to west (Beacon, Marlborough, Commonwealth, Newbury, Boylston, St. James, and Stuart), intersected by smaller residential cross streets arranged in alphabetical order (from Arlington to Hereford). This sensible and easily navigable scheme is indeed a welcome rarity in this town.

Comm Ave runs up the center of the Back Bay, which, unlike most other streets here, has two-way traffic—divided by a grassy, tree-lined, and statue-filled mall. In the winter, the mall comes alive with twinkling Christmas lights. Residents, particularly dog owners, stroll amidst the varied monuments honoring such figures as Alexander Hamilton and Phillis Wheatley.

The Back Bay presents a dream come true for architecture buffs, home to too many significant structures to give full due here. Let it suffice to say that most of the buildings survive from the Victorian era, inspired by various European styles of the time, particularly French and Italian. Coexisting with the quiet brownstones are such Boston greats as the Boston Public Library, a relic of the Italianate Renaissance style; the Prudential building, or "Pru," which was the Back Bay's first skyscraper, built in 1964; and of course, I.M. Pei's sleek, 790-foot-high John Hancock Tower. New England's tallest building overcame a tumultuous introduction to the cityscape. Besides the obvious difficulties associated with building a 60-story structure on top of landfill, when it was first constructed, its giant, 500-pound windowpanes would often come crashing down to the streets below during high winds. Problems sorted out, the John Hancock Tower now stands as the city's crowning jewel in Copley Square, reflecting the Romanesque beauty of neighboring Trinity Church in its shimmering blue glass, as well as its 26-story predecessor across the street, commonly known as the "Old Hancock Building." (The Old Hancock Building sports a still-used weather beacon on its rooftop—to interpret its signals, use this poem: *Steady blue, clear view / Flashing blue, clouds are due / Steady red, rain ahead / Flashing red, snow instead.* A flashing red light in the summertime doesn't forecast the end of the world, but close—the Red Sox game has been cancelled.)

While Comm Ave, Marlborough, and Beacon streets are predominantly residential, Newbury and Boylston streets act as commercial centers. Boylston Street has more offices to complement its selection of stores, restaurants, and bars, while Newbury Street is referred to as Boston's "Rodeo Drive," offering upscale shopping to hordes of people. Perhaps more visible here than Boston's moneyed residents is the concentration of wealthy and often flashy international tourists and college students who glide in and out of posh boutiques, private art galleries, and chic cafés.

When the Back Bay was first developed, many of Boston's wealthy relocated here from Beacon Hill and the South End, moving into what were then brand new mansions. It remains a coveted and pricey neighborhood. If you are lucky enough to be in the Back Bay price bracket, it poses a variety of living options, including transformed or preserved mansions on quiet and shady Comm Ave or Marlborough Street, apartments above the bustle and trendy stores of Newbury Street, or modern luxury condos found in the Pru or in high-rises on Beacon Street, which afford views of the city or the Charles River, respectively.

While the Back Bay is unquestionably one of the most desirable addresses in the city, there are still some things to keep in mind when house or apartment hunting here. The parking situation can be very difficult (as with anywhere else in the heart of the city), but the Back Bay's numerous public alleys mean some homes do come with a parking spot—for a price, to be sure, but at least it's an option. Resident sticker–only parking prevails on the streets, and the wider, planned layout means that, while tricky, it's easier for a resident to find parking here than in the North End or Beacon Hill. Also note that the Back Bay was no less affected than any of Boston's other neighborhoods during the city's post-WWII decline that lasted, by some accounts, into the 1980s. During these years, many of the magnificent mansions were purchased and converted into apartments, school dorms, and even fraternity houses for some of Boston's colleges. As a result, you may come across some apartments that tote a high Back Bay price, but reflect a more "student-ghetto" quality. Lastly, it's worth mentioning that during and after mild winters, mice and rats can become a problem; this is especially apparent in the alleys behind Newbury and Boylston streets, where restaurant dumpsters double as rodent bistros.

By car and public transport, the Back Bay is one of the most convenient locations in the city. Drivers have easy access to the rest of downtown, Storrow Drive (to I-93), and the Mass Pike. Follow Comm Ave straight into Allston-Brighton, Beacon Street into Brookline, or simply cross the Mass Ave Bridge to reach Cambridge. The Green Line makes four stops here, while the Orange Line and most trains in and out of South Station stop at Back Bay Station.

In addition to its shopping and dining delights, the Back Bay has all the standard amenities, including a Shaw's supermarket in the Pru and a Trader Joe's on Boylston for the value-minded grocery gourmet. The city's best parks (the Public

Garden, Boston Common, and Charles River Esplanade) are all a short walk away, and nearby institutions like Symphony Hall, the Boston Ballet, and the French Library complement Newbury Street's art galleries to please the culture-conscious. No matter what your taste, if you want to live comfortably smack dab in the middle of the action, the Back Bay is a good choice.

Area Code: 617

Zip Codes: 02115, 02116, 02117, 02199

Post Offices: 207 Mass Ave; 31 St. James St; Prudential Center, 800 Boylston St

Police: District D-4, 650 Harrison Ave, 617-343-4250, www.cityofboston. gov/police

Emergency Hospitals: Mass General Hospital, 55 Fruit St, 617-726-2000, www. massgeneral.org; Boston University Medical Campus/Boston Medical Center, 88 E Newton St and 771 Albany St, 617-638-5000, www.bumc.bu.edu

Libraries: Central Library, Copley Square, 700 Boylston St, 617-536-5400, www. bpl.org; Goethe Institute, 170 Beacon St, 617-262-6050; French Library and Cultural Center, 53 Marlborough St, 617-912-0400, www.frenchlibrary.org

Parks & Open Space: Clarendon Street Playground; Comm Ave Mall; Boston Common; Public Garden; Charles River Esplanade and Charles River Reservation; Charlesgate; Copley Square; www.mass.gov/dcr, www.cityofboston. gov/parks

Community Publications: *Boston Courant,* 617-267-2700; *Back Bay Sun,* 617-523-9490, www.backbaysun.com

Community Resources and Web Sites: www.cityofboston.gov; www.boston backbay.com; Community Boating, 21 David Mugar Way, 617-523-1038, www. community-boating.org; Back Bay Chorale, 617-730-7430, www.backbay chorale.org; Blackstone Community Center, 50 W Brookline St, 617-635-5162; Gibson House Museum, 137 Beacon St, 617-267-6338; BosTix (half-price ticket outlet), Copley Sq, www.artsboston.org; Hynes Convention Center, 900 Boylston St, 617-954-2000; Prudential Center, 800 Boylston St, 800-746-7778, www.prudentialcenter.com; Copley Place, 100 Huntington Ave, 617-369-5000, www.simon.com; Lyric Stage, 140 Clarendon St, 617-437-7172; Boston Architectural Center, 320 Newbury St, 617-262-5000, www.the-bac.edu; Neighborhood Association of the Back Bay (NABB), www.nabbonline.com; for area colleges and universities, see the **Childcare and Education** chapter.

Public Schools: Boston Public Schools, 26 Court St, 617-635-9000, www.boston publicschools.org

Public Transportation: *Trains:* Green Line at Arlington, Copley, Hynes, and Prudential (all trains go to Arlington and Copley, all but the E train go to Hynes, and only the E train goes to Prudential); Orange Line, Commuter Rail, and Amtrak service at Back Bay Station.

Buses: for MBTA route and schedule information contact the MBTA Traveler's Information Center: 617-222-3200, 800-392-6100, or go to www.mbta.com.

BEACON HILL/WEST END

Boundaries: *Beacon Hill*: **North**: Cambridge St; **East**: Bowdoin St; **South**: Beacon St; **West**: Storrow Dr; *West End*: **North**: Nashua St; **East**: Staniford St; **South**: Cambridge St; **West**: the Charles River

Former home to such notable figures as Louisa May Alcott, Nathaniel Hawthorne, Daniel Webster, John Hancock, and Henry James, there is perhaps no place more quintessentially Boston than Beacon Hill. This neighborhood has the dubious distinction of being the only one of Boston's three original hills to remain, although at the end of the 18th century its top 60 feet were removed for the construction of North Station. Initially referred to as Sentry Hill for the guards who stood watch, its name eventually changed to reflect the 65-foot-tall beacon pole complete with a flame pot that was positioned on its crest in 1634, to be lighted in the event of an enemy attack. So well preserved is this neighborhood, with its gorgeous brick row houses, gaslights, redbrick sidewalks, and occasional cobblestone street, that one is virtually transported back to America's earlier days. Horses and carriages come to mind in this neighborhood of opulence. Architectural styles in Beacon Hill include Federal, Greek, and Victorian revivals, mixed in with early 20th-century colonial revivals and tenements. Thanks to the birth of the Beacon Hill Historic District in 1955 and the strict architectural restraints it imposes upon residents, Beacon Hill's distinct historical architecture will be preserved.

An area that measures barely one square mile, Beacon Hill consists of the South Slope, the North Slope, and the Flat of the Hill. The **South Slope**, developed for Boston's wealthiest families in the early 19th century, is what most people imagine when they think of Beacon Hill. Its carefully laid-out streets of townhouses, window boxes, ornate doorways, pear trees, and hidden courtyards rise up from Charles Street, the neighborhood's main commercial thoroughfare and home to a variety of unique and upscale restaurants and stores. Between Charles Street and Storrow Drive is the **Flat of the Hill**, a landfill that was originally part of the Charles River. Some larger homes in this area look as though they would make apt settings for an Edith Wharton novel. Toward the top of the hill between Pinkney and Mount Vernon streets lies the pride of Beacon Hill, **Louisburg Square**—a privately-owned grassy park surrounded by a cobblestone way and townhouses. On the other side of the hill descends the **North Slope** and its more colorful history. Over the years, Bostonians of simpler means have called this area home, including freed slaves and immigrants from Eastern and Southern Europe. Significant sites along the Black Heritage Trail are found here. Although slightly less fancy than the South Slope, this side of the hill still fetches otherworldly prices for its brick walk-ups and tenement-style buildings.

Home to the Bulfinch-designed Massachusetts State House at the top of Beacon Street, with its imposing structure and golden dome, Beacon Hill has always been Boston's premier seat of wealth, power, and prestige. In years past, area residents represented a stronghold of Boston's most elite social aristocracy, collectively entitled the "Brahmins" by Dr. Oliver Wendell Holmes in 1860. More recently, money has spoken louder than pedigree, and most of the Brahmin caste has moved off the Hill in search of greener and more suburban pastures, replaced by successful newcomers.

Your money will buy decidedly less (space-wise) in Beacon Hill than it would elsewhere in an already pricey town. The amount you might pay for a decent-sized apartment outside of Beacon Hill may only be enough to fetch a cramped, Manhattan-esque closet in this neighborhood—albeit a safe, well-located closet with a gorgeous exterior. When house hunting here, be aware that building interiors can vary from lovely redone homes worth every penny to shoddily built money pits whose exterior majesty hides major, original design flaws—or just centuries of wear and tear. While many residences have been updated to support modern conveniences, if the abundance of laundromats in the area is any indication, many buildings have not been fully modernized. The neighborhood itself, however, has moved into the current century in terms of amenities, if not aesthetics. Drug stores, a Whole Foods, ethnic and upscale restaurants, bars, coffee shops, and other services are all within walking distance. Beacon Hill is Boston's hub, with the Theater District, Chinatown, the Back Bay, North Station, City Hall Plaza, Boston Common, the Public Garden, and the Esplanade only minutes away on foot. Yet, despite being positioned amidst the most bustling areas of Boston, the seat of local government, and nearby major roadways, Beacon Hill is startlingly residential, quiet, and homogeneous.

Depending on where you live on the hill, getting to public transportation might require a slight walk. But that is clearly preferable to searching for on-street parking, which is as bad as it gets in the city and requires a resident permit sticker (see **Getting Settled** for more information about residential parking permits). Most homes here lack garages, making Beacon Hill one of the few places in the US where you can find millionaires cleaning snow off their cars on cold winter mornings. A parking garage underneath the Boston Common supplements the few street spots for residents.

The North Slope of Beacon Hill runs down to include parts of Boston's **West End**. This former neighborhood was razed during the massive urban renewal Boston experienced in the late 1950s and early '60s under Mayor John B. Hynes. Like so many of Boston's neighborhoods, for years this area was home to the newly arrived: in the late 1800s, the Irish edged out the African-Americans, and they then gave way to Italians and a mix of Jews, Greeks, Polish, Armenians, and Syrians. It was 1958 when the city, hoping to create a business center here, wrote the area off as blighted and ruthlessly razed the West End via eminent domain, displacing thousands of residents. A few historic buildings were preserved at the last minute, such as the first Harrison Gray Otis House and the Vilna Shul, but much of the rest was wiped out. Although the West End still officially exists, some Bostonians would give you a puzzled look if you asked for it by that name.

The area, flanked by Government Center and Cambridge Street as it runs to the Charles, is mostly devoted to Massachusetts General Hospital, the Mass Eye & Ear Infirmary, and a few high-rise apartment complexes like Charles River Park—with its infamous billboard that, facing suburban commuters trapped in traffic on Storrow Drive, reads, "If you lived here, you'd be home now." In terms of culture and local amenities, however, the West End as a residential enclave is no longer.

Area Code: 617

Zip Codes: *Beacon Hill*: 02108, 02114; *West End*: 02114

Post Offices: 136 Charles St; 25 New Chardon St; State House, 24 Beacon St, Room 2

Police: District A-1, 40 New Sudbury St, 617-343-4240, www.cityofboston. gov/police

Emergency Hospital: Mass General Hospital, 55 Fruit St, 617-726-2000, www. massgeneral.org

Libraries: West End Branch, 151 Cambridge St, 617-523-3957; Kirstein Business Branch, 20 City Hall Ave, 617-523-0860, www.bpl.org; Boston Athenaeum (private membership for proprietors and shareholders), 10-1/2 Beacon St, 617-227-0270, www.bostonathenaeum.org; Congregational Library, 14 Beacon St, 617-523-0470, www.14beacon.org

Parks & Open Space: Boston Common; Public Garden; Esplanade and Charles River Reservation; Louisburg Square; www.mass.gov/dcr, www.cityofboston. gov/parks

Public Schools: Boston Public Schools, 26 Court St, 617-635-9000, www.boston publicschools.org

Community Publication: *The Beacon Hill Times*, 617-523-9490, www.beaconhill times.com

Community Resources and Web Sites: www.cityofboston.gov; www.beaconhill online.com; Community Boating, 21 David Mugar Way, 617-523-1038, www. community-boating.org; Museum of Science, Science Park, 617-723-2500, www.mos.org; Museum of African American History, 46 Joy St, 617-725-0022, www.afroammuseum.org; Black Heritage Trail and Boston African American National Historic Site, 617-742-5415, www.nps.gov/boaf; Boston City Hall, City Hall Plaza, Congress St; Massachusetts State House, 24 Beacon St, 617-727-3676; Beacon Hill Civic Association, www.bhcivic.org; for area colleges and universities, see the **Childcare and Education** chapter.

Historical Sites in this area are too numerous to list, but a few of import are: First Harrison Gray Otis House, 141 Cambridge St, 617-227-3956; African Meeting House, 46 Joy St and 8 Smith Ct, 617-742-5415; Old Historic Vilna Synagogue, 14 Phillips St; Charles Nichols House Museum, 55 Mount Vernon St, 617-227-6993; Granary Burying Ground, Tremont and Bromfield Sts; King's Chapel and Burying Ground, 58 Tremont St, 617-227-2155; Park Street Church, One Park St, 617-523-3383.

Public Transportation: *Beacon Hill*: *Trains*: Red Line at Charles/MGH and Park St; Green Line at Park St, Government Center, and Science Park; Blue Line at Government Center and Bowdoin; www.mbta.com.
Buses: for MBTA route and schedule information contact the MBTA Traveler's Information Center: 617-222-3200, 800-392-6100, or go to www.mbta.com.

CHARLESTOWN

Boundaries: **North**: Mystic River; **East**: Boston Harbor; **South**: Charles River; **West**: roughly, I-93

Charlestown, just across the Charles River from downtown, was settled even before Boston in the late 1620s, and served as the first capital of the Massachusetts Bay Colony. It was also the departure point for Paul Revere's famous "Midnight Ride," an event reenacted here each April 17th. However, it is probably best known, at least historically, for the Battle of Bunker Hill. In 1775, one of the first and bloodiest battles of the Revolutionary War took place here on Breed's Hill (not Bunker Hill), and the American patriots lost. But no matter! The battle served as an important moral victory for the revolutionary forces because, despite being overmatched and outnumbered, the ragtag colonial militia inflicted heavy casualties on the superior British army. The 221-foot-tall Bunker Hill Monument was erected in the early 19th century to commemorate this brave stand, and residents are treated to a Bunker Hill Day parade each June.

After the battle, the British burned the eastern section of the town to the ground, and so the oldest surviving buildings in Charlestown date back to the 1780s, when post-war reconstruction began. The Warren Tavern on Pleasant Street, built in 1780 and named after one of the patriots who died at Bunker Hill, is the oldest tavern in New England. A national historic district, Charlestown has many homes dating from the 18th and 19th centuries representing the Federal, Greek Revival, and Queen Anne styles. Its look is similar to that of Beacon Hill, with masonry and wooden clapboard row houses and gas-lit cobblestone sidewalks, but it costs much less to live here. Apartments and homes are nice, many have been redone, and they tend to be significantly larger than their downtown counterparts—not to mention the fact that parking here, though regulated by resident permit in the "downtown" portion, is substantially less aggravating.

Long a working-class neighborhood with a substantial and close-knit Irish-American population that dates back to the 1800s, Charlestown experienced a rapid gentrification in the 1980s and '90s. As an example, the Charlestown Navy Yard, which employed thousands of local blue-collar workers from its opening in 1801 to its closure in 1974, now houses a National Historic Park and luxury waterfront condominiums. Today, long-time "townies" share their neighborhood with a burgeoning Latino population near the Bunker Hill housing development and young professionals and families seeking a safe urban setting with colonial charm.

Newcomers may feel most comfortable residing in the areas closest to the Bunker Hill Monument, namely Monument Square, City Square, and Thompson Square—enclaves that are designations in name more than in distinct characteristics. **Monument Square** is, as you might expect, the area directly surrounding the Bunker Hill Monument. As you head down the western slope of the hill you will come to **Thompson Square** and **City Square**, the northern and southern ends, respectively, of Main and Warren streets. These one-way streets run parallel to each other in opposite directions and form the main drags through the heart of Charlestown. Here you will find the area's largest cluster of small businesses and restaurants. On the more southerly side of the hill is **Winthrop Square** or **Training Field**, a plot of green set aside in 1632 for the local militia to practice drills that is now surrounded by rather desirable housing. Heading down the other side of the hill is Bunker Hill Street. It's in this direction where you will find the less attractive areas of northwestern Charlestown, including the Schraffts Building and **Sullivan Square**—a traffic circle on the Somerville border where much of Charlestown's public transportation converges.

As mentioned, the **Navy Yard** is an option for those seeking high-end luxury condos in one of the gray slate buildings on Charlestown's historic waterfront. The Freedom Trail cuts right through the site where, for close to two centuries, thousands of warships were constructed, repaired, or launched to serve in the US Navy. Tourists flock to the USS *Constitution* (dating from 1797, the oldest commissioned ship still afloat in the world), its museum, and the Charlestown Visitor's Center. But the Navy Yard is also a working port with ferries to Boston, the Courageous Sailing School, and restaurants and bars such as the Tavern on the Water, whose two floors and balcony positively bust at the seams in the summer. In the Navy Yard, a pretty penny will buy you a dreamlike view of Boston and the Harbor, with modern conveniences like high-speed internet access, fitness rooms, concierge service, and garage parking. Beware of parking near the Navy Yard, though, especially on 1st Avenue (parallel to Route 1), as petty car breaks can be a nuisance.

For some, a downside of Charlestown is that while charming, safe, clean, and residential, it can also feel a little isolated. Charlestown may afford divine views of Boston, but you are looking at the city from a distance and are distinctly not in it. Instead, it has more of a friendly little village feel, with only a few restaurants and bars. There is a full size Foodmaster supermarket, and Todd English (Boston's biggest restaurateur) established two of his trademark restaurants here: Figs and Olives. The Orange Line provides T access to downtown, but its infrequency is legendary, and neither of its local stops is especially close to the major residential areas. Then again, in nice weather you can simply walk across the Charlestown Bridge and reach the North End in about 15 minutes, and driving into the city or to the northern suburbs via I-93 or Route 1 is easy. But if you are someone who needs to be in the thick of things, Charlestown might just be a little too quiet and out of the way for you.

Area Code: 617

Zip Code: 02129

Post Office: 23 Austin St

Police: District A-5, 40 New Sudbury St, 617-343-4240; www.cityofboston. gov/police

Emergency Hospital: Mass General Hospital, 55 Fruit St, 617-726-2000; www. massgeneral.org

Library: Charlestown Branch, 179 Main St, 617-242-1248, www.bpl.org

Parks & Open Space: Monument Square; Charlestown Naval Shipyard Park; City Square; John Harvard; Training Field/Winthrop Square; Barry Playground; www.mass.gov/dcr, www.cityofboston.gov/parks

Community Publication: *Charlestown Patriot-Bridge,* 617-241-8500, www. charlestownbridge.com

Community Resources and Web Sites: www.cityofboston.gov; http://charles town.ma.us; Charlestown Community Center, 255 Medford St, 617-635-5169; Golden Age Center, 382 Main St, 617-635-5175; Kent Community Center, 50 Bunker Hill St, 617-635-5177; Bunker Hill Burying Ground; Bunker Hill Monument, 617-242-5641, www.nps.gov/bost/Bunker_Hill.htm; USS Constitution Museum, Charlestown Navy Yard, 617-426-1812, www.ussconstitution museum.org; Navy Yard Visitor Center and Bunker Hill Pavilion, Outside Gate 1, Constitution Rd, 617-242-5601, www.nps.gov/bost/Navy_Yard.htm; for area colleges, see the **Childcare and Education** chapter.

Public Schools: Boston Public Schools, 26 Court St, 617-635-9000, www.boston publicschools.org

Public Transportation: *Trains:* Orange Line at Community College and Sullivan Sq

Buses: for MBTA route and schedule information contact the MBTA Traveler's Information Center: 617-222-3200, 800-392-6100, or go to www.mbta.com.

Boats: Charlestown Navy Yard (Pier 4)–Long Wharf; www.mbta.com

DORCHESTER

Boundaries: North: Columbia Rd; **South:** Neponset River and Cummins Hwy; **West:** Harvard St and Franklin Park; **East:** Dorchester Bay and Boston Harbor

Dorchester is the city's largest neighborhood in terms of both population and size, and perhaps the quintessential embodiment of rough-around-the-edges, working-class Boston—not unlike its most famous native son, actor Mark Wahlberg. Long reputed as one of Boston's dodgier areas, Dorchester is enjoying a renaissance of sorts. Not that it is without its rough patches, but by and large "Dot" is quite livable and worth thinking about if you'd like to live in Boston but are of modest means. The cost of housing here is markedly below the city's average: you can rent a three-bedroom apartment here for the cost of a one-bedroom in the more glamorous addresses of downtown Boston, Brookline, or Cambridge.

Founded in 1630 when a group of Puritans landed at what is now **Columbia Point** (where the Kennedy Library and UMASS-Boston are located), Dorchester was annexed by Boston in 1870. Some of the region's oldest historical sites are here, including the city's oldest standing house, the 1648 Blake House on Columbia Road, and the Dorchester North Burying Ground, which dates back to 1633. On Parish Street, on top of **Meeting House Hill**, is the Mather School—founded in 1639, it is the nation's oldest elementary school.

Today, Dorchester Avenue, also known as "Dot Ave," is the neighborhood's main drag, home to Irish pubs, bakeries, Southeast Asian markets, and West Indian grocers selling fragrant curries and spices. Downtown Boston is minutes away via either the Red Line or car—which you won't mind having in Dorchester since it is not too difficult to find parking. (Then again, the main route into the city, I-93, is pretty much the last place you'll want to be during rush hour.) There are some parks and open spaces, and waterfront access as well—Malibu Beach, while no match for its Californian cousin, nonetheless offers a marina, baseball field, playground, and pleasant promenade. The most significant outdoor area is along Dorchester's eastern border, where you will find Franklin Park (the final link in Olmsted's **Emerald Necklace**—more about that in the **Greenspace** chapter) and the Franklin Park Zoo.

Dorchester has a racially diverse population that includes well-established Vietnamese and Haitian communities. The Vietnamese population is concentrated between the **Savin Hill** and **Fields Corner** sub-regions of east Dorchester. Residents run the gamut socio-economically, from those living below the poverty line, to working-class families, to upwardly mobile professionals. Given the cultural and economic diversity—and the only very recent move toward gentrification here—housing is affordable.

With its large size and such a vast range in population demographics, it should come as no surprise that Dorchester is comprised of many smaller sub-neighborhoods. Many of these are generally safe, but some are still in transition and others far worse than that. The volunteer citizen patrol group, the Guardian Angels, returned to Boston in 2007—after fifteen years of absence—in response to a recent surge in violence centered in Dorchester and neighboring Roxbury; Boston also had to revive the Operation Ceasefire program here, an attempt to reduce inner-city violence by breaking up gangs. Specifically, trouble spots include Blue Hill Avenue and the Washington Street corridor, which runs through Dorchester Center and includes the **Codman Square** and **Four Corners** neighborhoods. The area around **Dudley Street** in north Dorchester and Roxbury is one of Boston's most economically depressed neighborhoods.

Despite these rougher areas, some of Boston's most beautiful Victorian homes are in Dorchester, mingling with a proliferation of wooden triple-deckers from the early 1900s on quiet side streets. There are too many sub-neighborhoods with their own nuances to list, and it will be a personal choice as to which area is most suitable, but as a general rule, newcomers may be more comfortable in the areas with train service, including (from north to south, roughly around Dorchester Avenue) the **JFK/UMASS**, Savin Hill, Fields Corner, **Shawmut**, and **Ashmont** neighborhoods. Primarily residential in nature, the JFK/UMASS area sees a lot of students and tourists, and its eponymous T stop also provides access to Morrissey Boulevard, a highly commercial and not-so-pedestrian-friendly strip. Other sub-regions in southern Dorchester worth considering include **Adams Village,** around the intersection of Adams Street and Gallivan Boulevard, and **Neponset**, in southeast Dorchester by the Neponset River Reservation.

Area Code: 617
Zip Codes: 02121, 02122, 02124, 02125
Post Offices: 554 Washington St; Fields Corner, 218 Adams St; 647 Warren St; Uphams Corner, 551 Columbia Rd
Police: District C-11, 40 Gibson St, 617-343-4330, www.cityofboston.gov/police/c11.asp
Emergency Hospitals: Carney Hospital, 2100 Dorchester Ave, 617-296-4000, www.carneyhospital.org; Boston Medical Center, One Boston Medical Center Pl, 617-638-8000, www.bmc.org
Libraries: Lower Mills Branch, 27 Richmond St, 617-298-7841; Uphams Corner, 500 Columbia Rd, 617-265-0139; Codman Square Branch, 690 Washington St, 617-436-8214; Adams Street Branch, 690 Adams St, 617-436-6900; Fields Corner Branch, 1520 Dorchester Ave, 617-436-2155; www.bpl.org
Parks & Open Space: Tenean Beach; Columbia Point; Savin Hill/Malibu Beach; Dorchester Park; Franklin Park, Franklin Park Golf Course, and Franklin Park Zoo (www.zoonewengland.com); Neponset River Reservation; Ronan Park; www.mass.gov/dcr, www.cityofboston.gov/parks
Community Publications: *Boston Irish Reporter*, 617-436-1222, www.bostonirish.com; *Dorchester Community News*, 617-282-3543; *The Dorchester Reporter*, 617-436-1222, www.dotnews.com; *Boston Haitian Reporter*, 617-436-1222, www.bostonhaitian.com
Community Resources and Web Sites: www.cityofboston.gov; www.bostonmainstreets.com; www.ashmonthill.org; www.scidorchester.org; John F. Kennedy Presidential Library & Museum, Columbia Point, 877-616-4599, www.jfklibrary.org; Bayside Expo Center, 200 Mt. Vernon St, 617-474-6000, www.baysideexpo.com; Cleveland Community Center, 11 Charles St, 617-635-5141; Holland Community Center, 85 Olney St, 617-635-5144; Marshall Community Center, 35 Westville St, 617-635-5148; Murphy Community Center, 1 Worrell St, 617-635-5150; Perkins Community Center, 155 Talbot Ave, 617-635-5146; Louis D. Brown Peace Institute, 1452 Dorchester Ave, 617-825-1917, www.louisdbrownpeaceinstitute.org; Bird Street Community Center, 500 Columbia Rd, 617-282-6110, www.birdstreet.org; Jones Hill Neighborhood Association,

www.joneshill.com; Columbia–Savin Hill Civic Association, www.columbia savinhillcivic.org; Popes Hill Neighborhood Association, www.popeshill.org; Dorchester Historical Society, www.dorchesterhistoricalsociety.org; for area colleges and universities, see the **Childcare and Education** chapter.

Public Schools: Boston Public Schools, 26 Court St, 617-635-9000, www.boston publicschools.org

Public Transportation: *Trains*: Red Line at JFK/UMASS, Savin Hill, Fields Corner, Shawmut and Ashmont; Commuter Rail at JFK/UMASS

Buses: for MBTA route and schedule information contact the MBTA Traveler's Information Center: 617-222-3200, 800-392-6100, or go to www.mbta.com.

DOWNTOWN

Boundaries: *Financial District/Downtown Crossing*: **North**: State St; **East**: Atlantic Ave; **South**: Essex St; **West**: Tremont St; *Chinatown*: **North**: Essex St; **East**: Lincoln St/I-93; **South**: E Berkeley St; **West**: Tremont St; *Leather District*: **North**: Essex St; **East**: Atlantic Ave; **South**: Kneeland St; **West:** I-93/Surface Rd

A few places you may not have considered include those in the downtown area, such as Chinatown, the Leather District, and the Financial District/Downtown Crossing. Depending on your needs, they may be worth more than a passing thought.

Like so much of Boston, **Chinatown** and its lesser-known sub-neighborhood the **Leather District** are landfill areas dating from the 1800s. From the 1840s to the 1890s, immigrants from around the world poured into the area; eventually it was the Chinese who stayed, forming what is now one of the largest Chinatown neighborhoods in the US. Many had worked temporarily on the transcontinental railroad or as strikebreakers in Lawrence factories, and gained employment here laying phone lines for the nearby central office of Bell Telephone Company. Further immigration was greatly limited by the Chinese Exclusion Act of 1882, but Boston's slowly growing Asian population gained steam when some of those stringent immigration laws were repealed during the 1940s. Recent censuses indicate that Boston's Asian population is growing at an annual rate of over 10%.

With immigrants comprising more than half its residents, Chinatown is an active community with a long history of standing up to city-wide projects that threatened its survival, such as the development of the Central Artery, Mass Pike, and New England Medical Center. Residents here were also crucial to the success of cleaning up the (now defunct) "Combat Zone," a red light district of porn shops, strip clubs, and other tawdry businesses. Today, Chinatown concerns itself with the business of welcoming not only tourists, but immigrants from all over Asia, including Japan, Vietnam, Korea, and Thailand, and helping them adapt to life here.

Like the North End, Chinatown is full of three- to five-story buildings with ground-level storefronts and restaurants, topped by densely packed apartment space above. But unlike Boston's other famous ethnic enclave, many buildings have a more utilitarian look about them, and the gentrification of recent years has brought a number of new luxury apartment towers, such as the 28-story Archstone high-rise. Chinatown restaurants have the uncommon distinction of literally burning the midnight oil: not only do Bostonians frequent Chinatown for the most authentic Asian cuisine at 7 p.m., but they also flock in at 2 a.m., since it is one of the few areas in the city where restaurants are open late. Parking is difficult here, but Interstate 93 and the Mass Pike are easily accessible, and so is the rest of downtown Boston (especially the Common and the Theater District), by car, foot, T, or bus.

Just east of the Chinatown Gate, across Surface Road, is the small, up-and-coming **Leather District**. After a good portion of Boston was wiped out by the Great Fire of 1872, the leather industry established itself in this corner, and remained here until the 1940s and '50s when the Central Artery construction threw the neighborhood into chaos. In more recent years, artists have been moving into the somewhat revitalized Leather District, using the 19th-century brick warehouses as galleries, studios, and loft space. Restaurants have cropped up to cater to new residents, and with South Station, Boston's main bus and train terminus, just across the street, as well as I-93, Route 1, and the Mass Pike, it's a convenient place to live. Although some lofts are priced for struggling artists, others are more expensive, attracting professionals who work in the nearby financial district.

The **Financial District/Downtown Crossing** and areas in between are just what you would expect: non-residential and devoted mostly to office workers and tourists. As its name implies, the Financial District is home to a lot of the city's suits scuttling in and out of the tall buildings that hover around Post Office Square. During weekdays and weeknights, the many bars and restaurants are bustling with lunch and post-work crowds, but on weekends the area is almost deserted. Downtown Crossing is an adjoining open-air shopping zone centered on the pedestrian-only portions of Washington, Summer, and Winter streets. Once a thriving retail hub, the area has floundered a bit of late, as some large stores have closed or relocated; many remain however, as do the pushcart vendors. The Freedom Trail cuts through here, taking tourists past the Old State House and the Old South Meeting House, and the newly restored Opera House and state-of-the-art AMC Loews Boston Common Movie Theater bring both culture and crowds. Though these areas of Boston are almost entirely commercial, luxury developments like the Devonshire in the Financial District, and upscale buildings along the Common on Tremont Street, provide homes for those who can afford them. Obviously, there's no real sense of neighborhood here, but some find the views, the location, the doormen, and the luxurious living satisfying enough to call it home. Parking is a challenge, but if you can afford to live in the Ritz-Carlton apartments on Tremont, then you can probably handle the additional cost for a private garage space.

Area Code: 617

Zip Codes: 02101-02111, 02208-02210

Post Offices: 7 Avenue de Lafayette; 25 Dorchester Ave; 31 Milk St

Police: District A-1, 40 New Sudbury St, 617-343-4240; www.cityofboston.com/police

Emergency Hospitals: New England Medical Center, 750 Washington St, 617-636-5000, www.nemc.org; Mass General Hospital, 55 Fruit St, 617-726-2000, www.massgeneral.org

Libraries: Chinese Cultural Center, 30 Kneeland St, 617-426-9881; Kirstein Business Branch of the Boston Public Library, 20 City Hall Ave, 617-523-0860 (this branch is specialized toward business reference and research; your closest and best bet for a general library is the Central Library at 700 Boylston St, 617-536-5400, www.bpl.org)

Parks & Open Space: Boston Common; Public Garden; Post Office Square Park; www.mass.gov/drc, www.cityofboston.com/parks

Public Schools: Boston Public Schools, 26 Court St, 617-635-9000, www.bostonpublicschools.org

Community Publications: *Banker and Tradesman,* 617-428-5100, www.bankerandtradesman.com; *Boston Business Journal,* 617-330-1000, www.boston.bizjournals.com; *Boston Chinese News,* 617-338-1170, www.bostonchinesenews.com; *The Jewish Advocate,* 617-367-9100, www.thejewishadvocate.com; *Sing Tao Newspaper,* 617-426-9642, www.singtaousa.com; *World Journal–Chinese Daily News,* 617-423-3347, www.worldjournal.com

Community Resources and Web Sites: www.cityofboston.gov; Boston Chinatown Neighborhood Center, 38 Ash St, 617-635-5129, www.bcnc.net; Leather District Neighborhood Association, 617-482-1239, www.leatherdistrictboston.com; Old State House and Museum/Bostonian Society, 206 Washington St, 617-720-1713, www.bostonhistory.org; Old South Meeting House, 310 Washington St, 617-482-6439, www.oldsouthmeetinghouse.org; King's Chapel and Burying Ground, 64 Beacon St, 617-227-2155, www.kings-chapel.org; Orpheum Theatre, 1 Hamilton Pl, 617-679-0810; Granary Burying Ground, Tremont and Bromfield Sts; Park Street Church, 1 Park St, 617-523-3383; Asian American Civic Association, 200 Tremont St, 617-426-9492, www.aaca-boston.org

Public Transportation: *Trains*: Orange Line at Chinatown, State, Downtown Crossing, and New England Medical Center; Blue Line at Government Center and State; Red Line at South Station, Park St and Downtown Crossing; Green Line at Boylston, Park St, and Government Center

Buses: for MBTA route and schedule information contact the MBTA Traveler's Information Center: 617-222-3200, 800-392-6100, or go to www.mbta.com.

EAST BOSTON

Boundaries: North: Suffolk Downs and the Chelsea River; **East:** Logan Airport, Bells Isle Inlet, Boston Harbor; **West:** Boston Harbor; **South:** Boston Harbor and Logan Airport

East Boston, or "Eastie," as residents call it, is another of Boston's neighborhoods built on landfill. Once upon a time, East Boston, which paradoxically in no place touches Boston proper and is only connected to the city by tunnels, was actually five separate islands in Boston Harbor. Who knew? For the first two centuries after Boston was settled, Noddle's Island, Hog (or Breed's) Island, Governor's Island, Apple Island, and Bird Island were primarily under private ownership and used for farming, grazing, and military fortifications. In 1833, General William H. Sumner, owner of Noddle's Island, got caught up in the landfill craze that swept Boston and formed the East Boston Company. Sumner and his company filled in the marshes between Noddle's Island and Hog Island to form the major commercial and residential portion of East Boston. In 1923, the company disbanded, but construction of Logan International Airport began when the waters surrounding the three remaining islands were filled in.

East Boston's ample waterfront has greatly influenced its character over the years. Initially promoted as a resort community, the large Victorian homes built for vacationers changed hands and character when East Boston became a shipbuilding center. In came people to work in the shipyards. Eastie was also transformed into an immigrant processing center second only in this region of the country to New York's Ellis Island. Between the Civil War and WWI, Eastie welcomed waves of Canadians, Irish, Italians, and Russian and Eastern European Jews to its industrial areas along the waterfront for work. Single-family homes were converted into multi-family units, and brick apartment buildings and triple-decker tenements were built. To this day, Eastie maintains a strong Italian-American heritage, intermixed with new waves of immigrants who have been arriving since the 1960s: South Americans, Central Americans, Haitians, Southeast Asians, and Eastern Europeans. The variety of shops and restaurants that line the narrow streets are evidence of Eastie's diverse population.

Today, Eastie is a densely populated district that lacks the aesthetic charm of other downtown neighborhoods—though some sections, like Piers Park, do boast a spectacular view of the city skyline. The proliferation of the functional triple-deckers and homes with multi-colored stone fronts that survive from Eastie's shipbuilding years makes it feel more working-class than many areas of Boston. Though laid out in a grid pattern, the streets converge at angles in the main squares, creating traffic nightmares. Despite its less than polished environs, Eastie is a fairly safe, family-oriented neighborhood, home to many long-time residents. Women with babies in strollers and other children tagging along are plentiful, and there are still strong Italian and Hispanic Catholic communities. Amidst the triple-deckers, some large Victorian homes in predominantly Greek and colonial revival styles have survived. These are particularly evident in **Eagle Hill**, the section at the northwest tip of Eastie accessible from Meridian Street; **Jeffries Point**, at the southwest end of the residential area along Sumner Street; and **Brophy Park** (formerly Belmont Square), along Sumner Street between **Maverick Square** on Eastie's southwest end and Jeffries Point. Brownstones can be found on Webster Street, and the **Orient Heights** section in northeast Eastie has single-family homes with lawns clustered on its hill.

Those who live in Eastie are greatly affected by the presence of Logan International Airport and Suffolk Downs. Logan, one of the country's busiest airports, takes up an entire third of East Boston. While noise pollution is a concern to nearby residents, the Massachusetts Port Authority has instituted a project to reduce the effects on area homes in East Boston, Winthrop, Revere, and South Boston. Call MassPort's Noise Abatement Office for details at 617-561-1636. For those who like to play the ponies, Suffolk Downs offers live horse racing and closed circuit television broadcasts of cards from other tracks around the country.

While home prices in Eastie have increased dramatically in the last decade, it is still one of the most affordable neighborhoods in Boston; in fact, the Boston Housing Authority just completed an acclaimed new mixed-income housing development at Maverick Landing, steps from Boston Harbor, making over 300 rental units available to low- and middle-income families. Residents benefit from natural resources such as waterfront parks, Constitution Beach, and the Belle Isle Marsh, a large wetland area that gives some idea of what East Boston looked like before the landfill arrived. Despite its location across the harbor, it's just two or three stops from downtown on the Blue Line. Parking is relatively easy, and there is quick access to Route 1A heading north; however, drivers to and from the city are wholly dependent on the Sumner, Callahan, and Ted Williams tunnels. While it's a short (if claustrophobic) drive, and their steep tolls are discounted for local residents, traffic doesn't discriminate.

Area Code: 617

Zip Codes: 02128, 02228

Post Offices: 50 Meridian St; 139 Harborside Dr

Police: District A-7, 69 Paris St, 617-343-4220, www.cityofboston.gov/police

Emergency Hospitals: East Boston Neighborhood Health Center, 10 Grove St, 617-569-5800, www.ebnhc.org; offers urgent care service.

Libraries: East Boston Branch, 276 Meridian St, 617-569-0271; Orient Heights Branch, 18 Barnes Ave, 617-567-2516, www.bpl.org

Parks & Open Space: Belle Isle Marsh Reservation; Constitution Beach; Piers Park; Paris Street Pool, 113 Paris St, 617-635-5122; Brophy Park; www.mass.gov/dcr, www.cityofboston.gov/parks

Community Publications: *East Boston Sun Transcript*, 617-567-9600, www.eastie times.com; *Eastie Latino Magazine*, 617-233-5168, www.eastielatino.net

Community Resources and Web Sites: www.cityofboston.gov; www.eastbos

ton.com; www.ebmainstreets.com; East Boston Chamber of Commerce, 296 Bennington St, 617-569-5000, www.eastbostonchamber.com; Harborside Community Center, 312 Border St, 617-635-5114; Orient Heights Community Center, 86 Boardman St, 617-635-5120; Paris Street Community Center, 112 Paris St, 617-635-5125; Piers Park Sailing Center, 95 Marginal St, 617-561-6677, www.piersparksailing.org; Jeffries Yacht Club, 565 Sumner St, 617-567-9656, www.jeffriesyachtclub.com; East Boston Social Centers, 68 Central Sq, 617-569-3221, www.ebsoc.org; Italia Unita (Italian-American cultural organization), 617-562-3201, www.italiaunita.org; East Boston Artists Group, 617-569-4907; Neighborhood of Affordable Housing, www.noahcdc.org; East Boston Foundation, 617-561-6336, www.eastbostonfoundation.com

Public Schools: Boston Public Schools, 26 Court St, 617-635-9000, www.boston publicschools.org

Public Transportation: *Trains*: Blue Line stops at Maverick, Airport, Wood Island, Orient Heights, and Suffolk Downs

Buses: #112 (Wellington–Wood Island via Central Ave, Mystic Mall and Admiral's Hill); #114/116/117 (Wonderland-Maverick via Revere St), #120 (Orient Heights–Maverick via Bennington St, Jeffries Point, Waldemar Loop); #121 (Wood Island–Maverick via Lexington St); for MBTA route and schedule information contact the MBTA Traveler's Information Center: 617-222-3200, 800-392-6100, or go to www.mbta.com

Ferries: Logan Airport–Long Wharf–Quincy Shipyard; Logan Airport–Pemberton Point, Hull; www.mbta.com

FENWAY/MISSION HILL

Boundaries: *Fenway*: **North**: Storrow Dr/Charles River; **East**: Charlesgate East & Mass Ave; **South**: Tremont and Ruggles Sts; **West**: BU Bridge, St. Mary St and the Riverway; *Mission Hill*: **North**: Huntington Ave; **East**: Ruggles St; **South**: Heath St; **West**: the Riverway and Jamaicaway

Home to many of Boston's educational, cultural, and sporting institutions, residentially the Fenway is often overlooked, particularly by newcomers. It is, in fact, similar to the South End in terms of population and socio-economics, but without all the flash it rarely gets due press. Thirty-three thousand call the Fenway home, and it is about one and a quarter square miles in size, radiating outwards from the Back Bay Fens, the first of Frederick Law Olmsted's parks. A latecomer to Boston's landfill and development projects, until the 1870s the area was yet another plot of stinky marshland. It was drained and Olmsted was commissioned to design the Fens, part of a seven-mile system of connected green space. The Fens consists of a reedy park around the man-made Muddy River, the Victory Gardens (public gardening plots made in 1942 of landfill excavated when the Kenmore T stop was constructed), the James P. Kelleher Rose Garden, and the baseball and basketball lots of Roberto Clemente Field.

Throughout the Fenway you will find a population of varying ethnic backgrounds, incomes, professions, and lifestyles. This neighborhood is minority-friendly, with significant gay and immigrant populations. Nearly half of its residents are students who attend one of the several major colleges located here.

With this mix of people comes a range of living options. Newly built and affordable housing developments (that is, complexes where at least one quarter of the units are made affordable to households earning less than 80% of the area's median income) stand shoulder to shoulder with luxury units. While there is some brand new construction here, like the Trilogy complex of luxury condos and shops on Brookline Avenue, most of the residential buildings reflect turn-of-the-century styles. You'll see a little more stonework mixed in with the brick bow fronts here, reminiscent of New York's Upper West Side. Rents are in the mid to high range for the city: slightly less than Beacon Hill, but more than Brookline or Jamaica Plain. A look at a building's exterior upkeep will usually tell you if it houses students or professionals, and the conditions of the apartments therein.

According to the active Fenway Community Development Corporation, the Fenway actually consists of five sub-neighborhoods: East Fenway, West Fenway, Kenmore Square, Longwood, and Audubon Circle. Roughly covering the area between the Fens, Mass Ave, and Tremont Street, **East Fenway** encompasses the big hitters of Boston's cultural and educational offerings. Here lies Northeastern University, Berklee College of Music, the Boston Conservatory of Music, the New England Conservatory of Music, Horticultural Hall, the Massachusetts Historical Society, and BU's Huntington Theatre. As such, East Fenway is crawling with academics, musicians, and sundry artist types, making their way to classes or concert halls. Visitors come from around the city, country, and globe to marvel at the gargantuan stone headquarters and reflecting pool of the Christian Science Church, to take in world-class exhibitions at the Museum of Fine Arts, and to hear the renowned Boston Symphony Orchestra perform in the perfect acoustics of Symphony Hall. Tiny tree-lined streets such as St. Botolph, which runs just behind the Christian Science Center, are quaint and unexpectedly quiet.

West Fenway stretches from the Park Drive side of the Fens northwards, and includes Lansdowne Street, a strip of loud and glitzy clubs and bars across from Fenway Park—the nation's oldest baseball stadium and home to the city's beloved Red Sox. While game days can mean hordes of oft-drunken fans, difficult-to-impossible parking, and gridlock traffic in most of West Fenway, the area between unsightly Boylston Street and scenic Park Drive is actually a lovely little neighborhood, home to a few of its own shops, restaurants, and bars.

Kenmore Square surrounds the T stop of the same name, where Brookline and Commonwealth avenues intersect with Beacon Street and Charlesgate. The Boston University campus dominates the Kenmore area, stretching west down Comm Ave all the way to Allston-Brighton. Once a gritty headquarters of Boston's underground scene, Kenmore Square is hardly recognizable to fans of its seedier days. Many local shops and bars have given way to national chains such as Barnes and Noble and Uno's, and longtime local standbys like the Deli-Haus keep disappearing as the gentrification process progresses. Housing in Kenmore Square reflects this transition, as you're likely to encounter shoddy student-variety digs or gleaming luxury condos, without much in between. The new 150-room Hotel Commonwealth in the heart of the square, for instance, can run upwards of $300 a night, but has also housed freshman BU students during dorm room shortages. Unless you are a student yourself, you'll probably want to look elsewhere in the Fenway for neighbors more accustomed to a nine-to-five schedule.

The BU population thins out somewhat toward **Audubon Circle**, roughly between Beacon Street and Brookline Avenue between Kenmore Square and Brookline. Although the area is mostly residential, the old Sears Building at the intersection of Brookline Avenue and Park Drive was recently converted into the Landmark Center. The complex now holds a number of mall-style megastores and the Fenway 13, a large movie theater with stadium seating and ample garage parking. A few privately owned restaurants and bars line Brookline Avenue between the Landmark Center and Kenmore Square.

Continuing southwest down Brookline Avenue across the Fenway will bring you to **Longwood**, or the **Longwood Medical Area**, so named for the cluster of hospitals located here. In addition to Beth Israel Deaconess, Children's Hospital, Dana-Farber, Brigham & Women's, and the Joslin Diabetes Center, Longwood also completes Fenway's educational and cultural offerings with Wheelock College, Emmanuel College, Simmons College, Mass College of Art, Mass College of Pharmacy, and Wentworth Institute of Technology. Longwood is also home to the extravagant Isabella Stewart Gardner Museum. An active and unconventional woman of the Victorian era who is rumored to have marched down Tremont Street with a lion, Isabella Stewart Gardner (nicknamed "Mrs. Jack") used her inheritance to construct a palatial home. She first opened her doors to the public in 1903, and upon her death in 1924, generously bequeathed her three-story Venetian palazzo and extensive art collection to the city.

All in all, the Fenway makes for a positive living experience. The most frequently heard complaint is, of course, the parking (or lack thereof), which is mostly on-street, regulated by resident sticker, and impacted by the large student population. Parking is even worse for those living near Fenway Park; aside from the flood of fans, there are also numerous game-day parking restrictions, so it's a good idea to take note of the Red Sox home schedule.

The Fenway is well served by the T, and offers fairly easy access to the area's major highways. Drivers can take Storrow Drive east at Charlesgate to reach Routes 93 and 1, and an entrance to the Mass Pike westbound is just up the road on Mass Ave. There is an additional (eastbound only) entrance to Storrow Drive near BU, and Jamaica Plain, Brookline, Allston-Brighton, and Cambridge (via the BU Bridge) are easy trips. It is also a safe neighborhood, with the exception of the

Fens at night—by day a lovely park for the community to enjoy, at night the Fens can be trouble and should be avoided.

Mission Hill, encompassing the three-quarter mile area just south of Longwood, and bordering Jamaica Plain (JP) and Brookline, is in the process of figuring itself out. Geographically, some official city groups lump Mission Hill in with the Longwood area, others group it with Roxbury, and still others consider Mission Hill an entity unto itself. In terms of neighborhood characteristics, simply put, Mission Hill is a community in progress: not quite up-and-coming, but slowly taking its fledgling steps toward that status. During Revolutionary War times, Mission Hill was made up of farms and large estates, followed by the establishment of breweries and a mass of German and Irish immigrants who worked in them. Long called Parker Hill after a man named John Parker who'd built his home at its peak, the name eventually changed to Mission Hill for the mission that German Redemptorist priests established in 1869. In 1876, they built the Mission Church, a twin-spired Romanesque basilica. Today the breweries are gone, but the cathedral remains. A national historic landmark, it is also a functioning church with services in Spanish and English. Parker Hill Avenue climbs up from Huntington to the actual hill, which is densely covered in homes. Much of the housing in Mission Hill dates from the late 1800s: Queen Anne homes coexist with triple-deckers, brick row houses, and some low-cost housing projects from the last century. In parts of Mission Hill, housing is notably dingy, but some buildings, such as those along the Riverway, are quite attractive and your dollar will buy a lot more space here than it would downtown.

For the better part of the 20th century, Mission Hill struggled with a reputation for crime and failed residential development projects. But post-2000, crime is down and the area is being revived. Organizations such as Mission Hill Main Streets and Empowerment Zone are dedicated to generating sustained community revitalization, and the city has invested $15 million to make Huntington Avenue more pedestrian-friendly and commercially viable. The student population has risen dramatically in recent years; students, like many families, young professionals, and medical staff from the neighboring Longwood area, are drawn to Mission Hill for its reasonable rents and convenient services. With the E train running down Huntington Avenue, residents can get to downtown in 10 to 20 minutes.

Despite recent efforts, safety is still an issue here. Reports of break-ins, drug dealing, and other crimes are common. Is Mission Hill safer than it was ten years ago? Absolutely. Should you leave your doors unlocked at night? No. Those accustomed to an edgier urban environment should have no problem feeling at home here.

Area Code: 617
Zip Codes: 02115, 02215, 02120
Post Offices: 207 Mass Ave; 11 Deerfield St; 1575 Tremont St

Police: *Fenway:* District D-4, 650 Harrison Ave, 617-343-4250; *Mission Hill:* District B-2, 135 E Dudley St, 617-343-4270; www.cityofboston.gov/police

Emergency Hospitals: Beth Israel Deaconess Hospital, 330 Brookline Ave, 617-667-7000, www.bidmc.harvard.edu; Brigham & Women's Hospital, 75 Francis St, 617-732-5500, www.brighamandwomens.org; Children's Hospital, 300 Longwood Ave, 617-355-6000, www.childrenshospital.org

Libraries: Central Library, Copley Sq, 700 Boylston St, 617-536-5400; Parker Hill Branch, 1497 Tremont St, 617-427-3820; www.bpl.org

Parks & Open Spaces: Back Bay Fens; Charles River Reservation; Charlesgate; Evans Way Park; Forsyth Park; Lee Playground–Clemente Field; Victory Gardens; Kelleher Rose Garden; Riverway; Southwest Corridor Park

Community Publications: *The Fenway News,* 617-266-8790; *The Boston Courant,* 617-267-2700; *Mission Hill Gazette,* 617-524-2626, www.missionhillgazette.com; *The Daily Free Press,* 617-232-6841, www.dailyfreepress.com

Community Resources and Web Sites: www.cityofboston.com; www.missionhillmainstreets.org; Symphony Hall, 301 Mass Ave, 617-266-1492, www.bso.org; Isabella Stewart Gardner Museum, 2 Palace Rd, 617-566-1401, www.gardnermuseum.org; Fenway Park, 4 Yawkey Way, 617-482-4SOX, www.redsox.com; Massachusetts Horticultural Society, 300 Mass Ave (Horticultural Hall), 617-933-4900, www.masshort.org; Massachusetts Historical Society, 1154 Boylston St, 617-536-1608, www.masshist.org; Museum of Fine Arts, 465 Huntington Ave, 617-267-9300, www.mfa.org; Huntington Theatre Company, 264 Huntington Ave; Fenway Cultural District, 617-437-7544, www.fenwayculture.org; Colleges of the Fenway, 475 Longwood Ave, 617-632-2729, www.colleges-fenway.org; Fenway Community Development Corporation, www.fenwaycdc.org; Tobin/Mission Hill Community Center, 1481 Tremont St, 617-635-5216; Mission Hill Neighborhood Housing Services, 1530 Tremont St, 617-442-5449, www.missionhillnhs.org; Mission Hill Artists Collective, www.geocities.com/mhacollective; for area colleges and universities, see the **Childcare and Education** chapter.

Public Schools: Boston Public Schools, 26 Court St, 617-635-9000, www.bostonpublicschools.org

Public Transportation: *Trains:* Green Line B, C & D trains to Hynes and Kenmore Sq; B train stops at Blanford St, BU East, BU Central, BU West; D train stops at Fenway and Longwood; E train stops at Prudential, Symphony, Northeastern, MFA, Longwood Medical Area, Brigham Circle, Fenwood Rd, Mission Park, Riverway, Back of the Hill, and Heath St; Orange Line at Ruggles

Buses: for MBTA route and schedule information contact the MBTA Traveler's Information Center: 617-222-3200, 800-392-6100, or go to www.mbta.com.

JAMAICA PLAIN

Boundaries: North: Heath St; **East:** Columbus Ave and Franklin Park; **South:** VFW Pkwy and Arnold Arboretum; **West:** Jamaica Pond and Brookline (Riverway and Chestnut St areas)

Welcome to Jamaica Plain! A one-time summer resort area for Boston's colonial and Federal-era rich and famous, "JP," as the locals call it, has become one of Boston's most ethnically, politically, and socio-economically diverse neighborhoods. Scenic Jamaica Plain, once called the "Eden of America," has four community centers, strong neighborhood associations, and lots of open space.

Different accounts exist as to how Jamaica Plain acquired its name, but sources at its historical society believe the area is named after a Native American woman named Jamaica who lived in the area. Settled in 1639 as a farming community, during the 1800s JP was transformed to accommodate the area's burgeoning industry, including breweries like those in neighboring Mission Hill. Along with German and Irish immigrant workers, Boston's elite came and set up summer homes along Jamaica Pond, lending a resort quality to the area. By 1874, Jamaica Plain, along with neighboring West Roxbury and Roslindale, was annexed by Boston.

In addition to the establishment of Boston's privileged on Jamaica Pond's shores, JP benefited greatly from Boston's parks and greenspace planning of the late 1800s. A major portion of Olmsted's park system is either in or adjacent to JP, including Olmsted Park, Jamaica Pond, the Arnold Arboretum, and Franklin Park. The posthumously named Olmsted Park consists of 180 acres of parkland with pedestrian and bike paths that connect the man-made Muddy River and Leverett Pond to the north with the naturally occurring Jamaica Pond to the south. This glacial kettle hole, which also happens to be the largest body of water within Boston's city limits, is so pristine it serves as the city's back-up reservoir. It's a popular outdoor recreation area where locals come to canoe, fish, jog, and sunbathe. The Arnold Arboretum came into being after 1842 when Benjamin Bussey left 250 acres of land to Harvard. The arboretum has over 15,000 trees and shrubs, and on the third Sunday of every May (Lilac Sunday) over 20,000 visitors come to see the many blossoms. Franklin Park, which Olmsted believed to be some of his best work, lies to the south and west of JP, and features a woodland preserve, golf course, and zoo. Not part of the Olmsted system, but still green and inviting, is the Forest Hills Cemetery just south of Franklin Park.

Today Jamaica Plain is a neighborhood with a strong sense of community identity. Artists and artisans sell their wares in front of the Arts Center on Centre Street, left-leaning political activists and locals alike help organize community-wide, multicultural festivals and parades, and long-time residents tend community gardens and take pride in their vibrant neighborhood. With brightly painted murals scattered about, the nation's oldest community theater group, and an art gallery at the Green Street T stop, the arts are a positively integral part of the JP experience. In terms of day-to-day life, you will probably find this neighborhood more like the Harvard and Central Square areas of Cambridge than any other area of Boston. Once home to e.e. cummings, Eugene O'Neill, and Anne Sexton, today JP has a large number of artists, writers, musicians, and graduate students from Harvard Medical School, Northeastern University, and Boston University. There is a thriving gay and lesbian population (especially lesbian), and, in addition to its considerable African-American populace, JP is home to Boston's largest Hispanic community.

Housing is relatively affordable in Jamaica Plain, but you will no longer find the bargains that were available here a decade ago. Apartment options mostly consist of triple-deckers or large single-family homes that were broken up into separate units. Condominiums and single-family homes are average-priced for the city as well. Whatever you are seeking, housing stock in JP is substantially roomier than that in downtown Boston, and you are far more apt to find other perks such as a lawn, garden, deck, and easy parking. Many of the homes and public structures in JP have survived from as early as the 18th century, and the intermingling of 200 years' worth of architecture contributes to the area's eclectic and colorful appearance. Triple-deckers, 1960s-style apartment complexes, live-in artists' studios, and shiny new cookie-cutter condos mix with large Federal, Gothic Revival, Queen Anne, Italianate, Greek Revival, Georgian, stick style, Second Empire, shingle style, and classic revival houses and mansions. There are also row houses along Centre Street, some public housing, and one luxury high-rise, the Jamaicaway Tower on Perkins Street.

JP's commercial spine is in the **Eliot Square** area along **Centre Street** and **South Street,** a charming stretch of one-of-a-kind shops and small businesses. Here you'll find an array of neighborhood pubs, like the laid-back James's Gate—an Irish pub with a full menu and cozy fireplace—ethnic restaurants, cafés, boutiques, and any other services you might need, including a Harvest Co-op market and the original J.P. Licks ice cream shop. **Hyde Square**, near the intersection of Centre and Perkins streets, is an up-and-coming area (to which realtors insist on attaching a "hip" moniker) with a higher concentration of ethnic grocers, including the large Hi Lo Hispanic supermarket, another beloved Irish pub, Brendan Behan's, and a combination dance club/bar/bowling alley/eatery, the Milky Way Lounge and Lanes. As you progress farther eastward on Centre Street, there is a large public housing project near the Jackson Square T stop, and the surrounding area is still in the midst of transformation; freshly painted, remodeled homes stand alongside beaten-up triple-deckers and neglected lots.

Like the South End, JP is generally safe, but not without some criminal activity. Small crimes and housebreaks sometimes occur, and women especially should take care not to walk alone at night. As a general rule, newcomers may feel more comfortable in the west of JP along the Brookline border, particularly the pond-side area, and the western section of central Jamaica Plain, the area between the Arboretum and South Street, as well as **Sumner Hill** or **Forest Hills.**

Although JP does feel somewhat distant from downtown, it's not as far as you might think, and its relaxed, green, and friendly atmosphere more than makes up for the distance. For those with pets, JP is probably a good option to consider due to the space (both in the homes and greenspace outside) and the higher likelihood of finding a pet-friendly building. There are a number of public transportation options that can get you downtown fairly quickly, including the Orange Line, buses, and the Green Line's E Train. If you have a car, parking in JP is not too difficult; sometimes it is regulated by resident sticker, although winter parking can be difficult along the more densely populated streets.

Area Code: 617

Zip Code: 02130

Post Office: 655 Centre St

Police: District E-18, 1249 Hyde Park Ave, 617-343-5600; District E-13, 3347 Washington St, 617-343-5630, www.cityofboston.gov/police

Emergency Hospitals: Faulkner Hospital, 1153 Centre St, 617-983-7000, www.faulknerhospital.org; Beth Israel Deaconess Medical Center, 330 Brookline Ave, 617-667-7000, www.bidmc.harvard.edu; Brigham & Women's Hospital, 75 Francis St, 617-732-5500, www.brighamandwomens.org; Children's Hospital, 300 Longwood Ave, 617-355-6000, www.childrenshospital.org; Lemuel Shattuck Hospital, 170 Morton St, 617-522-8110, www.mass.gov/dph/hosp/lsh.htm

Libraries: Connolly Branch, 433 Centre St, 617-522-1960; Jamaica Plain Branch, 12 Sedgwick St, 617-524-2053; www.bpl.org

Parks & Open Space: Arborway; Arnold Arboretum, www.arboretum.harvard.edu; English High Athletic Fields; Forest Hills Cemetery; Jamaica Pond/Jamaica Park; Olmsted Park; Franklin Park, Franklin Park Golf Course, and Franklin Park Zoo (www.zoonewengland.com); Riverway; Southwest Corridor Park; www.mass.gov/dcr, www.cityofboston.gov/parks

Community Publication: *Jamaica Plain Gazette*, 617-524-2626, www.jamaicaplaingazette.com

Community Resources and Web Sites: www.cityofboston.gov; www.jamaicaplain.com; www.boston-online.com/jp; Agassiz Community Center, 20 Child St, 617-635-5191; Curtis Hall Community Center, 20 South St, 617-635-5193; English High Community Center, 144 McBride St, 617-635-5244; Hennigan Community Center, 200 Heath St, 617-635-5198; Footlight Club, www.footlight.org; Green Street Gallery, www.greenstreetgallery.com; Samuel Adams Brewery, 30 Germania St, 617-522-9080, www.samadams.com; Arborway Coalition, www.arborway.net/coalition; Emerald Necklace Conservancy, 617-232-5374, www.emeraldnecklace.org; Arborway Committee, 617-222-3085, www.arborway.net/lrv/; JP Historical Society, 617-524-5992, www.jphs.org; JP Community Center, 617-635-5201, www.alri.org/ltc/jpalp; JP Neighborhood Development Corporation, www.jpndc.org; Hyde Square Task Force, 375 Centre St, 617-524-8303, www.hydesquare.org

Public Schools: Boston Public Schools, 26 Court St, 617-635-9000, www.boston publicschools.org

Public Transportation: *Trains*: Orange Line at Stony Brook, Green St and Forest Hills; Green Line E train at Riverway, Back of the Hill, and Heath St; Commuter Rail at Forest Hills Station

Buses: for MBTA route and schedule information contact the MBTA Traveler's Information Center: 617-222-3200, 800-392-6100, or go to www.mbta.com.

NORTH END/WATERFRONT
(NORTH END AND DOWNTOWN PORTIONS)

Boundaries: *North End*: **North**: Commercial St; **East**: Commercial St and Atlantic Ave; **South**: Cross St; **West**: Cross St and N Washington St; *Waterfront*: **North and East**: Boston Harbor; **South**: Fosters Wharf; **West**: Commercial St and Atlantic Ave

Boston's first residential neighborhood, the North End was home to wealthy merchants and tradesmen of the Revolutionary era before it gave way to the booming shipping and mercantile industries in the early 1800s. During this period of rapid economic growth and physical expansion—nearly 70 acres of unusable marshland and mudflats were reclaimed through landfill projects, allowing the construction of new wharves and waterfront warehouses—the neighborhood also degenerated into a hotbed of disrepute, attracting drunken sailors, gamblers, criminals, and prostitutes. By the mid-19th century, the area had deteriorated into a slum, and so began the North End's relationship with the newly arrived. This tiny, impoverished corner of the city welcomed, in succession, African-Americans fleeing slavery, thousands of Irish fleeing the Great Famine, Jews fleeing persecution in Eastern Europe, and, finally, the Italians who would make this neighborhood what it is today: the epicenter of Boston's ethnic Italian community, our own Little Italy.

By its peak in 1930, there were more than four times as many Italians living in the North End as there are *total* residents in the neighborhood today. More and more long-time inhabitants have either moved or been forced out by rising rents—its location in the heart of the city, quaint narrow streets, abundance of restaurants, and tight-knit sense of community make the North End a desirable place for young professionals to live. Still, almost half of the residents remain of Italian descent, and you will still be greeted by vestiges of the Old World: singing in the streets, clotheslines strung between alleyways, and the smell of garlic in the air.

The North End's dense concentration of restaurants (almost all of which specialize in Italian cuisine), cafés, and charm, combined with historical sites along the Freedom Trail such as the Old North Church and Paul Revere's House, make it one of the most visited sections of Boston. Its latticework of narrow streets is filled day and night with tourists and locals, young and old, and on several summer weekends the community sponsors ornate parades and festivals to honor the feast days of various patron saints.

Isolated from the rest of the city for years by the monstrosity that was the Central Artery—a looming, congested, double-decker highway running through the center of the city—the North End is finally reaping the benefits of the Big Dig's completion. With I-93 now beneath the city, the site of the old highway is being landscaped into the Rose Kennedy Greenway, making it a peaceful and easy stroll from the North End to Faneuil Hall and all of downtown. This has also served to make the neighborhood a more attractive living option—for a long time, noise, air pollution, and other side effects of Big Dig construction kept rents and home prices somewhat in check. Rents here are still slightly more reasonable than those in the Back Bay or Beacon Hill neighborhoods, though. Apartments can run the gamut from old, dark, and confined labyrinths to nicely refurbished units, and many buildings have roof decks with city views. Those who can afford to live in town are drawn to the North End by its lively character, central location, and reputation as one of Boston's safest neighborhoods.

The North End's main strip is the densely populated Hanover Street, with its three- and four-story brick walk-ups, many of which have ground-level storefronts and restaurants. During the warmer months, wonderful smells from hundreds of Italian kitchens combine with the friendly and animated conversations in the street, many of which are even in Italian, creating a warm and inviting atmosphere. There are no large stores here—there's no room for them—so grocery shopping is done as it is in Europe, in little butcher shops, produce shops, and bakeries that primarily run along Salem Street. (Those with cars can drive to the Whole Foods in Government Center or Foodmaster in Charlestown.) Street parking in the North End is unpleasant to say the least, and permitted with resident sticker. The situation grows even more desperate in the winter, when residents will defend parking spaces they've struggled to shovel out. There are parking provisions for visitors, but those spots are extremely hard to come by; regular visitors often head straight for one of several parking lots and garages in the area.

A word of caution: if it is peace and quiet you are looking for, the North End may not be for you. Many may find the constant hustle and bustle comforting, but with people constantly talking, singing or even yelling in the streets, trucks rumbling through even into the wee hours of the morning, and the occasional sirens of ambulances and fire engines, the North End is a little noisy. The side streets not directly surrounding Hanover Street are less clamorous.

Like many parts of the city, Boston's **Waterfront** neighborhood is being transformed by current city developments. While various city neighborhoods, including Charlestown, Southie, Eastie, and Dorchester, greet the Atlantic, when one hears reference to "the Waterfront," it usually means this region along the harbor running from the North End to downtown. Starting at the Charlestown

Bridge, the Waterfront is a mixed-use area with businesses, restaurants, upscale condos, and converted warehouses situated along wharves. Specifically, Constitution, Battery, Lincoln, Union, Sargent's, Lewis, and the North Commercial and South Commercial wharves make up the **North End Waterfront**. In addition to the stunning views across the harbor of the USS *Constitution* and Charlestown, the Waterfront is blessed with two nice parks. The North End Playground, at the northern end next to the Coast Guard Pier, includes tennis and bocce courts, baseball fields, and an outdoor swimming pool and skating rink. At the southern end, where the North End and Downtown waterfronts intersect, is Christopher Columbus Park, a patch of green along the water with a fountain and a picturesque wisteria and vine arbor.

Long, Central, India, Rowes, and Foster wharves pick up where the North End Waterfront leaves off, blending imperceptibly into the **Downtown Waterfront**. With the dust of the Big Dig finally settled, the Downtown Waterfront is a great place to call home, particularly if you work in the nearby Financial District, and it consistently attracts a social crowd of tourists, diners, and drinkers. With its gorgeous views, proximity to the Financial District, and happening restaurants, this area is popular with Boston's after-work crowd, especially in the summer. From the first warm night of the season until the last one, the Waterfront bubbles with a happy crowd.

Less residential and more tourist-oriented than other Boston enclaves, the Downtown Waterfront is home to a few of the city's more impressive hotels and restaurants. Here, amidst all the water traffic—tour boats, whale watches, water taxis, booze cruises—you will find the New England Aquarium, the stunning Boston Harbor Hotel, and the Marriott Long Wharf. And lest we forget the Custom House, the stately, 496-foot-tall clock tower dominates the cityscape and now houses, of all things, a Marriott.

Area Code: 617

Zip Codes: 02113, 02109, 02110

Post Offices: 217 Hanover St; Post Office Square, 90 Devonshire St; 25 New Chardon St; 7 Avenue de Lafayette

Police: District A-1, 40 New Sudbury St, 617-343-4240, www.cityofboston. gov/police

Emergency Hospital: Mass General Hospital, 55 Fruit St, 617-726-2000, www. massgeneral.org

Library: North End Branch, 25 Parmenter St, 617-227-8135, www.bpl.org

Parks & Open Space: North End Playground; Christopher Columbus Park; Paul Revere Mall; www.mass.gov/dcr, www.cityofboston.gov/parks

Public Schools: Boston Public Schools, 26 Court St, 617-635-9000, www.boston publicschools.org

Community Resources and Web Sites: www.cityofboston.gov; www.northend boston.com; Saint Leonard's Community Center, 44 Prince St, 617-523-0350;

Faneuil Hall, 15 State St, www.faneuilhallmarketplace.com; New England Holocaust Memorial, Carmen Park at Congress and Union Sts; Haymarket (open on Fridays and Saturdays); Paul Revere and Pierce/Hitchborn House, 19 North Sq, 617-523-2338, www.paulreverehouse.org; Old North Church, 193 Salem St, 617-523-6676, www.oldnorth.com; Copp's Hill Burial Ground, Charter St at Snowhill St; New England Aquarium, Central Wharf, 617-973-5200, www.neaq.org; TD Banknorth Garden, 100 Legends Way, 617-624-1050, www.td banknorthgarden.com

Public Transportation: *Trains*: Orange Line at Haymarket, State, and North Station; Green Line at Government Center, Haymarket, and North Station; Blue Line at Government Center, State, and Aquarium; Commuter Rail at North Station

Buses: for MBTA route and schedule information contact the MBTA Traveler's Information Center: 617-222-3200, 800-392-6100, TTY 617-222-5246 or go to www.mbta.com.

Boats: note: you must differentiate the public transportation listed here from the tour boats (cruises, whale watches, harbor tours) and privately owned water taxis that stop on many points along the harbor for a higher cost: Rowes Wharf–Hingham Shipyard; Long Wharf–Charlestown Navy Yard; Long Wharf–Pemberton Point, Hull; Long Wharf–Quincy Shipyard–Logan Airport; www.mbta.com

ROSLINDALE

Boundaries: **North**: VFW Pkwy and Arnold Arboretum; **East**: Forest Hills Cemetery and Mt. Hope Cemetery; **South**: Stony Brook Reservation; **West**: W Roxbury Pkwy and Centre St

Although Roslindale is not serviced by the subway (buses and commuter trains run here) and parts have a very suburban feel, it is a part of Boston. Like JP, Roslindale, referred to affectionately as "Rozzie" (or "Roslinopoulos" for its substantial Greek population) was annexed by Boston in 1874. A rural area until the late 1880s, Roslindale is a classic example of a streetcar suburb (minus the streetcars, these days), and many of its homes date from one of its two building booms: the first in the 1890s and the second in the 1920s and '30s. Public churches, schools and institutional buildings built during these times are all still extant and have been the focus of the Roslindale Village Main Street program, a project sponsored by the National Trust for Historic Preservation. Amongst the utilitarian triple-deckers and low-rises added in the 20th century are some impressive examples of Gothic Revival and Empire Baroque architecture, including an enormous "summer house" on Metropolitan Avenue built by William Fox of 20th Century Fox before he lost all his money (and the house) during the Great Depression.

Roslindale is a moderate-density residential area: over 75% of its housing stock consists of one- to four-unit buildings, usually with backyards. A good deal of housing, particularly along Washington Street, which runs the length of the neighborhood, is of the triple-decker variety with stacked balconies. An example of function over form, these homes can pack in three families but are distinctly plain, and many, especially those closer to Jamaica Plain, could use some upkeep. Then again, the **Centre Street** side of the neighborhood, closer to West Roxbury, is lined with some lovely homes. Housing options here are similar to what you might find in JP—lots of room for a good price.

Residents love Roslindale most for its quiet feel, cultural diversity, and ample greenspace. To the south, the Stony Brook Reservation is a 500-acre forest in the city, next to which is the George Wright golf course. To the north and east, Roslindale is bordered by the Arnold Arboretum and Mt. Hope Cemetery, respectively. **Roslindale Square** or **Roslindale Village** (either is correct) is the heart of the community, and its cluster of small businesses—including restaurants like the cozy, Mediterranean-themed Sophia's Grotto, and bakery cafés like Fornax—offer Rozzie residents the charm of a small town within city limits. The only thing lacking is a nightlife scene—and many consider this a plus. By far the most active (and perhaps attractive) part of Roslindale's real estate market is the area between Roslindale Village and the Arboretum.

While most homes here have driveways, making parking much less of a hassle than in other parts of the city, there is no direct route into Boston, so trips downtown will be marked by back roads, traffic lights, and stop-and-go traffic. Public transit options here are not great; the Commuter Rail's Needham Line stops at Roslindale Village and brings riders downtown in just 16 minutes, but even at rush hour it only comes by each half hour, and on Sundays it doesn't operate at all. There is also bus service to the Orange Line at Forest Hills, but most residents still find it difficult to live in Roslindale without a car.

Area Code: 617
Zip Code: 02131
Post Office: 16 Cummins Hwy
Police: District E-5, 1708 Centre St, W Roxbury, 617-343-4560, www.cityofboston. gov/police
Emergency Hospitals: VA Hospital, 1400 VFW Pkwy, 617-323-7700, www.va.gov; Faulkner Hospital, 1153 Centre St, JP, 617-983-7000, www.faulknerhospital. org
Library: Roslindale Branch, 4238 Washington St, 617-323-2343, www.bpl.org
Parks & Open Space: Arnold Arboretum, www.arboretum.harvard.edu; Fallon Field; Franklin Park, Franklin Park Golf Course, and Franklin Park Zoo, www. zoonewengland.com; George Wright Golf Course, www.georgewrightgolf course.com; Healy Playground; Hillside Street Play Area; Metropolitan Avenue Urban Wild; West Roxbury Parkway; Stony Brook Reservation, www.mass.

gov/dcr, www.cityofboston.gov/parks

Community Publication: *West Roxbury and Roslindale Transcript*, 617-327-2608, www.townonline.com/roslindale

Community Resources and Web Sites: www.cityofboston.gov; www.roslindale. net; Archdale Community Center, 125 Brookway Rd, 617-635-5256; Flaherty Pool, 160 Florence St, 617-635-5181; Roslindale Community Center (with pool), 6 Cummins Hwy, 617-635-5185

Public Schools: Boston Public Schools, 26 Court St, 617-635-9000, www.boston publicschools.org

Public Transportation: *Trains*: Needham Line Commuter Rail at Roslindale Village

Buses: for MBTA route and schedule information contact the MBTA Traveler's Information Center: 617-222-3200, 800-392-6100, TTY 617-222-5246 or go to www.mbta.com.

SOUTH BOSTON

Boundaries: **North**: Boston Harbor; **East**: Boston Harbor, Pleasure Bay and Castle Island; **West**: Fort Point Channel and I-93 (Southeast Expressway); **South**: Dorchester Bay and Columbus Park

One of Boston's most famous neighborhoods, South Boston, or "Southie," as it's commonly known, has an identity and pride all its own. This Irish-Catholic enclave, long notorious for its rough streets and high concentrations of white poverty and housing projects—not to mention its ties to the Irish mafia—has come a long way in recent years, emerging as an increasingly popular (and expensive) place to live. Close to downtown, relatively safe, and chock full of pubs, restaurants, and beaches, Southie has a lot to offer the young professionals who have flocked here. Besides increasing property values, this trend has changed the area's personality somewhat—many old, dingy pubs have either revamped themselves or given way entirely to more upscale establishments one wouldn't have ever expected to see here. As is the case with the North End, many locals bemoan the transition, and would have the neighborhood remain entrenched in its solid ethnic heritage and customs.

The city of Boston originally annexed South Boston in 1804, building a bridge to connect it with downtown, and laid out the community on a grid, naming the streets by letters and numbers—a hallmark that denotes a Southie address to this day. As the 1800s rolled on, industry grew in the area and in came the immigrant laborers, most notably the Irish, who stayed and made South Boston their own. The rise and reign of the Irish in local politics throughout the 20th century ensured there were plenty of civil service jobs available to Southie men, and the neighborhood, despite gentrification, still reflects its working class roots.

Essentially, South Boston can be divided in half: between the **South Boston Waterfront**, also known as the **Seaport District** (both names are bandied about for this developing neighborhood), and then the rest of South Boston—what most people mean when they say "Southie." The South Boston Waterfront/Seaport District covers the northern portion of South Boston and lies just across the channel from downtown and South Station, bordered by Boston Harbor to the north and Fort Point Channel to the west. The city has been trying to encourage mixed-use development of this largely industrial area; recently completed are the Boston Convention Center and Seaport Hotel, the new Institute of Contemporary Art, and a number of hotels, offices, and luxury condominium complexes. More planning is in the works, and a few restaurants have begun filling in the gaps as the area attracts increasing numbers of residents and tourists, but much of it remains a blank slate. The Museum Wharf between the Congress Street and Northern Avenue Bridges is a well-established tourist destination, with the Children's Museum and the Boston Tea Party Ship and Museum. To the north along the harbor you will find the US Federal Courthouse on Fan Pier, the World Trade Center on Commonwealth Pier, and the Bank of America Pavilion (waterfront concert venue) on Wharf 8. Fish Pier is where much of the local catch comes in each day. Many restaurants here capitalize on their waterfront location, attracting locals and tourists alike with their selections of fresh seafood; the view at Anthony's Pier 4 and the happy-hour buzz of the Barking Crab keep both regularly packed. The sub-section of the South Boston Waterfront/Seaport District that abuts the channel is sometimes referred to as **Fort Point Channel**, which is similar to the Leather District with which it is virtually contiguous. Those who move here often use the warehouses for both work and living space; it's particularly popular with artists.

The rest of South Boston is less glitzy than the Waterfront area. Here is the long-time stronghold of Boston's Irish population, and, accordingly, home of the city's annual St. Patrick's Day Parade. Like East Boston, Southie is full of triple-deckers and row houses, but somehow the buildings seem to have weathered the years better here than in Eastie. The main strip, Broadway, is host to a healthy mix of commercial and residential activity. West Broadway covers "**Lower Southie**," closer to downtown Boston, where the homes are packed more tightly together and parts appear very industrial. If you travel east on Broadway (until it becomes East Broadway), you will encounter more contemporary construction, including condos and apartment complexes from the 1960s, mixed in with lovely Victorian brick bow fronts and clapboard homes. Once you reach the **City Point** neighborhood by Pleasure Bay, the homes, most built in the last 100 years, are spacious and have lawns. Film buffs may enjoy knowing that the L Street Tavern here was the local bar in the film *Good Will Hunting*.

Southie is a practical and fairly safe place to live—most crime is limited to car breaks and bar fights. While apartments are priced a bit higher than in JP or Brighton, it is still quite affordable given its proximity to downtown. Parking is relatively easy, and all the services you need are nearby, including, of course, authentic Irish pubs. While it cannot rival JP's abundance of greenspace, Southie has cornered the market on ocean access with three miles of public beaches. Good for walks and safe for swimming, the oceanfront at City Point and Southie's south shore attracts local residents as well as those from elsewhere in the city. Every New Year's Day, the "L Street Brownies" depart from the Curley Recreational Facility (or "L Street Bathhouse") to one of these beaches for their yearly polar bear plunge. Pleasure Bay, at the eastern tip of Southie, offers a calm, enclosed lagoon for swimming, and affords walking access to Fort Independence on Castle Island. Originally constructed in 1779 at the command of George Washington (it was rebuilt in the pre–Civil War era), this five-bastioned granite fortification in the shape of a pentagon provided the inspiration for Edgar Allan Poe's "The Cask of Amontillado." It is open to the public, and there are guided tours every weekend during the summer. And lest you think Olmsted left this area of the city untouched, he is responsible for the Strandway, the green strip from Castle Island to Columbus Park.

In terms of public transportation, Southie is accessible, but a little complicated—the Red Line only services Lower Southie (at the Andrew and Broadway stops), and the Silver Line operates between the Seaport District and South Station. Buses cover the rest of the area fairly well, however, including the #9 and #10 routes, which run all the way from City Point to Copley Square in the Back Bay.

Area Code: 617

Zip Codes: 02210, 02127

Post Offices: 444 E 3rd St; 25 Dorchester Ave

Police: District C-6, 101 W Broadway, 617-343-4730, www.cityofboston. gov/police

Emergency Hospitals: Mass General Hospital, 55 Fruit St, 617-726-2000, www. massgeneral.org; New England Medical Center, 750 Washington St, 617-636-5000, www.nemc.org

Libraries: South Boston Branch, 646 E Broadway, 617-268-0180; Washington Village Branch, 1226 Columbia Rd, 617-269-7239; www.bpl.org

Parks & Open Space: Carson Beach; Castle Island; City Point Beach; Columbus Park; Independence Square; L and M Street Beaches; Marine Park; Thomas Park/Telegraph Hill; www.mass.gov/dcr, www.cityofboston.gov/parks

Community Publications: *The Irish Emigrant*, 617-268-8322, www.irishemigrant. com; *South Boston Tribune*, 617-268-3440, www.southbostoninfo.com

Community Resources and Web Sites: www.cityofboston.gov; www.south bostononline.com; Condon Community Center, 200 D St, 617-635-5100; Curley Community Center, 1663 Columbia Rd, 617-635-5104; PAL/Walsh McDonough Gym Community Center, 535 E Broadway, 617-635-5640; Tynan Community Center, 650 E 4th St, 617-635-5110; Boston Children's Museum, 300 Congress St, 617-426-8855, www.bostonchildrensmuseum.org; Boston Tea Party Ship and Museum (reopening in Fall 2008), Congress Street Bridge, 617-338-1773, www.bostonteapartyship.com; Seaport World Trade Center,

877-SEAPORT, www.seaportboston.com; St. Patrick's Day Parade, www.saint patricksdayparade.com/boston; Seaport Alliance for a Neighborhood Design, www.bostonseaport.com; Fort Point Arts Community, 617-423-4299, www. fortpointarts.org; South Boston Neighborhood House, 521 E 7th St, 617-268-1619, www.sbnh.org

Public Schools: Boston Public Schools, 26 Court St, 617-635-9000, www.boston publicschools.org

Public Transportation: *Trains*: Red Line at South Station, Broadway and Andrew; Commuter Rail at South Station

Buses: Silver Line at South Station, Courthouse Station, World Trade Center, and Silver Line Way; for MBTA route and schedule information contact the MBTA Traveler's Information Center: 617-222-3200, 800-392-6100, TTY 617-222-5246 or go to www.mbta.com.

SOUTH END/BAY VILLAGE

Boundaries: *South End (roughly)*: **North**: I-90 (Mass Tpke); **East and Southeast**: Albany St/I-93 (Fitzgerald Expy); **South**: Melnea Cass Blvd; **West and Southwest**: Huntington Ave/Mass Ave/Southwest Corridor; *Bay Village*: **North**: Stuart St; **East**: Charles St South; **South**: Cortes St and Marginal Rd; **West**: Berkeley St

A note to newcomers: when a Bostonian says "Southie," it is a reference to South Boston (see previous entry), *not* the South End. Home to an ethnically diverse population, the heart of Boston's gay community, and many of the city's trendiest cafés and restaurants, the South End is also the largest neighborhood of intact Victorian row houses in the US, according to the National Register of Historic Places. Like the neighboring Back Bay, the **South End** is the product of yet another of Boston's landfill projects initiated to cope with Boston's continuing expansion in the 1800s. In 1834 the city began filling in the mudflats around Boston Neck (used at the time as an execution ground). Developed as a neighborhood suitable for Boston's elite, the South End was designed with homes clustered around small parks in the style of redbrick Georgian bow fronts with grand stoops and latticework railings, balconies, and window boxes. Within a generation, however, the South End was no longer the chic spot for the wealthy. Residents, many of the rich mercantile class, moved from the South End to the more recently developed Back Bay, with its grand boulevards and French-style architecture. Thus began the South End's immigrant history. Over the next hundred or so years, Irish, Jews, Italians, Chinese, Greeks, Syrians, Lebanese, Hispanics, and African-Americans came to settle here, many attracted by the low- rent lodging houses into which the mansions had been converted. By the 1950s, an active African-American community gave birth to Boston's jazz scene. One remnant, Wally's Café, a hole-in-the-wall jazz club near the Mass Ave T stop, has survived since 1947 and still earns rave reviews from Boston's music aficionados.

These days the trendy and artsy South End is back in favor as one of Boston's most sought-after addresses, on par with the North End and just slightly less coveted than Beacon Hill or the Back Bay. Not your stereotypical Boston neighborhood, the South End is a visible amalgam of the phases it has experienced, managing to gentrify while maintaining the imprints of many who have come before. In a city that continues to be ethnically and socio-economically divided, the South End is a melting pot of residents. You'll find multigenerational families, artists, students, and professionals, not to mention the substantial GLBT population (of gay men in particular) which is largely credited with helping to transform this area from crime-ridden to chic over the last two decades. On busy Tremont Street, rainbow flags dominate, signaling the many gay-friendly stores, restaurants, bars, and services.

Many sub-regions actually comprise the South End, often evolving around the squares and parks they surround. At last count, 18 neighborhood associations claimed mini-sections. Newcomers should note that some of these sub-regions are distinctly safer than others; Tremont Street serves as a rough divider between the safer (north of Tremont, towards the Back Bay) and seedier (south of Tremont, towards Roxbury) sides of the South End. This also means that real estate south of Tremont is slightly more affordable than what you'll find north of it. The sub-neighborhoods north of Tremont Street include St. Botolph, Cosmopolitan, Claremont, Ellis, Pilot Block, and Rutland Square. **St. Botolph** corresponds to the upscale area of neatly manicured row houses just behind Copley and the Pru, around St. Botolph Street between Mass Ave and the Mass Pike. **Cosmopolitan** includes the blocks heading east from Back Bay Station between Carleton and West Newton streets and Columbus Avenue. **Claremont** covers the square section from Claremont Street to Tremont Street, between West Newton Street and Gainsborough Street, with the exception of **Rutland Square**, which is its own sub-neighborhood. Claremont, Cosmopolitan, and Rutland Square are all more expensive and desirable parts of the South End, although Claremont becomes slightly dodgier as you pass Mass Ave heading west. **Ellis** is the fashionable area between the Mass Pike to the east and West Canton Street to the west, bound by busy Columbus Avenue and Tremont Street on the north and south, respectively. This sub-region includes several of the hip South End commercial establishments, some of its most picturesque streets—such as the irresistible Appleton Street—and the substantial Boston Center for the Arts. Between Ellis and Claremont is **Pilot Block**, which encompasses more of the commercial attractions on these main streets.

Sub-sections south of Tremont include Castle Square, Eight Streets, Union Park, Old Dover, Bradford, Inquilinos Boriculas En Acción/Villa Victoria, Rutland Street, West Concord Street, Hurley Block, Chester Square, Worcester Square, and Franklin-Blackstone. **Castle Square**, between the Pike and East Berkeley Street, is a relatively industrial region near the Herald building on the South End's border with Chinatown. The area between East Berkeley and Waltham streets, bound by

Tremont Street and Shawmut Avenue, is the residential **Eight Streets**. Just west, around the oval-shaped park of the same name, is **Union Park**, from Tremont Street south to Harrison Avenue. The section of Union Park directly surrounding the park itself is reasonably sought after, but Washington Street, a block further, still seems a little stripped—an elevated transit system was torn down in the 1980s, and for years nothing was rebuilt in its place; however, New England's largest cathedral, the Catholic Cathedral of the Holy Cross, stands on Washington Street. The Boston Redevelopment Authority has instituted projects to revive this southern portion of the South End, and many of the old brick warehouse buildings in what realtors are now calling **SoWa** (south of Washington) have been converted into office space, artists' lofts, or condos. Small art galleries and cafés have begun to spring up here in response, and summer weekends bring the popular outdoor SoWa Open Market to Harrison Avenue, a good place to find handmade crafts, jewelry, or even antiques from a rotating cast of artisans and vendors. In addition, the T's Silver Line, an articulated bus system, now runs along the Washington Street corridor. Between Shawmut Avenue and I-93, from Waltham Street to the Mass Pike, is a fairly large, quiet, residential neighborhood called **Old Dover**, although the portion directly around Bradford Street is actually called **Bradford**. Next to Union Park is **Inquilinos Boriculas En Acción/Villa Victoria**. Bound roughly by Upton and West Newton streets between Tremont and Shawmut, **Villa Victoria** is home to a large Puerto Rican population, whose activism in the 1960s persuaded the city to give them control of their housing project's redevelopment; they found an architect who was able to model it after a typical Puerto Rican village, complete with a town plaza. Continuing in a southwesterly direction from Villa Victoria are three sub-neighborhoods, each only one street long: **Rutland Street**, **West Concord Street**, and **Hurley Block**. **Chester Square** surrounds Mass Ave's Chester Park, from West Springfield to Lenox Street, on the edge of Roxbury. Just south of Chester Square, at the southern-most tip of the South End, is **Worcester Square**. It encompasses the area around Worcester Park and the campus of the Boston University Medical Center, which illuminates Harrison Avenue. The final sub-region in the South End is **Franklin-Blackstone**, so named for the adjacent Franklin and Blackstone squares branching off in either direction from Washington Street. Franklin-Blackstone cuts into Worcester Square, bordering on the medical campus. Despite all of the hospital-related activity and greenspace, Worcester Square, Chester Square, and Franklin-Blackstone are sub-neighborhoods with an edgier reputation. Nonetheless, some medical staff and students do make their homes nearby.

Overall, the character of the South End varies from block to block, with some streets looking posh and gorgeous and others reminiscent of cramped and downtrodden late 19th-century row houses. Some blocks are pristinely quiet and residential, while others are decidedly more trafficked or commercial. However, thanks to the active South End Historical Society, in general the quality of the interior of the homes throughout the South End is good. A South End apartment or home means a majestic stoop, with ornate cast iron railings. Unfortunately, many of the single-family Victorian brownstones were separated into apartments. Some are spacious, however, with exposed brick walls, hardwood floors, and roof decks. It's not unheard of to find an apartment with working fireplace and original architectural detailing.

T service to the South End isn't as comprehensive as it is for other neighborhoods, and you may have a bit of a hike from the Back Bay Station or Mass Ave T stop. Bus service does supplement the T, as does the Silver Line's Washington Street route. Car owners are blessed with easy access to the Mass Pike and I-93, but not with an easy parking situation; the South End is a hassle and usually requires a resident permit, though it's not quite as difficult as in the Back Bay, Beacon Hill, or the North End.

The South End is home to plenty of greenspace, thanks to its English-inspired design. One park, Peters Park, is dog-friendly. The Southwest Corridor, a four-mile pedestrian/bike path offering access to public tennis and basketball courts, a children's playground, and public gardening plots, stretches from the Mass Ave T stop all the way through Roxbury to Jamaica Plain. Specialty boutiques, trendy eateries, and bars, many on Tremont Street, attract people from all over the city. In addition to having all the conveniences of city living—dry cleaners, hardware stores, drug stores, corner markets—Copley Square is just as accessible to the South End as it is to the Back Bay. And South Enders need not travel far for artistic inspiration. The Boston Center for the Arts, in the heart of the South End, attracts over 200,000 visitors each year to its galleries and theaters, which showcase works from acclaimed artists, residents, and small- to mid-sized theatre companies from all over New England. Beyond the BCA, local artists often organize Open Studios weekends for the public, and it is an easy walk to either the Theater District or Symphony Hall area.

Just north of the South End, stuffed between the Back Bay and the Theater District, lies little **Bay Village**, a neighborhood so tiny, quiet, and unassuming that most Bostonians would swear there is no such place. Almost entirely residential, Bay Village covers an expanse of just six blocks, with only about 700 residents. Bay Village has two notable claims to fame. First, it is the birthplace of Edgar Allan Poe, and second, Boston's worst disaster happened here. On November 28, 1942, fire burst out at a popular nightclub called the Coconut Grove. With a jammed revolving door, four locked exits, and two doors that opened inward, 492 of the club's patrons were trapped inside and perished. As a result, country-wide regulations were passed requiring all doors in public buildings to open outwards.

Today Bay Village looks like a mix of all of Boston's grander neighborhoods thrown together—a combination of sturdy colonials and grand Victorians. Red brick buildings with painted shutters and some wrought iron work are common here. Mostly the neighborhood is solidly residential, upscale, tucked away, and cozy, but the boundary with the Theater District around the vicinity of Charles

Street South and Stuart Street feels a little more exposed and edgy. Bay Village is privy to all the nearby amenities of the South End, Back Bay, and Chinatown.

Area Code: 617

Zip Codes: 02118, 02111

Post Offices: 59 W Dedham St; 207 Mass Ave

Police: District D-4, 650 Harrison Ave, 617-343-4250, www.cityofboston. gov/police

Emergency Hospitals: BU Medical Center, 88 E Newton St and 840 Harrison Ave, 617-638-8000, www.bumc.bu.edu; New England Medical Center, 750 Washington St, 617-636-5000, www.nemc.org

Libraries: South End Branch, 685 Tremont St, 617-536-8241; Central Library, Copley Sq, 700 Boylston St, 617-536-5400; www.bpl.org

Parks & Open Space: Blackstone Square; Chester Park; Franklin Square; Peters Park; Southwest Corridor Park; Union Park; Worcester Square; www.mass.gov/dcr, www.cityofboston.gov/parks

Community Publications: *Bay Windows*, 617-266-6670, www.baywindows.com; *South End News,* 617-266-6670, www.southendnews.com

Community Resources and Web Sites: www.cityofboston.gov; www.southend. org; www.bayvillage.net; Blackstone Community Center, 50 W Brookline St, 617-635-5162; Boston Center for the Arts (BCA), 539 Tremont St, 617-426-5000, www.bcaonline.org; Boston Center for Adult Education, 122 Arlington St, 617-267-4430, www.bcae.org; SoWa Open Market, www.southendopenmarket.com; South End Historical Society, 532 Mass Ave, 617-536-4445, www.southendhistoricalsociety.org; for area universities, see the **Childcare and Education** chapter.

Public Schools: Boston Public Schools, 26 Court St, 617-635-9000, www.bostonpublicschools.org

Public Transportation: *South End:* *Trains:* Orange Line at Back Bay Station or Mass Ave; *Buses:* #1 (Harvard/Holyoke Gate–Dudley Sq via Mass Ave and BU Medical Center), #8 (Harbor Point/UMASS–Kenmore Station via South End Medical Area and Dudley Station; #9 (City Point–Copley Sq via Broadway Station); #10 (City Point–Copley Sq via Andrew Station and Boston Medical Area); #39 (Forest Hills–Back Bay Station via Huntington Ave), #43 (Ruggles Station–Park and Tremont Sts); #47 (Central Sq, Cambridge–Broadway Station via South End Medical Center, Dudley Station and Longwood Medical Area); Silver Line Bus (Dudley Sq–Downtown Boston via Washington St); for MBTA route and schedule information contact the MBTA Traveler's Information Center: 617-222-3200, 800-392-6100, TTY 617-222-5246 or go to www.mbta.com.

Bay Village: Trains: Green Line at Arlington; Orange Line at New England Medical Center; *Buses:* #9 (City Point–Copley Sq via Broaday Station); #39 (Forest Hills–Back Bay Station via Huntington Ave); #43 (Ruggles Station via Park and Tremont Sts); #55 (Jersey and Queensberry–Copley Sq or Tremont and Park Sts via Ipswich St); for MBTA route and schedule information contact the MBTA Traveler's Information Center: 617-222-3200, 800-392-6100, TTY 617-222-5246 or go to www.mbta.com.

WEST ROXBURY

Boundaries: **North**: Allandale St; **East**: W Roxbury Pkwy and Centre St; **South and West**: Suffolk County Line

West Roxbury (also called, as you might have been able to surmise by now, "Westie") and Roslindale were once part of Roxbury. Initially the area was sparsely settled by farming families; later, wealthy Boston families built their summer estates here. In 1851, West Roxbury seceded from Roxbury, bringing Jamaica Plain and Roslindale along with it. In 1874, West Roxbury was officially annexed to Boston.

The Roxbury Latin School—a prestigious, private secondary school which, founded in 1645, is the oldest school in continuous existence in North America—is located here, as is Brook Farm, the utopian experimental community created in the 1840s by Bronson Alcott (Louisa May's father) and his following of transcendentalists. Today, West Roxbury is Boston's most suburban-feeling neighborhood. Its predominantly white population of middle- to upper-class means has a median age of just over 40—several years older than Boston's. Homes here are nice, the city services efficient, and the streets mostly crime-free. An unsung enclave, Irish Catholic residents here may well outnumber those in either Southie or Charlestown. More akin to Newton than Boston, West Roxbury is pricier than Jamaica Plain and Roslindale but less expensive than Newton or Brookline. West Roxburyans by and large live in single-family homes covering the gamut of architectural styles from the 1800s and 1900s: Queen Annes, Tudors, Gothic Revivals, etc., with backyards and ample parking. There are also some 1960s-style apartment complexes and cute condo developments interspersed throughout. Washington Street is where you'll find restaurant chains and gas stations, and Centre Street offers a quaint mix of new storefronts as well as a Roche Bros. Supermarket.

As in Roslindale, getting to downtown Boston from West Roxbury is not easy; residents must make use of the bus or the commuter rail (West Roxbury has three stops, as opposed to Roslindale's one), or else drive into the city through circuitous routes like the VFW Parkway or city roads like Centre and Washington streets.

Area Code: 617
Zip Code: 02132
Post Office: 1970 Centre St
Police: District E-5, 1708 Centre St, 343-4560, www.cityofboston.gov/police

Emergency Hospitals: Faulkner Hospital, 1153 Centre St, JP, 617-983-7000, www.faulknerhospital.org; VA Hospital, 1400 VFW Pkwy, 617-323-7700, www.va.gov

Library: West Roxbury Branch, 1961 Centre St, 617-325-3147, www.bpl.org

Parks & Open Space: Bellevue Hill Reservation; Billings Field; Westerly Burying Ground; West Roxbury Parkway; Stony Brook Reservation, www.mass.gov/dcr, www.cityofboston.gov/parks

Community Publication: *West Roxbury and Roslindale Transcript*, 617-327-2608, www.townonline.com/roslindale

Community Resources and Web Sites: www.cityofboston.gov; West Roxbury YMCA, www.ymcaboston.org; Draper Pool, 5275 Washington St, 617-635-5021; Ohrenberger Community Center, 175 W Boundary Rd, 617-635-5183; Roche Community Center, 1716 Centre St, 617-635-5066; West Roxbury Community Center and Swimming Pool, 1205 VFW Pkwy, 617-635-5066; Jim Roche Community Ice Arena, 1275 VFW Pkwy, 617-323-9512

Public Schools: Boston Public Schools, 26 Court St, 617-635-9000, www.boston publicschools.org

Public Transportation: *Trains*: Commuter Rail's Needham Line stops at West Roxbury, Highland and Bellevue.

Buses: #35 (Dedham Mall/Stimston St–Forest Hills via Belgrade Ave and Centre St); #36 (Charles River Loop or VA Hospital–Forest Hills via Belgrade Ave and Centre St); #37 (Baker and Vermont Sts–Forest Hills via Belgrade Ave and Centre St); #38 (Wren St–Forest Hills via Centre and South Sts); #51 (Cleveland Circle–Forest Hills via Hancock Village); for MBTA route and schedule information contact the MBTA Traveler's Information Center: 617-222-3200, 800-392-6100, TTY 617-222-5246 or go to www.mbta.com.

ALSO IN SUFFOLK COUNTY

The three other cities to share Suffolk County with Boston:

- **Chelsea** is a working-class, industrial inner urban suburb just three miles north of Boston over the Tobin Bridge, bordered by the Mystic and Chelsea Rivers. It wasn't long ago that this small city was in such bad shape it went bankrupt, prompting the state of Massachusetts to take over operations. However, with views of downtown Boston and pockets of classic brick row house architecture, a few young urban trendsetters priced out of Somerville and other former artistic enclaves have joined Chelsea's multicultural mix of residents. Indeed, in 2005 *Boston Magazine* named Chelsea "Best Place to Live for Hipsters," though it has yet to fully realize that title. It lacks a T stop, but there is Commuter Rail and bus service, and the drive to downtown or Logan Airport is quick. City homepage: www.ci.chelsea.ma.us; municipal offices: 617-466-4000.
- **Revere** is a large, working-class community just five miles north of Boston on the ocean. There is easy access to the airport and city via the Blue Line (Beach-

mont, Revere Beach, and Wonderland stops), and by car on Routes 1 and 1A. Revere Beach is the country's oldest public beach and a popular summertime cruising strip (if also the butt of some jokes). Also within its bounds is the Wonderland Greyhound Park and Suffolk Downs. City homepage: www.revere.org; community page: www.revere.com; municipal offices: 781-286-8100.

- **Winthrop,** on a peninsula jutting out into the Atlantic southeast of Revere, is home to a close-knit (and slightly isolated) working- to middle-class oceanside community. No major highways reach Winthrop—access is via Route 1A in Revere or East Boston—and public transit is limited to bus service. Beaches and waterfront property abound, and there is easy access to the airport, though noise from the planes can be an issue. City homepage: www.town.winthrop. ma.us; municipal offices: 617-846-1742

SURROUNDING COMMUNITIES

Over Boston's nearly four centuries of existence, the city has annexed many neighboring communities. However, while cities such as Chicago, New Orleans, and even London took over neighboring areas as they grew, in Boston, a significant number of metropolitan communities managed to resist annexation. Thus, Brookline, Somerville, Medford, Cambridge, and Watertown, while integral to the fabric of the Boston metropolitan area, maintain their political individuality. As a newcomer, you probably won't notice when you're crossing from one town to another. As a result, when locals refer to living, working, or going out in "Boston" or "the city," the statement warrants qualification: they may just as easily be referring to Cambridge as they are the Back Bay.

The cost of living can vary considerably between Boston proper and the surrounding communities. A neighboring town such as Arlington or Waltham may be, to a large extent, more affordable and just as feasible a living option, especially since subway service and bus lines make it a relatively easy commute into Boston. Since there isn't much rhyme or reason to community boundaries and layouts in the Boston area, we have divided the surrounding areas by county—Middlesex and Norfolk—and then listed the individual communities alphabetically for ease of reference. Cities and towns that share a significant border with Boston or Cambridge are profiled.

MIDDLESEX COUNTY

ARLINGTON

Boundaries: North: Winchester and Medford; **East:** Cambridge and Somerville; **South:** Belmont and Cambridge; **West:** Lexington

Arlington, located on the western perimete of metro Boston and covering only five and a half square miles, is a nice residential area with a dense population of over 40,000. Arlington is popular with those who don't want to live in downtown, but still want easy access to the city or Cambridge.

Originally part of Cambridge, Arlington was first known as Menotomy then West Cambridge, finally becoming Arlington in 1867. Mass Ave, Pleasant, Mystic and Medford streets are actually native trails adopted as highways in the mid-17th century. Many historically and architecturally significant homes survive in Arlington, which has seven historic districts. Along Battle Road are colonial houses with Revolutionary War connections. Arlington also features a variety of 19th-century housing, including Victorians along Mass Ave and Pleasant Street, and workers' cottages along Mill Brook. As with many of Boston's outlying communities, Arlington underwent a building boom in the late 1800s, spurred when public transportation was extended out from Boston's center.

From east to west, Arlington's three regions are known as **East Arlington**, **Arlington Center**, and **Arlington Heights**, which borders Lexington. Arlington is less expensive than Belmont and Lexington, and it is home to many renters who enjoy the safe, residential reputation. Newcomers seeking a raging night on the town should note that Arlington does not have any real bars, pubs, or clubs. For nightlife, residents generally head down Mass Ave to Cambridge. However, in the past few years a number of good, often high-end restaurants, many of which hold beer and wine licenses, have started popping up around Arlington. For moviegoers, the historic Capitol Theatre, located at 204 Mass Ave, shows a good mix of family-friendly films and independent productions for a lower price than your usual multiplex. There are also three malls in the immediate area: Meadow Glen Mall in Medford, Fresh Pond Mall in Cambridge and Arsenal Mall in Watertown (see **Shopping for the Home**).

With seven elementary schools, Arlington is an attractive choice for young families. The town also features a swimming area at Arlington Reservoir on the town border with Lexington between Mass Ave and Route 2A, Menotomy Rocks Park is just northwest of the intersection of routes 2 and 60, and the Minute Man Bike Trail goes right through town. Just northeast of the intersection of routes 2 and 50 and south of Mass Ave is the lovely kettlehole, Spy Pond.

Public transportation options include the Red Line terminus at the Alewife T Station on the Cambridge border, commuter rail stops in neighboring Belmont, and buses throughout town. Drivers have easy access to Route 2, and routes 16 and 60 can take you to I-93 via Medford. Overnight on-street parking is not allowed, so make sure your new place includes a parking spot.

Area Code: 781
Zip Codes: 02474, 02476
Post Offices: 10 Court St; 1347 Mass Ave; 240 Mass Ave
Police: Community Safety Building, 112 Mystic St, 781-316-3900, www.town.

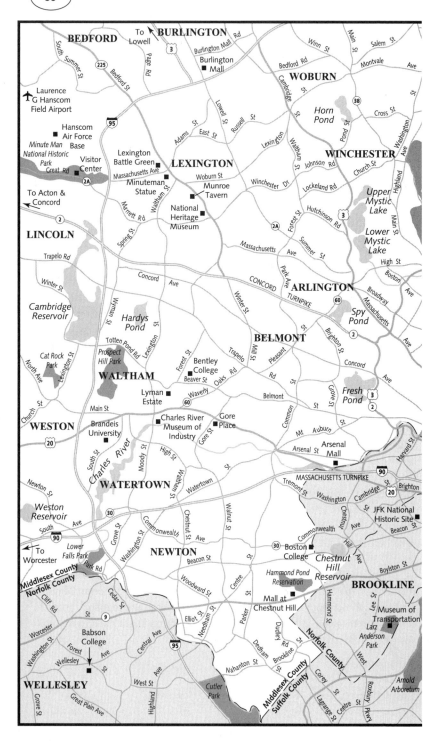

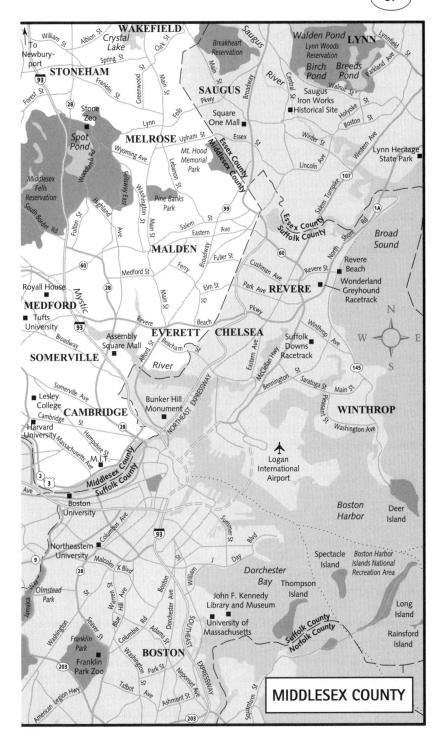

MIDDLESEX COUNTY

arlington.ma.us/Public_Documents/ArlingtonMA_Police/index

Emergency Hospitals: The Cambridge Hospital, 1493 Cambridge St, 617-665-1000, www.challiance.org; Mt. Auburn Hospital, 330 Mt. Auburn St, Cambridge, 617-492-3500, www.mountauburn.caregroup.org; Somerville Hospital, 230 Highland Ave, Somerville, 617-591-4500, www.challiance.org

Libraries: Robbins Library, 700 Mass Ave, 781-316-3200; Fox Branch, 175 Mass Ave, 781-316-3198; www.robbinslibrary.org

Parks & Open Space: Alewife Brook Reservation, www.mass.gov/dcr; Bishop Field; Hill's Hill; Lussiano Field; Menotomy Rocks Park; Minute Man Bike Trail; Spy Pond and Field; Arlington Heights Playground; Arlington Reservation; Turkey Hill Reservation; Robbins Farm Park, www.robbinsfarmpark.org

Community Publication: *The Arlington Advocate*, 781-643-7900, www.townon line.com/arlington.

Community Resources and Web Sites: www.arlington-mass.com, www.town. arlington.ma.us, Arlington Chamber of Commerce, 781-643-4600, www. arlcc.org; Arlington Historical Society, www.arlingtonhistorical.org; George A. Smith Museum/Jason Russell House, 7 Jason St, 781-648-4300; Menotomy Minute Men, www.menotomy.org; Old Schwamb Mill, 17 Mill Lane, 781-643-0554, www.oldschwambmill.org; Whittemore-Robbins House, 670R Mass Ave, 781-316-3260; Arlington Center for the Arts, www.acarts.org; Arlington Friends of the Drama, www.afdtheatre.org; Capitol Theater, 204 Mass Ave, 781-648-4340; Dallin Art Museum, One Wittemore Park, 781-641-0747, www. dallin.org; Regent Theater, 7 Medford St, 781-646-4849; Philharmonic Society of Arlington, www.psarlington.org; For area colleges and universities, see the **Childcare and Education** chapter.

Public Schools: Arlington Public Schools, 869 Mass Ave, 781-316-3501, www.ar lington.k12.ma.us

Public Transportation: *Trains*: Red Line at Alewife; Commuter Rail at West Medford or Belmont Center

Buses: nos. 62, 67, 77, 78, 79, 80, 84, 87, and 350; for MBTA route and schedule information contact the MBTA Traveler's Information Center: 617-222-3200, 800-392-6100, TTY 617-222-5146 or go to www.mbta.com.

BELMONT

Boundaries: **North**: Arlington/Route 2; **East**: Cambridge (at Fresh Pond); **South**: Watertown (along Belmont St); **West**: Waltham and Lexington

Once part of a larger settlement that included the present day towns of Watertown, Waltham, Weston, Lincoln, and parts of Cambridge, Belmont was officially born in 1859 after much debate over land. The new town was primarily fruit farms and market gardens, whose produce was sold in Faneuil Hall, making

Belmont known for its quality goods. Today, those farms are mostly gone, giving way to residential homes and neighborhoods.

The railway, which reached Belmont in the mid-1800s, was responsible for changing this neighborhood from an agricultural town to a Boston suburb. By the mid-1900s, Belmont's commercial cores had emerged: **Belmont Center** with a Victorian town hall and depot, **Waverly** (almost in Waltham) with its Victorian firehouse, and **Cushing Square** which features retail blocks. Further expansion occurred with the streetcar-based building boom in the early 1900s, resulting in multiple-family housing in the lowlands (southern area) and single-family estates on the high ground. Belmont is a good bet if you are looking for an old home: Victorians can be found in Belmont Center and Waverly Square; **Payson Hill** offers examples of revival styles; and the **Presidential** area (a neighborhood with streets named after presidents) has many well-kept colonials.

Today Belmont is a well-to-do, sleepy suburb, whose residents appreciate its quiet, low-key reputation; having a dry town helps keep it that way. If you're looking for wine at your romantic dinner, or to buy a six-pack on your way home from work, heading across the town line is a must. There are some shops and services, but a trip to Cambridge, Boston, or elsewhere is necessary for nightlife, fine dining, and definitely alcohol.

Although Belmont doesn't have as many rental properties as Arlington or Watertown, you can find some along the Watertown border. Many Harvard affiliates opt to live here, as it is more affordable than Cambridge. And if you are looking to raise a family or already have one, the town's public school system is excellent, with well-financed music and athletic departments.

Area Code: 617

Zip Codes: 02478, 02479

Post Offices: 405 Concord Ave; 492 Trapelo Rd

Police: Belmont Police, 460 Concord Ave, 617-484-1212, www.belmontpd.org

Emergency Hospitals: The Cambridge Hospital, 1493 Cambridge St, Cambridge, 617-665-1000; www.challiance.org; Mt. Auburn Hospital, 330 Mt. Auburn St, Cambridge, 617-492-3500, www.mountauburn.caregroup.org

Libraries: Belmont Public Library, 336 Concord Ave, 617-489-2000; Benton Branch, 75 Oakley Rd, 617-489-2000 ext. 2854; www.belmont.lib.ma.us

Parks & Open Space: Beaver Brook Reservation, www.mass.gov/dcr; Grove Street Playground; Habitat Education Center and Wildlife Sanctuary, 10 Juniper Rd, www.massaudubon.org/Nature_Connection/Sanctuaries/Habitat; Payson Park; Pequosette Park; Underwood Pool Area

Community Publication: *Belmont Citizen-Herald*, 617-484-2633, www.townonline.com/belmont/

Community Resources and Web Sites: www.town.belmont.ma.us, Watertown-Belmont Chamber of Commerce, 617-926-1017, www.wbcc.org; Arlington-Belmont Chorale, www.psarlington.org/chorale.htm; Belmont

Country Club, 181 Winter St, 617-484-5360, www.belmontcc.org; Belmont Studio Cinema, 376 Trapelo Rd, 617-484-1706, www.studiocinema.com; Powers Music School, 380 Concord Ave, 617-484-4696, www.powersmusic.org

Public Schools: Belmont Public Schools, 644 Pleasant St, 617-484-2642, www.belmont.k12.ma.us

Public Transportation: *Trains*: Commuter Rail at Belmont Ctr and Waverly Sq; Red Line at Alewife (Arlington)

Buses: nos. 62, 73, 74, 76, 78 and 84; for MBTA route and schedule information contact the MBTA Traveler's Information Center: 617-222-3200, 800-392-6100, TTY 617-222-5146 or go to www.mbta.com.

CAMBRIDGE

Boundaries: **North**: Arlington and Somerville; **East**: Boston Harbor; **South**: the Charles River; **West**: Watertown and Belmont

As pivotally and permanently as Boston and Cambridge are conjoined, the latter has its own distinct flavor. Cambridge is, first and foremost, an academic capital. Its attractive, low-key streets with quaint buildings, pretty green areas, and bookstores galore can obscure that important fact. The left-leaning "People's Republic of Cambridge," as it's jokingly called, is Boston's veritable fraternal twin—inextricably linked, but unmistakably different. The one-time capital of the Massachusetts Bay Colony, Cambridge has over 100,000 residents in its 6.5-square-mile area. Those numbers swell during the day as people flood in to work, study, visit, eat, and drink.

The city was founded as Newtowne in 1630, when John Winthrop and his band of Puritans settled just south of what is now Harvard University, near the Charles River. In 1636, Harvard was established with a grant of £400 from the Massachusetts General Court as a school to train young ministers, and not, as is commonly thought, by John Harvard. Assistant Pastor John Harvard entered the picture two years later when he died, bequeathing half his money and his entire library to the new school. It was in light of this act of generosity that Harvard was renamed—after its primary funder, not founder. When the school received Harvard's donation and subsequently named itself in his honor, the general court of Newtowne then renamed their town Cambridge, after the university in England, which many of them had attended.

For its first 150 years, Cambridge developed as a settlement fairly separate from Boston, establishing itself as a farming and college community. By the time of the Revolutionary War, most Cantabrigians were descendants of the first Puritan settlers, with the exception of a few British loyalists (Tories) whose homes clustered along Tory Row, now Brattle Street. At the advent of the Revolutionary War, the rebelling colonial government confiscated many of these estates, and General George Washington set up headquarters in one of them for nine months. The same house is now known as the Longfellow National Historic Site because Henry Wadsworth Longfellow lived there in the 1840s. General Washington also ordered the erection of several forts along the river, one of which, Fort Washington, remains today at 101 Waverly Street.

Just as the natural barrier of the Charles River protected the patriots from invasion during war, it also prevented easy access between Boston and Cambridge. The first bridge built across the Charles River was the Great Bridge, erected in 1662. Until then, the only way to get to Boston—short of taking a ferry from Charlestown, a long endeavor in itself—was to travel a time-consuming and indirect eight-mile route, starting with crossing the river via ferry at JFK Street, and following a path (now North Harvard Street) through Brookline and Roxbury into Boston. Over the years, eight bridges have been built, spanning the Charles at various points along the length of Cambridge. Their presence profoundly impacted the city's development, opening it up as a Boston community. In spite of the accessibility, Cantabrigians are known to balk at "crossing the river," preferring to keep close to home.

Today people representing many nations and lifestyles live in Cambridge. It is home to professors, scientists, students, artists, industrial workers, immigrants, "techies," and other young professionals. Its international flavor comes from the thousands of foreign students and professors who live here during the school year, as well as a strong immigrant community that includes many small business and restaurant owners. Not only are there people from every walk of life, but of every financial status as well. Many residents are of modest economic means, some living in area public housing. However, of all large cities in the nation, the 2000 Census showed Cambridge as having the largest concentration of homes (nearly 12% or one in eight) worth over $1 million, followed by San Francisco. As with housing prices, rents in Cambridge are relatively high, but some areas are more reasonable than others. Most homes date from pre-WWII, although triple-deckers, high-rises, chic urban apartments with exposed brick, pricey colonials, and contemporary single-family homes can also be found.

Accessibility to public transportation is one of Cambridge's major perks. The Red Line runs the length of the city with stops in the major squares (Kendall, Central, Harvard, and Porter), and the Green Line stops at Lechmere and Science Park. Areas not covered by the T are served by bus. If you do have a car, parking can be a problem, but generally not as bad as in Boston. There is easy access to routes 2, 16, I-93, and even the Mass Pike, while Mass Ave runs the length of Cambridge between Arlington and Boston's Back Bay. As for greenspace in Cambridge, while not expansive, there is Cambridge Common on the western end of Harvard Square, the entire bank of the Charles, and Fresh Pond by the border with Arlington, not to mention pocket parks, lawns, and Harvard Yard itself.

Like many university towns, Cambridge caters to academics, offering coffee shops, second-hand bookshops, and health food stores galore, as well as a thriving nightlife. Short of a few busy streets, including Mass Ave, the main commercial corridor that runs the length of Cambridge from Boston all the way to Arlington, Cambridge has plenty of sleepy, tree-lined side streets.

Cambridge can be broken up into 13 official areas: East Cambridge, MIT, Wellington-Harrington, Area Four, Cambridgeport, Mid-Cambridge, Riverside, Agassiz, Peabody, West Cambridge, North Cambridge, Cambridge Highlands, and Strawberry Hill, all of which have additional sub-neighborhoods. It's useful to know the sub-neighborhood names when reviewing real estate and rental listings.

EAST CAMBRIDGE (LECHMERE)

East Cambridge (with sub-neighborhoods Lechmere and Science Park) is the area between the Charles River on the east, the B&A railroad tracks to the west, and bounded by Main Street and Broadway to the south and Somerville to the north. In 1809, the Canal Bridge was built, opening eastern Cambridge for development and making it the city's major industrial area until the 1880s. Just a hop away from downtown Boston, furniture and glass factories opened here, establishing a working-class community of Irish, followed by Polish, Portuguese, and Italian immigrants. Today East Cambridge continues to be an ethnically diverse area (although the number of manufacturing jobs has declined), with some of the most affordable rents in Cambridge. It's conveniently located for easy access to Somerville, Charlestown, North Station, Beacon Hill, and routes 1 or I-93. The courthouse and prison are in East Cambridge, as well as upscale developments like the Cambridgeside Galleria Mall in the **Lechmere** neighborhood, near the Lechmere T stop (terminus for the Green Line).

MIT (KENDALL SQUARE)

Just south of East Cambridge, bounded by Main Street, Broadway, and the railroad on the north and sprawled along the Charles River, is the **MIT** neighborhood. Encompassing the Massachusetts Institute of Technology and Kendall Square, this region of Cambridge was defined in 1916 when MIT moved out of Boston. Today, this world-renowned technical institute commands 168 acres of land along the Charles River facing historic Beacon Hill and Back Bay. The Harvard Bridge, commonly known as the Mass Ave Bridge, runs through the center of campus and connects a traffic-heavy, stoplight-laden section of Mass Ave to Boston's Back Bay. Memorial Drive, Cambridge's less crowded alternative to Storrow Drive, curves between the greenspaces along the river and the campus buildings. It's a good back-up to consider during rush hour if Storrow is packed.

Beginning at the northern tip of MIT's campus is **Kendall Square**, where Broadway and Main Street branch off just west of the Longfellow (a.k.a. "Salt and Pepper") Bridge. Overrun with vast, stark, and sometimes unmarked buildings that house technology, biomedical, and pharmaceutical companies (yes, it is as eerie as it sounds!), it is no wonder Kendall all but shuts down at dusk when the nine-to-fivers head home. Just a few blocks away, 1 Kendall Square offers a little pocket of dining and entertainment options that stay open until midnight or so. Included here: the wonderful independent film theater Landmark Cinemas, Flattop Johnny's pool hall, the local Cambridge Brewing Company, and several popular restaurants. With the exception of a public housing complex on Main Street, there are few places to live throughout Kendall; most residents are students living in university housing. Faculty and staff are more apt to live elsewhere in Cambridge. The MIT population is, according to local police, generally well behaved. Unlike many university towns, most students here are probably too busy studying to wreak much havoc; however, MIT students have been known to pull elaborate pranks, or get in even more serious trouble computer hacking, counting cards during poker (read *Bringing Down the House*), and the like. The area is served by the Kendall/MIT T stop on Main Street—the first stop of the Red Line on the Cambridge side of the river.

WELLINGTON-HARRINGTON (INMAN SQUARE)

West of East Cambridge, north of Kendall Square, and south of Somerville is **Wellington-Harrington**, an area about half the size of East Cambridge, which extends to and includes **Inman Square**, where Cambridge and Hampshire streets intersect. Inman/Harrington is densely populated, with housing that ranges from single- to three-family homes and apartment complexes. Home to European immigrants in the 1800s and through the middle of the last century, today the trend of welcoming incoming foreigners continues. The mixed-use Cambridge Street is the main thoroughfare, connecting the Cambridgeside Galleria and Lechmere part of East Cambridge with Inman Square and then eventually Harvard Square. Because Inman Square is not directly served by the T, it feels like an out-of-the-way treasure, accessed mostly by bus or car—but for willing walkers, it's only about a 10–15 minute journey from Central Square, or 20 minutes from Harvard. Popular with 20-to-30-something hipsters who have no problem biking or walking, and young professionals willing to take buses or drive to work, Inman has become a neighborhood to live in. Save for a Taco Bell/KFC, it is densely packed with small, completely independent businesses: restaurants of all ethnicities, pubs like the Druid and the Thirsty Scholar, yoga studios, coffee shops like the 1369, retail stores that include a toy store and bookstore, a bakery, and of course, one divey rock club to round things out. Inman also borders Somerville, and is only a few blocks south of "hip" Union Square.

AREA 4

Bounded by Prospect Street to the west, Hampshire Street to the north, the B&A tracks to the east, and Mass Ave to the south, between MIT and Central Square lies **Area 4**. Comprised mostly of two- and three-family homes, with some large apartment complexes and two public housing developments, a large percentage of its occupants are families. Area 4 is home to *El Mundo*, Massachusetts' oldest Spanish newspaper, and has many specialty food markets and international restaurants. Sennott Park hosts free concerts and street fairs. Small businesses, including those that can only be seen in a place like Cambridge, such as the Garment District (an alternative department store) and the Miracle of Science bar (an MIT/techie hangout, which posts the menu in the form of a periodic table and serves the bill in beakers), can be seen scattered throughout Area 4. Residents enjoy easy access to Central Square and its T stop, located on its western edge, or the quick, clear shot eastward to Boston via either the Longfellow or the Harvard bridges. It should be noted that this area has Cambridge's highest proportion of low-income residents, and a higher than average crime rate.

CAMBRIDGEPORT

When the Longfellow Bridge (then called the West Boston Bridge) was built in 1793, **Cambridgeport** developed as people began to settle between Harvard and the bridge. Notable residents at the time included Margaret Fuller, the first woman to use the Harvard library, and William Lloyd Garrison, an abolitionist. It was also here, during the Revolutionary War, that George Washington had Fort Washington built to protect his troops during the siege on Boston.

Cambridgeport spreads south from Central Square to the Charles River between MIT to the east and River Street to the west. Once a popular settling place for immigrants, the 1980s brought area industry elsewhere. In recent years Cambridgeport has undergone a resettlement; buildings previously used for industrial purposes were revamped or demolished altogether, and the area is now predominantly residential, made up of single- to multi-family homes and large apartment complexes. Its population is a mix of artists, working class, young professionals, university faculty, and even some seasoned executives. Although Cambridgeport may have developed as a result of the Longfellow Bridge, residents now also have the BU Bridge and River Street Bridge right in their laps, making for easy access to Allston and the Mass Pike. Some large stores, gas stations, and hotels line Cambridgeport's tract of Memorial Drive, while a few small stores and restaurants begin to pop up as one approaches Central Square; truthfully, it can be a challenge to define where Central Square ends and Cambridgeport begins.

MID-CAMBRIDGE (HARVARD SQUARE AND CENTRAL SQUARE)

Bound by three of Cambridge's five major squares—Central Square on the east, Inman Square on the northeast, and Harvard Square on the west, between Mass Ave and the Somerville border—is **Mid-Cambridge**, the geographical and institutional heart of the city. Both Central Square and the main portion of the Harvard campus in Harvard Square are part of Mid-Cambridge, which also lays claim to Cambridge Hospital, city hall, the main branch of the Cambridge Public Library, and the Cambridge Rindge and Latin School. A great deal of the same multi-family homes and large apartment complexes seen throughout the city can be found in Mid-Cambridge, supporting the largest population in all of Cambridge.

Located on Riverside's eastern edge and Cambridgeport's northern, where Western Avenue and River and Magazine streets converge upon Mass Ave, is **Central Square**—Harvard Square's less touristy and grittier little sister. Central Square is one giant melting pot of ethnicities, cultures, socioeconomic status, and age, not to mention punk rockers mixed with the homeless blended with young urban teenagers; there is no sight too strange or crazy to encounter here. That being said, Central Square is also home to Cambridge's city hall, the main post office, the YMCA and YWCA, and a homeless shelter. For nightlife, Central Square has many options from which to choose: Irish pubs like the Phoenix Landing and The Field, the Soviet-themed People's Republik, the Cantab Lounge for bluegrass, funk, and blues lovers, and the Middle East—a complex of four restaurants and clubs serving up Middle Eastern food *and* some of the Boston area's best indie rock. Central Square is also known for its international cuisine, and celebrates its diversity by hosting the World's Fair every summer, displaying an assemblage of food and art from around the world. While most of the businesses here are independent, there are some larger chains, such as Starbucks and the Gap, that have moved in since the late 1990s; however, Central Square maintains a good deal of its beloved secondhand stores, particularly on its fringes. And it remains the center of Cambridge's progressive political scene.

West on Mass Ave is the famous **Harvard Square**. Served by the third Cambridge T stop on the Red Line, the area is the third Cambridge square located on Mass Ave, and covers ground in Mid-Cambridge, West Cambridge, Riverside, and Peabody/Neighborhood 9. The heart of Harvard's campus, Harvard Yard, and a good chunk of Harvard Square falls within Mid-Cambridge's bounds. Known for bookstores, street musicians, and university culture, Harvard Square is home to an amazing array of sights, sounds, shops, newspapers, events, restaurants, and history; however, in recent years, due to sky-high rent and the encroachment of larger chains, many of Harvard Square's more charming businesses and restaurants have disappeared. Regardless, the Square still teems with masses of tourists, locals, shoppers, performers, diners, university faculty, and students. As one can imagine, people-watching is a favorite Harvard Square activity. Coffee is abundant, as are bookstores, and so are homeless people, who you can just as easily spot playing chess with a Harvard professor as panhandling. On most nights you can find poetry readings, lectures, and earnest political discussions. The Square is also home to respected jazz and folk venues, and bars, movie houses, a repertory theater, and a wide array of museums. The city licenses a large number of street performers, which makes for inexpensive entertainment on summer evenings. Many famous performers, including Joan Baez, Tracy Chapman, and Guster, have played here early in their careers. People are often crowded on various corners or around "the pit"—the main entrance to the Harvard T stop—to watch and listen to the free music. Locals and tourists alike also gather outside of Cardullo's—an import delicatessen—to watch local sports games or political debates on the store's television, which they ever-so-nicely place in the front window facing the sidewalk. Bring your own folding chair if you plan to stay awhile!

The idea of moving to such a colorful enclave may be appealing, but the reality of finding a place to live here can be difficult—and expensive. If you are a student or a faculty member, the Harvard Housing Services office (www.hres. harvard.edu/rre.htm) is a good place to start. Parking is also a challenge for residents and visitors alike.

RIVERSIDE

Riverside is the section of Cambridge south of Mass Ave along the Charles between River Street and JFK Street—or easier, the area behind Central Square between Cambridgeport and Harvard Square. Like Cambridgeport, Riverside, one-time home to W.E.B. DuBois, is a transitional area between the Harvard-influenced western part of Cambridge and the lower-budget, industrial section to the east. A number of Harvard's dorms take up Riverside's western edge along the Charles, but the neighborhood loses its ivy influence as you head east. The dorms make the overall median age for the neighborhood young. There are sizable African-American and Asian populations here, creating a solid sense of community despite the influx of seasonal inhabitants. It is predominantly middle-class and residential, with just a few stores (including perhaps the city's best Whole Foods supermarket). The three final bridges spanning the Charles in Cambridge are in Riverside, connecting Cambridge to Lower Allston. The Western Avenue Bridge, at the southern tip of Harvard's Campus, provides a fairly straight shot to the Mass Pike, while the Anderson Bridge links Harvard University to its north campus in Lower Allston; the John Weeks Foot Bridge near Cowperthwaite Street provides pedestrian access to the other side. On summer Sundays, Memorial Drive can be enjoyed, but not driven on, as its Riverside and West Cambridge stretches are closed off for pedestrians and bike riders.

AGASSIZ

Agassiz (pronounced AG-uh-see) encompasses Mass Ave north of its inter-section with Cambridge Street and all parts east up to the Somerville border. Roughly, it is the area between Harvard and Porter squares. Lesley College as well as Harvard's Law and Divinity schools account for the southern portion of this triangular neighborhood. Agassiz is historically significant as African-Ameri-can headmistress Maria Baldwin lived here at the turn of the last century. After holding home-study classes for African-American students at Harvard (including W.E.B. DuBois) in 1889, Cambridge-native Baldwin was named headmaster of the Agassiz School. Dense, residential, and full of students and professors from Cam-bridge's schools as well as young professionals, Agassiz is a comfortable place to live. It includes brick-lined sidewalks and, due to the mixture of apartment buildings and multi- and single-family homes, isn't overwhelmingly upscale. The neighborhood is quiet and within walking distance of Harvard Square, Porter Square, and Davis Square in Somerville. Parking along this stretch of Mass Ave is easier than up the street in the center of Harvard Square. Commercial and retail offerings along Mass Ave, as well as a nearby portion of Beacon Street in Somer-ville, are more than adequate, and include several boutiques, restaurants, and bars.

PEABODY/NEIGHBORHOOD 9 (AVON HILL)

Peabody, a.k.a. **Neighborhood 9**, is shaped rather like an ice cream cone—Mass Ave on the east and Garden and Concord streets on the west stem out from the bottom of the cone to where they intersect, and the rounded top is formed by the boundary marked by the B&M railroad tracks. Here you will find the Radcliffe campus and the Longy School of Music, as well as access to the Cambridge Com-mon and Danehy Park. Peabody/Neighborhood 9 is separated into two distinct areas, with Upland Road serving as the divider. Just south of Upland is **Avon Hill**, one of the more desirable neighborhoods in Cambridge. In the shadow of Porter Square, it has a mixture of grand older homes (some single, some multi-family) and brick apartment complexes. To the north of Upland, housing options tend to be more diverse and readily available, and include large apartment buildings, a public housing development called Lincoln Way, and a mixture of single- and multi-family homes of varying styles, including triple-deckers—known endear-ingly as Irish battleships. Heading away from Harvard and Radcliffe, chances of getting parking (driveways!) increase greatly.

WEST CAMBRIDGE/NEIGHBORHOOD 10

Located south of Peabody/Neighborhood 9, bounded by JFK Street in Harvard Square on the east and Fresh Pond on the west, is the biggest neighborhood in

Cambridge, **West Cambridge**, which contains a good portion of Harvard Square. Brattle Street, called Tory Row during the Revolutionary War, still holds some of the lavish homes of that time. Those in the market for some of the oldest real estate in the country or just a beautiful mansion need look no further. The large and stately homes, most on large lots, make this some of the most desirable and expensive real estate in Cambridge. Aside from the aforementioned gorgeous historic housing, West Cambridge has more greenspace than any neighborhood in the city, even if much of it is for the deceased: the Mt. Auburn Cemetery, the Cambridge Cemetery, and the Old Burying Ground are all here. On its western edge, residents enjoy proximity to Fresh Pond, Kingsley Park, Mt. Auburn Hospital, and Buckingham Browne & Nichols School, not to mention easy access to Memorial Drive and Route 16. Note: West Cambridge, like Riverside, is apt to be affected by the summertime Sunday closures of Memorial Drive for pedestrian/bike use only. Residents on the east side can use the Harvard T stop; residents on the northwest side might be close enough to walk to the Alewife T stop; residents toward the southwest must rely on buses.

NORTH CAMBRIDGE (PORTER SQUARE)

Everything north of the railroad tracks—west of and including Porter Square to the borders of Arlington, Belmont, and Somerville—constitutes **North Cambridge**. In the mid-1800s, Irish immigrants, many of whom worked in North Cambridge's claypits and brickyards, moved here. They were followed by a wave of French Canadians around the turn of the 20th century. Largely a working class neighborhood until the late 1990s, North Cambridge is now gaining popularity with a host of young professionals and students who were forced to look to outlying areas such as Porter Square (and Davis Square in Somerville) during Boston's turn-of-the-millennium housing crunch. Homes here vary from triple-deckers to a public housing development to the large Fresh Pond Apartments high-rise complex. North Cantabrigians have good access to public transit, including two stops on the Red Line: Porter Square, which also has commuter rail service, and Alewife, the Red Line terminus, with an enormous commuter parking lot. There is easy access to Mass Ave and Route 16, and a good amount of greenspace, including the Clarendon Avenue Playground, Linear Park, Rindge Field, Gergin Playground, and the O'Callaghan Little League field.

Porter Square, the fourth Cambridge square as you progress westward along Mass Ave or the Red Line, is most visibly recognizable by the 46-foot stainless steel kinetic sculpture named "Gift of the Wind" outside its T station. Home to the Porter Square Shopping Mall and the Porter Exchange Mall (housed in the old Sears Building), this neighborhood is not to be overlooked, especially for those going to school or working along the Red Line. Although substantially farther from downtown Boston, Porter Square is safer and slower-paced than Central Square, but can be pricier. In Porter Square itself are restaurants, bars, health clubs, cute boutiques, chain stores, and some specialty Japanese shops and an Asian food court in the Exchange building. Either way down Mass Ave, toward Arlington or toward Agassiz/Peabody further into Cambridge, are even more commercial options. Within walking distance from Porter Square are Harvard and Davis squares, and downtown Boston is only about 15–20 minutes away via T.

CAMBRIDGE HIGHLANDS (FRESH POND)

Cambridge Highlands is the tiny area accounting for the northern portion of **Fresh Pond** bordered by the B&M railroad tracks (on the east, the tracks coincide with the Fresh Pond Parkway) and the Belmont border. There are fewer than 300 households in Cambridge Highlands, which coexist with some warehouses, the Fresh Pond (strip) Mall, Fresh Pond Cinema, and large, beautiful homes that line the busy Fresh Pond Parkway. In addition to commercial amenities, residents enjoy a low crime rate and easy access to the Alewife T stop and routes 2 and 16. Also in Cambridge Highlands is Cambridge's main water supply, Fresh Pond, which provides an expanse of greenspace for walking and jogging, especially popular with dog-owners.

STRAWBERRY HILL

Bound by the pond to the north, Aberdeen Avenue to the east, and the Watertown and Belmont town lines to the south and west, **Strawberry Hill** is yet another quiet little nook at the far end of Cambridge. With about four times the population of Cambridge Highlands, it too boasts a low crime rate. Here you will find mostly large, single-family homes on small lots, but there are some apartments, including a large complex at 700 Huron Avenue. Strawberry Hill and Cambridge Highlands are about as far from downtown Cambridge and downtown Boston as can be while still in Cambridge. Although Strawberry Hill isn't very near the Red Line, the Fresh Pond Parkway to Memorial Drive or Brattle Street is an easy route to Boston or the rest of Cambridge.

Area Code: 617
Zip Codes: 02138–02142
Post Offices: Main Post Office, 770 Mass Ave; 303 Cambridge St (East Cambridge); 125 Mt. Auburn St (Harvard Sq); 1311 Cambridge St (Inman Sq); 250 Main St (Kendall Sq); 84 Mass Ave (MIT); 1953 Mass Ave (Porter Sq)
Police: Cambridge Police, 5 Western Ave, 617-349-3300, www.cambridgema.gov/cpd; Harvard University Police, 1033 Mass Ave, 6th Floor, 617-495-1215, www.hupd.harvard.edu; MIT Police, 301 Vassar St, Bldg W89, 617-253-1212, http://web.mit.edu/cp/www/
Emergency Hospitals: The Cambridge Hospital, 1493 Cambridge St, 617-665-1000, www.cha.harvard.edu; Mt. Auburn Hospital, 330 Mt. Auburn St,

617-492-3500, www.mountauburnhospital.org

Library: Main Branch (Mid-Cambridge), 359 Broadway, 617-349-4030, TTY 617-349-4421, www.cambridgema.gov/~CPL

Parks & Open Space: Alewife Brook Reservation, www.mass.gov/dcr; Cambridge Common; Charles River; Danehy Park; Donnelly Field; Fresh Pond Reservation; John F. Kennedy Memorial Park; Magazine Beach; Mount Auburn Cemetery; Russell/Samp Field; Fresh Pond Municipal Golf Course, 617-349-6282, www.freshpondgolf.com; go to www.cambridgema.gov/DHSP2/outdoor.cfm for a complete list and a map, or call 617-349-6228 for information.

Community Publications: *Cambridge Chronicle*, 617-577-7149, www.townon line.com/cambridge; *El Mundo*, 617-522-5060, www.elmundoboston.com

Community Resources: www.agassiz.org, www.cambridgema.gov, www.cen tralsquarecambridge.com, www.eastcambridge.org, www.harvardsquare. com/, www.mcna.org, Chamber of Commerce, 617-876-4100, www.cam bridgechamber.org; Harvard Museum of Natural History, 26 Oxford St, 617-495-3045, www.hmnh.harvard.edu; Harvard University Art Museums (including the Fogg, Sackler, and Busch-Reisinger museums), 32 Quincy St, 617-495-9400, www.artmuseums.harvard.edu; Longfellow National Historic Site, 105 Brattle St, 617-876-4491, www.nps.gov/long; MIT Museum, 265 Mass Ave, 617-253-4444, http://web.mit.edu/museum; Museum of Science, Science Park, 617-723-2500, www.mos.org; Peabody Museum of Archaeology and Ethnology, 11 Divinity Ave, 617-496-1027, www.peabody.harvard.edu; Ameri can Repertory Theatre, 64 Brattle St, 617-547-8300, www.amrep.org; Brattle Theatre, 40 Brattle St, 617-876-6837, www.brattlefilm.org; Brazilian Cultural Center of New England, 310 Webster Ave, 617-547-5343, www.capoeira-an gola.com; Cambridge Multicultural Arts Center, 41 Second St, 617-577-1400, www.cmacusa.org; Harvard Film Archive, 24 Quincy St, 617-495-4700, www.harvardfilmarchive.org; Hasty Pudding Theatricals, 12 Holyoke St, 617-495-5205, www.hastypudding.org; Improv Boston, 1253 Cambridge St, 617-576-1253, www.improvboston.com; Jose Mateo Ballet Theatre, 400 Har vard St, 617-354-7467, www.ballettheatre.org; MIT List Visual Arts Center, 20 Ames St, 617-253-4680, http://web.mit.edu/lvac; Cambridgeside Galleria, 100 Cambridgeside Pl, 617-621-8666, www.cambridgesidegalleria.com; Fresh Pond Mall, 185 Alewife Brook Pkwy, 617-491-4431; for area colleges and uni versities, see the **Childcare and Education** chapter.

Public School Education: Cambridge Public Schools, Administrative Offices, 159 Thorndike St, 617-349-6400, www.cpsd.us

Public Transportation: *Trains*: Red Line stops at Kendall/MIT, Central Sq, Harvard Sq, Porter Sq, Alewife; Green Line D and E train stops at Lechmere

Buses: nos. 1, 47, 62, 64, 66, 70, 70A, 71-73, 74/75, 76, 77, 77A, 78-80, 83-88, 91, 96, 350/351, CT1, and CT2; for MBTA route and schedule information contact the MBTA Traveler's Information Center: 617-222-3200, 800-392-6100, TTY 617-222-5146 or go to www.mbta.com.

MALDEN

Boundaries: East: Revere; **South**: Everett; **West**: Medford; **North**: Stoneham and Melrose

Malden, about five square miles in size, lies five miles north of Boston. First settled in 1629 and then referred to as Mystic Side, the town was incorporated in 1649 and as a city in 1882. In the last century, its desirability has fluctuated somewhat—from a solidly middle-class suburb during the baby boom years of the 1940s, '50s, and '60s, to a more working-class area in a bit of economic decline during the 1970s, '80s and '90s. During its heyday, Malden was especially popular with Italian and Jewish families who moved here from the city in search of bigger homes and bigger lawns. When baby boomers came of age, however, those who could afford to leave went to the even greener suburbs of the North Shore. Today Malden is on the upswing, with young professionals, families, and newly arrived immigrants moving in. Many of those who cannot or perhaps do not want to pay the high rents in the city come here, enjoying Malden's proximity and easy access to the city, without the higher cost of living. Malden is an economically and racially diverse community; the Chinese and Vietnamese presence is especially visible in the many Asian establishments, particularly restaurants.

Maldonians, as residents are called, live mostly in one-, two- or three-family triple-deckers and Victorians. Although there are a few apartment complexes, such as the Granada Highlands (popular with the elderly community), Malden is noted for its large Victorian homes with lawns, turrets, porches, ambling stairways, and driveways. But, there is more of an urban outskirt–feel here than that of a green leafy suburb. Ten percent of Malden's housing stock is subsidized low- to moderate-income, which is more than can be found in some of Boston's other more strictly suburban communities.

Malden lacks the number of historical or cultural sites that dominate much of the greater Boston area. It has no major universities or theaters, nor is it a "destination," per se. But as far as housing goes, compared to Boston, Malden may offer better value for your dollar. It also offers quick access to downtown, with two Orange Line T stops, and routes I-93, 1, or 28 will get you to town in 10 to 20 minutes. New bars, storefronts, and restaurants, from the Ryan Family Amusement Center (bowling alley) on Main Street to Artichokes Trattoria on Florence Street, have opened up in response to the recent influx of residents. However, those wanting an exciting night out should head to Boston.

Area Code: 781
Zip Code: 02148
Post Offices: 664 Salem St; 109 Mountain Ave
Police: Malden Police Department, 200 Pleasant St, 781-397-7171, www.malden pd.com
Emergency Hospitals: Lawrence Memorial Hospital, 170 Governors Ave, Med-

ford, 781-306-6000, www.hallmarkhealth.org; Melrose-Wakefield Hospital, 585 Lebanon St, Melrose, 781-979-3000, www.hallmarkhealth.org; Whidden Memorial Hospital, 103 Garland St, Everett, 617-389-6270, www.cha.harvard. edu

Libraries: Main Library, 36 Salem St, 781-324-0218; www.maldenpubliclibrary. org

Parks & Open Space: Amerige Park; Bell Rock Park; Coytemore Lea Park; Devir Park; Fellsmere Pond and Park; Hunting Field; Middlesex Fells Reservation, www.mass.gov/dcr; Miller Park; O'Connell Park; Pine Banks Park; Roosevelt Park; Trafton Park

Community Publications: *Malden Evening News*, 781-321-8000; *Malden Observer*, 781-322-6957, www.townonline.com/malden/

Community Resources: www.ci.malden.ma.us; Malden Chamber of Commerce, 200 Pleasant St, 781-322-4500; Malden Historical Society, 36 Salem St, 781-338-9365; Chinese Culture Connection, 238 Highland Ave, 781-321-6316, www.chinesecultureconnection.com; Ideas 5 Artists' Studios, 183 Pleasant St, 781-322-8640, www.ideas5.com; Malden Access Television, 145 Pleasant St, 781-321-6400, www.matv.org; Malden Arts/Cultural Council, 200 Pleasant St, 781-388-0857; Window Arts Malden, 781-330-9053, www.maldenarts.com.

Public School Education: Malden Public Schools, 200 Pleasant St, 781-397-7204, www.malden.mec.edu

Public Transportation: *Trains*: Orange Line at Malden Center and Oak Grove, commuter rail at Malden Center

Buses: nos. 97, 99, 101, 104–108, 131, 132, 136/137, 411, 427, and 430; for MBTA route and schedule information contact the MBTA Traveler's Information Center: 617-222-3200, 800-392-6100, TTY 617-222-5146 or go to www.mbta. com.

MEDFORD

Boundaries: **East**: Everett and the Malden River; **South**: Mystic River and Somerville; **West**: Mystic Valley Pkwy and Upper and Lower Mystic Lake; **Northwest**: Stoneham and Middlesex Fells Reservation

Located five miles northwest of Boston off Interstate 93, Medford is home to Tufts University, an honor it shares with nearby Somerville. The presence of Tufts means that students, faculty, and staff make up a large contingent of Medford's almost 56,000 residents.

Medford's early commerce was of a mercantile nature; as a seaport situated on the tidewaters of the Mystic River, which runs into the Atlantic Ocean, the town was well located for trading. A man named Thatcher Magoun utilized the riverside location to commence a clipper shipbuilding industry. The seaport also enabled Medford to participate in the Triangle Trade Route, for its part distilling molasses into its then- famous "Medford Rum." Ships left Medford loaded with rum for West Africa, where the alcohol was traded for slaves. They then headed to the West Indies, where slaves were sold and molasses purchased, and finally back to New England, where the molasses was distilled into rum. By the 1800s, the brick-making industry also took hold in Medford, and immigrants, particularly Irish, moved in to work the local brickyards and the Medford granite quarry. Magoun's shipyard was booming in 1855, at which time it is said to have employed 1,100 people. Later in the century, with the decline of shipbuilding, the city's businesses expanded into textiles, shoe-making machinery, chemicals, and manufacturing.

In 1852, Charles Tufts, a brickmaker and descendant of one of the first settlers of neighboring Malden, gave 20 acres of land atop a hill straddling the Somerville and Medford line to the Unitarian church on the condition that it be used for a college. The school got its charter from the state of Massachusetts that same year and became Tufts University, named after its first benefactor. Subsequent land gifts boosted Tufts' property size up to 100 acres.

Beyond the areas around Tufts, which have an understandably collegiate feel, Medford is a working and middle-class enclave adjacent to Boston, and serves as a haven for those who want urban living, decent city access, and more affordable (than Boston) housing prices. Housing styles run the gamut, and include federal, Greek revival, and Victorian homes, as well as the ever-present triple-deckers, although most residences are packed close together and sit on small lots. There are some historic homes here, including the Isaac Royall estate, which holds the dubious title of being the only surviving building in the north with its attached slave quarters intact. There are older two- and three-family homes in **South Medford**, or newer (20th century) construction in **West Medford** off High Street. Other areas, such as **Wellington** (near the Orange Line T stop in southeast Medford), **Fulton Heights**, **Lawrence Estates**, and **Medford Hillside** (in West Medford, just north of Tufts) also tend toward 20th-century architecture, offering bungalows, cottages, ranches, colonials, and Cape Cods.

Medford's shopping amenities are basic, tending more toward grocery, variety, and liquor stores than luxury boutiques. Unlike many of the tree-lined residential areas, the shopping districts of Salem Street, Main Street, Riverside Avenue, and High Street in **Medford Square** and **West Medford** are fairly urban. For greater shopping pursuits, you can head to the Meadow Glen Mall along the Mystic River on Route 16. Medford residents who prefer the great outdoors to shoe shopping are in luck as well; the Middlesex Fells Reservation (better known simply as the Fells) contains 2,000 acres of meadows, wetlands, forests, and ponds, located along most of Medford's northern border. People come here, as well as to the Mystic River Reservation, to enjoy expanses of flora and fauna and to fish, hike, bike, and jog.

Boston is a quick and easy drive from East Medford down I-93, and Route 38 heads into the city as well, via Somerville. Routes 16 and 60 bring drivers to Cambridge or Arlington, where they can hook up with Route 2 leading west. For those without a car, living in Medford will be more of a challenge. T access is limited to an Orange Line stop at Wellington—on the eastern periphery of town—and a commuter rail stop at West Medford. A lucky few may be within walking distance of the Red Line stop at Davis Square in Somerville; bus lines are also available.

Area Code: 781

Zip Codes: 02153, 02155, 02156

Post Offices: 20 Forest St; 470 Boston Ave (Tufts University); 485 High St

Police: Medford Police, 100 Main St, 781-391-6404; www.medfordpolice.com

Emergency Hospitals: Lawrence Memorial Hospital, 170 Governors Ave, 781-306-6000, www.hallmarkhealth.org; Tufts University Health Service, 124 Professors Row, 617-627-3350, http://ase.tufts.edu/healthservices

Library: Medford Public Library, 111 High St, 781-395-7950; www.medfordlibrary.org

Parks & Open Space: Barry Park; Brooks Estate; Carr Park; Columbus Park; Harris Park; Hickey Park; Hormel Stadium Facility & Riverbend Park; Middlesex Fells Reservation, www.mass.gov/dcr; Morrison Park; Playstead Park; Thomas Brooks Park; Tufts Park; Victory Park; Wrights Pond/City Park; go to www.medford.org/Pages/MedfordMA_DPW/parks/parks for more information.

Community Publications: *Medford Transcript,* 781-396-1982, www.townonline.com/medford/index.html

Community Resources: www.medford.org, Medford Chamber of Commerce, 781-396-1277, www.medfordchamberma.com; Chevalier Memorial Auditorium and Gene Mack Gymnasium, 781-396-7773; Friends of the Middlesex Fells Reservation, 781-662-2340, www.fells.org; Grandfather's House, 114 South St; Isaac Royall House, 15 George St, 781-396-9032, http://royallhouse.org; Tufts (Cradock) House, 350 Riverside Ave; New England Storm (Women's Professional Football), Hormel Stadium, 781-395-TEAM, www.newenglandstorm.com; North Medford Club, www.northmedfordclub.org; Black Lab Craft and Fine Art Event, 781-395-1930; The Chevalier Theatre, 30 Forest St, 781-391-7469, www.chevaliertheatre.com; Mystic Players, 781-942-1340, www.mysticplayers.org; Springstep, 98 George P. Hassett Dr, 781-395-0402, www.springstep.org; West Medford Open Studios, 77 Monument St, 781-483-3605; Meadow Glenn Mall, 3850 Mystic Valley Pkwy, 781-395-6710, www.meadowglen.com; for area colleges and universities, see the **Childcare and Education** chapter.

Public School Education: Medford Public Schools, 489 Winthrop St, 781-393-2387, www.medford.k12.ma.us

Public Transportation: *Trains:* Orange Line at Wellington, Red Line at Davis Sq (Somerville); commuter rail at West Medford

Buses: nos. 80, 90, 94-97, 99-101, 106, 108, 110, 112, 134, 325, 326, 354 and 355; for MBTA route and schedule information contact the MBTA Traveler's Information Center: 617-222-3200, 800-392-6100, TTY 617-222-5246 or go to www. mbta.com.

NEWTON

Boundaries: **North, West, and South**: bordered by the Charles River; **East**: Middlesex County line, Brighton, Brookline, West Roxbury

Newton is Boston suburbia at its finest, comprising 13 villages: Auburndale, Chestnut Hill, Lower Falls, Newton Centre, Newton Corner, Newton Highlands, Newtonville, Nonantum, Oak Hill, Thompsonville, Upper Falls, Waban, and West Newton. The villages cover over 18 square miles of some of the most desirable and safe land (named the nation's safest city by research group Morgan Quitno from 2003 to 2005) in the greater Boston area.

Referred to as the "Garden City," Newton was originally part of the Cambridge land grant of 1630, incorporating as a separate town in 1688. By 1873, Newton had become a city, complete with a Mayor, Board of Aldermen, and Common Council. Also dating back to the 1630s, the **Newton Corner** area near the Newton-Brighton line was the original settlement. Sometimes just called "Newton," this neighborhood boasts Newton's own historic museum, Jackson Homestead. Sparsely populated in its earliest years, it served as a stagecoach stopping point. More came here to live in the 1830s and '40s when the Boston & Worcester Railroad brought commuter tracks here.

By the early 1700s, people were being drawn to the powerful glacial waterfalls and rapids along the Charles River, constructing the industrial villages of Newton Upper Falls and Newton Lower Falls. **Newton Upper Falls**, in southern Newton across the Charles River from Needham, saw a sawmill established in 1688, followed by a grist mill (1710), a woolen mill (1715), snuff and wire mills (late 1700s), and finally a cotton mill in 1823. Much of this area is now a historic district. The closest T access is the Green Line D train's Eliot stop, at Route 9 and Woodward Street. **Newton Lower Falls**, across the Charles, got its start in 1704 when John Hubbard and Caleb Church dammed the river to create an ironworks. By the 1800s, paper mills began cropping up in Lower Falls—by 1816, there were nine mills spread out over two dams. Sadly, the urban renewal of the 1970s destroyed much of this neighborhood's historic architecture, but a few remnants of the original mill village, including a Georgian mansion and some late 19th-century Victorian architecture, survive on Washington Street. Although it may not be within walking distance for many Lower Falls residents, there is still close access to the Woodland T stop on the Green Line D train at Washington Street northeast of Beacon Street, by the Newton-Wellesley Hospital.

Nonantum was also a site for waterpower generation. Considered Newton's own mini version of Little Italy, this tightly knit Italian community celebrates various saints, and the fire hydrants are painted with red, green, and white stripes. One of the most affordable neighborhoods in greater Boston, Nonantum welcomes all newcomers. Nonantum has no T access, but residents can head a bit south for the Newtonville commuter rail stop.

Newton Centre, the largest of the villages, is the area around Centre Street between Beacon Street and Comm Ave. Until the mid-1800s, this area was sparsely settled. In the 1850s, the Charles River Railroad came through, and in the 1870s it was upgraded to include commuter service to Boston, which turned Newton Centre into an affluent suburb. Hence, much of the architecture in this part of town is representative of late 19th- century suburban styles. Residents of this village also have T access: the Newton Centre stop on the Green Line's D train is on Union Street, between Herrick Street and Langley Road.

The Village of **Thompsonville**, just south of Newton Centre and east of Chestnut Hill, is the area roughly bound by Beacon and Boylston streets to the north and south, respectively, and the Hammond Pond Parkway and Parker Street to the east and west. One of the area's larger theological schools, the Andover Newton Theological Seminary, falls within Thompsonville's boundaries. Villagers use the Newton Centre T stop.

Railroad extensions through Newton that connected it with Boston were responsible for the development of many of the other villages, including Chestnut Hill (1850s), Newton Highlands (1870s) and Waban (1880s). **Chestnut Hill**, at Newton's eastern border with Brighton and Brookline, was once owned almost entirely by the Hammond Family, who settled there in 1665. The Charles River Railroad and Beacon Street were extended to this part of town in the early 1850s, piercing Chestnut Hill's isolation by connecting it to Boston and Brookline. By the late 1800s, settlement here began in earnest, and between 1880 and 1910 most of the land was segmented into private estates, building lots, and a farm. Thus, today's Chestnut Hill architecture is largely representative of that era, featuring Georgian, colonial revival, and shingle homes, in particular. Much of Boston College's campus, which straddles Newton and Brighton, is also located in Chestnut Hill. Residents have access to the Chestnut Hill T stop on the Green Line's D train, and those near the BC campus can ride into town from the BC stop at the end of the Green Line's B train.

The area just north of Route 9, where it intersects with Woodward and Walnut streets, belongs to the village of **Newton Highlands**. Much of this area once belonged to John Haynes, the governor of the Massachusetts Bay Colony in 1635. Newton Highlands was predominantly agricultural until the mid- to late-1800s, when the railroad-related population booms in neighboring Newton Corner and West Newton caused real estate developers to look toward the highlands. The Charles River Railroad cut through the area in 1850, but didn't present a commuter option until the 1870s. Before then, trains were used to haul dirt for the

Back Bay landfill project. Today's commuters have access to two Green Line stops: Newton Highlands at Lincoln and Walnut streets, near the village shopping district, and Eliot, near Route 9 and Woodward Street. Many homes in this area date back to the 1870s—examples of Victorian architecture abound, along with mansard, Italianate, and colonial revival styles.

West of Newton Highlands and along the Charles, across from Newton's border with Wellesley, is the village of **Waban**. Until 1855, the area was comprised of four large farms. During that year, Beacon Street was extended westward to the junction of Woodward and Washington streets—the intersection of the four farms. In 1886, the Charles River Railroad commuter service to Boston came through, and more development followed. Today, the private Brae Burn Country Club takes up a good portion of Waban's land. Modern commuters still enjoy the proximity to train lines: the D Line's Waban stop is on Beacon Street in Waban Square, and the Woodland stop is toward the boundaries of Waban, Newton Lower Falls, and Auburndale, on Washington Street.

Newtonville is the area around the intersection of the Mass Pike and Walnut Street. Previously a broad, well-watered plain used for agriculture, the environs seen today were partially created by the daily commuter trains along the Boston & Albany railroad that came through in the latter half of the 19th century. Developers first laid house lots on small plots near the railroad line in the 1840s, but the area didn't become popular until Newton built its first high school here in 1859. By the Civil War, Newtonville had arrived. As with other Newton villages that developed during the 19th century, Victorian architecture, Greek and colonial revivals, and friendly tree-lined parks are aplenty. While Newtonville residents have no T stop, there is bus service and a commuter rail stop between Harvard and Walnut streets by the Mass Pike. Of course, this village is also convenient for commuters who wish to take the Pike into Boston. And as a random (yet important!) side note, Newtonville is home to one of Boston's surviving independent bookstores, Newtonville Books.

At Newton's westernmost tip, just north of Newton Lower Falls, along the Charles River and boundary with Weston, lies **Auburndale**. Until the 1830s, this village was just a remote tract of farmland, marsh, and rolling wooded hills; even in 1831, Auburndale had only seven families. That all changed, however, by 1837 when the Boston & Worcester Railroad extended to this area. By the 1860s, Auburndale was a bona fide village with residents who enjoyed easy access to the Charles and the Stony Brook Reservoir. Like neighboring Newton Lower Falls, Auburndale was adversely affected by the construction of Route 128 and the Mass Pike. However, unlike Newton Lower Falls, Auburndale was able to hold onto some of its older housing stock. Look for homes from the 18th, 19th, and 20th centuries here, including farmhouses and colonial revivals. Auburndale retains its original roots as a commuter stop; today's commuters have easy access to the Pike, the Auburndale commuter rail stop (on Lexington Street at the Pike), and two T stops on the Green Line D train—Woodland (at Washington and Beacon streets) and Riverside (the D train terminus on Grove Street off Route 128).

Finally, just northeast of Auburndale is the village of **West Newton**, the final railway village located between the Mass Pike and Newton's northern border with Waltham. Like Auburndale, West Newton was once a thinly settled agricultural area full of forests and swamps. West Newton originally made the map in 1764, when it became the religious center for northwestern Newton with the construction of the West Parish (Congregational) Church. When the Boston & Worcester line was set up as a commuter rail line in 1834, the area began its life as a suburb. By 1850, new, year-round homes were going up on West Newton Hill, and Irish immigrants and other local workers were moving into modest cottages along the River Street flats. Today, West Newton residents enjoy easy access to the Pike and a small village center with shops, restaurants, and an independent art-house cinema. Some 19th-century construction remains, including simple Greek Revivals and Italianate homes with long front porches and bay windows. West Newton residents have no T access but, like Newtonville, they do have bus service, a commuter rail stop on Route 16, and easy access to the Mass Pike.

Oak Hill was created specifically as a neighborhood of affordable, modern homes for WWII veterans. In Newton's southernmost territory, this village is roughly bound by Mt. Ida College to the north, West Roxbury to the south, Dedham Street to the east, and the Charles River on the west. The City of Newton financed the construction of Oak Hill, formerly a sand and gravel pit. At the time, only veterans who were Newton residents before the war were allowed to move here. The village features a series of culs-de-sac and the houses themselves are small, modern cottages cut from six basic designs; each has a living room, dining area, kitchen, three bedrooms, bath, and utility room, but no basement. The original owners had their choice of clapboard, cedar shingle, or asbestos shingle siding, and hip or gable roofs, as well as garages, porches, and breezeways as the extras. When built, most of the homes faced public walkways, away from the street. However, over the years, many have been remodeled so the front doors now face the street. Additionally, many residents have added second floors. Northern Oak Hill was not part of the original housing development, and hence the architecture is slightly different; expect split-levels here. Streets throughout the original Oak Hill development are named after Newton residents who died during WWII. Oak Hill has no T or commuter rail access, but it does have bus service. The Charles River Country Club (private) is also here.

Today Newton's villages vary from enormous homes on sprawling greenery to more tightly packed, citified areas, like Route 9 and Newton Corner. Even so, during peak rush hours, this city is much quieter than Boston. A solidly residential enclave with good public schools, lovely parks, and easy access to Boston, Newton is one of Boston's priciest areas. The variety of housing is incredible. You'll find Victorians, colonials, Dutch Colonials, Brick Colonials, Tudors, 19th-century cottages, Craftsman bungalows, and picturesque Revivals.

It's probably easier to buy a house in Newton than to find an apartment, although its sought-after address will make for competition on the home-buying front. Those who rent will find Newton a much better deal than downtown. Most renters here are students at one of Newton's several small colleges or BC, but young professionals can be found in places like Newton Corner. Newton does have its commercial amenities, including bars, restaurants, movie theaters, and a major commercial stretch along Route 9. Most villages have all the necessary services and usually a good restaurant or pub to boot, but there is not an excess of entertainment or nightlife, so many head to Boston for a night out.

As a general rule of thumb, the more affordable homes are in West Newton, Newton Corner, Auburndale and Nonantum; pricier neighborhoods include Chestnut Hill, Newton Centre, Waban and Newton Highlands. Newton Corner and Chestnut Hill also offer high-rise apartments.

There is a substantial Asian population in Newton, and it also shares the title as the seat of Boston's Jewish community with neighboring Brookline. You'll find many active synagogues in Chestnut Hill, Newton Lower Falls, Oak Hill, Newton Centre and Newton Corner, as well as a great number of churches. Newton Centre also houses the Andover Newton Theological Seminary, and Catholic churches can be found in Waban and in Nonantum.

As for T access, there are many Green Line and commuter rail T stops and bus routes throughout, but Newton is so big that often residents do not have a stop within walking distance. Newton is a great place to live for car owners, however. Parking is aplenty by Boston standards, and most of Boston is accessible in about 15 minutes via the Mass Pike. Newton also has easy access to routes 9 and I-95/128.

Area Code: 617

Zip Codes: Auburndale, 02466; Chestnut Hill, 02467; Newton, 02458–02462; Newton Centre, 02459; Newton Highlands, 02461; Newton Lower Falls, 02462; Newton Upper Falls, 02464; Newtonville, 02458, 02460, 02462; Waban, 02468; West Newton, 02465

Post Offices: 2122 Comm Ave (Auburndale); 136 Comm Ave (BC); 12 Middlesex Rd (Chestnut Hill); 716 N Beacon St (Newton Center); 63 Lincoln St (Newton Highlands); 2344 Washington St, Suite 1 (Newton Lower Falls); 81 Oak St (Newton Upper Falls); 897 Washington St (Newtonville); 326 Watertown St (Nonantum); 83 Wyman St (Waban); 525 Waltham St (West Newton)

Police: Newton Police Headquarters, 1321 Washington St, 617-796-2100

Emergency Hospital: Newton-Wellesley Hospital, 2014 Washington St, 617-243-6000, www.nwh.org

Library: Newton Free Library Main Branch, 330 Homer St, Newton Centre, 617-796-1360, TTY 617-552-7154; www.ci.newton.ma.us/Library

Parks & Open Space: Auburndale Cove; Bullough Pond; Burr Park; Cabot Park; Chestnut Hill Reservation, 617-333-7404, www.mass.gov/dcr; Crystal Lake

Park; Davis Playground; Edmands Park; Forte Memorial Park; Gath Memorial Pool; Hamilton Playground; Hammond Pond Reservation, www.mass.gov/dcr; Hunnewell Park; Joanne C. Pellegrini Memorial Park; New Cold Spring Park; Newton Centre Green; Oak Hill Playground; Old Cold Spring Park; Hemlock Gorge, Friends of Hemlock Gorge, www.hemlockgorge.org

Community Publication: *Newton TAB,* www.townonline.com/newton, 617-969-0340

Community Resources: www.ci.newton.ma.us, www.newtoncitizens.com; Newton-Needham Chamber of Commerce, 281 Needham St, 617-244-5300, www.nnchamber.com; New Art Center, 61 Washington Park, 617-964-3424, www.newartcenter.org; New Philharmonic Orchestra, 617-527-9717, www.newphil.org; Newton Choral Society, 617-527-SING, www.newtonchoral.org; Newton Community Chorus, www.newtoncommunitychorus.org; Newton Country Players, 617-244-9538, www.newtoncountryplayers.org; Newton Symphony Orchestra, 230 Central St, 617-965-2555, www.newtonsymphony.org; Turtle Lane Playhouse, 283 Melrose St, 617-244-0169, www.turtlelane.org; West Newton Cinema, 126 Washington St, 617-964-6060, www.westnewtoncinema.com; Longyear Museum, 1125 Boylston St, 617-278-9000, www.longyear.org; Mary Baker Eddy House, 400 Beacon St, 617-566-3092; Newton History Museum at The Jackson Homestead, 527 Washington St, 617-796-1450, www.ci.newton.ma.us/jackson; Brae Burn Country Club, 326 Fuller St, 617-244-0680, wwwbraeburngolf.com; Charles River Country Club, 617-332-1320, 483 Dedham St, www.charlesriverccc.org; The Windsor Club, 1601 Beacon St, 617-527-9871, www.windsorclub.org; Atrium Mall, 300 Boylston St, 617-527-1400, www.atrium-mall.com; The Mall at Chestnut Hill, 199 Boylston St (Route 9), 617-965-3038, www.mallatchestnuthill.com; for area colleges and universities, see the **Childcare and Education** chapter.

Public School Education: Newton Public Schools, 100 Walnut St, 617-559-6100, www.newton.k12.ma.us

Public Transportation: *Trains*: Green Line D train at Chestnut Hill, Newton Centre, Newton Highlands, Eliot, Waban, Woodland, and Riverside; Commuter Rail at Auburndale, West Newton, and Newtonville

Buses: nos. 52, 57, 59, 60, 500-502, 504, 505, 553–556, and 558; for MBTA route and schedule information contact the MBTA Traveler's Information Center: 617-222-3200, 800-392-6100, TTY 617-222-5146 or go to www.mbta.com.

SOMERVILLE

Boundaries: **North**: Medford and the Mystic River; **East**: Charlestown; **South and Southwest**: Cambridge; **West**: Arlington

Once dubbed "Slummerville" and regarded as a grungy urban area that lacked the charm or cultural offerings of a Boston or Cambridge, Somerville has cleaned itself up, gone straight, and jumped on the gentrification wagon since the T extended its Red Line service to Porter and Davis squares in the mid-1980s. Today it is home to a mix of artists, long time Irish- and Italian-American residents, newly arrived immigrants, and young, mostly single, professionals (according to *Money* magazine, Somerville has the seventh highest concentration of single people in the nation). Somerville continues to draw those looking for the next cool, affordable place to live—housing is comparably inexpensive, though it does increase in price closer to Davis Square—and it is now said in the same breath as its more cultural and moneyed counterpart, Cambridge.

Somerville was included in the Charlestown land grant of 1630, but became an independent town in 1842 and incorporated as a city in 1872. John Winthrop, the first governor of the Massachusetts Bay Colony, made his home in Somerville during the 1600s. He lived in a neighborhood along Somerville's northern border with the Mystic River that today is called **Ten Hills**. The neighborhood features homes of old and new construction, as well as some light industrial land and parkland along the Mystic.

Originally Somerville was a grazing area for colonial dairy farms, and then served as an important military location for the Revolutionary Army. **Prospect Hill**, in the city center between Highland and Somerville avenues, was the site of military fortifications, some remnants of which still exist in Prospect Hill Park. Today the neighborhood boasts wide, tree-lined streets, older homes, many parks, and views of Boston. Other historical notes: the first American flag was raised here in January of 1776, and Major General Charles Lee used a house on Sycamore Street as his headquarters during the Revolutionary War.

By the early 19th century, Somerville was located right along the transportation corridor linking Boston to the northwest, thus positioning the town perfectly as an industrial center along the Mystic River. Although Somerville also had dairy, agriculture, pottery, and slate industries at the time, it was the brickyards that became its major source of commerce. During the mid-1800s, Irish immigrants came by the droves to labor in the brickyards, each year producing over one million bricks by hand, and even more after the development of a patent press. By 1842, Highland Avenue had become Somerville's civic center (the original Greek revival city hall survives and performs its original function), while **Union Square**, in southeastern Somerville, became its center of commerce. Bow Street in Union Square still features many well-preserved period commercial buildings.

Boston's extension of the trolley tracks in the late 19th century paved the way for the surrounding communities' expansion, and Somerville was no exception. In fact, between 1890 and 1910, almost 50% of Somerville's current housing stock was built. As a result, much of the architecture is devoted to sturdy triple-deckers and multiple-family housing, intended originally for those who came to work in the local brickyards, iron mills, tube works, and meat packing plants. The abundance of multiple-family housing in Somerville is responsible for its impressively high-density population: according to the 2000 Census, Somerville has almost 77,500 people living in just over four square miles. Peak occupancy was during WWII, when over 105,000 people lived here! Triple-deckers have roomy interiors, and renters can get a positively spacious multi-room apartment, with a lawn and possibly a parking space, for what one would spend for a "closet" in downtown Boston. For something more historic and aesthetically pleasing, early 20th-century brick apartment houses and tenements can be found, especially on Highland Avenue and around Union Square. There are a few historic districts, including Spring Hill, Mt. Vernon, and Westwood Road. Summer Street is made up predominantly of colonial revivals, with well-preserved Victorian churches. The retail areas of Davis Square feature the architecturally important Somerville Theatre, great coffee shops, an art-deco bank, and the Rosebud Diner.

Union Square, close to Cambridge's Inman Square, is located in a triangular area where Prospect Street, Webster Avenue, Somerville Avenue, and Washington Street all intersect. In addition to municipal buildings surviving from Somerville's earliest days, this area has many small businesses, pubs, and ethnic restaurants, including a Portuguese restaurant and bakery and many Indian eateries. Recently, Union Square emerged as the new "hip" place to live, due to cheaper rents and a thriving nightlife, but lock in rents or buy now—those places deemed cool become overrun and overpriced quickly (see Davis Square). For those without wheels, getting around will be an issue—there are no T stops within walking distance. There have been rumors that the MBTA will one day extend the Green Line through Union Square, but until that happens (don't hold your breath!), those living here will have to make due with bus service, a car, bike, or their own two legs.

Davis Square, located where College Avenue and Highland Street intersect with Holland Avenue, is the only Somerville square with a stop on the Red Line, and is the birthplace of Somerville's late 20th-century gentrification—hence, rents are higher here than elsewhere in Somerville. It is a bustling place, with one-of-a-kind stores, coffee shops, restaurants, and bars that draw a distinctly young (mid- to late-20s) crowd. In terms of artistic presence, Davis Square hosts Somerville Open Studios (an annual arts festival each spring) and houses the Somerville Theatre, which, in addition to mainstream, second-run movies, features international shorts and art films, and hosts the international animation festival each year.

Magoun Square, just off Medford Street, between Winter Hill and Powderhouse Circle, is an old-fashioned commercial area, with storefronts looking as they might have appeared in the 1950s and '60s. **Winter Hill**, once home to the Winter Hill Gang run by Irish mob boss "Whitey" Bulger, is just north of Highland Avenue in central Somerville, and is a predominantly residential neighborhood with several parks and somewhat affordable homes. In northern Somerville, **Powderhouse Circle**, between Highland and Boston avenues, Elm Street, and

Tufts University, is where you'll find gracious homes on large lots with views of the Tufts athletic fields. **Ball Square** is just past Trum Field on Broadway and is home to many small bakeries. **Teele Square**, which overlaps with **Tufts University**, is also on Broadway near Powderhouse Boulevard, and borders Route 16 near Arlington. Davis Square's nightlife spills out toward Teele Square, but Teele is more residential. Both Ball and Teele squares are located in the heart of Tufts' territory; their triple-deckers are overrun with coeds, and most stores in these areas cater to the college set.

Somerville's picturesque neighborhoods include West Somerville and Spring Hill. Due west of Davis Square along the Arlington border, **West Somerville** has some older Victorian homes and a suburban, residential feel. East of Cambridge's Porter Square, between Highland and Somerville avenues, is **Spring Hill**, another residential neighborhood with lots of lawns, gardens, and hills— and views of Boston and Cambridge. Spring Hill has the added convenience of being within walking distance of the Red Line's Porter Square T stop just over the Cambridge border.

Davis Square and, to a lesser extent, Porter Square in Cambridge, offer Red Line access to the southwestern portions of Somerville. The only other viable T station is the Orange Line's Sullivan Square stop, just beyond the fringe of Somerville's industrial border, alongside I-93 in Charlestown. Those in other areas must rely on bus service or cars. Parking in Somerville can be tight—the Tufts area being most difficult—but the multiple-family housing makes getting a parking space more likely. On-street parking is regulated by resident permit (obtainable for $10/year). And if you are looking to escape the city by car, Somerville offers easy access to routes I-93, 1, 2, 16, 28, and 38.

Area Code: 617
Zip Codes: 02143–02145
Post Offices: 237 Washington St; 58 Day St; 320 Broadway
Police: Somerville Police, 220 Washington St, 617-625-1600
Emergency Hospital: Somerville Hospital, 230 Highland Ave, 617-591-4500, www.cha.harvard.edu
Library: Somerville Public Library Central Branch, 79 Highland Ave, 617-623-5000; www.somervillepubliclibrary.org
Parks & Open Space: Alewife Brook Reservation, 617-727-9693, www.mass.gov/dcr; Alewife Linear Park; Conway Park; Corbett Park; Dilboy Field; Draw Seven Park; East Somerville Community Playground; Foss Park; Glen Park; Kenney Park; Lincoln Park; Marshall Street Playground; Mystic River Reservation, www.mass.gov/dcr; Osgood Park; Perry Park; Seven Hills Park; Shore Drive Parkland; Trum Field and Playground; Vinal Avenue Community Growing Center
Community Publication: *Somerville Journal*, 617-625-6300, www.townonline.com/somerville

Community Resources: www.somervillema.gov, www.bostonsquares.com/davis; Somerville Chamber of Congress, 2 Alpine St, 617-776-4100, www.somervillechamber.org; Jimmy Tingle's Off Broadway, 255 Elm St, 617-591-1616, www.jtoffbroadway.com; Loews Assembly Square, 35 Middlesex Ave, 617-628-7000; Somerville Arts Council, 50 Evergreen Ave, 617-625-6600 ext. 2985, www.somervilleartscouncil.org; Somerville Museum, 1 Westwood Rd, 617-666-9810, www.somervillemuseum.org; Somerville Open Studios, 617-623-5590, www.somervilleopenstudios.org; Somerville Theatre, 55 Davis Sq, 617-625-5700, www.somervilletheatreonline.com; Washington Street Art Center, 321 Washington St, 617-632-5315, www.washingtonst.org; for area colleges and universities, see the **Childcare and Education** chapter.

Public School Education: Somerville Public Schools, 181 Washington St, 617-625-0953, www.somerville.k12.ma.us

Public Transportation: *Trains*: Red Line at Davis Sq and Porter Sq (Cambridge); Orange Line at Sullivan Sq (Charlestown)

Buses: nos. 80, 83, 85-92, 94, 96, 101, 194, and CT2; for MBTA route and schedule information contact the MBTA Traveler's Information Center: 617-222-3200, 800-392-6100, TTY 617-222-5146 or go to www.mbta.com.

WALTHAM

Boundaries: North: Lexington; **East**: Belmont and Watertown; **Southeast**: Newton; **Southwest**: Weston; **West**: Lincoln

Waltham, named after Waltham, England, covers over 13 square miles in the westernmost part of metro Boston, inside Route 128. Bisected in the south by the Charles River, Waltham's proximity to Boston, good housing values, and commercial and entertainment venues has made it a popular place to live. Residents include wealthy sports stars on Boston's professional athletic teams, young professionals who work on Technology Highway (a section of Route 128 where many high-tech companies are headquartered), as well as young families, and college students and faculty of Brandeis University and Bentley College, both located within its bounds.

Originally a part of Watertown, Waltham became an independent town in 1738. Main Street (now also Route 20) was the post road from Boston and has served as the civic and commercial center of Waltham since the early 18th century. The northern section of Waltham got its start as an agricultural area, while industry, particularly watchmaking, developed along the Charles River in the south. In 1854, Aaron Dennison opened the Waltham Watch Company, which flourished for over 100 years, and today Waltham is nostalgically known as "Watch City." Two rural federal period estates survive and are open for tours: Gore Place, just south of Main Street in southeastern Waltham by the Watertown line, and The Vale (also known as the Lyman Estate) in central Waltham just north of Lyman Pond.

Although there are many sub-neighborhoods throughout the city (and corresponding neighborhood associations), most people think of Waltham in terms of north, southeast, west, and central. **Southeast Waltham** is a working-class area with many young families. From Beaver Street south to the town line you'll find affordable multiple-family housing. The westernmost portion of Southeast Waltham, adjacent to Auburndale in Newton and across the Charles from Angleside, is called the **Island**. It's a residential neighborhood of mixed housing, from multi-family structures to small cottages to large Victorians situated around Cram's Cove and Purgatory Cove, inlets of the river. To get here, you must go through a light industrial area that separates the Island from the rest of the residences of Southeast Waltham, either via Rumford or Woerd avenues. Residents have easy access to greenspace in Auburndale, including Norumbega Park.

Waltham Center, roughly the area where Main and Moody streets intersect just north of the Charles River, has surviving 19th-century factory complexes as well as brick Victorian and neo-classic civic and business buildings. This is the veritable city center, full of all the commercial offerings the local student set and young professionals could need. The northern section of Waltham Center houses a large population of mostly young professionals. Many live in expensive condo complexes and exclusive rentals in sub-neighborhoods like the **Highlands**, which is the area just east of Prospect Hill Park. The part of Waltham Center between Grove Street and the River is called the **Bleachery**, after the former Waltham Bleachery and Dye Works. The area around Pine Street and the river is called the **Chemistry**, after the Newton Chemical Company that used to be here. The Bleachery and the Chemistry are good examples of former factory areas along the riverbank that have been changed to support more modern uses, such as running and walking paths. Both neighborhoods feel virtually contiguous with the center of town. The area to the east of Waltham Center between the center and the Watertown border is **Warrendale**.

The middle and southwestern portion of the city is called the **West End**, taken up mostly by **Brandeis University's** 235-acre campus. The only nonsectarian Jewish college in the US—and a well-respected academic institution—Brandeis was founded in 1948. Brandeis centers around South Street, with a Victorian cemetery as its neighbor, and overlaps with the **Angleside**, the sub-neighborhood to the south at the city's southern tip, and **Robert's**, from South Street west to the river. Also in the vicinity, **Banks Square**, where Main Street and Weston Road intersect, forms the rough boundary between the West End and Waltham Center; and north of the Brandeis campus is the **Cedarwood** neighborhood. Angleside, Banks Square, Robert's, and Cedarwood all offer convenient housing for Brandeis students, faculty, and staff, and are all within walking distance of the school.

Route 128/I-95 runs north/south along Waltham's western boundary with Weston. It is this stretch of freeway that is sometimes referred to as "**Technol-**

ogy Highway" for all the tech businesses here. In fact, outside of Boston proper, Waltham has the most office space in the greater Boston area.

North Waltham is the most affluent section of the city, with grand estates and larger houses and apartment complexes, as well as the self-contained campus of the business school, **Bentley College**. Considering the long distance from Boston's subway system (outside of driving, Waltham-ites can only reach Boston via bus or commuter rail), available apartment complexes are on the pricey side—a two-bedroom here approaches Boston prices. However, some complexes offer residents private shuttle service to the Alewife T Station in Arlington, and many feel the swimming pools and tennis courts are worth the price. Also popular is the one-time resort area of **Lakeview**, located around Hardy Pond between Lake Street and the Lexington border. **Piety Corner** and **the Lanes**, north and south of the intersection of Totten Pond Road and Lexington Street respectively, have condominium complexes and exclusive rentals. These portions of Waltham are made up mainly of single, young professionals.

While Boston is about a 20-minute drive (without traffic) on the Pike, Waltham residents need not go far beyond their front door for services that range from chain stores, restaurants, and grocers, to one-of-a-kind eateries, farm stands, and quaint neighborhood markets. Moody Street is undergoing a gentrification of its own, with trendy new restaurants and bars cropping up to cater to the crowds. Places like the Watch City Brewing Company and Iguana Cantina are always full, and Campania, an Italian restaurant, and Solea, a tapas restaurant, actually draw diners in from the city. The Landmark Theatre, an independent movie theater on Pine Street, attracts out-of-town visitors as well. Overall, Waltham, with its low crime rate, local services, easy highway access, and minimal parking problems, is an appealing place to live.

Area Code: 781

Zip Codes: 02451–02455

Post Offices: 776 Main St; 415 South St (Brandeis U); 854 Lexington St; 38 Spruce St

Police: Waltham Police, 155 Lexington St, 781-314-3500; www.city.waltham. ma.us

Emergency Hospital: Deaconess-Waltham Hospital, 9 Hope Ave, 781-647-6000, www.waltham.caregroup.org

Library: Main Library, 735 Main St, 781-314-3425, TTY 781-314-3439, www. waltham.lib.ma.us

Parks & Open Space: Beaver Brook Reservation, 617-484-6357, www.mass.gov/ dcr; Cambridge Reservoir; Hardy Pond; Lazazzero Playground; Nipper Maher Park; Norumbega Park; Prospect Hill Park and ski area; Riverwalk Park; Stony Brook Basin; Waltham Woods

Community Publication: *Daily News Tribune*, 781-647-7898, www.dailynews tribune.com

Community Resources: www.city.waltham.ma.us, www.waltham-community.org, www.discoverwaltham.com; Waltham–West Suburban Chamber of Commerce, 781-894-4700, www.walthamchamber.com; Charles River Museum of Industry, 154 Moody St, 781-893-5410, www.crmi.org; Gore Place, 52 Gore St, 781-894-2798, www.goreplace.org; Lyman Estate, 185 Lyman St, 781-893-7232, www.waltham-community.org/Lyman; Paine Estate, 100 Robert Treat Paine Dr, 781-314-3290, www.waltham-community.org/Paine; Waltham Historical Society, 190 Moody St, 781-891-5815, http://walthamhistorical society.org; Waltham Museum, 25 Lexington St, 781-893-9020, www.waltham museum.com; Hovey Players, 9 Spring St, 781-893-9171, www.hoveyplayers.com; Landmark Cinema, 16 Pine St, 781-893-2500; Reagle Players, 617 Lexington St, 781-891-5600, www.reagleplayers.com; Spingold Theater Center, 415 South St (Brandeis campus), 781-736-3400; for area colleges and universities, see the **Childcare and Education** chapter.

Public School Education: Waltham Public Schools, 7 Lexington St, 781-314-5440, www.city.waltham.ma.us

Public Transportation: *Trains*: Commuter Rail at Brandeis/Roberts, Waltham and Waverly

Buses: nos. 70, 70A, 170, 505, 553, 554, 556, and 558; for MBTA route and schedule information contact the MBTA Traveler's Information Center: 617-222-3200, 800-392-6100, TTY 617-222-5146 or go to www.mbta.com.

WATERTOWN

Boundaries: **North**: Belmont; **East**: Cambridge; **South**: the Charles River; **West**: Waltham

Watertown, established in 1630, ceded much of its land to the surrounding communities of Waltham, Weston, Lincoln, Cambridge, and Belmont. Today the town covers only 4.1 square miles. Except for one small portion set off from Newton on the south side of the Charles, Watertown is located on the north shore of the Charles River.

A fairly unassuming place, Watertown history includes the following: it was the temporary seat of government during the Revolutionary War, home to patriot Paul Revere and where he printed Massachusetts' first paper currency, and the site of the Old Bemis Mills, weavers of the canvas sails for the USS *Constitution*. Today Watertown is a residential community with a mix of young singles and couples, many of whom move here for the Cambridge-type location without the Cambridge prices; and with one of the largest Armenian populations outside of Armenia itself, Watertown has earned itself the moniker "Little Armenia." Armenian markets are abundant (particularly around **Coolidge Square**), as well as restaurants, an Armenian Cultural Center, and a museum.

Watertown varies from moderately urban to downright suburban, with big houses on big lawns, easy street parking or better yet, driveways, and quiet streets. Many of Boston's young professionals are buying houses here while they're still affordable, enjoying close proximity to the city and major transportation routes, and convenient shopping at nearby big box stores like Best Buy, Target, and Home Depot.

Watertown Square, with its location along the river, developed, along with the mills, as the town's economic center. By the mid-19th century, Watertown Square was further established as a large industrial and commercial area when the railroads and streetcars linked it to Boston. Today, the Square retains Victorian and neo-classic retail blocks.

During the federal period, the **Arsenal Street** corridor was home to the US arsenal. Parts of it now comprise the recently revamped Arsenal Mall and its selection of chain stores. Many young professionals live along **Mt. Auburn Street**, where you can find interesting early diners and gas stations, as well as a number of greengrocers and Armenian markets. In addition, the area around the **Oakley Country Club**, which borders Belmont, has become a desirable place to live. It features brick, stone, clapboard and stucco colonials, and Victorians with wraparound porches.

Watertown is greener than many sections of Somerville and Cambridge, bordered by the Mt. Auburn Cemetery on the east and the running paths and parks and recreation facilities along the Charles River. There are playgrounds, tot lots, and an ice skating rink. Housing here is more affordable than in Arlington, and is mostly multi-family, with some apartment complexes and single family houses.

Watertown Square doesn't offer a lot of nightlife, although it does have a few chic restaurants and smart shops. There are pubs in Orchard Park and on the Waltham and Cambridge borders, but many residents head to Cambridge or Boston for their evening entertainment. In terms of transportation, the motto is: have car, will travel. Residents have easy access to the Mass Pike, Memorial Drive, Soldiers Field Road, and routes 16 and 20. There are no subway stations in Watertown, but there are express buses to downtown Boston, as well as regular bus service to the Red Line and Cambridge.

Area Code: 617
Zip Codes: 02471, 02472
Post Offices: 126 Main St; 589 Mt. Auburn St; 123 Galen St
Police: Watertown Police, 34 John "Sonny" Whooley Way, 617-972-6500, www.watertownpd.org
Emergency Hospital: Mt. Auburn Hospital, 330 Mt. Auburn St, Cambridge, 617-492-3500, www.mountauburn.caregroup.org
Library: Watertown Free Public Library, Main Branch, 123 Main St, 617-972-6431, TTY 617-926-4189, www.watertownlib.org

Parks & Open Space: Arsenal Park; Beacon Park; Filippello Playground; Mt. Auburn Cemetery; O'Connell Park; Saltonstall Park; Sullivan Playground

Community Publication: *Watertown TAB & Press*, 617-926-8897, www.townonline.com/watertown

Community Resources: www.ci.watertown.ma.us, www.watertown-ma.com, Watertown-Belmont Chamber of Commerce, 617-926-1017, http://wbcc.org/; Armenian Library and Museum of America, 65 Main St, 617-926-2562, http://armenianheritage.com/almindex.htm; Arsenal Mall, 485 Arsenal St, 617-923-4700, www.shopsimon.com; The Commander's Mansion, 440 Talcott Ave, 617-926-7755, www.commandersmansion.com; New Repertory Theatre, 321 Arsenal St, 617-923-8487, TTY 617-923-2067, www.newrep.org; Oakley Country Club, 410 Belmont St, 617-484-2400, www.oakleycountryclub.org; Perkins School for the Blind, 175 N Beacon St, 617-924-3434, www.perkins.pvt.k12.ma.us

Public School Education: Watertown Public Schools, 30 Common St, 617-926-7700, www.watertown.k12.ma.us

Public Transportation: *Buses*: nos. 52, 57, 59, 70, 71, 73; express buses 502 and 504; for MBTA route and schedule information contact the MBTA Traveler's Information Center: 617-222-3200, 800-392-6100, TTY 617-222-5146 or go to www.mbta.com.

NORFOLK COUNTY

BROOKLINE

Boundaries: North: Comm Ave (Boston), Brainerd Rd and Corey Rd; **East**: St. Mary's St, the Riverway, and the Jamaicaway; **South**: Jamaica Plain, West Roxbury, and Newton; **West**: Brighton and Newton

An independent town of 6.8 square miles and 57,000 residents nestled in the heart of western Boston, Brookline offers a unique, best-of-both-worlds blend of city convenience and suburban sanctuary; it is a beautiful, safe, middle- to upper middle–class town, with a healthy mix of high-density hotspots and quaint, quiet neighborhoods. Residences range from sprawling mansions on spacious estates to relatively affordable brick apartment buildings and upscale condos. Renters can get a little more space for their dollar here than in comparable Boston neighborhoods, and with its top-notch school system, suburban feel, and easy commute, it's no wonder many choose to settle here for good.

Well-known as the center of Boston's Jewish community, Brookline received Jewish immigrants from Germany and Eastern Europe throughout the 19th and 20th centuries, as well as an influx of Russian Jews in more recent years. There

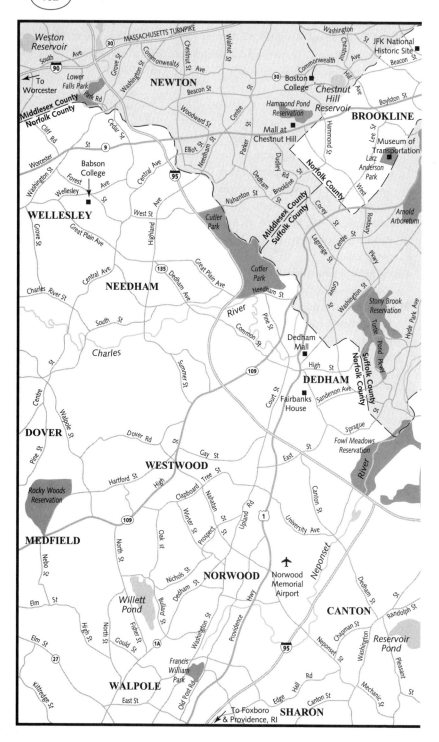

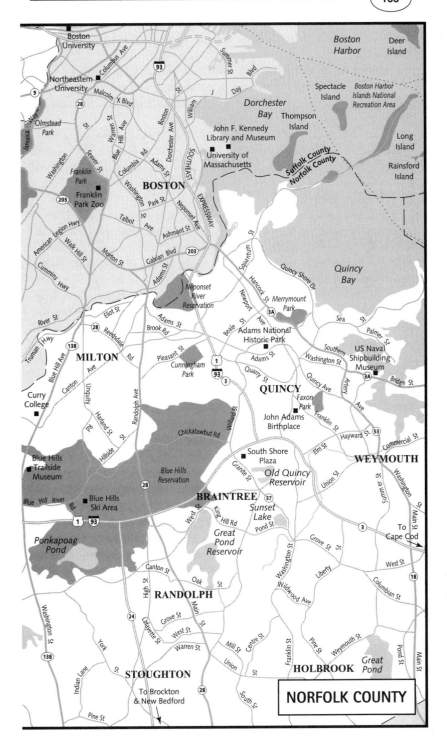

NORFOLK COUNTY

are prevalent Orthodox and Hassidic communities, as well as a small Sephardic presence.

Evidence of Brookline's thriving Jewish culture is ubiquitous. Harvard Street is lined with kosher delis, bakeries, and bagel shops, as well as Israeli import and Judaica shops. There are over a dozen temples in town, and where else could you find multiple kosher Chinese and Korean restaurants?

This is not to say that everyone in Brookline is Jewish. More recent immigration trends have spurred a growing Asian population of mostly Chinese and Japanese descent, and it is also a bastion for many area college students. Brookline consistently attracts young professionals with children; like Newton, it is a great place to raise a family.

Originally called the "Muddy River Hamlet," this area was mainly used as allotment farmland for Boston's citizens in the 1630s. After several failed attempts by its residents, Brookline was incorporated as an independent town in 1705, and has successfully resisted annexation by the city of Boston for over 300 years—unlike all other surrounding communities. While an integral part of the city, Brookline maintains its own separate government (a representative Town Meeting system), and goes to great lengths to differentiate itself from its urban neighbor where possible. For example, there is no overnight street parking permitted, lending even the busiest streets a quiet, small town feel.

Brookline's economy remained solidly agricultural until the early 1800s, when wealthy Boston merchants began building their summer homes here. Famous residents have since included Zabdiel Boylston (who introduced the smallpox vaccine to the US), Frederick Law Olmsted (landscape architect of Boston's Emerald Necklace and New York's Central Park), John F. and Robert F. Kennedy, late-night talk show host (and valedictorian of Brookline High School's class of 1981) Conan O'Brien, and former Massachusetts governor and 1988 Democratic Party presidential nominee, Michael Dukakis.

With Boston's mid-19th-century streetcar expansion came another building boom for Brookline that included construction of the picturesque (an architectural style) subdivisions of **Brookline Village**, the early gothic-style stone houses and churches in the **Longwood** area, and carefully landscaped, wealthy residential neighborhoods like **Fisher Hill**. The early 20th century brought **Coolidge Corner**, a welcoming assortment of brick and faced stone apartments along Beacon Street and extending toward Comm Ave, and the higher density blocks on **Aspinwall Hill**. More modern and utilitarian triple-deckers are found around the intersection of Cypress and Boylston streets, adjacent to the Brookline Hills T stop and Brookline High School.

Bisecting Brookline is Route 9 (a.k.a. Boylston Street), a thoroughfare that connects Boston to its western suburbs. Those areas of Brookline north of Route 9, closer to Boston, have a distinctly urban feel. Excepting some hidden enclaves of multi-million- dollar homes along the town line near Boston University, the housing stock in northern Brookline is fairly uniform: pre-WWII apartments and brownstone row houses similar to those in the Fenway, along with some newer high- and low-rise developments and colonial single families and condos. Apartments, stores, and restaurants line the busy but pedestrian-friendly Beacon Street corridor from stem to stern of its Brookline stretch between Boston and Newton. Running along here—besides over 20,000 of the world's most elite marathoners each April—is the Green Line C train, connecting Cleveland Circle (Brighton) to downtown. The D train—the fastest of the Green Line's routes—meanders through the area south of Beacon Street and north of Route 9, connecting **Longwood**, **Brookline Village**, and **Brookline Hills** with rapid access to the city. Although many side streets off of Beacon and Boylston quickly disseminate into more suburban-feeling neighborhoods, south of Route 9 is where true suburbia lies. One of Greater Boston's most well-to-do areas, this is where you're apt to find enormous, gorgeous, and expensive homes.

Although Brookline is mainly residential, it does have major commercial centers, several of which are tied to its most popular neighborhoods. These include St. Mary/Lower Beacon Street, Coolidge Corner, JFK Crossing, Brookline Village, Washington Square, Longwood, and Chestnut Hill. **St. Mary/Lower Beacon Street** (named after Beacon's cross street) sits just over the town line, within walking distance of Fenway Park. A cluster of small, independent businesses, restaurants, and even guesthouses flourish here.

Farther down Beacon Street, the next major neighborhood and commercial hub is **Coolidge Corner**, where Beacon and Harvard streets intersect. Coolidge Corner is Brookline's core shopping and dining district, a lively mix of chain and independent stores, some of the city's most popular ethnic restaurants, new and used bookstores, clothing shops, coffee shops, and toy stores. The art deco Coolidge Corner Theater offers a variety of second-run, international, independent and specialty films, as well as book readings in conjunction with the independently owned Brookline Booksmith across the street; both businesses are regular recipients of local awards for excellence. Given the abundance of nearby amenities, you'd expect parking here to be horrid, but there are just enough metered spots in the area to curb the issue. Higher rents in and around Coolidge Corner reflect its wide popularity.

Following Harvard Street north of Coolidge Corner (between Beals Street and the Brighton border) will lead you to **JFK Crossing**—John F. Kennedy was born at 83 Beals Street. Besides its place in history, JFK Crossing is most noted for its established Jewish community and conglomeration of kosher eateries, grocers, bookshops, and Judaica stores. Being about equidistant between Beacon Street and Comm Ave in Boston, residents may walk to either the B train or the C train.

South from Coolidge Corner on Harvard Street is **Brookline Village**, at the intersection of Boylston and Harvard streets and extending up Washington Street. Brookline Village is the town's civic center, home to the fire department, police station, and municipal court. A quick ride from downtown Boston on the

D train, this quaint neighborhood offers interesting stores and boutiques, eateries, antique shops, children's stores, and even a puppet theater called the Puppet Showplace. Most businesses are independently owned, although there are a couple of larger chains, including Bertucci's. Brookline Village has both a posh side—the antique shops and some of the restaurants are pricey—and a hipper side, with thrift stores, an old-fashioned barbershop, and a diner. Matt Murphy's, the celebrated local pub, manages to embody this dynamic: in a cozy, almost elegant candlelit room, gourmet culinary inventions coexist nightly with an eclectic array of live local music. Traffic around the main intersection can get a little congested, and parking around here is sometimes difficult.

Further down Beacon Street from Boston, at the intersection of Washington Street, is **Washington Square**. This commercial/residential neighborhood is smaller and less glamorous than Coolidge Corner or Brookline Village, but still has plenty of necessary services (dry cleaners, dentists, law offices), as well as a few restaurants, an ice cream parlor, coffee shops, Asian and Russian grocers, and a cat hospital. While the housing stock has remained fairly unchanged through the years, the neighborhood's commercial face has undergone recent restoration.

The **Longwood** area of Brookline, one stop nearer to the city on the D train than Brookline Village, is synonymous with Longwood in the Fenway of Boston—they are two halves of the same whole, named for the medical area that straddles the Boston/Brookline border. Technically, the boundary is the Riverway—everything east is Boston, and everything west is Brookline. Generally speaking, the medical buildings and many of the commercial buildings are on the Boston side, and most of the residences are in Brookline, home to medical students and hospital staff. Perhaps the most distinctive housing option in this area is Longwood Towers, originally built as a hotel in 1924, but converted into luxury residences, offering long- and short-term rentals.

The **Chestnut Hill** area of Brookline, accessible by the D train, is an extension of the Chestnut Hill Village of Newton. It spans the western edge of Brookline between the Hammond Pond Parkway and Hammond Street, just south of and including Route 9, and includes leisure institutions like the Country Club, the Putterham Meadows Golf Course, and the Longview Cricket Club. While Route 9 is heavily trafficked and built-up, it does mean easy driving access to restaurants like Legal Sea Foods and The Capital Grille, as well as smaller shops and services, the Atrium Mall, a large movie theater, and a Star Market. In terms of residential options, this is an up-market area; most of the housing stock is single-family, and ranges from well-manicured estates to upscale condominiums.

On the eastern edge of Chestnut Hill is Pine Manor College, and on the northern edge is Newbury College; the much larger Boston College lies just over the border. To the south is **Putterham Circle**, which, in terms of housing and commerce, is similar to Chestnut Hill. The **Westbrook Village** area in the southwest corner of Brookline is where you will find typical Brookline homes (read expensive), and not a lot of rental properties.

As mentioned, there is no overnight on-street parking in Brookline, not even for guests. If you have a car, you'll have to pay for a parking space, either at your building or at one of the several town lots, which, of course, have waiting lists. For more information on parking in Brookline, see the **Getting Settled** chapter.

Area Code: 617

Zip Codes: 02445–02447

Post Offices: 1295 Beacon St; 207 Washington St

Police: Headquarters, 350 Washington St, 617-730-2222; www.brooklinepolice. com

Emergency Hospitals: Beth Israel Deaconess Hospital, 330 Brookline Ave, 617-667-7000, www.bidmc.harvard.edu; Brigham & Women's Hospital, 75 Francis St, 617-732-5500, www.brighamandwomens.org; Children's Hospital, 300 Longwood Ave, 617-355-6000, www.childrenshospital.org

Library: Public Library of Brookline, Main Branch, 361 Washington St, 617-730-2375, www.brooklinelibrary.org

Parks & Open Space: Brookline Reservoir Park; Chestnut Hill Reservoir; D. Blakely Hoar Sanctuary; Fisher Hill Reservoir; Griggs Park; Hall's Pond Sanctuary; Larz Anderson Park; Longwood Mall; Lost Pond Reservation and Conservation Area; Lotta Bradburn Schick Park; Olmsted Park; The Riverway; www.townof brooklinemass.com/Conservation/Parks.html

Community Resources: www.townofbrooklinemass.com, Brookline Chamber of Commerce, 251 Harvard St, 617-739-1330, www.brooklinechamber. com; Allandale Farm, 259 Allandale Rd, 617-524-1531, www.allandalefarm. com; Brookline Arts Center, 86 Monmouth St, 617-566-5715, www.brookline artscenter.com; Brookline Historical Society, 347 Harvard St, 617-566-5747, www.brooklinehistoricalsociety.org; Brookline Neighborhood Associations, www.townofbrooklinemass.com/NeighborAssociations.html; Coolidge Corner Theater, 290 Harvard St, 617-734-2500, www.coolidge.org; The Country Club, 191 Clyde St, 617-566-0240, http://tcclub.org; Larz Anderson Auto Museum: The Museum of Transportation, 15 Newton St, 617-522-6547, www. mot.org; Kennedy Historic Site, 83 Beals St, 617-566-7937, www.nps.gov/jofi; Olmsted Historic Site, 99 Warren St, 617-566-1689, www.nps.gov/frla; Puppet Showplace Theatre, 32 Station St, 617-731-6400, www.puppetshowplace.org; for area colleges and universities, see the **Childcare and Education** chapter.

Community Publications: *Brookline TAB*, 617-566-3585, www.townonline.com/ brookline; *Boston Russian Bulletin*, www.russianmass.com

Public School Education: Brookline Public Schools, 5th Floor, Town Hall, 333 Washington St, 617-730-2401, www.brookline.k12.ma.us

Public Transportation: *Trains*: Green Line C trolley makes surface stops along Beacon Street from downtown to Cleveland Circle at St. Mary's St, Hawes St, Kent St, St. Paul St, Coolidge Corner, Summit Ave, Brandon Hall, Fairbanks, Washington Sq, Tappan St, Dean Rd and Englewood Ave; Green Line D trolley at Longwood, Brookline Village, Brookline Hills, Beaconsfield, and Reservoir

Buses: nos. 51, 60, 65, 66, and 86; for MBTA route and schedule information contact the MBTA Traveler's Information Center: 617-222-3200, 800-392-6100, TTY 617-222-5146 or go to www.mbta.com.

DEDHAM

Boundaries: **North**: Charles River, Needham, and West Roxbury; **East**: Boston (Readville); **South**: Canton, Islington, and Westwood; **West**: Westwood and Needham

To the southwest of Boston at the border of West Roxbury and Readville lies Dedham, population 24,000. Like Malden, Dedham is an example of a solid working-class town adjacent to the city and with good highway access. Founded in 1636, Dedham has been around almost as long as Boston, but has fewer historical points of interest. The town does have one relic however; the Fairbanks House, located near the center of town, dates back to 1737 as the oldest wooden-frame house in North America.

Initially an agricultural town, Dedham's character was forever changed with the digging of Mother Brook in 1637. Mother Brook connected the Charles River with the Neponset River, thus paving the way for industry, particularly mills. For over 200 years, the Neponset River's waterpower fed Dedham's mills (wool, cotton, corn, etc.), and supplied the power necessary to run the factories. Many arrived from Ireland and Germany in particular to work and settle in Dedham. Toward the end of the 19th century, many local industries closed shop; by the end of WWI, the remaining textile plants closed as well.

Today Dedham's affordability and safety make it a popular choice. Unfortunately, most of the architecture from its colonial days has not survived; the majority of the housing stock in town was built in the 20th century. Most Dedham residents live in sturdy, single-family homes and duplexes, although the dedicated home seeker may be able to find a more historic house. Dedham has a rather uniform feel with little architectural variation between neighborhoods, though the west side of town is more thinly settled and feels more rural, and the eastern half is fairly dense and more commercial. Houses are on good-sized lots, and are shaded by mature trees.

Ashcroft, on the eastern border with Readville, carries over the urban, developed flavor of Boston. You'll see a lot of small and relatively new single-family homes with siding. The **Endicott**, to the west of Ashcroft around the intersection of East and Sprague streets, and **Oakdale** (just north of that) neighborhoods are a little more upscale than Ashcroft. Homes are more expensive here compared with the rest of Dedham. At the town's northeast border with Boston and running over to Mother Brook is **East Dedham**, which houses affordable duplexes and inexpensively built homes. Only 20% of Dedham's residents are renters, and a good deal of its apartment stock is in East Dedham.

Commercial offerings include two movie theaters and the Dedham Mall on the Providence Highway. Dedham residents are quite proud of their handsome, historical municipal center made up of buildings in well-preserved architectural styles, including a granite Greek revival courthouse and a Romanesque revival public library. If you'd like to get outdoors, Dedham has several small ponds and waterways, including a segment of the Charles. Also nearby: the Stony Brook Reservation and the large Blue Hills Reservation.

Like Malden, Dedham has great highway access, but it's not quite as direct a route into the city. As Dedham borders Boston on its southwest side, it is relatively far from Boston's center, and to get there entails a trip through West Roxbury or Jamaica Plain—not too difficult, but not overly convenient. However, Dedham is perfectly poised to pick up routes 128 and I-95 to head north and south to the shores of Massachusetts. The Dedham portion of I-95 is also very close to its junction with I-93, another major route into Boston. Public transportation, sadly, is not so hot. The options are bus or commuter rail into the city. The Franklin line of the commuter rail has two stops in Dedham: Endicott (on Washington Avenue off East Street) and Dedham Corporate (East Street off Route 128).

Area Code: 781

Zip Codes: 02026, 02027

Post Offices: 611 High St; 280 Bussey St

Police: Dedham Police, 600 High St, 781-326-1212, www.dedhampolice.org

Emergency Hospital: Beth Israel Deaconess Hospital, 148 Chestnut St (Needham), 781-453-3000, www.glover.caregroup.org

Library: Dedham Public Library, 43 Church St, 781-751-9284, www.dedham library.org

Parks & Open Space: Charles River; Cutler Park, 617-333-7404, www.mass.gov/dcr; Stony Brook Reservation, www.mass.gov/dcr; Weld Pond; Wigwam Pond; Wilson Mountain Reservation, www.mass.gov/dcr

Community Resources: www.dedham-ma.gov; Neponset Valley Chamber of Commerce, 781-769-1126, www.nvcc.com; Dedham Community Theater, 580 High St, 781-326-0409, www.dedhamcommunitytheatre.com; Dedham Historical Society (Museum and Library), 612 High St, 781-326-1385, www. dedhamhistorical.org; Dedham Mall, 300 Providence Hwy, 781-329-1210; Fairbanks House, 511 East St, 781-326-1170, www.fairbankshouse.org; The Museum of Bad Art, 580 High St, 781-444-6757, www.museumofbadart.org; for area colleges and universities, see the **Childcare and Education** chapter.

Community Publication: *Daily News Transcript*, www.dailynewstranscript.com

Public School Education: Dedham Public Schools, 1106 High St, 781-326-5622, www.dedham.k12.ma.us

Public Transportation: *Trains*: commuter rail at Endicott and Dedham Corporate Center Stations

Buses: nos. 33, 34, 34E, 35, 36, and 52; for MBTA route and schedule information contact the MBTA Traveler's Information Center: 617-222-3200, 800-392-6100, TTY 617-222-5146 or go to www.mbta.com.

MILTON

Boundaries: **North**: Neponset River and Boston; **East**: Quincy; **South**: Blue Hills Reservation and Canton; **West**: Boston and Dedham

Just south of Dorchester across the Neponset River and bordering Hyde Park is the well-heeled town of Milton, which may best be summed up in one word: gorgeous. That is, if you find large, well-preserved colonial homes on roomy, green lots in a sylvan setting, with in-town amenities, and easy highway, forest, and city access appealing. A community of about 26,000 people, Milton is made up mostly of homeowners. If it's urban living you're looking for, then Milton is probably not your best choice. But if you want what could be considered the prototypical *Better Homes & Gardens*–sort of white picket fence American suburb, look no further.

The birthplace of former president George H. W. Bush, Milton was used by the British as a trading post as early as the 1620s, and was incorporated as a town in 1662. Like Dedham, starting in the last quarter of the 17th century, Milton was the site of many mills, which harnessed the Neponset River's ample water supply. The town also was home to what is thought to be the oldest piano factory in the US, established in 1800 by Benjamin Crahoe. It was the extension of the streetcar lines to Milton from Boston in the late 1800s that transformed the town into the streetcar suburb that you see today.

As Milton developed, large estates were built alongside farms, and although much of the original acreage was broken up and subsequently developed with smaller homes, this area is still unmistakably affluent. Today, Milton comprises 13 square miles of expensive homes in a setting that, while somewhat densely settled, still manages to feel pastoral. For a pretty penny you can have your pick of a colonial, a 19th-century country home, a New England farmhouse, a large Georgian estate, or a worker's cottage nicely offset from the street with a lawn.

Milton is sandwiched between the Blue Hills Reservation to the south and the Neponset River and Boston's Dorchester neighborhood to the north and thus tends to be more heavily settled the closer you are to Boston, particularly near Milton Village, Milton Center, and East Milton. **Milton Village**, located at the northeast border with Dorchester near where Adams Street and Central Avenue cross the river, and **Milton Center**, right in the center of town, are both made up of a cluster of streets, along which are colonial and Victorian homes, and a few commercial offerings. Residents often head over the river into Dorchester for more shopping and services. To the east of Milton Center are Milton Hospital, Milton Academy, and Fontbonne Academy campuses, and past these, toward Quincy, is **East Milton**. Resembling parts of Cambridge and Arlington, East Milton is toned down, although still very nice. It is slightly busier, with shops and some Victorian apartment blocks, and modest homes. The western and southern portions of Milton are more thinly settled and nicely shaded with thick maples and oaks. Here you will find the campus of Curry College, an independent liberal arts school, as well as the Blue Hills Reservation, a 7,000-acre park that offers horseback riding, hiking, skiing, and more. If that just isn't enough greenspace for you—or if, perhaps, you wind up in northern Milton—you can always head to the Neponset River Reservation, which has playgrounds, bird watching, fishing, bike trails, and much more.

Commuting to Boston from Milton is easily done by car. Interstate 93 (the Southeast Expressway) cuts right through East Milton; it circles the town to the south through the Blue Hills Reservation, where it meets I-95 and Route 128. If you don't feel like fighting the often wretched traffic on I-93, you can also just head through Hyde Park, Mattapan, and Dorchester via Hyde Park, Dorchester, or Blue Hills avenues. As for public transportation, aside from a commuter rail stop in neighboring Hyde Park and a couple of MBTA South Shore bus routes, the Red Line of the T is an option…sort of. It's really a trolley that costs extra and connects to the Cambridge/Dorchester Red Line at Ashmont.

Area Code: 617

Zip Code: 02186

Post Offices: 499 Adams St; 50 Adams St (Milton Village)

Police: Milton Police, 40 Highland St, 617-698-3800, www.miltonpd.com

Emergency Hospital: Milton Hospital, 199 Reedsdale Rd, 617-696-4600, www.miltonhospital.org

Library: Milton Central Library, 476 Canton Ave, 617-698-5757, www.miltonlibrary.org

Parks & Open Space: Andrews Park; Blue Hills Reservation, 695 Hillside St, 617-698-1802, www.mass.gov/dcr; Neponset River Reservation, 617-727-5290, www.mass.gov/dcr; Shields Park; Town Forest; Turners Pond

Community Resources: www.townofmilton.org; Bent's Cookie Factory, 7 Pleasant St, 617-698-5945, www.bentscookiefactory.com; Blue Hill Meteorological Observatory, summit of Great Blue Hill, 617-696-0389, www.bluehill.org; Blue Hills Trailside Museum, 1904 Canton Ave, 617-333-0690, www.mass.gov/dcr; Captain Forbes House Museum, 215 Adams St, 617-696-1815, www.forbeshousemuseum.org; Milton Historical Society, 1370 Canton Ave, 617-333-9700, www.miltonhistoricalsociety.org; The Milton Players, 90 Reedsdale Rd, 617-698-7469, www.miltonplayers.org; Wollaston Golf Club, 999 Randolph Ave, 617-698-0800

Community Publications: *Milton Record-Transcript*, 617-698-6563; *Milton Times*, 617-696-7758, www.miltontimes.com

Public School Education: Milton Public Schools, 1372 Brush Hill Rd, 617-696-4809, www.miltonps.org

Public Transportation: *Trains*: Mattapan/Red Line (trolley connector) at Milton, Central Ave, Valley Rd and Capen St

Buses: nos. 215, 217, 240, and 245; for MBTA route and schedule information contact the MBTA Traveler's Information Center: 617-222-3200, 800-392-6100, TTY 617-222-5146 or go to www.mbta.com.

QUINCY

Boundaries: **North**: Dorchester and Quincy bays and the Neponset River; **South**: Braintree and the Blue Hills Reservation; **West**: Blue Hills Reservation and Milton; **East**: Quincy Bay

Quincy, pronounced "Quin-zee," is so named and so pronounced because the original Quincy family that settled here at Mount Wollaston pronounced their name with a "z" rather than a "c" sound. Family members included Colonel John Quincy, the city's namesake and the grandfather of President John Adams. Also known as the "City of Presidents," Quincy has the distinction of having been the birthplace and home of the second and sixth presidents of the United States, the aforementioned John Adams and his son, John Quincy Adams—as well as John Hancock.

Originally part of Braintree (just to the south), Quincy became an independent town in 1792 and a city in 1888. In addition to having been an agricultural community and home to many famous early American colonists and political figures, Quincy saw early industry in shipbuilding and granite quarrying, which coincided with a wave of European immigration.

Almost 17 square miles in size, Quincy lies nine miles south of Boston, separated from it by the Neponset River. As it is situated between the Blue Hills and Quincy Bay, this city offers easy access to a great deal of Massachusetts' natural environs—in particular, beaches to the east and hilly forestland to the west—while still offering residents ample shopping and dining options and relatively quick access to Boston via car or public transit. While most choose to live in Quincy and commute to Boston for work, there is enough commerce here to sustain some office buildings, in addition to the usual town amenities. Quincy is a mix of suburban residential areas, local shopping developments, and seaside beaches along its ample waterfront. While the city has always been an Irish-American enclave—with an overabundance of pubs as proof—its population of 88,000 residents is becoming more heavily Asian-American. Now with your well-poured pint you can also get some of the best Asian food in Boston outside of Chinatown. The Fung Wah Bus, a Chinatown-to-Chinatown service, now also runs out of Quincy.

Whether you're looking for a modern apartment in a big complex or a single-family home in a grand old colonial, Quincy probably has something for you. Since the city was settled as early as Boston itself, a great deal of its homes reflect its status as one of America's oldest communities. Because of the time/distance factor in terms of getting to downtown Boston (you either have to fight the thick Southeast Expressway traffic or take a 25-minute T ride), housing is less expensive here than in Boston and other inner ring communities such as Cambridge and Somerville.

As Quincy is quite large, there is more than one commercial area and lots of strip malls. Quincy's bona fide municipal center of town, at the intersections of Hancock and Washington streets, **Quincy Center** is historic and charming, with a real Tudor structure and an art-deco Bank of America. **North Quincy**, between Hancock Street and Quincy Bay, is fairly middle-class, with busy shops, a few chain stores, and many brick homes. Because of a horse racing track that operated in this area during the 1800s, North Quincy wasn't developed until well after other areas of the city, and it wasn't until the early 1900s that this area was laid out with dense, single-family lots. Near the marina and **Quincy Point** you can find triple-decker homes, built around the turn of the 20th century.

The more upscale neighborhoods throughout Quincy include **Presidents Hill** at Furnace Brook Parkway and Adams Street, as well as Governor's Road in **West Quincy**, and **Wollaston Hill**, **Squantum**, and trendy **Marina Bay**. If you're looking for an old colonial or Victorian, check in **Wollaston** and **Wollaston Hill**, just north of the Furnace Brook Golf Course in central Quincy. Wollaston, named for Captain Wollaston, who first settled Quincy in 1625, is one of the older parts of Quincy, and is popular for its easy access to public transit. Wollaston presents a dense grid of residential streets, and has a good array of commercial offerings. Closer to the T stop you can find some apartments, and a short bus ride from there is **Wollaston Beach**—Boston Harbor's largest beach, with views of the Boston skyline, ample parking, a bathhouse, and some New England–style clam shacks like the Clam Box and Tony's Clam Shop, and the music venue, the Beachcomber.

Southwest of the golf course is **West Quincy**, where you'll find some truly impressive homes on lovely lots with positively enormous trees. Along with **South Quincy**, which is near the border with Braintree, West Quincy got its start with the quarrying industry and was initially home to many of the immigrant workers who came to work and then never left. The waterfront areas of Quincy, including **Squantum** (the finger of land jutting into the Bay in north Quincy), **Adams Shore**, and **Hough's Neck** (on the peninsula east of Quincy Center), provide beautiful views of Boston Harbor and the Boston skyline. These neighborhoods are somewhat reminiscent of Cape Cod, with their laid-back, beachfront feel, cottage homes, and shops. Squantum, once home to Native Americans of the same name, got its start as a summer vacation area for Bostonians. Over the last century, the summer cottages were converted into year-round homes, and Squantum was connected to the mainland by a causeway. Further south, Adams Shore shares a peninsula with Germantown and Hough's Neck, jutting out into Quincy Bay just east of Quincy Center. Similar to Squantum, Adams Shore went from summer resort to a year-round community with desirable beachfront property.

As the Harbor, and thus Quincy Bay, gets cleaner, these neighborhoods become even more sought after. Further out on this peninsula is Hough's Neck, which was developed a little later than other areas of the city. This neighborhood remained agricultural until the 1800s, when it became a summer destination for fishing and beaching. Today the cottages are year-round residences for "Neckers," as locals call themselves. This part of the peninsula, known as "God's Country," is home to many close-knit extended families, but it is still popular with newcomers who appreciate the ocean views and aren't put off from trying to carve out a new niche in this well-established neighborhood. Include **Marina Bay**, with its condos, restaurants, bars, and Nantucket-style boardwalk along the harbor, in this bunch as well. Marina Bay also has a "New Urbanist" development called Chapman's Reach—a collection of modern homes set up with porches and well-manicured lawns designed to foster a stronger sense of community. Area amenities include nearby pubs and the marina.

Germantown, on the peninsula between Adams Shore and Hough's Neck, is one of Quincy's more affordable neighborhoods. It is also one of the oldest—settled in the 1640s. Originally called Shed's Neck, this neighborhood became Germantown when German immigrants came in droves to seek work at nearby Fore River Shipyard. In recent years, Germantown has seen the building of single-family homes, and 900 public housing units. Still on the mainland, between Quincy Center and Adams Shore, is the neighborhood of **Merrymount**. Once home to a sizable Native American population, this hilly area became the property of the Adams family until it was sold for housing development during the 20th century. Most of Merrymount's housing stock was built before WWII.

Quincy is transforming from a Boston bedroom community to a workplace destination in and of itself for the corporate office park employee. Quincy has good public transit, including four major Red Line stations with large parking areas, as well as several bus routes to and from Boston. Via car, Route 3A connects to Route 93 for easy Boston access, at least in theory. Frustratingly, traffic on I-93 south of the city is often abysmal; getting through this stretch of highway, and not just during rush hour, is often arduous. Alternate methods of travel, such as commuter ferry to Long Wharf in Boston or taking the T, should be considered.

And finally, although the Fore River Shipyard closed in 1986, there is a renewed effort to revive shipbuilding in the Fore River area. Military enthusiasts can get a glimpse of one of the great warships, the USS *Salem*, a decommissioned heavy cruiser now anchored at the US Naval Shipbuilding Museum, near the Fore River Bridge. Other historical sites include the Adams' birthplaces, as well as their burial plots in the United First Parish Church.

Area Code: 617
Zip Codes: 02169–02171
Post Offices: 47 Washington St; 454 Hancock St; 5 Beach St
Police: Police Headquarters, 1 Sea St, 617-479-1212, http://ci.quincy.ma.us/police.asp

Emergency Hospital: Quincy Medical Center, 114 Whitwell St, 617-773-6100, www.quincymc.org

Library: Thomas Crane Public (Main) Library, 40 Washington St, 617-376-1301, www.thomascranelibrary.org

Parks & Open Space: Broad Meadows; Edgewater Drive Beach; Faxon Park; Forbes Hill Playground; Fore River Field; Kincaide Park; Labrecque Field; Merrymount Park; Nickerson Beach; Parkhurst Beach; Quincy Shore Reservation, 617-727-5290, www.mass.gov/dcr; Rhoda Beach; Wollaston Beach

Coummunity Resources: www.quincyonline.com,; http://ci.quincy.ma.us; www.quincymass.com; Adams National Historic Park, 135 Adams St, 617-770-1175, www.nps.gov/adam; Colonel Josiah Quincy House, 20 Muirhead Rd, 617-227-3956; Granite Railway Quarry, Ricciuti Dr, 617-698-1802; Quincy Art Association, 26 High School Ave, 617-770-2482, www.quincyart.org; Quincy Asian Resources, 1509 Hancock St, 617-472-2200, www.qari.info; Quincy Historical Society, 8 Adams St, 617-773-1144, http://ci.quincy.ma.us/qhs.asp; Quincy Homestead, 34 Butler Rd, 617-727-5250; United First Parish Church, 1306 Hancock St, 617-773-1290, www.ufpc.org; US Naval Shipbuilding Museum, 739 Washington St, 617-479-7900, www.uss-salem.org

Community Publication: *Patriot Ledger*, 617-786-7000, http://ledger.southofboston.com

Public School Education: Quincy Public Schools, 70 Coddington St, 617-984-8700, www.quincypublicschools.com

Transportation: *Trains*: Red Line at North Quincy, Wollaston, Quincy Center, and Quincy Adams; commuter rail at Quincy Center

Buses: nos. 210-212, 214-217, 220-222, 225, 230, 236, 238, and 245; for MBTA route and schedule information contact the MBTA Traveler's Information Center: 617-222-3200, 800-392-6100, TTY 617-222-5146 or go to www.mbta.com.

Boats: Fore River Shipyard–Logan Airport–Long Wharf (Harbor Express)

GREATER BOSTON AREA

Many people live in the surrounding suburbs, referred to collectively as the greater Boston area. Here are a few communities worth looking into, particularly if you don't need to commute into Boston every day. As is the case in the cities and towns outside major cities, housing in the greater Boston area tends to be more spacious and on bigger lots, and the communities offer either a suburban or small-town lifestyle. For towns not profiled below, you can get information on the web at www.mass.gov/cc/.

BRISTOL COUNTY

- **Attleboro** (population 42,000) is a manufacturing city with a small-town,

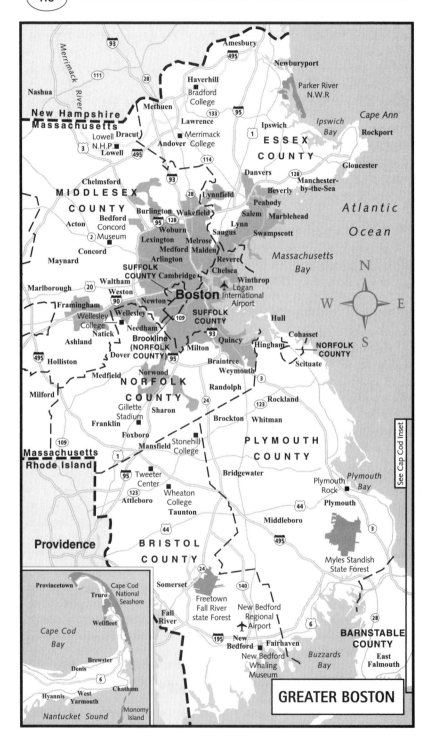

GREATER BOSTON

almost country atmosphere. At 32 miles southwest of Boston, Attleboro is actually closer to Providence, and borders Rhode Island. Homes are small to mid-sized, and mostly of 19th- and 20th-century construction—including post-WWII builds and some modern condos. Residents shop in strip malls downtown, and enjoy the Capron Park Zoo and the Industrial Museum. Easily accessible via routes I-95 and I-295, and there is a commuter rail stop at Attleboro station. City web site: www.cityofattleboro.us; municipal offices: 508-223-2222

- **Mansfield** is an unpretentious and unassuming suburb of 22,500, located 26 miles south of Boston at the intersection of routes 95 and 495. It is residential, save for the Tweeter Center, a major outdoor music venue. The commuter rail stop is at Mansfield station. Town web site: www.mansfieldma.com; municipal offices: 508-261-7370
- **New Bedford** (population 99,000) sits on the southern tip of Massachusetts near Rhode Island and Cape Cod, 54 miles south of Boston. Formerly a major whaling center (said to have inspired Herman Melville's *Moby Dick*), it is now an appealing oceanfront city with a vibrant community that is proud of its working waterfront, museums, theaters, shopping, dining, beaches, and festivals. It is home to a substantial Portuguese population. New Bedford is accessible via routes 140 and I-195. An extension of the commuter rail's Stoughton line has been proposed (to begin servicing New Bedford in 2016), but not approved. City web site: www.ci.new-bedford.ma.us; municipal offices: 508-979-1400
- **Taunton** is a quiet community of 56,000. A former mill town on the Taunton River, Taunton has a friendly rural feel, despite its industrial roots. The Weir neighborhood is the exception, with its higher density environs and rougher edges. In addition to several commercial areas, including a Federalist-looking town center, an industrial park, and the Silver City Galleria mall and movie theater, Taunton is known for its green areas, which include parklands, swamps, and Lake Sabbatia. Housing stock is mostly from the 19th and 20th centuries; there are some condos, and 40% of available housing is rentals. Taunton is located 33 miles south of Boston, close to Providence, and accessible via routes I-495 and 24, but has no commuter rail stop. City web site: www.ci.taunton. ma.us; municipal offices: 508-821-1000

ESSEX COUNTY

- **Andover** is an affluent suburb of just over 31,000 residents, located 22 miles north of Boston. Winding roads pass through wooded areas, interspersed more and more frequently with ever-larger homes; traditional farmhouses and modern mansions sit on equally expansive lots. There are some (well hidden) industrial parks occupied by such large companies as Raytheon and Gillette. Also in Andover is Phillips Academy, one of the most prestigious private high schools in the country. Highway access includes routes I-495 and I-93; the commuter rail stops at Andover Center and Ballardvale. Town web site: www. andoverma.gov; municipal offices: 978-623-8200

- **Beverly** was settled even before Boston. This mid-sized seaport community lies just 18 miles north of Boston. Once a major industrial center (particularly noted for shoemaking), Beverly now prides itself on being 85% residential, with a lot to offer in the way of commercial and social options. The North Shore Music Theatre is here, and the downtown area around Cabot Street is densely built up with stores, restaurants, and even a small movie house. Local industry includes high-tech and biotech businesses, and schools include Endicott College, North Shore Community College, and Montserrat College of Art. Life here is not too urban, not too rural. The downtown and waterfront areas, where you'll find some rentals, are heavily settled with not much in the way of greenspace or beaches, although the harbor does offer some respite. Northern Beverly and Beverly Farms offer greener environs and large homes and mansions. Drive to Boston and surrounding towns via routes 1A and 128, or take the Commuter rail from Beverly Farms, Prides Crossing, Montserrat, North Beverly, or Beverly Depot. Town web site: www.beverlyma.gov; municipal offices: 978-921-6000

- **Gloucester** (population 30,000) is the oldest seaport in America, located 31 miles northeast of Boston on Cape Ann. The homes of local fishermen, many of them of Italian and Portuguese descent, are modest, and contrast sharply with the tremendous estates that can be found elsewhere along the coast. While the sea defines Gloucester (as the famous Fisherman's Memorial will testify), it also has several office parks and a vibrant art scene that produced the likes of painters Winslow Homer and Edward Hopper, as well as Israel Horowitz's Gloucester Theatre Company. Tourists, drawn by the beaches, artists, and maritime history, swell the town's numbers by almost one third in the summer. Access to the rest of the region is available via Route 128; commuter rail stops are at Gloucester and West Gloucester. For a sneak preview, watch the locally filmed *The Perfect Storm*. City web site: www.ci.gloucester.ma.us; municipal offices: 978-281-9720

- Bisected by the Merrimack River, **Lawrence** is a densely populated, industrialized mill city 26 miles north of Boston. Priding itself on its history and continuing status as a multicultural gateway-city for new arrivals to the US, Lawrence refers to itself as "Immigrant City." Many of Lawrence's 72,000 residents are of Hispanic descent, although recent population influxes include newcomers from Laos and Cambodia. Over one third of local industry is still based in manufacturing, and over two thirds of the available housing stock consists of rentals—new condo conversions and lofts have begun to spring up along the river in former brick textile mills. Lawrence is accessible via Routes I-93 and I-495, and has a commuter rail stop at Lawrence station. City web site: www.ci.lawrence.ma.us; municipal offices: 978-794-5803

- Just nine miles north of Boston, **Lynn** is a city of 89,000. Historically known for shoemaking, Lynn continues as an urban manufacturing community. In addition to its very built-up business areas—strip malls and car dealerships galore line the Lynnway, while downtown is dense with brick buildings—Lynn has the campus of North Shore Community College, isolated greenspace in the Lynn Woods Reservation, and some of the greater Boston area's most affordable waterfront property along the Atlantic. However, be prepared to hear the familiar refrain: *Lynn, Lynn, the city of sin, you'll never come out the way you went in.* Routes 1, 1A, and 128 are accessible from the ends of town, and there are bus routes and a commuter rail stop at Lynn station. City web site: www. ci.lynn.ma.us; municipal offices: 781-598-4000

- **Lynnfield** (population 11,000) is a quiet, mostly residential, affluent suburb 16 miles north of Boston. Country roads, a small town square, and 18th-century farmhouses with wraparound porches make this an inviting place to live; in addition to its large percentage of families, Lynnfield is home to some prominent Boston-area athletes and wealthy restaurant owners. Town web site: www.town.lynnfield.ma.us; municipal offices: 781-334-3128

- Only four and a half square miles in size, **Marblehead** is a scenic waterfront town of 20,000 on Boston's North Shore. Originally a seafaring community dating back to the mid-1600s, today Marblehead still includes many historic colonial houses, complete with plaques commemorating the sailors and sea captains who built them. Marblehead Neck in particular is crowded with quaint historic homes on postage stamp–sized lots, with unbeatable views of the harbor. Although the town is technically not far from Boston (only 18 miles northeast), it isn't situated near the major highways, therefore daily commutes to the city are cumbersome. Local services are available and include upscale clothing and knick-knack shops and seafood restaurants. Neighboring Salem and Swampscott are also easily accessible. It is also home to one of the more sizable Jewish communities on the North Shore. Marblehead is accessible via routes 1A, 114, and 129; bus routes go into the city, but no commuter rail stops are in town. Town web site: www.marblehead.org; municipal offices: 781-631-0528

- Serving as the state capital before Boston and one of Massachusetts' smallest cities, **Newburyport** (population 17,000) is situated in the northeastern-most corner of the state at the mouth of the Merrimack River. Residents and tourists alike enjoy the town's quaint charm and attractions: gaslights, red brick sidewalks, a boardwalk along the harbor, wildlife sanctuaries, museums, theaters, restaurants, and coastal sites, including harbor cruises and whale watching. Despite being older than Boston, Newburyport's historic architecture, particularly in and surrounding downtown, tends more toward grand Federalist style homes and buildings built for wealthy whaling and clipper ship merchants. One third of the housing stock is rentals, and many apartments and condos come with alluring antique features such as functioning fireplaces. Though it is a 60-minute ride to Boston, many residents take the commuter rail from

Newburyport station each day; there is also easy access to routes 1 and I-95. City web site: www.cityofnewburyport.com; municipal offices: 978-465-4413

- Thirty-seven miles north of Boston, on the tip of Cape Ann, **Rockport** is an old and charming seafaring community. Eight thousand people call it home, including a small artists' colony. Houses here tend to be close together, and there are plenty of gray, weathered wood homes (as is typical both here on Cape Ann and south on Cape Cod). Rockport is made up of tiny art studios, museums, theaters, shops, restaurants, and inns, with a large coastal area that offers rocky and sandy beaches, lobster pots, and recreational boating. Residents range from young professionals who commute into the city to resident artists and retirees. Note: Rockport is a dry town; residents must buy alcohol in neighboring Gloucester, but are permitted to bring their own drinks to restaurants. The commuter rail stops here at Rockport Station. Town web sites: www. rockportusa.com, www.town.rockport.ma.us; municipal offices: 978-546-6894

- **Salem** is a historic coastal town 16 miles north of Boston, home to Nathaniel Hawthorne and infamous for the witch trials of 1692. Today's Salem is a city of over 40,000, with a state college, a charming, pedestrian-only shopping district, and many popular tourist attractions, including museums, wharves, witch-themed shops, and mystics. Although Salem has many surviving Colonial and Federalist buildings (especially evident in downtown, replete with brick and cobblestone structures and streets), many homes and condos are modern, and a full half of its residents are renters. Salem is a diverse community, with almost 20% of its population comprising minorities. The commuter rail stops in downtown Salem, and it's just a 26-minute ride to North Station; however, driving to Salem can be a bit tedious, via routes 1A, 107, or 114. City web sites: www.salem.com, www.salemweb.com; municipal offices: 978-745-9595

- **Swampscott** is a seaside bedroom community of only three square miles with about 14,500 residents. Fifteen miles northeast of Boston on the Atlantic, Swampscott was once home to Mary Baker Eddy, the founder of the Christian Science religion, and the summer retreat of President Calvin Coolidge. It is now home to a sizable Jewish community. This is a quiet, wealthy town with large, stunning homes on good-sized lots along the coast. There are five beaches and some commerce along the waterfront, although the major commercial amenities are restricted to an inland area called Vinnin Square. Swampscott is somewhat out of the way in terms of major highways; access is via Route 1A and the commuter rail stop at Swampscott station. Town web site: www.town. swampscott.ma.us; municipal offices: 781-596-8850

- **Manchester-by-the-Sea, Wenham, Essex,** and **Ipswich** are all scenic, small towns on the north shore, marked by a mix of coastal and colonial charm and wealth. Ipswich's Clam Box and Woodman's of Essex routinely vie for the honor of best seafood shack in Massachusetts, while Crane Beach in Ipswich and Manchester's Singing Beach are two of the most popular and picturesque beaches north of Boston. All except Essex have commuter rail stops; Manchester and Wenham are closest to Route 128. Manchester-by-the-Sea: www.manchester.ma.us, 978-526-2040; Wenham: www.wenhamma.gov, 978-468-5522; Essex: www.essexma.org, 978-768-6262; Ipswich: www.town.ipswich.ma.us, 978-356-6600

MIDDLESEX COUNTY

- **Acton** is a town of about 20,000 residents (and growing) next to Concord, just over 20 miles west-northwest of Boston. Acton's surroundings range from rural stretches resplendent with historic homes and the quintessential town green to mini-malls. Commuting to Boston can take from 45 minutes to an hour, either by car (via Route 2) or commuter rail (which stops in South Acton). Acton is a quaint, traditional community with local museums and a community theater, good services, and a solid educational system with some of the highest MCAS scores in the state (ranked 8th in the state among all communities in 2006). Town web site: www.town.acton.ma.us; municipal offices: 978-264-9615
- **Bedford** (population 12,500), home of "the oldest complete flag in the United States," sits 15 miles northwest of Boston and has good highway access to routes 3 and 128. This community prides itself on its colonial and Revolutionary War history, and its outdoor recreational amenities, such as bike and foot paths. There is a mixture of business and industry complementing the local Middlesex Community College and Hanscom Air Force Base. Town web site: www.town.bedford.ma.us; municipal offices: 781-275-0083
- **Burlington** is a community of about 23,000 residents, 13 miles northwest of Boston. After the construction of Route 128, Burlington experienced enormous growth, and it is now a major resource in the Massachusetts business economy. Its industrial zones and office parks are home to many major local, national, and international corporations, and hotels, chain restaurants, and retail centers like the well-known Burlington Mall bring in droves of visitors. Although there are no Burlington stops on the commuter rail, buses run from here to Boston, and it rests at the junction of two major highways, routes 3 and 128. Town web site: www.burlington.org; municipal offices: 781-270-1600
- **Concord,** a wealthy, historic suburb of roughly 17,000, is located 18 miles northwest of Boston. Famous for Revolutionary War battles (reenacted annually on Patriot's Day), as well as famous literary figures—the Alcotts, Emerson, Thoreau, Hawthorne—Concord draws a lot of tourists. Residents love their beautiful and somewhat staid New England town, with its well-preserved relics, colonial and Victorian homes, wooded greenspaces (including Walden Pond and the meeting of the Sudbury, Assabet, and Concord rivers), a non-commercialized town center, and a select private high school—Concord Academy. West Concord, a tad dressed down in comparison, is complete with a still-functioning Victorian Gothic–style prison. Access to Boston and Route

128 is a straight shot on scenic Route 2, and the commuter rail stops at Concord Station and West Concord. Town web sites: www.concordnet.org, www.concordma.com; municipal offices: 978-318-3080

• **Everett** (population 38,000) is a small, working-class industrial city just over the Mystic River from Charlestown and Somerville. Wedged between Malden, Chelsea, and Revere, Everett tends to get overlooked. While making a name for itself in the paint and chemical industries in the late 19th-century, Everett drew hordes of immigrants, and many of those long-time Irish and Italian families still live here. A more recent influx has brought immigrants from Central and South America, particularly Brazilians, who have opened up a number of stores and restaurants on Broadway. The southern portion of the city—where all the industrial plants are—and its border with Chelsea are fairly unattractive places to live, but north of Route 16 you'll find neighborhoods of triple-deckers that resemble the density and feel of pre-gentrified Somerville. The Gateway Center at the southwestern edge of town acts as a major shopping destination (with a Target, Home Depot, and that ilk), and just across the river is Wellington Station—with over 1,300 parking spots, it's a popular commuter point on the Orange Line. City web site: www.ci.everett.ma.us; municipal offices: 617-389-2100

• **Framingham,** 19 miles west of Boston, with close to 67,000 residents in its 25 square miles, is not just a bedroom community but also a working and shopping destination in its own right. It offers a wide variety of housing, including apartments, Victorians, and ranch style homes. Neighborhoods run the gamut, too, and include a number of villages like Saxonville and Framingham Center (dominated by the Framingham State College campus), as well as industrial parks and shopping malls. Framingham is mixed socio-economically and culturally, with a large Hispanic population. The Mass Pike and Route 9 offer direct pipelines to Boston, while the commuter rail stops at Framingham Station and local buses service the surrounding area. Town web site: www.framinghamma.org; municipal offices: 508-532-5520

• **Lexington,** forever linked to Concord through shared Revolutionary War experiences, is slightly closer to Boston, and also slightly more affordable. In this suburb of 30,000 residents, you can live in a colonial home dating to before the Battle of Lexington, a small Cape Cod, or a more modern option, while enjoying the greenspace of conservation lands and the Minuteman Bike Path, a town center with galleries and restaurants, and proximity to Boston, just 11 miles away. It is known for a school system so solid that, according to the *Boston Globe*, 93% of residents send their children to public schools here. Bound by routes 2 and 128, the town offers easy driving access, but there is no commuter rail stop—you'll need to drive, bike, or take a bus to the Alewife T station. Town web site: http://ci.lexington.ma.us; municipal offices: 781-862-0500

• **Lowell** is a large, densely populated (105,000) industrial city 25 miles north of

Boston on the Merrimack River. The birthplace of Jack Kerouac and a former mill town, Lowell endured some very hard times when textile manufacturing declined in the early 20th century. However, it has succeeded in restoring much of its luster: most of the old mills have been converted into office space or artists' studios, and tourist sites complement trolley and canal boat tours. Its cobbled downtown streets come alive with cultural festivals such as the Southeast Asian Water Festival and the three-day Lowell Folk Festival (which draws almost a quarter of a million attendees), and the city's arts and entertainment scene thrives thanks to the self-sustaining (and well regarded) Merrimack Repertory Theatre, concert halls, a Single-A Red Sox farm team, and two colleges, including UMASS-Lowell. The housing stock includes Victorians, colonials, Capes, ranches, and triple-deckers suitable for one to three families, as well as apartments and condos. Lowell is situated at the intersection of routes 3 and I-495, and the commuter rail will take you from Lowell Station to Boston in about 45 minutes. City web site: www.lowellma.gov; municipal offices: 978-970-4000

- **Maynard** is a small town (a little over five mostly rural square miles) of 10,000 that sits on the Assabet River about 22 miles northwest of Boston. While Maynard is without a commuter rail stop or a major local highway, it has nonetheless managed to put itself on the map as a commercial area, popular with high-tech and internet companies. Most notably, Monster.com keeps its worldwide headquarters here in a converted mill complex in the center of town. Outside of downtown, Maynard is fairly wooded and green, and residents live mostly in single- and multi-family housing. Town web site: http://web.maynard.ma.us; municipal offices: 978-897-1000

- **Melrose** (population 27,000) is a small city just seven miles north of Boston, tucked between I-93 and Route 1. A good choice for commuters, Melrose has benefited from Boston's continuing urban sprawl, and gentrification has brought unique storefronts and restaurants to the Victorian downtown area. Housing ranges from Victorians to 20th-century colonials, and a good selection of rentals, including some apartment complexes. To get your fill of nature, roam the 2,000+ acres of the Middlesex Fells Reservation at the western edge of town, or play 18 at the beautiful (and public) Mt. Hood golf course. Commuter rail service is available at Melrose Highlands, Cedar Park, and Wyoming Hill, and the Orange Line's Oak Grove T station is just over the town line in Malden. City web site: www.cityofmelrose.org; municipal offices: 781-979-4500

- **Natick** is a busy town of almost 32,000 residents, located 15 miles west of Boston. It is a middle- to upper-middle-class suburb—similar to Burlington and Framingham—complete with local industry, surrounding rural areas, greenspaces, old New England colonial charm, and expansive malls (the area around Speen St, between the Mass Pike and Route 9, is a mega-center of commerce). Housing is reflective of Natick's 350-year history: colonials, Victorians, post-war, and some apartments and condos. City access is via the Mass Pike and Route

9, and there are commuter rail stops at Natick and West Natick stations. Town web site: www.natickma.gov; municipal offices: 508-647-6400

- **Sudbury** is a popular suburb for families located 20 miles west of Boston. This town of 17,000 has a high per capita income, a strong educational system, and a rural feel with plenty of conservation land. Sudbury's roots date back to colonial times, and residents were active in the Revolutionary War (in fact, the zip code is 01776) and King Philip's War. One of the town's best-known landmarks is the Wayside Inn, which was immortalized in Longfellow's *Tales of a Wayside Inn* and is one of the oldest operating inns in the country. Sudbury and most of its shopping can be accessed along Route 20, although this can get fairly congested during rush hours; there is no commuter rail service in town. Neighboring **Lincoln** shares a high school with Sudbury, and while slightly closer to Boston, feels more pastoral and remote. Lincoln's current population is about 8,000, and historical homes and pastures dot the landscape. Points of interest include Drumlin Farm, which is a working farm open to the public, the DeCordova Museum and sculpture park, and the self-contained Hanscom Air Force Base. Lincolnites also have easy access to Walden Pond in nearby Concord. Lincoln can be accessed via routes 2 and 117, and the commuter rail stops at Lincoln Station. Sudbury: www.town.sudbury.ma.us, 978-443-8891. Lincoln: www.lincolntown.org, 781-259-2600

- **Wakefield** is a commuter suburb of 25,000, located 10 miles north of Boston, at the hub of routes 128 and I-93. Its location offers quick access into Boston via the highway, and the commuter rail makes stops at Wakefield and Greenwood. Although Wakefield is primarily residential, there is a central business district and some office and industrial park space in town. Lake Quannapowitt is the center of many community outdoor activities. Modern homes coexist with a variety of older historic ones: colonials, Georgians, Greek Revivals, gothic revivals, Italianates, and Queen Annes, among others. Town web site: www.wakefield.ma.us; municipal offices: 781-246-6383

- Twelve miles west of Boston, at the heart of what is perhaps the area's most desirable suburban region, **Weston** (population 11,500) consistently ranks as the wealthiest town per capita in Massachusetts. Mansion-like homes sit on secluded and expansive lots in this rural and seemingly out-of-the-way community. There are a good deal of outdoor recreation opportunities including golf, horseback riding, cross-country skiing, and plenty of forest trails for hiking. Weston is also home to Regis College, a Catholic liberal arts school that only recently began to admit male students. Access to Boston and surrounding areas is via the Mass Pike and routes 128 and 20; commuter rail stops are at Silver Hill, Hastings, and Kendall Green. Town web site: www.weston.govoffice.com; municipal offices: 781-893-7320

- **Winchester** is an upper-middle-class bedroom community that, at only 8 miles away, is closer to Boston than its small town charm would lead you to believe. Winchester's 20,000 residents can stroll through the welcoming town center, swim at Wedge Pond, or hike and bike the expansive Middlesex Fells Reservation at the eastern edge of town. It's a quick drive to Boston on I-93, while public transit includes commuter rail stops at Winchester Center and Wedgemere, and bus routes to nearby Arlington, Medford, and Cambridge. Town web site: www.winchester.us; municipal offices: 781-721-7130

- A suburban industrial city of 37,000, 10 miles north of Boston, **Woburn** has a long history as a manufacturing community, which has morphed into a business belt along Route 128. Though it is not without spots of historic beauty, its overall industrial nature does rob Woburn of some residential attractiveness compared with smaller neighboring communities; still, what it lacks in quaintness it gains in function and ease. Large office spaces, stores, restaurants, and a movie theater crop out from the highway. Woburn is contiguous to Burlington, and they feel similar. Renters here can find large, modern units that provide much more in the way of amenities than comparable apartments in Boston, and the city is only a short drive away on I-93. Commuter rail stops are at Mishawum and Anderson/Woburn. Town web site: www.cityofwoburn.com; municipal offices: 781-932-4400

NORFOLK COUNTY

- **Braintree** is a residential suburb of nearly 34,000, about 10 miles south of Boston. At the crux of routes I-93 and 3, with a Red Line T station and a commuter rail stop, one of the obvious benefits of living in Braintree is its easy access to both Boston and Cape Cod. Many residents are able to live and work here, rather than commute to Boston, as there are industrial parks, offices, and commercial space in town to complement its residential neighborhoods. In addition to a good public school system, there is also the private Thayer Academy and a Catholic high school. Other amenities include the South Shore Plaza (a shopping mall), an 18-hole municipal golf course, and a large AMC movie theater. Greenspace is prevalent throughout Braintree, and the sprawling Blue Hills Reservation extends from the northwest of town. Most homes here are mid-sized, single-family units built post-WWII, and sit on smallish lots, with a few condos and apartment complexes mixed in. Town web site: www.townofbraintreegov.org; municipal offices: 781-794-8000

- **Cohasset** is a classic, sylvan, seaside suburb of just over 7,000 residents, located on the South Shore. Named after the Conohasset tribe, the original inhabitants of this area, the name means "long rocky place." Life here is quintessential New England, with its lush greenery, boat-filled harbor and waterfront, and the colonial town common. Residents live in big homes, including colonials, Victorians, and contemporaries, all sitting nicely on large, well-kept, wooded lots. An active community, vibrant arts scene, four shopping areas, and the South Shore Music Circus all make Cohasset a desirable location. At 25 miles southeast of Boston, and fairly distant from the highway—Route 3A is as major as it gets—

Cohasset is a bit far flung for driving commuters. However, the commuter rail's long-awaited Greenbush Line, a resurrection of the Old Colony Railroad that will stop at Cohasset station, is slated to begin service in late 2007, and there is commuter boat service from neighboring Hingham. Town web site: www.townofcohasset.org; municipal offices: 781-383-4105

- **Dover,** 16 miles southwest of Boston, ranks alongside Weston as one of the wealthiest suburbs in the state. Here you'll find big homes, large lots, and hefty price tags in one of the most posh regions of the country. Originally an agricultural community during colonial times, Dover gained some milling industry after the damming of the Charles in the late 18th century, and became the site for some staggeringly large country estates by the late 19th and early 20th centuries. Dover is small—only 5,500 residents share the bucolic settings of horse farms and greenspaces. There are no major highways or commuter rail stops in town, although Dover is relatively close to Route 128. Town web site: www.doverma.org; municipal offices: 508-785-0032

- **Foxborough,** home of the New England Patriots and a community of 16,000, is about 25 miles south of Boston, halfway to Providence, RI. Despite Gillette Stadium and the accompanying heavy traffic and general mayhem surrounding its football games, soccer matches, concerts, and other events, Foxborough (or Foxboro) is a pleasant, small town with some forested areas and the noteworthy Orpheum Theater. Bound by routes I-95, I-495, and 1, the town enjoys excellent highway access, but the commuter rail services Foxborough only during stadium events. Town web site: www.townoffoxborough.us; municipal offices: 508-543-1200

- **Needham,** whose quarries helped fill in so much of Boston during the 19th century, is 12 square miles of rolling, middle- to upper-middle-class suburbia just over 10 miles from Boston. Aside from some office parks near the highway, the headquarters of ABC's Boston affiliate (Channel 5), and a few television transmitting towers, Needham on the whole is fairly residential. Most homes in town were built in the 20th century, though some Victorians and a few 18th-century summer homes remain interspersed. You'll find most of Needham's 28,000 residents living in clusters nearer to Route 128, where homes are close together and most lots are well-kept and small to mid-sized; to call this area a prototypical example of American suburbia is not an exaggeration. The western and southern portions of town are more rural, home to lovely rolling hills, forestland, and pricier real estate. The commuter rail's Needham line makes four stops in town (though it does not run on Sundays), and there is easy access to routes 128 and 9. Town web site: www.needhamma.gov; municipal offices: 781-455-7500

- **Norwood** is a town of 28,500, about 14 miles south of Boston. It is a standard suburb, with small to medium-sized 20th-century homes and a dignified urban downtown, complete with civic amenities, several churches (as well as one synagogue), and a town common that hosts a farmer's market and open-air concerts in the summer. Boston is easily accessible via routes 1 and 128/I-95, and the commuter rail makes stops at Norwood Depot, Norwood Central, and Windsor Gardens. Town web site: www.ci.norwood.ma.us; municipal offices: 781-762-1240

- **Sharon** is a woodsy suburb of 18,000, located 22 miles south of Boston. The town boasts of its natural beauty, and indeed it offers a number of outdoor recreational opportunities, including a berry farm, Massapoag Lake, the Borderland State Park, and an Audubon Society wildlife sanctuary. Indoor attractions include a movie theater and the Kendall Whaling Museum. Sharon has a reputation for being religiously and ethnically diverse: in addition to the traditional New England church spires in town, there is a substantial Jewish presence and the Islamic Center of New England. Many homes are modern and tend to be small to mid-sized on heavily wooded lots, though there are some more opulent options. Route I-95 passes nearby, and there is commuter rail service to Boston and Providence, RI. Town web site: www.townofsharon. net; municipal offices: 781-784-1515

- **Wellesley** is a lovely and exclusive suburb of 26,000. A small, picturesque community, it is home to Wellesley College (one of the prestigious "Seven Sisters") as well as Babson and Massachusetts Bay Community College. Famous past and current residents include three Nobel Prize winners: poets Anne Sexton and Sylvia Plath, and Alexander Graham Bell. Just 13 miles west of Boston, Wellesley is the halfway point of the Boston Marathon, and offers easy access to routes 9, 16, 128, and the Mass Pike. Commuter rail stops are at Wellesley Square, Wellesley Hills, and Wellesley Farms. Town web site: www.ci.wellesley. ma.us; municipal offices: 781-431-1019

- The hilly, coastal, middle-class town of **Weymouth** (population 54,000) lies 12 miles southeast of Boston. More urban than neighboring South Shore communities—its high school enrolls about 4,000 students—Weymouth is technically a city, but commonly referred to as a town. In addition to substantial commercial offerings, Weymouth benefits from the waterfront, a pond, and a beach. Some older colonial homes, as well as pre-WWII construction, are available. One third of Weymouth residents rent, and you'll find a variety of apartment buildings and townhouses. Near the epicenter of Dunkin Donuts, Weymouth is home to the busiest franchise in the entire country. As a suburb, it is well situated on routes 3 and 3A, and has a commuter rail stop at South Weymouth, as well as two stops on the new Greenbush Line at Weymouth Landing and East Weymouth. Town web site: www.weymouth.ma.us; municipal offices: 781-335-2000

PLYMOUTH COUNTY

- **Brockton** is an industrial city of 94,000 people about 20 miles south of Boston. Known for its dominance in the shoe manufacturing and leather industries between the Civil War and WWII, and more recently for its dominance in the boxing ring with native sons Rocky Marciano and "Marvelous" Marvin Hagler, today Brockton comprises a major urban area that can be rough in spots. There are plenty of triple-decker homes and all basic amenities, including grocers, restaurants, and city office space. Residents also enjoy the city's Fuller Museum of Art, and, like Lawrence, condos and lofts are available in former brick mills. Nearly 45% of Brockton residents are renters, and the minority population here is fairly substantial. Route 24 is the major highway, and there are commuter rail stops at Montello, Brockton, and Campello. City web site: www. brockton.ma.us; municipal offices: 508-580-7123

- Located 15 miles southeast of Boston, **Hingham** is a nice, affluent, seaside community, similar in nature to Weymouth, Cohasset, and Scituate. With 21 miles of shoreline, a harbor filled with boats, town beach, 18-hole municipal golf course, and small movie theater, owners of expensive waterfront properties enjoy more than just the views of Boston and the Atlantic. Primarily residential, this community of almost 20,000 is very proud of its colonial roots. The town has preserved its early buildings, has six designated historic districts, and many Cape Cod, Federalist, and colonial homes. Although downtown living is tight, farther out the lots are big and wooded, and the town has some affordable housing. Like neighboring Cohasset, Hingham is set back from the major highways, but is accessible via Route 3A. The commuter rail's new Greenbush Line—opposed by the Town of Hingham for years due to concern over its historic sites and town square—stops at West Hingham and Nantasket Junction, while MBTA commuter boats shuttle passengers between the Hingham Shipyard and Rowes Wharf in Boston. Town web site: www.hingham-ma.com; municipal offices: 781-741-1400

- **Hull's** 11,000 residents are packed onto a narrow strip of land only 3 square miles in size that juts out into the Atlantic. Housing styles are varied, and most homes are small to medium-sized on cramped lots. There is not much in the way of parks, but Nantasket Beach is one of the most popular beaches this side of Cape Cod, and virtually all homes here could be described as waterfront or water-view. One quarter of the housing market is rentals. Hull is set even farther back from major highways than other South Shore communities (off Route 228), so driving into the city takes time. There is no commuter rail, but the MBTA runs a ferry between Pemberton Point (at the tip of the peninsula) and Boston's Long Wharf. Town web site: www.town.hull.ma.us; municipal offices: 781-925-2000

- **Plymouth** is a pleasant, large (over 96 square miles), and safe town of nearly 52,000. A little more suburban and with pilgrims instead of witches, this town has a similar feel to Salem. This is the Plymouth of *Mayflower* fame and has several landmarks, museums, restaurants, hotels, shopping, and pilgrim-themed services that cater to tourists. Plymouth's seaside downtown is busy: among its sites are a working harbor, beaches, and an Ocean Spray cranberry bog. Houses consist of colonials, Cape Cods, and more recent postwar construction (ranches, capes). Thirty-seven miles southeast of Boston, Plymouth is very close to Cape Cod and accessible to both via Route 3; a commuter rail stop is at Cordage/Plymouth station. Town web sites: www.townofplymouth.org and www.key-biz.com/ssn/Plymouth; municipal offices: 508-747-1620

- The residential suburb of **Scituate** (pronounced SIT-chew-it) is home to about 18,000, though its numbers increase a bit in the summer. Scituated—har, har—23 miles south of Boston, it's known in some circles as the heart of the South Shore's "Irish Riviera." Inviting beaches, windy cliffs, lighthouses, and a working harbor mix with recently built modern homes and traditional New England styles. Like its neighboring oceanfront communities, Scituate is not immediately accessible to the major highways, but the commuter rail's new Greenbush line will terminate here and stop at Scituate station. Town web site: www.town.scituate.ma.us; municipal offices: 781-545-8700

NEWCOMERS TO THE BOSTON HOUSING AND RENTAL MARKET ARE likely to experience a bit of sticker shock, as the cost of living here rivals that of cities like New York and San Francisco. A small but popular city, there is only so much space to go around, and most of it was sold years ago. The good news is, after a solid decade of skyrocketing real estate prices and rents, the market has finally softened in what many experts believe is an overdue "correction." While home prices are still high, they have, at least for the time being, settled down to something resembling normalcy.

Another thing newcomers may discover is that, while there certainly is no shortage of new construction and modern condo developments, much available property is old—sometimes *very* old. In towns like Salem, it's not uncommon to find houses originally built in the late 1600s. While this means that charm abounds—you'll run across your share of elegant crown moldings, ornate fireplaces, exposed brick, and claw foot tubs—it also means you might encounter drafty windows, older plumbing, or cramped quarters better suited for five-foot-tall revolutionaries.

Still, there is certainly something for everyone here—new suburban homes with sprawling lawns and plenty of parking, student digs in old Victorian mansions, 19th-century brownstones in the bustling heart of the city… with the right information and attitude, you will be able to find the perfect home to rent or buy. While everyone's tastes and priorities are different, bear in mind that central location, good public transportation routes, and nearby historical sites will all add to the price tag of any property.

A good clearinghouse of information for prospective homeowners and renters is the **Massachusetts Housing Consumer Education Centers**. Call them at 800-224-5124 or check www.masshousinginfo.org.

RENTING

During the late 1990s, Boston's rental market was glutted. Apartment hunters faced a citywide vacancy rate of less than 1%, meaning rents climbed ever upwards, prospective tenants were expected to cover brokerage fees, and most apartments were snatched up as soon as they were listed. After the mild recession that followed the dot-com crash, however, rents finally began to level off, and even held relatively steady for a few years. For a time, landlords were even desperate enough to offer incentives to prospective renters, such as a break on the first month's rent, and were willing to cover the expensive real estate agent fees. Recently, rents have begun to rise again, but only just—and at a slower, steady pace.

No matter what the market conditions, the best apartments don't stay available for long, and by most standards, living in Boston is still quite expensive. Many renters cushion the cost by living with roommates, and as a newcomer to the area, it can be a quick and simple way to make new friends. (Of course, depending on you or your roommates, it can also be a quick and simple way to make new adversaries!) While the best-case scenario usually involves a friend of a friend or some other personal reference, the city of Boston has a high proportion of singles, meaning there is a steady and fairly respectful roommate culture; the prevailing attitude tends toward "you do your thing and I'll do mine." Many of the city's best rental bargains are found in large houses, where the lease is passed on year after year from one revolving group of tenants to another. In any event, cost will likely play the biggest role in determining whether you decide to live alone or with housemates—and how many.

APARTMENTS

When you begin your search for an apartment, first determine how much you can or are willing to spend each month on rent. The standard formula holds that rent should constitute no more than one-third of your salary. The more centrally located and/or historic and scenic neighborhoods, such as Beacon Hill and the Back Bay, are among the most expensive. Apartments farther out from the city center but still on the T, such as Allston-Brighton, Jamaica Plain, and Somerville, have more mid-range price tags. For the best Boston bargains, head to communities with only bus or commuter rail service but lots of parking, such as Roslindale or West Roxbury, or try the suburbs, where prices may be cheaper still.

Next, you'll need to figure out your space needs. A small, dark studio with a kitchen-cum-hallway located in one of Boston's prime neighborhoods may be worth it if your office is within walking distance or if you are rarely home. If you plan on working from your apartment, convenient location to the city center may not be as much of an issue, and instead you'll want space for a home office. A roommate situation may become more appealing when you compare paying

$1100/month for a small one-bedroom apartment to sharing an airy, light-filled, two-bedroom unit for $700 each—not to mention splitting the cable, internet, gas, and electric bills two ways. Keep in mind that, while you may have been able to afford to live alone in your previous home, a one-bedroom unit here may be out of your price range. (If a roommate sounds like a good idea, check the resources below under **Newspaper Classifieds** and **Online Resources—Renting**.)

Other considerations as you look for an apartment include the following:

- Do you prefer living in a quiet residential area, or a more active, densely populated urban area?
- Will you be happy surrounded by college students?
- If you have a car, will you be comfortable parking it on the street, or will you require a parking space, which may cost extra? Or will you rely on public transit?
- Boston's summers are hot and uncomfortably humid, so a major concern when you look for an apartment will be climate control. Obviously, central air is the most attractive option, but usually only available in newer buildings—window air conditioning units, or, if nothing else, electric fans, are other options. Even if you plan on being at work most of the day, think about how easy it will be to sleep—a sometimes difficult and uncomfortable task when it is a muggy 90 degrees in your apartment with no cross ventilation. Note that many basement/garden level apartments have iron bars to protect the windows, meaning it may be impossible to install a window A/C unit.
- Conversely, winter brings long cold spells, and heating systems—and costs—vary. Find out whether the apartment is heated by an oil burner, electric furnace, or natural gas, and ask the current residents how much they typically spend on heating bills. Older buildings often have just one thermostat serving all units, forcing landlords to include heat and hot water in the rent. With the rising cost of heating oil, this isn't a bad thing! However, it does mean that the temperature will be out of your control, and you may want to ask current tenants whether the landlord keeps the building at a comfortable level.
- If you have a dog, you'll likely want to find an apartment with at least a shared backyard or close proximity to a park, and of course, a large dog and small studio make a difficult match. If you do have a pet, be sure to mention it right away when inquiring about places. Those with pets, particularly dogs, will find the apartment search more challenging.
- If you are already employed, find a neighborhood that's convenient to your place of business. As with flights, direct routes are best: living close to the same T line as your office is ideal, but even a direct bus route, or bike path for that matter, will work. Commutes that entail two or more transfers get old quickly; the MBTA web site (www.mbta.com) has a trip planner feature that will help you determine the best route. Apartments not on the T tend to cost less, and typically offer easier parking. If your job is outside the city, or will entail driving,

that may be a better option for you. Lastly, a smart idea is to try out (and time) your commute once or twice from an area that you're considering, to determine if you could live with it on a day-to-day basis.

While Boston has its share of high-rises, rentals of two- and three-family dwellings, often in the form of triple-deckers built during the late 1800s, are abundant. They provide housing for three families—one per floor—and while not the most elegant of styles, tend to provide fairly spacious apartments.

As a general rule: the farther out you are from downtown Boston, the more living space you'll get for your money, although there are exceptions. Apartments in the city's most coveted neighborhoods, such as Beacon Hill, the Back Bay, and the North End, built between the colonial and Victorian eras, tend to be cramped. The South End and the Fenway, with housing stock dating back to similar time periods, tend to offer a little more space. Quarters in the so-called "student slums" are usually in varying states of neglect or disrepair, as one might expect. Cambridge has a little of everything, from triple-deckers, to brownstones, to Victorians, to modern buildings. A typical apartment in a triple-decker in Brighton, Jamaica Plain, or Somerville has two or three bedrooms and a foyer. Many have front and back porches, as well.

People often assume that most Boston apartments become available in the late spring, when area students graduate or leave for the summer, but that is a mistake. Most fixed-term leases in Boston are for a year and turn over in August/September. While the early summer months are a good time to find a sublet, the best time to hunt for an apartment is mid- to late summer.

Area police departments can supply you with safety information about a specific neighborhood. Call the community officer in your precinct (see the **Neighborhood Profiles** for these numbers) with questions about a prospective neighborhood and information about local crime watch organizations.

APARTMENT HUNTING

While the rental market in the greater Boston area is less daunting now than it has been in recent years, it still presents a challenge, particularly if you enter the market off-season. As mentioned, most leases follow the school year and begin in August or September, so apartment hunting in mid-summer will provide you with the most options—but also the most competition. The majority of landlords still list their units through rental agents, mainly for convenience, but also for their protection; agents usually require you to submit a detailed rental application with references from work and previous landlords, and you will be subject to a credit check. While real estate agents do present an upside, as they can show you many available properties at once, they also charge a finder's fee of up to one month's rent, payable by either you, the landlord, or some negotiated combination thereof.

You will typically be expected to pay first and last month's rent upon signing your lease, plus a security deposit that can range anywhere from $50 to an entire month's rent. When combined with a finder's fee, your upfront expenses might add up to the equivalent of four months' rent. If that sounds like a bankrupting proposition to you, read on for ways to avoid some of these upfront costs.

Online classifieds, particularly Craigslist, have by and large supplanted newspaper ads as the most popular way to find an apartment. Besides the obvious benefits of multiple color photos, more detailed descriptions, and free searchable listings, online classifieds also make it easier to locate apartments free from realtor fees. You might find units listed directly by landlords or property management companies; often you'll encounter tenants seeking someone to take over their lease, in which case you might only need to pay one month's rent upfront. Look for ads boasting "No Fee" to avoid the extra finder's fee.

There are many other tactics that may help you find an apartment without a rental agent. For example, if you re affiliated with a local college or university, check with their housing office. Also try pavement pounding: go to the neighborhoods that appeal to you and check for posted phone numbers of landlords or management agencies. You can also look for vacancy postings, but they re less common here than in other cities. Don t forget handwritten postings on bulletin boards in cafés, on college campuses, or at work.

NEWSPAPER CLASSIFIEDS

The first thing most people do when looking for an apartment in the greater Boston area is to search the classifieds, either online or in print form. If nothing else, a quick scan will give you an idea as to the price ranges in the various neighborhoods in and around the city. As mentioned previously, a good deal of these ads are placed through rental agents and it's not always clear who you will be reaching—the landlord or agent—when you call.

- **Boston Globe**, 617-929-2000, www.boston.com; especially the Sunday edition, easily the most popular periodical for apartment listings in greater Boston. Listings are posted online daily.
- **Boston Herald**, 617-426-3000, www.bostonherald.com; extensive apartment listings, especially on Saturday.
- **Boston Phoenix**, 617-536-5390, www.bostonphoenix.com; free alternative weekly, comes out on Thursday. Includes ads for Boston area rentals, sublets, and room shares.
- **Boston Metro**, boston.metro.us; free weekday commuter newspaper that includes daily apartment and roommate listings, as well as a special real estate section on Fridays.
- Neighborhood papers like the **Jamaica Plain Gazette**, 617-524-2626, www.jamaicaplaingazette.com, the **South End News**, 617-266-6670, www.southendnews.com, and the **Boston Courant**, 617-267-2700, also run apartment

ads. Information about additional community publications can be found after each individual neighborhood profile in the **Neighborhoods** chapter.

OTHER RENTAL PUBLICATIONS

In addition to the general local periodicals, there are a number of rental and/or housing publications. These are often free and available in newspaper boxes, grocery stores, cafés, and storefronts throughout the city. They cover area real estate, rentals, and sometimes roommates. Many of their listings come from rental companies and may therefore result in your paying a realtor's fee. Here are a few:

- *Boston Homes*, 888-828-1515, www.homefind.com; weekly publication geared towards the Boston real estate market (specifically the Back Bay, Beacon Hill, Charlestown, downtown, the Fenway, JP, South Boston, the South End, the North End, and the Waterfront). Its listings include apartments for rent and for sale, as well as rental agents.
- *Just Rentals*, 800-242-1335, www.bostonforrent.com; free rental guide to properties in the greater Boston area.

ONLINE RESOURCES—RENTING

As young and tech-savvy as Boston's population is, online apartment hunting is the norm. From simple free classified listings to paid membership sites, you're sure to find something helpful in your search. Here are a few places to start with:

- **ApartmentRatings.com**; not an apartment listing service but rather a nationwide rating service. Residents of the greater Boston area post assessments of where they live for the benefit of those in search of an apartment.
- **ABostonLoft.com**; free listings of lofts for rent and for sale in Boston, Cambridge, and Somerville.
- **Boston.Backpage.com**; free online classified ads, including apartments for rent and roommate ads; essentially a much smaller version of Craigslist, affiliated with the *Weekly Dig*.
- **BostonApartments.com** offers extensive free listings of apartments to rent (fee and no fee) and to buy, as well as roommate wanted/available ads, and short-term and furnished rentals; updated daily.
- **Boston.com**; visit www.boston.com/realestate for a guide to everything housing-related in the greater Boston area, including neighborhood facts and statistics, moving tips, and a free (and giant) database of apartments for rent and for sale.
- **Craigslist**, http://boston.craigslist.org; the Boston branch of this free community classifieds site is wildly popular, with hundreds of listings added every day. Includes both fee and no fee apartments for rent, roommate wanted/available

ads, sublets, property for sale, and more.

- **EasyRent.com**; for a flat rate, you can search no-fee apartments in the greater Boston area, and have new listings emailed to you daily; they will refund your payment if you find an apartment through someone else. Affiliated with www. easyroommate.com, a roommate-matching service.
- **JustRentals.com**; online rental listings for the greater Boston area. Free to renters.
- **Massachusetts Housing Finance Agency** (**MHFA**), www.mhfa.com; offers information about renting and buying from the state's affordable housing program (e.g., Section 8 housing).
- **MatchingRoommates.com** is the oldest roommate referral service in the country. Pay a flat rate of $75 and they will screen and match you with other applicants.
- **MIT European Club**, http://euroclub.mit.edu/; their popular bulletin boards offer apartment and roommate want ads.
- **Oodle.com**, an all-purpose online classified site that culls listings from thousands of web sites.
- **Rentzilla.com** is Gateway Realty's online database of rental listings throughout the city.
- **Roommates.com**; find a roommate or a room. You can create a profile, search listings, and send messages with a free membership; for a low flat rate you can read messages sent to you.
- **Tufts Off-Campus Housing Resource Center**, http://ase.tufts.edu/och/; Tufts University compiles for its students a list of apartments, houses, and rooms for rent in the Somerville, Medford, and Arlington area, as well as roommate want ads and sublets. The site is open to the public and also contains some useful information about tenants' rights and other resources.

SHORT-TERM RENTAL OPPORTUNITIES/SUBLETS

If you prefer to take your time finding just the right home, you might benefit from a **short-term sublet**. Most of the leases in Boston last one year, and many of them run from September 1 to August 31. It's particularly easy to find a summer sublet (from June through August), as many students have an extra three months on their lease when they leave town at the end of the spring semester.

If you are interested in finding a temporary housing arrangement, you should research many of the same avenues used by apartment seekers (above). In particular, local papers like the *Phoenix* and the roommate-matching web sites listed above are great resources for sublet listings. In addition, sublet seekers will do well to check for notices posted on college kiosks and neighborhood notice boards (at laundromats, cafés, T stops, etc.). Short-term rental opportunities might include a weekly or monthly rental situation. See the **Temporary Lodgings** chapter near the end of this guide for ideas.

;ENTS

In Boston, most apartments available for lease are brokered through a rental agent. While there is no set amount, a rental agent's commission generally runs one half to one month's rent, payable by either the tenant or the landlord, depending on the market.

Boston is overrun with rental agencies, and it is these agents that place most of the apartment classifieds found in the major newspapers and free weeklies. When you respond to these ads, more often than not you'll find a rental agent on the other end of the phone with several properties that match your requests. Many seekers choose to go directly to a rental office in their neighborhood of interest. Agents will have some paper work for you to fill out to help them determine your apartment specifications. Be clear about what you want: price range, amenities, preferred neighborhoods, etc. Good brokers won't waste your time taking you to apartments that don't meet your needs. As most agents focus their business on one or two neighborhoods, you'll quickly determine which agents will work best for you. Do not feel committed to just one agent. Call on as many rental agencies as you like, and view as many properties as you can, until you find the broker and apartment that suits you best. Usually, you arrange to meet the broker at an appointed location and time, and then he either walks or drives you around to other properties in the neighborhood.

The following list offers just a few rental agents (many also handle real estate sales as well):

- **Anzalone Realty**, 100 Prince St, 617-367-1300, www.bostonapartments.com/anzalone (North End/Waterfront)
- **Apartment Hub**, 66 Union Sq, Somerville, 617-440-6060, www.apartmenthub.com (Cambridge/Somerville)
- **Bayside Realty**, 843 Mass Ave, Cambridge, 617-868-7979, www.baysidecambridge.com (Boston/Cambridge)
- **Boston's Preferred Properties**, 57 Gainsborough St, 617-859-3838, www.liveinboston.com (Fenway/South End)
- **Boston Realty Source**, 51 Church St, 617-867-7771, www.bostonrealtysource.com (Boston/Cambridge)
- **Boston Realty Works**, 252 Newbury St, 617-236-2062, www.bosrealty.com (Back Bay/Beacon Hill)
- **Bremis Realty**, 1177 Broadway, Somerville, 617-623-2500, www.bremis.com (Somerville)
- **Brownstone Real Estate**, 330 Newbury St, 617-262-4250, www.brownstonere.com (Back Bay/Beacon Hill)
- **Cabot & Company**, 213 Newbury St, 617-262-6200, www.cabotandcompany.com (Back Bay/Beacon Hill)
- **Century 21**, 134 Tremont St, Brighton, 617-787-2121, www.c21shawmut.com

(Allston-Brighton); 284 Salem St, Medford, 781-395-2121, www.c21advance.com (Medford/Malden); 49 Beale St, Quincy, 617-472-4330, www.c21annex.com (Quincy/South Shore); 161 Mt. Auburn St, Watertown, 617-926-5280, www.century21west.com (Watertown)

- **Chobee Hoy Associates**, 18 Harvard St, Brookline, 617-739-0067, www.chobeehoy.com (Brookline)
- **City Link Realty**, 375 Harvard St, Brookline, 617-738-8500, www.citywideusa.com (Brookline/Brighton)
- **City Realty Boston**, 372 Chestnut Hill Ave (Brighton), 1231 Comm Ave (Allston), 418 Centre St (JP); 617-739-7000, www.cityrealtyboston.com
- **Coldwell Banker**, 171 Huron Ave, 617-864-8566 (Cambridge); 321 Columbus Ave, 617-266-8000 (South End); 635 Mass Ave, 781-643-6228 (Arlington); 702 Main St, 781-893-0808 (Waltham); 858 Walnut St, 617-965-7171 (Newton); www.newenglandmoves.com
- **East Coast Realty**, 1212 Comm Ave, 617-739-2211, www.eastcoastrealty.com (Fenway/Allston-Brighton)
- **Exit Realty Associates**, 1028 Comm Ave, 617-730-9800, www.exitboston.com (Boston)
- **First Choice Realty**, 1340A Comm Ave, 617-734-8200, www.firstchoiceboston.com (Allston-Brighton)
- **Gibson Sotheby's International Realty**, 227 Newbury St, 617-375-6900, (Back Bay/Beacon Hill); 553 E Broadway, 617-268-2011, (South Boston); 556 Tremont St, 617-426-6900, (South End); www.gibsondomaindomain.com
- **Greater Boston Realty Group**, 404 S Huntington Ave, 617-522-2120 (JP)
- **H&R Realty**, 1245 Hancock St, Quincy, 617-770-9636, www.quincyapartmentrentals.com (Quincy)
- **Justin Reynolds Associates**, 5 Banks St, Waltham, 781-891-7888 (Waltham)
- **JVT Realty**, 931 Mass Ave, Arlington, 781-643-1004, www.bostonapartments.com/jvt (Arlington)
- **McCormack & Scanlon**, 3494 Washington St, 617-522-7355, www.mccormackscanlon.com; (JP)
- **Newton Centre Associates**, 50 Union St, Newton, 617-965-3300, www.nca1.net (Newton)
- **Olde Forge Realty**, 175 Cambridge St, 617-227-6600 (Beacon Hill), 617-437-7000 (Back Bay/South End); www.oldeforgerealty.com
- **Otis & Ahearn**, 200 Newbury St, 617-267-3500, www.otisahearn.com (Back Bay/Beacon Hill/Charlestown/North End/Waterfront)
- **Preservation Properties**, 439 Newtonville Ave, Newton 617-527-3700, www.preservationproperties.com (Newton/Waltham/Watertown)
- **Real Estate 109**, 459 Common St, Belmont, 617-489-5110, www.realestate109.com (Belmont/Watertown)
- **Realty Resource Associates**, 1340 Comm Ave, 617-730-5300, www.realtyresource.net (Allston-Brighton)

- **SCS Realty Group**, 879 Beacon St, 617-388-5881, www.scsrealtygroup.com (Allston-Brighton)
- **Skyline Realty**, 10 Magazine St, Cambridge, 617-547-8700, www.skylinerealty. com (Cambridge/Arlington)
- **Werman Real Estate**, 617-497-7888, www.aptgods.com (Cambridge)

CHECKING IT OUT

Unless you're just looking for a temporary sublet to get you through a couple of months, you should be confident about a place before signing a lease. Yes, there will likely be competition from other renters, but you shouldn't feel pressured to commit to an apartment that isn't right for you.

When checking out prospective apartments, in addition to aesthetics and price, keep in mind some of the following:

- Outside the living areas, is there enough space, including closets and storage? Sometimes additional storage space is available elsewhere in the building, like a basement or a locker. In the kitchen, check that there are enough drawers, shelves, and cabinets. Some Boston apartments are so compact that they have little to no cupboard space, and no kitchen drawers! While in the kitchen, check that the stove works. Boston landlords are not required to supply a refrigerator with rental units, so find out who owns the refrigerator before you assume the apartment is equipped with one.
- If you're living with roommates, consider whether there are enough bathrooms for everyone to get ready for work on a weekday morning. Many older apartments in Boston have only one bathroom, though some apartments make it easier for multiple tenants by having the toilet and shower in one room, and the sinks in another. Run the faucets and the showerhead, and flush the toilet at the same time to check the water pressure. Ask how big the water tank is, and if it serves more than one unit.
- Are you comfortable in this neighborhood? Would you feel safe walking home at night? Is it too loud, particularly on weekend nights, or conversely, does it feel too isolated? Also consider building security and safety devices.
- Is there a second exit in case of fire? Old buildings have fire escapes that have been "grandfathered" into building inspection approval, but newer buildings must have two exits to meet code. Are there smoke or heat detectors, which alert you to a change in air or temperature in case of a fire, carbon monoxide detectors, fire extinguishers, and fire alarms?
- Are you close to the T, bus, or commuter rail? Your daily commute to work or school will play a huge role in whether you are happy in your new place. If you will be bringing a car, consider parking options and distance to a major thoroughfare or highway.

- Does the building allow pets? This is important to know if you have a pet, but also if you have an allergy to pet dander and can't tolerate living in a building where other tenants have them.
- Is there laundry in the building or hook-ups for a washer/dryer in the unit? If there are no facilities on site, see how close (or far) the neighborhood laundromat is.
- Do you see any signs of insects or vermin? Even nice buildings can have rat and mice troubles, and apartments over restaurants are particularly prone to cockroaches. Ask what the landlord does in terms of vermin prevention, and keep in mind that sometimes, despite a landlord's best efforts, pests might come back from time to time.
- Which monthly utility bills are covered in the lease, and which bills are you required to pay? In Massachusetts, landlords must pay for water, and many pay for heat. Consider asking for the past year's fuel bills—both heat and electric—to figure how much more in the way of monthly expenditures you will be faced with.
- How is the technology in the building? Is it wired for cable? DSL? And on a more basic note, are there enough electrical outlets?
- Is the apartment large enough for all your belongings—and more importantly, will you be able to get them inside? Many old apartment buildings, especially in the cramped quarters of the North End and Beacon Hill, are walk-ups, with tiny, winding staircases; try to picture whether your favorite couch will make it up that narrow staircase before you actually attempt it on moving day. Also, if there is no elevator, will you mind walking up four or five flights each day?
- Is there a landlord or building manager on the premises? If not, whom do you contact in case of an emergency? How far away are they, and can you call at all hours?

If you'd like to do some more pre–apartment hunting research, check Ed Sacks' *Savvy Renter's Kit*, which contains a thorough renter's checklist.

STAKING A CLAIM

While Boston's rental market isn't as white-hot as it was a few years ago, chances are still good that several people will be angling for the same place you're viewing. If the apartment you are considering fits your basic specs and is in the neighborhood where you want to live, don't dawdle—*take it!*

The process usually requires filling out an application wherein you'll need to supply information about your job, bank account, credit and personal references, and previous landlord(s). It's best to bring these documents with you when viewing prospective apartments. If you have bad credit, consider having your lease co-signed by a parent, spouse, or someone else who can vouch for your financial stability. In such a case, be sure your co-signer has his/her banking information and social security number. Most importantly, don't forget to bring your checkbook so you can put down a deposit.

If you do get the apartment, expect to pay your new landlord at least the first month's rent (and usually the last month's as well), a security deposit of up to one month's rent (like the realtor fee, this can be negotiated with the landlord), and sometimes a key deposit or fee to purchase and install new locks. This means that a one-bedroom apartment at $1,200 per month, for example, might require $2,400 for first and last month's rent, up to $1,200 for a security deposit, up to $1,200 for the realtor's fee, plus a key deposit—for a total upfront expenditure of over $4,800.

LANDLORDS AND TENANTS

LEASES

There are two types of rental situations in Massachusetts: fixed-term and tenant-at-will. A fixed-term lease, an agreement to rent a unit for a specified amount of time (typically one year), is the most common. During this time period, a landlord can neither raise your rent nor evict you, unless you violate specific lease clauses. At the end of the agreed-upon term, you can opt to renew or leave. If you need to leave before the end of the term, you will possibly need to pay out the remainder of the lease or find an acceptable subletter to take over your lease. A tenant-at-will scenario, called a month-to-month agreement in other parts of the country, is where you pay rent at intervals, usually monthly. The upside to this arrangement is that it is easy to move out. The downside is that your landlord can raise your rent or evict you at any time, providing he gives you 30 days' notice.

Always read a lease carefully. Many landlords use forms weighted in their favor. You can negotiate with your landlord, however, striking unacceptable clauses and adding others, if the landlord agrees to the changes. Do this before you sign, and be sure to have the landlord initial the changes. Typical issues can include sublet restrictions and pet clauses.

Some leases contain illegal clauses, but they are not enforceable, even if you don't catch them before signing. For example, a lease requiring the tenant to pay for water and sewage cannot be enforced. Also, some landlords will stipulate in a lease that if your rent is late, they will charge a penalty fee. This is legal, but only if the rent is over 30 days late. Landlords creating a penalty for rent that is less than 30 days past due are violating the law. Valid leases in Massachusetts include the following:

- The amount of monthly rent
- The date on which your tenancy begins and ends
- The amount of your security deposit and your rights concerning it (see

below)
- The names, addresses, and phone numbers of your landlord and any other person responsible for maintaining the property
- The tenant authorized to receive notices and court papers

Make sure you get all promises not included on the lease in writing, and that all blank spaces are filled out. Finally, make sure you can prove the state of your apartment when you moved in. The best thing is to insist on a walk-through with your landlord, creating an inspection checklist that you both sign. This could save you in case the landlord makes unjustifiable deductions from your security deposit to cover repairs upon your exit.

SECURITY DEPOSITS

In Massachusetts, a security deposit must be placed in an interest-bearing escrow account in a Massachusetts bank. Within 30 days, a landlord is required to give you a receipt for this deposit, indicating the bank's name and address, amount of deposit, and account number. Should he not do so, you are permitted to have your security deposit returned to you. Each year, on the anniversary of your tenancy, your landlord must tell you how much interest your deposit has accrued, and either pay you said interest or deduct it from your next month's rent. Security deposits must be returned within 30 days after the tenancy ends. Landlords may deduct any reasonable cost of repairs for damage caused by the tenant, but normal wear and tear expenses are *not* deductible. If your landlord does not return your deposit within 30 days, you can sue for up to three times the amount of the deposit plus court costs and attorney fees.

Be aware that some landlords tack on bogus costs such as "rental fees," "pet fees," "fees for credit checks," or "holding deposits." These pre-payments are illegal. If you choose to pay them rather than lose the apartment, you can consider subtracting the charges from your future rent payments; however, doing so might set up a rancorous landlord/tenant relationship, which no one wants. It is best to rent from a fair landlord who won't try to gouge you with illegal fees.

LANDLORD/TENANT RIGHTS AND RESPONSIBILITIES

As a tenant, it's a good idea to know your rights and responsibilities, as well as the landlord's rights and responsibilities.

- The State of Massachusetts requires that landlords **provide safe buildings**: doors to the building, the main entryway, and individual units must lock, as must all opening exterior windows. Landlords are responsible for maintaining all smoke detectors in the building, but not fire extinguishers or carbon monoxide detectors. Many apartments in the area still have lead paint, and it's against the law for children under six to live in them. If you have small children and are interested in a unit that still has lead paint, a landlord cannot refuse to rent it to you; instead, he must have the paint removed. See the **Safety** section in the **Childcare and Education** chapter for more information about the lead poisoning prevention program in Massachusetts.

- As mentioned earlier, refrigerators do not always come with a unit; however, if a landlord provides one initially, he must continue to do so. Other **kitchen appliances**, including sinks, dishwashers (if included in the unit), and stoves must be in good working condition.

- A landlord must keep the general living environment **clean and free of vermin**. If your building has three or more units, the landlord is responsible for the disposal of garbage, and he must make sure the common areas are free from refuse.

- Massachusetts tenants do not pay for **water**, and a landlord is required to make sure there is enough hot water (between 110° to 130°) available for normal tenant use. Some units, particularly renovated ones, have separate heating systems, in which case tenants will likely be responsible for their own hot water and heating fuel, unless specified in the lease. Most buildings in Boston are less modern, however, and have a common heating system (without individual meters). If that s the case, the landlord pays for hot water and heat. From September 16 to June 14, units must be heated to a minimum of 68° during the day, and 64° at night.

- In the winter, the landlord is responsible for **snow and ice removal**, including clearing all exits and fire escapes.

- Lease provisions allowing a landlord **legal access to a unit** include entrance to inspect (e.g., for insurance purposes), to make repairs, and to show the unit for rental or purchase, provided the tenant has been given notice and has given permission. As a tenant, you are obliged to allow your landlord "reasonable access," but unless the lease states otherwise, the landlord isn't even entitled to a key. All other entrance clauses that may appear on a lease are not legal. In emergency circumstances (i.e., fire, flood) a landlord may enter a unit without warning. He may also enter without warning if you appear to have abandoned your unit, so it's a good idea to alert your landlord if you are going away for an extended period of time.

- It is **illegal for a landlord to refuse to rent to you** based on your race, religion, gender, sexual orientation, age, marital status, military status, or disability. Nor may you be discriminated against based on whether you have children or your source of income; a landlord may require proof that you have enough income to make the rent, but he cannot discriminate regarding the source of those funds. In Massachusetts, there are some instances in which a landlord may refuse to rent to a person with children: if the landlord is leasing out his own unit for less than a year; if it's a two-family house and the landlord lives in the other unit; or if it's a three-family (or less) house, and one of the other tenants is elderly/infirm to the point that having children in the building would create undue hardship.

Massachusetts provides some **legal protection for tenants**. Boston, Worcester, and Springfield provide mediation services for landlords and tenants through their court systems. The following are some organizations and municipal departments that can offer you more information about your rights and may be able to help if you have a dispute with your landlord.

- **Action for Boston Community Development**, 178 Tremont St, Boston, 617-357-6000, www.bostonabcd.org
- **Boston College Legal Assistance Bureau**, www.neighborhoodlaw.org
- **Boston Fair Housing Commission**, City Hall, Room 966, Boston, 617-635-4408, www.cityofboston.gov/civilrights
- **Boston Inspectional Services**, 1010 Mass Ave, 5th Floor, Boston, 617-635-5300
- **Cambridge Eviction-Free Zone**, 55 Norfolk St, Cambridge, 617-354-1300
- **Cambridge Inspectional Services Department**, 831 Mass Ave, Cambridge, 617-349-6100, www.cambridgema.gov
- **Community Action Agency of Somerville**, 66-70 Union Sq, Somerville, 617-623-7370
- **Community Legal Services and Counseling Center**, 1 West St, Cambridge, 617-661-1010, www.clsacc.org
- **Greater Boston Legal Services**, 197 Friend St, Boston, 617-371-1234; 60 Gore St, Suite 203, Cambridge, 617-603-2700; www.gbls.org
- **Harvard Legal Aid Bureau**, 1511 Mass Ave, Cambridge, 617-495-4408, www.law.harvard.edu/students/orgs/hlab/
- *Legal Tactics: Tenant's Rights in Massachusetts, Private Housing*, published by the Massachusetts Law Reform Institute, 99 Chauncy St, 5th Floor, Boston, 617-357-0700, www.mlri.org. Cost is $20.
- **Massachusetts Bar Association Lawyer Referral Service**, 20 West St, Boston, 617-654-0400, www.massbar.org
- **Massachusetts Attorney General's Office Face-to-Face Mediation Program**, 100 Cambridge St, Boston, 617-727-2200, www.ago.state.ma.us; also publishes *The Attorney General's Guide to Tenants' Rights*. Other services are available through the **Consumer Protection Division**.
- **Massachusetts Commission Against Discrimination**, 1 Ashburton Pl, 6th Floor, Boston, 617-994-6000, TTY 617-994-6196, www.mass.gov/mcad
- **Massachusetts Department of Housing & Community Development**, 100 Cambridge St, Boston, 617-727-7765, www.mass.gov/dhcd
- **Massachusetts Office of Consumer Affairs and Business Regulation**, 10 Park Plaza, Suite 5170, Boston, 617-973-8787 or 888-283-3757, www.mass.gov/consumer; provides a list of applicable links for tenant/landlord rights and issues in the state. This office also puts out *The Tenant's Commandments*,

a pamphlet detailing tenants' rights, available from their office or online at www.tenant.net/Other_Areas/Massachusetts/. They also provide links to information about tenant and landlord rights and responsibilities, moving in Massachusetts, and the state sanitary code.

- **Massachusetts Rental Housing Association (Landlord Resources)**, 276 Washington St, Boston, 877-863-9665, www.massrha.com
- **Massachusetts Tenants' Organization**, 14 Beacon St, Boston, 617-367-6260
- **Rental Housing Resource Center,** 1 City Hall Plaza, Room 709, Boston, 617-635-RENT; www.cityofboston.gov/rentalhousing
- **Somerville Fair Housing Commission**, 50 Evergreen Ave, Somerville, 617-625-6600, ext. 2564, www.ci.somerville.ma.us (provides a helpful booklet called *The Tenant's Helper: A Handbook for Renters*)
- **Tenant Advocacy Project**, Harvard Law School, Austin Hall, Room 009, 1515 Mass Ave, Cambridge, 617-495-4394, www.law.harvard.edu/academics/clinical/tap/
- **Volunteer Lawyers Project**, 29 Temple Pl, Boston, 617-423-0648, www.vlpnet. org

Boston tenants with emergency landlord problems—no heat or threatened lockout—can call the Mayor's 24/7 hotline for intervention: 617-635-4500.

RENT AND EVICTION CONTROL

Put to voters in a 1994 statewide ballot was the issue of **rent control**. The outcome—by a narrow 51% to 49% vote—prohibited rent control in Massachusetts, effective December 1996, meaning landlords can legally increase rent as much as they want at the end of your lease. Since an initial spike in rents when the law first took effect, landlords have generally not abused this privilege, especially with tenants who have proven themselves to be reliable. You may be able to renew your lease at the same rate each year; more common is an annual rent increase of about $25–$50 per month.

In an effort to assist those heavily affected by the rent control decision, the **Rental Housing Resource Center** (617-635-RENT; www.cityofboston.gov/rentalhousing) provides mediation between landlords and tenants, legal advice for both landlords and tenants, and assistance in housing placement for elderly, handicapped, or low-income residents.

Eviction can occur only under certain circumstances—rules differ according to whether the tenant is in a fixed-term lease or is a tenant-at-will. If you are a tenant-at-will, a landlord can end your tenancy whenever he wants, provided you are given 30 days' notice and there is reason to evict.

Massachusetts landlords are forbidden from using eviction as a means of retaliating against their tenants. For instance, complaining to the landlord or a government agency about housing conditions, or joining a tenants' union is not grounds for eviction. Should your landlord try to evict you, raise your rent, or otherwise change the terms of your lease within six months after you've taken any of the aforementioned actions, his behavior will legally be assumed to be retaliation.

RENTER'S/HOMEOWNER'S INSURANCE

Even though Boston isn't in the Tornado Belt or on the Pacific Rim, bad things do happen here to good apartments and houses. For these reasons, renter's or homeowner's insurance is a good idea. Renter's insurance is usually quite affordable, and depending on the policy, it can protect you in the event of a number of catastrophes, including theft, fire, and water damage, and sometimes personal liability.

You can start researching policies through the **Massachusetts Division of Insurance**, 1 South Station in Boston, 617-521-7794, www.mass.gov/doi. They offer a host of information regarding renter's and homeowner's insurance, and can provide you with information about insurance rates by community and a list of insurance agencies in the state. **Insure.com**, **Insweb.com**, **NetQuote.com**, and **InsuranceFinder.com** all offer comparison shopping, instant quotes, and additional insurance information.

To order your CLUE (Comprehensive Loss Underwriting Exchange) report, write to **ChoicePoint Consumer Disclosure**, P.O. Box 105108, Atlanta, GA 30348-5108, or go to www.choicetrust.com. This national database of consumers' automobile and homeowner's insurance claims is used by insurers when determining rates or denying coverage. Contact ChoicePoint if you find any errors in your report.

A few of the major insurers in the greater Boston area include **Arbella** (www.arbella.com), **GEICO** (www.geico.com), **Hanover** (www.hanover.com), **Liberty Mutual** (www.libertymutual.com), and **MetLife** (www.metlife.com).

Renter's insurance is available through an insurance agent, or you can apply directly to the **FAIR** (**Fair Access to Insurance Requirements**) Plan. In Massachusetts, this program is administered by the Massachusetts Property Insurance Underwriting Association, located at 2 Center Plaza in Boston across from City Hall Plaza, 617-723-3800, 800-851-8978, www.mpiua.com.

BUYING A HOME

As with renting, buying a home in the greater Boston area can be a bit daunting. And unless you're from California or New York, you'll likely experience some sticker shock when you see how much (or rather, how little) your dollar will buy.

Many newcomers arrive with the intention of buying a house, but decide to rent, at least at first. This may be good if you are unsure of what location best suits you, or if you don't think you will be in the area longer than a couple of years.

But, if you can afford to, and you are positive about your location preference, buying real estate tends to be a good long-term investment. Monthly mortgage payments may not be that much more than monthly rent, plus you're building equity. There are also tax breaks to consider when purchasing a home.

Housing styles throughout Massachusetts vary widely. Most common is the triple-decker (sometimes called a three-decker or a three-family house), which is unique to Boston. Most were built during the 1800s when cheap housing was needed to shelter the city's growing number of immigrant workers. They consist of three floors, usually with one apartment to a floor. Aside from these, buyers have a range of choices, the most prevalent being colonials; Cape Cods; ranches; Gothic, Greek, and Tudor Revivals; and Victorians. Many homes in the greater Boston area are old enough to be on the National Register of Historic Places. When you drive or walk around town, you'll sometimes notice homes boasting small plaques with the name and date of the family who built them.

Aside from rental units, most housing options in Boston's city center are condos and co-ops, which are often in multiple-story colonial and Victorian buildings, though there are a few luxury condominiums in more modern high-rise type structures, particularly downtown. There are still many single-family residences (a.k.a., mansions) as well, particularly in Beacon Hill, the Back Bay, and the South End. These are most often brick Victorian row houses, which managed to escape the common fate of being chopped up and parceled into apartments during the mid-1900s.

In neighborhoods like Allston-Brighton, JP, West Roxbury, and the communities directly surrounding Boston (Brookline, Cambridge, Somerville), you'll encounter a mix of housing options. From efficiency studios to stately mansions—to enormous homes that *once* were stately, but have been inhabited by students for decades—there is something for everyone, including condos for sale in old brownstones and in big, practical complexes, as well as single- and multi-family houses of all styles. As you head further out of the city, you'll find stereotypical suburbia: bigger homes with lawns and driveways. These communities have more houses and fewer condos, co-ops, or rental options.

DECIDING WHAT, WHETHER, AND WHERE TO BUY

If you are **considering buying a home**, there are a few factors to keep in mind:

- Consider how long you plan to live in your potential home. On average, it takes three to four years for your home's value to appreciate enough to cover the purchasing and selling costs. If you plan on leaving after only two years, it may be in your best financial interest to rent.
- Consider your space needs. Are you planning on having children in the near future or are your children about to leave? Will four flights of stairs for a swank townhouse work for a retired couple?
- What kind of house do you want: old or new? An old Victorian can be an abso-

lute gem of a house when all the renovations are complete, but this is no easy task. Families with children, in particular, should take care with any housing renovations, as disturbing long-hidden lead paint is hazardous.

- Consider the neighborhood. This is particularly important if you have children. Consider nearby parkland, the quality of the schools, property values, heavy traffic, crime rates, and planned future construction in the community. Even if all of these factors aren't crucial to you personally, they can affect the appreciation of your home and thus the value of your investment. Most realtors agree that homes in good school districts are less vulnerable to slumps in the housing market.

- When looking at housing in a particular community, pay attention to how quickly homes sell, and if there are often large gaps between list prices and sale prices. Buying a place in an "up and coming" area can be a good investment, but keep in mind, not all "up and coming" areas actually come up. Pay attention to high-density streets (a lot of apartments), heavy traffic, poor public transportation, and an absence of neighborhood services.

- Generally, it's good to know that two-bedroom condos sell more easily than one-bedroom condos, two-bedroom/one-bath homes are less desirable than three-bedroom homes, and the nicest house on the block is not as easy to sell as the more middle-of-the-road house just two doors down.

CONDOMINIUMS (CONDOS) AND COOPERATIVES (CO-OPS)

Co-ops and condos are similar housing arrangements. Both tend to offer environments that are more social than what you'd experience in a single-family home, if for no other reason than the need to make decisions about upkeep and use of the communal parts of the property. Maintenance fees are common in both, and in addition to paying your assessment, from time to time you may be required to give more for unexpected repairs or capital improvements. Prospective buyers should take as much time to examine the condo's or co-op's financial reports as to view the available unit. Also look at recent capital improvements and have the grounds inspected to forewarn you of any upcoming repair needs—outside decks, recreation area, landscaping, roof, windows, etc.

In a **condo**, you purchase an individual unit, but the land and common areas are jointly owned by the condo association, of which you would be a part. When you live in a **cooperative** (**co-op**), you actually own a share of the corporation that owns the building, as opposed to the unit itself. In this situation each shareholding entity (i.e., tenant) has a unit reserved for his use. In the past, co-ops were more favorable to selling to those with substantial economic means, and tended not to allow financing, although that is no longer, necessarily, the case. Condos, on the other hand, did and do permit standard mortgage financing. Times have changed, and although some co-ops maintain the cash-only policy, others have revised their bylaws to allow in "desirable" buyers with high enough incomes but inadequate savings. Another thing to keep in mind when considering a co-op is that co-op units can take longer to sell due to the rigorous screening process of applicants and higher down payments, which is not good if you find yourself needing to sell quickly. When buying a unit in a co-op, be prepared to disclose your financial information to the board. A well-run co-op will be careful to make sure incoming tenants are financially dependable, and they may also scrutinize your personal life. On your end, you should be sure to get a prospectus, minutes of the last meeting of the board, and a financial statement from the co-op (or condo, for that matter) and go over them with your broker and your lawyer. If your purchase is rejected, expect no explanation. Be aware that co-op size may affect your ability to get a mortgage; in co-ops with fewer than 12 units, lenders may be more likely to reject a mortgage application because the relatively small number of shareholders in such buildings raises the collective risk of default. Also, keep in mind that co-op maintenance fees (the cost of upkeep for everything outside the walls of your apartment) can be steep, and only some of the maintenance fee (the portion of the fee that is allocated for property tax payments) is tax deductible.

Purchasing a condo is similar to purchasing a single-family home, the difference being you will have to contend with (annual or monthly) condo fees that cover the expenses of communal area upkeep and shared amenities, such as garage, laundry room, or pool. Again, obtain a copy of condo association records to determine not only how often association fees have gone up, but also by how much.

For more information about housing associations, visit the **Community Associations Institute** at www.caionline.org or the **American Homeowners Resource Center** at www.ahrc.com. Both are national organizations that offer information and tips on how to live in a community association.

FINDING A PLACE TO BUY

Tried and true methods of finding a place to buy include driving around a neighborhood looking for "For Sale" signs, working with a real estate agent, and perusing the newspapers. The Sunday *Boston Globe* and the Saturday edition of the *Boston Herald* are the primary source of print real estate ads for the region; both papers have extensive real estate sections, listing condos and houses and their respective agencies (see above under **Newspaper Classifieds**). However, more and more popular with buyers and sellers alike are online real estate classifieds and search engines, whether it's just the enhanced listings from the local paper (Boston.com), or dedicated sites like Craigslist, Trulia.com, and Realtor.com. Most of these are free to browse, offer multiple color photos, and will even map out the property for you, allowing you to do much of your research in advance and on your own. The web is particularly helpful for those seeking **For Sale By**

Owner (FSBO) properties; for more information, see the **Online Resources** section coming up.

Once you start viewing homes, several things will help make the process easier. First, make a list of your "must haves," and then make a list of "wants." Take a copy of them with you, and mark on the list which homes have which amenities. Brokers recommend that you seriously consider no more than three houses at a time. Of course, it will probably take lots of viewings before you find your top three. To help keep your memory fresh, keep a written log for each house, including the date you saw it, with which broker, and then make notes on the listing sheet. Take a digital camera along if possible, and photograph each home as you tour it; this will help you to remember and visually compare them all later on. You also can get a map of the neighborhood(s) in which you're looking and mark the homes you've seen. When a property you've looked at sells, ask your broker for the sale price or look it up online—this will give you a good idea of the current market and the price range in which you should be making an offer.

When touring homes, look for red flags. For example, if you see all the items in a basement resting on platforms, it's a good indication that the basement takes in water; a lot of armoires and chests may indicate inadequate storage space.

WORKING WITH A REAL ESTATE BROKER

Although you do not have to work with a real estate broker when buying a home, they can be very helpful. Even in this age of information—where online community classifieds allow sellers to advertise directly to prospective buyers for free and without commissions—more people than not choose to obtain a broker's services, whether it be on the buying or the selling end. In Massachusetts, real estate brokers are licensed and are legally bound to put their clients' interests first, maintain confidentiality about information provided, comply with clients' wishes, keep clients apprised of any useful information, and account for any money involved.

Because buying and selling homes is their daily business, realtors can be a great resource during your journey toward home ownership. Real estate brokers are qualified to advise you on how much you can afford to spend; how to find alternative financing or recommend a lender; what personal data you'll need when going for your loan approval; the property values, taxes, utilities costs, services, zoning ordinances in certain neighborhoods; and where to find a good inspector. Additionally, realtors can save you a lot of time and effort by showing you houses that are in your price range and in your preferred neighborhoods. Often a realtor will have access to homes that, while on the market, are not visibly advertised elsewhere. Most realtors in Massachusetts belong to the MLS (Multiple Listing Service) Property Information Network, which means the agent you work with will have shared access to essentially every property listed in the system (not just the ones listed through their own agency).

The first thing you should know when picking a real estate broker is that there is a difference between a seller's agent and a buyer's agent. A **seller's agent** represents the person trying to sell a house; a **buyer's agent** represents the person trying to buy the house. In Massachusetts, one person can legally be a broker for both sides of a real estate deal, called a "dual agent," if both the buyer and seller are aware of this and have given informed consent. But, since the seller is trying to get the highest price, and the buyer is trying to pay the lowest price—and the seller usually pays the realtor's commission—the likelihood is that the realtor will work harder, however unwittingly, for the seller. Therefore, you should think seriously about getting yourself a good buyer's agent, whose sole responsibility is to represent you.

Even real estate professionals recommend that you shop around a little before settling on a broker to represent you. Ideally, you want someone who knows the local market in depth, is able to find and manage listings well, and is assertive enough to negotiate on your behalf. Chemistry and compatibility are certainly important too.

A good place to start when looking for an agent is to visit open houses in your neighborhood(s) of choice and meet with the representing agent, or ask friends or co-workers for recommendations. Some things to think about when you're deciding on an agent are:

- Is she licensed and in good standing? What credentials does she have?
- Does she belong to a Multiple Listing Service or other online buyer's research service?
- Is this her full-time career? If not, her bigger priorities may lie elsewhere.
- How does she plan to help you get what you want in a home?

If you do find a buyer's agent, have her sign a written buyer's brokerage agreement to be your "Buyer's Agent." You will promise to work only with this agent for a specified amount of time (usually three months) and not buy from anyone else. The commission will still come from the seller, but your agent must present the offer. Also, it pays to be discreet when disclosing information to any realtor. Unless you've gotten him to sign on as a buyer's agent, you should presume that anything you say to a realtor will go straight to the seller, and that might not always be ideal.

The **Board of Registration of Real Estate** answers real estate–related questions, at www.mass.gov/reg/boards/re. If you're looking for a real estate agent, you might want to check with the **Massachusetts Association of Realtors** (www.marealtor.com), or the **Greater Boston Real Estate Board** (**GBREB**, 617-423-8700, www.gbreb.com). In addition to providing names of real estate agents, they also have a number of property listings and advice on obtaining financing. The GBREB site also offers downloadable software to help prospective homeowners figure out how they can fit a mortgage into their budget. Most of the rental brokers listed above also handle sales.

ONLINE RESOURCES—HOUSE HUNTING

Web sites for would-be homeowners include the following (also see **Additional Resources** below):

- **ABostonLoft.com**; free listings of lofts for rent and sale in Boston, Cambridge and Somerville.
- **BostonApartments.com**, in addition to their apartment rentals, compiles real estate sales listings throughout Massachusetts.
- **BostonCondos.com**; free listings of condos for sale throughout the greater Boston area, including full agent contact information and photos.
- **Boston.com/realestate**; the *Globe's* online guide to everything real estate in the greater Boston area: rentals, sales, mortgage calculators, community profiles, recent sales, moving tips, etc.
- **BostonRealEstate.com**; searchable property listings and other real estate resources such as community comparisons, mortgage calculators, etc.
- **Craigslist**, http://boston.craigslist.org/rfs/; the Boston branch of this free community classifieds site is wildly popular, with hundreds of local property listings added every day. Includes FSBO and agency listings alike.
- **FISBO Registry**, www.fisbos.com; registry of FSBO homes, with searchable listings, links to buyer's agents, and other resources such as moving, mortgage, and legal advice.
- **ForSaleByOwner.com**; FSBO listings and real estate resources for buyers and sellers.
- **HomeGain.com**; find a realtor, view homes for sale, or look up property value estimates.
- **HomePages.com**; searchable listings, aerial maps, and other resources.
- **Homes.com**; members can view property listings, community profiles, foreclosure listings, etc.
- **ISoldMyHouse.com**; FSBO listings and other services; does not give property addresses.
- **Move.com**; comprehensive real estate/moving site, partnered with Realtor.com.
- **Oodle.com**, an all-purpose online classified site that culls through property listings from thousands of web sites.
- **Owners.com** is the largest FSBO marketplace on the web.
- **Propsmart.com**; national real estate search engine, displays results on an interactive Google map.
- **Realtor.com**; the National Association of Realtors' web site is the largest online database of homes for sale in the US; does not include FSBO listings.
- **Trulia.com**; type in the town or city you're interested in, and this easy-to-use site will display area properties for sale on an interactive map. An excellent tool if you're particularly sensitive to location within a given neighborhood.
- **Zillow.com**; another useful site that incorporates a large database of agent

and FSBO listings, interactive maps, and property value estimates based on market conditions and recent sales—it will even offer you estimated values of listed homes to compare with their asking prices.

- **ZipRealty.com**; nationwide online realtor offering buyers cash back on commissions; must register (for free) to view full property details.

THE BUYING PROCESS

The first thing you need to consider when buying a house is how much you can spend. Start with your gross monthly income. Then tally up your monthly debt load: credit cards, student loans, car payments, personal debt, child support, alimony, etc. For revolving debt (like credit card debt), use your minimum monthly payment for the calculation, and ignore any debts you expect to have paid off entirely within six months' time. As a rule, mortgage lenders don't want your monthly housing costs to exceed 28% of your total monthly income, and your debt load shouldn't exceed 36% of it. Some lenders might make an exception to the 28/36 formula, depending on your situation (assets, liability, job, credit history); but be careful about overextending yourself. In recent years, the rise in home prices has far out-paced wage increases, making affordable housing hard to find and threatening to drive middle-income buyers out of the real estate market entirely. To prevent that, lenders have developed several "creative" alternatives to the standard home loan, including low (or even zero) down payment loans, "interest-only" mortgages, and negative amortization mortgages. All of these loans help buyers purchase more home than they would normally qualify for; however, they also carry disadvantages. Buyers who use these tools are not building equity in their homes, and are exposing themselves to financial ruin should the real estate market collapse, leaving them with a house that is worth less than they still owe on it.

When calculating your budget, don't forget to factor in closing costs, which include appraisals, attorney's fees, transfer taxes, title insurance, points, and myriad other fees, and must be paid upon closing. (*Points* are fees you might pay the bank upfront in order to gain a lower long-term interest rate; each point is equal to 1% of the mortgage amount.) Closing costs vary by lender—some banks offer their customers reductions or even full discounts—but tend to average nearly $3,000. Likewise, when determining your budget, consider additional monthly expenses such as homeowner's insurance, property taxes, utilities, condo fees, and maintenance.

Lenders suggest that you **"pre-qualify"** or, better still, get **"pre-approved"** for a loan. **Pre-qualification** is, in essence, an educated guess as to what you'll be able to afford for a loan. With **pre-approval**, your financial claims are verified, and thus your ability to pay the stated amount is guaranteed by the lender. To be pre-approved, your loan officer will review your financial situation (by running a credit check, going over your proof of employment, savings, etc.) and then you will be given a letter documenting that the bank is willing to lend you a particular amount based on your proven financial situation. Pre-approval is more labor-intensive for you and the lender, but putting in the effort ahead of time demonstrates to sellers and real estate agents that you are a serious buyer, and thus may give you a competitive edge over other prospective buyers. Also, in the end, you'll know for sure what you can (and cannot) afford, and you will be ready to act if you find a home you really love.

If you are planning to get pre-qualified or pre-approved for your loan, go to your lender prepared with documentation of your financial history, including recent pay stubs and cancelled rent checks, and contact the three major credit bureaus listed below to make sure your credit history is accurate. You will need to provide your name, address, previous address, and Social Security number with your request. You are entitled to one free credit report per year from each credit bureau (additional reports will cost a nominal fee); contact each company for specific instructions, or visit www.annualcreditreport.com or call 877-322-8228 for access to all three. A credit report will show your credit activity for the past seven years, including your highest balance, current balance, and promptness or tardiness of payments. After seven years, the slate is wiped clean for any credit transgressions, except in the case of bankruptcy, which will appear on your record for 10 years. Fortunately, lenders are more concerned with your most recent track record than how you behaved seven years ago. It's best to try to pay all your bills in full and on time for at least a year before you apply for a loan. Even if you pay your bills on time, having too much credit can be a problem. Generally, you can get away with a couple of "blemishes" on your record and still get low rates. And even if your credit report isn't stellar, you will likely still be able to get a loan, though your rates (interest and fees) may be higher. Also, saving up a lot of money can counteract credit flaws to make you a more appealing financial risk to a lender.

The major credit bureaus are:

- **Experian**, 888-397-3742, www.experian.com
- **TransUnion**, P.O. Box 6790, Fullerton, CA, 92834, 877-322-8228, www.trans union.com
- **Equifax**, P.O. Box 740241, Atlanta, GA 30374, 800-685-1111, www.equifax.com

It's best to get a copy of your credit report from each bureau, as each report may be different. If you discover any inaccuracies, contact the service immediately and request that it be corrected. By law they must respond to your request within 30 days. If you are insecure about your credit record, call Fannie Mae's nonprofit credit counseling service at 800-732-6643 before you apply for a mortgage. Be aware that too many credit record inquiries can lower your credit status.

Most buyers need a **mortgage** to pay for a house. A typical house mortgage is for either 15, 20, or 30 years and consists of four parts, commonly referred to as "PITI" (principal, interest, taxes, and insurance). The **principal** is the flat sum of money that you borrowed from the lender to pay for the property. The larger the down payment, the less you will need to borrow to meet the total purchase price of your home. The lender charges **interest**, a percentage of the principal, as repayment for the use of the money that you've borrowed. It is how lenders make their money. Your community charges you **taxes** based on a percentage of your property value; you'll continue paying these even after your mortgage is paid off. The final component of PITI is home **insurance** against calamities such as fire, theft, and natural disasters. It is a requisite to buying a house. In many cases, people deposit funds to cover insurance and taxes into an escrow or trust account.

There are many loan programs around. Search the internet, newspapers, and books, and speak with financial planners, real estate agents, and mortgage brokers to find out what's available. Direct lenders (banks) and mortgage brokers are the most common places to go for a loan. A **direct lender** is an institution with a finite number of in-house loans, whose terms and conditions are controlled by the lender. A **mortgage broker**, on the other hand, is a middleman who shops around to various lenders and loan programs to find what's best for your needs. Because brokers shop around for the best interest rates, it's often worth paying their fee. Most major lenders and brokers have their own web sites. For a list of local banks, look in the **Money Matters** chapter.

When educating yourself about mortgages, be sure to take the time to re-search institutions' loan costs and restrictions: interest rates, broker fees, points, prepayment penalties, loan term, application fees, credit report fees, and cost of appraisals. The Bank Rate Monitor (www.bankrate.com) offers pages of infor-mation on mortgages and interest rates at over 2000 banks. It can pay to shop around.

Traditionally, a lender will expect a **down payment** of 20% of the purchase price; if less, you will be required to get the loan qualified by an outside party (such as the Veterans Administration or Federal Housing Authority) or pay for private mortgage insurance (PMI). (Once your loan balance reaches 78% of the purchase price, you are no longer required to pay PMI). However, as mentioned, lenders have instituted new programs that require as little as 5%—or even 3%—down, such as Fannie Mae's three/two loan program, which gives a first-time buyer 95% of the price of a home. The buyer is required to supply 3% of the down payment; the other 2% can be a gift from family, a government program, or a non-profit agency. First-time homebuyers may also qualify for a number of state-backed programs that feature lower down payment requirements and below-market interest rates. **MassHousing** offers a number of popular low-to-no down payment loans, including the MassAdvantage programs for first-time homebuyers, and the Municipal Mortgage Program, designed to help civic em-ployees such as teachers and firefighters purchase a home in the community they serve; visit www.masshousing.com for information on eligibility and the application process. Massachusetts also sponsors a "**SoftSecond**" mortgage program for low- to moderate-income residents, which effectively lends you money toward your down payment, sometimes at below market interest rates. This allows you to avoid paying PMI, even if you can't afford to put a full 20% down. The SoftSecond program is available in cooperation with various local lenders; visit the web site of the **Massachusetts Housing Partnership** (www.mhp.net/home ownership) for details.

Although some believe that Massachusetts' officially defined **affordable housing** (below market rate) is not as available as it should be, even in the suburbs, the state does have housing assistance programs. The biggest portal for this information is through the **Massachusetts Department of Housing and Community Development**, www.mass.gov/dhcd. Also check with the **Citizens' Housing and Planning Association** (617-742-0820, www.chapa.org) and the **Massachusetts Affordable Housing Alliance** (617-822-9100, www.mahahome. org), nonprofits devoted to the issues of affordable housing and community development in Massachusetts. The **Boston Redevelopment Authority** (www. cityofboston.gov/bra) is a decades-old organization devoted to development projects, including affordable housing in Boston. The local branch of the **Department of Housing and Urban Development** (**HUD**, www.hud.gov/local) may also be of use.

To take advantage of most national and state-sponsored affordable housing programs, buyers are often required to attend a **first-time homebuyers course**; they are usually inexpensive (sometimes free), and extremely valuable resources to anyone preparing to buy a home.

When filling out the **final paperwork for your loan approval**, keep in mind that intentionally offering incorrect information on a loan application is a federal offense. Within three business days of applying for your loan, your lender must give you a "good faith estimate" of how much your closing costs will be. Once you are approved, you can make an offer on the house (even if you are not formally approved, but are pre-qualified, you can make an offer—but it will have to be contingent on funding). If you want your offer to be seriously considered, particularly in a tight market, be sure to offer a fair market price, include a bank statement on the source of your down payment, your pre-approval letter, and even a note to the seller about why/how much you want the house. If cost is an issue, try to do your house hunting during the off-season (November to January), when competition will not be as intense. **Note**: in Massachusetts, it is customary for the buyer to make a good faith deposit of 5% to 10% of the total purchase price at the time of the offer. The deposit is usually held in escrow until the seller accepts the offer, at which time the funds are transferred.

Once you have made the offer, the house will need to be appraised, and the title will need to be sent to the lender for a **title search**.

Offers, which should be submitted in writing to the seller, may mention the following:

- Address and legal description of the property
- Price you will pay for the home
- Terms (how you will pay)
- Seller's promise to provide clear title
- Target date for closing (when the property is actually transferred to you, and the funds are transferred to the seller)
- Down payment accompanying the offer—how much and in what form
- Plan for prorating utilities, taxes, etc., between buyer and seller
- Provisions: who will pay what extra costs (e.g., insurance, survey)
- Type of deed
- Contingencies

Many people hold the misconception that the closing is the most important part of the home buying process, but, in fact, it is the offer that is most crucial. This variable and negotiable document is your chance to spell out, in detail, your terms of purchase, including any contingencies you wish to attach. **Common contingencies** can protect you, the buyer, from being legally bound to the purchase agreement if, for example, you cannot qualify for a loan, you are unable to sell the house you currently live in, the house you are buying fails its inspection(s), or the seller is not able to give you possession by a certain date. For homes built before 1978, buyers in Massachusetts are entitled to a housing inspection within 10 days of the offer's acceptance; if the house fails inspection (i.e., does not meet the state's structural, mechanical, or environmental building code standards), the seller must fix the defects, or you may back out of (or lower) your offer. Offers on newer homes traditionally include the 10-day inspection period as well, although state law does not automatically give buyers the right to a home inspection, so a seller must approve that contingency in the offer. Another common contingency to consider is "on terms to be approved by the buyer's attorney." This clause gives you the freedom to have the purchase agreement reviewed by your lawyer before it becomes binding.

Once you make an offer, the buyer will accept it, reject it, or make a counteroffer, at which point you may accept, reject, or change the counteroffer—and so on. Some items you may negotiate include many of the transaction costs and who pays them, including brokers' commissions, inspection costs, escrow or attorneys' fees, title search, owner's title insurance, transfer taxes, and recording fees. You can also negotiate on which items or appliances in the house you might want to purchase. While in theory anything attached to or installed in a home constitutes part of the house, in practice it doesn't always work this way—so clarify in writing whether or not you're entitled to the washer/dryer. When both parties agree, a legally binding **purchase and sale (P&S) agreement** is drawn up. If you default on this contract, you can lose your deposit money. If the seller defaults, you can sue him to force the sale to which he agreed in writing.

As mentioned, **inspections** are crucial, particularly for older homes—of which there are plenty in Massachusetts. This is your protection against losing your deposit—or worse, actually going through with the purchase—in the event that the building is structurally damaged or infested. The standard home inspection costs under $400, though it depends on the neighborhood and size of the house, and should take about two hours; plan on accompanying the inspector so you can ask questions about repair costs or the extent of possible problems. He or she will examine the structural and technical condition of accessible portions of the property, including the roof, attic, walls, windows, foundation, ceilings, floors, doors, basement, insulation, ventilation, heating/cooling systems, interior plumbing, electrical systems, and septic tanks, and provide you with a full written report. An **environmental inspection,** usually separate, is also worth considering—particularly because it is legal in Massachusetts to sell a residence with onsite environmental hazards. Typical environmental problems to check for include unsafe drinking water, radon, pests, airborne asbestos, lead (very common), urea formaldehyde foam insulation (UFFI), and oil spillage. As of 2001, housing inspectors in Massachusetts must pass an examination and meet state standards to become licensed; however, do not confuse a license with home inspector "certifications," which are designations from trade societies or companies—while not bad, they are not part of the state's licensing requirement. To find an inspector, like anything else, it's best to get a recommendation from a friend if possible; failing that, you can also ask your buyer's agent, or simply look in the Yellow Pages under "Building Inspection Services." The **American Society of Home Inspectors** (800-743-ASHI) and the **Division of Professional Licensure** (617-727-4459, www.mass.gov/reg/boards/hi) can also steer you to a qualified inspector. Feel free to ask for references, and if you're in doubt about an appraisal or safety inspection, get a second opinion.

Assuming the inspection goes well and/or all issues are resolved to your satisfaction, it is time for **closing** (also known as "settlement" or "escrow"). It is at this time that payments such as transfer taxes, closing costs, legal fees, and the rest of your down payment are due. It is a brief process in which the title to the property is transferred from seller to buyer; the seller gets his payment, you get the keys, and the closing agent officially records your loan. If you balk at anything at this point and refuse to sign and complete the process, you'll probably end up in court.

Your lender will require you to buy insurance to protect their investment (your home); you will need title insurance, homeowners' insurance, and possibly flood insurance. **Title insurance** is a one-time fee, paid at the time of closing. It protects you in case the title to the property somehow turns out to be invalid. Most lenders generally require title insurance up to the amount of the loan, but you can opt for an owners' policy, which protects the mortgage amount as well as the down payment value. Mandatory **homeowners' insurance** covers your home and belongings against most disasters such as fire, storm damage, and break-ins, but usually not flood damage. Separate **flood insurance**, issued by the federal government, may be a requirement in high-risk areas; contact the

National Flood Insurance Program at 888-CALL-FLOOD. Finally, buyers of new construction might consider **home warranties**—one-year service agreements that you buy from a third party (not the seller, builder, or lessor) to cover any costs to repair defects in your home. They are not insurance policies, and you should be sure to check that any home warranty coverage you buy doesn't cross over with your insurance. While there are laws to protect consumers who have purchased a home with shoddy workmanship, home warranties usually cover the structural, appliance, or utility problems that crop up in the day-to-day business of having a home, as opposed to pre-existing defects or conditions. For additional information on home insurance, including a list of providers in the state, go to www.mass.gov/doi/.

ONLINE RESOURCES—MORTGAGES

The following sites might help you on your quest to finance a home:

- **Bankrate.com**; everything about mortgages and lending.
- **Countrywide Financial**, www.countrywide.com; nationwide mortgage rates, credit evaluations, etc.
- **Dirs.com**; links and information on mortgages, home equity loans, and credit management.
- **Fannie Mae**, www.fanniemae.com; national organization dedicated to helping lower- and middle-income Americans achieve home ownership.
- **FreddieMac.com**; provides information on low-cost loans, a home inspection kit, and tips to help avoid unfair lending practices.
- **Interest.com**; shop for mortgages and rates.
- **Massachusetts Housing Finance Agency** (**MHFA**), www.mhfa.com; information about renting and buying from the state's affordable housing bank.
- **Massachusetts Mortgage Clearing House**, www.mmch.com
- **The Mortgage Professor**, www.mtgprofessor.com; demystifies and clarifies the confusing and often expensive world of mortgage brokers, helpfully written by an emeritus Wharton professor who even answers readers' questions! Includes a number of helpful spreadsheets and calculators.
- **QuickenLoans.com**; home to all things mortgage-related.

ADDITIONAL RESOURCES—BUYING A HOME

Finally, consider the following resources and publications:

- *100 Questions Every First Time Homebuyer Should Ask: With Answers from Top Brokers from Around the Country*, 2nd edition (Three Rivers Press) by Ilyce R. Glink
- *The 106 Common Mistakes Homebuyers Make (And How to Avoid Them)*, 4th edition (Wiley) by Gary W. Eldred
- **City of Boston Assessing Department**, www.cityofboston.gov/assessing/;

the City of Boston's web site offers an easy-to-fill-out form to find out the official assessed value of a property.

- **City of Boston Taxpayer Referral and Assistance Center** (**TRAC**), www. cityofboston.gov/trac/; this portion of the City of Boston web site offers information on residential exemptions and other tax breaks.
- The **Commonwealth of Massachusetts** provides information for potential homebuyers at www.mass.gov/consumer/.
- **Community Associations Institute**, www.caine.org; New England chapter of this alliance of condo, co-op, and homeowner associations.
- *The Co-Op Bible: Everything You Need to Know About Co-Ops and Condos: Getting In, Staying In, Surviving, Thriving* (St. Martin's Griffin) by Sylvia Shapiro
- **Scorecard.org**; if you're particularly concerned about environmental toxins at your new property, check out this site sponsored by the Environmental Defense Fund.
- *Your New House: the Alert Consumer's Guide to Buying and Building a Quality New Home* (Windsor Peak Press) by Alan and Denise Fields

MOVING AND STORAGE

BEFORE YOU CAN START YOUR NEW LIFE IN BOSTON, YOU AND your worldly possessions have to get here. How difficult that will be depends on how much stuff you've accumulated, how much money you're willing (or able) to spend on the move, and from how far away you're coming.

If you will be renting upon your arrival, most fixed-term leases in Boston run yearly from September through August. Moving on September 1st is both a rite of passage and a dizzying foray into the depths of urban chaos, particularly in neighborhoods near colleges or universities. During this yearly free-for-all you may find moving trucks double-parked in the wrong direction on one-way streets (blocking traffic entirely for hours), backed onto sidewalks, or, reliably, wedged under the low overpasses on Storrow Drive. While misery loves company—you'll certainly find opportunity to bond with your new neighbors—you may wish to consider a different day for your move if your schedule allows it.

TRUCK RENTALS

The first question you need to answer: am I going to move myself, or will I have someone else do it for me? If you're used to doing things for yourself, by all means, rent a vehicle and head for the open road. It may well be the best way to get your belongings where you're going—and it will save you from the risk and stress of entrusting your things to a moving company. So look in the Yellow Pages under "Truck Rental," then call around and compare prices. Below, we list four national truck rental firms and their toll-free numbers and web sites, but for the best information you should call a local office. Note that most truck rental companies now offer "one-way" rentals (don't forget to ask whether they have a drop-off/return location in or near your destination) as well as packing accessories and storage facilities. Of course, these extras are not free and, if you're cost-conscious, you may want to scavenge boxes from liquor stores or purchase them from discounters and arrange for storage yourself. (See **Moving Supplies** and **Storage** sections below.)

If you're planning on moving during the peak season of May through September, call well in advance of when you think you'll need the vehicle—at least a month. It's not unheard of for truck rental companies to "have no record" of your reservation, leaving you high and dry on your scheduled moving day. To avoid this inconvenience, it's a good idea to double or triple check on your truck reservation the week before your moving date. And consider timing your move for the middle, rather than the end, of the month, if possible, because availability and prices will likely be better.

Speaking of price: cheapest is not always best, and some companies in this industry do have a history of unresolved complaints with the **Better Business Bureau**, so be sure to contact your local BBB and request a report (www.bbb.org, or, for the Massachusetts branch, call 508-652-4800, www.boston.bbb.org). The following are national truck rental companies with offices in Boston:

- **Budget**, 800-527-0700, www.budget.com
- **Penske**, 888-996-5415, www.penske.com
- **Ryder**, 800-BY-RYDER, www.ryder.com
- **U-Haul**, 800-GO-U-HAUL, www.uhaul.com

Once you're on the road, keep in mind that your rental truck full of furniture, TVs, and stereo equipment may be a tempting target for thieves. If you must park it overnight or for an extended period (more than a couple of hours), try to find a safe place, preferably somewhere well-lit and easily observable by you, and do your best not to leave anything of particular value in the cab. Use a steering wheel lock if possible, and make sure the back door of the truck is padlocked.

Also remember that you are driving a truck, a vehicle with considerable more height and bulk than you're likely used to. Pay close attention to those "low clearance" signs—in particular, while it may be the easiest or quickest route to your new home, **trucks are NOT ALLOWED on Storrow Drive** in Boston. Each year it seems someone is daft enough to take their moving truck down Storrow... and slam it straight into one of the low underpasses, ripping the roof right off!

Not sure that you want to drive the truck yourself? Commercial freight carriers, such as **ABF** (800-355-1696, www.upack.com) and **PODS** (1-866-767-PODS, www.PODS.com) offer an in-between service: they deliver a trailer or container to your home, you pack and load as much of it as you need, and they drive the vehicle or deliver your container to your destination.

MOVERS

While moving *can* be affordable and problem-free, the chances of that happening certainly diminish if you're hiring a mover.

Let us begin with a word of caution: watch out for shakedown schemes that begin with a lowball bid off the internet and end with the mover holding your belongings hostage for a high cash ransom. Despite the fact that federal law forbids movers from charging more than 10% over any written estimate, it is not unusual for unscrupulous movers to charge you several times their written estimates—and with your possessions in *their* possession, you may find yourself paying anyway, since companies that operate this way also won't tell you where they're holding your stuff. It's fraud. It's extortion. And sometimes there isn't a lot the police can do to help you… So protect yourself. For help finding a reputable mover, check out **MovingScam.com**, a web site dedicated to improving consumer protections in the moving industry, and providing solid, impartial consumer education. Loaded with valuable articles, information, and other resources (it even maintains a "Black List"), its message boards are staffed around the clock with experienced volunteers who answer moving-related questions promptly and at no cost to the consumer.

A similar web site run by the **Federal Motor Carrier Safety Administration (FMCSA)** is www.protectyourmove.gov. This site provides one-click checking to make sure that an interstate mover is properly registered and insured. It also posts details about regulations governing professional moving companies together with news of recent criminal investigations and convictions. In addition, the site contains information about how to spot a rogue mover before trouble strikes, and offers links to local Better Business Bureaus, consumer protection agencies, state attorneys general, state moving associations, and the **FMCSA Safety Violation and Consumer Household Goods Complaint Hotline** (1-888-DOT-SAFT [1-888-368-7238], www.1-888-dot-saft.com). Don't expect much from this hotline, however. It is essentially just a database and you will only hear from the DOT if it looks at your complaint and determines that enforcement action is warranted.

INTERSTATE MOVES

Like anything else, the best way to find a mover is by **personal recommendation**. Absent a friend or relative who can recommend a trusted moving company, you can turn to what surveys show is still the most popular method of finding a mover: the **Yellow Pages**. You could also try asking a local realtor, who may be able to steer you toward a good mover—or at least tell you which ones to avoid. American Automobile Association (AAA) members receive a 60% discount at **Consumers Relocation Services** (800-839-MOVE, www.consumersrelocation.com), a company that assigns you a personal consultant to handle every detail of your move. And then there's the internet: just type in "movers" on a search engine, and you'll be directed to hundreds of more (or less) helpful moving-related sites.

But beware! Since 1995, when the Interstate Commerce Commission was eliminated, the interstate moving business has degenerated into a wild and virtually unregulated industry with thousands of unhappy, ripped-off customers annually. (There are so many reports of unscrupulous carriers that we no longer list movers in this book.) Since states do not have the authority to regulate interstate movers, and since the federal government won't, you are pretty much on your own when it comes to finding an honest, hassle-free interstate mover. That's why we can't emphasize enough the importance of carefully researching and choosing who will move you.

To aid you in your search for a fair and problem-free **interstate** mover, we offer a few general recommendations.

- Make sure the mover is licensed. State law requires that licensed movers be insured, have licensed vehicles that meet certain safety and other requirements, and provide for a system in which complaints can be made and dealt with properly. See that the carrier has a Department of Transportation MC ("Motor Carrier") or ICC MC number; it should be displayed on all advertising and promotional material as well as on the truck. With the MC number in hand, contact the **Department of Transportation's Federal Motor Carrier Safety Administration** at 800-832-5660, or check online at www.fmcsa.dot.gov or www.protectyourmove.gov, to see if the carrier is licensed. If the companies you're interested in are federally licensed, the next step is to contact the Better Business Bureau (www.bbb.org), Attorney General's office, or consumer protection board in the state in which the company is licensed, and find out if there are records of any complaints against them. Although most companies are reputable, one call to the BBB could steer you away from the few who are not.

- Assuming you find no negative information, go on to the next step: asking for references. Particularly important are references from customers who did moves similar to yours. If a moving company is unable or unwilling to provide references, or tells you they can't because their customers are all in the federal Witness Protection Program, eliminate them from your list. Unscrupulous movers have even been known to offer phony references that falsely sing the mover's praises—so talk to more than one reference and ask questions. If something feels fishy, it probably is. One way to learn more about a prospective mover is to ask them if they have a local office (they should), and then walk in to check it out.

- Once you have at least three movers you feel reasonably comfortable with, it's time to ask for price quotes. Get several written estimates from companies that have actually sent a sales representative to your home to do a visual inspection of the goods to be moved. Don't worry about cost here; estimates should always be free. Don't do business with a company that charges for an estimate—ever—or wants to give you an estimate over the telephone. Make sure each company is giving you an estimate for approximately the same poundage of items to be moved and the same services, and only accept estimates written on a document containing the company's name, address, phone number, and signature of the salesperson. Note that estimates can be either binding or non-binding. A binding "not-to-exceed" quote guarantees the total cost of the move based upon the quantities and services shown on the estimate. A non-binding estimate is what your mover believes the cost will be, based upon the estimated weight of the shipment and the extra services requested; it is not binding on the mover, however, and you may be required to pay up to 10% more. Whatever you do, *do not* mislead a salesperson/estimator about how much and what you are moving. And make sure you tell a prospective mover about how far they'll have to transport your stuff to and from the truck, as well as any stairs, driveways, obstacles or difficult vegetation, long paths or sidewalks, etc. The clearer you are with your mover, the better he or she will be able to serve you.

- Follow-up with your State Department of Transportation to find out if the estimate the mover gave you is based on the hourly rate they have filed with the Department of Transportation. Some movers may *quote* below this rate and then, at your destination, attempt to *charge* the higher rate they filed with the state.

- Be sure you understand the terms of the moving contract. Get everything in writing, including the mover's liability to you for breakage or loss. Consider whether to buy additional replacement insurance to cover loss or damage. Check your homeowner's or renter's insurance policy to see what, if any, coverage you may already have for your belongings while they are in transit. If the answer is none, ask your insurer if you can add coverage for your move. If necessary, you can purchase coverage through your mover, but their coverage is normally based on the weight of the items being insured, not the value. If you want to cover the actual value of your belongings, you will need to purchase "full value" or "full replacement" insurance. Though it's the most expensive type of coverage offered, it's probably worth it. Trucks get into accidents, they catch fire, they get stolen—if such insurance seems pricey to you, ask about a $250 or $500 deductible. This can reduce your cost substantially while still giving you much better protection in case of a catastrophic loss.

- You should pack and transport all irreplaceable possessions, such as jewelry, important documents, or sentimental items, yourself. Do not put them in the moving van! That way you can avoid the headache and heartache of possible loss or breakage of your most valuable possessions. You might also consider sending less precious items that you're reluctant to send on the truck via the US Postal Service or UPS.

- Compile an inventory of all items shipped and their condition when they left your house. Even though movers will put numbered labels on all your possessions and *should* issue you a "bill of lading," or manifest, you should make your own numbered list of every item and every box that is going in the truck. Detail box contents and photograph anything of particular value. Also be sure to check the mover's inventory sheet to make sure you agree with their evaluation of existing damage on your belongings. Once the truck arrives at the other end, you can check off every piece and know for sure what did (or did not) make it, and if anything was damaged—which brings us to another important moving tip: be present for both the loading and unloading of your things. At the loading end, you can direct the movers to load the truck in reverse order to how you want things to come off, and at the unloading end, you can not only check your items, but you can probably ensure that more care is taken with your things than might otherwise happen. Finally, since checking every item as it comes off the truck is probably impossible when you're moving the contents of an entire house, write "subject to further inspection for concealed loss or damage" on the moving contract to allow for damage you may discover as you unpack.

- File a written claim with the mover immediately if any loss or damage occurs—and keep a copy of your claim, as well as all the other paperwork related to your move. If your claim is not resolved within a reasonable time, file complaints with the Better Business Bureau and appropriate authorities as well. (See **Consumer Complaints—Movers**, below.) To learn more about your rights and responsibilities with respect to interstate moving, check out the United States Department of Transportation (USDOT) publication "Your Rights and Responsibilities When You Move," which you can download from www.protectyourmove.gov.

If you've followed the steps above and succeeded in hiring a reputable mover, here is some further general advice:

- Listen to what the movers say; they are professionals and can give you expert advice about packing and preparing. Also, be ready for the truck on both ends—don't make them wait. Not only will it irritate your movers, it may cost you. Understand, too, that things can happen on the road that are beyond a carrier's control (weather, accidents, etc.) and your belongings may not get to you at the time, or on the day, promised.
- Treat your movers well, especially the ones loading your stuff on and off the truck. Offer to buy them lunch, and tip them if they do a good job.
- Be prepared to pay the full moving bill upon delivery. Cash or a cashier's check may be required. Some carriers will take VISA and MasterCard, but it's a good idea to get it in writing that you will be permitted to pay with credit card, since the delivering driver may not be aware of this and demand cash. Unless you routinely keep thousands of dollars of greenbacks on you, you could have a problem getting your stuff off the truck.
- Consider keeping a log of every expense you incur for your move, i.e., phone calls, trips to Boston, etc. In many instances, the IRS allows you to claim these

types of expenses on your income taxes. (See **Taxes**, below.)

• Finally, before moving pets, attach tags to their collars with your new address and phone number in case your pets accidentally wander off in the confusion of moving. For more help in this area, you might want to look into *The Pet-Moving Handbook* (First Books, www.firstbooks.com).

INTRASTATE MOVES

Intrastate moves (moves within Massachusetts) are regulated by the **Transportation Division** of the **Massachusetts Department of Public Utilities**. Intrastate movers must apply for authority to transport passengers or property for hire, through chapters 159A and B of Massachusetts law. You can contact the department for more information at 617-305-3559, or visit their web site at www. mass.gov/dpu.

Those **moving within the greater Boston area** with minimal belongings (renters, singles, etc.) probably won't need a huge truck to complete the task. If you (and all of your friends) are not interested in loading and unloading a rented truck, you may want to consider hiring a local mover. **Local movers** generally charge by the hour, not by the size and weight of your shipment. When shopping around for a local mover, you will be given a "not to exceed price" based on how much stuff you want them to move, and the ease or difficulty of getting it out of your old apartment and into the new one. The minimum charge is usually at least 2 hours, and this includes time spent driving from their origin to your apartment. Other contributing cost factors include how many men will be needed to move your belongings, the size of the van needed, and the distance traveled. This "not to exceed" price should be in written form, and cover all services. If your move goes faster than the salesperson estimated, you should be charged less.

CONSUMER COMPLAINTS—MOVERS

To file a complaint about an interstate mover, contact FMCSA's Household Goods Consumer Complaint web site at http://nccdb.fmcsa.dot.gov or call 888-DOT-SAFT. Also, be sure to register your complaint with the Attorney General's office and Better Business Bureau of the state where the mover is located.

For problems with an intrastate move that you are unable to resolve directly, you can talk to the Transportation Division of the Massachusetts Department of Public Utilities. Call them at 617-305-3559 or visit www.mass.gov/dpu. The Massachusetts Office of Consumer Affairs and Business Regulation can be reached at 888-283-3757, 617-973-8787, or online at www.mass.gov/consumer. If satisfaction still eludes you, begin a letter writing campaign: to the state Attorney General, to your congressional representative, to the newspaper—the sky's the limit. Of course, if the dispute is worth it, you can hire a lawyer and seek redress the all-American way.

ROAD RESTRICTIONS

Given Boston's old and narrow streets, you won't necessarily be able to just roll in with a big moving truck without some pre-arrangements (though people still do—hazard lights will get you just about anywhere in this town). In particular, those who are moving into an older building without a loading zone might want to get a **Street Occupancy Permit** to park a moving van on the street. First, you must be bonded with the City of Boston Public Works Department. To do this, go to Room 714 of City Hall. Then, to apply for the Street Occupancy Permit, go over to the Boston Transportation Department office in Room 721. You will need to tell them why you need the permit, how long you need it for, how vehicular and pedestrian access will be allowed, and a copy of your bond. You'll pay a small fee; the exact amount will depend on how many signs you will need and how much space you'll be taking up.

After you get the permit, it is your responsibility to notify neighbors and area businesses by posting signs in the area at least 48 hours in advance, noting the time and date of the restricted access—even more notice is courteous, especially in residential parking areas, as your neighbors' cars may be towed for violating the permit restrictions. For more information, go to www.cityofboston. gov/transportation/streetoccupancy.asp, or call the **Boston Transportation Department** at 617-635-4675.

STORAGE

If your new pad is too small for all of your belongings, or if you need a temporary place to store your stuff while you find a new home, self-storage may be the answer. Most units are clean, secure, insured, and inexpensive, and you can rent anything from a locker to your own mini-warehouse. You may need to bring or buy your own padlock, and be prepared to pay first and last month's rent upfront—though many companies will offer special deals to entice you, such as a free month's rent or waived deposit.

Probably the easiest way to find a storage facility is to look online, whether through a search engine, online yellow pages, or a moving and relocation specialty site such as **Move.com**. Alternatively, look in the Yellow Pages under "Storage—Self Service" or "Movers & Full Service Storage." Your mover may offer storage, and while this may be easier than storing it all yourself, it may also be more expensive. As mentioned earlier, there are also companies such as PODS and ABF that will drop off a large storage bin at your house, and come pick it up for you (or even drive it cross-country) when you've packed it full of your belongings.

When looking for a storage unit, price, convenience, security, fire sprinklers, climate control, and accessibility are all considerations. Ask, too, what your payment options are, and whether a deposit is required.

Keep in mind that demand for storage surges from May through September, so try not to wait until the last minute to reserve a unit. Also, if you don't care about convenience, your cheapest storage options may be outside of Boston. You just have to figure out how to get your stuff there and back.

A word of warning: unless you no longer want your stored belongings, pay your storage bill and pay it on time. Storage companies may auction the contents of delinquent customers' lockers.

STORAGE FACILITIES

Listing here does *not* imply endorsement by First Books. For more options check the Yellow Pages, or search online for "self-storage Boston."

- **Brighton Self-Storage**, 1360 Comm Ave, Allston, 617-739-4401, www.bright onselfstorage.com; offers free use of their van when moving your belongings *into* storage (but not moving out).
- **Castle Self-Storage**, 39 Old Colony Rd, South Boston, 617-268-5056, www.cas tleselfstorage.com; also has locations in Braintree and Weymouth.
- **Extra Space Storage**, 800-895-5921, www.extraspace.com; national chain with storage facilities throughout greater Boston.
- **Fetch Storage**, 888-610-1684, www.fetchstorage.com; a unique option, they will come pick up your belongings and store them for you, and deliver them back to you at your convenience—even if it's just one box—eliminating trips to the storage facility.
- **Planet Self-Storage**, 100 Southampton St, Boston, 617-445-6776, www.planet selfstorage.com
- **Public Storage**, 877-788-2028, www.publicstorage.com; has facilities throughout the Boston area.
- **The Storage Bunker**, 420 Rutherford Ave, Charlestown, 617-242-6400, www. storagebunker.com

CHILDREN

Studies show that moving, especially frequent moving, can be hard on children. According to an American Medical Association study, children who move often are more likely to suffer from such problems as depression, low self-esteem, and aggression. Often their academic performance suffers as well. Aside from not moving more than is necessary, there are a few things you can do to help your children through this stressful time:

- Talk about the move with your kids. Be honest but positive. Listen to their concerns. To the extent possible, involve them in the process.
- Make sure children have their favorite possessions with them on the trip; don't pack "blankey" in the moving van.
- Make sure you have some social life planned on the other end. Your children may feel lonely in your new home, and such activities can ease the transition. If you move during the summer you might find a local camp (check with the YMHA or YMCA) in which they can sign up for a couple of weeks in August to make some new friends.
- Keep in touch with family and loved ones as much as possible. Photos and phone calls are important ways of maintaining links to the important people you have left behind.
- If your children are school age, take the time to involve yourself in their new school and in their academic life. Don't let them fall through the cracks.
- Try to schedule a move during the summer so they can start the new school year at the beginning of the term.
- If possible, spend some time in the area prior to the move doing fun things, such as visiting a local playground or playing ball in a local park, or checking out the neighborhood stores with teenagers. With any luck they will meet some other kids their own age.

For younger children, there are dozens of good books on the topic. Just a few include *Max's Moving Adventure: A Coloring Book for Kids on the Move* by Danelle Till; *Alexander, Who's Not (Do You Hear Me? I Mean It!) Going to Move* by Judith Viorst; *Goodbye/Hello* by Barbara Hazen; *The Leaving Morning* by Angela Johnson; *Little Monster's Moving Day* by Mercer Mayer; *Who Will Be My Friends?* (Easy I Can Read Series) by Syd Hoff; *I'm Not Moving, Mama* by Nancy White Carlstrom; *Gila Monsters Meet You at the Airport* by Marjorie Weinman Sharmatand; and *The Berenstain Bears' Moving Day* by Jan and Stan Berenstain.

For older children, try *The Moving Book: A Kid's Survival Guide* by Gabriel Davis; *Amber Brown is Not a Crayon* by Paula Danziger; *The Kid in the Red Jacket* by Barbara Park; *Hold Fast to Dreams* by Andrea Davis Pinkney; *Flip Flop Girl* by Katherine Paterson; and *My Fabulous New Life* by Sheila Greenwald.

For general guidance, read *Smooth Moves* by Ellen Carlisle; *Will This Place Ever Feel Like Home?*, New and Updated Edition; *Simple Advice for Settling in After You Move* by Leslie Levine; and Clyde and Shari Steiner's *How To Move Handbook*.

TAXES

If your move is work-related, and your employer is not reimbursing you, some or all of your moving expenses may be tax-deductible—so you need to keep your receipts. Though eligibility varies, depending, for example, on whether you have a job or are self-employed, generally the cost of moving yourself, your family, and your belongings is tax deductible, even if you don't itemize. In order to take the deduction, your move must be employment-related, your new job must be at least 50 miles farther away from your former residence than your old job location, and you must be at your new location for at least 39 weeks during the first 12 months after your arrival. If you're self-employed, you must continue to work in the new location (as a self-employed person or as an employee) for at least 78 weeks during the 24 months following the move; at least 39 weeks of that total must be in the first 12 months.

In general, you can deduct the costs of transportation and hauling to your new residence, moving your belongings from a place other than your old residence (such as a summer home), storage-in-transit and valuation (limited to 30 consecutive days), shipping your car, moving your pets, and your entire family's trip to your new place of residence (including lodging, but not meals).

If you take the deduction and then fail to meet the requirements, you will have to pay the IRS back, unless you were laid off through no fault of your own or transferred again by your employer. Consulting a tax expert for guidance about the IRS's rules with respect to moving is probably a good idea. However, if you're a confident soul, get a copy of IRS Form 3903 (www.irs.gov) and do it yourself!

RELOCATION AND MOVING INFORMATION

- **American Car Transport**, 866-322-3169, www.American-Car-Transport.com.
- **Best Places**, www.bestplaces.net, compares quality-of-life and cost-of-living data of US cities.
- **BostonApartments.com** hosts a modest directory of local movers, truck rentals, and storage companies in addition to its extensive apartment listings.
- **Employee Relocation Council**, www.erc.org, a professional organization, offers members specialized reports on the relocation and moving industries.
- **FirstBooks.com**; relocation resources and information on moving to Atlanta; Boston; Chicago; Los Angeles; Minneapolis/St. Paul; New York; Portland; San Francisco; Seattle; Texas; Washington, D.C.; and London, England. Also publisher of the *Newcomer's Handbook for Moving to and Living in the USA; The Moving Book: A Kids' Survival Guide; Max's Moving Adventure: A Coloring Book for Kids on the Move; the Pet-Moving Handbook;* and *Furniture Placement and Room Planning Guide*.
- ***How to Move Handbook*** by Clyde and Shari Steiner, an excellent general resource.
- **Move.com** provides relocation resources in addition to their real estate listings, including a handy salary calculator that will compare the costs of living in various US cities.
- **Moving.org**; members of the American Moving and Storage Association.
- **The Riley Guide**, www.rileyguide.com/relocate.html; online moving and relocation clearinghouse, including Moving/Relocation Guides, Cost of Living and

Demographics, Real Estate Links, and School and Health Care Directories.

- **www.usps.com**; helpful relocation information from the United States Postal Service.

OPENING A BANK ACCOUNT IS ONE OF THE FIRST THINGS YOU WILL need to take care of upon arriving. Many landlords and rental agents will not accept a tenant who does not have a checking account—and often, it's difficult to open an account without a permanent address—so it's probably wise to keep your old bank account active for at least a short time after moving.

FINANCIAL INSTITUTIONS

BANKS

Boston has its share of financial giants and small local banks, both of which offer online and telephone banking, mortgage services, and ATM/debit cards for use anywhere in the world. Bigger banks tend to have ATM coverage that spans virtually everywhere (often owing to their having bought out smaller competitors), but will typically penalize you harshly for using an outside ATM. Meanwhile, many smaller banks in the Boston area only have a few branches, but belong to the wide-ranging SUM network of community banks. This allows their customers fee-free ATM access at any member bank throughout New England. Moreover, it's often easier to talk to a real person, either at the bank or over the phone, when dealing with a smaller bank.

For a complete list of local banks, you can visit the **MassHome Directory of Banks** at www.masshome.com/banks.html or the **Massachusetts Division of Banks** at www.state.ma.us/dob. Local and national banks serving the Boston area include:

- **Bank of America**, 800-900-9000, www.bankofamerica.com
- **Brookline Bank**, 877-668-2265, www.brooklinebank.com
- **Cambridge Savings Bank**, 888-418-5626, www.cambridgesavings.com

- **Cambridge Trust Company**, 800-876-6406, www.cambridgetrust.com
- **Century Bank**, 866-8-CENTURY, www.century-bank.com
- **Citizens Bank**, 800-922-9999, www.citizensbank.com
- **The Cooperative Bank**, 617-325-2900, www.thecooperativebank.com
- **East Boston Savings Bank**, 800-657-EBSB, www.ebsb.com
- **Eastern Bank**, 800-EASTERN, www.easternbank.com
- **Hyde Park Cooperative Bank**, 888-722-1191, www.hydeparkcoop.com
- **Peoples Federal Savings Bank**, 617-254-0707, www.pfsb.com
- **Sovereign Bank**, 877-SOV-BANK, www.sovereignbank.com
- **TD Banknorth**, 800-747-7000, www.tdbanknorth.com
- **Watertown Savings Bank**, 800-207-2525, www.watertownsavings.com
- **Wainwright Bank & Trust**, 888-428-BANK, www.wainwrightbank.com

You may want to shop around, as fees, products, and quality of service vary. Typically, these fees are added to consumer services such as non-interest-bearing checking accounts, stop-payment orders, overdrafts, and ATM use.

CREDIT UNIONS

According to the **National Credit Union Administration** (**NCUA**), "A federal credit union is a nonprofit, cooperative financial institution owned and run by its members. Organized to serve, democratically controlled credit unions provide their members with a safe place to save and borrow at reasonable rates. Members pool their funds to make loans to one another. The volunteer board that runs each credit union is elected by the members." Your place of work or your alma mater may offer membership in a credit union—which could be your best banking deal of all. These nonprofit, cooperative financial institutions offer almost all the same products that banks do, usually with fewer fees and higher interest rates. Your employer will be able to tell you if you are eligible for membership in any credit unions through your work; local trade unions and churches sometimes offer membership as well. Because credit unions limit membership based on set criteria, you'll need to investigate a few for a match.

Here are a few credit unions in the Boston area:

- **Alpha Credit Union**, for employees of various medical institutions in the Longwood area, 617-632-8164, www.bidmc.harvard.edu/alpha/
- **Cambridge Portuguese Credit Union**, for Portuguese people in Massachusetts, 617-547-3144, www.cpcu.org
- **City of Boston Credit Union**, for Commonwealth of Massachusetts employees and their families, 617-635-4545, www.cityofbostoncu.org
- **Industrial Credit Union**, for anyone living or working in the greater Boston area, 617-742-1616, www.icu.org
- **Tremont Credit Union**, for many area employers and schools, 781-843-5626, www.tremontcu.org
- **University Credit Union**, for current and former employees of many local

schools, medical institutions, and others, 617-739-7447, www.universitycu.org

For a complete list of local credit unions or information about them, you can visit the **MassHome Directory of Credit Unions** (at www.masshome.com/cr unions.html), the **Massachusetts Division of Banks** (www.state.ma.us/dob), the **National Association of Credit Union Service Organizations** (www.nacuso. org), or the **National Credit Union Administration** (www.ncua.gov), which is an independent federal agency that supervises and insures credit unions, and maintains a searchable database. You can also use this site to file a complaint. Other resources include the **Credit Union Match Up** service (www.howtojoin acu.org), and **Credit Unions Online** (www.creditunionsonline.com).

ONLINE BANKING

Virtually every bank offers online banking, making it easy to track your account activity, pay all of your bills automatically, or even apply for a loan—all from the comfort of your own home. You'll also have 24-hour-a-day access to your account and never have to write another check, lick an envelope, or buy a stamp—although services vary from bank to bank, and some charge a fee for automatic bill-paying features. See **Bank Accounts and Services,** for area banks' web addresses. Three national internet banks you might want to check out are **ING Direct** (www.ingdirect.com), **NetBank** (www.netbank.com), and **Presidential** (www.presidential.com). All advertise significantly higher-yielding interest rates than their so-called "brick and mortar" competitors.

Today, it is rare when a bank does not offer online banking. Generally this includes simple balance and other account information, making transfers, paying bills, and even applying for loans from the comfort of your own home. Security should be a chief concern when accessing your private financial information over the internet. While banks should encrypt your personal information and password, the user should also take standard precautions as well. Don't share your password with anyone, and change it often; don't send confidential information through e-mail or over unsecured web space; and restrict your banking interactions to private computers, not a work computer with a shared network or at an internet café.

Online access services and fees may vary from bank to bank, so check with individual institutions for information. Sometimes access is directly through the bank's web site; sometimes you'll first need to download a program or use specialized banking software.

CHECKING AND SAVINGS ACCOUNTS

It's easy to open checking or savings accounts—all you need is identification, an address and, of course, money. Today, some banks will even open a new account over the phone. You will need a social security number, identification, and employment information.

For fee-free checking, you may need to maintain a certain monthly balance or have direct deposit; however, most fee-free accounts are not normally interest-bearing accounts. Some opt to connect checking with savings for overdraft protection. Other products and services to inquire about: debit cards, online or telephone banking, certificates of deposit, safe deposit boxes, hours, and fees.

CONSUMER COMPLAINTS—BANKING

Federal and state government regulate bank policies on discrimination, credit, anti-redlining, truth-in-lending, etc. If you have a problem with your bank, you should first attempt to resolve the issue directly with the bank; you may need to contact senior bank management or the bank's customer service representative. Should you need to **file a formal complaint** against your financial institution, you need to find the appropriate regulator (knowing the type of financial institution you're complaining about will be a tremendous help). Here is a list of regulators and whom they regulate:

- Nationally chartered commercial banks—banks with "national" in the name— go through the **US Comptroller of the Currency**, 800-613-6743; www.occ. treas.gov.
- For federally chartered and state-chartered savings associations contact the **US Office of Thrift Supervision**, 800-842-6929, www.ots.treas.gov.
- State-chartered banks that are members of the Federal Reserve System: **Board of Governors of the Federal Reserve System**, Division of Consumer and Community Affairs, 202-452-3693, www.federalreserve.gov/pubs/complaints/.
- For state-chartered banks that are *not* members of the Federal Reserve System: **Federal Deposit Insurance Corporation** (**FDIC**), 877-275-3342, www. fdic.gov.
- For federally chartered credit unions: **National Credit Union Administration**, 703-518-6330, www.ncua.gov.
- For state-chartered credit unions: **Massachusetts Division of Banks and Loans**, Consumer Assistance Office, 800-495-2265, www.state.ma.us/dob.
- Finance companies, stores, auto dealers, mortgage companies, and credit bureaus go through the **Federal Trade Commission**, 877-382-4357, www.ftc. gov/ftc/consumer.htm.

CREDIT CARDS

If you're one of the few Americans whose mailbox isn't flooded with unwanted credit card offers—it's estimated that over 4 billion direct mail solicitations are delivered each year—you can compare various card rates and apply online through a number of web sites, including **CreditCards.com**, **CardTrak.com**, and

BankRate.com. **Consumer Action (CA**, www.Consumer-Action.org) offers rate comparisons as well, but also provides some helpful consumer information and tips, such as the downloadable brochure entitled "Credit Cards: What You Need to Know." CA also suggests appropriate complaint-handling agencies. And if you'd like put an end to all that junk mail, you can dial 888-5-OPT-OUT or visit www.optoutprescreen.com; this will keep the major credit bureaus from releasing your credit profile to unsolicited banks.

To request a specific credit card application, you can also contact any of the following:

- **American Express**, 800-THE-CARD, www.americanexpress.com
- **Diner's Club**, 800-2-DINERS, www.dinersclubus.com
- **Discover Card**, 888-DISCOVER, www.discovercard.com
- **VISA** and **MasterCard** can be obtained through banks and other financial service associations. Check first with your bank, and shop around for the best combination of low interest rates, annual fees, and rewards. If you are diligent about paying your bill on time, you can rack up frequent flyer miles or other rewards without worrying about a high interest rate; however, if you're just looking to transfer an already unwieldy balance, you'll definitely want to pay more attention to getting a low fixed rate.
- **Department and clothing store credit cards** are one of the best ways to begin building credit if you have none. They are usually easy to qualify for and easy to come by, as they are marketed at the checkout counter; often the store will offer an incentive for you to fill out an application immediately, such as a discount off that day's purchases. Aside from establishing your credit, you might also benefit from coupons, members-only sales, and free shipping.

A word of warning to credit card users: the biggest revenue sources for credit card issuers are penalty charges for late payments. If you want to avoid high finance charges, check to see what your grace period is—the period between the end of a billing cycle and the payment due date during which no interest is charged if the account balance is paid off in full. Try to pay off your balance within this period. In some cases, however, grace periods have been eliminated altogether, and some companies actually start charging you interest from the date of your purchase, so watch out! Since credit card issuers are always coming up with new ways to improve their profits, be sure to read the fine print in your contract, and don't necessarily be taken in by low interest rates.

IDENTITY THEFT AND CREDIT REPORTS

In this new world of technological wonder—as debit cards begin to replace cash, strangers share their life's stories on countless blogs and social networking sites, and customers pay more and more bills over wireless internet connections—it's easier than ever for crafty criminals to gather information on you without your knowledge. In Massachusetts alone—in 2006 alone!—*The Boston Globe* accidentally distributed the personal check routing information and credit card numbers of thousands of subscribers, and TJX, the parent company of T.J. Maxx and Marshalls, unwittingly compromised the credit and debit card numbers of over 45 million customers during a security breach.

While the notion of credit card fraud or identity theft sounds awful enough on paper, it's even worse if it actually happens to you. A fraud such as identity theft can nearly ruin your life. Victims spend an average of 600 hours trying to repair their credit; it's a daunting task, but there are protections in place to help you, if you take action. By law, consumers are not held responsible for any unauthorized charges on their credit cards. The trick is to check your monthly statements carefully and notify your credit card company *immediately* if you notice any incorrect or suspect charges. So what else can you do to protect yourself? Security experts say there are several things. First, don't print your full name and Social Security number on your checks, and don't carry your Social Security card in your wallet or purse. Second, as silly as these may seem, don't let your mail sit in your mailbox any longer than necessary, and shred personal documents—even that pile of unsolicited credit card offers—before putting them into the recycle bin. Third, think twice before you make a financial transaction over the internet, particularly on public computers or over Wi-Fi. Convenient and secure as it usually is, security failures still occur from time to time.

Finally, check your credit rating periodically. You are entitled to one free credit report per year from each of the three major credit bureaus, so if you request a report every four months from a different credit reporting company, you'll be able to keep tabs on your credit rating—for free. If you discover any inaccuracies in a report with your name on it, contact the service immediately and request that it be corrected. By law they must respond to your request within 30 days. Reports are also free if you've been denied credit based on your credit report within the last 30 days.

Visit **www.annualcreditreport.com** for online access to all three national credit bureaus, or you can contact them directly:

- **Equifax**, P.O. Box 740241, Atlanta, GA 30374, 800-685-1111, www.equifax.com
- **Experian**, P.O. Box 2002, Allen, TX 75013, 888-EXPERIAN, www.experian.com
- **TransUnion Corporation**, P.O. Box 1000, Chester, PA 19022, 800-888-4213, www.transunion.com

For more information on credit card fraud and identity theft, including steps you should take if you think you've been victimized, contact the **Federal Trade Commission** (877-ID-THEFT or www.ftc.gov/idtheft/), or the **Identity Theft Resource Center** (858-693-7935 or www.idtheftcenter.com).

TAXES

In 1789, Benjamin Franklin said, "in this world nothing can be said to be certain, except death and taxes." A history of high taxes in Massachusetts—sales tax, use tax, state income tax, property tax, excise tax, cigarette tax, etc.—as well as additional fees and tolls long ago earned the state of Massachusetts the nickname "Taxachusetts." While the moniker may be an exaggeration, many Bostonians still cross the border to New Hampshire from time to time to make purchases free of sales tax—particularly large-ticket electronic and home-good items, or alcohol at the state liquor store—and some even prefer to live in New Hampshire and commute to work in Massachusetts. Ironically, Britain's practice of over-taxing the colonists was one of the primary catalysts of the American Revolution.

According to the Massachusetts Executive Office of Administration and Finance, 64% of the state's revenue comes from taxes. The rest comes from lottery revenues, federal reimbursements, rainy day reserves, and fines and fees (mostly from the Registry of Motor Vehicles). Lots of taxes means lots of government services: taxes go to fund schools, transportation, roads, health programs, human services, public safety, environmental protection, health insurance for state employees, housing and community development, assistance to low income families, and economic and workforce development, among other state services and programs.

City of Boston residents have an excellent resource at their disposal: the **Taxpayer Referral and Assistance Center** (TRAC, www.cityofboston.gov/TRAC, 617-635-4287), which provides information and answers to nearly all city-specific tax questions.

SALES AND USE TAXES

Sales tax in Massachusetts is 5% on all retail sales of tangible personal property, and on certain telecommunications services rented in the Commonwealth—mostly cell phone transmissions. Goods purchased out of state or out of country that will be used or consumed in Massachusetts require a "use tax" of 5%—this includes mail order items and automobiles purchased out of state, and, technically, that sofa you bought in New Hampshire last April.

Many items, gratefully, are **exempt from sales and use tax**, including food, clothing, periodicals, health care items, small household items, admission to events, utilities, heating fuel to residences and small businesses, telephone services to residences, personal or professional services, and transportation charges. Luxury items, however, including clothing items over $175 and restaurant dining, are taxed. Big-ticket household items, like appliances and furniture, are also taxed, as are cars, gas, and cigarettes.

While you pay sales tax at the register, you must report and pay use tax on your personal income tax returns. However, if itemizing every last thing you've bought off eBay and Amazon.com in the last year seems difficult or even impossible, you can opt to pay a flat "safe harbor" amount of use tax each year, between $0 and $45, depending on your income. This option is only applicable to items purchased for less than $1,000; if you bought your car out of state, you'll still have to report and pay the full 5%.

For more detailed information on Massachusetts sales and use tax, visit the **Commonwealth of Massachusetts Department of Revenue** at www.mass.gov/dor/, or call 617-887-MDOR. They publish a booklet entitled *A Guide to Sales and Use Tax* that you may find helpful; it is accessible online.

PROPERTY TAX

Massachusetts residents pay **property taxes** on residences, commercial and industrial property, and personal property. As a general rule, property taxes finance local government and city services, such as public schools, fire and police protection, roads, health programs, parks, city streets, sewer systems, garbage removal and recycling, and public libraries. Cities and towns obviously differ in their property tax rates. At present, Boston's residential property tax is 1.099%, while commercial and industrial properties are taxed at almost 2.7%. By comparison, Cambridge taxes residential property at 0.748% and commercial property at 1.83%, and Brookline's rates are 0.973% and 1.588%. Boston residents are eligible for an exemption, however, which lowers their property tax rate significantly if the house they own is their primary residence (this is essentially to penalize absentee landlords). To compare property tax rates in towns and cities throughout Massachusetts, visit www.mass.gov/dor/, click "For Individuals and Families," and then select "Municipal Information." For specific questions regarding your property taxes, contact the Assessor's office of your city or town hall.

MOTOR VEHICLE TAX

All residents who own a car registered in Massachusetts must pay a **motor vehicle excise tax**. The Registry of Motor Vehicles demands $25 per thousand dollars of vehicle's value each year. This excise tax is due thirty days from the date the notice is mailed. Excise tax also applies to trucks, motorcycles, and trailers. If you don't pay the excise tax, your registration and driver's license can be suspended.

For more information call the RMV at 617-351-4500, or go to www.mass.gov/rmv.

FEDERAL INCOME TAX

You can find federal tax forms in most public libraries and post offices come tax season, and of course they are always available for download online at www.irs.gov. Alternatively, you can request tax forms by calling 800-TAX-FORM from

Monday through Friday, 7 a.m. to 10 p.m. Here are some additional resources to help you file:

- **IRS Tax Help Line,** 800-829-1040, www.irs.gov
- **IRS Boston Branch**, 25 New Sudbury St, JFK Bldg, Room 775, Boston, 617-316-2850
- **Federal Tele-Tax Information Line**, 800-829-4477

STATE INCOME TAX

In addition to state sales, use, and property taxes, residents must also pay state income tax, currently at a flat 5.3% rate. Massachusetts voters approved an income tax rollback (to 5%) in 2000, but this has yet to be accomplished by the legislature. Among other standard deductions, Massachusetts allows you to deduct half of what you paid in rent over the course of the year, up to $3,000.

Newcomers with questions on income taxes should contact the **Customer Service Bureau of the Massachusetts Department of Revenue** at 617-887-MDOR or 800-392-6089, or go online to www.mass.gov/dor/. Contact this office to find out which forms you'll need (especially if you haven't lived in Massachusetts for the whole tax year) or for other income tax questions. Forms are available through the Massachusetts Department of Revenue, or at public libraries, post offices, and some banks during tax season. The Department of Revenue's Boston office is located at 100 Cambridge Street in Boston.

For additional income tax help, the **Boston Bar Association** has a **Volunteer Income Tax Program** that is generally held at the Boston Public Library's Copley Square branch; trained volunteers offer free tax preparation assistance to low- to moderate-income taxpayers. Check with the library (www.bpl.org) or the Bar Association (617-742-0615, www.bostonbar.org) for exact dates, times, and locations.

ELECTRONIC INCOME TAX FILING

One of the easiest and most accurate ways to file both your federal and state tax returns—and, if you're anticipating a refund, the quickest way to get it—is by e-filing online. Most e-file services will charge a small fee for this convenience, but if your Adjusted Gross Income is under $52,000, you might be able to e-file your federal return for free—the **IRS's e-file site** (www.irs.gov/efile) can direct you to dozens of participating services. Two of the most popular, **TurboTax.com** and **HRBlock.com,** offer several e-filing options, whether you want to buy and download their tax preparation software, or simply go through the process completely online; you can even save your session and pick up where you left off at a later date. Most e-file services will walk you through each portion of your tax return; explaining the directions in simple terms, they make the process relatively painless. (Well, unless you owe money!)

Massachusetts also encourages e-filing. Once you've finished with your federal return, you can opt to have the tax program transfer all of your information onto your state return for a fee—a huge time savings. Some residents may qualify for free state e-filing, and many more are eligible to Telefile their state return via touch-tone phone. Go to the **Massachusetts Department of Revenue** web site, www.mass.gov/dor/, for a full list of options, including approved e-file agencies and software.

STARTING OR MOVING A BUSINESS

If you choose to open a new business or move your existing business to Boston, you may want to hire an attorney who is familiar with the process. To do some legwork on your own, the following resources will be helpful:

- **Boston Bar Association**, 16 Beacon St, Boston, 617-742-0615, www.boston bar.org
- **Commonwealth of Massachusetts**, www.mass.gov, has a portal with all sorts of helpful information regarding opening a business, including links to various important state agencies, a step-by-step guide to getting started, and information on licenses, permits, and regulations. From the main Mass.gov page, click "For Businesses" and then "Getting Started."
- **Internal Revenue Service**, 800-829-1040; where you need to go to get an employer tax ID number.
- **Massachusetts Bar Association**, 20 West St, Boston, 617-338-0500, www. massbar.org
- **Massachusetts Small Business Development Center Network**, 413-545-6301, www.msbdc.org
- **US Small Business Administration Home Page**, 800-827-5722, www.sba. gov

ONCE YOU'VE FOUND A PLACE TO CALL HOME, YOU'LL NEED TO get your basic utilities hooked up and other services like cable or internet connected. If you own a car, you should get it registered in Massachusetts and apply for a new driver's license; you might also need to figure out where and how you're going to park it. Other orders of business might include signing up for a local library card, finding a physician, or getting a license for your dog and finding a vet.

City web sites providing online information about municipal services in the greater Boston area are listed following the **Neighborhood** profiles. In addition, the Commonwealth of Massachusetts runs an excellent web site, www.mass.gov, which may solve any of your unanswered questions as you settle in.

UTILITIES

Your landlord, building manager, or real estate agent should be able to point you in the right direction when it's time to set up your utilities; to give you a head start, local distribution companies and the areas they serve are listed here. Services vary from town to town, and utility to utility. For example, each community generally has only one gas provider, but residents may buy heating oil from any number of independent suppliers. The **Massachusetts Department of Utilities** (DPU, 617-305-3500, www.mass.gov/dpu) oversees the service, pricing, safety, and structure of energy utilities statewide. A handy feature on their web site can provide you with the gas, electric, and cable companies designated to serve your town or city: http://db.state.ma.us/dpu/qorders/frmCityUtilities.asp.

ELECTRICITY

Electricity was deregulated in Massachusetts in 1998; this means that while a regulated **distribution company** (such as NSTAR) provides power to your home or business and handles your account, you have the option of purchasing electricity from a number of separate **competitive power suppliers** who set their own prices (not regulated by the DPU). You can choose to receive a separate bill from each company, or a single bill from your distributor divided into two separate charges. For a complete guide to the state's electric utility restructuring, call the Office of Consumer Affairs and Business Regulation at 617-973-8700, or visit www.mass.gov/thepower/.

Generally landlords don't turn off the electricity at the end of the prior lease, so usually you just have to call your distribution company to transfer the account to your name. Customer service representatives will ask you standard questions over the phone when you call to set up your account; no deposit is required. If electric service wasn't extended throughout the vacancy, it should only take a day or two for the distribution company to turn on service.

In addition to federally sponsored tax incentives for the installation of renewable energy systems in your home or business, Massachusetts offers state tax breaks. For information on both programs, or about purchasing renewable energy credits, contact the Division of Energy Resources at 617-727-4732 or visit www.mass.gov/doer/.

To report a complaint, call the **Department of Public Utilities** at 800-392-6066 or 617-305-3531. For fraud or unfair practices, you can also call the **Office of the Attorney General** at 617-727-2200.

The following is a list of **distribution companies for Boston area** communities:

- **NSTAR Electric (formerly Boston Edison)**, 800-592-2000, www.nstaronline. com, for electric service in Boston (all neighborhoods), Arlington, Brookline, Cambridge, Chelsea, Dedham, Milton, Needham, Newton, Somerville, Waltham, and Watertown.
- **National Grid (formerly Mass Electric)**, 800-322-3223, www.nationalgridus. com, services to Everett, Malden, Medford, Melrose, Quincy, and Winthrop.
- Belmont's electric service is run through its Municipal Light Department: **Belmont Municipal Light Department**, 40 Prince St, Belmont, 617-484-2780, www.town.belmont.ma.us/

GAS

Next, you might need to set up gas service for your stove or water heater. Like local electric service, gas in Massachusetts is also regulated by the DPU. There are ten investor-owned and four municipal gas utilities in the state. Call in advance to set up service, especially during the busy months of August and September, when it could take days or even weeks to get an appointment to have your gas service connected. Connection may require a home visit, especially if service has been turned off before you move in, in which case you'll need to schedule a time when you or your landlord can be around to provide the gas company access to your apartment and your meter.

Here are the major **Boston area gas providers** and the communities they serve:

- **KeySpan Energy Delivery** (formerly **Boston Gas**), 800-732-3400, www. keyspanenergy.com; covers Arlington, Belmont, Boston, Brookline, Malden, Medford, Newton, Quincy, Waltham, and Watertown.
- **NSTAR Gas** (formerly **Commonwealth Gas**), 800-592-2000, www.nstaronline. com, provides gas service to residents of Cambridge, Dedham, and Needham.

In **Milton** and **Somerville**, both NSTAR and KeySpan are providers. Call and ask which one serves your address.

Gas utilities have energy savings plans that may help you save on your bills. Contact your gas company for details.

OIL

According to the Energy Information Administration, the Northeast accounts for over three quarters of all the US households that rely on oil for heat, and oil is the primary home heating fuel in most of New England. Oil distribution is not controlled by any one utility, so residents can choose their own supplier. In an apartment situation, your landlord may already have a service agreement with an oil supplier who will also maintain the furnace burners and filters. If you need to find a supplier, there are many listed in the Yellow Pages; you can also check out www.orderoil.com, a site that allows you to compare local oil dealers' prices, available delivery times, and customer satisfaction ratings, and schedule and purchase an oil delivery online. Some companies only service certain areas, such as just the north shore or south shore. You might also consider an oil cooperative; for a membership fee of $10 to $15, your oil will cost less per gallon than normal rates from non–co-op suppliers. The Boston area has two oil cooperatives:

- **Mass Energy Consumers Alliance** (formerly Boston Oil Consumers Alliance), 617-524-3950, 800-287-3950, www.massenergy.com, offers a renewable energy (solar, wind, etc.) program in addition to the oil cooperative.
- **Ecological Innovations Oil Buying Network**, 617-349-6247, 800-649-7473

TELEPHONE

The **Department of Telecommunications and Cable** (DTC) regulates the telecom industry in Massachusetts. This industry includes local carriers, long distance carriers, area codes, cellular phones, pagers, and some internet services.

AREA CODES

Due to the exponential increase of phone, fax, and particularly mobile numbers over the last decade, many states across the nation have exhausted available exchanges. Consequently, telecommunications officials continue to augment the existing area codes with new ones to handle the ever-increasing volume. In 1998, the number of area codes in Eastern Massachusetts was doubled from two to four: to 617 and 508 were added 781 and 978. In 2001, those four area codes split again, bringing the total to eight. Basically, two area codes serve each region, the original (such as Boston's 617) and an overlay area code (such as 857) that acts as an overflow catchall for new numbers. Specifically, 617/857 covers Boston and its immediate surrounds, including Cambridge, Somerville, Brookline, Belmont, Watertown, Milton, Quincy, Newton, Everett, Chelsea, and Winthrop; 781/339 serves the inner suburban ring that falls generally on and within the 128 belt, including Arlington, Waltham, Medford, Malden, and many others; 508/774 spans across southern Massachusetts, including Cape Cod, Martha's Vineyard, Nantucket, and the south central portion of the state out to Worcester; and 978/351 covers the northern and north central portion of the state. The entirety of western Massachusetts is in the 413 area code. Eleven-digit dialing (one, plus the area code, plus the phone number) is always required, whether you are dialing your neighbor who has the same area code, or someone in Bar Harbor, Maine.

To verify the area code(s) for your community, go to www22.verizon.com/AreaCodes.

CONVENTIONAL AND LOCAL LONG DISTANCE

While it's entirely possible, and even fairly common, to live without a landline these days—relying on your cell phone is completely feasible in a dense urban setting like the Boston area—it's not a bad thing to have either. For one thing, a local number is handy, not just so your friends can call you without paying long distance, and not simply because pizza delivery shops sometimes balk at an out-of-state number, but because—along with getting your name in the phone book—newspapers, credit cards, and other companies routinely use your telephone number to track your account.

The most recent in a long line of telecom behemoths to provide local service to the Boston area is **Verizon**. You arrange for new local phone service long before you arrive; call Verizon at 800-870-9999 between 8 a.m. and 6 p.m., Monday through Friday, or open an account and schedule your new service online anytime at www.verizon.com. Verizon offers a variety of calling plans that range from basic flat rate service with available add-ons to bundled packages of unlimited local, long distance, wireless, digital TV, and high-speed internet service, with every manner of combination in between.

When researching **long distance plans**, as with everything else, make sure to read the fine print; low per minute rates often mean higher flat fees, and vice versa, so finding the right plan depends on how, and how often, you will use the service. To compare long distance plan pricing, check out **SmartPrice.com** or call 877-550-5317. They will ask you questions regarding your phone usage, your area code, and the first three digits of your phone number, and then provide a free instant cost analysis of carriers available in your area. You can also find help making an informed decision by visiting the **Telecommunications Research and Action Center** (**TRAC**) web site (www.trac.org). The TRAC staff researches telecommunications issues and publishes rate comparisons and useful consumer tips.

Major long distance service providers in the area include:

* **AT&T**, 800-222-0300, www.att.com
* **GTC Telecom**, 800-486-4030, www.gtctelecom.com
* **IDT**, 800-CALL-IDT, www.idt.net
* **MCI-WorldCom**, 800-444-3333, www.mci.com
* **Sprint**, 800-877-7746, www.sprint.com
* **Verizon**, 800-870-9999, www.verizon.com
* **Working Assets**, 800-362-7127, www.workingforchange.com

In this modern age, there are of course other options, such as **Voice over Internet Protocol (VoIP)** services, which allow users to make calls via high-speed internet for a flat monthly fee, or even for free. The two biggest are **Vonage** (1-VONAGE-HELP, www.vonage.com), which lets you transfer your current phone number to a new Vonage account, and **Skype** (www.skype.com), which is a good option for international newcomers, or those with family or friends abroad, as it allows for free international calling to other Skype users. Also read on to the **Cable Television** section for a selection of companies offering bundled packages of various services.

If you have problems with your phone service, or find you have been "slammed" (an illegal practice in Massachusetts, where a company changes your long distance service without your consent), read ahead to the **Utility Complaints** section of this chapter for advice. **Phone solicitations** can be curbed by going to the government's **do not call registry** (www.donotcall.gov) and registering your phone number—or call 888-382-1222, TTY 866-290-4236.

CELLULAR PHONES

Trying to imagine life before the advent of the cell phone age can boggle the mind. How did people find each other in a crowd? What if you were running late, or lost? According to a survey performed by The Mobile World, a UK-based company specializing in telecom analysis, as of 2007, more than 1,000 new customers worldwide were signing up for mobile phone service *every minute*. The per capita saturation rate in Western Europe is already over 100%, meaning that for every single person—including newborn babies—there is a cell phone in use (some people use more than one).

While the US has lagged behind Western Europe somewhat, chances are still very good that you have a cell phone already. If your provider services the Northeast, and you find you get good reception when you arrive, you may not have to change a thing. If you do need to switch carriers, you can at least keep your old number if you (and your friends or clients) have grown accustomed to it—since 2003, cellular companies must permit you to transfer your old cell phone number to a new carrier.

Boston being a major urban area, cellular coverage in the city and its surrounding areas is very good, though some providers have spottier coverage than others, and a few outlying towns are certainly prone to poor reception. When heading to the mountains of Vermont or New Hampshire for the weekend, be prepared for pockets of little or no signal strength. Also note that while Massachusetts has not yet followed New York and Connecticut's example of banning hand-held cell phone use while driving, it is under consideration; the state does allow local municipalities the option, and as of 2007, Brookline is the only town that has enacted the ban.

With such a staggering number of customers, there is an equal amount of competition in this mega-industry, which means you should be able to find a phone and plan that suits your needs. Many offer unlimited in-network calling, so if most of your friends and family members use the same carrier, it can make sense to join them. A cell phone dealer will typically be able to offer you a heavily discounted phone, or even a full rebate, when you either sign up or renew your contract. Speaking of contracts, they often come with a hefty early termination fee attached, so be sure you know what you're getting into. For help choosing a cell phone and plan, visit the **Cellular Telecommunications and Internet Association (CTIA)** at www.wow-com.com, or try the previously mentioned TRAC (www.trac.org). Boston.com, *Consumer Reports*, and other publications also offer cell phone reviews.

The following are the Boston area's largest cellular providers:

- **AT&T** (formerly Cingular Wireless), www.wireless.att.com
- **Sprint**, 800-SPRINT-1, www.sprint.com
- **T-Mobile**, 800-937-8997, www.t-mobile.com
- **Verizon Wireless**, 800-870-9999, www.verizonwireless.com

With only slightly higher rates and no year-long contract commitments, monthly service charges, credit checks, or deposits, **prepaid cellular** is easily worth the small amount of inconvenience associated with continually replenishing minutes. Available at numerous stores around Boston, phones come with a card representing a certain financial value ranging from $15 to $100. Activate the card and, when the money runs out, replenish it with another payment—this is called "topping up." **T-Mobile Prepaid Mobile To Go** starter kits are available at T-Mobile outlets, 7-Eleven convenience stores, and CVS pharmacies, online at www.t-mobile.com, or by calling 877-677-5505. Other options are **Verizon's** pay-as-you-go plan, **FreeUp**, which includes text messaging (available at Verizon outlets or at www.verizonwireless.com), and **AT&T's GoPhone** (888-4-GO-PHONE, www.wireless.att.com).

DIRECTORY ASSISTANCE

For local and national telephone directory assistance, dial 411. Most calling plans include a certain number of calls to 411 per month, but if you exceed the limit, you might be charged. Alternatively, make use of free online yellow and white page directories like www.switchboard.com, www.411.com, www.whitepages. com, AT&T's www.anywho.com, http://people.yahoo.com, or www.yellowbook. com.

INTERNET SERVICE PROVIDERS (ISP)

Internet service varies from traditional dial-up access over phone lines to much faster broadband service via cable modems or DSL (digital subscription lines). Cable modem and DSL availability can vary from town to town, or even from building to building, depending on whether service has been extended to your area and by whom. Also available in most areas are **bundled telecommunications**: digital cable, telephone, and internet services that are grouped into one package plan (read on to **Cable Television** for more information).

Depending on your ISP, and whether you opt for old school dial-up or a broadband option like DSL or high-speed cable internet, you can expect to pay anywhere from $10 to $60 per month. When looking at plans, compare the per second download speeds. A traditional dial-up modem operates at about 56 Kbps (kilobits per second), whereas the bulk of broadband options fall between 756 Kbps and 6 Mbps (megabits per second), or 15 to 100 times faster than dial-up. At the high end, Verizon's fiber-optic service tops out at over 30 Mbps in its most competitive regions (of which Boston is one). If you're simply sending a few text-rich emails, dial-up may suit your needs, but if you or your kids plan on downloading MP3s or video files, consider how much time you want to devote to watching status bars.

There are certainly alternatives to paying for internet access, especially if you own a computer or laptop with **Wi-Fi** capability. Many area businesses, including bars, coffeeshops, and even laundromats, offer their customers free Wi-Fi access, and some neighborhoods benefit from local benefactors that have banded together to ensure free wireless internet access for residents and visitors alike, such as **Newbury Street** (www.newburyopen.net). The **Boston Public**

Library provides computer stations with free internet access and free Wi-Fi at all locations (with a valid library membership), and the City of Boston is working to create a free citywide Wi-Fi network; as of 2007, operational Wi-Fi zones include Roslindale Village and portions of Washington Street in the South End, with more zones already in the works for West Roxbury, Mission Hill, and Hyde Park. Visit www.mainstreetswifi.com for information.

While we don't recommend **piggy-backing** onto your neighbor's wireless connection, due to the increased vulnerability to viruses or identity theft and the questionable legality involved, Boston's densely clustered apartment buildings certainly make it possible to do so.

Because broadband service usually requires access to existing telephone lines or a cable connection, ISPs that offer high-speed internet are often limited to the big players; those serving the Boston area are listed below. A few communities—Braintree, Norwood, and Shrewsbury—maintain municipally run cable and ISP services; see the **Cable Television** section. For the lowest priced internet access, there are a number of dial-up ISPs to choose from, from locally-run **The World** (617-783-9753, www.theworld.com) to national companies like **PeoplePC** (877-947-3327, www.peoplepc.com), **Earthlink** (800-327-8454, www.earthlink.net), **Compuserve** (800-848-8990, www.compuserve.com), **Juno** (800-390-5866, www.juno.com), **NetZero** (877-665-9995, www.netzero.net), **MSN** (877-564-6676, www.msn.com), and of course, **America Online** (888-265-8003, www.aol.com).

BROADBAND INTERNET SERVICE PROVIDERS

- **Comcast**, 800-COMCAST, www.comcast.com; high-speed cable internet from 6 to 8 Mbps
- **RCN**, 800-RING-RCN, www.rcn.com; dial-up and high-speed internet up to 1.5 to 20 Mbps
- **Verizon**, 877-483-5898 (for high-speed internet) or 888-GET-FIOS (for FiOS fiber optic service), www.verizon.com; DSL and FiOS available from 756 Kbps to 30 Mbps

WATER

WATER SERVICE

The **Massachusetts Department of Environmental Protection (DEP)** estimates that more than six million residents drink tap water every day. Most communities get their drinking water from reservoirs. Although there are several primary and back-up reservoirs around the state, most of Massachusetts' water supply origi-nates in the **Quabbin Reservoir** in western Massachusetts.

If you're renting, your water bill will be taken care of by your landlord. Homeowners are responsible for their monthly water bill. Water service in Mas-sachusetts is organized in the same way as electrical service—with suppliers and distributors. Since 1984, the **Massachusetts Water Resources Author-ity** (**MWRA**) has been the public water and sewer wholesale service provider for the greater Boston area, brokering Quabbin Reservoir water to 2.5 million people, 5,500 large industrial users, and 61 metro Boston communities. MWRA provides water and sewer service to Arlington, Belmont, Boston, Brookline, Mal-den, Medford, Milton, Newton, Quincy, Somerville, Watertown, and Waltham. A "middleman" then distributes the water to your community, and this is the entity you should contact to set up your water service (read on).

Residents of Cambridge get their water from the MWRA only in special situations. Otherwise, their water comes from **Fresh Pond**, and the municipally owned Cambridge Water Department (www.ci.cambridge.ma.us/~Water, 617-349-4770) provides their water utility service. Dedham residents have a similar back-up emergency arrangement with the MWRA, but otherwise their water comes from local wells, provided through the **Dedham-Westwood Water Dis-trict** (www.dwwd.org, 781-329-7090). In **Needham**, residents should contact the **Department of Public Works' Water and Sewer Division**, 781-455-7547.

If you are moving to a community farther out, call 617-660-7971 or go on-line to www.mwra.com to find out if your new home is served by the MWRA. You can also check with your local city hall.

Distributors may vary from community to community, but water is mostly distributed by each town's Department of Public Works. In Boston, it's the **Boston Water and Sewer Commission** (**BWSC**). Here's a contact list to get you started, including the MWRA and the individual community distributors:

- **MWRA**, 100 First Ave, Charlestown Navy Yard, Boston, 617-660-7971, www.mwra.com
- **BWSC**, 980 Harrison Ave, Boston, 617-989-7000, www.bwsc.org; serves Boston proper.
- **Arlington DPW**, Water & Sewer Division, 780 Mass Ave, Arlington, 781-316-3108, www.town.arlington.ma.us/
- **Belmont DPW,** Water Division, 35 Woodland St, Belmont, 617-993-2700, www.town.belmont.ma.us
- **Brookline DPW,** Water and Sewer Division, 44 Netherlands Rd, Brookline, 617-730-2170, www.townofbrooklinemass.com/Dpw
- **Malden Department of Engineering, Planning, and Waterworks**, 200 Pleas-ant St, Malden, 781-397-7040, www.ci.malden.ma.us/
- **Medford Water and Sewer Division**, 52 Swan St, Medford, 781-393-2420, www.medford.org

- **Milton Water and Sewer Department**, 525 Canton Ave, Milton, 617-898-4878, www.townofmilton.org
- **Newton DPW**, Water and Sewer Utilities Division, 1000 Comm Ave, Newton, 617-796-1040, www.ci.newton.ma.us/dpw
- **Quincy DPW**, 55 Sea St, Quincy, 617-376-1918, www.ci.quincy.ma.us
- **Somerville DPW**, Water Division, 1 Franey Rd, 617-625-6600, ext. 5850, www.ci.somerville.ma.us
- **Waltham Water and Sewer Department**, 781-314-3250, www.city.waltham.ma.us
- **Watertown DPW**, Water Department, 124 Orchard St, Watertown, 617-972-6420, www.ci.watertown.ma.us

WATER QUALITY

The DEP rates Boston's drinking water as "very safe." In 2005, the MWRA began treating its water with ozone (as opposed to chlorine) at a new facility in Marlborough, which eliminates more germs and bacteria than chlorine without producing as many byproducts—water quality complaints have reached an all-time low since this process was introduced. Additional steps taken against bacterial contamination include added chloramine (a mixture of chlorine and ammonia) and increased pH levels. While this is not harmful to humans, it is bad for aquatic pets, so those with fish tanks need to add specific agents to the water or use a high-grade granular activated carbon filter to make the water gill-friendly. The MWRA also fluoridates the water in 135 communities.

Common complaints about tap water in Massachusetts include occasional yellow-tinged water, cloudy-white water, and rusty water. Yellowish water is probably the result of iron in the pipes, which the EPA says is not a threat to your health. Rusty water or "red water" occurs from time to time as a result of a change in water flow in the pipes, as in the event of a water main break. The rust should clear up within a couple of hours; in the meantime, you should try not to use the water for drinking, bathing, or washing. Cloudy water or "white water" is a harmless scenario caused when very cold weather causes air bubbles to be trapped in the water.

If your tap water smells or tastes funny it might be due to certain algae in the reservoirs that tend to crop up when the seasons change. According to the MWRA, "different types of algae can cause your water to smell fishy, moldy, grassy, or even like cucumbers or violets." Fortunately, these microorganisms are not harmful. The MWRA suggests refrigerating the water to deodorize it and putting in some lemon to spruce up the taste. Chlorine-scented water is a result of the chlorine used to disinfect the water from bacteria. Residents living near reservoirs are most apt to have this problem; leaving the water in an open container can help the odor subside.

Water that stains your fixtures green probably does so because of copper piping, which is most likely to occur in communities upstream from an MWRA treatment facility. Unlike the aforementioned water issues, copper contamination can be harmful. In 1996, the MWRA began treating drinking water to make it less corrosive, which in turn keeps it from absorbing as much copper—and the more dangerous **lead**—from pipes. While water is safe when it leaves the reservoirs, lead pipes were not banned until 1940, and even some brass and copper fixtures used lead soldering until 1986. Lead in these pipes or fixtures can leach into the water en route to your tap, and pose a danger to your health. The good news is lead levels in "worst case" homes have dropped significantly over the last 15 years. The City of Boston has replaced most—but not all—of its lead water pipes, but some communities are not so proactive. Even if the public plumbing is safe, lead pipes are still a danger in older houses. Boston.com maintains a list of addresses in the city, sortable by neighborhood, that are known to be fed by lead water pipes, and it's never a bad idea to get your water tested, especially if you are pregnant or have young children. The MWRA maintains a list of labs certified to perform lead testing at www.mwra.com/04water/html/testinglabs.html; expect to pay $15 and up for the service.

If you do have lead pipes in your home, there are programs that will help you to replace them, such as the BWSC's **Lead Replacement Incentive Program**, which offers homeowners up to $1,000 in financial assistance toward replacing their old lead plumbing. Visit their web site (www.bwsc.org) or call 617-989-7000 for details.

If you would like more information on the quality of your tap water, contact the **Massachusetts DEP Drinking Water Department** (617-556-1165, www.mass.gov/dep); the **Massachusetts Department of Public Health** (617-624-6000, www.mass.gov/dph); the **EPA's Safe Drinking Water Hotline** (800-426-4791, www.epa.gov/safewater); the **Water Quality Association** (800-749-0234, www.wqa.org); or check out the **National Water Quality Assessment Program** of the US Geological Survey online at http://ma.water.usgs.gov.

CONSUMER PROTECTION–UTILITY AND OIL COMPLAINTS

If you have problems with your utility company, you should try to resolve them with the company first. If satisfaction eludes you, call the consumer division of either the **Department of Telecommunications and Cable (DTC)** for telecom or cable issues, or the **Department of Public Utilities (DPU)** regarding electric, gas, water, or transportation issues. Alternately, you can also turn to the Consumer Protection Division of the Massachusetts Attorney General's Office or the Division of Energy Resources. Some water issues can be handled through the Massachusetts DEP.

- **Massachusetts DPU and DTC**, Consumer Division, 1 South Station, Boston, 617-305-3531 or 800-392-6066, www.mass.gov/dpu, www.mass.gov/dtc

- **Massachusetts Attorney General's Office**, Consumer Protection Division, 1 Ashburton Pl, Boston, 617-727-8400, www.ago.state.ma.us
- **Massachusetts Division of Energy Resources**, 100 Cambridge St, Boston, 617-727-4732, www.mass.gov/doer
- **Massachusetts DEP**, 1 Winter St, Boston, 617-292-5500, www.mass.gov/dep

Additionally, if you look at your phone bill and think you've been "**slammed**" (your long distance provider or established services were changed without your consent) or "**crammed**" (calls you didn't make were added to your bill), and you can't get help from your local service provider or from the Attorney General's Office, you can file a complaint with the **Federal Communication Commission's Consumer Center** (888-CALL-FCC, www.fcc.gov); or the **Federal Trade Commission** (202-FTC-HELP, www.ftc.gov).

GARBAGE AND RECYCLING

If you're a renter, the most you're going to need to know about garbage is where and when to put it out, and how to handle your recycling—questions your landlord can answer. For homeowners within the city of Boston, garbage and recycling pick-up is free (free in as much as it's included in your taxes!), and you can contact the **Sanitation Division of the DPW** (1 City Hall Plaza, Room 714, Boston, 617-635-4900, www.cityofboston.gov/publicworks/Sanitation.asp) to find out the pick-up schedule for your street. Depending on where you live, refuse will be picked up between one and three times per week. Trash may be left curbside beginning at 5 p.m. the night before pick-up, and must be stored in covered barrels (or otherwise protected from hungry street rodents) until that time. Perhaps because of all the college students—who can be, shall we say, less than diligent in keeping house—the city actively enforces this rule by issuing tickets at least a couple of times per year.

Yard waste collections occur on Saturdays in the spring and fall, and Christmas trees are picked up the first two weeks in January. Large items like dishwashers, stoves, and washing machines are okay to put out curbside—they are recycled. Refrigerators, air conditioners, televisions, and computer monitors need to be picked up separately; call the Sanitation Division at 617-635-7574 to schedule a pick-up, or you can arrange for one online.

In buildings of more than six units, landlords or building management agencies must purchase large recycling receptacles and then coordinate a pick-up program with the city—so as a resident of one of these buildings, your recycling schedule may be somewhat irregular. In buildings with six or fewer units, the city does free curbside recycling. Contact the DPW at 617-635-4959 to request the requisite blue bin, and then put your recycling out according to the following schedule: the same time as your garbage if you only have one pick-up day per week; on the first day if your trash is picked up twice weekly; and on the middle day if your garbage is picked up three times a week. Put plastic containers, metals, and glass in the designated blue box (no plastic bags); recycle paper, cardboard (no pizza boxes), and phone books in brown paper bags. The city hosts paint and motor oil recycling programs and hazardous waste drop-offs at various Public Works Yards on Saturdays from May to October. There is also a drop-off center for reusable building materials, such as old doors, windows, or bathroom fixtures, at the Boston Building Materials Co-op and Resource Center (100 Terrace Street, Mission Hill, 617-442-2262/617-442-8917, www.bbmc.com, www.bostonbmrc. org). For further recycling questions, you can call the **DPW's Recycling Hotline** at 617-635-4959 or go to www.cityofboston.gov/publicworks/recycling/.

Outside the City of Boston, use the following resources to find out about your sanitation and recycling services:

- **Arlington DPW**, 780 Mass Ave, 781-316-3108, www.town.arlington.ma.us
- **Belmont DPW**, Highway Division, 19 Moore St, 617-993-2690, www.town.bel mont.ma.us
- **Brookline DPW**, Highway and Sanitation, 80 Hammond St, 617-730-2156, www.townofbrooklinemass.com/dpw
- **Cambridge DPW**, 147 Hampshire St, 617-349-4800, www.cambridgema.gov
- **Dedham DPW**, Recycling, Trash, and Solid Waste Services, 55 River St, 781-751-9350, www.dedham-ma.gov
- **Malden DPW**, 356 Commercial St, Malden, 781-397-7160, www.ci.malden. ma.us
- **Medford DPW**, Highway Division: 781-393-2417; Recycling: 781-393-2419; www.medford.org
- **Milton DPW**, 629 Randolph Ave, Milton, 617-898-4868, www.townofmilton. org
- **Newton DPW**, 1000 Comm Ave, Newton, 617-796-1000, www.ci.newton. ma.us/DPW
- **Quincy DPW**, 55 Sea St, 617-376-1953, www.ci.quincy.ma.us
- **Somerville DPW**, Sanitation Department, 1 Franey Rd, 617-666-3311, www. ci.somerville.ma.us
- **Waltham DPW**, 167 Lexington St, 781-314-3855, 781-314-3390 (recycling), www.city.waltham.ma.us
- **Watertown DPW**, 124 Orchard St, 617-972-6420, www.ci.watertown.ma.us

BROADCAST AND PRINT MEDIA

TELEVISION

Fewer than 10% of homes in the Boston area lack cable television, but even viewers with old-fashioned rabbit ears can pick up affiliates from New Hampshire and Rhode Island, as well as Boston. If you have cable, ask your provider for a channel guide, as local stations are often relegated to unexpected places.

BOSTON

Channel 2, WGBH-TV, PBS (www.wgbh.org)
Channel 4, WBZ-TV, CBS (www.cbs4boston.com)
Channel 5, WCVB-TV, ABC (www.thebostonchannel.com)
Channel 7, WHDH-TV, NBC (www.whdh.com)
Channel 25, WFXT-TV, FOX (www.fox25.com)
Channel 27, WUNI-TV, UNIVISION (Spanish)
Channel 38, WSBK-TV (www.tv38.com)
Channel 44, WGBX-TV, PBS
Channel 56, WB56-TV, CW (www.cw56.com)
Channel 68, WBPX-TV, PAX

EXTENDED REGION

Channel 6, WLNE-TV (ABC out of Rhode Island)
Channel 9, WMUR-TV (ABC out of New Hampshire)
Channel 10, WJAR-TV (NBC out of Providence/New Bedford)
Channel 11, WENH-TV (PBS out of New Hampshire)
Channel 12, WPRI-TV (FOX out of Providence)
Channel 50, WNDS-TV (independent out of Derry, NH)
Channel 60, WGOT-TV (independent out of Merrimack, NH)

CABLE TELEVISION

Cable television (basic cable only) is regulated in Massachusetts through the **Department of Telecommunications and Cable** (1 South Station, Boston, 617-305-3580, www.mass.gov/dtc). Expanded, premium, and pay-per-view services are unregulated. There are eleven licensed cable carriers throughout the commonwealth, though most communities receive service from only one or two, and the mighty Comcast takes up the lion's share of subscribers. Comcast, Charter, Verizon, Braintree Electric Light Department, and RCN provide **bundled telecommunications** packages—that is, digital cable, internet, and phone, all from one provider, on one bill, and at a bulk discount. In Boston, the **Office of Cable Communications** is at 43 Hawkins Street, Boston, 617-635-3112, www.cityofbos ton.gov/cable.

Check with the following list to find the cable carrier(s) in your town or city. If your community isn't mentioned, contact your city hall to find out who your carrier is, or visit www.mass.gov/dtc/catv for a complete list of all cable systems in Massachusetts, whom they serve, and how to contact them.

• **Adelphia Cable**, 877-227-9658, www.adelphia.net, serves Cape Ann, Martha's Vineyard, the Berkshires, Plymouth and other south shore communities, and some areas of the north shore.

- **Braintree Electric Light Department**, 617-388-2353, www.beld.com, serves, as you might expect, the town of Braintree.
- **Comcast**, 800-COMCAST, 888-633-4236, www.comcast.com, serves Boston, Brookline, Arlington, Cambridge, Dedham, Malden, Medford, Milton, Needham, Newton, Quincy, Somerville, Waltham, Watertown, and a great deal of the state.
- **Charter Communications**, 888-GET-CHARTER, www.chartercom.com, covers the Worcester area, Pioneer Valley, and some rural areas of central Massachusetts.
- **Norwood Municipal Light System**, 781-948-1150, www.norwoodlight.com; serves the community of Norwood.
- **RCN**, 800-746-4726, www.rcn.com, shares territory as a competitor to Comcast, serving Boston, Arlington, Brookline, Burlington, Dedham, Framingham, Lexington, Natick, Needham, Newton, Somerville, Wakefield, Waltham, Watertown, and Woburn.
- **Shrewsbury Community Cablevision**, 508-841-8500, www.shrewsbury-ma.gov/cable/
- **Time Warner**, 888-633-4266, www.timewarnercable.com, serves only the far western portion of the state, including Pittsfield.

RADIO STATIONS

Here's a rundown of a few of the major players in the local radio market. Depending on where you are, you'll pick up signals from New Hampshire, Cape Cod, Rhode Island, or Worcester, along with many small (or even pirate) stations. Some smaller stations or college stations, such as those from Tufts and Wellesley, share a frequency.

The main players as you scan the Boston FM dial include:

- **88.9 FM WERS** (Emerson College radio)
- **89.7 FM WGBH** (public radio/classical)
- **90.9 FM WBUR** (National Public Radio)
- **91.9 FM WUMB** (UMASS-Boston, folk)
- **92.5 FM WXRV** (indie/acoustic)
- **92.9 FM WBOS** (adult alternative)
- **94.5 FM WJMN** (hip-hop/urban/dance)
- **96.9 FM WTKK** (talk)
- **98.5 FM WBMX** (top 40)
- **99.5 FM WCRB** (classical)
- **100.7 FM WZLX** (classic rock)
- **101.7 FM WFNX** (alternative/indie)
- **102.5 FM WKLB** (country)
- **103.3 FM WODS** (oldies)

- **104.1 FM WBCN** (rock)
- **105.7 FM WROR** (classic hits)
- **106.7 FM WMJX** (soft rock)
- **107.3 FM WAAF** (hard rock/metal)
- **107.9 FM WXKS** (top 40)

And on the AM dial, where there's something for everyone, including a number of small stations that air mostly foreign language and ethnic programming, the following stations have the biggest presence.

- **590 AM WEZE** (religious)
- **680 AM WRKO** (talk/Red Sox games)
- **850 AM WEEI** (sports talk)
- **890 AM WAMG** (ESPN Radio)
- **1030 AM WBZ** (news)
- **1260 AM WMKI** (Radio Disney)
- **1510 AM WWZN** (sports)

NEWSPAPERS AND MAGAZINES

The two major dailies in the Boston news market are **The Boston Globe** (www.boston.com, 617-929-2000), and **The Boston Herald** (www.bostonherald.com, 617-426-3000).

Boston Magazine (www.bostonmagazine.com, 617-262-9700) offers an elegant, monthly account of life in the metropolitan area, featuring local events, news, commentary, entertainment, and the best in places to live, work, study, shop, eat, and play. Pick it up at newsstands, or subscribe for $10 per year.

Boston's demographic mix of students and young professionals—many of whom make for a captive audience as they ride the T each day—are particularly attractive to advertisers. Accordingly, there are many free daily, weekly, and monthly publications available in newsboxes, stores, and T stations all over the city—the following are a few you're sure to run into.

- The **Metro**, www.metrobostonnews.com, 617-357-5706; Boston's edition of the largest and fastest growing international newspaper in the world is both an inescapable and indispensable part of any commuter's morning. It is what it is: a free and brief daily newspaper comprised mostly of national wire feed from the AP and Reuters, with a few original columns and local features to round things out. It's meant to be digested in fifteen minutes on your way to or from work, but hey, there's a crossword and a Sudoku puzzle if your train ride is longer than that!
- The **Boston Phoenix**, www.thephoenix.com, 617-536-5390; Boston's first alternative weekly (akin to *The Village Voice*), the *Phoenix* was founded in the 1960s and owns WFNX 101.7 FM, the station credited for breaking Nirvana in the Boston area. The traditional go-to guide for music, arts, and entertainment listings,

the *Phoenix* also offers a surprising amount of in-depth reporting and editorial content. While it certainly paved the way for Boston's thriving alt-weekly industry, the *Phoenix* never misses a chance to remind you of it. Comes out on Thursdays; they also publish editions in Providence, RI, and Portland, ME.

- The **Weekly Dig**, www.weeklydig.com, 617-426-8942; once the little weekly that could, the *Dig* gradually earned a spot amongst the most beloved publications in the city under former editor Joe Keohane, now a writer for *Boston Magazine*. Unashamedly city-centric and routinely hilarious, the *Dig* offers irreverent, outspoken—and, often, unexpectedly insightful—commentary and local news features to complement its full line-up of music, arts, film, food, and comedy listings. Published on Wednesdays.
- **Barstool Sports**, www.barstoolsports.com, 617-262-6882; founded just a few years ago by a group of friends looking to start a paper written "by the common man, for the common man." Whether it's the humorous (Bill Simmons–influenced) columns, cover models, or special issues like "Boston's 25 Sexiest Bartenders," *Barstool Sports* has proved its staying power in this sports-crazed city.
- The **Improper Bostonian**, www.improper.com, 617-859-1400; this free, glossy fortnightly covers local lifestyle, trends, dining, and entertainment, and gears itself toward the city's upscale and fashion-minded, particularly 20- to 30-something women. Available every other Wednesday; residents in the Back Bay, Beacon Hill, North End, and South End find it delivered to their door.
- **BostonNOW**, www.bostonnow.com, 617-482-3669; this upstart free daily launched in 2007 with an aim to cut into the *Metro*'s enormous commuter readership. *BostonNOW* differentiates itself by incorporating "citizen journalism," i.e., excerpts from local blogs, and allowing the public to sit in on, and even participate in, online editorial meetings that determine the content of the next day's paper.

Most neighborhoods or communities have their own papers. Some are free, some charge, and many of them are run by Gatehouse Media, Inc. Hence, a great deal of them can be found online through the same web site: www.townonline.com. Below are a few of the local papers serving metro Boston towns and communities.

- **Allston-Brighton TAB**, 617-254-7530, www.townonline.com/allston
- **Arlington Advocate**, 781-643-7900, www.townoline.com/arlington
- **Bay State Banner**, 617-261-4600, www.baystatebanner.com; weekly newspaper for the African-American community.
- **Bay Windows**, 617-266-6670, www.baywindows.com; weekly newspaper for the gay and lesbian community
- **Beacon Hill Times**, 617-523-9490, www.beaconhilltimes.com
- **Belmont Citizen-Herald**, 617-484-2633, www.townonline.com/belmont
- **Boston Haitian Reporter**, 617-436-1222, www.bostonhaitian.com

- **Boston Irish Reporter**, 617-436-1222, www.bostonirish.com
- **Brookline TAB**, 617-566-3585, www.townonline.com/brookline
- **Cambridge Chronicle**, 617-577-7149, www.townonline.com/cambridge
- **Christian Science Monitor**, 617-375-4000, www.csmonitor.com; daily (Monday–Friday)
- **Dorchester Reporter**, 617-436-1222, www.dotnews.com
- **El Mundo**, 617-522-5060, www.elmundoboston.com; the area's largest and longest-running Spanish-language publication has served greater Boston's Latino community for over 35 years.
- **El Planeta**, 617-232-0996, www.elplaneta.com; weekly Spanish-language newspaper founded in 2004 to compete with *El Mundo*
- **Jamaica Plain Gazette**, 617-524-2626, www.jamaicaplaingazette.com
- **Jewish Advocate**, 617-367-9100, www.thejewishadvocate.com; weekly newspaper for the Jewish community
- **Malden Observer**, 781-322-6957, www.townonline.com/malden
- **Medford Transcript**, 781-396-1982, www.townonline.com/medford
- **Newton TAB**, 617-969-0340, www.townonline.com/newton
- **Quincy Patriot Ledger**, 617-786-7000, www.patriotledger.com
- **Roslindale/West Roxbury Transcript**, 617-327-2608, www.townonline.com/roslindale
- **Somerville Journal**, 617-625-6300, www.townonline.com/somerville
- **South Boston Tribune**, 617-268-3440, www.southbostoninfo.com
- **South End News**, 617-266-6670, www.southendnews.com
- **Watertown TAB & Press**, 617-926-8897, www.townonline.com/watertown

AUTOMOBILES

Expensive parking and high insurance premiums (crowded, narrow streets + assertive drivers + panic-prone tourists = increased likelihood of dings and dents) make Boston one of the most expensive cities in the nation in which to own a car. If you bring your car to Boston or buy one here, you'll want to make sure you're square with the state's legal requirements. Aside from obtaining a local operator's license, you will need to secure a title, registration, and insurance for your vehicle, and have it inspected. As with licenses, the RMV web site is very helpful for answering questions about automobile registration.

DRIVER'S LICENSES AND STATE IDS

In an automotive sense, life here is more New York than LA: public transportation is good, parking is a hassle, and insurance is expensive, the end result being many choose to live here without a car. For those coming with an automobile, the **Massachusetts Registry of Motor Vehicles** (**RMV**, 617-351-4500 or 800-

858-3926, www.mass.gov/rmv) is the source for most legal information and requirements for owning and operating an automobile or motorcycle in Massachusetts. (Parking permit requirements will vary depending upon your city.) The RMV's comprehensive web site can answer virtually all your vehicular questions, and you can complete many transactions online—a fabulous service, given the notoriously long lines at RMVs, DMVs, and secretaries of state across the country. If you still have to go in person, you can look up the current waiting times at various branches online to save yourself some aggravation.

The web site **www.DMV.org**, while *not* affiliated with the actual Registry of Motor Vehicles (or any governmental agency for that matter), is nonetheless an easy to follow, comprehensive source of information, advice, and links for Massachusetts automobile owners.

DRIVER'S LICENSES

Technically, Massachusetts residents are legally required to have a valid Massachusetts license to drive here, which means you should convert your out-of-state license right away. Of course, many people (particularly students who only live here part of the year) don't bother changing their license until their out-of-state one is about to expire…or they get caught.

Whether you're converting an old license, getting your first one, replacing a lost license, or just getting a state ID, you'll do it through the RMV. Go to www.mass.gov/rmv for a complete list of the types of documentation you should bring when registering your vehicle and for a list of fees.

The **Boston RMV**, located at 630 Washington Street in Chinatown, is the main full-service office in the city. Hours are 8:30 a.m. to 5 p.m., Monday–Friday, with extended hours on Thursday to 7 p.m. Additional full-service branches are located in Quincy and Watertown, and there is a limited service "License Express" branch in the Cambridgeside Galleria Mall, 100 Cambridgeside Place (Lechmere T), open Monday to Friday, 10 a.m. to 7 p.m. License Express offices can take care of quick and simple licensing needs, such as license or registration renewals, changes, duplicates, and plate returns. There are dozens of RMV and License Express offices throughout the state; check www.mass.gov/rmv/branches, or call 800-858-3926 for a complete list and contact information.

Massachusetts licenses are valid for up to five years and expire on the birthday of the license holder. You can **renew** your license anytime during the year preceding the expiration date. The state may refuse to renew your license if you have outstanding parking or abandoned vehicle tickets, unpaid excise tax or Fast Lane toll violations, or outstanding warrants and child support obligations.

In Massachusetts, everyone under 18 years of age is subject to the **Junior Operator License Law**, a graduated license law that requires young drivers pass through a number of phases before getting full driving privileges. Check with the RMV for complete details.

To convert your out-of-state license to a Massachusetts driver's license, you'll have to pay for all application, testing, and license fees. If your out-of-state license is current or has been expired for less than a year, you will not have to take a written or road test to convert your license. A standard Class D license will cost you $90. Go to an RMV or License Express with either your Social Security card or current passport in tow, and three additional pieces of ID (check online at www.mass.gov/rmv for acceptable forms of identification). Also bring a form of payment (check, money order, or credit card), your current out-of-state photo license, and proof of Massachusetts' residency (such as a local utility bill in your name).

The requirements for **converting a foreign license** to a Massachusetts driver's license will depend upon which country issued your license. To convert a current Canadian, Mexican, or US Territory license, you will have to obtain a certified driving record no more than a month old from the country in which you're licensed, as well as pass an eye exam. Requirements for lapsed Canadian, Mexican, or US Territory licenses are the same as for out-of-state ones. Newcomers hailing from any other country must take the full licensing exam from scratch and may require a sponsor; International Driving Permits cannot be converted.

If you're planning on riding a **motorcycle**, you'll have special requirements to complete for your licensing. Check with the RMV for specifics.

STATE IDs

Massachusetts ID cards look like driver's licenses and are available to state residents 16 years old or older who do not have a driver's license. Bring your social security card or valid passport, and other documents proving your date of birth, signature, state residency, and parental consent (for minors) to a full service RMV. IDs cost $15 and expire after 5 years, although you may wish to upgrade to a liquor ID card when you turn 21. **Massachusetts Liquor ID cards** cost $25 and also expire every five years.

AUTOMOBILE REGISTRATION, TITLING, INSPECTION, AND INSURANCE

TITLES

In Massachusetts, you must have the title to your automobile, which proves ownership and documents the vehicle's history. The state's **Title Law** requires that all vehicles and trailers be titled within 10 days of purchase. Exemptions include dealer cars, cars owned by the government, and cars owned by non-residents. A car will get a "clear title" if it is new or has not been in an accident. If you have a car that was totaled it gets a "salvage title." There is also a "memorandum" title, which means that the car was brought in from out of state with a lien on it, and the lien holder is in possession of the out-of-state title. Check www.mass.gov/rmv/titles for complete details. Expect to pay $50 to title your car plus any applicable sales tax.

REGISTRATION

If you are bringing your car from another state, by law you are required to register your car immediately; there is no grace period. If the car has been registered elsewhere for more than six months the car is exempt from Massachusetts state sales tax. To convert your out-of-state registration, go to a full service RMV and complete form MVU-29 (the Affidavit in Support for Exemption from Sales or Use Tax for Motor Vehicle Purchased Outside of Massachusetts. You can also download it online from the Massachusetts RMV site). Then, set up an insurance policy with a Massachusetts insurance agent and have him or her stamp and sign the application for registration and title (form RMV-1). Verify that all the information is correct, sign it, and bring it to a full service RMV, along with your out-of-state title, out-of-state registration, and completed MVU-29 form. Fees are the same as for newly purchased vehicles, minus the 5% sales tax. If your car was registered elsewhere for less than six months, skip the MVU-29 step, head to the insurance agent, and proceed as before, bearing in mind that you'll have to pay the sales tax at the RMV when you register. (See the **Money Matters** chapter for more information about state and use tax.)

To register a new vehicle in Massachusetts, you must first insure it with a Massachusetts insurance agent. Regardless of whether you purchased the car here or in another state, have your dealer fill out a RMV-1 form. Then set up an insurance policy with an agent licensed in Massachusetts; he or she must also stamp and sign off on the RMV-1. Verify that all the information is correct before you put your own signature on it, and then bring the form and a Certificate of Origin, which you get from the dealer and acts in place of a title, to a full-service RMV. For a standard (non-commercial) vehicle, you'll pay $36 for the registration plus a $50 title fee and 5% sales tax.

Note: all new passenger vehicles sold and registered in Massachusetts are subject to the **Low Emission Vehicle Program**. Specifically, new vehicles with less than 7,500 miles on them must meet cleaner California emission standards, i.e., have factory-installed California-certified advanced emission control systems.

If you're buying a used car from a dealership, you follow most of the same channels: have the dealer fill out the RMV-1, get an insurance policy with a Massachusetts insurance agent and have him or her sign the RMV-1, check it over to make sure all the information is correct, sign it yourself, and then bring it along with either the previous owner's title (if the vehicle is titled) or the bill of sale and proof of last registration (if non-titled) to a full service RMV. The fees are the same as for new cars purchased from a dealer.

For instructions on **vehicles purchased from a non-dealer, or acquired from family or friends,** visit the RMV site at www.mass.gov/rmv/regs.

Upon completing the registration transaction for all types of vehicles, the RMV will give you the registration certificate, new license plates, and the year of expiration decal, which goes on the rear plate. The RMV will process your new title and mail it to you (or to the lien holder if you have a loan); it should arrive in six to eight weeks.

SAFETY AND EMISSIONS INSPECTIONS

Once your vehicle is registered with the RMV, you have **one week** (seven calendar days, not seven business days) to take your vehicle in for a state **safety inspection.** Safety inspections cost $29 and are valid for one year. Go to www.massstationlocator.com for a complete directory of participating stations. Inspectors will check your registration and plates, windshield, windshield wipers, headlights, taillights, brake lights, turn signals, hazards, horn, exhaust system, tires, body panels/fuel tank, emergency brake, seat belts, ball joints, steering, and suspension. They won't check airbags or anti-lock braking systems (although regular brakes must work), but a crack in any of your lights or windows could fail you, as will neon lights (they're illegal) and after-market glass tinting above 35%. Check with the RMV for state regulations.

Every other year, at your state inspection, your car will also have to pass an **emissions test,** unless the model is pre-1983 or brand new, in which it is exempt for the first two years. Regardless of the last two caveats, if (visible) smoke pours out of your exhaust pipe during the emissions inspection, the car won't pass.

If your car fails the safety inspection, it is not legally allowed on the road until the problem is fixed; if it is something small, like a broken tail light, the service station performing the test will likely offer to repair it for you on the spot. If your vehicle fails the emissions test, you have 60 days to fix the problem. In either case, your car will be branded with a *Scarlet Letter*–style "R" (rejected) sticker until it achieves a passing inspection. If you bring it back to the same station that performed the initial test within 60 days, you won't be charged again.

When you pass the safety and emissions tests, the inspector will put a color-coded Certificate of Inspection sticker on the lower right hand corner of your windshield, bearing the inspection date. It is valid for one year, and should be taken seriously. Meter maids can and will ticket for an outdated sticker, and if you are found driving without a valid inspection sticker, the citation for non-compliance is $50. Failure to complete inspection can also result in a suspended registration. You have until the last day of whatever month your inspection expires to get it re-inspected each year. (Note that, people being people, there can be significantly longer wait times at inspection stations on the last day of each month.)

AUTOMOBILE INSURANCE AND ACCIDENTS

Automobile insurance is required in Massachusetts. Coverage must include bodily injury to others, personal injury protection, bodily injury caused by an uninsured auto, and damage to someone else's property. **Compulsory coverage** includes:

- **Bodily injury to others** at $20,000 per person (maximum $40,000 per accident) for damages to anyone hurt or killed by your car in Massachusetts.
- **Personal injury protection** offers $8,000 for medical expenses; replacement services; and 75% of lost wages for you, passengers, and pedestrians, regardless of who is at fault for an accident.
- **Bodily injury caused by an uninsured auto** covers $20,000 per person and $40,000 per accident.
- **Damage to someone else's property** covers up to $5,000 for property damage in an accident.

You can, of course, opt for more coverage; look in the Yellow Pages or online for a complete listing of insurance carriers. You'll find that some well-known national discount insurers do not offer coverage in Massachusetts, and that rates don't vary much from one company to another. This is because the state, not private companies, sets insurance premiums each year. Massachusetts also offers the **Safe Driver Insurance Plan** (**SDIP**), a program that rewards low-risk drivers (those with cleaner driving records) with lower insurance rates. Essentially, the SDIP employs a point system to tally how risky a driver you are, factoring in such things as at-fault accidents and moving violations to adjust your insurance premium accordingly.

If you do get into an accident, don't leave the scene. Always call the police to make a report, no matter how minimal the accident might seem.

The following may be useful as you try to track down an insurer:

- **Massachusetts Office of Consumer Affairs and Business Regulation**, insurance information, www.mass.gov/doi/consumer
- **Citizen Information Service**, auto insurance discount information, www.sec. state.ma.us/cis/
- **Automobile Insurers Bureau for Massachusetts**, www.aib.org
- **Commonwealth Automobile Reinsurers**, www.commauto.com
- **Massachusetts RMV**, www.mass.gov/rmv

- **Better Business Bureau**, www.bbb.org; use their search feature to locate BBB-approved auto insurers in your area.
- **ChoicePoint Asset**, P.O. Box 105108, Atlanta, GA 30348-5108, www.choicetrust.com; order your CLUE (Comprehensive Loss Underwriting Exchange) report. This national database of consumers' automobile and homeowner's insurance claims is used by insurers when determining rates or denying coverage. Contact ChoicePoint if you find any errors.

AUTOMOBILE SAFETY

Most Bostonians will own up to their reputation as being some of the worst drivers anywhere. Well, worst as in *best*, if you value the ability to cut across three lanes of traffic without notice, reverse up one-way streets for entire blocks, and fit into nonexistent parking spots with only a few love taps to the car in front of you—all while navigating the city's unruly maze of narrow and congested roadways without causing an accident. In short, Boston's streets are a driving jungle, subject to the rules of the wild, and as such, local driving customs have evolved in Darwinian fashion. As the City of Boston's web site posts, "Boston drivers have created quite a name for themselves—and for good reason. If you choose to join the mayhem and drive a car on the streets of Boston, good luck and be careful."

Despite the aggressive driving habits of its residents, Boston routinely ranks at or near the top of the Surface Transportation Policy Project's reports on **pedestrian safety** in the fifty largest US metro areas. Boston is, by and large, a walking city, as more people walk to work here than in any other major American city—not to mention the thousands of students who live here without a car. Massachusetts state law requires that, if there are no traffic signals in place, drivers must yield to pedestrians in a crosswalk—you may be fined $100 if you fail to do so.

Driving under the influence of drugs or alcohol is illegal in Massachusetts. The legal blood alcohol limit is .08. If you are pulled over for driving under the influence, you will likely be arrested, have your car towed, and be given a breathalyzer test. (Refusing a breathalyzer in Massachusetts will result in an automatic license suspension of at least 180 days.) If you fail the breathalyzer test, on your first offense you will be fined, your license will be suspended for between 30 days and a year, and you may spend a night (or longer) in jail. A second offense carries a minimum thirty-day jail sentence, in addition to a two-year license suspension and heavy fines; a third offense is a felony charge. For more details go to www.mass.gov/ghsb/ or www.dui.com/states/massachusetts/.

Massachusetts is a **seatbelt** state. All occupants of a vehicle—be it a car, truck or van—including children in safety seats, must be properly buckled in. To enforce this rule, Massachusetts instigated its "Click it or Ticket" campaign to promote increased safety belt use. All children under the age of five or older ones up to 40 pounds are legally required to be in a safety seat. For older children, seatbelts must be used (child safety seats for all children up to 80 pounds are encouraged but not required.) A police officer can pull you over if he or she sees there is a child riding in the car without proper restraint. To learn more about Massachusetts' rules for driving with kids, visit the Governor's Highway Safety Bureau page at www.mass.gov/ghsb/. Also check the National Highway Transportation Safety Administration's web site (www.nhtsa.gov) for tips on what to look for in a child safety seat.

Boston is subject to all sorts of variations in weather, the most dangerous of which are **wintertime snow**, **sleet**, **freezing rain**, and **ice**. Black ice—basically invisible ice—is particularly treacherous. It's a good idea to check your tire treads and get your car tuned before the snow begins to fly. If your car has rear-wheel drive, well...good luck with that! For some excellent winter driving tips, check out www.cartalk.com/content/features/WinterDriving/. Lastly, consider taking the T. It runs in any weather, and while waiting in the cold isn't all that appealing, neither is skidding into a telephone pole.

For up-to-the-minute **traffic alerts**—crucial given the number of daily traffic jams in Boston—visit SmarTraveler.com, Boston.com/traffic/, or www.wbztv. com/traffic/ before you hit the road. You can also dial SmarTraveler at 617-374-1234, or listen to WBZ 1030 AM for traffic reports every 10 minutes.

Helpful auto safety web sites:

- **NHTSA.gov**; National Highway Transportation Safety Administration (NHTSA)
- **Mass.gov/ghsb**; State of Massachusetts Highway Safety Bureau
- **SafeKids.org**; National SAFE KIDS Campaign

CONSUMER PROTECTION—AUTOMOBILES

When you buy a car in Massachusetts, it's good to know about state lemon laws, which include the New and Leased Car Lemon Law, Used Vehicle Warranty Law, and Lemon Aid Law. These are intended to protect buyers from the misfortune of buying a car that is a dud. Legally, vehicle companies, after being given a fair crack at fixing the damage, have to replace their product. In Massachusetts, the **New and Leased Car Lemon Law** protects consumers who have bought or leased a new vehicle, motorcycle, van, or truck from a new-car dealer for personal or family purposes. It's good for up to one year or 15,000 miles, whichever comes first. State law defines a lemon as "a new or leased motor vehicle that has a defect which substantially impairs the use, market value, or safety of the vehicle, and which has not been repaired after a reasonable number of attempts," i.e., three times for the same problem or 15 business days out of service for any combination of problems. Then, you must give the manufacturer a formal seven business days "final repair attempt" to fix the problem. Because the law doesn't have an exact requirement as to what constitutes a "substantial" defect, it can be tricky to provide proof. Be sure to keep a record of all repair attempts, number of days in the shop, and any comments from the mechanics who worked on your vehicle. If your car is indeed a lemon, you are entitled to either a refund or a replacement vehicle. The Massachusetts Office of Consumer Affairs and Business Regulation provides more information at www.mass.gov/consumer/.

The **Used Vehicle Warranty Law** protects used car buyers; it covers pre-owned cars, vans, trucks, and demonstration vehicles sold by a Massachusetts dealer or private party. Vehicles purchased from dealers must cost $700 or more. The amount of coverage on a dealer-sold vehicle depends on the mileage on the odometer at the time of sale, and the warranty only covers defects that substantially impair the vehicle's use or safety. You can view full details online on the Massachusetts Office of Consumer Affairs and Business Regulation's web site at www.mass.gov/consumer/. If you want to make sure the used car you're buying was never designated a lemon, or if you suspect it was stolen, run the vehicle identification number through Carfax (888-422-7329 or www.carfax.com). On the National Highway Traffic Safety Administration's site (www.nhtsa.gov), you can perform a vehicle recall search through the Office of Defects Investigation database. For more legal tips on buying a used car in Massachusetts, check out the National Consumer Law Center's guide at www.neighborhoodlaw.org/cat/81/.

Last but not least, the coy but appropriately named **Lemon Aid Law** covers your new or used car or motorcycle, whether bought from a dealer or private individual, if it fails inspection within seven days of the sale date, and the estimated costs of repairs exceed 10% of the purchase price. Since this law covers you for only the first seven days following purchase, you should have your inspection done right away. For more information, go to www.mass.gov/consumer/.

If you need to have your car worked on, Massachusetts requires that auto mechanics provide fair customer service. First and most importantly, repairs not made "in a good and workman like manner, in accordance with accepted trade standards" must be corrected promptly and free of charge. Second, it's illegal for a shop to con you into paying for repairs that aren't necessary by telling you that they are; they must represent the necessity of the suggested work honestly. Always ask for a written estimate on work to be done on your car; mechanics must provide this, and they cannot charge you for repairs made without your permission. If repairs are going to exceed the projected price, the mechanic must get your authorization (verbal or written) before proceeding; otherwise, you don't have to pay the extra amount.

Here are some helpful resources for further consumer protection information:

- The **Massachusetts Trial Court Law Libraries** web site hosts a helpful collection of links pertaining to automobile law in Massachusetts: www.lawlib.

state.ma.us/auto.html.

- **Massachusetts Consumers' Coalition**, 617-349-6152, www.massconsumers. org; publishes a guide called "Car Smart," which covers purchasing a vehicle and consumer rights.
- **Massachusetts Attorney General's Office**, 617-727-2200, www.ago.state. ma.us; has a consumer affairs division, which includes a subsection on auto sales and repair that offers guides on car buying and the lemon aid law.
- **Massachusetts Office of Consumer Affairs and Business Regulation**, 617-973-8787, www.mass.gov/consumer; the state department in charge of all things consumer-related, they provide links on their web site to general auto information and lemon laws in particular.
- **Massachusetts Registry of Motor Vehicles**, 617-351-4500, www.mass. gov/rmv
- **Better Business Bureau,** 508-652-4800, www.bosbbb.org; provides a good deal of tips and publications on automobiles for the consumer.
- **National Highway Traffic Safety Administration**, 888-DASH-2-DOT, www. nhtsa.gov; provides information on vehicle recalls, crash tests, and all things safety related.
- **Federal Trade Commission Bureau of Consumer Protection**, 877-FTC-HELP, www.ftc.gov/bcp/menu-auto.htm

PARKING

Most cities suffer from too many cars trying to park in too few parking places, and Boston's old, narrow streets only exacerbate this common urban problem. Finding parking is particularly difficult in the historic districts such as downtown, the Back Bay, Beacon Hill, the North End, and Charlestown. Parking spaces are scarce during the spring, summer, and fall, and are almost nonexistent in the winter, when piles of snow cover many choice spots.

As the City of Boston's snow policy is one of snow repositioning rather than snow removal, parking wars are common. When city trucks come through to clear a path, they simply plow the center of the streets, which pushes masses of snow off to the sides of the street, burying any parked cars along the way. Hence, residents who have to shovel their cars out when it's time to drive to work the next day often become very protective of "their" spot. So, be advised: if you value your car's paint job or tires, think twice before removing a trash can, milk crate, or orange cone meant to designate someone's shoveled-out parking space. Also, if a street sign says no parking during a **snow emergency**, take heed; all cars on the street *will be towed* in the event of a winter storm.

BOSTON

Finding a legal place to leave your car in the city can be as confusing as it is difficult. When you find a spot, make sure you read all the nearby signs on your side of the street—even if you're obeying one sign, you might be violating another. For instance, resident sticker or not, everyone has to move their car for street cleaning, which occurs regularly between April 1 and November 31, or risk being ticketed or towed. Signs on your street will indicate the street-sweeping schedule in your neighborhood, or you can find it at www.cityofboston. gov/publicworks/.

Most parking meters in Boston operate Monday through Saturday, from 8 a.m. to 8 p.m., and only take quarters (there are a few multi-space meters—curbside kiosks that accept credit/debit cards, dollar bills, and coins, and give you a receipt to display in your car's window). During these hours, the parking rate is 25 cents per 15 minutes, with a maximum of 2 hours; there is a 1 hour time limit at all out-of-order meters. There is no fee or time limit at night or on Sundays. Meters with red caps have certain restrictions that are posted both on the meter and on a street sign; for instance, it may mean that you cannot park there during rush hours. Yellow-capped meters indicate that at certain times of the day (often in the morning), the spot is a commercial loading zone only—this is also posted both on the meter and on a street sign. For more information about parking rules and restrictions, check out www.cityofboston.gov/transportation/.

RESIDENT PARKING STICKERS

Many areas of Boston, particularly in densely populated neighborhoods and near T stops, require that cars display neighborhood-specific resident parking stickers to take advantage of legal on-street parking. The stickers are free, and the process to get them isn't terrible, but you must be a city resident, and your sticker is only valid for your own neighborhood. First, you must insure and register your car in Boston. Then, bring your vehicle's registration documents and proof of residency to Boston City Hall, Room 224, Office of the Parking Clerk, between 9 a.m. and 4:30 p.m., Monday–Friday. Be sure to pay any parking tickets *before* you get there, because you won't get a sticker if you have any outstanding citations. Proof of residence can be a recent utility bill, bank statement, water/sewer bill, credit card bill, or your signed lease; just be sure it has your name and address on it. After filling out the form, you'll receive a sticker, which you should affix to the inside of your rear window. Parking permits are now renewed every two years—when your sticker is about to expire, you will receive a notice from the Transportation Department, and you can renew by mail or online. For more information call **Resident Permits** at the **Office of the Parking Clerk** (Boston Transportation Department), 617-635-4682, or go to the City of Boston's web site, www.cityofboston.gov/transportation. You can download application and renewal forms online, and fill them out before visiting the parking clerk.

PARKING TICKETS AND TOWING

Boston's parking enforcement officials are so zealous that some Boston residents include a parking ticket fund in their monthly budgets. Tickets start at $15 and can exceed $100, depending on the offense. Parking at an expired meter ($25) or in a resident permit-only space ($40) will usually just yield a ticket; failing to move your car for street cleaning, or parking in certain restricted spots, like hand-icapped spaces, private lots, or construction zones, will often result in towing. If a ticket goes unpaid for more than 21 days, the fine will increase, and once you accumulate five or more overdue tickets, your car may be booted or towed.

To pay a parking ticket, mail your payment using the accompanying gar-ish orange envelope, go in person to Boston City Hall, or pay online by debit or credit card at www.cityofboston.gov/parking (you'll need the violation num-ber). Methods of payment include cash, check, Visa, MasterCard, or money order. If you wish to appeal the ticket, you may state your case in a letter (be sure to include any photographs or other evidence), or go in person to the Office of the Parking Clerk at City Hall to request a hearing. For more information, visit www.cityofboston.gov/transportation/appeal.asp. If you walk outside to find your car shackled with the dreaded boot, you'll need to pay $56 for the boot removal *and* all of your outstanding parking violations; personal and business checks are *not* accepted for boot removals. Once payment is received at either Boston City Hall or the Boston Transportation Department (BTD) tow lot (200 Frontage Road, 617-635-3900), your car should be released within an hour and a half.

To find out if your car has been towed by the city for parking tickets or any other reason (such as a snow emergency) call **Public Information/Ticket Infor-mation** at 617-635-4410. If it has been towed, you're going to have to follow the same procedure as if your car were booted. You will be responsible for all out-standing tickets, a towing fee, and a storage fee of $15 per day. For directions to the tow lot, go to www.cityofboston.gov/transportation/towdirections.asp.

If a private company has towed your car (for parking in a private lot, say), the city might not have a record of the towing. Before you panic and file a stolen car report, check the area where you parked for posted signs bearing the name and number of a towing company. Getting your car out of a private tow lot will cost you upwards of $100—and a piece of your sanity—so beware of Private Parking signs.

COMMUTER PARKING

Parking in Boston and its surrounding communities is both difficult and expen-sive, so unless your office offers a parking space, commuting here by car should be a last resort. Boston's public transit is good and many people outside of Boston drive each day to an MBTA commuter lot or T station and head into downtown on a bus, commuter rail, T train, or commuter boat. Lots vary in price, but are usually just a few dollars or less per day. Depending on size, location, and popularity with commuters, lots may fill up quickly. For example, the Alewife station lot, at the end of the Red Line, has almost 2,600 spaces, while Oak Grove has fewer than 1,000 spots and can fill up even before the morning rush is over. To check current parking rates at the MBTA lot nearest you, visit www.mbta.com. As an incentive to get commuters to use public transportation, you can receive a discount on auto insurance if you use monthly T (subway or bus) passes. Provide your insurance company with 11 out of 12 of them annually as proof, and you'll get 10% off collision and property damage insurance, up to $75.

Failing public transportation, there are parking lots and garages all over the city, many of which offer monthly rates. They vary in terms of price, security, and convenience; smaller lots, where you may have to leave your keys, and your car may be blocked in for part or most of the day, run from $12 to $20, while garage parking typically costs between $20 and $35 per day.

Persons with disabilities may park at any parking meter in the city of Boston, for free and without the usual 2-hour time limit, provided they display a valid HP/V license plate or placard.

STOLEN AUTOMOBILES

Auto theft isn't quite an epidemic in Boston, but that's not to say it doesn't happen, and fairly often. Always lock your doors, close your windows, and hide anything of value from plain sight, especially laptop bags. Many Boston car owners invest in some sort of anti-theft device, whether it's a simple steering wheel lock, an electronic alarm, LoJack, or a system that shuts off your engine if a secret code isn't entered once the car has been started.

If your car is missing, first make sure you know which town you parked in (boundaries can be blurry for newcomers) before you call to find out if it has been towed. Once you're sure it hasn't been towed, you must go to the police precinct with jurisdiction over the area from which the car was stolen, and fill out a report (see the **Neighborhood** sections for precinct addresses and phone numbers). You will need your vehicle ID number, the title, and the license plate number. It goes without saying that if you have photocopied your title, registration, and proof of insurance, your task will be much easier.

The Governor's Auto Theft Strike Force runs a toll-free anonymous tip line, 1-800-HOT-AUTO, to help stop car thieves, in addition to their Vehicle Identification Number (VIN) Etching program. Etching your VIN into the windows is quick, costs only $10, and can reduce your auto insurance rate by 15%, while making your car far less appealing to thieves who would have to replace the windows.

PARKING—BEYOND BOSTON PROPER

Outside of Boston, check with your local police or traffic department for specifics on parking citations, overnight street parking guidelines, snow restrictions, visitor permits, and towing details:

- **Arlington**: Parking Clerk, 781-316-3035; Police Department, 781-316-3900; www.town.arlington.ma.us; no overnight street parking (between 1 a.m. and 7 a.m.)
- **Belmont**: Parking Clerk, 617-993-2770; Belmont Police Traffic Department, 617-993-2530; www.town.belmont.ma.us; no overnight street parking (between 1 a.m. and 7 a.m.)
- **Brookline**: Transportation Department, 617-730-2177; Police Department, Traffic and Parking Clerk, 617-730-2230, www.townofbrooklinemass.com, www.brooklinepolice.com (to pay tickets online); no overnight street parking (2 a.m. to 6 a.m.), though the town has started to make overnight spaces in its public lots available for rent at $100 per month.
- **Cambridge**: Traffic, Parking, and Transportation Department, 617-349-4700, www.cambridgema.gov/traffic/; Police tow line, 617-349-3300; Cambridge has a resident permit program similar to Boston's ($8 fee), and also offers visitor parking passes (one per household).
- **Dedham**: Police Department, 781-751-9300; www.dedham-ma.gov
- **Malden**: Traffic Commission, 781-397-7190; Police Department, 781-397-7171; www.ci.malden.ma.us; resident permit parking in some areas, visitor passes available.
- **Medford**: Police Department, 781-391-6404, www.medfordpolice.com; overnight parking allowed on one side of street only from December through April; resident parking permits cost $10.
- **Milton**: Parking Clerk, 617-898-4876; www.townofmilton.org
- **Newton**: Parking Department, 617-796-1344, www.ci.newton.ma.us; overnight (2 a.m. to 6 a.m.) on-street parking prohibited from November through April.
- **Quincy**: Parking Clerk, 617-376-1060; Traffic Department, 617-376-1406; www.ci.quincy.ma.us
- **Somerville**: Somerville Office of Traffic and Parking, 617-666-3311, www.ci.somerville.ma.us; resident parking permits are available for $10; during a declared snow emergency, parking is allowed on odd-numbered side of the street only; if your car has been towed in Somerville, call Pat's Towing Service directly at 617-776-5810.
- **Waltham**: Transportation and Parking, 781-314-3400, www.city.waltham.ma.us; unless posted, no overnight (2 a.m. to 6 a.m.) on-street parking—enforced more strictly in winter.
- **Watertown**: Watertown Police Traffic Department, 617-972-6547, www.watertownpd.org; no overnight (1 a.m. to 6 a.m.) on-street parking, strictly enforced from November through April.

VOTER REGISTRATION

You can register to vote a number of ways: at your local election office, city or town hall, when you get your driver's license, or by mail. Residents of Massachusetts who are US citizens and at least 18 years of age on Election Day are eligible to vote. If you'd like a mail-in registration form, call 617-727-2828 or 800-462-VOTE to have one sent to you, or go online to www.sec.state.ma.us/ele/elestu/stuidx.htm. You may also sign up in person at your city or town hall, or any Massachusetts RMV office. To vote in an upcoming election, you must be registered 20 days in advance. You will need proof of residence, which can be a lease, utility bill, or driver's license. For a comprehensive link to all things voting-related in the Commonwealth, go to the **Citizens' Information Service** at www.state.ma.us/sec/ele/eleidx.htm.

Boston and other cities have their own local elections, but in many towns, New England–style **town meetings** (either open or representative) are still the form of local governance. To get involved, contact your town or city hall to find out about meeting schedules and agendas.

Following is a listing of voter registration information:

- **Boston**, Election Department, 1 City Hall Plaza, Room 241, 617-635-4635, www.cityofboston.gov/elections
- **Arlington**, Town Hall, 730 Mass Ave, 781-316-3076
- **Belmont**, Town Hall, 455 Concord Ave, 617-993-2600
- **Brookline**, Town Clerk's Office, 11 Pierce St, 617-730-2010; town meeting information available at www.mybrookline.com.
- **Cambridge**, City Hall, 795 Mass Ave, 617-349-4260; www.cambridgema.gov
- **Dedham**, Town Hall, 26 Bryant St, 781-751-9145
- **Malden**, City Hall, 200 Pleasant St, Room 323, 781-397-7116
- **Medford**, City Hall, 85 George P. Hassett Dr, 781-393-2425
- **Milton**, Town Hall, 525 Canton Ave, 617-898-4859; go to www.townofmilton.org for town meeting information.
- **Newton**, Election Commission, City Hall, 1000 Comm Ave, Room 106, 617-796-1350
- **Quincy**, Elections Commission, City Hall, 1305 Hancock St, 617-376-1141
- **Somerville**, Election Department, City Hall, 93 Highland Ave, 617-625-6600
- **Waltham**, City Clerk's Office, City Hall, 610 Main St, 781-314-3120
- **Watertown**, Town Clerk's Office, Town Hall, 149 Main St, 617-972-6486

Outside of the greater Boston area, you can find your town hall address at www.state.ma.us/sec/ele/eleclk/clkidx.htm.

Political parties with offices in the area include:

- **Massachusetts Democratic Party**, 617-776-2676, www.massdems.org
- **Massachusetts Republicans**, 617-523-5005, www.massgop.com

- **Libertarian Party**, 800-JOIN-LPM, www.lpmass.org
- **Green–Rainbow Party**, 978-688-2068, www.massgreens.org

For voter information from the **Massachusetts League of Women Voters**, call 617-723-1421 or visit www.lvwma.org. For questions about or to report ethical issues (voter fraud, illegal contributions, etc.), contact the **State Ethics Commission** at 617-371-9500 or go to www.mass.gov/ethics.

SOCIAL SECURITY

All information for new and replacement Social Security Cards can be found on the Social Security Administration's (SSA) web site, www.ssa.gov. You can download the application form (Form SS-5), and then either mail it or take it to the nearest Social Security office with the proper supporting documentation. You don't need an appointment and it doesn't cost anything.

The main Social Security office in Boston is at 10 Causeway Street, Room 148, in the Tip O'Neill Building by North Station. However, there are other offices in the greater Boston area that might be more convenient; find one by entering your zip code on the SSA web site. If you don't want to go online, you can call 800-772-1213 and get all the same information and forms.

PASSPORTS

As of 2007, Americans are required to carry passports when traveling between the US and Mexico or Canada; the ensuing demand has overburdened the system, and at this point it's a wise idea to begin your passport application process several months before a planned trip, no matter where you're going.

To get a passport or renew an old one, you may apply at a number of local passport acceptance facilities, such as libraries, post offices, courts, and county and municipal offices. Depending on your needs, you may apply either in person or through the mail. You *must* apply in person if: you are applying for a passport for the first time; your previous passport was lost or damaged; your previous passport was issued over 15 years ago and has expired, or was issued before you were 16; your name is different than it was on your last passport and you don't have any legal proof of the change; or you are between the ages of 14 and 17 years old. Otherwise, you may apply or renew through the mail. Either way, a new passport costs $97 ($82 for those under 16), and renewals are $67.

Passport application forms are available at the National Passport Information Center web site (NPIC, www.travel.state.gov), or from passport acceptance facilities. When you apply for your passport, you'll need to fill out the application form (DS-11), and bring proof of US citizenship, proof of identity, two passport photos, money, and a social security number. Acceptable documents proving your citizenship include a previous passport, certified birth certificate, consular report of birth abroad, naturalization certificate, or certificate of citizenship. Acceptable documents proving your identity include a previous passport; naturalization certificate; certificate of citizenship; or a current and valid ID (driver's license, state ID, military ID). Passport photos, two identical 2" x 2" color headshots, can be obtained at photo shops, pharmacies, or AAA offices.

You can apply for a passport at any number of official **passport acceptance facilities** throughout the city, all of which operate on weekdays only, including the Back Bay Post Office (31 St. James St, 617-236-7800); Boston City Hall (Room M5, 617-635-4488); JFK Station Post Office (25 New Chardon St, 617-523-6566); Milk Street Post Office (31 Milk St, 617-482-1956); as well as most other post offices in the city and town clerk's offices in surrounding communities. To find the passport acceptance facility most convenient for you, visit http://iafdb.travel.state.gov and enter your home or work address.

You should allow *at least* six weeks for processing—if you don't have that much time, the State Department offers expedited service for $60, which should take about two weeks. Boston is one of the few cities in the US that has its own passport agency, so you may go directly to the **Boston Passport Agency** in the Tip O'Neill Federal Building, 10 Causeway St, Room 247; they only service customers who are traveling within 14 days, and by appointment only. Bring your tickets or itinerary showing your short-notice trip schedule along with the standard passport-related documents. Hours of operation are Monday–Friday, 9 a.m. to 4 p.m., and the nearest T stop is North Station. Schedule an appointment at any time by calling 877-487-2778.

Regardless of which office processes your application, all passports originate in the same place: the US Department of State. For a first-line source of information regarding your application needs, current processing times, and the status of your passport, go to www.travel.state.gov.

LIBRARY CARDS

Boston's main library at Copley Square was the first large city library in the US opened to the general public. Today, most of the greater Boston area libraries are networked, so if you have a library card in one city or town, you will be able to check out books from other libraries or even at neighboring colleges. Public library memberships are free.

The **Boston Public Library** has branches in every neighborhood in Boston, and shares borrowing privileges with the communities of Chelsea and Malden through the **Metro Boston Library Network**. If you are a member of this network, you can use any of the Boston neighborhood branches, the libraries in the Boston public school system, the State Transportation Library, and the public libraries in Chelsea and Malden. The **Minuteman Library Network** links many major communities surrounding Boston and to the west, including Cambridge, Somerville, Wellesley, Arlington, Concord, Weston, Needham, Dedham, Medford, Brookline, Watertown, Waltham, Newton, Belmont, a few colleges, and more. To see the complete listing of linked communities and libraries, visit www.mln.lib. ma.us. Further out from the city are the **North of Boston Library Exchange** (www.noblenet.org), which links several north shore communities such as Peabody, Lynnfield, Beverly, Swampscott, Salem, Gloucester, and Marblehead; the **Merrimack Valley Library Consortium** (www.mvlc.org), which includes libraries closer to the New Hampshire border like Burlington, Andover, Newburyport, Lawrence, and Haverhill; and the **Old Colony Library Network** (www.ocln.org), which links south shore communities like Hingham, Hull, Milton, Plymouth, Sharon, and Cohasset.

You will find exact library locations listed in the **neighborhood profiles** in this book, so check there for the library closest to you. If you live further out from the city, you can check with the **Massachusetts Board of Library Commissioners** (www.mblc.state.ma.us, 617-725-1860 or 800-952-7403), or click "Other Networks" on the Old Colony Library Network web site (www.ocln.org), to find links to other major library networks throughout the state.

Boston's main library is at 700 Boylston Street, 617-536-5400, www.bpl.org. To get a library card, the **Boston** library system requires proof of Massachusetts residence and some sort of ID with your signature on it (it doesn't have to be a photo ID). Most cities require one proof of residence in the form of a driver's license, check book, bill, etc., which shows both your name and an address in that town. Others require two forms of identification showing your name and local address, one being a photo ID. Call your local library or check their web site for membership requirements before you go down there to apply. (See **Literary Life** in the **Cultural Life** chapter for more on area libraries.)

FINDING A HEALTH CARE PROVIDER

Finding a new doctor isn't something one looks forward to when moving to a new city—but neither is braving an unexpected health emergency without a physician you know and trust. The good news is Boston has some of the most well-renowned medical institutions in the world. People come from all over to see specialists at Mass General or the Dana-Farber Cancer Institute, and many hospitals are affiliated with top area medical schools: BU is partnered with the Boston Medical Center, Tufts with the New England Medical Center, and Harvard with Boston's Longwood medical campus, which includes Dana-Farber, Children's Hospital, Beth Israel/Deaconess, Brigham and Women's, and the Joslin Diabetes Center. So where to begin? Like anything else, the best recommendation might come from a friend or coworker. Short of that, the following list of resources may help steer you in the right direction.

- **American Board of Medical Specialties Certification Verification**, 866-ASK-ABMS, www.abms.org; check to see if your specialist is certified by the national board.
- **Massachusetts Board of Registration in Medicine**, http://profiles.massmed board.org; get the full skinny on a physician's profile, including where they went to school, where they performed their residency, and any malpractice claims.
- **Division of Professional Licensure**, 617-727-3074, www.mass.gov/reg; here you can verify licenses to practice medicine, dentistry, therapy, nursing, speech therapy, physical therapy, podiatry, nutrition, while also being informed of any recent disciplinary actions.
- **Massachusetts Dental Society**, 508-480-9797, www.massdental.org; find a dentist who is a member of this professional association.
- **Massachusetts Department of Public Health**, 250 Washington St, Boston, 617-624-6000, www.mass.gov/dph; a good starting point for all health issues in the state.
- **HealthGrades.com** allows visitors to search their free hospital ratings or purchase a complete report on a physician or facility.

Those with health insurance through an HMO or PPO generally have a smaller pool of doctors, dentists, etc., to choose from. For more information on Massachusetts HMOs, go to the Department of Insurance web site, www.mass.gov/doi/.

As of July 1, 2007, **all Massachusetts residents are required to maintain health insurance**. If you are not eligible for coverage through your employer, **Commonwealth Connector**—the state agency in charge of the mandatory health care initiative—operates two basic programs to assist you: Commonwealth Care (www.macommonwealthcare.com), which offers subsidized plans for lower income residents, and Commonwealth Choice, for those who don't qualify for financial assistance. Visit the Commonwealth Connector web site at www.mahealthconnector.org or call 877-MA-ENROLL to learn about eligibility information, to compare plans, or to enroll.

If you are not insured, the **Massachusetts League of Community Health Centers** (**CHS**, 100 Boylston Street, Boston, 617-426-2225, massleague.org) can put you in touch with a community health center in your neighborhood. Community Health Centers provide comprehensive health services, such as primary care, OB/GYN, dermatology, and elder care, to the under-served (i.e., low-income, underinsured, high-risk patients). One in nine Bay State residents goes to a CHC; there's a community health center in the North End, for example, staffed with Mass General doctors and utilized by many neighborhood residents. The Department of Public Health's **Division of Primary Care and Health Access** provides family planning services, including STD testing, birth control, pap smears, and pregnancy testing, to low-income, uninsured Massachusetts residents and all residents under the age of 20. Contact them for information or the family planning program site closest to you at 617-624-6012 or www.mass.gov/dph.

In the event that either you or a loved one need emergency inpatient psychiatric care, the Boston area is also home to McLean Hospital (115 Mill Street, Belmont, 617-855-2000, www.mcleanhospital.org), one of the most prestigious psychiatric hospitals in the world. Located on a hilly campus outside of the city, it is affiliated with Harvard University and Mass General. Another mental health resource is the **Massachusetts Department of Mental Health** (25 Staniford Street, Boston, 617-626-8000, www.mass.gov/dmh).

Should you run into problems with your health care provider, start with the DPH's **Office of Patient Protection**. Call 800-436-7757 or visit www.mass.gov/dph/opp.

PETS

While Boston, like most large cites, isn't perfectly pet-friendly, it did top Dog-Friendly.com's 2007 list of best dog-friendly vacation cities in North America. Leashed dogs are allowed on the subway, and there are plenty of parks in which to walk your pooch, if not a lot of backyard space. It can be difficult to find a rental apartment that is large enough for a big dog, or that permits them in the first place, but it doesn't seem to deter dog lovers—Boston Animal Control claims there are approximately 65,000 dogs in the city, equivalent to 10% of the city's human population! Finding a suitable place to live with a dog-friendly greenspace nearby may take a little extra effort on your part; as anywhere, cat lovers are apt to have an easier time finding an accommodating landlord.

A helpful guide to living in Boston with a dog is *The Dog Lovers Companion to Boston* by Joanna Downey and Christian J. Lau. You can also check www.dogfriendly.com, a national listing of pet-friendly places and businesses, or www.doggeek.com, which offers tips on choosing, obtaining, and caring for a dog, as well as local information.

ADOPTING A PET

If you'd like a pet, you can't beat adopting from a local shelter. Pets come spayed or neutered, many have been housebroken, and the cost is reasonable. The main headquarters of the **Massachusetts Society for the Prevention of Cruelty to Animals** (**MSPCA**, 617-522-7400, www.mspca.org) is in Jamaica Plain at 350 South Huntington Avenue. They have adoption hours for dogs, cats, rabbits, birds, and other more exotic animals from Tuesday through Saturday. They are also the best resource for animal information, including education, tips on renting an apartment if you have a pet, and vet recommendations. Affiliated shelters are located throughout the state on the north and south shores, western Massachusetts, Cape Cod, Nantucket, and Martha's Vineyard. There are also several private, volunteer **no-kill shelters** in the area including: the **Quincy Animal Shelter** (617-376-1349, www.quincyanimalshelter.org); the **Melrose Humane Society** (781-662-3224, www.melrosehumanesociety.org); **Baypath Humane Society of Hopkinton** (508-435-6938, www.baypathhumane.org); and the **Scituate Animal Shelter** (781-545-8703, www.town.scituate.ma.us/animalshelter/).

Additional pet adoption resources include:

- **Alliance for Animals Metro Action Clinic**, 232 Silver St, South Boston, 617-268-7800, www.afaboston.org; pet adoption center, low-cost veterinary services, and animal rights advocacy.
- **Animal Rescue League of Boston**, 10 Chandler St, 617-426-9170, www.arl boston.org; adoption center open daily, and runs affiliated adoption centers in Dedham and East Brewster (Cape Cod).
- **Boston Animal Control** (includes dog licenses), Boston City Hall, Room 811, 617-635-5348, www.cityofboston.gov/animalcontrol
- **City of Boston Adoption Center**, 26 Mahler Rd, Roslindale, 617-635-1800
- **Boston.craigslist.org**; the local branch of this popular online classifieds site has a thread devoted to pets—including adoption, pet sitting, dog walking, and other services—with dozens of new posts daily.
- **Doggeek.com**; offers links and informational resources on dog sitting, pet care, veterinary services, adoption, parks, kennels, and much more.
- **Massachusetts Ferret Friends**, 781-224-1098, www.maferrets.org
- **Massachusetts House Rabbit Society**, 781-665-9962, www.mahouserabbit. org
- **Petfinder.com**; search for pets at shelters around the city and country.

PET LAWS AND SERVICES

Check with **Boston Animal Control** (1 City Hall Plaza, Room 811, Boston, 617-635-5348, www.cityofboston.gov/animalcontrol) for information about dog licenses, vaccines, adoptions, advice, pet abuse prevention, and more. If you have **lost your pet**, contact the shelter at 617-635-1800 (they hold an animal for between seven and 10 days).

Massachusetts requires dog owners to have their dogs licensed annually; non-compliance may result in a $50 fine. To obtain a **dog license**, bring or mail your application (available for download from their web site), check/money order, and proof of rabies inoculation to Boston City Hall, Animal Control, Room 811, Boston, MA 02201. The fee is $17 for unspayed or unneutered dogs; $6 if they are spayed or neutered; and $50 for Pit Bulls. In 2004, the City of Boston passed an ordinance requiring Pit Bull owners to spay or neuter their pets, to post warning signs outside their homes, and to muzzle their dogs while in public areas (violation of the ordinance carries a $100 fine).

All dogs are required by law to be leashed in public areas at all times. While it's not uncommon to see owners of well-behaved dogs breaking this rule in more pet-friendly parks, they still run the risk of getting a citation. In the state campgrounds where pets are permitted, dogs must be leashed, supervised, and wearing proof of their rabies vaccination. *No matter where you are, you must clean up after your dog.*

VETERINARIANS AND PET EMERGENCY SERVICE

Boston boasts one of the country's top animal hospitals, the **MSPCA Angell Memorial Animal Hospital** (350 South Huntington Avenue, Jamaica Plain, 617-522-7282, www.angell.org). Come here for 24-hour emergency services or contact them for a referral to other veterinary clinics.

Veterinarians abound throughout the city and the suburbs; you'll find many listed in the Yellow Pages. Doggeek.com also maintains a list of vets statewide at www.doggeek.com/Vets/Massachusetts.shtml. The best source is generally through a referral, so talk with your neighbors, go for a walk in the park, or call the **MSPCA**. You can also check out a veterinarian's record with the **Division of Professional Licensure** (617-727-3074, www.mass.gov/reg). Here are a few to get you started:

- **Boston Cat Hospital** in Kenmore Square, 665 Beacon St, 617-266-7877, specializes in felines.
- **East Boston Animal Clinic**, 1007 Saratoga St, 617-567-0101, www.bostonvet.com
- **Fresh Pond Animal Hospital**, 15 Flanders Rd, Belmont, 617-484-1555
- **Boston Veterinary Associates**, www.bostonvet.com; South Boston Animal Hospital: 659 E Broadway, 617-269-0610; East Boston Animal Hospital: 1007 Saratoga St, 617-567-0101
- **Brookline Animal Hospital**, 678 Brookline Ave, Brookline, 617-277-2030
- **Parkway Veterinary Hospital**, 18 Spring St, West Roxbury, 617-469-8400, www.parkwayvethospital.com

OFF-LEASH AREAS AND DOG-FRIENDLY PARKS

- **Armory Playground** on Armory St in Brookline; off-leash hours from dawn to 1 p.m.
- **Arnold Arboretum** in JP (leashed); expansive park.
- **Back Bay Fens**, in the Fenway (leashed).
- **Belle Isle Reservation**, for dogs in Eastie (leashed).
- **Boston Common**; owners of well-behaved dogs may let them run off-leash in the Common, on the lawn at the corner of Beacon and Charles streets. Be careful, though, as the area is not fenced in, and cars whiz past on the adjacent streets.

- **Brookline Avenue Playground,** almost 4 acres of fenced-in lawn in Brookline; off-leash hours from dawn to 1 p.m. in summer, and dawn 'til dusk in winter.
- **Cambridge Dog Park,** at the intersection of Mt. Auburn and Hawthorne streets, is an off-leash park for dogs under voice control.
- **Carleton Court Dog Park,** off-leash, fenced-in area resembling an old tennis court on Holyoke St in the South End (by the Southwest Corridor Park).
- **Carson Beach** in Southie, between Labor Day and Memorial Day (leashed).
- **Charlesgate Dog Run** in the Back Bay; small but serviceable fenced-in dog park on the corner of Mass Ave and Beacon St.
- **Charles River Esplanade,** a favorite for joggers with dogs (leashed)--be careful of the bicyclists.
- **Comm Ave. Mall,** where all the Back Bay residents walk their dogs (leashed).
- **Dorchester Park,** Tenean Beach off Morrissey Blvd in Dorchester (leashed).
- **Fort Independence,** big castle and beach walk in Southie (leashed).
- **Fort Washington Park,** on Waverly St in Cambridge, offers an off-leash run for dogs under voice control.
- **Kingsley Park** in Cambridge at Huron Ave and Fresh Pond Pkwy (leashed); parking is for Cambridge residents only.
- **Larz Anderson Park** in Brookline; strictly on-leash.
- **Peters Park,** www.peterspark.org, is a popular off-leash dog park in the South End, at E Berkeley and Washington streets.

Further out of the city, there is obviously more space to roam; try the **Blue Hills Reservation,** a huge state park at the edge of Milton (leashed), the **Middlesex Fells Reservation,** which offers 2,000 dog-friendly acres of forest (dog owners usually enter via the Sheepfold parking lot in Medford), or the **Stodders Neck Dog Park** in Hingham, an off-leash, 3/4-mile looped trail that runs along the water.

SAFETY AND CRIME

As in any other major American city, crime is a fact of life in Boston. A decade of steadily sinking crime levels at the end of the 21st century prompted envious city leaders from around the country to come study the "Boston Miracle"—when murders in the city plunged from a peak of 152 in 1990 to 39 in 1999. The early years of this decade brought crime levels creeping back, however, and in 2005 the murder rate shot up significantly. That year's 75 murders represented a ten-year high and a 17% increase over the year before; 2006 didn't fare much better, with 74 murders. In addition, nonfatal shootings doubled in those two years, and reported rapes, vehicle theft, and aggravated assault rates all remain higher than average. There are a variety of reasons for the increase in crime, depending on whom you ask: police funding has been steadily decreasing, after-school programs have been cut, the city's population of teenagers has risen dramatically, and many former gang members—arrested during the clean-up efforts of the '90s—are now being released from jail, looking to pick up where they left off.

While this trend is discouraging to say the least, the majority of violent crime in Boston tends not to be random, and is largely isolated in the poorer areas of the city like Roxbury, Mattapan, and Dorchester. The T is generally safe (the Orange Line has the highest levels of incidents; be wary in the early afternoon, after high school gets out). And adjacent communities like Cambridge, Brookline, and Newton make the Boston metropolitan area as a whole feel much safer. As you look for your new home, Boston.com's community profiles include a helpful crime index rating (where 100 is the national average), if you'd like to compare towns and neighborhoods in terms of crime. There is also an interactive map of reported crimes in the city of Boston (including brief descriptions from the police reports) at www.boston-online.com/crime, which can be useful in identifying riskier areas of the city. The Boston Police Department also posts updated crime data at www.bpdnews.com. For more safety resources in the state of Massachusetts, go to www.mass.gov and click "For Residents" and then "Safety."

If you find yourself the victim of a crime, you should first call the police (911), and then check with the **Massachusetts Office for Victim Assistance** (MOVA, 1 Ashburton Place, Suite 1101, Boston, 617-727-5200, www.mass.gov/mova), which offers a variety of resources and support services.

Those with concerns about domestic abuse should first contact the **Massachusetts Department of Transitional Assistance**, which runs a **Domestic Violence Unit** (www.mass.gov/dta/). Their mission is to help battered women and children live self-sufficient, violence-free lives. They have safety assessment specialists who can put you in touch with appropriate resources and agencies. **MOVA** also has a similar list of resources on their web site.

The Massachusetts Department of Public Health (DPH) takes care of the state's **Sexual Assault Prevention and Survivor Services** office, and provides a list of rape crisis centers. They are located at 250 Washington Street, in Boston. Go to www.mass.gov/dph/fch/sapss/ or call 617-624-5457 for more information. To contact the main **Boston Area Rape Crisis Center** (99 Bishop Allen Drive, Cambridge), call 617-492-RAPE or visit www.barcc.org. If you need information from the state's **Sex Offender Registry Board** about victim services, resources, or safety tips, go to their web site at www.mass.gov/sorb, or call them at 978-740-6400 or 800-93-MEGAN.

Massachusetts has been sponsoring the **Safe Neighborhood Initiative** (**SNI**), a collaboration of the State Attorney General's office, the Boston Police Department, the City of Boston, and other offices, since 1993. SNI is a forum where community residents voice their concerns and advise their local police, neighborhood prosecutors, and city government about the crime and safety issues that confront them. The goal of the SNI is to coordinate law enforcement, revitalize neighborhoods, and prevent crime by intervening and treating high-risk offenders. If you'd like more information about SNI, or would like to initiate an SNI in your neighborhood, visit the Attorney General's web site at www.ago. state.ma.us and click on "School and Community Safety," or call 617-727-2200. In addition, the Boston Police Department has headed the **Boston Neighborhood Crime Watch Program** since 1985. Contact them at 617-343-4345 or visit www. bostoncrimewatch.com for safety tips, citizen alerts—or if you'd like to join or form a crime watch in your neighborhood. The BPD also sponsors Crime Stoppers, a program that highlights unsolved violent crimes in the local news media. Viewers or readers with information can call the tip hotline at 800-494-TIPS or text the word "TIP" to CRIME (27463); it is 100% anonymous, and if the information you provide yields an arrest, you will be eligible for a reward of up to $1,000.

In any urban setting, there are some common sense steps everyone should take:

- Trust your intuition when something doesn't feel right.
- When outside, keep your eyes and ears open; always remain alert and aware of your surroundings.
- Avoid walking alone at night—your vulnerability to street crime decreases by as much as 70% just by being in a group. If you must walk alone, avoid poorly lit areas, alleys, shortcuts, or unfamiliar neighborhoods, and refrain from talking on your cell phone or listening to headphones—so you can hear if anyone is approaching you. If you feel you are being followed, do your best to stay in a well-lit public place, and call 911 with your location.
- Never let a stranger get in your car, and don't get in a car with a stranger. Studies show that once you are in a vehicle with a would-be criminal, your chances of survival decrease dramatically.
- Don't move into a neighborhood where you don't feel comfortable. Before you accept an apartment, walk around the neighborhood at different times of day to get an impression of what the area is like.
- Protect your apartment or home from potential intruders. For example, in a ground floor or garden apartment, you should probably have sturdy bars on your windows. Check your door for a deadbolt. If it doesn't have one, request that your landlord install one for you. Always err on the side of caution when assessing your risk.
- On public transportation, try to sit in a car with other people. On a bus, sit up front near the driver.
- Strap purses and bags across your chest, not over your shoulder, so they're more difficult to steal.
- Don't leave bags on the passenger seat of your car when you're driving; they're easy for someone to reach in and grab. Lock your car when you park it, and put any items out of sight or in the trunk so as not to tempt thieves. Also, visible auto theft deterrent items, such as a steering wheel lock, make a car less inviting.
- Report a crime by calling 911. (From a cell phone, 911 will dial the State Police,

who can transfer you to the local authorities if necessary. You can dial the Boston Police directly from a cell phone at 617-343-4911 in an emergency.) For non-emergency police questions, call the BPD at 617-343-4200; they can tell you the location of your nearest District or Area police headquarters.

SETTING UP YOUR HOME MAY REQUIRE HIRING OUT FOR A FEW SER-vices. Some of the services you'll find in this chapter are those designed to make your life easier, like house cleaning and pest control. Other services detailed, such as **Services for People with Disabilities, International Newcomers,** and **Gay and Lesbian Life**, are relevant to specific communities of people.

DOMESTIC SERVICES

Sometimes a little help goes a long way, particularly around the house. Some of the following services are luxuries and some of them are must-haves, but regardless, they're all sure to make adjusting to life in your new home smoother.

DIAPER SERVICES

Diaper services, while on the decline, do still exist in the area:

- **Baby's Laundry and Diaper Services**, 135 Boston St, Salem, 978-744-4162
- **Changing Habits Diaper Service**, 588 Greenfield Rd, Deerfield, 800-286-6622, www.changinghabits.com
- **Dede's Dide's Diaper Service**, 0 Hillcrest Ave, Peabody, 978-532-5901

DRY CLEANING DELIVERY

Dry cleaners aren't too difficult to come by; generally you should be able to find one within walking distance. If you prefer to have pick-up and delivery service, the list is smaller. Here are a few:

- **Charlesbank Cleaners**: 17 Myrtle St, Beacon Hill, 617-523-6860; locations also in Allston, Cambridge, and Newton.

- **Lapel's Dry Cleaning**, 866-695-2735, www.lapelsdrycleaning.com; various locations in Boston metro area, including Boston, Brighton, Concord, Framingham, Quincy, and Salem.
- **Pressed 4 Time**, 978-823-8301, www.pressed4time.com; serving locations around metro Boston; also does laundry service, shoe repair and alterations.
- **Sarni Cleaners of Greater Boston**, 617-742-1311; locations throughout Boston.
- **Stavros Cleaners**, 1292 Beacon St, Brookline, 617-277-1215
- **Zoots Dry Cleaning**, www.zoots.com; locations around the metro area including Cambridge, Quincy, and Newton.

HOUSE CLEANING SERVICES

In addition to regular house cleaning, most services also offer special one-day cleaning arrangements for moving days (either in or out) or for fire restoration. Look in the Yellow Pages under "House Cleaning Service" for a complete list, or ask around for a recommendation. For added security, make sure the company is bonded and insured.

- **Boston Cleaning**, Boston, 617-539-9099
- **Chapman Home Cleaning Services**, 158-R Chestnut Hill Ave, Brighton, 617-782-4979, www.chapmancleaning.com
- **Clean & Green**, Jamaica Plain, 617-522-2122
- **MaidPro**, Boston, 617-742-8080, www.maidpro.com
- **The Maids Home Service**, Boston, 617-267-0101
- **Mass Maids Services**, South Boston, 617-269-6767, www.massmaidsservices.com
- **Merry Maids**, locations throughout the metro area, including Waltham, Dorchester, West Roxbury, and Brighton. Call 800-891-1598, or go online to www.merrymaids.com for the nearest location.
- **Rent-A-Maid**, Boston, 617-536-333
- **Trust Cleaning Services**, throughout the greater Boston area, 877-547-4800, www.cleaningwell.com

PEST CONTROL

Depending on where you live, you might experience a variety of pest problems—from cockroaches in apartments above restaurants in the North End to rats and mice, particularly in the Back Bay, the Fenway, and Beacon Hill. Further out from the city, the critters can be bigger—raccoons in the chimney, skunks tearing up your yard and going after neighborhood pets, and bats in your attic. Ants, termites, and wasps can also be an issue.

Check the Yellow Pages under "Pest Control Services" or try one of these:

- **Atlantic Pest Control**, greater Boston area, 866-989-0731
- **Bay State Wildlife Management**, 866-953-5433, www.baystatewildlife.com; specializes in removing squirrels, skunks, bats, raccoons, birds, moles, and more.
- **Brothers Pest Control**, 781-329-4600 or 508-583-1611, www.brotherspest control.com
- **City Wildlife Control**, 617-635-5348, www.cityofboston.gov/animalcontrol
- **Environmental Health Services**, 888-737-8646, www.pest-mgmt.com; non-chemical pest management solutions for Boston and all of Eastern Massachusetts.
- **John D**. **Lyon Co**., 617-241-9166 or 781-643-1592, www.johndlyon.com; 24-hour, same-day service.
- **NW Pest Control**, 877-522-7123, www.nwpestcontrol.com; several locations around greater Boston.
- **Security Pest Elimination**, 800-362-2687, www.securitypest.com; several locations around greater Boston.
- **Target Pest Co.**, 800-649-9602; Medford, Somerville, and Wakefield.
- **Terminix**, 800-233-5917, www.terminix.com

MAIL DELIVERY AND SHIPPING

Boston's main postal hub is the **Fort Point Channel Station** at 25 Dorchester Avenue near South Station. They are open seven days a week, 24 hours per day. Contact them at 617-654-5302.

Smaller branch post offices can be found throughout Boston in every neighborhood. For more information on your local postal annex, check the resources listed after the neighborhood profiles at the beginning of this book, or go to "Locate a Post Office" on the USPS web site (www.usps.com), where you can also ask about postal rates, services, zip codes, make consumer complaints, and more.

JUNK MAIL

Junk mail will surely follow you to your new locale. In order to curtail this kind of unwanted mail we suggest you register with the Direct Marketing Association's Mail Preference Service by going to www.dmaconsumers.org/cgi/offmailing and either registering online, or printing and mailing the registration form they provide. Some catalogue companies will need to be contacted directly with a purge request. Another option is to call the "opt-out" line at 888-567-8688, and request that the main credit bureaus not release your name and address to interested marketing companies. (**Curb phone solicitations** by going to the government's "do not call registry," www.donotcall.gov, and registering your phone number.)

The **Massachusetts Office of Consumer Affairs and Business Regulation** offers a few more tips on decreasing your junk mail flow on their web site, www. mass.gov/consumer. Or for a dime a day you can stop your junk mail and have trees planted on your behalf by joining **Green Dimes**, www.greendimes.com.

MAIL RECEIVING SERVICES

If you're in between addresses but need a place to receive mail, you can rent a box at the post office. Most local branch post offices have boxes, but if they're full, you can call the main Fort Point Channel station to request a box (dial 617-654-5302), or try a private service. Here are a few:

- **Delta Letter Drop**, 58 Batterymarch St, Boston, 617-423-3543
- **HQ Global Workplaces** has locations throughout Boston, Cambridge, and Waltham. Check the Yellow Pages or visit www.hq.com, for the nearest location.
- **UPS Stores** (formerly **Mail Boxes, Etc.**) offer mail box rentals and shipping services. Check the Yellow Pages or www.mbe.com for details.

SHIPPING SERVICES

- **Boston Craters & Freighters**, 7 Perry Dr, Foxboro, 866-894-0123, www.crater sandfreighters.com; for especially heavy or bulky items.
- **DHL Worldwide Express**, 800-CALL-DHL (800-225-5345), www.dhl-usa.com
- **FedEx**, 800-GO-FEDEX (800-463-3339), www.fedex.com/us/
- **UPS**, 800-PICK-UPS (800-742-5877), www.ups.com
- **US Postal Service Express Mail**, 800-ASK-USPS (800-275-8777), www.usps. com

AUTOMOBILE REPAIR

Should your vehicle need to be towed, there are many towing companies listed in the Yellow Pages. However, many find it practical to join an auto club. The local branch of the American Automobile Association is **AAA Southern New England**, and the standard yearly membership fee covers roadside assistance, car jumps, towing, free traveler's cheques, personalized route maps, passport photos, discounts on travel services (like car rentals and train tickets), insurance services, and more. For membership details, contact them at www.aaa.com or 800-JOIN-AAA; for roadside assistance (members only) dial 800-AAA-HELP.

Many of us feel at a loss when it comes time to take the car to the shop. To find an auto mechanic, check with friends, acquaintances, or co-workers for a reputable shop, try the "mechanic files" link on the Car Talk web site, or try your chances in the Yellow Pages. You can always check with the **Better Business Bureau** (508-652-4800, www.bosbbb.org) to find out if any complaints have been filed against an auto repair shop. Dealers are usually reliable, and often have the parts necessary to fix your car in stock, but can be more expensive than a small independent shop. When all else fails, try calling **Car Talk** (888-CAR-TALK), the popular NPR radio show where the entertaining Click and Clack brothers (Boston locals Tom and Ray Magliozzi) try to diagnose and solve your car's problems from your descriptions over the phone. Tune in Saturdays at 11 a.m. for the live show and listen to repeats on Sunday nights at 6 p.m. on 90.9 FM, WBUR, or go to http://cartalk.cars.com to listen to the weekly podcast.

For information about the Massachusetts Lemon Laws, refer to **Consumer Protection—Automobiles** in the **Getting Settled** chapter.

CONSUMER PROTECTION—RIP-OFF RECOURSE

If you find yourself in the unfortunate situation of having been swindled or ripped off, there may be something you can do about it. A number of private organizations in Massachusetts provide information about business practices and consumer issues, and some will assist you in resolving your complaints. No matter what, it's always a good idea to check up on any service before you enter into an agreement. But if you've discussed terms with the proprietor, read the fine print, and still find yourself with a cubic zirconia when you were promised a diamond, there are some places you can turn for help. First go to www.mass.gov (click on "Consumer" under "For Residents") or check with the following:

- **Better Business Bureau**, 235 W Central St, Suite 1, Natick, 508-652-4800, www. bosbbb.org; offers general information on products and services, reliability reports and background information on local businesses and organizations, and consumer guidance.
- *A Citizen's Guide to Massachusetts State Services*, available at the State Bookstore, 617-727-2834, is a state publication that provides information on state matters of business/economy, children, consumer, education, arts, employment, environment, energy, health, housing, community development, licenses/paperwork, law enforcement, public safety, recreation, senior citizens, transportation, utilities, welfare, and more.
- **Consumer Product Safety Commission**, 800-638-2772, www.cpsc.gov
- **Federal Trade Commission**, 877-FTC-HELP, www.ftc.gov; is responsible for working against fraudulent, unfair business practices.
- **Federal Citizen Information Center (FCIC)**, 888-878-3256, www.pueblo.gsa. gov; provides information about federal agencies and common consumer issues. They also publish the *Consumer's Action Handbook* for tips on finding the right services. For a free copy, fill out the form on www.consumeraction.gov.
- **Massachusetts Attorney General's Office**, 1 Ashburton Pl, Boston, 617-727-2200, www.ago.mass.gov; protects the public's interest in the areas of

healthcare, environment, consumer issues, civil rights, the elderly, children, the workplace, charity, high-tech, and criminal enforcement. Has several hotlines: consumer hotline, 617-727-8400; elder hotline, 888-AG-ELDER; fair labor, 617-727-3465; insurance fraud, 617-573-5330; utilities, 888-514-6277; insurance consumer helpline, 888-830-6277.

- **Massachusetts Office of Consumer Affairs & Business Regulation**, 10 Park Plaza, Suite 5170, Boston, 617-973-8700, www.mass.gov/consumer; consumer hotline: 617-973-8787 or 888-283-3757; offers assistance with automobiles, banking, cable TV and telecommunications, credit and debt, energy and fuel, fitness, health and medical care, home buying and construction, identity theft, insurance, investing, jewelry, junk mail, licensing, consumer groups, privacy, shopping issues, small claims court, tenant and landlord relations, travel, and worker's comp.
- **MassPIRG (Massachusetts Public Interest Research Group)**, 44 Winter St, Fourth Floor, Boston; 617-292-4800, www.masspirg.org; a non-profit advocacy and research organization committed to protecting consumers and the environment. Provides information and referral on a variety of consumer and environmental issues. Reports are available for download.

MEDIA-SPONSORED CALL FOR ACTION PROGRAMS

Sometimes it can't hurt to have the power of the press behind you. The following are local consumer advocacy programs operated by Boston-area TV and radio stations:

- **Help Me Hank**; WHDH (Channel 7) local reporter uses the local news to fight consumer battles for viewers in need; helpmehank@whdh.com.
- **WBZ Call for Action**, 1170 Soldiers Field Rd, Boston, 617-787-7070, www.wbz1030.com; telephone information and referral for individuals with consumer problems. Sponsored by WBZ-AM 1030 radio.
- **WBZ-TV A-List**, www.wbztv.com/consumer; consumer guide to the "best" of Boston's services from watch repair to martial arts studios. Visit the web site or listen to the news to learn about the winners, or go to http://wbztv.cityvoter.com to vote for your favorites.

LEGAL MEDIATION/REFERRAL PROGRAMS

If you need legal advice or referrals, try one of the following:

- **Massachusetts Bar Association**, 20 West St, Boston, 617-338-0500, www.massbar.org; on the first Wednesday of each month call 617-338-0610 between 5:30 p.m. and 7:30 p.m. for free basic legal advice from a Massachusetts attorney.

- **National Consumer Law Center**, 77 Summer St, 10th Floor, Boston, 617-542-8010, www.consumerlaw.org. For the complete listing of **state information for the elderly**, go to www.mass.gov/elders. Or call or visit AgeInfo: 800-AGE-INFO (800-243-4636), www.800ageinfo.com.

SMALL CLAIMS COURTS

For legal disputes of less than $2,000 that you are unable or unwilling to settle through negotiation or mediation, you can always take it to small claims court. The **Massachusetts Office of Consumer Affairs & Business Regulation** (10 Park Plaza, Suite 5170, Boston, 617-973-8787, www.mass.gov/consumer) offers information and guidance regarding the ins and outs of taking a case to small claims court. For additional help contact the **Small Claims Advisory Service** (Phillips Brooks House, Cambridge, 617-497-5690, http://hcs.harvard.edu/~scas).

The following is a list of local small claims courts in the Boston metro area:

BOSTON

- **East Boston District Court** (also covers **Winthrop**), 37 Meridian St, 617-569-7550
- **Municipal Court of the City of Boston** (all of **Suffolk County**), Edward W. Brooke Courthouse, 24 New Chardon St, Boston, 617-788-8411
- **Municipal Court of Brighton District** (also covers **Allston**), 52 Academy Hill Rd, Brighton, 617-782-6521
- **Municipal Court of Charlestown District**, 3 City Sq, Charlestown, 617-242-5400
- **Municipal Court of Dorchester District,** 510 Washington St, Dorchester, 617-288-9500
- **Municipal Court of the West Roxbury District** (also covers **Hyde Park, Jamaica Plain**, parts of **Mattapan, Readville, Roslindale**), 445 Arborway, Jamaica Plain, 617-971-1200
- **Roxbury District Court**, 85 Warren St, Roxbury, 617-427-7000
- **Trial Court of the Commonwealth-District Court Department South Boston Division**, 535 E Broadway, South Boston, 617-268-8305

SUFFOLK COUNTY

- **Chelsea District Court** (also covers **Revere**), 120 Broadway, Chelsea, 617-660-9200

NORFOLK COUNTY

- **Brookline Municipal Court**, 360 Washington St, Brookline, 617-232-4660
- **Quincy District Court** (covers **Braintree, Cohasset, Holbrook, Milton, Randolph, Weymouth**), 1 Dennis F. Ryan Pkwy, Quincy, 617-471-1650

MIDDLESEX COUNTY

- **Cambridge District Court** (covers **Arlington, Belmont**), 40 Thorndike St, Cambridge, 617-494-4315
- **Framingham District Court** (covers **Ashland, Holliston, Hopkinton, Sudbury, Wayland**), 600 Concord St, Framingham, 508-875-7461
- **Newton District Court**, 1309 Washington St, West Newton, 617-244-3600
- **Somerville District Court** (also covers **Medford**), 175 Fellsway, Somerville, 617-666-8000
- **First District Court of Eastern Middlesex** (covers **Everett, Malden, Melrose, Wakefield**), 89 Summer St, Malden, 617-322-7500
- **Waltham District Court** (covers **Watertown, Weston**), 38 Linden St, Waltham, 781-894-4500

SERVICES FOR PEOPLE WITH DISABILITIES

Since the passage of the federal Americans with Disabilities Act in 1990, Boston has made great strides to serve the needs of disabled residents and visitors. Curbs have been rebuilt for easy wheelchair accessibility, and most public buildings have special disabled-friendly entrances. There is a well-coordinated effort within the public and private sector that works to meet the needs of the disabled here. Perhaps most notably, Boston has a substantial blind population; its small size, walkability, and good T service make it a particularly comfortable city for those with visual impairments.

Following are services, organizations, and resources to help make life easier for new Bostonians with special needs.

GETTING AROUND

- **The RIDE** is a shared-ride, wheelchair-accessible, door-to-door paratransit program operated by the **MBTA**, and offered to all Massachusetts residents who can't use regular trains, subways, or buses. The fare for the RIDE is a one-way $2 flat fee within the zone you're located; personal care assistants are not charged. You must apply to become a registered RIDE user, which you can do through the T's web site or by contacting The RIDE, 10 Park Plaza, Room 5750, Boston 02116, 617-222-5123, 800-533-6282, TTY 617-222-5415, www.mbta.com/riding_the_t/accessible_services. Out-of-state and/or out-of-area travelers visiting the area may use the RIDE with proper ADA documentation.

- **Bus Service**: all MBTA buses are 100% handicap-accessible. Older buses are equipped with rear door lifts, and newer, low-floor buses are equipped with a front door ramp.

- **Subways and Commuter Rails**: about half of the MBTA's subway and commuter rail stations are handicap-accessible with elevators and car-level platforms; the **Orange Line** is the only subway line where every stop is completely accessible. To see if the station you want to use is one of them, visit www.mbta.com/schedules_and_maps/subway. In the true fashion of all things mechanical, elevators and handicap lifts can break often; to check if they are in working order (and we suggest you do), call the **MBTA Elevator Update line** at 617-222-2828, 800-392-6100, or TTY 617-222-5146.

- **Service animals** are allowed on MTBA systems at all times, provided they are wearing their work gear (harness, etc.) and are under control.

- **TTY Public Pay Phones** are available in many different MBTA stations. Go to www.mbta.com/riding_the_t/accessible_services, or call 617-222-3200, TTY 617-222-5146 for a complete list.

- **The MBTA's Senior Pass Program and Access Pass Program** offer reduced-fare passes to persons 65 years old or older, or to those with disabilities. Applications available at MBTA Back Bay and Downtown Crossing Stations, or call 617-543-8287, TTY 617-222-5854.

- **Disability Plates, Placards, and Disability Veteran Plates** are issued to Massachusetts residents on a temporary or permanent basis. An application, available through the Medical Affairs Branch of the Registry of Motor Vehicles, has to be filled out by a physician before it's submitted for approval at a full service RMV branch office or sent through the mail to P.O. Box 199100, Boston 02119, 617-351-9222. For more information on plate prices, eligibility requirements, etc., or to download applications, visit www.mass.gov/rmv, or call 617-351-4500, TTY 617-536-7534. In the city of Boston, disability plates or placards allow you to park at any meter, **free of charge**, for as long as you need.

- **Taxis**: many Boston taxi companies have accessible cabs. **Veterans Taxi** specializes in accessible transportation. Check the Yellow Pages, or call 617-527-0300 for their downtown Boston location.

COMMUNICATION

Verizon offers a range of equipment for people in Massachusetts who are blind, deaf, hard of hearing, vision- or speech-impaired, and/or mobility-impaired. Services include amplified phones, big-button or memory-button phones, TeleTYpewriters (TTY), and cordless and speakerphones. Massachusetts residents who are Verizon customers with state-certified cognitive, hearing, motion, speech, or vision impairments may qualify for free or reduced-rate equipment. Call the **Verizon Center for Customers with Disabilities** at 800-974-6006 or e-mail vccd@verizon.com for an application.

Massachusetts Relay is an operator service that connects TTY with voice service and vice versa. Voice service is 800-439-0183. TTY service is 800-439-2370.

HOUSING

- **Boston Center for Independent Living**, 60 Temple Pl, Fifth Floor, Boston, 617-338-6665, TTY 617-338-6662; www.bostoncil.org; nonprofit that promotes civil rights for all people with disabilities.
- **Citizens' Housing and Planning Association**, 617-742-0820, www.chapa.org; keeps track of housing and vacancy information.
- **Housing Court Department**, Edward W. Brooke Courthouse, 24 New Chardon St, Sixth Floor, Boston, 617-788-6500, www.mass.gov/courts; the hub of legal jurisdiction regarding housing discrepancies.
- **Mass Access**, http://massaccesshousingregistry.org; an accessible-housing registry to help those with disabilities look for rental housing.
- **Massachusetts Architectural Access Board**, 1 Ashburton Pl, Room 1310, Boston, 617-727-0660 or TTY 617-727-0019, www.mass.gov/aab; a regulatory agency in place to make sure public buildings are handicapped accessible.
- **Massachusetts Department of Housing and Community Development**, 100 Cambridge St, Suite 300, 617-573-1100 or TTY 617-573-1140, www.mass.gov/dhcd; the center for state housing information's web site includes a program book for tenant rules in state-aided housing that covers handicap housing.
- **Massachusetts Office on Disability**, 617-727-7440 or 800-322-2020 (voice and TTY), www.mass.gov/mod; offers information on disability access and home modification funding, as well as service systems, and disability laws regarding housing.
- **Massachusetts Rehabilitation Council's Home Modification Loan Program**, 617-204-3636, www.mass.gov/mrc/; offers loans for home modifications.
- **Massachusetts Rehabilitation Commission Adult Supported Living Program**, 27-43 Wormwood St, Boston, 617-204-3600, Voice/TTY 617-245-6543, www.mass.gov/mrc/; independent living support for young adults with physical disabilities.
- **Special Needs Housing/Supported Living** is available through the **Massachusetts Department of Mental Health**, 617-626-8000, www.mass.gov/dmh, and the **Massachusetts Department of Mental Retardation**, 617-727-5608, www.mass.gov/dmr

ADDITIONAL RESOURCES

Massachusetts provides a variety of public and private services for physically or mentally challenged residents. Following is a list of **governmental and private agencies**:

- **Association of Late Deafened Adults,** www.alda.org
- **Braille and Talking Book Library at the Perkins School for the Blind,** 175 N Beacon St, Watertown, 617-924-3434, www.perkins.org
- **Cambridge Commission for Persons with Disabilities,** 51 Inman St, Cambridge, 617-349-4692, TTY 617-492-0235, www.cambridgema.gov/ DHSP2/disabilities.cfm
- **Governor's Commission on Mental Retardation,** 2 Boylston St, Fourth Floor, Boston, 617-988-3200, www.mass.gov/gcmr
- **Disabled Persons Protection Commission,** 50 Ross Way, Quincy, 617-727-6465, 800-426-9009 (voice/TTY hotline), www.mass.gov/dppc; protects disabled individuals from caregiver abuse through public awareness, investigation, oversight, and prevention activities.
- **Massachusetts Commission for the Blind,** 48 Boylston St, Boston, 617-727-5550, TTY 800-392-6556, www.mass.gov/mcb
- **Massachusetts Commission for the Deaf and Hard of Hearing,** 150 Mount Vernon St, Boston, contact by videophone: 617-265-8447 or use the IP address 70.22.152.162, www.mass.gov/mcdhh; handles requests for interpreters and computer-aided real time translation (CART) reporters.
- **Massachusetts Department of Mental Retardation,** 500 Harrison Ave, Boston, 617-727-5608, TTY 617-624-7783, www.mass.gov/dmr
- **Massachusetts Department of Public Health, Division for Special Health Needs,** 250 Washington St, Boston, 617-624-6060, www.mass.gov/dph/topics/ specialhealth.htm
- **Massachusetts Developmental Disabilities Council,** 1150 Hancock St, Quincy, 617-770-7676, TTY 617-770-9499, www.mass.gov/mddc; establishes state priorities in regards to individuals with developmental disabilities.
- **Massachusetts Law Reform Institute,** 99 Chauncy, Suite 500, Boston, 617-357-0700, www.mlri.org; nonprofit statewide legal services support center for low-income, minorities, immigrants, elders, and people with disabilities.
- **Mental Health Legal Advisors Committee,** 399 Washington St, Boston, 617-338-2345, www.mass.gov/mhlac; protects legal rights through advocacy, legal advice, referrals, etc.
- **Museums** in the Boston area have an access coordinator for the disabled: **Museum of Fine Arts,** 617-267-3189, TTY 617-267-9703, or go to www.mfa. org; **Museum of Science,** 617-723-2500, TTY 617-589-0417 or go to www.mos. org.
- **National Association of Guide Dog Users,** www.nfb-nagdu.org, 508-673-0218

- **New England ADA Technical Assistance Center**, 180-200 Portland St, Suite 1, Boston, 800-949-4232 (voice/TTY), www.adaptiveenvironments.org
- **Perkins School for the Blind**, 175 N Beacon St, Watertown, 617-924-3434, www.perkins.org
- **VSA Arts Massachusetts**, China Trade Center, 2 Boylston St, Boston, 617-350-7713, TTY 617-350-6836, www.vsamass.org; a non-profit organization that helps make it possible for people with disabilities to participate in Boston's arts and culture scene.

WHEELCHAIRS AND SCOOTERS

If you need to rent a motorized wheelchair or scooter, here are a few places:

- **Scooter Store**, 800-391-7237, www.scooterstore.com
- **American Ramp System**, 202 W First St, South Boston, 617-269-5679 or 800-649-5215, www.americanramp.com
- **Gary Drug Co.**, 59 Charles St, Boston, 617-227-0023

INTERNATIONAL NEWCOMERS

Boston has been the home for immigrants since the days of the Mayflower, and in recent years the immigration population has seen a resurgence that, according to the Boston Redevelopment Authority, is rising faster than both the national and state rates.

In 2005 the Boston Redevelopment Authority put together the **New Bostonians Report** (www.cityofboston.gov/newbostonians/pdfs/demo_report_2005.pdf), which stated that there are over 8,000 immigrant-owned businesses that employ more than 37,000 people. Boston's largest numbers of immigrants hail from Haiti, the Dominican Republic, and China; and although the Irish aren't arriving in large numbers like the good old days, they *are* still arriving and remain a dominant force in this city, as can be noted by the vast number of Irish pubs that pour a good Guinness and have brogue-laden bartenders.

If you are coming to Boston from afar, you will not be alone. According to the 2000 census, 26% of Boston is foreign born; however, Boston is still very much an American city, and navigating its bureaucracies, legalities, and idiosyncrasies can be baffling. For advice on legal matters, your best resource may be your embassy or consulate. There are over 20 consulates in Boston; go to www.state.gov/s/cpr/rls/fco for a complete and updated list.

IMMIGRATION AND NATURALIZATION SERVICE

A variety of helpful information can be found online at the **US Citizen and Immigration Services** web site (www.uscis.gov). If you have specific questions, you can also contact the USCIS national customer service center at 800-375-5283,

TTY 800-767-1833. Once you know what you need to do, you'll undoubtedly have to fill out paperwork. To get the proper forms call 800-870-3676 or look on the USCIS web site.

For further assistance, you can schedule an appointment with US Citizen and Immigration Services by calling 800-375-5283. The local satellite office for Boston is the **Boston Field Office** (John F. Kennedy Federal Building, Government Center, Room E-160); please note they are closed on the third Friday of every month.

PUBLICATIONS

You can download a useful guide, "Welcome to the United States: A Guide for New Immigrants" free at http://uscis.gov/files/nativedocuments/M-618.pdf. The booklet includes information on your rights and responsibilities as well as the steps to take to become a US citizen.

International newcomers experiencing culture shock can get a quick overview of American culture, etiquette, expectations, and quirks in the *Newcomer's Handbook for Moving to and Living in the USA* by Mike Livingston, published by First Books (www.firstbooks.com).

MOVING PETS TO THE USA

- *The Pet-Moving Handbook* (First Books) covers domestic and international moves, via car, airplane, ferry, etc. Primary focus is on cats and dogs.
- **Cosmopolitan Canine Carriers** out of Connecticut, 800-243-9105, www.caninecarriers.com, has been shipping dogs and cats all over the world for over 25 years. Contact them with questions or concerns regarding air transportation arrangements, vaccinations, and quarantine times.

GAY, LESBIAN, BISEXUAL, AND TRANSGENDER (GLBT) LIFE

In 2003, the Massachusetts Supreme Court ruled that same-sex couples have the legal right to marry, allowing such couples the benefits and protections previously awarded only to heterosexual married couples, a great victory for Massachussetts' gays and lesbians. In Boston, a substantial and active GLBT population centers around the South End, with a satellite population in Jamaica Plain. In the summer, everyone who is anyone heads to Provincetown on Cape Cod. There are many organizations, including sport and social groups, support groups, businesses, and publications that exist solely for Boston's GLBT community. Here are a few to give you a place to start:

- **BGL Advertising**, www.bgladco.com; links to Boston-area GLBT resources, including health, social, religious, athletic, and entertainment groups and venues.

- **Bisexual Resource Center**, P.O. Box 1026, Boston 02117, 617-424-9595; www. biresource.org; huge collection of local bisexual resources, including pamphlets, news, pride products, and support groups.
- **GLBT-friendly places of worship** at www.johnrpierce.com/bostonglc.html
- **GLBT-friendly AA meetings** at www.geocities.com/dallasuapace/aa.html
- **GayBoston**, www.gayboston.ws; Boston guide.
- **Calamus Bookstore**, 92B South St, Boston 02111, 617-338-1931, www.cala musbooks.com
- **Edge**, www.edgeboston.com; online news and information for the GLBT community.
- **Greater Boston Business Council**, 866-594-4222, www.gbbc.org; the council of the GLBT business community.
- **MLGBA (Massachusetts Lesbian and Gay Bar Association)**, 617-984-0535, www.mlgba.org

NEWSPAPERS, NEWSLETTERS, AND OTHER PUBLICATIONS

For frequently updated current events, information, and club listings from the pulse of Boston's GLBT community, try these publications:

- *Bay Windows*, 46 Plympton St, Boston, 617-266-6670, www.baywindows. com; "New England's leading gay and lesbian newspaper." Published every Thursday.
- *In Newsweekly*, 450 Harrison Ave, Suite 414, Boston 02118, 617-426-8246, www.innewsweekly.com; "New England's premier GLBT news and entertainment weekly." Published in all six of New England's states every Thursday.
- *Pink Pages*, 800-338-6550, www.pinkweb.com; GLBT yellow pages for New England and beyond.

HOUSING

If you're looking to live with like-minded neighbors, there are a few options. The heart of Boston's gay community is, without question, the **South End**, where neighbors form a friendly, tight-knit community. Here you'll find GLBT-geared and owned businesses, restaurants, and housing. **Jamaica Plain** is where the girls are, although, you won't find as many GLBT-friendly services as you will in the South End. Finally, lest we forget, the gay mecca is **Provincetown**, on the tip of Cape Cod. P'town, as it is affectionately called, is quite a ways away from Boston—you have to drive all the way around the arm of Cape Cod or take a two-hour ferry ride to get there.

SUPPORT AND ACTIVIST GROUPS

Everyone can use a little help. Fortunately, if you need support with issues pertaining to your sexual orientation, there are area organizations and groups at the ready. Check *Bay Windows* or the *Pink Pages* for support group listings. Here are just a few:

- **Boston Gay and Lesbian Adolescent Social Services (GLASS) Center**, 39 Mass Ave, 3rd Floor, Boston, 617-266-3349, www.bostonglass.org; drop-in center for GLBT teens, located in the Back Bay.
- **Citizens Against Homophobia**, 324 Shawmut Ave, Boston, 617-576-9866, www.actwin.com/cahp; group using mass media to fight homophobia.
- **Coming Out Group**, Fenway Community Health Center, 7 Haviland St, Boston, 617-927-6202; a short-term group (10 weeks) for men and women in the process of coming out or questioning their sexuality.
- **Dignity/Boston**, 617-421-1915, www.dignityboston.org; GLBT Catholic support group that meets every Sunday at 5:30 p.m. at the Church of St. John the Evangelist, 35 Bowdoin St, Boston.
- **Gay and Lesbian Helpline**, 617-267-9001 or 888-340-GLBT; toll-free national hotline providing information and support for GLBT callers.
- **Gay and Lesbian Advocates and Defenders**, 294 Washington St, Suite 301, Boston 02108, 617-426-1350, www.glad.org
- **Gay Men's Domestic Violence Project**, 955 Mass Ave, Cambridge, 617-497-7317, toll free hotline 800-832-1901, www.gmdvp.org
- **Greater Boston PFLAG**, 866-GBPFLAG or 781-891-5966, www.gbpflag.org; local chapter of the national support group for Parents and Friends of Lesbians and Gays. Go to the web site or call to learn about PFLAG meetings in your community.
- **The History Project**, 29 Stanhope St, Boston, 617-266-7733, www.historyproject.org; researches and documents Boston's LGBT history.
- **Keshet**, 284 Amory St, Jamaica Plain, 617-524-9227, www.boston-keshet.org; support group for the local Jewish GLBT community.
- **Peer Listening Line**, 800-399-PEER; trained GLBT volunteers provide assistance.
- **Speak Out**, 31 Heath St, Boston, 617-238-2470, www.speakoutboston.org; GLBT speakers bureau.

WHEN MOVING TO A NEW AREA, ONE OF THE MOST IMPORTANT tasks parents face is finding good childcare and/or schools for their children. The results of this search can be a deciding factor in, among other things, choosing a community in which to purchase a home. Key factors to consider when looking for a daycare center or school are affordability, convenience, safety, and, most importantly, the quality of care and instruction. Please note: listing in this book is merely informational and is **not** an endorsement. When entrusting your child to strangers, always err on the side of safety and caution.

The Boston area also offers a dazzling array of options for higher learning, from public and private colleges and universities to non-credit classes, all addressed in the final section of this chapter.

DAYCARE

In a city where many two-income families have small children, locating quality childcare can be a competitive and expensive proposition. Expecting parents should include the daycare search as part of their prenatal activities, as it can take a year or more to get your child into your preferred facility. And be prepared: full-time care in a childcare center is expensive. According to Runzheimer International, in 2006 Boston ranked second to NYC nationwide for monthly full-time daycare expenses, with an average cost of $1006.94.

The **Massachusetts Department of Early Education and Care** (EEC, 51 Sleeper Street, Fourth Floor, Boston, 617-988-6600, www.eec.state.ma.us) can assist with your childcare search. The EEC exists to make sure Massachusetts' children are getting quality education and childcare, and is responsible for licensing and training childcare providers, running background checks, setting policy, and investigating complaints. Contact the EEC to receive information on licensed childcare providers in your area, or go to the EEC web site to use their database.

Other **referral agencies** include the following:

- **Child Care Choices of Boston**, 105 Chauncy St, 2nd Floor, Boston, 617-542-5437, www.childcarechoicesofboston.org, provides many services, including referrals to childcare resources in Boston, Brookline, Chelsea, Winthrop, and Revere.
- **Child Care Resource Center**, 130 Bishop Allen Dr, Cambridge, 617-547-9861, www.ccrcinc.org; provides information and referrals on daycare programs in Cambridge, Arlington, Belmont, Brookline, Newton, Somerville, and Watertown.
- The **City of Cambridge** also has a **Childcare and Family Support Division** in its Human Services Department. Call 617-349-6254 to speak with the childcare enrollment coordinator or visit www.cambridgema.gov/DHSP2/childcare.cfm.
- The **Brookline Community Partnership for Children**, Sperber Education Center, 88 Harvard St, Brookline, 617-264-6404, www.townofbrooklinemass.com/bcpc, offers a guide to programs, services, and places for young children and their families in the town, including childcare and preschool referrals.
- **Community Care for Kids**, 1509 Hancock St, Quincy, 800-637-2011 or 617-471-6473, www.communitycareforkids.org; operated by Quincy Community Action Programs, connects parents with childcare providers in 20 South Shore communities.

Additional resources include *The Boston Parents' Paper* (www.boston.parenthood.com), a free publication with childcare-related listings and advertisements. Look for it in stores, cafés, and public libraries. The Community Newspaper Company publishes *Parents and Kids* (www.townonline.com/parentsandkids), an online guide for Boston-area parents. And don't forget the **Yellow Pages**: check under "Child Care," "Nanny Service," and "Baby Sitting Service."

If you only need **occasional daycare**, try **Bright Horizons Family Solutions**, which offers full-time care as well as back-up and vacation care. They have offices all over Boston and Cambridge, and you can contact them at 617-673-8000 or www.brighthorizons.com for more information. You can also get back-up care from **Parents in a Pinch** (617-739-KIDS, www.parentsinapinch.com); a childcare provider will come to your house, day or night.

WHAT TO LOOK FOR IN DAYCARE

One of the first credentials you will want to consider is whether or not a daycare facility is licensed by the EEC, which proves the provider meets state-sanctioned health, safety, and educational levels. The EEC license should be visibly posted at the provider's place of business. There are three types of licensed daycare in Massachusetts:

- **Group Childcare** provides center-based care for infants, toddlers, or preschoolers, and includes part-time nursery schools and private kindergartens. Head Start programs, which provide free, part-time care for children from low-income families—or with disabilities—between ages three and five, also fall under this category.
- **School Age Childcare** programs are extended day or after-school programs that provide care for children outside of school hours and during vacations.
- **Family Childcare** licenses authorized care in the provider's home for up to six children, including those of the provider. Under this licensing there is also **Large Family Childcare**, which allows for up to 10 children in the home with the assistance of an approved assistant, and **Family Childcare Plus**, which allows six children plus two school-age children.

In-home childcare provided by a nanny or sitter, childcare provided by a relative in the relative's home, or care provided by private and public preschools or after-school programs *do not require* special childcare licensing.

When investigating prospective daycare centers, visit each center at least a couple of times, preferably unannounced. Consider the following:

- Examine the kitchen, play area, bathroom, and grounds for safety and cleanliness: Is disinfectant used in the kitchen and bathroom? Are toys age-appropriate and in good condition? Are there any potential hazards lying around?
- Check for indoor and outdoor play areas.
- Watch the children at the center: do they seem happy, well behaved, and well supervised? Do they respond well to the attendants? Observe the caregivers with the children.
- Review the daily schedule to make sure the kids have what you think is an appropriate balance of active time and quiet time, and age-appropriate activities.
- You should also determine the employees' qualifications and ask about the staff turnover rate. Also, ask for references—names and phone numbers of other parents whose children are enrolled, whom you can contact.

ONLINE RESOURCES—DAYCARE

There are many parents' organizations in the greater Boston area. Consulting them online is a quick way to hook into a network of peers with knowledge about local childcare agencies, regulations, and child-related events.

- **GoCityKids** has a Boston portal, www.gocitykids.com/choose, which provides links to local services, stores, childcare, after-school activities, and more.
- **MaChildCare.com**, www.machildcare.com, bills itself as "the online resource for childcare information."
- **Parents' P.L.A.C.E. (Parents Learning About Children's Education)**, 1135 Tremont St, Boston, 617-236-7210, www.pplace.org, is the Massachusetts

statewide Parent Information and Resource Center (PIRC). Offers individual referrals, workshops, bulletins, and a resource library.

- **Parentzone** has a Boston portal, http://boston.parentzone.com, where you can find information about local events, resources, healthcare, daycare, and parenting classes.
- **Warmlines**, 225 Nevada St, Newtonville, 617-244-INFO, www.warmlines.org, is a parenting organization in Newton that links local families.

In addition to the specific Boston-area sites, there are several useful resources you can access online to help you on your hunt for good, safe childcare and schools.

- **National Child Care Information Center**, www.nccic.org; provides links to childcare sites on the web.
- **Child Care Aware**, www.childcareaware.org, 800-424-2246; referrals to childcare agencies.
- **US Maternal and Child Health Bureau**, www.mchb.hrsa.gov, 800-598-KIDS; national resource center for health and safety in childcare, providing information about health and safety, state licensing regulations, national health and safety standards, and links to other agencies.

NANNIES

While often the most expensive daycare option, hiring a nanny can be very convenient. You can expect to pay more for an experienced nanny, and you will find that most nannies are not US born. While a cultural exchange with a foreign-born nanny can be wonderful, be sure she is legally authorized to work in the US and speaks enough English to communicate well with you and your child. If you are hiring a nanny without the help of an agency, you'll want to do a background check, which can be done online. Go to any search engine and type in "employment screening." A host of companies are available to research criminal records, driving records, and credit information for you. Check local parent magazines or newspaper classifieds for listings of available nannies.

Nanny services in Boston, which will handle employment screening, include the following (inclusion here does not imply endorsement by First Books):

- **American Nanny Company**, P.O. Box 600765, Newtonville, 800-262-8771, www.americannannycompany.com
- **Beacon Hill Nannies, Inc.**, 825 Beacon St, Suite 19, Newton, 617-630-1577 or 800-736-3880, www.beaconhillnannies.com
- **Boston Nanny Centre, Inc.**, 135 Selwyn Rd, Newton, 617-527-0114 or 800-456-2669, www.boston-nanny.com
- **Minute Women, Inc.**, 781-862-3300, www.minutewomen.net
- **Nannies Nook, Inc.**, P.O. Box 220, Accord, 781-523-1454, www.nanniesnook.com

NANNY TAXES

For those hiring a nanny directly (not using a nanny agency) there are certain taxes you will be responsible for calculating, specifically social security and Medicare, and possibly unemployment. For help with such issues, check the **Nanitax** web site, www.4nannytaxes.com, or call 800-NANITAX. Nanitax provides household payroll and employment tax preparation services. You can also check with **The Nanny Tax Company** (800-747-9826, www.nannytaxprep.com), or the IRS's household employer page (www.irs.gov/taxtopics/tc756.html), which discusses taxes for household employees (topic 756).

You also might want to enlist the aid of **Eisenberg Associates** (800-777-5765, www.eisenbergassociates.com), a group that provides health insurance and other fringe benefits for nannies.

AU PAIRS

The US Information Agency oversees and approves the organizations that offer au pair service. Young women, between the ages of 18 and 26, provide a year of in-home childcare for a maximum of 10 hours a day, and 45 hours a week, in exchange for room and board, airfare, a portion of the au pair's medical insurance, a $139 weekly wage for families with children over two and $164 for families with children under two, and $500 towards their required six hours of academic credit. The program is certainly valuable for the cultural exchange that goes on between the host family and the (usually European) au pair. The downside of the program is that it lasts only one year and the au pairs don't have the life or work experience of a career nanny. Any of the following national agencies will connect you with a local coordinator who will match up your family with the right au pair.

- **Cultural Care Au Pair**, 800-333-6056, www.culturalcare.com
- **Au Pair in America**, 800-928-7247, www.aupairinamerica.com
- **Au Pair USA**, 800-287-2477, www.interexchange.org

Good to know: the placement agencies charge additional fees, including an application fee, placement fee, and/or a program fee. These extra costs can add up; however, au pairs are still one of the lowest-cost, full-time childcare options available.

BABY SITTERS

So, you are new to town and need a night out. What to do with the little ones? If you're lucky, maybe you have family members or an already-established network of friends or neighbors to help you out—either to watch the kids for you or who will give you their coveted list of trusted sitters. If not, and there are no available high school or college students in your neighborhood (check area college employment offices), you can check with **Sittercity** (www.sittercity.com), a group that unites parents and college sitters. Or call **Parents in a Pinch** (617-739-KIDS, www.parentsinapinch.com) for a day, evening or overnight sitter.

CHILD SAFETY

Local hospitals host emergency training classes for infant and child CPR. You can also get helpful safety information from **Massachusetts Citizens for Children** (617-742-8555, www.masskids.org), who offer parental stress hotlines and abuse hotlines, **The Childproofer** (800-374-2525, www.childproofer.com), and a cornucopia of other tips at **SafeKids** (www.safekids.org) and **Boston Parentzone** (http://boston.parentzone.com).

LEAD POISONING

According to the EPA, lead is one of the most pervasive toxic substances in the country today. Lead paint, which children ingest by eating paint chips or inhaling paint dust, can result in serious and permanent damage to the brain, kidneys, bones, nervous system, and red blood cells. In the 1990s, the Massachusetts Department of Public Health reported that over 90% of all the cases of childhood lead poisoning in the state were a result of exposure in the home. And because Boston is such an old city, at least by American standards, a lot of its housing has lead paint. As the report says, "the older the house, the more likely it is to contain lead paint, and the higher the lead concentration is likely to be." Specifically, houses built before 1978 (the year lead was taken out of residential paint) are the primary culprits of lead paint poisoning in children. With almost 50% of Massachusetts' total housing stock built before 1950, it ranks second in the nation for its volume of old housing.

To protect children from lead exposure, the **State of Massachusetts Lead Law** mandates that any house built before 1978 with occupants younger than six must have its lead paint hazards removed or covered, whether it's a rental unit (cleanup would be done at the landlord's expense) or a single-family home. To determine if your house has lead paint, have your home inspected by a licensed lead inspector. Once the de-leading work is finished and the house has been reinspected, an inspector will send a letter of compliance to the homeowner.

For more information about lead poisoning and prevention in Massachusetts, contact the **Childhood Lead Paint Poisoning Prevention Program** (CLPPP, 250 Washington Street, Boston, 617-624-5757 or 800-532-9571, www.mass.gov/dph/clppp). Or to learn about a particular building in Boston, go to www.leadsafehomes.info.

SCHOOLS

Our nation's educational system has been undergoing a great deal of reform in recent years, and Boston-area schools are certainly no exception to the rule. In addition to the national No Child Left Behind Act, there are statewide initiatives being put into practice in an attempt to improve the quality of education for Massachusetts' children. The biggest challenge has been the introduction of the **MCAS**, or **Massachusetts Comprehensive Assessment System** test. The MCAS (pronounced "em-kas") are standardized aptitude tests for English language arts, math, and science (as well as pilot tests in history and social science in high school) that are required of third- through tenth-grade students. Many find the MCAS tests challenging, which is in line with the Massachusetts Department of Education's (DOE) desire to make Massachusetts' schools among the best in the country. To find out more about area schools and where they fall in regards to the National Assessment of Educational Progress, visit http://nces. ed.gov/nationsreportcard.

All children in the Massachusetts public school system must pass the MCAS in order to graduate, including those in charter schools, educational collaboratives, students receiving publicly funded special education in private schools, those with disabilities who have an established Individual Education Program (IEP) or Section 504 instructional accommodations, and those with limited proficiency in English (assuming the student has been in the state at least three years and is ineligible for the Spanish version). Home-schooled students, however, are exempt, as they are not considered part of the public school program.

All this said, there are many groups that oppose the MCAS, fearing it will actually increase the dropout rate, as opposed to increasing the quality of public education. For more about the MCAS, including testing schedules, sample questions, resources, and test results, visit www.doe.mass.edu/mcas or www.boston.com/mcas. If your child will have to take the MCAS and you think extra tutoring is in order, you can turn to the services of **MCAS Mentor** (781-780-2175, www.mcasmentor.com), an organization that provides workbooks, workshops, and counseling to help children pass the MCAS. You can find MCAS scores for a given town or region by checking the DOE's web site, www.doe.mass.edu/mcas/results.html. You can also research school and district profiles at http://profiles.doe.mass.edu. You can reach the **MCAS Parent Information Hotline** at 866-MCAS220.

More follows about how to investigate prospective schools, the public school enrollment process, and listings of parochial and private schools.

CHOOSING A SCHOOL

Massachusetts requires that in September all children over age six must be enrolled in a school. When choosing a school there are many factors to consider.

According to PBS Parents (www.pbs.org/parents/), it may be helpful to consider the educational apporoach or philosophy of the school, class sizes, the learning environment, coursework, curriculum, and policies on social-emotional issues, discipline, and homework. You also want to look at teacher turnover rate; how many students take advanced placement exams and how they perform; other test scores, including MCAS, SAT, and ACT; college acceptance rate; and graduation/dropout rate. You should be able to find at least some of this information at the Massachusetts Department of Education site, which posts "report cards" for its schools. When viewing school rankings, keep in mind that, while smaller schools tend to have lower dropout rates, higher attendance rates, and fewer discipline problems, larger schools tend to have more resources, including a bigger selection of courses and extracurricular activities. And safety records can be deceptive; if a school has a low number of suspensions, expulsions, etc., it *can* mean a quiet, safe school, but it can also mean a lax principal.

When looking for a school, your best research will be firsthand. Visit with the principal and discuss the school's mission, staff motivation, staff autonomy, and teacher accomplishments. Ask yourself, "Can I see my child fitting in here and being successful?" Also talk to the teachers and interview fellow parents. Find out about available technology, including computers and Internet access. When visiting the principal, tour the school, looking into classrooms, the library, and bathrooms.

SCHOOL RESOURCES

A good place to start for all public school–related information is the **Massachusetts Department of Education**, 350 Main Street, Malden, 781-338-3000, www.doe.mass.edu. Also, most cities and towns within Massachusetts have a municipal web site with a link to education (check the neighborhood profiles in this book, or visit www.mass.gov/cc). For more information on public schools in Boston, check with **Boston Public Schools** (26 Court Street, Boston, 617-635-9000), or go to www.bostonpublicschools.org.

Besides the Boston School Department and the Boston School Committee, there are other ways to gain information about the school choices available. One of them is **School Match** (800-992-5323), a private company that offers ratings of public schools through their web site, www.schoolmatch.com. **School Wise Press** (www.schoolwisepress.com) offers free school rankings, profiles, and news articles, and in-depth reports for a fee. Also, each Boston public school zone has a **Family Resource Center** to answer your questions: West Zone is 617-635-8040; East Zone is 617-635-8015; North Zone is 617-635-9010.

BOSTON PUBLIC SCHOOLS

If you are sick of hearing about Boston having the first, oldest, and most famous of everything, you may want to skip to the next paragraph, but it truly *does* have all those things! As we were saying, Boston is the birthplace of the nation's first public school system. **Boston Latin School**, renowned as one of the country's best public high schools, is also the country's first ever (general) public school, having opened in 1635 and graduated such celebrated Bostonians as John Hancock, Samuel Adams, Benjamin Franklin, Ralph Waldo Emerson, and Leonard Bernstein. The nation's oldest public elementary school is Mather, which opened in 1639.

About 57,000 kids (K–12) are enrolled in Boston's 145 public schools. Classroom sizes range between 22 and 31 students. If your child, like many kids, is worried about what to wear on their first day, please note that while there is no required uniform for Boston Public Schools, many individual schools, especially elementary and middle schools, now have uniforms and/or dress codes (e.g., no baseball hats or hooded sweatshirts). So check with the particular school at which your kids are registered.

Of the unique offerings available to students through Boston Public Schools is the **Boston Arts Academy**, the city's first public high school for students showing strong interest in dance, music, theater, and visual arts (admission based on interview and portfolio). There are also the **Boston Latin Academy** and the **John D. O'Bryant School of Mathematics and Science**; both require a qualifying entrance exam. At the elementary school level, full-day kindergartens are available for five-year-olds.

In addition to the traditional public schools, there are also a number of **charter schools**, publicly funded schools headed by boards of educators and parents instead of cities or towns. As of 2007 there were 17 charter schools in Boston. For information on the charter school program in Massachusetts and listings of charter schools throughout the state, contact the DOE at www.doe.mass.edu/charter.

SCHOOL APPLICATION AND ENROLLMENT

Boston Public Schools' elementary and middle grades are divided into three zones: North, East, and West. The **North Zone** covers the Back Bay, Charlestown, downtown Boston, East Boston, Mission Hill, the North End, the South End, and Allston-Brighton; the **West Zone** covers Jamaica Plain, Roslindale, Roxbury, and West Roxbury; and the **East Zone** covers the neighborhoods of Dorchester, Hyde Park, Mattapan, and South Boston.

Parents can apply to send their child to a school in the zone in which they live, schools in other zones that are still within their "walk zone," or citywide K–8 and middle schools open to all students. Whether or not you get the school of your choice depends on several variables, such as whether your child has a sibling in the school, whether your child lives within walking distance, and random lottery. Please note that 50% of each school's seats are set aside for applicants with walk zone priority, which means those living within one mile from an elementary school, within 1.5 miles from a middle school, or within two miles of a high school.

Five schools are **open to all students regardless of their zone** (admission is based on a lottery): Hernandez School (K–8) in Roxbury, M.L. King, Jr. Middle School in Dorchester, Mission Hill School (K–8) in Roxbury, Trinity Middle School in Roxbury, and Young Achievers Science & Mathematics School (K–8) in Jamaica Plain. All high schools are open to students citywide. For more information, call **Boston Public Schools**, 617-635-9000, or go to www.boston.k12.ma.us/schools/assign.asp. Also, check the Massachusetts Department of Education web site at www.info.doe.mass.edu.

Newcomers to Boston Public Schools will want to get a copy of Boston Public's *Introductory Guide*. It should answer many of your questions regarding selecting a school and registration, including when, how, and where to get started. All **students who are new to Boston Public must first *apply* to enroll** in school; applications are available at **Family Resource Centers**: Campbell Resource Center, 1216 Dorchester Avenue, Dorchester, 617-635-8015 for the East Zone; Jennie Barron Building, 515 Hyde Park Avenue, Roslindale, 617-635-8040 for the West Zone; and Madison Park Complex, 55 Malcolm X Boulevard, Roxbury, 617-635-9010 for the North Zone. School applications are not available online—you must visit the school during the appropriate registration period; however, you can preregister and get other school assignment information at http://boston.k12.ma.us/register/. You also *must apply* if your child will be starting kindergarten, will be entering grade six or nine, is in grade one at an Early Education Center or Early Learning Center, will be transferring zones, or is in a special program (e.g., ESL, interdisciplinary learning). If your child is already enrolled at one of the schools, you can pick up the application at your school. Enrollment deadlines vary depending on what grade your child is in, but are usually in the winter.

To apply, bring the application form; two preprinted proofs of address, such as a bank statement, utility bill, or lease; your child's birth certificate or passport; and your child's immunization record. School applications require that you list your three top choice schools. Those already in the Boston Public School system will have a leg up on newcomers as far as receiving their first choice of schools, because students not in transition grades (entering kindergarten, six, or nine) are automatically reassigned to their same school, and those with siblings already enrolled in a school are given priority. The earlier you apply, the better.

After applying, you will receive a notice in the mail of your child's assignment. If your child doesn't get his or her first-choice school you will be put on the waiting list for it. If he or she doesn't make it into the second choice school, then you will be on the waiting list for both of them.

IMMUNIZATIONS

By kindergarten, children should be up to date on their diphtheria, tetanus, pertussis, polio, mumps, measles, and hepatitis B vaccines. You must also show proof your child has been vaccinated against or has already had the chicken pox. By the seventh grade a measles, mumps, rubella (MMR) booster is required. Even students who come to Massachusetts for college must show proof of two MMR shots, a recent tetanus shot (within the last ten years), and the full three doses of hepatitis B vaccine. Public school students new to the system must also present evidence of a complete physical within the past year; without one, children will be banned from participating in any athletic activity. You can contact the **Boston Public Schools Health Service** at 617-635-6788 with any questions about vaccinations or waivers for religious or medical purposes.

GREATER BOSTON AREA PUBLIC SCHOOLS

There are a great many towns and cities throughout the greater Boston area, and an equal number of school districts. **The Massachusetts Department of Education**'s web site catalogs and profiles these schools through a wonderful, interactive map that shows every county, and then every school district within the whole of Massachusetts. This site provides phone numbers and contact information for all the schools in each district. Instead of listing each school here, we urge you either to go to the site mentioned (www.profiles.doe.mass.edu), check out your town or city's web site, visit the closest school to your home, or check the yellow pages for more information on your local school district.

PRIVATE/PAROCHIAL/RELIGIOUS SCHOOLS

About one quarter of school-aged children living within Boston's city limits do not attend a public school, opting instead for private or parochial schools, charter schools, suburban public schools (through the METCO program), or home schooling.

There are a number of well-regarded private schools in the area, including the famous **Phillips Academy** in Andover, about 20 miles north of Boston, and **Milton Academy** in Milton, just south of Boston. To find out more, contact **The Association of Independent Schools in New England** (222 Forbes Road, Braintree, 781-843-8440, www.aisne.org), which has listed over 175 member schools throughout the six-state region, beginning with preschools.

MONTESSORI SCHOOLS

The Montessori educational movement, founded by Maria Montessori in the early 1900s, prizes the development of a child's individual initiative, sense and muscle training, and freedom, through prepared materials and games. For more information about the Montessori method or to find a listing of schools, visit the **Montessori Foundation** web site, www.montessori.org.

WALDORF SCHOOLS

Waldorf schools employ an idiosyncratic, arts-oriented approach to education developed by Austrian Rudolf Steiner in 1919 and based on his spiritual philosophy, Anthroposophy. For more information on Waldorf Schools, and to locate those in the Boston area, contact the **Association of Waldorf Schools of North America**, www.awsna.org, 612-870-8310.

PAROCHIAL SCHOOLS

Religious schools in Boston have a long history of providing quality education, so much so that they are even popular with non-religious parents. In recent years, due to the ever- notorious scandals of the Catholic church, many schools have closed their doors; however, the **Boston Archdiocese** (www.rcab.org) still operates an extensive parochial school system of about 49 schools in the greater Boston area. Contact their **Department of Education** (www.abcso.org, at 617-298-6555) for more information or call 800-SCHOOL-4 to obtain a directory of schools. In addition to Catholic schools, there are also Christian (non-Catholic), Jewish, and Islamic programs. Here are a few religious schools in the region:

- **Al-Noor Academy**, 20 Church St, Mansfield, 508-261-7077, http://anahs.org/; Islamic high school.
- **Austin Prep**, 101 Willow St, Reading, 781-944-4900, www.austin.mec.edu; coed (Augustinian) Catholic high school.
- **BC High School**, 150 Morrissey Blvd, Dorchester, 617-436-3900, www.bchigh. edu; Jesuit high school for boys.
- **Cambridge Friends School**, 5 Cadbury Rd, Cambridge, 617-354-3880, www. cambridgefriendsschool.org; coed, Quaker, pre-K–8.
- **Cohen Hillel Academy**, 6 Community Rd, Marblehead, 781-639-2880, www. cohenhillel.org; coed, Jewish, K–8.
- **Fontbonne Academy**, 930 Brook Rd, Milton, 617-696-3241, www.fontbonne academy.org; Catholic, college prep (high school) for girls.
- **Islamic Academy of New England**, 84 Chase Dr, Sharon, 781-784-0400, www. iane.org; K–8.
- **Jewish Community Day School**, 57 Stanley Ave, Watertown, 617-972-1733, www.jcdsboston.org; coed, K–8.
- **Malden Catholic High School**, 99 Crystal St, Malden, 781-322-3098, www. maldencatholic.org; high school for boys.

- **Rashi School**, 15 Walnut Park, Newton, 617-969-4444, www.rashi.org; reform Jewish day school; coed, K–8.
- **St. Stephen's Armenian Elementary School**, 47 Nichols Ave, Watertown, 617-926-6979, www.ssaes.org, K–5 Armenian elementary school.
- **Torah Academy**, 11 Williston Rd, Brookline, 617-731-3196, http://torahacademy.us; orthodox Jewish day school, pre-K–8.

HOMESCHOOLING RESOURCES

Massachusetts children are required to be in school from ages 6 to 16, be it a private, parochial, public, or home school. According to the ***Worldwide Guide to Homeschooling*** (Broadman & Holman, 2002) by Brian Ray, between 1.6 and two million children are homeschooled nationwide.

If you wish to homeschool your child, the state requires you provide 900 hours of elementary education and 990 hours of secondary education in the areas of reading, writing, English language and grammar, geography, arithmetic, drawing, music, history, the US *Constitution*, citizenship, health (including CPR), physical education, and good behavior. You must get approval from the local school committee or superintendent to operate a home school and must officially withdraw your child from the public school system. There are no specifically required standardized tests a homeschooled child must take, but the school committee or superintendent is authorized to make such tests a stipulation for granting you the authority to homeschool your child. Also, homeschooled children do not need to take the MCAS.

For assistance with homeschooling, you can contact:

- **Home School Legal Defense Association**, 540-338-5600, www.hslda.org; their web site explains laws regarding homeschooling in each state and offers links to necessary forms. They also will send you a free introductory guide to homeschooling called *Home Schooling: Start Here*.
- **Homeschool.com**, www.homeschool.com; resources, guides, local links.
- ***Homeschooling Today***, 276-628-7730, www.homeschooltoday.com; a major "trade" publication that will keep you informed of all the important trends, events, and contacts.
- **Massachusetts Home Learning Association**, 617-497-6732, www.mhla.org; resources, guides, support groups.

HIGHER EDUCATION

Boston is a student's dream. The number of colleges and universities in the city is astonishing. You'd be hard pressed to find another metropolitan area with such a large number of higher education institutions. Along with the quantity of schools, there is also the quality. Within Boston and its environs are some of the world's top colleges and universities, including Harvard, MIT, Brandeis, Boston College, Boston University, Wellesley, and Tufts. Needless to say, bar trivia competition can be fierce.

From September through June, Boston is packed to the hilt with the 18- to 22-year-old set, on top of the year-round presence of graduate students. It is only during the summer that the city returns to the hands of the older folks for a few, albeit fleeting, months.

If you're moving to Boston to attend college or university, the higher education options are a-plenty. For those who can't afford the high prices of private universities, and/or are in a state of general Northeast sticker shock, you may want to look into Massachusetts' many state-funded schools. The **Massachusetts Board of Higher Education** (www.mass.edu) lists and profiles the state's fifteen community colleges, five campuses of the University of Massachusetts (UMass), including one in Boston, and the nine state colleges, six of which are comprehensive and three that are specialized.

Perhaps you are more interested in non-credit classes? Maybe you've always dreamed of speaking French, learning to knit, or being able to taste the difference between a $10 bottle of wine and a $30 bottle. Adult education centers are a great way to broaden your horizons, meet people, and learn a new skill. For the **Boston Center for Adult Education**, go to www.bcae.org, or for the **Cambridge Center for Adult Education**, click over to www.ccae.org. If you and/or your child are interested in taking art classes, check out the **Eliot School** in Jamaica Plain, 617-524-3313, www.eliotschool.org. Opened in 1676, it is one of the oldest continually run educational institutions in the country.

As for private universities and colleges, there is a wide and diverse selection from which to choose. The prices for these schools range from "possibly affordable" to through-the-roof expensive, and just as the tuitions vary, so do the schools' size, focus, and even vibe. To find a comprehensive list of Boston's colleges and universities, check out the directory posted by the Massachusetts Library Information Network, http://mblc.state.ma.us. Also check the Yellow Pages under "Schools" for a complete list of colleges and universities in and around Boston.

Following is a sampling of the area's private colleges and universities:

- **Babson College**, 231 Forest St, Wellesley, 781-235-1200, www.babson.edu; independent school of business and management education.
- **Bentley College**, 175 Forest St, Waltham, 781-891-2000, www.bentley.edu; four-year college, emphasizing careers in business.
- **Berklee College of Music**, 1140 Boylston St, Boston, 617-266-1400, www.berklee.edu; one of the best modern music schools in the country, offering degrees and diplomas in all areas of music, from performance to production to music therapy. Alumni include Quincy Jones, Melissa Etheridge, Kevin Eubanks, John Mayer, Aimee Mann, Gillian Welch, Susan Tedeschi, and Natalie Maines.
- **Boston Architectural College**, 320 Newbury St, Boston, 617-262-5000, www.

the-bac.edu; offers undergraduate and graduate degrees in architecture, interior design, landscape, and more.

- **Boston College (BC)**, 140 Comm Ave, Chestnut Hill, 617-552-8000, www. bc.edu; coed, Jesuit-affiliated university located six miles from downtown Boston. Home to 8,500 undergraduates and 4,000 graduate students.
- **Boston Conservatory**, 8 The Fenway, Boston, 617-536-6340, www.boston conservatory.edu; private college offering undergraduate and graduate programs in music, dance, and musical theater.
- **Boston University (BU)**, 121 Bay State Rd, Boston, 617-353-2300, www.bu.edu; nonsectarian, coed university located on the banks of the Charles River. BU has 15 schools and colleges, and over 30,000 students, many of whom are international.
- **Brandeis University**, 415 South St, Waltham, 781-736-2000, www.brandeis. edu; nonsectarian Jewish university that offers a range of undergraduate and graduate degrees.
- **Emerson College,** 120 Boylston St, Boston, 617-824-8500, www.emerson.edu; a four-year school of communications and performing arts overlooking Boston Common; graduate programs and continuing education as well.
- **Emmanuel College**, 400 The Fenway, Boston, 617-735-9715, www.emmanuel. edu; Catholic, coed, liberal arts and sciences college that offers undergraduate, graduate, and professional programs, located near Fenway Park.
- **Fisher College**, 118 Beacon St, Boston, 617-236-8818, www.fisher.edu; liberal arts and sciences college that offers two- and four-year degrees, situated in the heart of Boston's Back Bay.
- **Harvard University**, Harvard Sq, Cambridge, 617-495-1000, www.harvard.edu; America's first and most prestigious university. Offers summer programs, Radcliffe programs, and continuing ed through the Harvard Extension School.
- **Lesley University**, 29 Everett St, Cambridge, 617-868-9600, www.lesley.edu; located between Harvard and Porter squares, Lesley offers degrees in education and a wide range of human services, management, and the arts, combining internships with classroom work.
- **Longy School of Music**, 1 Follen St, Cambridge, 617-876-0956, www.longy. edu; small, classical music conservatory in Harvard Square.
- **Massachusetts College of Art**, 621 Huntington Ave, Boston, 617-879-7000, www.massart.edu; public, four-year fine arts college located in the Fenway.
- **Massachusetts Institute of Technology (MIT)**, 77 Mass Ave, Cambridge, 617-253-1000, www.mit.edu; premier science university that draws top graduate and undergraduate students from around the world. Also offers degrees in the arts, humanities, and social sciences.
- **Mount Ida College**, 777 Dedham St, Newton, 617-928-4500, www.mountida. edu; founded in 1899, Mount Ida offers more than 25 areas of study.
- **New England Conservatory of Music**, 290 Huntington Ave, Boston, 617-585-1100, www.newenglandconservatory.edu; graduate, undergraduate,

preparatory, and continuing education divisions offering instruction in classi-cal music, jazz, and contemporary improvisation.

- **New England Institute of Art**, 100 Brookline Pl W, Brookline, 800-903-4425, www.artinstitutes.edu/boston/; offers two- or four-year degrees in media, art, and design.
- **Northeastern University**, 360 Huntington Ave, Boston, 617-373-2000, www.northeastern.edu; located near the Museum of Fine Arts in the Fenway, North-eastern offers a unique co-op internship program in field study for undergrads. Has graduate programs, including a law school, and continuing education courses.
- **Regis College**, 235 Wellesley St, Weston, 781-768-7000, www.regiscollege.edu; a Catholic liberal arts and sciences college. Formerly a women's college, Regis began admitting men in 2007.
- **Simmons College**, 300 The Fenway, 617-521-2000, www.simmons.edu; four-year women's college focusing on liberal arts and sciences and professional education; also offers coed graduate programs.
- **Suffolk University**, 8 Ashburton Pl, Boston, 617-573-8000, www.suffolk.edu; located on Beacon Hill in the heart of the city's business, technology, law, medical, and government centers. Suffolk offers undergraduate and graduate degrees in liberal arts and sciences, as well as business and law.
- **Tufts University**, Medford, 02155, 617-627-3170, www.tufts.edu; well-regarded liberal arts, science, and medical programs for graduates and undergraduates. Their medical and dental school campus is in downtown Boston.
- **Wellesley College**, 106 Central St, Wellesley, 781-283-1000, www.wellesley.edu; elite four-year women's college.
- **Wentworth Institute of Technology**, 552 Huntington Ave, Boston, 617-989-4590, www.wit.edu; located on 30-acre campus across from the Museum of Fine Arts in the Fenway, offering bachelor's degrees in architecture, design, engineering, technology, and management of technology.

L IKE MANY LARGER CITIES, BOSTON'S SHOPPING OFFERS SOMETHING for everyone. You'll find everything from upscale boutiques to chain stores within city limits, and the few stores you might be missing are only a short car ride away in the larger metro area. If you're from out of state, make note that Massachusetts has a 5% sales tax, though that excludes items deemed necessities—meaning clothes and groceries. This is great for those used to paying tax at retail clothing stores. To avoid sales tax on all other purchases, especially big-ticket items like TVs or furniture, many locals take the short ride into New Hampshire, where they make good on their "Live Free or Die" motto!

SHOPPING DISTRICTS

In the city's center, **Downtown Crossing** is an outdoor, pedestrian-only area that once reigned as the prime shopping spot in Boston. Recently, as some big stores (Filene's Department Store, Barnes & Noble, etc.) have pulled out, the once-happening shopping district has been floundering. There are still a number of stores, including Macy's (who bought Filene's and shut it down), some discount shopping (H&M, Marshalls, the original Filene's Basement, DSW Shoe Warehouse), urban wear (Manhattan Clothing), a few traditional mall chain stores (Express, Bath and Body Works), and lots of little vendor carts hawking purses, sunglasses and the like. If you drive here, the parking garages are plentiful, but pricey. If you're smart and take the T, get off at Park Street or Downtown Crossing.

Faneuil Hall/Quincy Market, like Downtown Crossing, is a cobblestoned pedestrian shopping area, but with a more upscale feel. Though tourists abound here—the Freedom Trail cuts through it, and many families stop to watch the street performers—locals also enjoy browsing the 70+ mid-sized shops like Ann Taylor and Urban Outfitters, as well as the smaller independent stores and the fleet of 43 unique pushcarts selling a variety of wares. If you get hungry, try any one of the 40+ food vendors or 17 restaurants and pubs. There are a few parking garages in the area, and while they aren't cheap, some provide a discount with shopping validation. By T, it's a short walk from either Government Center or Haymarket—just follow the crowds. Visit www.faneuilhallmarketplace.com for more information.

With the opening of a Filene's Basement, H&M, Borders, and others in the **Newbry Building**, which has entrances on both Boylston and Newbury Streets, and the continued dominance of the small boutique and designer clothing stores that line Newbury Street from the Boston Public Garden to Mass Ave, the **Back Bay of Boston** has stolen Downtown Crossing's proverbial crown as THE place to shop. Many stores on **Boylston Street** are surprisingly large, including a big Crate and Barrel, Anthropologie, Marshalls, and EMS, all of which are mixed in with restaurants, bars, and some designer stores, including Hermès, Escada, and the chic Priscilla of Boston bridal store. **Newbury Street** is packed with little one-up, one-down street level shops in three- or four-floor Victorian brownstones, many of which have apartments in the upper floors. Virtually anything you desire, shopping-wise, can be found here: restaurants (chic and low-key), salons/spas, and a thorough mix of big-name stores (Gap, Banana Republic, French Connection, Armani Exchange, Louis Boston), smaller boutiques (Whim, Stil, Mudo, Intermix), and others (The Hempest, Shambala Tibet). Beyond clothing, Newbury Street offers art galleries, new and used music stores, shoes, books, etc. For more information, go to www.newbury-st.com. Newbury and Boylston are accessible by three different stops on the Green Line—you can get off at Arlington, Copley, or Hynes Convention Center. Parking on Newbury is always difficult, but if you can't find a metered spot, there are discounted parking garages nearby at Copley Place and the Prudential Center just a couple streets over—read on.

Copley Place and the **Shops at the Prudential Center** (www.prudential center.com) are two upscale malls connected by covered pedestrian bridges. In addition to repeats of many stores you'll find just blocks away on Newbury, there are also big department stores like Lord & Taylor, Saks Fifth Avenue, and Barneys New York.

Head a few blocks southwest of Copley and the Pru, and you'll hit **Tremont Street** in the South End, a once sketchy area that has been somewhat gentrified but still maintains an out-of-the-mainstream feel. The South End is now packed with funky unique shops and eateries. In the summer, the **South End Open Market** sets up every weekend from April through October with over 120 vendors selling artisan wares, antiques, homemade baked goods and more. They even have free parking! For more information, check out www.southendopenmarket.com.

Charles Street, the main drag of Beacon Hill, has a nice selection of one-of-a-kind and often pricey shops, including Wish (clothes), Moxie (shoes), Koo di Kir (homegoods), and a string of antique shops. Those driving here can check for a metered spot on Cambridge or Beacon streets or park under the Common; sans car, you can take the Red Line to the Charles/MGH stop.

In **Cambridge**, Mass Ave between Central and Porter squares is packed with all kinds of shops; the heaviest concentration is found in the **Harvard Square** area. Banks, ATM lobbies, and mall chain stores (Gap, Urban Outfitters) have taken over some of the charm of Harvard Square, but look closer and you can still find some fabulous independent shops that have managed to survive. If you haven't been there in years, it is quite possible your favorite store (like Wordsworth Books) is long gone. Still standing strong are a number of shoe stores (Berk's, The Tannery), bookstores, for which the square is famous (Harvard Bookstore, Curious George bookstore, Grolier Poetry Shop, Shoenhoffs, Revolution Books), newsstands (Out of Town News), specialty shops, cafés, and ethnic restaurants. Metered parking can be difficult to find and will only allow you an hour; however, many parking garages in Cambridge can be validated at local stores, and there are some free municipal lots. To utilize public transportation, take the Red Line to the appropriately named stop—Harvard Square for Harvard Square, etc.

The **Harvard Street/Coolidge Corner** area of Brookline also offers a variety of outdoor shopping, with chain shops such as Bowl and Board, Magic Beans, Pier 1, TJ Maxx, and Barnes & Noble, and a few smaller independent stores, including some specializing in Judaica.

MALLS

In the greater Boston area, there are a variety of malls ranging in size and price. (For a list of anchor stores see **Department Stores**.) Here are a few malls to get you started:

- **Arsenal Mall/Watertown Mall**, 485 Arsenal St, Watertown, 617-923-4700, www.shopsimon.com; has a food court, restaurants, and over 65 stores in the old Civil War arsenal.
- **The Atrium Mall**, 300 Boylston St, Newton, 617-527-1400, www.atrium-mall. com; smaller, ultra-upscale mall with only a few restaurants and 35 specialty shops.
- **Burlington Mall**, 75 Middlesex Tpke, Burlington, 781-272-8667, www.shop simon.com; large mall with a food court, restaurants, and over 155 stores.
- **Cambridgeside Galleria**, 100 Cambridgeside Pl, Cambridge, 617-621-8666, www.cambridgesidegalleria.com; big, urban, multi-level mall with 120 specialty boutiques, kiosks, and restaurants. Parking is discounted, or accessible from the Lechmere T stop (Green Line).
- **Copley Place**, 2 Copley Pl, Boston, 617-369-5000, www.shopcopleyplace.com; Smaller, upscale mall with a few restaurants and 100 stores, connected by a skywalk to the Prudential Center. Discounted Parking, or accessible from the Copley T stop (Green Line).
- **Fresh Pond Mall**, 185 Alewife Brook Pkwy, Cambridge, 617-491-4431; strip mall of a few clustered stores and a movie theater.
- **Liberty Tree Mall**, 100 Independence Way (routes 114 and 128), Danvers, 978-

777-0794, www.simon.com; includes a food court, an arcade, a 20-plex movie theater, and big name stores.

- **The Mall at Chestnut Hill**, 199 Boylston St, Chestnut Hill, 617-965-3038, www. mallatchestnuthill.com; upscale sister-mall to The Atrium, with 60 specialty boutiques and three restaurants.
- **Meadow Glen Mall**, 3850 Mystic Valley Pkwy, Medford, 781-395-6710, www. meadowglen.com; includes a food court and over 50 stores and kiosks in an urban setting.
- **Natick Mall**, 1245 Worcester St, Natick, 508-655-4800; www.natickmall.com; over 170 stores, a food court, and child-friendly amenities like PlaySpace and kiddie rides.
- **North Shore Mall**, routes 114 and 128 in Peabody, 978-531-3440; www.shop simon.com; over 120 stores.
- **Porter Exchange Mall**, 1815 Mass Ave, Cambridge; not necessarily a "mall," but has a large collection of Japanese restaurants, as well as City Sports and Lesley University's bookstore. Accessible from the Porter T stop (Red Line).
- **Shops at the Prudential Center**, 800 Boylston St, Boston, 800-SHOP-PRU, www.prudentialcenter.com; over 75 shops and restaurants, and a large food court. Attached to Copley Place, and accessible from the Copley T stop.
- **South Shore Plaza**, 250 Granite St, Braintree, 781-843-8200, www.shopsimon. com; standard mall with a food court, restaurants, and 180 specialty shops.
- **Square One Mall**, Route 1 South, Saugus, 781-233-8787; www.shopsimon. com; standard mall, with a food court, restaurants, and 115 specialty shops.

OUTLET MALLS

If you are willing to leave the city, outlet shopping can satisfy those shoppers seeking bargains and quality. Along with the few outlets in the greater Boston area, North Conway, NH, and Kittery and Freeport, Maine (a few hours drive north), are well-known outlet towns. Freeport, in particular, is a great day trip if only for the L.L. Bean Outlet, which is open 24 hours, 7 days/week. The following are outlets in the surrounding Boston area:

- **Bourne Outlet Center**, Route 6, Bourne, MA, 800-406-8435
- **Cape Cod Factory Outlets**, One Factory Outlet Rd, Sagamore, 508-888-8417; www.capecodoutletmall.com
- **Tower Outlet Mall**, 657 Quarry St, Fall River, 508-678-6033
- **VF Factory Outlets**, 375 Faunce Corner Rd, North Dartmouth, 508-998-3311; www.vfoutletmall.com
- **Wrentham Village Premium Outlets**, One Premium Outlets Blvd, Wrentham, 508-384-0600; www.premiumoutlets.com/wrentham

DEPARTMENT STORES

Department stores are often the best places to find everything you need under one roof.

- **Barneys New York**, a Manhattan institution known for being high-end and very chic. Upscale Bostonians were positively beaming when Barneys recently came to their city; Copley Place, 617-385-3300; The Mall at Chestnut Hill, 617-969-5354.
- **Bloomingdale's**, The Mall at Chestnut Hill, 617-630-6000, www.blooming dales.com; an upscale national department store chain that got its start in New York's Lower East Side in the 1860s. Personal shoppers or interior designers are available.
- **Harvard/MIT Cooperative Society**, known as "the Coop" (pronounced as in chicken), has two main locations: Harvard Square, 1400 Mass Ave, 617-499-2000, and Kendall Square, 3 Cambridge Center, 617-499-3200; www.thecoop. com. The Coop is a cooperative that students, faculty, alumni, and employees of Harvard, MIT, Wheelock, and the Massachusetts College of Pharmacy can join. Members earn a rebate annually that is based on what they've spent throughout the year. It sells everything from appliances to deodorant.
- **JCPenney**; chock full of all the usual department store stuff for you and your home. There are no locations within the city, but a few in the surrounding suburbs: Natick Mall, 508-651-7041; North Shore Mall, 978-977-3050; Hanover Mall, 1775 Washington St, Hanover, 781-826-2096; 121-177 Concord St, Framingham, 508-820-7059; www.jcpenney.com.
- **Kohl's**, nearest store to Boston is at 3850 Mystic Valley Pkwy in Medford, 781-395-6001, www.kohls.com. Other locations in the suburbs: Burlington, Chelmsford, Danvers, Framingham, Hingham, North Andover, Pembroke, Plymouth, Saugus, Stoughton, Walpole, and Woburn.
- **Lord & Taylor** is the oldest department store in the United States. Federated Department Stores (owner of Macy's) had bought Lord & Taylor, but after closing several locations, sold the chain to NRDC, which is still running many stores across the country and selling quality fashions. Boston area locations: Prudential Center, 617-262-6000; South Shore Plaza, 781-848-1970; Burlington Mall, 781-273-1461; Natick Mall, 508-651-0744; www.lordandtaylor.com.
- **Macy's** is a solid, mid-range store with a large variety of items. Since taking over Filene's (a well-established local chain) Macy's seems to be everywhere. Locations include Downtown Crossing, 617-357-3000; Belmont Center, 75 Leonard St, Belmont, 617-484-3800; Cambridgeside Galleria, 617-621-3800; South Shore Plaza, 781-848-1500; Burlington Mall, 781-272-6000; North Shore Mall, 978-531-9000; Natick Mall, 508-653-3800; www.macys.com.
- **Neiman-Marcus**, this posh department store offers an elegant collection of home goods, clothing, shoes, beauty items, gifts, shoes, etc., from the best designers. Come here for Manolo Blahnik shoes, Prada bags, Dolce and Gabbana

dresses, and more; 5 Copley Pl, Boston, 617-536-3660, Natick Mall, 508-620-5700; www.neimanmarcus.com.

- **Nordstrom** is a Seattle-based retailer that started as a shoe store in 1901, and now offers high-end shopping with some more affordable fashion alternatives. Nordstrom had been looking at the Boston market for years; the first store is in the newly expanded Natick Mall. Plans for other stores in the upcoming years include the Burlington Mall, the North Shore Mall, and by 2010, the South Shore Mall. www.nordstrom.com.
- **Saks Fifth Avenue**, located downtown at the Prudential Center, 617-262-8500, www.saksfifthavenue.com; another of the nation's finest department stores, Saks has a big selection of upscale goods.
- **Sears**, the original department store; this is *the* place for refrigerators, lawnmowers, toolkits, washers and dryers, etc. And don't forget the automotive centers. Greater Boston area locations: Cambridgeside Galleria, 617-252-3500; Square One Mall, 781-231-4595; Dedham Mall, 300 Providence Hwy, Dedham, 781-320-5125; South Shore Plaza, 781-356-6000; Burlington Mall, 781-221-4992; www.sears.com.

DISCOUNT DEPARTMENT STORES

Everyone loves a good deal. Newcomers to Boston's bargain-shopping scene, home to Filene's Basement, will not be disappointed. The quality and the style of the goods vary from store to store, often reflecting the surrounding community. The discount shops in the more upscale communities often carry the best designer names.

- **DSW Shoe Warehouse** is a gigantic multi-floor shoe emporium—shoe addicts will think they've died and gone to heaven here. Not the place to find Jimmy Choo's, but still quite a lot of really good stuff. Greater Boston area locations: Downtown Crossing, 385 Washington St, Boston, 617-556-0052; Dedham Mall, 344 Providence Hwy, Dedham, 781-329-6310; 1 Worcester Rd, Framingham, 508-270-0091; for more store locations go to www.dswshoe.com.
- **Filene's Basement**; the original discount store, it opened in 1909 in the basement of Filene's Department store in Downtown Crossing. Come here for amazing markdowns, but be prepared: the Basement (particularly the original one) is not for the meek. It's crowded and sometimes messy. The Basement carries mostly clothing and shoes, but the second level has housewares, linens, and home decorations. Greater Boston locations include: Downtown Crossing, 426 Washington St, Boston, 617-348-7848; 497 Boylston St, Boston, 617-424-5520; South Shore Plaza, 781-849-0031; 215-227 Needham St, Newton, 617-332-1295; Arsenal Mall, 617-926-4474; for a full list of stores go to www.filenesbasement.com.

- **Kmart**; even staid Bostonians can't resist the lure of the blue light specials; some Greater Boston locations include: 77 Middlesex Ave, Somerville, 617-628-9500; 180 Main St, Saugus, 781-231-0404; 350 Grossman Dr, Braintree, 781-843-5400; check out www.kmart.com for more store locations.
- **Macy's Furniture Gallery**, Shoppers World Mall, routes 9 and 30, Framingham, 508-650-6000; unsold merchandise is sent here where it is marked down even further. You can find electronic equipment, beds, and furniture.
- **Marshalls**; one of the most popular discount shopping chains in the nation, it offers designer clothes, shoes, and other items for a good a bargain. Many locations throughout the area: 500 Boylston St, Boston, 617-262-6066; Downtown Crossing, 350 Washington St, Boston, 617-338-6205; 8D Allstate Rd, Dorchester, 617-442-5050; 3850 Mystic Valley Pkwy, Medford, 781-391-1331; Twin City Plaza, 22 McGrath Hwy, Somerville, 617-776-0674; 1399 North Shore Rd, Revere, 781-289-3217; 455 Arsenal St, Watertown, 617-923-1004; for additional store locations go to www.marshallsonline.com.
- **Target**; you name it, it's here: clothes, games, CDs, books, housewares, food, toys, etc. Greater Boston area locations include 7 Allstate Rd, Dorchester, 617-602-1921; Arsenal Mall, 550 Arsenal St, Watertown, 617-924-6574; 180 Somerville Ave, Somerville, 617-776-4036; 1 Mystic View Rd, Everett, 617-420-0000; 36 Furlong Dr, Revere, 781-922-6030; for additional stores near you, visit www.target.com.
- **T.J. Maxx** is another national bargain bastion, similar to Marshalls in terms of goods, size, and atmosphere. Locations include Downtown Crossing, 350 Washington St, Boston, 617-695-2424; 525 Harvard St, Brookline, 617-232-5420; 198 Alewife Pkwy, Cambridge, 617-492-8500; 105 Middlesex Ave, Somerville, ,617-628-1275; 100 Granite St, Quincy, 617-328-1763; 846 Lexington St, Waltham, 781-893-2968; for more store locations go to www.tjmaxx.com.
- **Wal-Mart**; come here for electronics, clothes, sporting goods, music, video games, toys, books, jewelry, etc. The five closest locations to Boston are all in the suburbs: 780 Lynnway, Lynn, 781-592-4300; 301 Falls Blvd, Quincy, 617-745-4390; 450 Highland Ave, Salem, 978-825-1713; 740 Middle St, Weymouth, 781-331-0063; 55 Avalon Village Way, Danvers, 978-777-6977; for more locations, go to www.walmart.com.

HOUSEHOLD SHOPPING

APPLIANCES, ELECTRONICS, COMPUTERS, AND SOFTWARE

Bostonians needing to augment or repair their home entertainment centers, upgrade their computer systems, or create home offices will find local proprietors eager to assist, as well as the more "self-service oriented" national chains. Check the Yellow Pages under "Appliances," "Electric Appliances," "Electronic Equipment & Supplies," and "Computers & Equipment" for a complete listing, or try one of the following:

- **Best Buy**; locations throughout the city and the suburbs: Cambridgeside Galleria, 617-577-8866; Landmark Center, 401 Park Dr, Suite 4, Boston, 617-424-7900; 14 Allstate Rd, Dorchester, 617-445-5361; Arsenal Mall, 617-926-0142; for additional locations, check out www.bestbuy.com.
- **Cambridge Sound Works**, 68 Highland Ave, Needham, 781-449-6442; www.cambridgesoundworks.com
- **Circuit City**, 8 Allstate Rd, Dorchester, 617-541-4120; 65 Mystic Ave, Somerville, 617-623-3400; suburban locations in Braintree, Burlington, Danvers, Hanover, Medford, Natick, Salem, and Saugus; www.circuitcity.com.
- **Mystic Appliance**, 135 Cambridge St, Charlestown, 617-242-9679
- **Radio Shack**; locations throughout the city and suburbs; visit www.radioshack.com for details.
- **Tweeter**, 350 Boylston St, Boston, 617-262-2299; 14 Needham St, Newton, 617-964-4414; 805 Providence Hwy, Dedham, 781-329-7300; www.tweeter.com

BEDS, BEDDING, AND BATH

Locals call Cambridge the futon capital of Massachusetts. For a complete list of stores, check the Yellow Pages under "Mattresses" and "Futons." In the meantime, here's a list to get you started:

- **Bed, Bath, & Beyond**, Landmark Center, 401 Park Dr, Boston, 617-536-1090 (take advantage of their rare, in-city parking lot); 8 Allstate Rd, Dorchester, 617-442-2422; 119 Middlesex Ave, Somerville, 617-629-4423; suburban locations in Braintree, Burlington, Danvers, Everett, and Framingham; for more locations and information, go to www.bedbathandbeyond.com.
- **Boston Bed Co.**, 1113 Comm Ave, Boston, 617-782-3830; www.bostonbed.com
- **Boston Futon**, 97 Mass Ave, Boston, 617-266-8970
- **Bedworks**, 15 Western Ave, Cambridge, 617-547-6000, www.bedworks.net
- **Dream On Futon–Futonair**, 299 Prospect St, Cambridge, 617-864-6000
- **Jennifer Convertibles**, 1 Porter Sq, Cambridge, 617-661-0200; 1524 VFW Pkwy, West Roxbury, 617-325-4891; 376 Boylston St, Boston, 617-375-9083; go to www.jenniferfurniture.com for more showroom locations.
- **Linens 'n Things**, Arsenal Mall, 617-924-8800; 260 Needham St, Newton, 617-964-0051; locations throughout the metro area include Braintree, Burlington, Danvers, Dedham, Framingham, and North Weymouth, to name a few; www.lnt.com.
- **Sleep-A-Rama**, 1007 Mass Ave, Cambridge, 617-354-6993; 97 Mass Ave, Boston, 617-266-8970; www.sleeparama.com.

FURNITURE

A small area of Cambridge between Harvard and Central squares where Mass Ave and Mt. Auburn Street intersect is called the "furniture district." This is a good place to start, but if you don't find what you want, there are many other furniture stores throughout the region, and you can always check the selection at your favorite department store.

- **Adesso**, 200 Boylston St, Boston, 617-451-2212; www.adesso-boston.com
- **Bernie & Phyl's Furniture**, local furniture store with catchy advertising and five showroom locations in the Boston suburbs—Braintree, Nashua, NH, Raynham, Saugus, Westboro, and Weymouth. Go to www.bernieandphyls.com for more location details.
- **Boston Interiors**, 31 Boylston St, Brookline, 617-731-6038; 10 Worcester Rd, Natick, 508-650-9539; and other locations throughout Greater Boston; go to www.bostoninteriors.com for more information.
- **City Schemes**, 1050 Mass Ave, Cambridge, 617-497-0707; 22 Kent St, Somerville, 617-776-7777; 395 Worcester Rd, Route 9 West, Natick, 508-655-3434; 799 Broadway, Saugus; www.cityschemes.com
- **Cocoon**, 170 Tremont St, Boston, 617-728-9898
- **Crate & Barrel**, 140 Faneuil Hall, Boston, 617-742-6025; 777 Boylston St, Boston, 617-262-8700; 48 Brattle St in Harvard Square, Cambridge, 617-876-6300; 1045 Mass Ave, Cambridge, 617-547-3994; The Mall at Chestnut Hill, 617-964-8400; suburban locations in Braintree, Burlington, Hingham, Natick, and Woburn; www.crateandbarrel.com.
- **Domain Home Fashions**, 7 Newbury St, Boston, 617-266-5252; 6 Wayside Rd, Burlington, 781-273-2288; 575 Worcester Rd, Natick, 508-907-6560; www.domain-home.com
- **Eastern Butcher Block**, 281 Concord Ave, Cambridge, 617-497-9100; suburban locations in Braintree, Danvers, and Framingham; www.butcherblock.com.
- **Ethan Allen**, 840 Willard St, Quincy, 617-471-3331; 636 Broadway, Saugus, 781-233-5663; 34 Cambridge St, Burlington, 781-273-2515; for additional store locations in Greater Boston, go to www.ethanallen.com.
- **Ikea**; nothing made Boston shoppers happier than to finally have the famous Swedish furniture store within their reach; 1 Ikea Way, Stoughton, 781-344-4532; www.ikea.com.
- **Jordan's Furniture**, local furniture retailer that has been operating for almost 100 years; they are famous for great deals, good customer service, recognizable advertising, and unique stores. All stores are in Boston suburbs: 1 Underprice Way (Route 9), Natick, 508-424-0088, includes an IMAX 3D Theater; 100 Stockwell Dr, Avon, 508-580-4900, includes Motion Odyssey (3D) Movie Ride and a colossal clearance center; 50 Walker's Brook Dr, Reading, 781-944-9090. For more stores and information, go to www.jordans.com.

- **Maverick Designs**, 1117 Comm Ave, Boston, 617-783-0274, www.boston wood.com
- **The Oak Gallery**, 201 Mass Ave, Lexington, 781-861-1500; www.oakgallery.com
- **Pottery Barn**, 122 Newbury St, Boston, 617-266-6553; Atrium Mall, 617-964-4001; South Shore Plaza, 781-849-8510; Burlington Mall, 781-229-2993; North Shore Mall, 978-532-5179; for additional store information, go to www.potterybarn.com.
- **Restoration Hardware**, 711 Boylston St, Boston, 617-578-0088; Atrium Mall, 617-641-6770; North Shore Mall, 978-532-1714; www.restorationhardware.com
- **Roche Bobois**, 2 Avery St, Boston, 617-742-9611; 579 Worcester Rd, Natick, 508-650-5844; www.roche-bobois.com
- **Shoomine**, 8 Park Plaza, Boston, 617-227-2021; www.shoomine.com

HOUSEWARES

If you love to browse, you'll enjoy discovering the many talented artists who sell their unique housewares in small shops throughout the area. However, if you're in a rush to outfit your kitchen fast, you may want to try a department or discount store, or check Bed, Bath, & Beyond, Crate & Barrel, Linens 'n Things, or Pottery Barn. Here are a few other establishments you might try:

- **Abodeon**, 1731 Mass Ave, Cambridge, 617-497-0137, www.abodeon.com
- **Bowl & Board**, small local chain with a decent variety of cool housewares and furniture: 1354 Beacon St, Brookline, 617-566-4726; 1063 Mass Ave, Cambridge, 617-661-0350; www.bowlandboard.com.
- **China Fair**, 2100 Mass Ave, Cambridge, 617-864-3050; 70 Needham St, Newton Highlands, 617-332-1250; www.chinafairinc.com
- **City Housewares**, 434 Harvard St, Brookline, 617-278-6333
- **Home Goods**, 978 Boylston St, Newton, 617-965-5055
- **Kitchen Arts**, 161 Newbury St, Boston, 617-266-8701
- **Lavender**, 173 Newbury St, Boston, 617-437-1102, www.lavenderhomeandtable.com
- **Pier 1 Imports**, 15 Mystic View Rd, Everett, 617-389-2445; 1 Porter Sq, Cambridge, 617-491-7626; 1351 Beacon St, Brookline, 617-232-9627; 120 Granite St, Quincy, 781-848-4933; for a listing of additional stores, go to www.pier1.com.
- **Placewares**, 796 Beacon St, Newton Centre, 617-527-9170; 59 Leonard St, Belmont Center, 617-489-3555; 68 Central St, Wellesley, 781-237-2860; 13 Walden St, Concord, 978-369-1590; www.placewares.com
- **Red River Trading Co.**, 1313 Washington St, Boston, 617-542-2223, www.redrivertradingco.com

- **Williams-Sonoma**, Copley Pl, 617-262-3080; Atrium Mall, 617-969-7090; South Shore Plaza, 781-365-0515; Burlington Mall, 781-273-1114; North Shore Mall, 978-531-9623; Natick Mall, 508-647-4007; for more store locations and information, go to www.williamssonoma.com.

HARDWARE AND GARDEN CENTERS

You should be able to find a hardware store in your neighborhood no matter where you live. For your local **Ace Hardware** go to www.acehardware.com, and for **True Value affiliates** visit www.truevalue.com. The two competing mega chains also have stores in the Greater Boston area:

- **Home Depot**, 75 Mystic Ave, Somerville, 617-623-0001; 5 Allstate Rd (South Bay), Boston, 617-442-6110; 1 Mystic View Rd, Everett, 617-389-2323; 1213 VFW Pkwy, West Roxbury, 617-327-5000; 615 Arsenal St, Watertown, 617-926-0299; go to www.homedepot.com for a complete listing of stores.
- **Lowe's** 1500 Broadway, Saugus, 781-417-1027; 306 Providence Hwy, Dedham, 718-355-3780; 729 Bridge St, Weymouth, 781-340-5964; 350 Cochituate Rd, Framingham, 508-309-1183; go to www.lowes.com for a complete listing of stores.

SECOND-HAND SHOPPING

Rack-rummaging at thrift stores and looking for treasures at flea markets are hobbies for many, and Boston definitely has some quality antique shops offering old New England wares. If you want to jump on the shabby chic bandwagon, consider the following suggestions.

ANTIQUE SHOPS AND DISTRICTS

Those newcomers who are up on their Limoges and Hummels should be pleased with the local antiquing scene. To get started, check the Yellow Pages under "Antiques" or go to www.antiquing.com or www.antiqueinfo.com for recommendations of shops in your area. The following are area antique districts or markets:

- **Antique Alley**; if you're in the mood for a day trip, this stretch of Route 7 between Great Barrington and the Connecticut border (mostly in Sheffield) is loaded with antique dealers.
- **Beacon Hill**; this area is paradise for many, particularly the stretch along **Charles Street**, where antique shops dominate.
- **Brimfield, MA**, home of the Brimfield Antique Shops; this is the largest out-

door antique show in New England, held over a one-mile stretch of Route 20 during the warmer months. Visit www.brimfield.com for details.

- **Cambridge Antique Market**, 201 Msgr. O'Brien Hwy, Cambridge, 617-868-9655, www.marketantique.com/cambridg.htm; over 150 dealer spaces on five floors, open 11 a.m. to 6 p.m. Tuesday–Sunday. Located across the street from the Lechmere T stop.
- **Essex, MA,** is referred to as "America's Antique Capital" for its 35+ antique shops. Don't forget to stop off at Woodman's for fried clams.
- **Haverhill Antique Market**, 90 Washington St, Haverhill, 978-374-6644, www.marketantique.com/haverhil.htm; come here for 80+ dealer spaces on two floors. Not open Mondays.
- **Provincetown Antique Market**, 131 Commercial St, Provincetown, 508-487-1115, www.marketantique.com/province.htm; P-town, at the tip of Cape Cod, has a big antique market on weekends, Memorial Day through November.

THRIFT AND VINTAGE SHOPS

Not only can you find some really cool, cheap stuff at thrift shops, but charities and hospital programs frequently benefit from the proceeds. What could be better than shopping for a cause? You might also want to check the weekly paper for listings of local flea markets, garage sales, and auctions. For those who like the challenge and the value of finding a diamond in the rough, try one of the following:

- **American Family Thrift Store**, 1698 Comm Ave, Brighton, 617-232-9694
- **Beacon Hill Thrift Shop**, 15 Charles St, Boston, 617-742-2323
- **Beth Israel–Deaconess Medical Center Thrift Shop**, 25 Harvard St, Brookline, 617-566-7016
- **Boomerangs**, 716 Centre St, Jamaica Plain, 617-524-5120
- **Christ Church Thrift Shop**, 17 Farwell Pl, Cambridge, 617-492-3335, www.cccambridge.org/thriftshop.html
- **The Garment District**, 200 Broadway, Cambridge, 617-876-5230, www.garment-district.com
- **Goodwill Stores**, 1010 Harrison Ave, Boston, 617-541-1270; 520 Mass Ave, Cambridge, 617-868-6330; 230 Elm St, Somerville, 617-628-3618; 315 W Broadway, S Boston, 617-307-6367; for more retail store locations, go to www.goodwillmass.org.
- **Oona's**, 1210 Mass Ave, Cambridge, 617-491-2654
- **Proletariat**, 36 JFK St (the Garage), Cambridge, 617-661-3865; www.arevolt.com
- **Salvation Army Thrift Stores**, 483 Broadway, Somerville, 617-395-9783; 328 Mass Ave, Cambridge, 617-354-9159; for more information and store locations, go to www.salvationarmyusa.org.
- **Second Time Around Collections**, 176 Newbury St, Boston, 617-247-3504;

219 Newbury St, Boston, 617-266-1113; 99 Charles St, Boston, 617-227-0049, 8 Eliot St, Cambridge, 617-491-7185; Atrium Mall, 300 Boylston St, Brookline, 617-928-0100; for more information and store locations, check out www.sec ondtimearound.net.

- **St. Gerard's Guild Thrift Shop**, 251 Washington St, Somerville, 617-666-3754
- **Thrift Shop of Boston**, 17 Corinth St, Roslindale, 617-325-5300
- **Urban Renewals**, 122 Brighton Ave, Allston, 617-783-8387; well loved by the alternative crowd.

FOOD

Boston's large immigrant population means you can find all sorts of international delicacies, and of course, fresh seafood is everywhere. For more about supermarkets, warehouse shopping, farmers' markets and community gardens, ethnic enclaves, and specialty grocers, read on.

SUPERMARKETS

Major grocery store chains in metro Boston are **Shaw's/Star Market, Stop & Shop**, and **Foodmaster**. Star Market and Shaw's are now under the same ownership, so you can use the same discount card at either of them. Foodmaster offers fewer gourmet items and tends to be less expensive. Outside the city, you'll find **Demoulas Market Basket**, which offers considerably lower prices than its competitors. Beyond the larger chains, most neighborhoods in the city have a corner mom and pop market where you can get most of your basic needs.

- **Demoulas Market Basket**, 400 Somerville Ave, Somerville, 617-666-2420; 160 Everett Ave, Chelsea, 617-884-0646; for more store locations, look up "Market Basket" in your local white pages.
- **FoodMaster**, 105 Alewife Brook Pkwy, Somerville, 617-660-1342; 45 Beacon St, Somerville, 617-660-1322; 51 Austin St, Charlestown, 617-660-1372; go to www.foodmasterinc.com for a complete listing of stores.
- **Shaw's (Star Market)**, 53 Huntington Ave, Boston, 617-262-4688; 33 Kilmarnock St, Boston, 617-267-4684; 1065 Comm Ave, Allston, 617-783-5878; 246 Border St, E Boston, 617-567-4116; 14 McGrath Hwy, Somerville, 617-625-4070; 20 Sidney St, Cambridge, 617-494-5250; 275 Beacon St, Somerville, 617-354-7023; 299 Broadway, Somerville, 617-776-7733; go to www.shaws.com for a complete listing of both Shaw's and Star Market stores.
- **Stop & Shop**, 155 Harvard St, Brookline, 617-566-4559; 713 E Broadway, S Boston, 617-269-7989; 1620 Tremont St, Boston, 617-232-3572; 460 Blue Hill Ave, Roxbury, 617-427-6752; go to www.stopandshop.com for the additional store locations.

HOME DELIVERY

Until recently, Boston had numerous home delivery services. These days there is one major grocery delivery service in Boston, **Peapod** (www.peapod.com), which is run by Stop & Shop. It's an internet service, and when you place your order you choose the day you would like your groceries delivered and a two-hour delivery window. If you're unhappy with the quality of the produce, you can send it back. Tipping is optional, and satisfaction is guaranteed. Visit them online to arrange for service.

WAREHOUSE SHOPPING

What warehouse stores (a.k.a. shopping clubs) lack in glamour, they make up for in affordability. You have to join and get a membership card to shop at them, but if you have a big family and go through lots of paper towels and milk, this may be a good option.

- **BJ's Wholesale Club**, 278 Middlesex Ave, Medford, 781-396-0451; 688 Providence Hwy, Dedham, 781-326-2697, 26 Whittier St, Framingham, 508-872-2100; for more store locations, go to www.bjs.com.
- **Costco**, 400 Commercial Circle, Dedham, 781-251-9975; 2 Mystic View Rd, Everett, 617-544-4806; and 71 Second Ave, Waltham, 781-622-3883; www.costco.com
- **Sam's Club**, 500 Colony Pl, Plymouth, 508-747-2047, www.samsclub.com

SPECIALTY GROCERS

Whole Foods Market is an upscale, supermarket-sized natural food chain. Similarly, **Roche Brothers Wild Harvests**, which are owned by Shaw's/Star Market and are usually in or next to one of those stores, offer natural food selections. **Trader Joe's** is another specialty chain, with a reputation for good prices. **Harvest Cooperative** is a community-owned co-op that buys products that support fair trade, sustainable agriculture, and supports local farmers and food producers.

- **The Harvest Co-op Markets**, 581 Mass Ave, Cambridge, 617-524-1664; 57 South St, Jamaica Plain, 617-524-1667; www.harvestcoop.com
- **Roche Bros.**, 377 Chestnut St, Needham, 781-444-0411; Granite Crossing, 101 Falls Blvd, Quincy, 617-471-0500; 1800 Centre St, West Roxbury, 617-469-0757; for a complete listing of stores, go to www.rochebros.com.
- **Savenor's Market**, 160 Charles St, Boston, 617-723-6328; high-end specialty market known for its selection of quality meats and cheeses.
- **Trader Joe's**, 899 Boylston St, Boston, 617-262-6505; 748 Memorial Dr, Cambridge, 617-491-8582; 1317 Beacon St, Brookline, 617-278-9997; 958 Highland

Ave, Needham, 781-449-6993; 1121 Washington St, Newton, 617-244-1620; for a complete listing of stores, go to www.traderjoes.com.

- **Whole Foods Market**, 15 Westland Ave, Boston, 617-375-1010; 181 Cambridge St, Boston 617-723-0004; 15 Washington St, Brighton, 617-738-8187; 15 Prospect St, Cambridge, 617-492-0070; 340 River St, Cambridge, 617-876-6990; for a complete listing of stores, go to www.wholefoodsmarket.com.

FARMERS' MARKETS

Local farmers' markets are a great way to buy fresh, often organic, produce and meats, while also supporting your local farmer. According to the Massachusetts Department of Food and Agriculture (MDFA), there are over 100 farmers' markets throughout Massachusetts, many of them in the metro Boston area. For a listing of markets, try out www.massfarmersmarkets.com. You'll notice most are open only during warmer months, but Boston's famous **Haymarket** is open year-round. For exact schedules either call your town hall, or contact the MDFA at 617-626-1700, www.state.ma.us/dfa. Haymarket is not a farmers' market in the truest sense; open on Fridays and Saturdays, the Haymarket is where wholesalers try to sell produce that they couldn't sell to area retailers or restaurateurs. Everyone should experience the Haymarket at least once, but keep your wits about you and carry lots of singles. The Haymarket is a good place to go if you have specific bulk items in mind, for example, a case of limes or lemons for a margarita party, or strawberries for making jam. Bostonians who frequent the Haymarket can get to know the sellers, and thus learn who has good produce, who will give a good deal, and who will take back their goods if they don't meet expectations. Fresh fish is sometimes available.

COMMUNITY GARDENS

Why pay someone else for fresh greens when you can grow them yourself? But where is that possible if you live in a densely populated neighborhood like Beacon Hill or the South End? A community garden is the answer. Over 200 community gardens exist in the greater Boston area. Perhaps two of the most visible in Boston proper are the community plots in the **Fens** (500 plots in the Richard Parker Memorial Victory Gardens, including some for children and special needs gardeners) and those in the **Southwest Corridor**, of which there are 15. Among other tasks, the **Boston Natural Areas Network** protects and supervises the local community gardens. To find out more about where the community gardens are, or to sign up for a place to exercise your green thumb, contact them at 617-542-7696, www.bostonnatural.org/garden_list.php.

RESTAURANTS

Boston's dining opportunities run the gamut from expensive, high-end dining rooms like Locke-Ober or the next creation by Todd English—easily the city's most famous restaurateur—to hole-in-the-wall gems like small Italian eateries, sushi bars, and low-key (but amazingly good) fried seafood shacks on the water. And when in doubt, you can almost always find a pub that serves decent fish and chips.

If you'd like a little guidance as you explore area eateries, try the *Boston Globe, Phoenix,* or *Herald* for restaurant reviews. *The Weekly Dig* and *The Improper Bostonian,* both free newspapers, also feature reviews, and are full of ads for local establishments. *Boston Magazine* puts out a yearly list of the "Best of Boston"; you can browse past years at www.bostonmagazine.com/best_of/. General restaurant advice can be found in the ubiquitous annual *Zagat Survey of Boston Restaurants* (www.zagat.com), or for short, digestible, "best of" lists, try *Phantom Gourmet: Guide to Boston's Best Restaurants* (www.phantomgourmet.com).

ETHNIC DISTRICTS

You can find the standard Chinese, Mexican, Indian, Vietnamese, Italian, French, and Middle Eastern restaurants spread throughout greater Boston. However, because Boston's distinct ethnic and immigrant groups tend to stick together, going to specific areas in the city will offer a selection of restaurants, bakeries, and grocers of the same cultural ilk.

Of course, the most obvious neighborhood in this respect is **Chinatown**, where you will find a well-rounded selection of not just Chinese, but **Asian foods** of many different types, including Thai, Vietnamese, and Korean. Chinatown is packed with independently owned restaurants, and you can also shop for specialty groceries if you like to cook with Asian ingredients. Many of the restaurants stay open later than in the rest of the city, so not only is Chinatown a great place to head with the family for dinner on a Sunday night, but it's also good during the wee hours of Sunday morning after a night out on the town. The Asian supermarket **Super 88** can be found not only in Chinatown, but also in **Allston, Malden, Quincy,** and **Dorchester**. Go to www.super88market.com for more location details.

Although we're about as far as you can get from the Pacific Rim within the US, Boston does have decent sushi options. The biggest concentration of sushi bars and **Japanese** restaurants is in **Coolidge Corner** in Brookline. If you want to shop for specialty Japanese ingredients, you will need to cross over the Charles and head to the **Porter Exchange** building in Porter Square, where there is a Japanese supermarket and a number of Japanese restaurants.

Because it is home to a large Jewish population, **Brookline** is also *the* place to go for **Jewish** food, particularly Coolidge and JFK corners. Delis, butchers, kosher kitchens, falafel joints, and bagel bakeries dot Harvard Street between Beacon Street and Comm Ave. You can even get kosher Chinese food at a restaurant near Brookline Village. If you are in Cambridge and you crave a knish and some matzo ball soup, try the **S&S Deli** in Inman Square, but be prepared for a long line during weekend brunch.

The **Russian** community is also prevalent in Brookline (especially **Washington Square**), where you can find a few Russian restaurants and grocers. For more Russian foodstuffs, check out Harvard Avenue in **Allston**, in particular the **Moscow International Food Store**, where you can find Russian food, gifts, and local community news. As for **Armenian** food, head over to **Watertown**, home to one of the largest Armenian populations in the US.

While **Italian** restaurants are plentiful throughout the state, nothing beats the **North End** when you're looking for food from the old country. Over 40 restaurants and cafés take up the first floors of a significant number of buildings. Some are big enough to take up two floors; some are so tiny they don't even have 10 tables; and some, like Giacomo's, are so popular they always have a line out the door, even on the coldest winter nights. There are also a number of small Italian grocers, or salumerias, which specialize in imported items from Italy. Keep in mind, parking in the North End is not an easy task. For other Italian enclaves, you might want to check out **Eastie** (specifically Sabatino's), although the Italian population there continues to decrease.

For newcomers in dire need of a good **German** wiener schnitzel, try **Jacob Wirth's**, an unassuming pub in the Theater District. And if you have a car, take the 15-minute drive up Route 1 North to **Karl's Sausage Kitchen**, a small, specialty German grocer and deli along a particularly gaudy stretch of highway in Saugus that draws pilgrims from all over the area.

Irish culture is everywhere in Boston, but if you are looking for where the true Irish hang out, complete with brogue-laden bartenders, afternoon sessions, hurling matches on the television, and grocers selling Heinz beans, head to **Southie, Dorchester, Brighton Center, Canton** (home to the Irish Cultural Centre of New England), or **Quincy**.

If **Greek** is your preference, you might want to hop in the car and check out Roslindale. You will also be interested to know that many Greek families own and run the pizza places/sub shops (a.k.a. submarine sandwich, grinder, hoagie, foot long, etc.) around the region. This means that when you stop into your neighborhood sub shop for a chicken-parmesan sub, you'll likely encounter pretty framed pictures of the Greek islands and be able to order a doner kabob as well.

For various types of **Latin** cuisine, your best bet may be to head to **Allston, East Boston,** or **Cambridge**, all of which have many immigrants from Central and South America. Cambridge has a number of **Brazilian** and **Portuguese** residents, and you can find some awesome restaurants serving those types of food between **Inman Square** and **East Cambridge**, particularly along Cambridge Street.

Cambridge itself is a melting pot where you will find ethnic foods of all sorts. This is best evidenced by Central Square, which has an array of ethnic cuisines. So if you are hankering for something exotic but don't know what, take a stroll around. Check out **Cardullo's** in **Harvard Square**, a specialty grocer that imports goods from all over the world; go there to find your English digestive biscuits or Australian Vegemite.

SEAFOOD

One market New Englanders have cornered is seafood. The abundance here is so great that in the old days there were laws restricting the number of times per month a wife could serve her husband lobster! First, a quick primer on local seafood culture. 1) There is a lot of fish on the menu here, and you will undoubtedly encounter something called "scrod." Scrod is *not* a type of fish, but rather the local term for the whitefish catch of the day, usually cod or haddock. 2) There is even more shellfish; options include shrimp, clams, scallops, mussels, oysters, and lobster. Crab is available, but it is not a local specialty. 3) Locals like their shellfish breaded and fried. Boston's nickname may be Beantown, but fried clams, fried shrimp, and fried scallops (all served with tartar sauce) are truly local dishes. Clams, in particular, come two ways: strips, which are just the necks, and then whole clams, which include the bellies along with the necks (whole clams are more desirable). Note: when you order a clam roll (or other type of shellfish roll), you'll be getting a fried helping of that shellfish on a hot dog roll; an exception is the lobster roll, which is regular lobster meat, not fried. 4) The other local dish is clam chowder. Undoubtedly you've eaten it before, but it is better here. New England clam chowder is the white kind; the red kind is Manhattan clam chowder. 5) And finally, the *pièce de resistance* of local shellfish is lobster. Some feel that eating lobster equals a whole lot of effort for only a little meat, but regardless, it is comfortably ensconced at the top of the shellfish chain in desirability and price. It is commonly the most expensive item on any menu, and often it will be listed at "market price," which means the price varies daily. You can have lobster boiled, steamed, Newberg, in bisque, in pie, or in a casserole, and when you eat it, the locals at nearby tables will be very, *very* excited if you've never had it before—there's nothing that can get a Bostonian to chat like asking for help cracking open your lobster. If you'd like to make it at home, it is easy and cheaper than ordering it at a restaurant. Throughout the region, grocery and seafood stores sell live lobsters.

Most seafood in Boston restaurants and grocery stores is bought daily from distributors at the fish pier in South Boston. If you'd like to experience this yourself, get there before dawn and you might see boats unloading their catch and buyers haggling for wholesale bargains. For a smaller version at more reasonable hours, go to Haymarket on Friday or Saturday and follow your nose to the few fish vendors.

One type of restaurant unique to New England is the **clam shack**, which serves lobster and fresh fried shellfish along the coast near beaches and harbors. They may look dodgy, but they're generally very good. Locals' opinions on the best around are as varied as their locations, but some of the better known establishments are **Woodman's of Essex**, the **Clam Box** in Ipswich, and **Kelly's** in Revere (also famous for their hot roast beef sandwiches). There are lots of more medium-range and upscale (not to mention healthier) seafood options around, too. **Legal Sea Foods**, with locations throughout the city, has built a legendary reputation for freshness and quality, and **Anthony's Pier 4**, by the South Boston wharves, is also a local favorite. While it is a bit of a tourist trap, you'll be tempted to try the **Union Oyster House** right next to Faneuil Hall. The oldest continuinously operating restaurant in the US, its ambiance, location, and décor are fabulous, and JFK himself used to eat there.

LIQUOR STORES

Because of the so-called "blue laws" that regulate the sale of alcohol, buying a bottle of wine is likely going to be more complicated than you are used to; however, in recent years, those laws have been loosened somewhat, especially with the 2004 lift on the Sunday alcohol ban. In Massachusetts you can't buy alcohol in grocery stores, gas stations, or convenience stores, though there is one exception: a clause allows supermarket chains to sell alcohol at three of their locations. If your local supermarket isn't one of these few, there are plenty of liquor stores around—a.k.a. package stores, or "packies"—where you can buy beer, wine, and spirits. Tip: when driving through New Hampshire, many locals stop at the New Hampshire State Liquor Store (numerous locations) to take advantage of their lower consumer taxes on wine and liquor (no beer sold).

CULTURAL LIFE

ONCE DUBBED THE "ATHENS OF AMERICA" FOR ITS VARIETY OF cultural offerings, Boston continues to uphold this weighty moniker. Options include music, movies, theater, opera, comedy, museums, lectures, children's events, and just about anything else you can think of to pass the time and broaden your horizons. On top of it all, lower-priced (or even free) student events abound in every category as well.

Institutions such as the Boston Symphony Orchestra and the Museum of Fine Arts are among the oldest and best-regarded in the nation. The local music scene, with distinguished alumni such as Aerosmith, the Cars, and the Pixies, continues to thrive in the city's bars and clubs, industry events, and college radio. An important outpost of the stand-up and improv circuits, Boston has produced a wealth of well-known comedians, from Dane Cook and Dennis Leary to talk-show hosts Conan O'Brien and Jay Leno.

The varied venues of the theater district host everything from grand-scale touring productions to edgy black-box dramas and student operas. New Broadway hits often debut with a trial run in Boston the week before their New York opening—big star casts included. Outside the theater district, and even outside of the city, quality theater options abound with venues like the American Repertory Theatre in Harvard Square, the Merrimack Repertory Theater in Lowell, and the Gloucester Stage Company (founded by world famous playwright Israel Horowitz).

During the warmer months, events in Boston are often staged outside. Summers are spent with the Boston Pops and other musical artists—from small local orchestras to major international bands—performing for free along the Charles River at the **Hatch Shell** on the Esplanade. On Friday nights Bostonians arrive in droves with chairs, blankets, and snacks to take advantage of the **Free Friday Flicks** series of family-appropriate movies that take place at sundown. Also, for about a week each summer, the Citi Performing Arts Center presents **Free**

Shakespeare on the Common, where you can lie on a blanket or in the grass and enjoy the poetic words of Will himself. Or for something more carefree and full of tempo, join the Tango Society of Boston for **Tango by Moonlight**; every full moon they tango on the Weeks Footbridge near Harvard Square.

Local newspapers are the best source for upcoming events. The *Boston Globe*'s "Calendar" is in the Thursday paper, and the "Sidekick" appears Monday through Saturday; the *Boston Herald*'s "Scene" arrives on Friday. Both papers offer extensive entertainment sections on Sundays as well. Additional free sources are the *Phoenix*, the *Weekly Dig*, and the *Improper Bostonian*.

TICKETS

Specifics on ticket information are usually included in newspaper listings. Depending on the venue, you'll either get your tickets from the theater or box office or through a ticket agency (usually Ticketmaster). If you cannot live without seeing an upcoming concert and the event is sold out, never fear, there are plenty of ticket resellers. Check http://boston.craigslist.org/tix for scalpers, or look in the Yellow Pages under "Ticket Sales Entertainment and Sports." Otherwise, try one of these options:

- **ArtsBoston/BOSTIX,** 617-262-8632, www.artsboston.org, is a non-profit umbrella group partially funded by the Massachusetts Cultural Council. They sell discounted theater, music, and dance tickets online and via mail order, and promote upcoming events through their newsletter *ArtsMail*. Call to get on their mailing list, or sign up online. ArtsBoston also operates BOSTIX (www.bostix.org) booths in Faneuil Hall Marketplace and Copley Square. In addition to full-price advance tickets, you can also get half-price day-of-show tickets and other bargains. The Copley Square booth is open Monday–Saturday from 10 a.m. to 6 p.m., and 11 a.m. to 4 p.m. on Sundays; the Faneuil Hall location follows the same schedule but is closed on Mondays. Cash only.
- **Berklee Performance Center,** 136 Mass Ave, Boston, 617-747-2261, www.berkleebpc.com; check with them at 617-747-8890 for recorded concert listings. Phone orders are through Ticketmaster, onsite sales are cash, MasterCard, or VISA only. The ticket booth is open Monday–Saturday, 10 a.m. to 6 p.m.
- **Boston Symphony Orchestra** offers 24-hour concert information; call 617-266-2378, or go to www.bso.org.
- **Live Nation,** www.livenation.com; promoter site with ticketing links to most area shows; often the exclusive ticket source for shows at the Paradise, Avalon, and Axis.
- **Ticketmaster** most likely will have what you need, for a steep fee. You can order tickets by phone at 617-931-2000 or online at www.ticketmaster.com.
- **World Music/CRASHarts** is a nonprofit group dedicated to bringing traditional, contemporary, and international performing arts to venues throughout the city; season is concentrated in the spring. Membership and subscrip-

tions available; call 617-876-4275 or visit www.worldmusic.org for tickets and information.

MUSIC

Imagine seeing the next up-and-coming Branford Marsalis, Juliana Hatfield, or Melissa Etheridge—all alumni of the Berklee College of Music. To catch current students' performances, head to the Berklee Performance Center. In various coffeehouses and small clubs around town, you can listen to modern folk singers. You can even find some bluegrass or line dancing in this Yankee bastion if you look hard enough. If more timeless fare is what you're after, there is certainly no shortage of world class jazz, blues, opera, and classical music to be found here.

PROFESSIONAL—SYMPHONIC, CHORAL, OPERA, CHAMBER

- Founded just 30 years ago, the **Boston Baroque**, 617-484-9200, www.boston baroque.org, was actually the first Baroque orchestra in all of North America, and has been nominated for several Grammys. Like the Boston Philharmonic, seasonal shows take place at New England Conservatory of Music's Jordan Hall and Harvard's Sanders Theater; however, you should contact the Boston Baroque's own box office to buy individual tickets or season subscriptions.
- **Boston Camerata**, 617-262-2092, www.bostoncamerata.com; this 50-year-old ensemble presents European and American medieval, renaissance and early baroque vocal and instrumental concerts at various locations around the metro area. On occasion they also perform 18th- and 19th-century American folk music.
- **Boston Chamber Music Society**, 617-349-0086, www.bostonchamber music.org, an ensemble of eight, has been performing chamber music to local audiences for over 20 years. Performances are held at NEC's Jordan Hall on Friday night and at Harvard's Sanders Theater on Sunday night, with additional events at the Longy School of Music in Cambridge. Buy a subscription or tickets to individual concerts and special events through their box office.
- Performing as a gay community–based chorus for 25 years, the acclaimed **Boston Gay Men's Chorus**, 617-542-SING, www.bgmc.org, is a 175-voice ensemble. They perform diverse musical works covering the gamut of genres—from classical, to popular, to showtunes. Subscription series and individual tickets are available to the shows at Jordan and Symphony halls, as well as Northeastern's Blackman Auditorium and various special engagements around the region.
- Since 1958, students aged 6–18 from all six New England states have been learning and performing with the highly esteemed **Greater Boston Youth Symphony Orchestras** (**GBYSO**), 617-353-3348, www.gbyso.org. With three full orchestras, a string orchestra, four chamber orchestras, and a preparatory

wind ensemble, GYBSO has performed all over the world, including in Europe, Israel, South America, and the White House. Locally, GYBSO usually performs its season at Symphony Hall, the Tsai Performance Center, BU Concert Hall, Sanders Theater (Harvard), and the Gardner Museum. Call the venue to purchase individual tickets or contact GBYSO for a subscription.

- Boston's major opera company, **Boston Lyric Opera**, 617-542-4912, www.blo. org, has been around since 1976, and performs at the regal **Shubert Theatre** at 265 Tremont Street in the theater district. Shows by the company's talented casts present all the visual splendor and vocal acrobatics one would expect of any established, well-funded opera company. The curtain is at 7:30 for evening performances and at 3 p.m. for Sunday matinees. English translations are provided on screens to either side of the stage for every show.

- **Boston Modern Orchestra Project** (**BMOP**), 617-363-0396, www.bmop.org, is one of the few full-size professional orchestras in the country devoted to performing works from only the 20th and 21st centuries. Look for between five and seven show series per year. Performances are held at various venues throughout the city, including Jordan Hall, Club Café in the South End, Harvard's Sanders Theater and John Knowles Paine Hall, and at other colleges. BMOP has a free tickets program for Boston area schools.

- The **Boston Philharmonic**, 617-236-0999, www.bostonphil.org, is a traditional classical orchestra that performs at NEC's Jordan Hall and Sanders Theater. It's smaller than the Boston Symphony Orchestra, but still wonderful, with talented soloists and a repertoire that ranges from classical to modern works. Tickets are available through their web site, or at each theater's box office.

- **Boston Symphony Orchestra and the Boston Pops**; in 1881, music-lover and philanthropist Henry Lee Higginson helped create the Boston Symphony Orchestra (BSO); by the turn of the century it had moved to its current home, Symphony Hall, located at 301 Mass Ave, Boston. Acoustically, Symphony Hall is considered one of the world's finest concert halls, designed with the help of a Harvard assistant professor of physics, Wallace Clement Sabine, who, after visiting other acoustically lauded concert halls, including Vienna's Musikvereinssaal and Leipzig's Neues Gewandhaus, chose a narrow, rectangular shoebox-like shape for the hall. It takes the echoes in Symphony Hall an intentionally precise 1.8 seconds to die down with a packed house. The Boston Pops, first known as Boston Promenade, then as Popular Concerts, began in 1885, evolving out of Higginson's desire to keep the BSO musicians occupied during the summer. With a winter season only, many musicians were forced to tour Europe in the summers to stay financially solvent—and sometimes they didn't return to Boston. Today, the Pops orchestra and the BSO no longer share musicians. Beloved BSO musical director and conductor Seiji Ozawa recently retired after a 29-year stint with the orchestra—the longest tenure of any conductor with a major orchestra in the US. Pops conductor Keith Lockhart is still going strong, however. Every summer, the BSO travels to Tanglewood in Lenox,

Massachusetts, where patrons come *en masse* to enjoy outdoor concerts in the Berkshires. From May through July, the Boston Pops takes over Symphony Hall, and chairs are replaced with small tables for a festive, nightclub-like atmosphere. Each July, Boston Pops presents a series of free concerts at the Hatch Shell on the Esplanade.

- **Tickets** for all Pops and BSO concerts are available online at www.bso.org, or by phone at 888-266-1200, 617-266-1200, or TTY/TDD 617-638-9289; disabled patrons may call 617-638-9431. Groups of 25 or more receive a discount; call the Group Sales office at 617-638-9345. Three-show to full season subscriptions are available, including the Repartee Series for 21- to 38-year-olds, which includes pre-concert receptions; check online, or call the Subscription office at 888-266-7575. Tickets are also available for purchase in person at the Symphony Hall box office during the BSO season, or at the Tanglewood box office during summer. To take in the BSO at a discount, there are a couple of options. A limited number of **rush tickets** are sold to performances on Tuesdays, Thursdays, and Friday afternoons; tickets are released the day of the show, beginning at 5 p.m. on Tuesday and Thursday, and 10 a.m. on Friday—one per person, cash only. Another inexpensive option is to attend one of the BSO's **open rehearsals** throughout the season; these are the final rehearsals before BSO concerts. Seating is general admission; call the concert line, 617-266-2378, to find out dates and times. Lastly, you can still purchase BSO tickets by mail if you desire. Send orders with a check and an SASE to the Symphony Hall Box Office, Symphony Hall, 301 Mass Ave, Boston 02115 before June 1. If you are buying Tanglewood tickets after June 1, send your orders to Ticket Office, Tanglewood, 207 West Street, Lenox, MA 01240.

- **Handel & Haydn Society**, 617-266-3605, www.handelandhaydn.org, is the BSO's older brother by 66 years. H&H was founded in 1815 to improve the choral music performance in Boston, and is the oldest continuously performing arts organization in the US. It is closely associated with such historical personages as Julia Ward Howe, better known as the composer of the "Battle Hymn of the Republic." Classical choral enthusiasts may subscribe to H&H's annual series, split between Jordan and Symphony halls, or attend any of their other concerts around Boston and Cambridge. Musical seasons cover classical masterworks for choral and period orchestra.

- **The New England Conservatory of Music** (**NEC**), 290 Huntington Ave, 617-585-1100, www.newenglandconservatory.edu, since its founding in 1867, has awarded undergraduate and graduate degrees to many prize-winning musicians, some of whom do nationwide concert tours even before graduation, and many of whom go on to perform in the BSO. The school hosts over 400 concerts, many free, by faculty, students, and guests at varying locations on campus. NEC's **Jordan Hall** (box office: 617-536-2412) is on the National Register of Historic Places and boasts an acoustically superior performance facility. It's a little newer than Symphony Hall—turn of the 20th century—and features a pitched balcony and the traditional ornate decorations of all of Boston's old concert and theatrical halls. Unlike Symphony Hall, there is no room for concessions during intermission. Over 100 free concerts are given at this hall each year by NEC students and faculty. The hall also hosts a number of performances by the Boston Philharmonic, Handel & Haydn Society (H&H), Boston Gay Men's Chorus, and Boston Baroque. Jordan Hall seats 1,000 and is located at the corner of Huntington Avenue and Gainsborough Street in Boston.

COMMUNITY—SYMPHONIC, CHORAL, OPERA, CHAMBER

If you're interested in singing recreationally, your first stop should be the **Greater Boston Choral Consortium** (www.bostonsings.org). This association of choral organizations in the greater Boston area will help you find the chorus that most closely matches your interests and geographical location. Other community musical groups include:

- **Boston Bel Canto Opera**, 617-424-0900, www.geocities.com/Vienna/3385/; presents operatic masterworks with the North Shore Philharmonic Orchestra at Jordan Hall.
- **Newton Symphony Orchestra**, 617-965-2555, www.newtonsymphony.org
- **Philharmonic Society of Arlington**, www.psarlington.org; includes the Arlington-Belmont Chorale, Arlington Philharmonic Orchestra, and the Arlington-Belmont Chamber Chorus.
- **Pro Arte Chamber Orchestra**, 617-661-7067, www.proarte.org; freelance musician–run cooperative orchestra bringing a progressive mix of classical and new chamber music to the stage.

CONTEMPORARY MUSIC

With all the young people here, Boston's modern music scene is hopping. Musicians and audiences fill the innumerable clubs on a nightly basis. Generally, Boston's club scene is split into four key areas: **Central Square** in Cambridge; **Harvard** and **Brighton Avenues** in Allston/Brighton; the **North Station** and **Faneuil Hall** areas in downtown Boston; and **Kenmore Square/Landsdowne Street**.

CONCERT FACILITIES

The following play host to the big shows:

- **TD Banknorth Garden**, 100 Legends Way (North Station), Boston, 617-624-1000, www.tdbanknorthgarden.com
- **Bank of America Pavilion**, 290 Northern Ave, Boston, 617-728-1600, www.

livenation.com; while the Pavilion (formerly called Harborlights) is actually located along the South Boston waterfront, you can buy tickets at the Orpheum Theatre's box office, or through Ticketmaster at 617-931-2000.

- **Gillette Stadium**, 1 Patriot Pl, Foxboro, event line: 508-543-3900; tickets: 800-543-1776, www.gillettestadium.com
- **Tweeter Center**, 885 S Main St, Mansfield, 508-339-2333, www.tweetercenter. com; large outdoor summer concert venue about an hour south of Boston, formerly known as Great Woods.
- **Agganis Arena**, 625 Comm Ave, Boston, 617-353-GOBU, www.agganisarena. com; BU's new hockey arena also hosts concerts; tickets available at the box office or through Ticketmaster.
- **Orpheum Theatre**, 1 Hamilton Pl, Boston, 617-679-0810; right across from the Park Street T stop.
- **Somerville Theatre**, 55 Davis Sq, Somerville, 617-625-4088, www.somerville theatreonline.com
- **DCU Center**, 50 Foster St, Worcester, 508-755-6800, www.dcucenter.com
- **North Shore Music Theatre**, 62 Dunham Rd, Beverly, 978-232-7200, www. nsmt.org; musicals, celebrity concerts, and concerts for children.
- **South Shore Music Circus**, 130 Sohier St, Cohasset, 781-383-9850, www. themusiccircus.org; concerts, musicals, and comedy; also runs the Cape Cod Melody Tent, in Hyannis.
- **Tsongas Arena**, 300 Arcand Dr, Lowell, 978-848-6938, www.paultsongasarena. com; although it's up near the campus of UMASS-Lowell, it's a popular and relatively convenient general admission venue for many tours coming to Boston. Parking is easy.

NIGHTCLUBS

Boston's club circuit showcases a deep roster of local and New England–based talent, along with national headliners who choose to tour smaller venues. While a few bars and clubs have a reputation for certain types of music, many aren't too rigid about the styles of artists they book; that is to say, you might see a folk singer on Tuesday and an '80s cover band on Wednesday. With that in mind, call the venue, check their web site, or pick up the *Weekly Dig* or *Boston Phoenix* to find out about upcoming performers. For a list of all upcoming shows in the area, big and small, check out www.pollstar.com.

ROCK, BLUES, JAZZ, AND REGGAE

- **Abbey Lounge**, 3 Beacon St (Inman Sq), Somerville, 617-441-9631, www.abbey lounge.com; despite a small makeover, this ultimate rock dive keeps it gritty and real; acoustic acts perform early on the pub stage.
- **Alchemist Lounge**, 435 S Huntington Ave, JP, 617-477-5741, www.alchemist

lounge.com; local songwriters and rock bands on Thursday nights, rockabilly on Sundays.

- **All Asia**, 334 Mass Ave, Cambridge, 617-497-1544, www.allasiabar.com; diverse range of live music in an Asian restaurant setting.
- **Atwood's Tavern**, 877 Cambridge St, Cambridge, 617-864-2792, www.atwoods tavern.com
- **Avalon**, 15 Landsdowne St, Boston, 617-262-2424, www.avalonboston.com; mostly a dance club, it attracts all the best DJs and also some big-name musicians; most live shows are either all ages or 18+, and start and end early to allow the club crowd in afterward.
- **Berklee Performance Center**, 136 Mass Ave, 617-747-2261, www.berkleebpc. com; this 1,200-seat performance hall at the Berklee College of Music hosts an array of concerts in all genres.
- **Bill's Bar**, 9 Lansdowne St, Boston, 617-421-9678, www.billsbar.com; "Boston's dirty rock club" is one of the only places to catch live bands in the club district next to Fenway Park. Live indie rock every night.
- **Bullfinch Yacht Club**, 234 Friend St (North Station), Boston, 617-723-0800, www.byc.com
- **The Burren**, 246 Elm St (Davis Sq), Somerville, 617-776-6896, www.burren.com; Irish sessions 7 nights a week in the front room; back room features everything from singer-songwriter nights to '80s bands.
- **Cambridge Elks Lodge**, 55 Bishop Allen Dr (Central Sq), Cambridge, www. myspace.com/cambridgeelks; DIY punk and hardcore bands regularly rent out the hall to stage shows; 17+.
- **The Cantab Lounge**, 738 Mass Ave (Central Sq), Cambridge, 617-354-2685, www.cantab-lounge.com; popular dive for a bit of everything, whether its open mics, bluegrass nights, blues, rock, and jazz jams, improv comedy, or dancing to live classic soul and funk bands.
- **Common Ground**, 83 Harvard Ave, Allston, 617-783-2071, www.common groundbarandgrill.com; reggae and roots bands some weekend nights.
- **The Good Life**, 28 Kingston St, 617-451-2622; occasional live jazz.
- **Great Scott**, 1222 Comm Ave, Allston, 617-566-9014, www.greatscottboston. com; live bands nightly, interspersed with famed hipster DJ nights like The Pill (www.thepillboston.com).
- **Harper's Ferry**, 158 Brighton Ave, Allston, 617-254-7380, www.harpersferry boston.com; roots rock and blues.
- **Hennessy's/Hennessy's Upstairs**, 25 Union St (Faneuil Hall), Boston, 617-742-2121, www.somerspubs.com, www.myspace.com/hennessysupstairs; upstairs indie rock venue hosts local and touring acts, while downstairs Irish pub features the usual mix of acoustic duos and cover bands.
- **Johnny D's**, 17 Holland St (Davis Sq), Somerville, 617-776-2004, www.johnnyds. com; live music every night, including weekend jazz brunch and Sunday blues jam.

- **Kennedy's Midtown**, 42 Province St, Boston, 617-426-3333, www.kennedys midtown.com
- **Les Zygomates**, 129 South St, Boston, 617-542-5108, www.winebar.com; wine bar and bistro with regular live jazz.
- **The Lizard Lounge**, 1667 Mass Ave, Cambridge, 617-357-5825, www.lizard loungeclub.com; intimate club with good reputation for music, underneath the Cambridge Common restaurant. Nightly entertainment ranges from rock bands to Americana to poetry slams; free acoustic sets before 9 p.m.
- **Lucky's Lounge**, 355 Congress St (Fort Point Channel), Boston, 617-357-LUCK, www.luckyslounge.com; live jazz, soul, and funk; pays particular homage to Sinatra.
- **The Middle East**, 472 Mass Ave (Central Sq), Cambridge, 617-864-EAST, www. mideastclub.com; literally a cornerstone of the Boston music scene—its venues and restaurants take up the entire corner of Mass Ave and Brookline St—The Middle East is a hub of live music. Its Upstairs and Downstairs rooms each host four or five bands nightly—**Downstairs** brings local acts with large followings and national headliners, while bands in the smaller **Upstairs** room play to about 200 people. In between the two, the wine bar **ZuZu** features an eclectic mix of music, from DJs to Latin ensembles. **The Corner** restaurant and bar features belly dancing, open mics, jazz, and more, often for free.
- **Midway Café**, 3496 Washington St, JP, 617-524-9038, www.midwaycafe.com
- **Milky Way Lounge and Lanes**, 403-405 Centre St, JP, 617-524-3740, www. milkywayjp.com; Latin, karaoke, rock, alternative—really anything goes here.
- **O'Briens Pub**, 3 Harvard Ave, Allston, 617-782-6245, www.obrienspubboston. com; small, gritty bar hosts bands of any genre, though mostly rock and metal, seven nights a week.
- **PA's Lounge**, 345 Somerville Ave, Somerville, 617-776-1557, www.paslounge. com
- **The Paradise Rock Club**, 969 Comm Ave, Boston, 617-562-8800, www.thedise. com; legendary Boston rock venue has essentially hosted everyone you've ever heard of on their way to stardom. The **Paradise Lounge** is a smaller venue in the front, showcasing original rock and acoustic acts.
- **Plough and Stars**, 912 Mass Ave (Central Sq), Cambridge, 617-441-3455, www. ploughandstars.com; blues, jazz, folk, and rock in this tiny Irish pub.
- **Regattabar**, Charles Hotel, 1 Bennett St (Harvard Sq), Cambridge, 617-661-5000, www.regattabarjazz.com; respected jazz venue on the third floor of this swank hotel.
- **Revolution Rock Bar**, 200 High St (Faneuil Hall), Boston, 617-261-4200, www. revolutionrockbar.com
- **Roxy**, 279 Tremont St, Boston, 617-338-ROXY, www.roxyplex.com; this ball-room-turned-club is better known for its Chippendales and Latin nights, but occasionally hosts big name bands and DJs.
- **Ryles Jazz Club**, 212 Hampshire St (Inman Sq), Cambridge, 617-876-9330,

www.rylesjazz.com; jazz, Latin, and salsa, and a Sunday jazz brunch.

- **Sally O'Briens**, 335 Somerville Ave (Union Sq), Somerville, 617-666-3589, www. sallyobriensbar.com; anything from comedy to jazz to roots rock, depending on the night.
- **Scullers Jazz Club**, Doubletree Guest Suites, 400 Soldiers Field Rd, 617-562-4111, www.scullersjazz.com; 200-seat venue routinely attracts the biggest names in jazz.
- **Sky Bar**, 518 Somerville Ave, Somerville, 617-623-5223, www.skybar.us
- **Sweetwater Café**, 3 Boylston Pl, Boston, 617-351-2515, www.sweetwater cafeboston.com
- **Toad**, 1920 Mass Ave (Porter Sq), Cambridge, 617-497-4950, www.toad cambridge.com; free (and good) live music seven nights a week in this tiny neighborhood bar.
- **TT the Bear's**, 10 Brookline St (Central Sq), Cambridge, 617-492-BEAR, www. ttthebears.com; next-door alternative to The Middle East, with a capacity of about 350.
- **Wally's Café**, 427 Mass Ave, Boston, 617-424-1408, www.wallyscafe.com; one of Boston's least assuming but most respected jazz clubs. Live music 365 days/year.
- **The Western Front**, 343 Western Ave, Cambridge, 617-492-7772, www. thewesternfrontclub.com; the area's premiere reggae club, also features hip hop, jazz, and Latin.

FOLK/COFFEEHOUSES

Check out the **Boston Area Coffeehouse Association** (www.bostoncoffee houses.org) or the web site of 91.9 FM, UMASS-Boston's folk radio station (www. wumb.org), for a comprehensive listing of area folk concerts and venues.

- **Amazing Things Arts Center**, 55 Nicolas Rd, Framingham, 508-405-ARTS, www.amazingthings.org; multi-purpose arts space hosts regular acoustic and jazz performances.
- **Club Passim**, 47 Palmer St (Harvard Sq), Cambridge, 617-492-7679, www.club passim.org; coffeehouse with an illustrious past showcases the best in local and national folk acts nightly.
- **Homegrown Coffeehouse**, First Parish in Needham, Unitarian Universalist, 23 Dedham Ave, Needham, 781-444-7478, www.uuneedham.org/Coffeehouse
- **Fox Run Music Series**, 978-443-3253, www.foxrun.org; intimate acoustic house concerts, tickets by reservation only.
- **Jamaica Plain Unplugged**, 12 South St, JP, at the historic Loring-Greenough House.
- **Joyful Noise Coffeehouse**, First Baptist Church, 1580 Mass Ave, Lexington, 781-861-0142, www.joyfulnoisecoffeehouse.org
- **Me and Thee Coffeehouse**, 8 Mugford St, Marblehead, 781-631-8987, www.

meandthee.org

- **Nameless Coffeehouse**, First Parish Church, 3 Church St, Cambridge, 617-864-1630, www.namelesscoffeehouse.org
- **Oasis Coffeehouse**, First Presbyterian Church in Waltham, 34 Alder St, Waltham, 781-795-1041, www.oasiscoffeehouse.org

IRISH AND CELTIC

Boston's tremendous Irish population and influence means there's no shortage of Celtic music in pubs all over town. Still, traditional Irish sessiuns often come and go as freely as the musicians who play in them, so call ahead to confirm. The pubs below are fairly good bets to provide some jigs and reels:

- **The Black Rose**, 160 State St (Faneuil Hall), Boston, 617-742-2286, www.irish connection.com; tourist-oriented Irish music—i.e., you will hear "The Wild Rover" two or three times—every night.
- **Brendan Behan**, 378 Centre St, JP, 617-522-5386; has a good sessiun on Saturday afternoons.
- **The Burren**, 246 Elm St (Davis Sq), Somerville, 617-776-6896, www.burren. com; Irish sessiuns every night.
- **The Druid**, 1357 Cambridge St, (Inman Sq), Cambridge, www.druidpub.com, hosts regular Friday night sessiuns and the occasional touring Irish musician.
- **Green Briar**, 304 Washington St, Brighton, 617-789-4100, www.greenbriarpub. com; sessiuns every Monday night.
- **The Kinsale**, 2 Center Plaza (Government Center), Boston, 617-742-5577, www. classicirish.com
- **Mr. Dooley's Tavern**, 77 Broad St, Boston, 617-338-5656, www.somerspubs. com; Sunday evening sessiuns and Irish folk.
- **The Skellig**, 240 Moody St, Waltham, 781-647-0679, www.theskellig.com; the Burren's sister pub also features live Irish music seven nights a week.
- **Tir na nÓg**, Union Sq, Somerville, 617-628-4300, www.thenog.com

DJS/SPINNING AND LOUNGES

In the wake of Boston's gentrification, it seems that every month a beloved-but-crusty old dive bar reinvents itself as an upscale lounge. Swank but sociable, these establishments have a reputation for spinning hip and inventive mixes at a conversation-friendly volume.

- **Alchemist Lounge**, 435 S Huntington Ave, JP, 617-477-5741, www.alchemist lounge.com; rotating cast of DJs on Friday and Saturday nights.
- **Caprice**, 275 Tremont St, Boston, 617-292-0080; pricey lounge that appeals to the Euro set.
- **Enormous Room**, 567 Mass Ave (Central Sq), Cambridge, 617-491-5550, www. enormous.tv; upstairs from Central Kitchen, just an elephant logo marks the

door. Good drinks and small plates, great DJs, opulent atmostphere—get there early for seats on the plush Oriental carpets or couches.

- **Felt**, 533 Washington St (Downtown Crossing), Boston, 617-350-5555, www.feltboston.com
- **Foundation Lounge**, 500 Comm Ave (Kenmore Sq), Boston, 617-859-9900, www.thefoundationlounge.com; high-end decorum, mixed beats, and gourmet Asian small plates…it's a long way from Kenmore's grittier days.
- **Middlesex Lounge**, 315 Mass Ave, Cambridge, 617-497-4308, www.middlesexlounge.com; wide open, loft-style lounge with an excellent line-up of DJs.
- **The Mission Bar**, 734 Huntington Ave (Brigham Circle), Boston, 617-566-1244, www.themissionbar.com
- **The Modern**, 36 Lansdowne St, Boston, 617-351-2581; lounge alternative to the Lansdowne dance scene.
- **Rise**, 306 Stuart St, Boston, 617-423-7473, www.riseclub.us; membership-only nightclub is one of Boston's only after-hours hangouts, open from 1:30 a.m. to 6:30 a.m. on weekends. Focus is on music and acceptance, with a wide range of guest DJs and diverse clientele; never a dress code.
- **River Gods**, 125 River St, Cambridge, 617-576-1881, www.rivergodsonline.com; an Irish pub with a remarkable twist, from its eccentric, dazzling décor to its varied spinning—home of weekly DJ showdowns among other theme nights. Low key but often crowded.
- **Saint**, 90 Exeter St, Boston, 617-236-1134, www.saintnitery.com; super-chic lounge dining offers trademark "communal mini-cuisine"—including caviar—amidst live jazz and guest DJs.
- **Wonder Bar**, 186 Harvard Ave, Allston, 617-351-2665, www.wonderbarboston.com; still hosts occasional live jazz, but has evolved into more of a DJ scene.

KARAOKE, PIANO BARS, CABARET

- **Courtside Pub**, 291 Cambridge St, Cambridge, 617-547-4374, www.courtsidekaraoke.com; self-proclaimed "King of Karaoke," this bar takes it pretty seriously.
- **Do Re Mi Music Studio**, 442 Cambridge St, Allston, 617-783-8900; unassuming place with private karaoke booth rentals and huge song catalog.
- **Encore Lounge**, 275 Tremont St, Boston, 617-338-7699, www.roxyplex.com/encore; cabaret and piano lounge attached to the Roxy Ballroom.
- **Jacques Cabaret**, 79 Broadway (Theater District), Boston, 617-426-8902, www.jacquescabaret.com; drag show revues and cheap, strong well drinks make this a popular venue with the gay crowd, bachelorette parties, Emerson students, and just about anyone else seeking a fun night.
- **Jake Ivory's**, 9 Lansdowne St, Boston, 617-247-1222, www.jakeivorysboston.com; dueling piano bar. Cheesy for sure, but still popular, especially with bachelorette parties.

- **Limelight**, 204 Tremont St, Boston, 617-423-0785, www.limelightboston.com; live, full-band karaoke on the main stage, and karaoke studios for private parties.

DANCE CLUBS

Boston is chock full of crowded bars and even low-key pubs spinning pop, rock, and dance music, meaning there's no shortage of places to get your groove on. When it comes to clubs, however, proprietors and club goers alike take themselves *very* seriously—long lines, steep cover charges, and strict dress codes are the norm. The larger clubs routinely change hands or reinvent themselves, but whatever the name, you can count on finding a chic place to dance on **Lansdowne Street**, in the **Theater District,** or in **The Alley** (across from the Boylston Street T stop). Here are a few standbys:

- **Aria**, 246 Tremont St (Theater District), Boston, 617-338-7080; small Euro-style club.
- **Avalon/Axis/Embassy**, 13–15 Landsdowne St, Boston, 617-262-2424, www.avalonboston.com; the mainstay of the Lansdowne Street club scene, Avalon attracts big-name DJs and is popular with the young set and BU students. The owners are currently considering a reconstruction that would make the complex larger than ever, even offering a terrace overlooking Fenway Park.
- **Felt**, 533 Washington St (Downtown Crossing), Boston, 617-350-5555, www.feltboston.com
- **Gypsy Bar**, 116 Boylston St, Boston, 617-482-7799, www.gypsybarboston.com; music ranges from house to Latin; often hosts celebrity DJs, themed parties, and fashion shows.
- **Hurricane O'Reilly's**, 150 Canal St, Boston, 617-722-0161, www.irishconnection.com; no pretense here, just blaring (and often cheesy) pop music for those who love to dance to it.
- **Liquor Store**, 1 Boylston Pl (The Alley), 617-357-6800, www.liquorstoreboston.com; a young clientele flocks here to ride the only mechanical bull in Boston.
- **Mojito's**, 48 Winter St, Boston, 617-988-8123, www.mojitosboston.com; everything from live Latin music and lessons in the lounge to thumping dance parties on the club level.
- **The Quarter**, 36 Lansdowne St, Boston, 617-536-2100, www.thequarterboston.com; Mardi Gras– themed nightclub.
- **Venu/Rumor**, 100 Warrenton St (Theater District), 617-338-8061, www.venuboston.com; one of the city's most popular dance clubs with an international influence, spinning hip-hop, old school, Latin, and techno for Boston's beautiful people.

DANCE

BALLET, JAZZ, MODERN, FOLK, RELIGIOUS

The Boston area is home to a number of dance companies, from the prestigious Boston Ballet to small, independent dance studios offering classes and occasional performances. In the summer, don't forget to check out **Jacob's Pillow** (www.jacobspillow.org), a season-long dance festival held in the Berkshires. For more information on the local dance scene, taking classes, or joining a company, try the nonprofit **Boston Dance Alliance** (www.bostondancealliance.org, 617-482-4588) or check out the **Sports and Recreation** chapter.

THE BOSTON BALLET

Founded over 30 years ago, this ballet company and its school enjoy a reputation as among the country's finest. The Boston Ballet performs both full-length classics and modern works, including an acclaimed production of Tchaikovsky's *The Nutcracker*. Devoted subscribers come to see the ballet's lovely, world-caliber shows every season at the impressive Wang Theatre and the restored Boston Opera House; both halls are known for their luxurious and ornate 1920s architecture. **For tickets,** call TeleCharge at 800-447-7400 or go to www.telecharge.com. Contact the Boston Ballet directly for **Group Sales** (617-456-6343) and **Season Tickets** and **Subscription Packages** (617-695-6955), or visit their web site, www.bostonballet.org. To purchase tickets in person, go to the Wang Theatre box office at 270 Tremont Street in Boston (Theater District). Cash only, day-of-show rush tickets are also available at the box office for all performances except *The Nutcracker*.

ADDITIONAL DANCE TROUPES AND STUDIOS

- Founded in 1992 by its namesake choreographer, **Anna Myer and Dancers,** 617-547-9699, www.annamyerdancers.org, has met with much critical acclaim in both Boston and New York. Shows display the choreographer's unique brand of dance, described as a mix of classical, modern, and post-modern influences. The company performs at various venues throughout the region.
- The **Boston Liturgical Dance Ensemble**, 617-552-6130, www.blde.org, presents Christian-inspired dance performances, including the spiritual exercises of St. Ignatius Loyola, mostly at BC and other Catholic-affiliated universities across the region.
- **Commonwealth Ballet**, 978-263-6533, www.commonwealthballet.org, based in Acton, performs at venues and schools in and west of Boston.
- **The Dance Complex**, 563 Mass Ave, Cambridge, 617-547-9363, www.dance

complex.org, is an all-purpose haven servicing the dance community from its Central Square location, offering a myriad of classes, workshops, studio space, and performances.

- **Green Street Studios**, 185 Green St, Cambridge, 617-864-3191, www.green streetstudios.org, is a small Cambridge-based center for movement and dance, which includes a concert series and some special events.
- While many go to the **Jeannette Neill Dance Studio**, 261 Friend St, 5th Floor, Boston, 617-523-1355, www.jndance.com, for lessons, the studio also stages performances, including twice-yearly repertory shows at the Tsai Center for Performing Arts.
- **Prometheus Dance**, 617-576-5336, www.prometheusdance.org, is a modern dance ensemble that takes on social and psychological issues. They perform throughout New England, and often tour the world. Visit their web site or call to find out about their current season.
- **Rainbow Tribe**, 617-769-9400, www.rainbowtribe.org, is in its 15th year as an inclusive, contemporary jazz dance company that stages energetic shows throughout Boston and the east coast.
- **Snappy Dance Theater**, 617-718-2497, www.snappydance.com, now in its tenth year, has grown to be the largest contemporary dance company in Greater Boston. For more information on the company's busy roster of shows throughout the region and far beyond, visit their web site.
- **Springstep**, 98 George P. Hassett Dr, Medford, 781-395-0402, www.springstep. org; nonprofit group celebrating traditional dance from around the world, offering classes, community partnerships, social dances, workshops, and an annual performance series at their Medford Square facility.

THEATER

Boston's theater district officially covers a three- to four-block area near both Boston Common and Chinatown, but theaters flourish all over the greater Boston area. You can find everything from longstanding favorite shows like Shear Madness and The Blue Man Group to national touring productions, to shows doing a pre-Broadway test run, to locally produced musicals, comedies, and dramas—not to mention the college and community theater productions.

Aside from checking the current events sections of the local papers, visit the **Theater Mirror** web site (www.theatermirror.com) which includes listings of current shows, theaters, and audition dates around the city. If you're more interested in performing, check with **StageSource** (617-720-6066, www.stagesource. org), the local "alliance of theater artists and producers" in New England. Their book, *The Source*, is an invaluable resource that lists Boston-area theater companies, upcoming auditions, head shot photographers, acting lessons, and more.

In the summers, you can take advantage of the summerstock productions and festivals put on in western Massachusetts, such as **Shakespeare & Company** (www.shakespeare.org); the **Berkshire Theatre Festival** (www.berkshiretheatre. org); and the mother of them all—the **Williamstown Theater Festival** (www.wt festival.org).

PROFESSIONAL THEATER

Many of the following theaters and performance centers stage a wide range of events in addition to plays. Theater junkies should consider getting a subscription to a particular house. Not only is it good for the theater, but also your year membership tends to come with perks like reduced prices on tickets and flexibility in seating and attendance dates.

BOSTON

- **Berklee Performance Center**, 136 Mass Ave, 617-747-2261, www.berkleebpc. com
- **Boston Center for the Arts**, 539 Tremont St, 617-426-ARTS, www.bcaonline. org; hosts a multitude of theater productions by nearly 20 different producing companies in four theaters—the BCA Plaza Theatre, the BCA Plaza Black Box, and the Calderwood Pavilion, which includes the Roberts Studio Theatre, and the Wimberly Theatre.
- **Boston Opera House**, 539 Washington St, www.bostonoperahouse.com; originally built in 1928, the Opera House hosts rock shows, Broadway musicals, the Boston Ballet's *Nutcracker*, and the occasional opera.
- **Boston Playwrights' Theatre**, 949 Comm Ave, 617-353-5443, www.bu. edu/bpt
- **Charles Playhouse**, 74 Warrenton St, 617-426-6912, www.broadwayinboston. com
- **Charlestown Working Theatre**, 442 Bunker Hill St, Charlestown, 617-242-3285, www.charlestownworkingtheater.org
- **Colonial Theatre**, 106 Boylston St, 617-880-2460, www.broadwayinboston. com
- **Cutler Majestic Theatre at Emerson**, 219 Tremont St, 617-824-8000, www. maj.org
- **Hatch Memorial Shell**, Charles River Esplanade, 617-727-5114; free concerts and other performances from mid-June to mid-September.
- **Huntington Theatre Company**, 264 Huntington St, 617-266-0800, www.hun tingtontheatre.org
- **Lyric Stage Company**, 140 Clarendon St, 617-585-5678, www.lyricstage.com; this is a more modern, albeit cramped, space on the second floor of the YMCA between the Back Bay and the South End, but it has a great atmosphere and produces some important, fine-tuned pieces.

- **Publick Theatre**, Christian Herter Park, 1175A Soldiers Field Rd, Brighton, 617-PUBLICK, www.publicktheatre.com; classic outdoor summer theater, including Shakespeare productions.
- **Shubert Theatre**, 265 Tremont St, 617-482-9393, www.wangcenter.org; like a smaller Wang Center, the Shubert's old, rococo house stages some of the biggest productions that pass through Boston.
- **The Wang Center for the Performing Arts**, 270 Tremont St, 617-482-9393, www.wangcenter.org; a splendid theater dating back to the 1920s, with gold leaf dripping from the mural-covered ceilings. Like the Shubert, it is also home to some of the biggest shows (dance and theater) in the city.
- **The Wheelock Family Theatre**, 200 The Riverway, 617-879-2000, www.wheelock.edu/wft
- **The Wilbur**, 246 Tremont St, 617-423-4008, www.broadwayinboston.com

BOSTON METRO AREA

- **American Repertory Theatre** (**ART**), Loeb Drama Center, 64 Brattle St, Cambridge, 617-547-8300, www.amrep.org
- **Cambridge Multicultural Arts Center**, 41 Second St, Cambridge, 617-577-1400, www.cmacusa.org
- **Gloucester Stage Company**, 267 E Main St, Gloucester, 978-281-4433, www.gloucesterstage.com; summer only.
- **New Repertory Theatre**, Arsenal Center for the Arts, 321 Arsenal St, Watertown, 617-923-7060, www.newrep.org
- **Orpheum Regional Performing Arts Center**, 1 School St, Foxboro, 508-543-ARTS, www.orpheum.org; in addition to productions, they offer special events, films, and classes.
- **Sanders Theatre**, Harvard University's Memorial Hall, 45 Quincy St, Cambridge, 617-496-4595, box office, 617-496-2222, www.fas.harvard.edu/memhall/sanders.html
- **Stoneham Theatre**, 395 Main St, Stoneham, 781-279-2200, www.stonehamtheatre.org
- **Theatre Cooperative**, Elizabeth Peabody House, 277 Broadway, Somerville, 617-625-1300, www.theatrecoop.org; offers high-caliber plays despite its small size and funding level. The theater is hard to find, but parking is easy.
- **Turtle Lane Playhouse**, 283 Melrose St, Newton, 617-244-0169, www.turtlelane.org
- **Underground Railway Theater**, 41 Foster St, Arlington, 781-643-6916, www.undergroundrailwaytheater.org; national touring and local performing company presenting a synthesis of theater, puppetry, and music, in productions ranging from adult cabaret to full-length plays.

In addition to the above professional productions, the large number of colleges and universities ensure a variety of interesting, cheap, progressive student productions. Emerson and BU, in particular, are known for the quality of their theater departments, and Harvard's Hasty Pudding club puts on a new, student-written, all-male show (famous for their traditional bawdy humor and cross-dressing) every year, in addition to the highly publicized roast of Hollywood icons. Check with individual schools to see what shows are going up at any given time.

FILM

Look in the paper to find today's listings of the biggest Hollywood blockbusters showing at the nearest 20-plex. Those in search of the harder-to-find flicks and art films can check with the following.

ALTERNATIVE AND ART FILM HOUSES

For art, revival, foreign, independent, classic, and second-run films, check the following venues:

- **AMC Loews Cineplex Harvard Square**, 10 Church St, Cambridge, 617-864-4580
- **Belmont Studio Cinema**, 376 Trapelo Rd, Belmont, 617-484-1706, www.studiocinema.com
- **Brattle Theatre**, 40 Brattle St (Harvard Sq), Cambridge, 617-876-6837, www.brattlefilm.org
- **Coolidge Corner Theatre**, 290 Harvard St, Brookline, 617-734-2500, www.coolidge.org
- **Harvard Film Archive**, 24 Quincy St (Harvard Sq), Cambridge, 617-495-4700, www.hcl.harvard.edu/hfa/
- **Kendall Square Landmark Theaters**, 1 Kendall Sq, Cambridge, 617-499-1996, www.landmarktheatres.com
- **Landmark Embassy Cinema**, 16 Pine St, Waltham, 781-893-2500, www.landmarktheaters.com
- **MIT Film Series**, 77 Mass Ave, Cambridge, 617-258-8881
- **Museum of Fine Arts**, 465 Huntington Ave, Boston, 617-369-3300, www.mfa.org/film
- **Somerville Theater**, 55 Davis Sq, Somerville, 617-625-5700, www.somervilletheatreonline.com
- **West Newton Cinema**, 1296 Washington St, W Newton, 617-964-6060, www.westnewtoncinema.com

Boston also has two venues for the popular **IMAX films**; be sure to arrive early as many showings sell out.

- **Mugar Omni Theater**, Museum of Science, Science Park, Boston, 617-723-2500, www.mos.org.

- **Simons IMAX Theater**, New England Aquarium, Central Wharf, Boston, 617-973-5200, www.neaq.org/visit/imax

FILM FESTIVALS

Boston offers a wide range of festivals, many of which are supported by the Museum of Fine Arts. Most festivals utilize the various art film houses around town; some of these theatres are not within walking distance from each other, so if you plan on seeing back-to-back films, check their locations and plan accordingly. Here are a few annual film events:

- **Boston Asian American Film & Video Festival**, www.aarw.org/film_website/index.html
- **Festival of Films from Iran**, www.mfa.org/film; all films are produced in Iran and in Persian with English subtitles.
- **Boston Film Festival**, www.bostonfilmfestival.org; 10-day festival every fall that serves as the US or world premiere festival for many major films.
- **Boston French Film Festival**, www.mfa.org/film; all films are produced in France and are in French with English subtitles.
- **Boston Gay & Lesbian Film Festival**, www.mfa.org/film
- **Boston Independent Film Festival**, www.iffboston.org; takes place every spring.
- **Boston Irish Film Festival**, www.irishfilmfestival.com, celebrates Ireland and the Irish on screen every April.
- **Boston Jewish Film Festival**, 617-244-9899, www.bjff.org; takes place every November with the support of the MFA.
- **Boston Underground Film Festival**, www.bostonundergroundfilmfestival.com, features work that pushes the envelope in form, style, and content.

MUSEUMS

Boston is blessed with world-class museums, and U.S. history buffs will be thrilled to call this area home. Indeed, Boston's history is that of our nation, and virtually nowhere else in the country offers such a vivid portal to our nation's past. Many of the historical sites are right in the thick of downtown Boston, and are connected along the not-quite-three-mile **Freedom Trail**. Taking a few hours to walk it is a great way to gain an appreciation of the rich local history and to familiarize yourself with the city. Before you go anywhere, look into getting a **citypass** (www.citypass.com, 888-330-5008). If you're planning to go to many museums and attractions within a short time period (nine days), you can save up to 50% on admission into the Aquarium, MFA, Harvard Museum of Natural History, JFK Library & Museum, Museum of Science, and the Skywalk Observatory at the Pru.

ART AND CULTURE MUSEUMS

In addition to all the museums in and around Boston, patrons of the arts will enjoy taking advantage of the multitude of small galleries dedicated to fine art and photography. Many galleries are concentrated along Newbury Street and in Fort Point Channel, but others can be found throughout the metro area, in Cambridge, Brookline, Somerville, and elsewhere. Boston's **Open Studios** are another way to take in, enjoy, and be a part of the local art scene. Twelve neighborhoods host open studio weekends at different times during the year. To check this year's schedule or to find more information on city art events, go to www.cityofboston. gov/arts/visual. Pick up a *Weekly Dig, Boston Globe* or others for more information on upcoming art events.

In the meantime, here is a listing of the **major art museums** for the greater Boston area:

- **Davis Museum and Cultural Center**, Wellesley College, 106 Central St, Wellesley, 781-283-2501, www.davismuseum.wellesley.edu
- **DeCordova Museum and Sculpture Park**, 51 Sandy Pond Rd, Lincoln, 781-259-8355, www.decordova.org; the museum is a castle-style building on 35 acres of parkland with an amphitheatre that can seat 1,800.
- **Harvard University Art Museums**, 617-495-9400, www.artmuseums.harvard. edu; open seven days a week, Monday–Saturday, 10 a.m. to 5 p.m.; Sundays, 1 p.m. to 5 p.m. The following museums, all of which are in Harvard Square, Cambridge, hold Harvard's art collections: **Arthur M. Sackler Museum**, 485 Broadway, offers fine arts and sculpture in the Indian, Asian, Islamic and Ancient traditions; **Busch-Reisinger Museum**, 32 Quincy St, for German Expressionists; and **Fogg Art Museum**, Werner Otto Hall on Prescott St, for European and American masters in all media.
- **Institute of Contemporary Art** (**ICA**), 955 Boylston St, Boston, 617-266-5152, www.icaboston.org; contemporary art, includes painting, sculpture, photography, film, video, and live performances. Free admission Thursdays after 5 p.m.
- **Isabella Stewart Gardner Museum**, 280 The Fenway, 617-566-1401 (617-734-1359 for concert information), www.gardnermuseum.org; the eccentric Mrs. Gardner built this Venetian-style palazzo at the turn of the 20th century to house the results of a lifetime spent collecting European art. A concert series runs from September through June. Free to all students on Wednesdays.
- **Mass MoCA**, 87 Marshall St, N Adams, 413-664-4481, www.massmoca.org; Massachusetts does have a museum of modern art, it just so happens to be way out in the western part of the state. If you've got a car and a penchant for progressive art, you'll find it well worth the trip. Open 11 a.m. to 5 p.m., except Tuesdays.
- **McMullen Museum of Art**, Boston College, 140 Comm Ave, Devlin Hall 108, Chestnut Hill, www.bc.edu/bc_org/avp/cas/artmuseum; open weekdays, 11

a.m. to 4 p.m., weekends, noon to 5 p.m. Free admission and parking.

- **MIT List Visual Arts Center**, 20 Ames St, Bldg E15/Wiesner Bldg, Atrium Level, Cambridge, 617-253-4680, web.mit.edu/lvac; contemporary art. Admission is free.
- **Museum of Fine Arts Boston**, 465 Huntington Ave, Boston, 617-267-9300, www.mfa.org; extensive collections of Asian, Egyptian, Classical Greek, and Roman art; and European and American sculpture, textiles, furniture and paintings. Excellent traveling exhibits. Classes, concerts, singles events, lectures, films, etc. Open seven days, starting at 10 a.m.
- **Museum of the National Center of African-American Artists**, 300 Walnut Ave, Roxbury, 617-442-8014, www.ncaaa.org; changing exhibitions of contemporary and historical African, African-American, and Caribbean art.
- **New England Quilt Museum**, 18 Shattuck St, Lowell, 978-452-4207, www.nequiltmuseum.org.
- **Peabody Essex Museum**, East India Sq, Salem, 978-745-9500, www.pem.org.
- **Rose Art Museum**, Brandeis University, 415 South St, Waltham, 781-736-3434, www.brandeis.edu/rose; "largest" and "finest" collection of modern and contemporary 20th-century art in New England, the museum got a big boost in the form of a $3.5 million gift from arts patrons Henry and Louis Foster.
- **Semitic Museum at Harvard University**, 6 Divinity Ave, Cambridge, 617-495-4631, www.lternet.edu/hfr/mus; features Near Eastern archeological and artistic exhibits. The museum was founded in 1889. Admission is free.

HISTORY MUSEUMS/SITES, CULTURAL CENTERS

FREEDOM TRAIL

The Freedom Trail is a walking tour of Boston covering 300 years of history by linking 16 of the city's most significant historical sites and museums on one relatively easy to follow, two-and-a-half mile path. The **National Park Service** offers guided tours, but you can walk the Freedom Trail on your own if you prefer. For detailed information about the Freedom Trail, go to www.cityofboston.gov/freedomtrail.

The trail begins at the information kiosk on Boston Common. Following the painted red line along the sidewalk (sometimes the line is brick) will take you to the **Statehouse**, recognizable by its imposing size, classic architecture, and regal gold dome. Head back out to Park Street to see the **Park Street Church** and then the **Granary Burying Ground**, which serves as the final resting place for such patriots as John Hancock, Samuel Adams, Paul Revere, Mary Goose (better known as Mother Goose to parents and children), and the parents of native son Benjamin Franklin. A statue of Franklin stands further down the trail at 45 School Street, by the site of the **first public school**, which you'll get to after you pass the **King's Chapel** and accompanying **Burying Ground**. Other downtown sites include the **Old South Meeting House** on Washington at Milk Street, the **site of the Boston Massacre**, and the **Old Corner Bookstore**, which now houses the Boston Globe Bookstore. After you finish with this downtown section, the Freedom Trail heads toward the North End, but not without making a run through **Faneuil Hall**. The trail then heads past the **Holocaust Memorial**, through **Haymarket** (which will be chaos if you're visiting on a Friday or Saturday), and then into the North End. A tour through the **North End** brings you past the **Old North Church**, where the famous signal was sent out to Paul Revere, "One if by land, two if by sea," to issue the warning that the Redcoats were coming. You'll also see **Paul Revere's house**, which happens to be the oldest standing home in Boston, and the **Copp's Hill Burying Ground**. Finally, the Freedom Trail heads over the slightly scary Charlestown Bridge to the **Charlestown Navy Yard**, not far from the **Bunker Hill Monument**. The nation's oldest commissioned war ship, **the USS *Constitution***, a.k.a. "Old Ironsides," is anchored in the Navy Yard, and it was at Bunker Hill, then known as Breed's Hill, that General Israel Putnam urged his troops not to fire on the British soldiers until they saw "the whites of their eyes."

HISTORIC SITES, TRAILS, AND CULTURAL CENTERS

While, for obvious reasons, the Freedom Trail is the first stop for many tourists and those exploring their new city, there is so much else to visit in Boston that isn't directly accessible from the trail's path. A lesser-known trail, the **Black Heritage Trail**, details the rich history of Boston's African-American community. It's located on the north slope of Beacon Hill, once known as the West End. The attractions include a memorial to a white aristocrat, **Robert Gould Shaw**, who led the all-black 54th Regiment during the Civil War, and the **African Meeting House** (76 Joy Street, 617-725-0022).

Don't forget to head out of Boston to see what other historical sites the area has to offer. Many famous New England authors lived right around here, so you can visit places like **Longfellow's house** in Cambridge, **Emerson's house** in Concord, Thoreau's **Walden Pond**, and Hawthorne's **House of Seven Gables**, as well as Salem's **Custom House**. In Brookline is the **Olmstead Museum** in the house where Frederick Law Olmstead, father of modern landscape architecture and designer of the Emerald Necklace, lived, as well as **JFK's birthplace**. If you head south to Plymouth you can see historical pilgrim sites, like **Plymouth Rock**, re-creations of the Mayflower and pilgrim life at the village, and a living history museum village called **Plimoth Plantation**.

If you want to feel historic while eating a fine dinner or drinking a pint, stop by **The Union Oyster House**, established in 1826, at 40 Union Street near Faneuil Hall; it claims to be America's oldest restaurant. A series of back streets nearby offers a view of what colonial Boston looked like. It is along this cobblestone nook where you can also visit the **Green Dragon Tavern** (11 Marshall Street), where patriots drank ale and plotted the uprising that became the Revolutionary War. In Charlestown, the **Warren Tavern** (2 Pleasant Street), which dates back to 1780, was one of the favorite watering holes of General Washington and Paul Revere. Or for more recent history, stay at the **Omni Parker House Hotel**, where JFK gave his first speech at seven years old, Ho Chi Minh worked in the bakery, and Malcolm X was a busboy.

Another contact for area history is the **Greater Boston Convention & Visitors Bureau** (888-SEE-BOSTON, www.bostonusa.com).

Following is a list of some of the many **historical museums and sites** in the greater Boston area:

- **Adams National Historic Site**, 135 Adams St, Quincy, 617-770-1175, www. nps.gov/adam; the birthplaces and homes of presidents John Adams and John Quincy Adams.
- **Boston Historical Society & Museum/Old State House**, 206 Washington St, Boston, 617-720-1713, www.bostonhistory.org; open daily, 9 a.m. to 5 p.m.
- **Boston Tea Party Ship and Museum**, Congress St Bridge, Boston, www.bos tonteapartyship.com
- **Concord Museum**, 200 Lexington Rd, Concord, 978-369-9763, www.concord museum.org; dedicated to Concord's history, including Revolutionary War, Thoreau, and Emerson exhibits.
- **Essex Shipbuilding Museum**, 66 & 28 Main St, Essex, 978-768-7541, www. essexshipbuildingmuseum.org; local shipbuilding artifacts from a proud and significant local industry. Tours available May–October.
- **Frederick Law Olmstead National Historic Site**, 99 Warren St, Brookline, 617-566-1689, www.nps.gov/frla; visit the home and office of the founder of American landscape architecture. Open for full tours on Fridays, Saturdays, and Sundays. Limited visitor services on weekdays.
- **Gibson House Museum**, 137 Beacon St, Boston, 617-267-6338, www.the gibsonhouse.org; Victorian house museum right in the Back Bay.
- **House of Seven Gables**, 115 Derby St, Salem, 978-744-0991, www.7gables. org; oldest surviving 17th-century wooden mansion in New England, which inspired the Hawthorne book. Includes Hawthorne's birthplace, gardens, and tour guides dressed in period garb on the property. Open daily year round, except during the first three weeks of January when it is closed.
- **The John F. Kennedy Library and Museum**, Columbia Point off Morrissey Blvd, Dorchester, 617-514-1600, www.cs.umb.edu/jfklibrary; exhibits that'll take you back in time, dedicated to perhaps the most beloved president of the 20th century.
- **Longfellow National Historic Site**, 105 Brattle St, Cambridge, 617-876-4491, www.nps.gov/long; Longfellow's home for more than 50 years.
- **Lowell National Historical Park**, 67 Kirk St, Lowell, 978-970-5000, www.nps. gov/lowe; textile mills, canals, worker housing, Suffolk Mill Turbine, and Boot Cotton Mills Museum.

- **Mary Baker Eddy Library for the Betterment of Humanity—Mapparium**, 200 Mass Ave, Boston, 617-450-7000 or 888-222-3711, www.marybakereddy library.org; the Christian Science complex in the Fenway section of Boston is remarkable. You'll be impressed by the outside of the buildings—the grand dome and reflecting pool. But inside the library is the pièce de resistance, the Mapparium—a three-story, stained-glass globe from the 1930s. Closed Mondays.
- **Minute Man National Historical Park**, 174 Liberty St, Concord, 978-369-6993, www.nps.gov/mima; American Revolution sites like Concord Green, as well as the homes of Alcott and Hawthorne.
- **Mt. Auburn Cemetery**, 580 Mt. Auburn St, Cambridge, 617-547-7105, www. mountauburn.org; one of the nation's most famous cemeteries and the resting grounds for Charles Bullfinch, Oliver Wendell Holmes, Dorothea Dix, B.F. Skinner, Mary Baker Eddy, Winslow Homer, and many others. Peaceful and beautiful place to go for a walk.
- **Museum of African American History**, 46 Joy St on Beacon Hill, Boston, 617-725-0022, www.afroammuseum.org; for the preservation and exhibition of contributions by African-Americans during the colonial period in New England. Includes the African-American Meeting House and Abiel Smith School.
- **New Bedford Whaling Museum**, 18 Johnny Cake Hill, New Bedford, 508-997-0046, www.whalingmuseum.org; offers a visual history of whaling.
- **Old South Meeting House**, 310 Washington St, Boston, 617-482-6439, www. oldsouthmeetinghouse.org; open daily.
- **Old State House**, 206 Washington St, Boston, 617-720-1713, www.boston history.org
- **Orchard House**, 399 Lexington Rd, Concord, 978-369-4118, www.louisamay alcott.org; home to the Alcott family.
- **Paul Revere House**, 19 North Sq (North End), Boston, 617-523-2338, www. paulreverehouse.org
- **Sleepy Hollow Cemetery**, Bedford St and Court Lane near Concord center; where Thoreau, Emerson, Alcott, and Hawthorne are buried, on "Author's Ridge."
- **Spellman Museum of Stamps & Postal History**, Regis College, 235 Wellesley St, Weston, 781-768-8367, www.spellman.org; open Thursday–Sunday, noon to 5 p.m.
- **The USS Constitution Museum**, Charlestown Navy Yard, 617-426-1812, www. ussconstitutionmuseum.org; interesting, lengthy tour given by well-informed naval officers who can tell you exactly how miserable life was on Old Ironsides and all about her history.
- **Walden Pond/Thoreau Exhibit**, 915 Walden St, Concord, 978-369-3254, www. state.ma.us/dem/parks/wldn; use the pond and walk the woods for free. Has a nice summer swimming hole and gorgeous fall foliage. Dogs welcome.

SCIENCE MUSEUMS

- **Harvard Collection of Historical Scientific Instruments**, 1 Oxford St, Cambridge, 617-495-2779, www.fas.harvard.edu/~hsdept/chsi.html
- **Harvard University Museum of Natural History**, 26 Oxford St, Cambridge, 617-495-3045, www.hmnh.harvard.edu, is the public institution of three Harvard museums: **Mineralogical and Geological Museum**, 24 Oxford St, worldwide collection of rocks and ores; **Harvard University Botanical Museum,** 26 Oxford St, houses the **Garden in Glass** (affectionately known as the "Glass Flowers"); and the **Museum of Comparative Zoology**, 26 Oxford St, 150-year-old museum covering twelve different areas of zoology.
- **MIT Museum**, 265 Mass Ave, Bldg N52, Cambridge 617-253-4444, http://web.mit.edu/museum; has collections in science, technology, architecture, nautical history, and holography. There are also two satellite galleries: **Compton Gallery**, 77 Mass Ave, Bldg 10/MIT campus, Cambridge; **Hart Nautical Gallery**, 55 Mass Ave, Bldg 5/MIT campus, Cambridge.
- **Museum of Science**, Science Park, Boston, 617-723-2500, www.mos.org; in addition to the permanent and traveling exhibits that make this over-170-year-old museum a local favorite, the Museum of Science also features changing IMAX shows in its **Mugar Omni Theater**, and laser shows and planetarium shows in the **Charles Hayden Planetarium**. Open daily. Easy access to the Green Line on the T and parking, although the garage fills up on holidays and weekends.
- **New England Aquarium**, Central Wharf (off Atlantic Ave), Boston, 617-973-5200, www.neaq.org; beautiful central tank for viewing sea life, captivating penguin pool, special shows (sea lions, etc.), and Simons IMAX Theatre. Open daily. Nearby parking or take Blue Line T to Aquarium stop.
- **Peabody Museum of Archeology and Ethnology**, 11 Divinity Ave, Cambridge, 617-496-1027, www.peabody.harvard.edu

LITERARY LIFE

In addition to Boston's extensive network of public and academic libraries, there are several special interest private libraries, including the Boston Athenaeum and the Mary Baker Eddy Library, where researchers can find scores of rare and exceptional books on their particular subject matter.

Boston is a hotbed of well-attended lecture tours, book signings, and poetry readings. Some are hosted by area bookstores, others by small coffeehouses or on university campuses. Check the *Globe* on Thursdays and the *Herald* on Fridays for listings, as well as the *Weekly Dig* and the *Harvard Gazette*. For more about past and present local writers, see the **Boston Reading List** chapter.

BOOKSTORES

In many towns and cities in America, you can be hard pressed to find an indie bookstore; in Boston, this is hardly the case. Boston—and, in particular, Cambridge's Harvard Square—is known for its large concentration of smaller, specialty bookstores, many of which have been in business for decades. As in most areas of the country, some of Boston's favorites did not survive the big chains and Amazon.com—but many stores are still giving the big guys a run for their money! And, while internet shopping has a lot going for it in terms of convenience, for those newcomers wanting to browse a cozy specialty bookshop or even a large chain, your options are varied. Check with the bookstores listed below to find a first-edition Robert Louis Stevenson, to pre-order a hot upcoming title, or to find out when your favorite author is coming to town. You'll also want to check for stores affiliated with local universities. Here are a few notable area bookstores to get you started:

- **Barnes & Noble Booksellers**, 325 Harvard St, Brookline, 617-232-0594; 170 Boylston St, Chestnut Hill, 617-965-7621; and there is another Barnes & Noble store that doubles as university bookstore at BU, 660 Beacon St, Kenmore Sq, 617-267-8484. www.barnesandnoble.com
- **Borders Books & Music**, 10-24 School St (Downtown Crossing), Boston, 617-557-7188, is a three-level book emporium, with the Irish Potato Famine memorial in front of it; 100 Cambridgeside Pl, in the Cambridgeside Galleria, Cambridge, 617-679-0887, www.borders.com
- **Boston Book Annex**, 906 Beacon St, 617-266-1090, www.rarebooks.com; a large selection of rare used books with an especially strong stock of political history, literature, and art books.
- **Brattle Bookshop**, 9 West St, Boston, 617-542-0210, www.brattlebookshop. com; one of the country's largest and oldest (started in 1825) antiquarian bookstores.
- **Brookline Booksmith**, 279 Harvard St (Coolidge Corner), Brookline, 617-566-6660, www.brooklinebooksmith.com; popular little bookseller with a wide selection of titles, and a staff that knows their stuff. Hosts a great many popular author readings and signings.
- **Children's Book Shop**, 237 Washington St, Brookline Village, 617-734-7323; large selection of children's books and teacher resources.
- **Comicopia**, 464 Comm Ave #3, Boston, 617-266-4266, www.comicopia. com; comic bookstore providing "highbrow, lowbrow...and everything in between."
- **Commonwealth Books**, 134 Boylston St, Boston, 617-338-6328
- **The Coop**, MIT, 3 Cambridge Center (Central Sq), Cambridge, 617-499-3200; Harvard, 1400 Mass Ave (Harvard Sq), Cambridge, 617-499-2000, www.the coop.com; started by students in 1882, it is now managed by Barnes & Noble, but is still a cooperative.

- **Curious George Shop**, 1 JFK St, Cambridge (Harvard Sq), 617-498-0062, www. curiousg.com; offers a large selection of children's books and artisan toys with a friendly staff to help you with all your questions, and to give you recommendations based on age and interest.
- **Grolier Poetry Bookshop**, 6 Plympton St (Harvard Sq), Cambridge, 617-547-4648, www.grolierpoetrybookshop.com; stocks over 15,000 volumes of trade, small press, and university poetry.
- **Harvard Bookstore**, 1256 Mass Ave (Harvard Sq), Cambridge, 617-661-1515, www.harvard.com; a large selection of titles, a basement full of used and remainder books, a knowledgeable staff, and host to many author readings, Harvard Bookstore is a favorite among locals.
- **Israel Bookshop**, 410 Harvard St, Brookline, 617-566-7113, www.israelbookshop.com; offers a full line of Judaica books and textbooks.
- **Kate's Mystery Books**, 2211 Mass Ave (Davis Sq), Cambridge, 617-491-2660, www.katesmysterybooks.com; a large selection of mystery books, and host to mystery author readings and signings.
- **Lorem Ipsum Books**, 157 Hampshire St (Inman Sq), Cambridge, 617-497-7669, www.loremipsumbooks.com
- **Lucy Parsons Center**, 549 Columbus Ave, Boston, 617-267-6272, www.lucyparsons.org; collectively run radical bookstore and meeting center that also hosts radical movie night every Wednesday.
- **McIntyre and Moore Bookstore**, 255 Elm St (Davis Sq), Somerville, 617-629-4840, www.mcintyreandmoore.com; source for scholarly used books.
- **Million Year Picnic**, 99 Mt. Auburn St (Harvard Sq), Cambridge, 617-492-6763
- **MIT Press Bookstore**, 292 Main St (Kendall Sq), Cambridge, 617-253-5479, http://mitpress.mit.edu/bookstore
- **New England Mobile Book Fair**, 82 Needham St, Newton, 617-527-5817, www.nebookfair.com; books stacked floor-to-ceiling at discounted prices in a warehouse-like setting.
- **Newtonville Books**, 269 Walnut St, Newton, 617-244-6619, www.newtonvillebooks.com; great selection of titles, and host to the award-winning author event series "Books and Brews."
- **Pandemonium Books and Games**, 4 Pleasant St, Cambridge, 617-547-3721, www.pandemoniumbooks.com; science fiction specialty store.
- **Petropol**, 1428 Beacon St (Coolidge Corner), Brookline, 617-232-8820, http://petropol.com; Russian language bookstore.
- **Porter Square Books**, 25 White St (Porter Sq Shopping Center), Cambridge, 617-491-2220, www.portersquarebooks.com; wide selection of books, helpful staff, and author readings and signings.
- **Quantum Books**, 4 Cambridge Center (Kendall Sq), Cambridge, 617-494-5042, www.quantumbooks.com; devoted solely to advanced level technical books.
- **Raven Books**, 52B JFK St (Harvard Sq), Cambridge, 617-441-6999; used bookstore with a great selection.

- **Revolution Books**, 1156 Mass Ave (Harvard Sq), Cambridge, 617-492-5443; radical bookstore.
- **Rodney's Bookstore**, 698 Mass Ave, Cambridge (Central Sq), 617-876-6467; 1362 Beacon St, Brookline, 617-232-0185; used bookstores with a ton of great books from which to choose.
- **Sasuga Japanese Bookstore**, 7 Upland Rd (Porter Sq), Cambridge, 617-497-5460, www.sasugabooks.com
- **Schoenhof's Foreign Books**, 76 Mt. Auburn St #A (Harvard Sq), Cambridge, 617-547-8855, www.schoenhofs.com; the place for books printed in whatever language you desire.
- **Seven Stars**, 731 Mass Ave (Central Sq), Cambridge, 617-547-1317; new and used bookstore devoted to spirituality, religious philosophy, Magik books, and science fiction.
- **Trident Booksellers & Café**, 338 Newbury St, Boston, 617-267-6888; half café, half bookstore, with a wide selection of magazines.
- **Village Books**, 751 South St, Roslindale, 617-325-1994; www.village-books. net

LIBRARIES

There are public and private libraries galore in Boston. For listings of public library branches, check the resources following the **Neighborhood Profiles**, and for information on obtaining a library card, check the **Getting Settled** chapter. Many popular **private libraries** are open to the public, others are by membership only.

- **Arnold Arboretum Library**, 125 Arborway, JP, 617-524-1718, www.arboretum. harvard.edu/library; over 40,000 volumes on such topics as botany, dendrology, horticulture, floras of the world, forestry, and taxonomy.
- **Boston Athenaeum**, 10-1/2 Beacon St, Boston, 617-227-0270, www.boston athenaeum.org, is a nearly 200-year-old private library. First floor is open to the public; membership allows you full use of (sometimes very old) reference materials, special collections, events, and more.
- **Boston Globe Library**, P.O. Box 55819, Boston, MA 02205, http://bostonglobe. com/newsroom/News/OtherServices/library; the library services of the *Globe* are not open to the public, but you can contact them with written requests about information that has appeared in the paper. Requests take a minimum of 10 days to fulfill.
- **Boston Historical Society Library**, 15 State St, 3rd Floor, Boston, 617-720-1713 ext. 12, www.bostonhistory.org; artifacts, books, photographs, and documents relating to the history of Boston, for use during weekdays by appointment.
- **Boston Psychoanalytic Society and Institute's (BPSL's) Hanns Sachs Li-**

brary, 15 Comm Ave, Boston, 617-266-0953, www.bostonpsychoanalytic. org/library; historical and contemporary psychoanalytic literature and journals, for use by BPSI members as well as unaffiliated scholars and students—free onsite use, borrowing privileges for an annual subscription fee.

- **Boston Public Library**, Central Library, 700 Boylston St, 617-536-5400, www. bpl.org, was founded in 1848, and was the country's first large free municipal library. Today it holds over 6.1 million books, 1.2 million rare books and manuscripts, and a number of maps, musical scores and prints. The library also displays a magnificent collection of John Singer Sargent paintings, as well as works by other famous painters and sculptors. Tours are available every day but Wednesday. For information on the 27 neighborhood branches, go to www.bpl.org/branches/index.htm.

- **Brookline Public Library**, 361 Washington St, Brookline, 617-730-2370, www. brooklinelibrary.org

- **Cambridge Public Library**, Main Branch, 359 Broadway, Cambridge, 617-349-4040, www.ci.cambridge.ma.us/CPL; local library with six neighborhood branches.

- **Congregational Library and Archives**, 14 Beacon St, Boston, 617-523-0470, www.14beacon.org; contemporary and classical religious studies material open to all researchers free of charge.

- **Federal Reserve Bank of Boston's Research Library**, 600 Atlantic Ave, Boston, 617-973-3397, www.bos.frb.org/economic/resource/library.htm; 65,000 volumes of economic and monetary policy and 400 banking and economics periodical titles. ID required for admission.

- **The French Library and Cultural Center/The Alliance Française of Boston and Cambridge**, 53 Marlborough St, Boston, 617-912-0400, www.frenchlib. org; large collection of French books, audiotapes, videos, CDs, courses, and cultural activities.

- **Goethe Institute Library**, 170 Beacon St, Boston, 617-262-6050; new German books, videos, audiocassettes, journals, magazines, etc.; free use, but no borrowing privileges.

- **JFK Library and Museum**, Columbia Point (South Boston), 617-514-1600, www.jfklibrary.org; one of eleven presidential libraries administered by the National Archives and Records Administration, this is a library devoted to all things Kennedy.

- **Mary Baker Eddy Library for the Betterment of Humanity** (see above, under **History Museums**)

- **Massachusetts Historical Society Library**, 1154 Boylston St, Boston, 617-536-1608, www.masshist.org/library; a collection of personal papers for the families and individuals who have lived in the commonwealth, free to the public.

- **Museum of Fine Arts Libraries (William Morris Hunt Memorial Library and W. Van Alan Clark, Jr. Library)**, MFA, 300 Mass Ave, 2nd Floor, Boston, www.

mfa.org; Hunt Memorial, 617-369-3385; Clark Library, 617-369-3650; holdings of art and art history literature corresponding to the museum's collections and the museum school, respectively; free admission to the public, but the holdings are non-circulating.

- **New England Historic Genealogical Society** (**NEHGS**) Research Library, 101 Newbury St, Boston, 617-536-5740, www.newenglandancestors.org/libraries
- **Newton Free Library**, Main Branch, 330 Homer St, Newton, 617-796-1360, www.ci.newton.ma.us/Library; local library with four neighborhood branches.

As far as **college and university libraries** go, unless you're a student of the school or in an affiliated library network, at best you may be able to go into the library and look at books, but generally you will not be allowed to check out materials. If you have an interest in using a particular library, check with the individual college or university to learn about its policies. If you are a student, your school library may be part of a network; for example, Emerson College, Emmanuel College, Lesley University, Mass. College of Art, Mass. College of Pharmacy, the MFA, the New England Conservatory, Wentworth Institute of Technology, and Wheelock College are all linked through the **Fenway Libraries Online** system, which allows students to borrow from any of the member libraries: http://flo.org, 617-442-2384.

CULTURE FOR KIDS

Boston has a great many attractions that are educational as well as fun. Area museums, theaters, zoos, historical sites, and others are good for the whole family, and some are targeted to a younger audience.

MUSEUMS

- **The Children's Museum**, 300 Congress St, Boston, 617-426-8855, www.boston kids.org
- **Pirate Museum**, 274 Derby St, Salem, 978-741-2800, www.piratemuseum.com; relive the adventures of famous pirates. Open from May through October, and some nights in November.
- **Salem Witch Museum**, 19-1/2 Washington Sq, Salem, 978-744-1692, www.salemwitchmuseum.com; dramatic overview of the Salem Witch Trials, with lights, narration, and life-sized figures. Open daily.

ZOOS/AQUARIUMS

- **Franklin Park Zoo**, 1 Franklin Park Rd, Dorchester, 617-541-LION, www.zoo newengland.com; 72-acre zoo nestled in Franklin Park, part of Boston's Emerald Necklace. Open daily.

- **New England Aquarium**, Central Wharf (off Atlantic Ave), Boston, 617-973-5200, www.neaq.org; beautiful central tank for viewing sea life at all levels from above-surface to underwater, captivating penguin pool, special shows, and Simons IMAX Theatre. Open daily. Nearby parking or take Blue Line T to Aquarium stop.
- **Stone Zoo**, 149 Pond St, Stoneham, 781-438-5100, www.zoonewengland.com; open daily.

SPORTS

See **Sports for Kids** in the **Sports and Recreation** chapter.

THEATER

- **Boston Baked Theatre**, 255 Elm St, Somerville, 617-628-9575, www.basic theatre.org
- **North Shore Music Theatre**, 62 Dunham Rd, Beverly, 978-232-7200, www.nsmt.org; musicals, celebrity concerts, and concerts for children.
- **Puppet Showplace Theatre**, 32 Station St (Brookline Village), Brookline, 617-731-6400, www.puppetshowplace.org; the first puppetry center in New England. Shows are appropriate for children five and up.
- **Turtle Lane Playhouse**, 283 Melrose St, Newton, 617-244-0169, www.turtle lane.org
- **Underground Railway Theater**, 41 Foster St, Arlington, 781-643-6916, www.undergroundrailwaytheater.org; national touring and local performing company presenting a synthesis of theater, puppetry, and music ranging from adult cabaret to full-length plays.

T'S IMPOSSIBLE TO OVERSTATE THE ROLE SPORTS PLAY IN MOST Bostonians' lives. Fans obsess about the fortunes of their professional teams, which range from famed franchises like the Red Sox and Celtics to modern day dynasties like the Patriots, and the abundance of universities provides a wealth of collegiate athletics. Add to that a wide array of participant sports, bountiful hiking and greenspace, and several mountain ranges within driving distance, and spectator or participatory sporting activities are easy to come by in any season.

Sports fans may be interested in **The Sports Museum of New England** at the TD Banknorth Garden. Call 617-624-1234 or go to www.sportsmuseum.org for more information.

PROFESSIONAL

The Boston area is mecca for New England's professional sports teams, with the **Red Sox**, **Celtics**, and **Bruins** all playing in Boston, and the **Patriots** and **Revolution** headquartered just 30 miles away in Foxborough. Residents of Vermont, New Hampshire, Maine, Rhode Island, Connecticut, and western Massachusetts have to make quite a trek to root for the home team, but they do it, and in droves. To better acquaint yourself with the ins and outs of area sports franchises, simply check the sports sections of the *Globe* or the *Herald* for the latest, or pick up the free bi-weekly *Barstool Sports*.

BASEBALL

From spring training in March until the last out of the season in October, the **Boston Red Sox** of the American League East dominate this city; they often steal headlines even in the off-season. Boston's fans are notoriously well educated when it comes to baseball—ESPN's Peter Gammons, who revolutionized baseball reporting with his "Diamond Notes" column in the *Globe* for 20 years, hails from Boston—and it is nearly impossible to make it through a summer day without discussing the state of Red Sox Nation. While the fandom's trademark cynicism and sense of futility eased somewhat in the wake of 2004's World Series Championship (the first since 1918), and even evolved into something resembling confidence after a follow-up World Series sweep in 2007, you can still get by with the familiar lament, "They're ruinin' my summah!" The Sox play at **Fenway Park**, located right in Kenmore Square. Built in 1912, it is the oldest professional stadium in the country, boasting a fabled history, intimate confines, and the most expensive ticket prices in baseball. The new ownership has been steadily improving the park since 2002, finding creative new ways to increase its limited seating capacity (and revenues). Tickets in 2007 ranged from $12 upper bleachers to $312 premium seats. The Red Sox currently have the second-longest sellout streak in baseball history (four years and counting), so getting to the game can be difficult, and there is a waiting list for season tickets; check www.redsox.com or call 877-REDSOX9 for ticket information. Alternatively, scalpers congregate outside the park on game days; if it's nice out, expect to pay $10–$50 over face value, and far more for Yankees games and Opening Day. To get to Fenway, take any Green Line train (except the E Line) to Kenmore Square, or the D Line to the Fenway stop. Then just follow the crowd.

Baseball fans outside of Boston can root for the Red Sox **minor league baseball** affiliates for a fraction of Major League prices. The Triple-A **Pawtucket Red Sox** play just over the Massachusetts border at McCoy Stadium (Division Street, Pawtucket, Rhode Island); visit www.pawsox.com or call 401-724-7300 for tickets and information. A couple of hours north in Portland, Maine, the popular AA **Portland Sea Dogs** play at Hadlock Field (271 Park Avenue); visit www.seadogs.com or call 800-936-3647 for information. And just outside the city, the Single-A **Lowell Spinners** play a shorter season at LaLacheur Park (450 Aiken Street, Lowell); call 978-459-2255 or visit www.lowellspinners.com.

BASKETBALL

The storied **Boston Celtics** of the NBA's Eastern Conference are a long way from their glory days, when Larry Bird, Kevin McHale, and Robert Parish brought deafening cheers to the Boston Garden, and even farther removed from the 1957–69 dynasty that won 11 championships in 13 years behind Bill Russell, Bob Cousy, and coach Red Auerbach. The beloved old "Gahden" was replaced by the Fleet Center in 1995 (later renamed the **TD Banknorth Garden**), and playoff runs are no longer a guarantee, but Celtic Pride still remains. The season runs from November through April, when the playoffs begin, and 2007 ticket prices ranged from $10 in the upper balcony to $1,500 floor seats. Individual tickets are available at the Garden box office, at www.ticketmaster.com, or by calling 800-4NBA-TIX; for season tickets, visit www.celtics.com or call 866-4CELTIX. To reach the TD Banknorth Garden, take the Green Line, Orange Line, or commuter rail to North Station. There are parking garages nearby if you're willing to endure heavy pre- and post-game traffic.

For information about other **TD Banknorth Garden events**—including concerts, professional wrestling, figure skating, gymnastics, the annual college hockey Beanpot tournament, Disney shows, and the circus—visit www.td banknorthgarden.com. You cannot call the box office directly; instead you must purchase tickets in person (the box office is open daily from 11 a.m. to 7 p.m.) or through Ticketmaster (617-931-2000 or www.ticketmaster.com).

FOOTBALL

Long-time underdogs, now perennial contenders, the AFC East's **New England Patriots** play at state-of-the-art **Gillette Stadium** in Foxborough (capacity 68,000)—about a half-hour south of Boston. Since Brookline native and lifelong fan Robert Kraft purchased the flailing franchise in 1994, the Patriots' successes and popularity have skyrocketed, culminating in Super Bowl victories in 2002, 2004, and 2005. There is a hefty waiting list for season tickets; call the Patriots at 800-543-1776 or go to www.patriots.com for information. Individual game tickets sell out quickly, and are available through Ticketmaster. Parking at Gillette Stadium is decent, with 16,500 spaces, and commuter rail service is available on game days; check www.mbta.com or call 617-222-3200 for event-specific schedule and fare information.

HOCKEY

The **Boston Bruins** play in the NHL's Eastern Conference, and carry a long, proud tradition as members of the "Original Six" (the six founding teams of the NHL). Hockey's season runs almost concurrently with basketball's, from October to April, and the Bruins share the TD Banknorth Garden with the Celtics. Even in down years, the Bs have a mighty and loyal following, creating a steady demand for tickets. To order season tickets, or to put your name on a waiting list should they sell out, call 617-624-BEAR or visit www.bostonbruins.com. For single game tickets, which in 2007 ranged from $10 to $176, stop by the Garden box office (see above) or order by phone or online through Ticketmaster (again see above). During evening games, you can purchase tickets from the Advance Ticket Sales Booth located at the southwest corner of Level 4.

The AHL has three **minor league hockey** franchises in the area, offering exciting and less expensive nights out. The **Providence Bruins** play at the Dunkin' Donuts Center at One La Salle Square, Providence, RI (www.providencebruins. com or 401-273-5000); tickets range from $15 to $40. San Jose's affiliate **Worces-**

ter **Sharks** play in the DCU Center at 105 Commercial Street in Worcester; $10–$16 tickets are available by calling Ticketmaster or online at www.sharksahl. com. The **Lowell Devils**, affiliated with New Jersey's NHL team, play at the Tsongas Arena at 300 Arcand Drive in Lowell (www.lowelldevils.com, 978-458-PUCK); tickets are in the $10–$18 range and are available at the Tsongas Arena box office or through Ticketmaster. All three AHL franchises offer season pass programs.

LACROSSE

The **Boston Cannons** of Major League Lacrosse's Eastern Conference have bounced around the area since their 2001 inception, most recently finding a home at Harvard Stadium on North Harvard Street in Allston. For tickets, which range from $15 to $20, call 888-847-9700 or visit www.bostoncannons.com.

RACING

Newcomers who like to spend a day at the track—for horses or greyhounds—will not be disappointed here. Attempts to ban greyhound racing in Massachusetts have been unsuccessful. Both parks are T accessible.

- **Horse racing: Suffolk Downs**, 111 Waldemar Ave, Route 1A, East Boston, 617-567-3900, www.suffolkdowns.com; admission is $2 for grandstands or clubhouse. There's free parking, or you can take the Blue Line to the Suffolk Downs stop.
- **Dog racing: Wonderland Greyhound Park**, 190 VFW Pkwy, Revere, 781-284-1300, www.wonderlandgreyhound.com; live races five nights a week. Lots of parking, or take the Blue Line to the Wonderland (last) stop.

SOCCER

The **New England Revolution**, Boston's Major League Soccer team, shares Gillette Stadium with the Patriots, and has made two straight appearances in the MLS Cup. Soccer season runs from April to October, and while Gillette Stadium's seating capacity is reduced during soccer season, tickets are still relatively easy to come by. For season ticket information call 877-GET-REVS or go to www.revolutionsoccer.net; single game tickets, ranging in price from $18 to $34 for the 2007 season, are available through Ticketmaster.

The **Boston Renegades** of the USL Women's League won the national championship in 2001 and 2002. The Renegades play at Bowditch Stadium, 475 Union Ave in Framingham. Individual tickets cost $8 for adults and $5 for children, and can be purchased at the field on game nights. For more information or to get season passes, call 781-891-6900 or visit www.bostonrenegades.com.

COLLEGE SPORTS

If college sports are more your style, you will find plenty of school teams to follow. Harvard University alone has 40 different varsity teams. Tickets for some college events can be as hard to come by as tickets to professional games—in particular, the final round of the **Beanpot** (a varsity hockey tournament between Harvard, Northeastern, BU, and BC) and the annual **Harvard vs. Yale football game** are both hot tickets.

Obviously there are too many colleges in Boston to list them all, but here are a few with popular athletic programs:

- **BC Eagles:** since moving to the Atlantic Coast Conference, BC's Division I basketball and football games have become regular sellouts, especially against nationally recognized programs like Duke, UNC, Florida State, and arch-rival Notre Dame. Their ice hockey program offers exciting games in the Hockey East Conference, and BC fields competitive men's and women's programs in over a dozen other sports. For tickets or information, call 617-552-GOBC, or visit http://bceagles.cstv.com.

- **BU Terriers:** While BU's ice hockey program—which boasts 28 Beanpot titles and a number of alumni in the NHL—is the pride of the school, they also sport men's and women's basketball, crew, cross-country, golf, soccer, swimming and diving, tennis, indoor/outdoor track, men's wrestling, and women's lacrosse, field hockey, and softball. For tickets or information, call 617-353-GOBU, or visit www.bu.edu/athletics.

- **Harvard Crimson:** Harvard claims the nation's largest Division I athletic program. Football tickets are still relatively inexpensive, and you also have your choice of men's and women's basketball, crew, cross country, fencing, golf, ice hockey, lacrosse, sailing, soccer, squash, and swimming, as well as baseball, field hockey, skiing, and softball. For information and tickets, call 877-GO HARVARD or visit www.gocrimson.com.

- **MIT Engineers/Beavers:** in addition to their very visible sailing program on the Charles River, teams at the varsity level include baseball, basketball, crew, cross country, fencing, field hockey, football, golf, gymnastics, ice hockey, lacrosse, pistol, rifle, skiing, soccer, squash, swimming, tennis, track and field, volleyball, water polo, and wrestling, as well as many club sports. For more information, call 617-253-1000, or visit http://mitathletics.cstv.com.

- **Northeastern Huskies:** varsity teams in men's and women's basketball, crew, cross-country, ice hockey, soccer, and track, as well as men's baseball and football, women's field hockey, and dozens of club sports. For tickets and information, call 617-373-GoNU or visit www.gonu.com.

- **Tufts Jumbos:** varsity teams in baseball, basketball, crew, cross-country, fencing, football, golf, ice and field hockey, lacrosse, sailing, soccer, softball, squash, swimming and diving, tennis, track and field, and volleyball. Call 617-627-3232 or visit http://ase.tufts.edu/athletics for information.

- **UMASS-Boston Beacons:** Division III basketball, played at Clark Athletic Center at the Columbia Point campus, is probably the best deal in town. Also baseball, cross country, soccer, ice hockey, tennis, volleyball, and lacrosse games and meets. Call 617-287-7800 or visit www.athletics.umb.edu.

OTHER SPECTATOR SPORTING EVENTS

The world-famous **Boston Marathon** goes from Hopkinton to Copley Square on Patriot's Day—a state holiday commemorating the April 19, 1775 "shot heard around the world," held the third Monday in April. The oldest annual marathon in the world, it is also one of the most prestigious. Because of this, runners must either qualify by completing another marathon under a certain time, or "pay" to run by gaining official sponsorship and raising money for charities such as the American Cancer Society, Dana-Farber, or American Liver Foundation. (Charitable runners typically have to raise more than $3,000 to qualify, and even those spots are difficult to come by.) The **Boston Athletic Association** (40 Trinity Place, 4th Floor, Boston, 617-236-1652, www.baa.org) has been in charge of the marathon since it was first run in 1897; check their web site for sign-up information, race details, or to track a runner's progress. To watch the fun, just bring a blanket and a portable radio and locate a suitable spot along the 26-mile route. Note: as you might expect, the popularity of the event, coupled with numerous road closings and detours, leads to awful traffic in the city.

In June of each year you can watch the annual **John F. Kennedy Regatta** in Boston Harbor. For information call 617-847-1800. And don't miss the **Head of the Charles Regatta**, held the second-to-last weekend in October, when college and club crew teams from all over the nation converge in Cambridge and Boston to compete in the world's largest rowing event. The 3-mile course runs from the BU Boathouse to Artesani Park in Brighton. Find a spot along the Charles to enjoy the spectacle; the Cambridge side features live music and vendors. Note: Memorial Drive is closed to traffic, and parking is difficult. Take the Red Line to Harvard or Central Square, or the Green B Line to BU Central. Call 617-868-6200 or visit www.hocr.org for information.

PARTICIPANT SPORTS AND ACTIVITIES

One of the easiest ways to meet people in your new town is by joining an intra-mural-type sports league—and it has the added benefit of getting you fit.

Check newspapers or ask friends, neighbors, and coworkers for recommendations of sports clubs, or check with www.active.com to find out about local leagues and events. You can also see if a **Boston Community Center** near you (617-635-4920, www.cityofboston.gov/bcyf) has facilities or leagues for adults or children. These community centers—called Boston Centers for Youth and Families—are located throughout the city and are open to everyone, not just those with a Boston address.

PARKS AND RECREATION DEPARTMENTS

The **Department of Conservation and Recreation** (**DCR**) serves Massachusetts through its many subdivisions in matters of recreation and individual sports, and maintains public rinks, playgrounds, beaches, pools, golf courses, parks, watersheds, reservations, and general nature space.

The DCR has several **Urban Parks & Recreation district offices**. If you need additional information on any event or facility in your neighborhood, call 617-626-1250 or go to www.mass.gov/dcr.

- **Charles District** covers Arlington, East Boston, Brighton, Cambridge, Charlestown, North End, JP, Somerville, Waltham, Watertown, Wellesley, and Weston.
- **Mystic District** covers Chelsea, East Boston, Everett, Malden, Melrose, Nahant, Revere, Saugus, Stoneham, Winthrop, Winchester, and Wakefield.
- **Harbor District** covers South Boston, Dorchester, Quincy, Weymouth, Hingham, Hull, and Cohasset.
- **Neponset District** covers Canton, Dedham, Hyde Park, Mattapan, Roslindale, Braintree, Dover, Weston, Milton, Randolph, and West Roxbury.

Although Massachusetts is one of the smaller states, it has one of the largest state park systems, offering plenty of places to go for camping, hiking, swimming, and other outdoor recreation. The most popular state park closest to Boston is the **Walden Pond State Reservation**. The small freshwater pond is a 103-foot-deep glacial kettle that sees lots of swimmers during the summer months, despite its pebbly shores. A walking path and welcoming green forest surrounds the pond and displays a gorgeous show of color each fall. For state parks, reservations, forests, and watersheds, contact **MassParks** (251 Causeway Street, Suite 600, Boston, 617-626-1250, www.state.ma.us/dcr).

The **Boston Parks and Recreation Department** oversees over 2,000 acres of greenspace within Boston proper, including 215 parks and playgrounds, the Emerald Necklace, and two golf courses. For more information on the parks that fall under this jurisdiction contact the Boston Parks and Recreation Department, 1010 Mass Ave., 3rd Floor, 617-635-4505, www.cityofboston.gov/parks.

What follows are leagues and individual sports and recreational activities that can be found throughout the greater Boston area. For children, see **Sports for Kids** at the end of this chapter.

BASKETBALL

For when a game of horse just isn't enough:

- **BSSC Basketball**, 617-789-4070, www.bssc.com; Boston Ski & Sports Club runs coed and men's year-round leagues throughout Greater Boston for all ability levels.
- **Cambridge Racquet & Fitness Club Basketball**, 617-491-8989, www.crfc basketball.com; men's and women's leagues of all levels for members and non-members.
- **Never Too Late Basketball**, 781-488-3333, www.nevertoolate.com; year-round clinics, camps, and scrimmages open to adults of all ages and abilities throughout the Boston area.
- **T's League**, 508-498-7845, www.tsleague.com; men's and women's leagues in Waltham.

BASEBALL, SOFTBALL, CRICKET

To join a **baseball** or **softball** league, call your town's recreation department. Some municipalities are strict about requiring proof of residence to play on a town league. You can also ask around in neighborhood bars or sporting goods stores to find out who sponsors teams, or try one of the following:

- **Beantown Softball League**, 617-937-5858, www.beantownsoftball.com, is a GLBT softball league that's been running for over 25 years.
- **Boston Men's Baseball League**, 9 Blossom Ln, Wayland, 617-BASEBALL, www. bostonbaseball.com, is New England's largest amateur baseball league; ages 18 and up.
- **Boston Park League Baseball**, www.bostonparkleague.org; America's oldest amateur baseball league, with games in Eastie, Hyde Park, Brighton, Rozzie, and Dorchester.
- **Boston West Coed Softball**, www.bostonwestcoedsoftball.com; adult coed league with games throughout the Greater Boston Area.
- **Brookline Adult Softball League**, www.scorebook.com/brooklinesoftball/; email leagueoffice@brooklinesoftball.com for sign-up information.
- **BSSC Softball**, 617-789-4070, www.bssc.com; coed, indoor and outdoor games throughout Greater Boston.
- **M Street Softball League**, www.sbsports.com; softball league based in South Boston.
- **Massachusetts State Cricket League**, www.mscl.org; matches in the Greater Boston area from May to September.
- **Metro Boston Amateur Softball Association**, 414 Main St, Melrose, 781-665-5665, www.asaboston.com; coed, men's, women's, and youth leagues in the Boston area.

BICYCLING

There are a number of bike paths in the Boston area as well as bicycling organizations that arrange trips around New England. The hills, mountains, woods, and waterfront areas of New England provide gorgeous views that many feel are best enjoyed when you're pedaling around. Because Boston and its environs are hilly, biking even on paved paths can be more challenging and strenuous than in many other US cities. Also keep in mind that the area's old, narrow, and sometimes cobbled streets can make city cycling particularly difficult and dangerous—as a bicyclist in the Boston area, be *very* careful. While only children 12 and under are legally required to wear helmets while biking, you shouldn't even think about riding in this city without one.

Bay State cyclists are subject to the same rules of the road as drivers are, with one exception: bicycles are not allowed on the major highways such as I-93, I-90 (the Mass Pike), Route 1A, etc. While Cambridge is already quite bicycle-friendly—many main streets like Mass Ave and Broadway have designated bike lanes—Boston is still working on it; however, the Boston Bicycle Plan has led to a number of improvements this decade. In terms of parking, riders will find provisions like bike racks and bike-friendly parking garages throughout the metro area. Bikes are allowed on most T and commuter line trains (with the exception of the Green Line and the Mattapan High-Speed Line) outside of rush hour. Contact the **Boston Bicycle Advisory Committee** at 617-635-4680 with questions, concerns, or complaints regarding bicycling in Boston.

If you are concerned about your bike being stolen, you can register it with the **National Bike Registry**. If police find a bike, they check with the registry to match it to its proper owner; $10 will get your bike registered for the next 10 years. Call 800-848-BIKE or visit www.nationalbikeregistry.com for more information. Lastly, if you want to make a buck while you bike, opportunities abound here. As in many congested cities, cycling tends to be the quickest means of transport available, creating demand for year-round bike messengers and seasonal pedicab drivers.

The Charles River has an 18-mile multi-use paved path between Science Park and Watertown Square known officially as the Dr. Paul Dudley White Charles River Bike Path (www.mass.gov/dcr), typically referred to as simply the **Charles River Bike Path.** This path is probably the most highly used recreation space in the city. It's filled with runners, cyclists, in-line skaters, and people just out for a stroll. The path is separated from the city's streets, but connects at several points by ramped pedestrian bridges so there's plenty of access.

Many parks in the Emerald Necklace provide green and peaceful places to ride: the **Arnold Arboretum** (www.arboretum.harvard.edu) is now open to cyclists, as are some non-zoo areas of **Franklin Park**. There is a mini-trail called the **Jamaicaway Bikepath** running from Jamaica Pond through Olmstead Park and along the Riverway/Route 9 to Leverett Pond, and the nearby **Muddy River**

Bikepath begins near the Fens and runs along Park Drive. And the **Stony Brook Reservation Bike Path** (www.mass.gov/dcr) includes some wilder terrain as it runs for four miles along Turtle Pond Parkway, starting at Hyde Park's River Street and ending at Washington Street in West Roxbury.

Aside from the Emerald Necklace, another of Boston's most popular bike paths is the Pierre Lallement Southwest Corridor Bikepath, a.k.a. the **Southwest Corridor**. Here you can ride for four miles parallel to the Orange Line through the South End, Roxbury, and Jamaica Plain. Originally, planners proposed putting a high-speed roadway here, but instead it became a closed-in park with separate bike and pedestrian paths, community gardens, playgrounds, and more. Where the Southwest Corridor intersects with the Ruggles T stop, you can split off onto the **Melnea Cass Bikepath** and head toward South Boston. Be forewarned: while the signs on this last path are easy to follow, the roads aren't so great. Some local cyclists enjoy riding around the historic and unquestionably beautiful **Forest Hills Cemetery** (www.foresthillstrust.org) in Jamaica Plain; no bikes are allowed in Cambridge's lovely Mt. Auburn Cemetery however. "America's most celebrated bike path," the **Minuteman Bikeway** (www.minutemanbikeway.org), is a 12-mile path from the Alewife T Station in Cambridge to Bedford. Residents of Somerville, Arlington, Cambridge, Lexington, Concord, and Bedford all have easy access to this rail trail, which takes cyclists back through American Revolutionary history. There are many places along the way to catch up with the trail, which is also popular with in-line skaters, and an extension called the **Red Line Linear Park Bikepath** runs through Davis Square. **Millennium Park** in West Roxbury is a 250-acre greenspace that was once a landfill, and features miles of paved pedestrian and bicycle paths. And along much of the waterfront you'll find the **Boston HarborWalk** (www.bostonharborwalk.com), a steadily expanding system of pathways aiming to connect the city's waterfront to existing public greenspace.

Farther out of the city, the 150-mile-and-growing **Bay Circuit Trail** (www.baycircuit.org) winds through 34 towns in an outer ring around Boston, from Newburyport to Duxbury. **Wompatuck State Park** in Hingham (off Route 228) has 12 miles of bike trails, and the **Mass Central Rail Trail** (www.masscentralrailtrail.org) comprises about 15 miles of the former railway, open for cycling between Boston and parts west. Another former railroad, the scenic **Cape Cod Rail Trail**, follows the protected Cape Cod National Seashore for much of its 22 miles.

The mountains and ski resorts north and west of Boston offer plenty of **mountain biking** options, but many locals just take a short ride north to the **Middlesex** and **Lynn Fells** (www.fellsbiker.com). The **Mystic River Reservation Bike Path** runs for approximately three and a half miles between Somerville and the Wellington Bridge in Everett. The **Lower Neponset River Trail** provides over two miles of bike paths on a former railroad bed along the Neponset River from Dorchester to Milton, while cyclists in Quincy take advantage of the DCR's

Squantum Point Park. You can find information online on all of these mountain biking paths through the DCR's web site, www.mass.gov/dcr. For mountain biking news, events, and trail information throughout New England, check out the **New England Mountain Bike Association** (800-57-NEMBA, www.nemba.org).

Contact your local town or city hall for information about bicycle advisory committees or advocacy groups in your area. The **Massachusetts Bicycle Coalition (MassBike)** at 171 Milk Street, Suite 33, in Boston (617-542-BIKE, www. massbike.org), is a great resource for information on all things in the Massachusetts bicycling world, including maps of current trails and updates on future projects.

If you're interested in bicycling with a group or participating in races and other events, you'll probably get your best tips from the folks at your local bike shop. In the meantime, you could start with one of these **bike clubs**:

- **Boston Bicycle Club**, 67 Jar Brook Rd, Holliston, www.bostonbicycleclub.org; riding, racing, and discounts on bike gear.
- **Boston Brevets**, www.bostonbrevets.com; a series of long distance training and qualifying rides.
- **BSSC Biking**, 617-789-4070, www.bssc.com
- **Charles River Wheelmen**, www.crw.org; over 1200 members of all skill levels get together for weekly rides and social events.
- **Rage On Boston Mountain Biking Club**, www.ragemtb.com; laid-back, loosely structured, off-road riding club for people of all skill levels. No membership fee.

BOATING, SAILING, WINDSURFING, KAYAKING & CANOEING

With the harbor, the Mystic and Charles rivers, and the miles of coastline to the north and south of the city at their disposal, area residents spend a lot of time on or near the water. If boating is your pleasure, perhaps the best place to dip your toes is at **BostonBoating.com**, a site devoted to water sports, sailing, and power boating in New England.

Boston's backyard waterway, the **Charles River**, is over 80 miles long and runs through many communities and neighborhoods mentioned in this guide. If you run, walk, bike, skate, or go to concerts, you will likely spend some time along the Charles. And if you sail or row, you'll be on it—though you should probably avoid spending too much time *immersed* in it. Pollution in the Charles reached legendary proportions during the latter part of the 20th century due to sewage and waste dumping between 1930 and 1970. Water quality is much better after a 1990s plan to clean up the river was set into motion; fish and other wildlife have returned, good indicators of its improving health. Boats of any type (except inflatables)—canoes, kayaks, rowboats, and powerboats—are allowed on the

Charles and in Boston Harbor. During the appropriate seasons, you can see the Harvard, MIT, and BU sailing and crew teams practicing and racing along the river. And on good weather days, it's littered with pleasure boaters. On the Fourth of July, the Charles swarms with boaters taking in the city's annual Independence Day celebration, when the Boston Pops play at the Hatch Shell to throngs of people along the Esplanade, and the fireworks barge anchors right in the middle of the river.

Obviously, **Boston Harbor**, being part of the Atlantic Ocean, is a much rougher body of water than the Charles. Except during the coldest weather (when the harbor can become spotted with ice chunks barring the safe passage of even large boats), recreational crafts mix right in here with commercial vessels, including fishing boats, whale watching ships, water taxis, and ferries.

Motorized boating is allowed in some of the **state parks and reservations** throughout Massachusetts. Visit www.state.ma.us/dcr or call **Massachusetts State Parks and Recreation** at 617-626-1250 for more information.

Before you head out on the water at all, it's probably a good idea to take a boating safety course. The **Massachusetts Environmental Police** run a Boating Education Program, where you can take courses in boating basics. For information, call 617-727-8760 or visit www.mass.gov/dfwele/dle/courselist.htm for a course directory. They also recommend the following **boating safety course providers**:

- **Boatwise**, 800-698-7373, www.boatwiseclasses.com
- **Duxbury Bay Maritime School**, 781-934-7555, www.duxbayms.com
- **New England Maritime**, 508-790-3400, www.nemaritime.com
- **US Coast Guard Auxiliary**, 800-848-3942 ext. 8309, www.uscgaux.org/~013
- **US Power Squadrons**, 800-336-2628, www.usps.org

The DCR and the City of Boston run boating and sailing programs for both children and adults. Depending on the sailing club's affiliation, children's lessons can be inexpensive or even free, thanks to government subsidies or charitable donations. Perhaps most popular is **Community Boating, Inc.** (617-523-1038, www.community-boating.org), which offers sailing, windsurfing, and kayaking lessons for all levels; summer youth memberships are only $1. The welcoming boathouse is located on the Charles River Esplanade between the Longfellow Bridge and the Hatch Shell. If sailing the Charles seems tame to you, the **Boston Sailing Center** (www.bostonsailingcenter.com) and **Boston Harbor Sailing Club** (www.bostonharborsailing.com) both offer more rigorous (and expensive) sailing classes on the waters of the harbor. There are many other clubs and sailing centers offering public lessons and classes, both inside and outside the metro area; check **BostonBoating.com** for a comprehensive list.

Boat owners will need to get the proper **licenses** and **registration**, as dictated by the Massachusetts Environmental Police and the Department of Fisheries, Wildlife, and Environmental Law Enforcement (www.state.ma.us/

dfwele/dle/). Massachusetts requires that all boats with motors (including jet-skis and sailboats with motors in them—even electric) be registered, no matter how infrequently you may use the motor. All boats longer than 14 feet with a motor must have a certificate of title, which costs $25. Registrations vary from $40 to $100, depending on the size of your boat. Once you get your paperwork, paint your boat's registration number on the forward half of the hull in block letters at least 3 inches high. The registration decal goes on the port side of the boat, lined up with and three inches sternward of the registration number. For more information and to download forms, visit www.state.ma.us/dfwele/dle/sptapps.htm, or contact the **Division of Law Enforcement**, Registration and Titling Bureau, Boston Licensing Office, 251 Causeway Street, 1st Floor, 617-626-1610. You can renew your motorboat license through the department's online licensing site, **MassOutdoors**, at www.sport.state.ma.us.

Although there are marinas galore within Boston proper, many boat owners choose to tie up at marinas outside the city; there is plenty of boat storage in traditional maritime towns all the way from the New Hampshire border to Cape Cod and the islands. Check BostonBoating.com or www.marinas.com for a list of public launch ramps and marinas that will be most accessible for you if you are looking outside the city. The DCR also runs a number of **small boat launches** in Boston, Medford, and Nahant. Call the Boston Harbor Master (34 Drydock Avenue, 617-343-4721), or the DCR for details and locations.

If **rowing** or **crew** calls you, **Community Rowing** is one of the largest public rowing clubs in the US. After over 20 years at the Daly Skating Rink on the Charles in Newton, they are moving their seasonal (April to October) operations—which include all manner of programs for adults, youths, and people with disabilities—to a new boathouse in Brighton in 2008. Visit www.communityrowing.org or call 617-923-7557 for information. **Boston Bay Blades** (www.bayblades.org) is a nonprofit rowing and sculling organization for Boston's GLBT community. For a more leisurely rowing experience, you can rent small boats at **Charles River Canoe & Kayak** (www.bostonpaddle.com), located in Artesani Park in Brighton, from May through September.

Finally, for **whitewater rafting**, you'll need to get a ways outside the city, if not the state, to find suitable rapids. Maine's Penobscot and Kennebec rivers are two popular destinations, with a number of local outfitters serving each; visit www.raftmaine.com. **BSSC Outdoor Adventure** (627-789-4070, www.bssc.com) organizes group weekend trips to western Massachusetts, Maine, and Canada.

BOWLING

The first thing to know about bowling in Boston is that much of it is of the "candlepin" variety, instead of the traditional ten pin (or as Bostonians call it, "big-ball") bowling you're likely used to. Invented in Worcester in 1881, candlepin bowling differs from its big brother in a number of ways: the balls are much smaller (and have no finger holes), the pins are quite slimmer, bowlers get three turns per frame instead of two, and fallen pins remain in play. There are a growing number of ten pin lanes in the city, but they can be hard to find elsewhere. Below are a few local bowling alleys, and unless otherwise noted, assume they are candlepin-only.

- **Boston Bowl**, 820 Morrissey Blvd, Dorchester, 617-825-3800; open 24 hours a day, with 30 ten pin lanes, 14 candlepin lanes, and billiards.
- **Central Park Lanes**, 10 Saratoga St, East Boston, 617-567-7073
- **King's Lanes**, Lounge & Billiards, 10 Scotia St, Boston, 617-266-BOWL, www.kingsbackbay.com; upscale ten pin alley also offers billiards and swank restaurant/lounge.
- **Lanes and Games**, 195 Concord Tpke, Cambridge, 617-876-5533, www.lanesgames.com; offers both ten pin and candlepin, near the Fresh Pond T station.
- **Lucky Strike Lanes**, 145 Ipswich St, Boston, 617-437-0300, www.luckystrikeboston.com; upstairs at Jillian's, the giant bar/pool hall across from Fenway Park; ten pin only.
- **Milky Way Lounge & Lanes**, 405 Centre St, JP, 617-524-3740, www.milkywayjp.com; seven candlepin lanes tucked at one end of this fun bar, which features live music, dance floor, and more.
- **Needham Bowl-A-Way**, 16 Chestnut St, Needham, 781-444-9614, www.needhambowlaway.com
- **Olindy's Quincy Avenue Lanes**, 170 Quincy Ave, Quincy, 617-472-3579
- **Sacco's Bowl Haven**, 45 Day St, Somerville, 617-776-0552, www.saccosbowlhaven.com
- **Town Line Ten Pin**, 665 Broadway, Malden, 781-324-7120; ten pin lanes and billiards.
- **Twentieth Century Bowling Lane**, 1231 Hyde Park Ave, Hyde Park, 617-364-5274; better known as the home of Ron's Gourmet Ice Cream.

If you're interested in joining a bowling league, simply inquire at your local alley or check with the **Massachusetts Bowling Association** (www.masscandlepin.com). In addition, there are two long-running GLBT leagues: **Beantown Bowling** (www.beantownbowling.com) does ten pin, and the **Monday Night Bowling League** (www.mnbl.net) bowls candlepin.

BOXING

The **Boston Sport Boxing Club** (125 Walnut Street, Watertown, 617-926-0362, www.bostonboxing.com) hosts amateur to Olympic-style boxing lessons for all ability levels, and is open Monday–Saturday, 2 p.m. to 10 p.m.

CHESS

There is definitely a solid chess scene in Boston, or rather, Cambridge—maybe having something to do with all the Harvard and MIT students. As glamorized in *Good Will Hunting*, the Au Bon Pain courtyard in Harvard Square is perhaps the most notable place to play a competitive pick-up game of chess.

College and graduate students can take advantage of their school chess clubs. The rest of us might want to join one of these:

- **Boylston Chess Club**, 240 Elm St, Suite B9, Somerville, 617-629-3933, http://world.std.com/~boylston
- **Massachusetts Chess Association**, www.masschess.org
- **MetroWest Chess Club**, 117 E Central St, Natick, 508-788-3641, www.metrowestchess.org
- **United States Chess Federation**, 800-903-USCF, www.uschess.org

CURLING

Evidently cold air masses are not the only thing we get from Canada. If you'd like to capture the spirit of the great white north with a game of curling, try one of these venues:

- **Broomstones Curling Club**, 138 Rice Rd, Wayland, 508-352-2412, www.broomstones.com; over 300 members of all ages compete in tournaments and leagues on their four sheets of ice.
- **Canadian Club of Boston**, www.canadianclubofboston.com. Supporting all things Canadian—especially curling—but open to all. Matches played at The Country Club in Brookline.

DANCE

Dance classes and dance parties are a fun way to stay fit and meet friends. Clubs, groups, and dance studios offer everything from classes to private lessons to dance nights in salsa, swing, African, etc.

- **Boston Dance Alliance**, 617-482-4588, www.bostondancealliance.org
- **Boston Swing Dance Network**, 617-924-6603, www.bostonswingdance.com; different bands play a variety of swing music, from big band to jump blues, one Saturday per month from September to June. Dances are held at the St. James Armenian Church in Watertown and admission is $13, which includes a beginner's lesson. Singles and couples welcome.
- **Dance Complex**, 536 Mass Ave, Cambridge, 617-547-9363, www.dancecomplex.org; a popular place for workshops, classes, and programs in the

metro area. Ballet, African, jazz, salsa, hip hop, modern, tango, flamenco, belly dancing, and more.

- **DanceNet**, www.havetodance.com, swing dance in Boston and New England, detailing lessons, dance nights, event calendar, etc.
- **Dance New England**, www.dne.org, a consortium of barefoot freestyle dancing.
- **Folk Arts Center of New England**, 42 W Foster St, Melrose, 781-662-7475, www.facone.org; teaches and promotes international folk dance, and publishes Folk Dancing 'Round Boston, a bi-monthly calendar of local dance events.
- **Impulse Dance Company**, 261 Friend St, Boston, 617-523-1355, www.impulsedance.com; ongoing classes in ballet, hip hop, jazz, modern, movement, and choreography.
- **Massachusetts Amateur Ballroom Dance Association**, www.massabda.org
- **New England Folk Festival Association**, www.neffa.org
- **SalsaBoston**, www.salsaboston.com, portal for Boston's salsa scene.
- **Swing City Dance Club**, Bishop Mackenzie Center, 1337 Centre St, Newton, 617-566-7111, www.wannadance.com; all ages dancing every Friday night.
- **Swingtime Boston**, 617-364-7207, www.swingtimeboston.com; monthly swing, Latin, and ballroom dance for Boston's GLBT community at Brookline Academy of Dance, 185 Corey St, Brookline.
- **Tango Society of Boston**, 617-669-OCHO, www.bostontango.org; instruction and dance nights.
- **Tap Boston**, http://tapboston.havetodance.com; listings of tap classes and events around the city.
- **Tempo Dance Center**, 380 Washington St, Brighton, 617-783-5467, www.havetodance.com/tempodancecenter; weekly lessons and classes in swing, Latin, hustle, etc., and bi-monthly Friday dance parties.
- **Topf Center for Dance Education**, 551 Tremont St, Boston, 617-482-0531, www.topfcenter.org; community outreach, interracial understanding, and dance instruction.

FENCING

If you want to get a touché from an epee, the **New England Division of the USFA** (www.neusfa.org) offers contact information for a number of Greater Boston fencing clubs, including the **Bay State Fencers** (www.baystatefencers.com), the **Boston Fencing Club** (www.bostonfencingclub.org), and the **Worcester Fencing Club** (www.worcesterfencing.com).

FISHING

The state's fishing and wildlife agency, **MassWildlife** (www.mass.gov/dfwele/dfw/), is a subsection of the **Massachusetts Department of Fisheries, Wildlife, and Environmental Law Enforcement**. Founded in 1866, this office should be the first government agency to contact with questions regarding where you can fish and what the requirements are. They can give you details about seasons, limits, regulations, stocking schedules, and where to get maps. MassWildlife's Boston office is at 251 Causeway Street, Suite 400, 617-626-1590.

Saltwater fishing is free, and freshwater fishing licenses in Massachusetts range from about $11 to $38; no charge for seniors (age 70 or over) and some people with disabilities. You can pick up a fishing license at various locations around the state, including town and city clerks, sporting goods stores, and bait and tackle shops; check with MassWildlife. Or, for maximum ease, you can get them online from **MassOutdoors** (www.sport.state.ma.us). Note: if you want to trap lobsters, you'll need a special permit, also available through this web site.

Fishermen and women who want to bring their catch home to their families should note that the EPA, FDA, and Massachusetts Department of Public Health advise young children and pregnant or breastfeeding women against eating shark, swordfish, king mackerel, tuna steak, and tilefish, as well as any Massachusetts freshwater fish, due to mercury pollution. Furthermore, be careful fishing in the Charles River or in Boston Harbor (despite its reputation for good bluefish and striper). The state cautions children and childbearing women against eating flounder and shellfish from Boston Harbor, and moving farther south doesn't remedy the problem either: fish and shellfish from New Bedford Harbor have an elevated level of polychlorinated biphenyl compounds (PCBs) that they pick up from toxic substances in the water. Despite these precautions, there are many places in and around Boston to catch safe-to-eat fish; in particular, freshwater fish caught in lakes and streams stocked by the Massachusetts Department of Fisheries and Wildlife such as trout, broodstock salmon, northern pike, and tiger muskie are fine. DCR- and MassWildlife-run fishing areas close to Boston can be found at www.mass.gov/dcr.

Those interested in a fishing club can check with the **Massachusetts Striped Bass Association** (Viking Club, Route 53, Braintree, 617-984-0530, www.msba.net). While **ice fishing** is not as popular here as it is in a place like Minnesota, the lakes of New Hampshire and Maine are dotted with ice shacks come wintertime, and the DCR allows ice fishing in some areas of the Charles. Call them at 617-727-7090, or Bear's Bait Shop, in Waltham, at 781-647-040 for information on permits.

FOOTBALL, RUGBY

For those newcomers who like the rough stuff:

- **BSSC Flag Football**, 617-789-4070, www.bssc.com; coed indoor leagues play at Sports World in Tewksbury from November to April; coed and men's leagues play throughout the city on spring and fall weekends. Individuals and teams of all abilities welcome.
- **Boston Irish Wolfhounds Rugby**, 617-254-9732, www.bostonirishwolf hounds.com; all abilities welcome, training in JP, games in Canton.
- **Boston Ironsides Rugby Football Club**, www.bostonironsidesrfc.org; rugby league for gay men.
- **Boston Rugby Club**, 617-566-2732, www.brfc.org; national-level team.
- **Boston Women's Rugby Football Club**, 617-824-4294, www.bwrfc.org; traveling team with home games in Brookline and Cambridge. All ages and skill levels welcome.
- **Charles River Rugby Football Club**, www.crrfc.com; men's and women's traveling teams, with practices at Boston English High School in JP and home games at Moakley Park in Southie.
- **FLAG Flag Football**, www.flagflagfootball.com; GLBT flag football league, with games on spring and fall weekends; all skill levels welcome.
- **Mystic River Rugby Club**, 617-267-5221, www.mysticrugby.com; Division I competitive men's rugby, based in Malden.
- **Old Gold Rugby Club**, 617-742-9648, www.oldgoldrugby.com; all levels, games on Saturdays.

FRISBEE

Frisbee isn't just a game you play with your dog. Ultimate Frisbee turns freestyle disc throwing into a structured and fun team sport, especially popular with the twenty- to thirty-something set.

- **BSSC Ultimate Frisbee**, 617-789-4070, www.bssc.com; coed weekly games in Charlestown and Waltham from May to November.
- **Boston Ultimate Disc Alliance (BUDA)**, P.O. Box 79242, Waverly, 617-484-1539, www.buda.org; runs several Ultimate Frisbee leagues and tournaments in the Boston area (Spring, Summer, Fall, Beginner, Open/Corporate)—most coed. Their site also has information on regular pick-up games.

GOLF

The Boston area offers dozens of public 18-hole golf courses to choose from, as well as the 36-hole **Ponkapoag Golf Course** (www.ponkapoaggolf.com) at the **Blue Hills Reservation**. Most courses are open from dawn to dusk and require reservations on weekends and holidays; it's always best to call ahead. Check with

www.golfboston.com, www.golfingnewengland.com, or the **Massachusetts Golf Association** (www.mgalinks.org) for area course listings and information.
Public courses closest to the city include:

- **Brookline Golf Club at Putterham**, 1281 W Roxbury Pkwy, Brookline, 617-730-2078, www.brooklinegolf.com; 18-hole course adjacent to The Country Club; season passes and discounts available for Brookline residents.
- **Fresh Pond Golf Course**, 691 Huron Ave, Cambridge, 617-349-6282, www.freshpondgolf.com; beautifully landscaped 9-hole course, with discount for Cambridge residents.
- **William Devine Golf Course at Franklin Park**, Dorchester, 617-265-4084; 18-hole course, discount for city of Boston residents.

There is no shortage of private courses in the Boston metro area; in fact, Brookline's The Country Club was the first in the US. If you're interested in applying for membership at a private golf club, check the Yellow Pages under "Golf Courses–Private." For a different (and less exclusive) kind of club, **BSSC Golf** (617-789-4070, www.bssc.com) offers scrambles, weekend outings, and lessons during the spring, summer, and fall.

HIKING, ROCK CLIMBING, AND MOUNTAINEERING

Great hiking can be found throughout New England, particularly as you head north into the less populated and wilder areas of Vermont, New Hampshire, and Maine. Mountain climbers find life here very satisfactory as well. For example, New Hampshire's Mount Monadnock claims to be the second most climbed mountain in the world. When climbing, use common sense and be extremely cautious during the winter season; reports of people freezing to death on the icy peak of Mount Washington in New Hampshire are, sadly, not uncommon.

On a more local scale, the DCR maintains hiking trails at several area reservations. Go to www.mass.gov/dcr for details.

- **Blue Hills Reservation**, Milton and surrounding towns, 617-698-1802; hiking, rock climbing and bouldering at the Quincy Quarries in Quincy.
- **Beaverbrook Reservation**, Mill St, Belmont and Waltham, 617-484-6357; 59 acres of open fields, wetlands, and woodlands.
- **Belle Isle Reservation**, Bennington St, East Boston, 617-727-5350; Boston's last remaining salt marsh.
- **Boston Harbor Islands**, www.bostonislands.com; there are many islands in the harbor, each of which offers a slightly different experience, and many offer hiking and camping. Three of them—George's, Peddock's, and Lovell's—are run by the DCR (see **Greenspace and Beaches** for more information).
- **Breakheart Reservation**, Forest St, Saugus, 781-233-0834; 640-acre hardwood forest with rocky hills, two lakes, and one river.

- **Hammond Pond Reservation**, Hammond Pond Pkwy, Newton/Brookline, 617-698-1802; open year-round, dawn to dusk, rock climbing and bouldering.
- **Hemlock Gorge/Cutler Park**, Needham and Newton, 617-698-1802
- **Middlesex Fells Reservation,** 2500 acres of parkland in Medford, Malden, Melrose, Stoneham, and Winchester, 781-662-2340, www.fells.org.
- **Neponset River Reservation**, Dorchester and Milton, 617-727-5290; one large park and a main trail.
- **Stony Brook Reservation**, Turtle Pond Pkwy, West Roxbury and Hyde Park, 617-361-6161; hills, valleys, rocky outcroppings, and wetlands.

For more ideas on where to go hiking in New England, you can always pick up guidebooks such as *Hiking Southern New England* and *National Geographic's Guide to America's Outdoors: New England*. Investigate the numerous **state parks** through the MassParks web site (www.massparks.org).

If you are interested in **rock climbing**, you should try the **Quincy Quarries** in the Blue Hills Reservation and **Menotomy Rocks Park** in Arlington. You can keep your rock climbing skills honed year-round by joining the **Boston Rock Gym**, an indoor facility with climbing walls, located at 78 Olympia Avenue in Woburn. Call 781-935-7325 or visit www.bostonrockgym.com for information.

Area hiking and climbing organizations include:

- **Appalachian Mountain Club**, 5 Joy St, Boston, 617-523-0655, www.amc boston.org; conducts hiking and skiing tours and trips and maintains a cabin system in the White Mountains.
- **Boston Hiking Guide**, www.geocities.com/Yosemite/Trails/1171; provides links to the best hiking areas and walking paths in the Greater Boston Area.
- **New England Bouldering**, www.newenglandbouldering.com
- **BSSC Hiking and Climbing**, 617-789-4070, www.bssc.com; guided day and weekend trips during the spring, summer, and fall. Year-round indoor and outdoor rock climbing lessons available.

HOCKEY—FLOOR, FIELD, ROLLER

There are a number of intramural **hockey leagues** and teams around, but it can be hard to break in as a newcomer. Some area bars sponsor teams, so try asking around at pubs in your neighborhood, visiting ice rinks, or checking the local sports pages for ads—sometimes organizations will advertise for players in the *Globe*. Below are some leagues to look into:

- **AM Hockey League**, 978-505-7377, www.amhl.com; ice hockey league with three seasons per year, all skill levels. Games held at 6:30 a.m. at Valley Sports Arena in Concord.
- **Boston Pride Hockey**, www.bostonpridehockey.org; GLBT ice hockey league, games at rinks throughout the greater Boston area.
- **BSSC Coed Floor Hockey**, 617-789-4070, www.bssc.com; open to individuals

and teams of all levels, indoors in Newton and Brighton or outdoors in North Reading.

- **Hockeytown USA in Saugus**, 781-233-3666, www.hockeytownsaugus.com, hosts a number of leagues and tournaments, including the Friday morning Blades and Breakfast ice hockey league, www.bladesandbreakfast.com, and the Eastern Mass Roller Hockey League, 978-922-2185, www.emrhl.com, on Saturdays and Tuesday nights.
- **The Roller Hockey League**, Newton Indoor Sports Center, 617-964-0040, www.therhl.com

HORSEBACK RIDING

A number of area stables offer both lessons and rentals, but you're definitely going to have to break away from the city. If you're interested in taking a lesson or renting a horse, try www.horserentals.com, www.northhorse.com, www.justhorses.com, or www.horsemensguide.com. Or check the Yellow Pages under "Horse Riding Stables."

Horseback riding is allowed on some **DCR reservation trails**:

- **Blue Hills Reservation**, Milton/Canton/Quincy/Braintree/Randolph/Dedham/Boston; horses from a number of private stables, 617-698-1802, www.mass.gov/dcr.
- **Middlesex Fells Reservation**, Malden/Medford/Winchester/Stoneham/Melrose, 617-727-1199 or 781-662-2340, www.mass.gov/dcr or www.fells.org

There are also trails at state parks where horseback riding is permissible. For more information, check with MassParks (617-626-1250) or visit www.mass.gov/dcr for a full list of all the parks where you can ride throughout Massachusetts. Parks with **riding trails in the greater Boston area**:

- **Ames Nowell State Park**, Linwood St, Abington, 781-857-1336
- **Borderland State Park**, 259 Massapoag Ave, Easton/Sharon, 508-238-6566
- **Bradley Palmer State Park**, Asbury St, Topsfield, 978-887-5931
- **Callahan State Park**, Millwood St, Framingham, 508-653-9641
- **F. Gilbert Hills State Forest**, Mill St, Foxborough, 508-543-5850
- **Georgetown Rowley State Forest**, Route 97, Georgetown, 508-887-5931
- **Great Brook Farm State Park**, 984 Lowell Rd, Carlisle, 978-369-6312
- **Harold Parker State Forest**, 1951 Turnpike St, Rte 114, North Andover, 978-686-3391
- **Lowell-Dracut-Tyngsboro State Forest**, Trotting Park Rd, Lowell, 978-453-0592
- **Maudslay State Park**, Curzon Mill St, Newburyport, 978-465-7223
- **Willowdale State Forest**, Linebrook Rd, Ipswich, 978-887-5931
- **Wompatuck State Park**, Union St, Hingham, 781-747-7160

ICE SKATING

The DCR maintains more than twenty ice rinks in the area, open from mid-November to mid-March. Check www.mass.gov/dcr/recreate/skating.htm for information about public skating hours, rates, and rink rentals. In addition, Brookline's **Larz Anderson Park** (23 Newton Street, Brookline, 617-730-2069, www.town.brookline.ma.us/recreation/LarzAnderson.html) offers an outdoor rink during winter months, Watertown runs the **Ryan Skating Arena** (One Paramount Place, Watertown, 617-972-6468, www.ci.watertown.ma.us/index.asp?nid=22), and **Community Skating Kendall Square** (617-492-0941, www.kendallsquare.org) hosts a public outdoor rink in Cambridge; all have skate rentals available on site. But perhaps the quintessential Boston experience is skating on the **Frog Pond** in the **Boston Common**. There may be nothing quite as charming or romantic as skating in the middle of the Common on a crisp winter night, with the State House and Beacon Hill's bowfront homes rising around you. For information on hours, rates, skate rentals, and renting the rink itself, call 617-635-2120 or visit www.bostoncommonfrogpond.org.

Skating clubs in the area include:

- **New England Figure Skating Club**, 121 Donald Lynch Blvd, Marlborough, 508-229-2700 ext. 212, www.newenglandfsc.com
- **Skating Club of Boston**, 1240 Soldiers Field Rd, Boston, 617-782-5900, www.scboston.org; general public skating on Tuesdays and Saturdays.
- **North Shore Skating Club**, 51 Symonds Way, Reading, 781-944-5874, www.nsskating.net

IN-LINE/ROLLER SKATING

In-line skating is popular in Boston, and if you're not daring enough to skate in the streets, there are many paths where you can use your blades. For fun hills, try the Arnold Arboretum. For distance, try the Charles River Bicycle Trail, the Minute Man Bicycle Trail, or Marine Park in Southie. On Sundays from May to November, 1.5 miles of **Memorial Drive** in Cambridge are closed to traffic, offering four wide lanes of smooth skating and cone courses. Some community and adult-education centers offer lessons, classes, and rentals, including **Beacon Hill Skate In-Line** (135 Charles Street, Boston, 617-482-7400).

A $20 annual membership with **The Inline Club of Boston** (www.sk8net.com) gets you weekly group skate nights, parties, scenic skate tours, and more; see the **Hockey** section for information on roller hockey leagues. The last standing roller rink in the city is the **Chez Vous Disco Rink** (11 Rhoades Street, Dorchester, 617-825-6877, www.chezvousskate.com); efforts are under way to keep it from closing down. An option north of the city is **Roller World** (425 Broadway, Saugus, 781-231-1111, www.roller-world.com), and while it's still in the planning and approval stages, you can check www.charlesriverskatepark.org for updates on the proposed **Charles River Skatepark** under the Zakim Bridge in East Cambridge, which would be the largest skatepark on the East Coast.

KICKBALL

- **BSSC Kickball**, 617-789-4070, www.bssc.com; individuals and teams welcome, summer and fall sessions, weekly games in Charlestown, Brighton, and Newton.

RACQUET SPORTS—TENNIS AND SQUASH

A number of area health clubs offer racquetball, squash, handball, and tennis courts that you can use if you have a membership. However, the DCR does maintain public tennis courts where you can play for free. (See the **Parks and Recreation Departments** section above for contact information.) The unlit courts are open until dusk; lighted courts are open until 10 p.m.

Additionally, the City of Boston operates tennis courts at some of its community centers. For example, the **Stillman Tennis Center**, part of the **Charlestown Community Center** (255 Medford Street, Boston, 617-635-5173), offers three indoor and seasonally open-air courts. The **Paris Street Community Center** (112 Paris Street, East Boston, 617-735-5125), **Harborside Community Center** (312 Border Street, East Boston, 617-635-5114), and **Curley Community Center** (1663 Columbia Road, South Boston, 617-635-5304) all offer racquetball courts. **Boston Common** and the **Esplanade** have outdoor tennis courts, and there are a number of public courts in Cambridge as well. Check the Yellow Pages for a list of private tennis clubs.

Squash is also popular among some Bostonians; many clubs have squash courts, as do the colleges. Probably the most famous of all is the private **Harvard Club** (374 Comm Ave., Boston, 617-536-1260, www.harvardclub.com). The **Allston-Brighton Squash & Fitness Club** (15 Gorham Street, Allston, 617-731-4177) is a public squash court. You may also contact the **Massachusetts Squash Racquets Association** (www.ma-squash.org) if you're interested in playing with the state's competitive league. Check the Yellow Pages for a list of private squash courts.

If you're interested in joining a **racquet sport league**, here are a few:

- **Boston Boasts Squash Club**, www.bostonboasts.com; the nation's oldest and largest GLBT squash league.
- **BSSC Tennis**, 617-789-4070, www.bssc.com; indoor and outdoor clinics, mixed double tennis parties, and more.
- **New England Badminton**, www.geocities.com/Colosseum/Loge/7554

RUNNING

In Boston there are many beautiful areas in which to run. For interesting paths or trails, see above under **Hiking**, **In-line Skating**, and **Biking** for various types of terrain. The most popular places to run within Boston proper are the paths around the Charles River (www.mass.gov/dcr). If you jog on running paths or the winding streets of Boston, a handy site to track how far you've run is www. gmap-pedometer.com.

If you aim to run competitively, there are many annual races, including the mother of them all—the Boston Marathon. For the complete skinny on running in the region, including a calendar of races and track and field events, go to **New England Runner** (www.nerunner.com) or contact the **Boston Athletic Association** (617-236-1652, www.baa.org). The calendar sections of the local papers and the *Improper Bostonian* also list race details.

If your iPod doesn't provide enough companionship, consider one of the following **running clubs**:

- **Boston Athletic Association Running Club**, 617-236-1652, www.baa.org; competitive weekly workouts with the best of the best.
- **Boston Hash House Harriers**, 617-499-4835, www.bostonhash.com; "serious drinkers with a running problem." Year-round weekly runs on Wednesdays or Sundays.
- **Cambridge Running Club**, www.cambridgerunning.org; weekly runs and workouts on tracks in Cambridge and Allston, also weekend long runs and social events.
- **Cambridge Sports Union**, www.csurun.org/csu.htm; join 200 men and women for coaching, races, and weekly workouts at the Harvard race track and around Fresh Pond.
- **Community Running**, 617-542-2RUN, www.communityrunning.org; three coached workouts weekly, year-round, for all ages and abilities.
- **Frontrunners Boston**, www.frontrunnersboston.org; GLBT running club for runners and walkers of all levels. Includes both shorter and longer runs/walks on weekdays and weekends.
- **Greater Boston Track Club**, www.gbtc.org; "friendly, competitive, team-oriented environment" for runners "who compete at the local, regional, and national levels." Check their web site for an extensive list of running clubs in areas not listed here.
- **Heartbreak Hill Striders**, www.heartbreakhill.org; short and long runs west of the city, in Wellesley and in Chestnut Hill by Heartbreak Hill.
- **Irish American Track Club**, www.iatc-boston.org; competitive and social runs and workouts, long and short, tracks and all terrain, Malden, Medford, JP. Not just for the Irish.
- **L Street Running Club**, www.lstreet.org; runs for the recreational runner to

the serious competitor in South Boston.

- **North Medford Club**, www.northmedfordclub.org; second oldest running club in the US—no frills, low cost, winter and summer races.
- **Parkway Running Club**, www.parkwayrunning.org, in West Roxbury.
- **Somerville Road Runners**, www.srr.org; fun group based in Somerville, $20 annual fee; sponsors of the Khoury's Thursday Night 4.13 Miler, a free weekly run at 7:15 p.m. in East Somerville.
- **Stellar Running Club**, www.stellarrunning.org; distance training, Belmont.
- **Thirsty Irish Runners Club**, www.thirstyirishrunners.org; a mix of serious and recreational runners with an embracing family attitude.

SKIING—CROSS COUNTRY

Snowfall in the Boston area varies from year to year; if the winter is a good one— that is, if you like snow—you can cross-country ski in the city, especially along the **Emerald Necklace** (see **Greenspace** chapter). The Arnold Arboretum offers both flat stretches and hills.

Cross-country skiing is permitted in all DCR reservations and many state parks throughout Massachusetts, but the Middlesex Fells, Blue Hills Reservation, and Charles River Reservation are the most popular near the city. Check the section on **Hiking** or www.mass.gov/dcr for a complete listing. For more information on the greater Boston cross-country scene, visit www.nensa.net, home of the New England Nordic Ski Association. If you're interested in joining a cross-country skiing club, try the Boston branch of the **Appalachian Mountain Club**, www.amcboston.org.

Here are a few favored **cross-country venues** within reach of the city:

- **Blue Hills Reservation**, Milton/Canton, 617-698-1802, www.mass.gov/dcr; open to the public during daylight hours.
- **Great Brook Farm State Park** in Carlisle, 978-369-6312, www.state.ma.us/dcr
- **Middlesex Fells Reservation**, 617-727-1199, www.mass.gov/dcr; six-mile trail with two loops, for a variety of skill levels. Free and open to the public during daylight hours.
- **Walden Pond State Reservation**, Concord, 978-369-3254, www.state.ma.us/dcr
- **Weston Ski Track**, at the Martin Golf Course, Weston, 781-891-6575, www.skiboston.com; lighted and groomed trails, lessons, rentals, snowmaking, refreshments, showers, lockers, snowshoeing, equipment repairs and maintenance. Open daily from December.
- **World's End, Boston Harbor Islands**, www.bostonislands.org

SKIING—DOWNHILL AND SNOWBOARDING

If you need a quick alpine ski fix, head to the **Blue Hills Ski Area** (www.thenew bluehills.com) in the Blue Hills Reservation. It sports eight trails, night skiing, snowmaking, a ski school, ski patrol, rentals, ski shop, restaurant, rope tows, and a double chair lift. There are several other small mountains in Massachusetts, the most popular being **Wachusett Mountain** (978-464-2300, www.wachusett. com), about an hour away in Princeton.

If you're looking for more serious skiing, you'll have to travel north a bit. Many mountain resorts in Vermont, New Hampshire, and Maine stand upwards of 4,000 feet above sea level and offer significant vertical drops—biggies like Killington (Vermont), Loon Mountain (New Hampshire), and Sunday River (Maine) offer multiple peaks, glade skiing, and seemingly endless miles of trails. Snow conditions aren't very reliable here—though they do improve farther north, where mountains like Stowe average 260 inches of natural snowfall per year—so it's common for local ski areas to compensate by making their own.

Many local weekend warriors go in together to buy or rent condos or houses near the slopes, most of which are within a two- to four-hour drive of Boston. Some southern Vermont resorts also attract quite a few New Yorkers, so if skiing like you're on the Brooklyn-Queens Expressway doesn't appeal to you, try heading farther north or deeper into New Hampshire and Maine. To find a complete listing of New England's ski mountains and their offerings, visit www.neweng landskiresorts.com.

Joining a **ski club** can be a great way to meet friends, or to catch a ride north if you don't own a car:

- **Appalachian Mountain Club Boston Chapter Ski Committee**, www.amc boston.org
- **Boston Ski Party**, www.bostonskiparty.org; African-American skiing and snowboarding club.
- **BSSC Skiing**, 617-789-4070, www.bssc.com; day trips, weekends, full-on vacations, and racing.
- **Outryders**, www.outryders.org; GLBT skiing and snowboarding club.

SOCCER

Public, high school, and university soccer fields abound; check www.mass.gov/ dcr for a complete list of DCR-managed soccer pitches in Greater Boston or to reserve a field.

Area **soccer leagues** include:

- **BSSC Indoor and Outdoor Soccer**, 617-789-4070, www.bssc.com; individuals and teams welcome to sign up for multiple leagues all over the Boston area.

- **Boston Strikers**, www.bostonstrikers.com; GLBT soccer club, with indoor and outdoor games.
- **Fun Sport & Social Group**, www.fssgboston.com; coed, six on six, indoor recreational soccer league. Games in Revere.
- **Los Guapos Football Club**, www.losguapos.org; coed soccer club based in Boston.

SWIMMING

Boston has many beaches within the city limits, and there are plenty more on the north and south shores, reachable by car, T, and commuter rail. Serious beach enthusiasts take day trips or rent summer houses on Cape Cod, Martha's Vineyard, or Nantucket. See the **Greenspace and Beaches** chapter for more details.

For those afraid of fish nibbling their toes, there are many **public pools** throughout the Boston area. For example, the DCR maintains a number of swimming pools and spray pools (see below under **Sports for Kids**) open from the end of June to Labor Day. Call the DCR office that covers your neighborhood for rates and hours of operation:

Charles and Mystic districts: 617-727-4708

- **Allied Veterans Memorial Pool**, Elm St, Everett
- **Brighton/Allston Pool**, N Beacon St, Brighton
- **Connors Memorial Pool**, River St, Waltham
- **Dealtry Memorial Pool**, Pleasant St, Watertown
- **Dilboy Field Memorial Pool**, Alewife Brook Pkwy, Somerville
- **Hall Memorial Pool**, N Border Rd, Stoneham
- **Holland Memorial Pool**, Mountain Ave, Malden
- **Latta Brothers Memorial Pool**, McGrath Hwy, Somerville
- **Lee Memorial Pool**, Charles St (West End), Boston
- **McCrehan Memorial Pool**, Rindge Ave, Cambridge
- **Veterans Memorial Pool**, Memorial Dr, Cambridge
- **Vietnam Veterans Memorial Pool**, Carter St, Chelsea

Harbor and Neponset districts: 617-727-8865

- **Cass Memorial Pool**, Washington St, Roxbury
- **Connell Memorial Pool**, Broad St, Weymouth
- **Olsen Memorial Pool**, Turtle Pond Pkwy, Hyde Park; has spray pool.
- **Phelan Memorial Pool**, VFW Pkwy, West Roxbury
- **Reilly Memorial Pool**, Cleveland Circle, Brighton

In addition to the DCR pools, the City of Boston operates a number of indoor pools year round and two outdoor pools seasonally, maintained by the **Boston Centers for Youth and Families**. You need not be a Boston resident to use the community centers, though entrance rates may be a little higher. For general information, including rates and hours of operation, call 617-635-4920 or visit www.cityofboston.gov/bcyf/. For pools in neighboring communities, check with your city or town hall or recreation department.

If you'd like to find out more about group and **competitive swimming** in Massachusetts, you might want to check out NEswim.com. To swim competitively or to just get a weekly workout doing laps with a team, try one of the following groups:

- **LANES** (Liquid Assets New England Swim Team), www.swim-lanes.org, is a team for the local GLBT community and friends, open to swimmers of all ability levels.
- **Bernal's Gator Swim Club**, 978-443-4584, www.bernalsgator.com; swimmers ranging in age and ability from young children to former Olympians. Participates in US Swimming–sponsored meets throughout the country, with primary training facility at Bentley College in Waltham.
- **Cambridge Masters Swim Club**, 617-484-0550, www.cambridgemasters. com; for all levels of dedicated masters swimmers and triathletes. Uses pools at Harvard and BU.
- **New England Masters Swimming**, 888-SWIMNEM, www.swimnem.org; not as intimidating as it sounds, for swimmers over 19 of all abilities.

VOLLEYBALL

Here are a few local leagues with enough options to keep you rotating year-round:

- **BSSC Volleyball League**, Boston Ski & Sports Club, 617-789-4070, www.bssc. com; coed teams and individuals of all abilities welcome to play in Cambridge, Watertown, Brookline, and Newton.
- **Boston Volleyball Association**, 617-332-2320, www.bostonvolleyball.com; indoor and outdoor coed volleyball league for players of all abilities. Games in Allston, Brighton, and Newton.
- **Cambridge-Boston Volleyball Association**, 617-522-2882, www.gayvolley ball.net; long-running volleyball league for Boston's GLBT community, part of the National Gay Volleyball Association. Indoor games for all abilities on Sundays at the Amigos School in Cambridge; September through May, $35/season or $7/session. Free outdoor games at various locations from June through August.
- **Spike Boston Volleyball**, 617-821-4013, www.spikebostonvolleyball.com; organizes over 25 tournaments per year in New England for all levels of play.
- **Yankee Volleyball Association**, 617-491-7102, www.yankee.org; indoor men's, women's, and coed tournaments from September to May.

YOGA

Most gyms (see **Health Clubs and Gyms** below) offer yoga classes to members, and there is a wide variety of yoga studios in and around the city. The well-reputed **Kripalu Center for Yoga & Health** (866-200-5203, www.kripalu.org) in the Berkshires offers weekend- to semester-long retreats in nearly every discipline. Check out www.bostonyoga.com for a full listing of local yoga studios and workshops, or start with these:

- **The Arlington Center**, 369 Mass Ave, Arlington, 781-316-0282, www.arling toncenter.org
- **Back Bay Yoga Studio**, 1112 Boylston St #3, Boston, 617-375-0785, www.back bayyoga.com
- **Baptiste Power Vinasa Yoga**, www.baronbaptiste.com; 139 Columbus Ave, Boston, 617-441-2144; and 2000 Mass Ave, Cambridge, 617-661-YOGA
- **Bikram Yoga**, 617-742-6334, www.bikramyogaboston.com, studios in Boston and Cambridge.
- **Blissful Monkey Yoga Studio**, 663 Centre St, JP, 617-522-4411, www.blissful monkey.com
- **Mystic River Yoga**, 196 Boston Ave, Suite 3900, Medford, 781-643-0117, www. mysticriveryoga.com
- **Newton Yoga**, 1135 Walnut St, Newton, 617-928-6080, www.downunderyoga. com
- **O2 Yoga Studio**, 288 Highland Ave, Somerville, 617-625-0267, www.o2yoga. com
- **Yoga for You**, 1854 Centre St, West Roxbury, 617-325-3244, www.yogaforyou. net
- **Yoga in Harvard Square**, 1151 Mass Ave, Cambridge, 617-864-YOGA, www. yogainharvardsquare.com
- **The Yoga Studio**, 74 Joy St, Boston, 617-523-7138, www.theyogastudio.org
- **Zen Athletica Yoga Studio**, 1065 Comm Ave, Allston, 617-789-3733, www. zenathletica.com

HEALTH CLUBS AND GYMS

There are hundreds of health clubs in the metro Boston area. No doubt, you will choose one based on convenience and services. Get a tour, and if possible a free pass or two, before signing on the dotted line—you may decide that the reality of exercising to skull-pounding music is not so healthful after all. When you're told that the club you're visiting is having a "sale," take it with several grains of salt; with few fixed prices, words like "special," and "discount" are next to meaningless in the fitness business. That means the person on the treadmill next to you may have paid double or half what you paid. Ask at your place of work if they offer an employer-sponsored program, or if your health insurance provides partial reimbursement for a gym membership. Finally, don't let yourself be pressured into signing up for a long-term commitment—unless you're *really* sure you want that multi-year membership.

A few area clubs are:

- **Bally Total Fitness**, www.ballyfitness.com; locations at Downtown Crossing, 617-338-9001; Brighton Landing, 617-779-7200; Porter Square in Cambridge, 617-868-5100; and Medford, 781-393-3500.
- **Beacon Hill Athletic Club**, www.beaconhillathleticclubs.com; locations in Beacon Hill, 617-367-2422; the North End/Waterfront, 617-742-0055; North Station, 617-720-2422; Brookline Village, 617-277-8600; Brighton, 617-562-0202; and Newton, 617-332-0008.
- **Boston Athletic Club**, 653 Summer St, Boston, www.bostonathleticclub.com
- **Boston Sports Club**, www.mysportsclubs.com; over a dozen locations in Greater Boston.
- **Cambridge Athletic Club**, 215 First St, Cambridge, 617-491-8989, www.cambridgefitness.com
- **Fitcorp**, www.fitcorp.com, numerous locations.
- **Healthworks Fitness Center for Women**, www.healthworksfitness.com; locations in Back Bay, 617-859-7700; Brookline, 617-731-3030; Chestnut Hill, 617-383-6100; and Porter Square in Cambridge, 617-497-4454.
- **The Sports Club/LA**, 4 Avery St at Tremont, 617-375-8200, www.thesportsclubla.com
- **Waverly Oaks Athletic Club**, 411 Waverly Oaks Rd, Waltham, 781-894-7010, www.waverlyoaks.com
- **Wellbridge Athletic Club**, 5 Bennett St, Cambridge, 617-441-0800, www.wellbridge.com

For one of the best fitness deals in town, the **YMCA** is always an option; check the White Pages under "YMCA" or visit www.ymca.net for a complete list of Boston area locations. The **Oak Square YMCA**, in Brighton (617-782-3535), is the newest (and perhaps nicest) facility; other area Ys include:

- **YMCA of Greater Boston**; numerous locations in and around the city, www.ymcaboston.org
- **Cambridge Family YMCA**, Central Sq, Cambridge, 617-661-9622, www.cambridgeymca.org
- **Malden YMCA**, 781-324-7680, www.ymcamalden.org
- **Somerville YMCA**, 617-625-5050

SPORTS FOR KIDS

For many, the first choices for children's sports programs are the **Boston Centers for Youth and Families** (community centers) located throughout the city. Programming and facilities vary from center to center, and you're likely to find a diverse group of kids who go there. For more information, call 617-635-4920 or go to www.cityofboston.gov/bcyf. Another resource is **GoCityKids** (www. gocitykids.com), an activities-based city guide for parents. They profile several cities across the country, including Boston, offering information on outdoor adventures, camps, parks, playgrounds, and sports. Then there are the **Boys & Girls Clubs of Boston** (50 Congress Street, Suite 730, Boston, 617-994-4700, www. bgcb.org) and your local **YMCA**.

The **Boston Youth Zone** (www.bostonyouthzone.com/sports/) has information on neighborhood leagues all over the city, from Pee-Wee Basketball to Lacrosse (www.metrolacrosse.com). You can also contact your town or city recreation department for information on **Little League Baseball and Softball** (www.littleleague.org), **Pop Warner Football and Cheerleading** (www. popwarner.com), or youth soccer leagues such as **Boston Area Youth Soccer** (www.bays.org), **Brookline Soccer Club** (www.brooklinesoccer.org), **Cambridge Soccer** (www.cambridgeyouthsoccer.org), **Watertown Youth Soccer** (www. watertownyouthsoccer.org), or the FIFA-associated **Massachusetts Youth Soccer Association** (www.mayouthsoccer.org).

If your little tyke wants to cool off on a hot summer day, you can take him to the **splash fountain** at the Christian Science Center Reflecting Pool, the **Frog Pond** in Boston Common (open for wading from July through August), or to one of the **spray pools** operated by the DCR (go to www.mass.gov/dcr for a complete list):

- **Allied Veterans Memorial Pool**, Elm St, Everett
- **Beaver Brook Reservation**, Trapelo Rd, Belmont
- **Lee Memorial Pool**, Charles St (West End), Boston, at the Artesani playground.
- **McCrehan Memorial Pool**, Rindge Ave, Cambridge

BOSTON IS TRULY BLESSED WITH AN ABUNDANCE OF GREENSPACE. The city and surrounding communities are replete with parks, waterways, forests, reservoirs, reservations, beaches, and arboreta. In fact, Boston was the final home to Frederick Law Olmsted, the father of American landscape architecture, who was responsible for many of the nation's foremost parks and park systems, including New York City's Central and Prospect parks. To Boston he contributed the Emerald Necklace, an interlaced system of several parks equivalent to six miles of connected linear greenspace. Even the area cemeteries are spectacular.

The following is an overview of greater Boston's larger green areas and beaches. Of course, there are many smaller neighborhood parks and pocket parks, which you are sure to stumble across as you explore your new environs.

Contact information for area parks and nature areas includes:

- **City of Boston Parks and Recreation Department**, 1010 Mass Ave, 3rd Floor, 617-635-PARK, www.ci.boston.ma.us/parks
- **Emerald Necklace Conservancy**, 617-232-5374, www.emeraldnecklace.org
- **Island Preserves**, 617-233-8666, www.bostonislands.com
- **Massachusetts Audubon Society**, 800-AUDUBON, www.massaudubon.org
- **Massachusetts Department of Conservation and Recreation (DCR)**, 251 Causeway St, Suite 600, Boston, 617-626-1250, www.mass.gov/dcr; now includes the former Division of Urban Parks and Recreation, the Division of Water Supply Protection, and the Division of State Parks and Recreation. (For a list of district offices which run the parks programs in communities around Boston, see "Participant Sports and Activities" in the **Sports and Recreation** chapter.)
- **Trustees of Reservations**, 978-921-1944, www.thetrustees.org

BOSTON COMMON, BOSTON PUBLIC GARDEN, COMMONWEALTH AVENUE MALL

The heart of Boston is **Boston Common**, established in 1634. Originally, the common was functional open pasture for grazing livestock. There was a military component to the common as well: the colonial militia trained for the Revolutionary War here, and the Redcoats occupied the common for eight years beginning in 1768. Anti-slavery meetings were also held here before and during the Civil War.

Today, people come to the common with their dogs and children instead of their pigs and cows, and it is smaller (its original four hills have been leveled), but it is still Boston's most popular outdoor space. The common's location in the heart of downtown makes it a neighborhood park for those who live on Beacon Hill, Back Bay, and Chinatown. There are also tennis courts and a baseball field for use in the summer, and the ever-popular Frog Pond for winter ice skating. An annual Christmas tree lighting takes place on the common every holiday season. Two T stops serve Boston Common—Park Street (Red and Green lines), and Boylston (Green Line).

Next to Boston Common is the **Public Garden**, established in 1837. The 24-acre Victorian-style park, designed by George V. Meacham, is reminiscent of those found in London (think Kensington Gardens) and was created as a public botanical garden. In the summer, many stop in for a ride on one of the Swan Boats (call 617-591-1150 or visit www.swanboats.com for information). Bicycling and in-line skating are not permitted in the Garden. The Arlington T stop (Green Line) is just across the street from the southwest corner of the Garden, but you can also get off at the Boylston T stop and walk.

The **Commonwealth Avenue Mall** is a formal avenue with 35 acres of green space running the length of the Back Bay. Until the mid-1800s, the Back Bay really was a bay—or rather, tidal flats—of the Charles River. Starting in 1857, gravel from quarries in West Needham was shipped in trains and dumped into the flats to create a landfill that eventually became a neighborhood. The Back Bay's unique layout—French-influenced Victorian—still survives. Streets were laid out in a grid around a central promenade, the Comm Ave Mall, which was created by Arthur Gilman. Today, the mall is lined with sweet gum, maple, green ash, linden, Japanese pagoda, zelkova, and elm trees, which in the winter twinkle with holiday lights. Local residents come here to relax or walk their dogs. The Comm Ave Mall links Boston Public Garden to the **Back Bay Fens** at Charlesgate, commencing the Olmsted-designed portion of Boston's six-mile park system known as the Emerald Necklace.

EMERALD NECKLACE

The **Emerald Necklace** is managed by the Emerald Necklace Conservancy. It ends roughly by Brookline Avenue, where the Muddy River and the Riverway begin. Boston Common, the Public Garden, and the Comm Ave Mall are the only parks in the necklace's string that Frederick Law Olmsted did not create for Boston. Including these three, there are nine parks in all, making it possible to walk nearly seven miles across Boston without leaving the parks.

Olmsted created the **Fens** section of the necklace in response to problems that arose from damming the Charles River (necessary in order to make the Back Bay). To be quite blunt, it stank. The area that is now called the Fens was a saltwater marsh, which, because it didn't have tidal flushing after the damming of the Charles, became stagnant—and a public health issue. Olmsted flushed out the waterways by building water gates to regulate the tidal flow and tried to create a semblance of the original tidal marsh ecosystem. It didn't work—the damming of the Charles a mile downstream from the Fens changed the water from brackish to fresh, and all the saltwater vegetation there died. Today the Fens is a mixture of greenspace surrounding a decidedly pleasant marsh area. While the greenery in the Fens is different from Olmsted's original vision, the park is still much used and appreciated. In it are the **WWII Victory Gardens** (community gardens for which you can apply for a plot of your own to grow flowers and vegetables), the **James P. Kelleher Rose Garden,** and **Roberto Clemente Field,** which has two baseball diamonds and basketball courts. Note: while the Fens are generally deemed perfectly safe and lovely during the day, they are not the safest place to be after dark. Tall reeds make good cover for illicit activities and the occasional spot of violence after hours. To get to the Fens, you'll have to walk a bit from any of the following Green Line T stops: Hynes/ICA (B, C, and D trains), Symphony, Northeastern, or Museum on the E train.

The Riverway is the result of Olmsted's rerouting of the manmade Muddy River that coincided with flushing of the Fens. With its steep, tree-filled banks and gently flowing water, this park gives you the sense that you really are in the woods. The carriage roads and bridle paths are now used as bike paths. What may be most interesting about this park is that on one side the trees are native to the area, and on the other Olmsted selected trees from Europe and Asia. The Riverway (the road) bisects the park system just northeast of where the Muddy River starts. This portion of the park runs south to the border of Brookline until the Muddy River joins up with Leverett Pond in Olmsted Park. You can access the Riverway best from the Longwood and Fenway stops on the Green Line D train.

Olmsted Park is sort of an informal boundary between Boston and Brookline. Olmsted's original vision was to have the park serve as an educational display with small pools used as natural history exhibits. Today, however, the pools are filled in, and the park's 180 acres are popular for walks and bike rides. Olmsted Park does feature the manmade Wards Pond and Leverett Pond, and

Daisy Field, a community softball diamond. All are peaceful retreats from the busy medical area nearby. The park begins where Route 9 bisects the parks, and continues south to JP (between Pond Avenue and the Jamaicaway), where it is cut off by Perkins Street. Your best bet for getting to Olmsted Park is at any of the four final stops on the Green Line E train: Mission Park, Riverway, Back of the Hill, and Heath Street.

From Perkins Street to the southern border with the Jamaicaway is **Jamaica Park**, important because it houses Jamaica Pond. The "pond," a 60-acre, 90-foot-deep kettle hole, was formed by an ancient glacier, and because of this and its natural springs, it is the largest and purest body of water in Boston. Once upon a time, JP was a summer retreat for Boston's wealthiest citizens and Jamaica Pond was the site of their summer homes. In the 1890s, the city bought the land and removed the houses (save for a few stunning mansions that still survive) and used the area for the ice-cutting industry. Today Jamaica Pond is a vibrant part of Jamaica Plain's community life. Locals come for free concerts, children's programs, and other community events at the boathouse. Runners, skaters, dog walkers, fishers, and strollers enjoy looping the pond's one-mile circumference. Jamaica Pond is also Boston's back-up reservoir, so no swimming allowed. To get to Jamaica Pond, take the Orange Line to either Stony Brook or Green Street and head west into JP—about a 10-minute walk.

South and west of Jamaica Pond, connected by the Arborway, is the 265-acre **Arnold Arboretum**. It is bound by Center and Washington streets and the Jamaicaway, and is shared by the communities of JP and Roslindale. For this "jewel" in the Emerald Necklace, Olmsted collaborated with Charles Sprague Sargent, a scientist who collected thousands of specimens of trees, flowers, and shrubs. The Arboretum features a remarkable collection of maples, laurels, azaleas, crabapples, lilacs, rhododendrons, and more. The 7,000-plus plants are identified and documented, and can be found in their computerized database, which not only gives you the botanical name, but the location of that plant within the Arboretum. Go to www.arboretum.harvard.edu for more information. In a unique agreement, Harvard University has leased the Arboretum from the city at the cost of $1 per year for 1,000 years. Harvard maintains the greenery and the city maintains the roads and walls. Take the Orange Line to the Forest Hills stop and you will be within close walking distance.

And finally, the last link in the chain, also accessible by the Forest Hills T stop, is **Franklin Park and Zoo**. It lies south and slightly east of the Arboretum, connected by the Arborway, and bound by Seaver and Morton streets, the American Legion Highway, and Blue Hill Avenue. Franklin Park consists of 527 acres, making it the largest park in the necklace. It is accessible to Roxbury, Dorchester, JP, and Roslindale. Olmsted created it as a "country park." It includes a woodland preserve, a 72-acre zoo, and a golf course. For information about the zoo, call 617-541-LION or visit www.zoonewengland.com.

CITY/NEIGHBORHOOD PARKS

The Emerald Necklace is by no means the only greenspace around. There are plenty of smaller parks throughout the city, many with playground structures. The **City of Boston Parks & Recreation Department** oversees 2,200 acres of park land throughout the city, including parks, playgrounds, city squares, urban woodlands, historic burying grounds, golf courses, and the aforementioned parts of the Emerald Necklace. The **Charles River Reservation** (617-722-5436, www. mass.gov/dcr), run by the DCR, provides 17 miles of riverfront green space accessible to many communities. Boston's Beacon Hill, the Back Bay, Allston-Brighton, and the communities of Cambridge, Watertown, Newton, and Waltham all border the river. There are bike and pedestrian trails for walking, running, pedaling, and in-line skating, a number of playgrounds, outdoor theaters, boathouses, and ice rinks along the Charles. Residents also use the river itself for sailing, canoeing, kayaking, and rowing. The part of the Charles parallel to the Back Bay and Beacon Hill, bound by Storrow Drive, is called the **Esplanade** and is where you'll find the Hatch Memorial Shell. On the Cambridge side, bound by Memorial Drive, is the five-mile-long **JFK Park**. Further west, on the north side of the river in Waltham, is **Landry Park** and the **Lakes District**. The riverbanks west of downtown are part of the Upper Charles River, and are where you will find Newton and Needham's **Hemlock Gorge**, a 23-acre wild area along the banks of the river. Also here is **Brook Farm**, 179 acres of rolling fields and wetland in West Roxbury; **Cutler Park**, a large freshwater marsh in the middle of the Charles in Dedham and Needham; and **Village Falls Park** in Needham.

Waterfront Park (also known as **Christopher Columbus Park**) is located right at the edge of Boston Harbor, between the Waterfront and the North End. As if its incredible view of the harbor weren't enough, it features a rose garden, fountain, and a wisteria-covered trellis. It's close to the Haymarket (Orange and Green lines), Government Center (Green and Blue lines), and Aquarium (Blue Line) T stops.

Boston's Charlestown has several smaller parks: the Navy Yard, Monument Square, Berry Playground, City Square, John Harvard Mall, and the Training Field. After nearly 175 years of serving the fleet, the **Navy Yard** (www.nps.gov/bost/Navy_Yard.htm, 617-242-5601) is now preserved by the National Park Service as part of Boston National Historical Park. Truth be told, it's a bit of a concrete jungle, but the views are gorgeous and many people come here to visit the USS *Constitution*, one of the last stops on the Freedom Trail. **Monument Square** is a small green park surrounding the unmistakable Bunker Hill Monument (also on the Freedom Trail), bound by Tremont, High, Lexington, and Pleasant streets. The **Training Field**, a.k.a. Charlestown Common, is bound by Adams, Winthrop, and Park streets. And further south, in the shadow of the remaining artery and Charlestown Bridge on the shore of the Harbor, is another wee green patch called **City Square**. The closest T stop is Community College on the Orange Line, but it's a bit of a walk.

Boston residents of West Roxbury, Roslindale, and Hyde Park, and neighboring Dedham have immediate access to the 475-acre **Stony Brook Reservation**, bound primarily by East and West Boundary streets and bisected by the Turtle Pond and West Roxbury parkways and Washington Street. The reservation offers hiking, biking, baseball fields, tennis courts, a swimming pool, tot lot, and skating rink. You can fish in Turtle Pond or climb 330 feet to the top of Bellevue Hill. It's accessible by the Orange Line Forest Hills T stop.

At the southernmost part of Dorchester and running over into Mattapan, Hyde Park, and neighboring Milton is the **Neponset River Reservation**, which offers 750 acres along the Neponset River and includes marsh and wetlands. Inside the reservation are playgrounds, community gardens, a concert venue (the Martini Shell), and several separate parks, including Kennedy Park in Mattapan, home to a community garden, Lower Neponset River Trail, Pope John Paul II Park, and Squantum Point Park.

An old drive-in theater and landfill was converted into **Pope John Paul II Park**, which connects Dorchester with the Neponset River estuary, and now boasts a restored saltwater marsh and replanted native flora. Locals come here to enjoy the picnic and playground facilities, soccer fields, and walking and jogging paths. It is also a good location for bird watching, particularly black ducks, mergansers, snowy egrets, and great blue herons. To get here, take the Red Line Ashmont train to Fields Corner and then take the #20 bus to either the Neponset Circle or Hallet Street entrance.

The **Lower Neponset River Trail** is a 2.4-mile trail for bikes and pedestrians along the Neponset River. At present it runs from Port Norfolk in Dorchester, through Pope John Paul II Park, across Granite Avenue, through the Neponset Marshes and Lower Mills, ending up on Central Avenue in Milton. You can pick up the trail at any of the following Red Line (Ashmont) stops: Butler, Milton Village, or Central Avenue.

You can also pay a visit to **Squantum Point Park**, on the site of a former Navy airfield. People come for bird watching, picnicking, fishing, canoeing, inline skating, running or walking. To get there, take the Red Line Braintree train to North Quincy Station and pick up the #211 bus.

The **Belle Isle Marsh Reservation**, in East Boston, is 152 acres of the city's last remaining saltwater marsh left standing after all the landfill projects of the 1800s. There are pathways, benches, an observation tower, and guided walks provided by the DCR. You can get here by taking the Blue Line to Suffolk Downs and entering off Bennington Street.

For more specifics about these or other parks scattered throughout the greater Boston area or the State of Massachusetts, contact your local parks district (city web sites are listed with the community profiles) or the DCR, at 617-626-1250, www.mass.gov/dcr.

CEMETERIES

Boston is home to sixteen historic burying grounds; some of which have grave-stone markers for Revolutionary War heroes, and men and women of national and international fame. Three of the grounds—Granary, King's Chapel and Copp's Hill—are along the Freedom Trail. These burying grounds and others are a great testimony to the city's early landscape and its rich history. Two of the most beautiful cemeteries in terms of greenspace, are the following:

- Some take advantage of the lovely and historic **Forest Hills Cemetery**, www.foresthillstrust.org, which forms the boundary with JP, Roslindale, Roxbury, and Dorchester. Henry Dearborn, then governor of Roxbury and the first president of the Massachusetts Horticultural Society, founded this 275-acre garden burial ground in 1848. Visitors come to see the final resting places of such famous figures as poets Anne Sexton and e.e. cummings, and playwright Eugene O'Neill. Locals come here for walks, picnics, and jogs, and dogs and bikes are welcome. In the summer, Forest Hills holds the annual, Buddhist-inspired Lantern Festival, a lovely tribute by those who want to remember lost ones by releasing candle-lit lanterns with personal messages onto Lake Hibiscus at sundown. As with the Stony Brook Reservation, get off the Orange Line at the Forest Hills T stop.
- The **Mt. Auburn Cemetery**, www.mountauburn.org, an arboretum in its own right with a collection of over 5,000 trees and shrubs, is located on Mt. Auburn St between Watertown and Cambridge. It is the smaller, but slightly older cousin of the above-mentioned Forest Hills Cemetery, and was founded in 1831 by the Massachusetts Horticultural Society. Today, this gorgeous 175-acre site draws people for many reasons, including hiking and tours. Many famous Bostonians, such as Mary Baker Eddy, Oliver Wendell Holmes, Charles Bullfinch, Henry Wadsworth Longfellow, Fannie Farmer, Isabella Stewart Gardner, and B.F. Skinner, are buried here. Bird watching is popular; during peak migration periods you may see up to 100 different species in a day and the cemetery posts a daily list of sightings at their entrance gate. Note: pets, horseback riding, picnicking, and biking are strictly forbidden. Gates close at 5 p.m. Buses #71, 72, and 73 stop here.

NATURE PRESERVES

STATE

Travel a little outside of Boston for more natural preserves. **Walden Pond** and **Walden Woods** in Concord (978-369-3254) are part of the state park system and are only about 20 minutes away. You can learn about Henry David Thoreau, visit a re-creation of his cabin, go on a walking tour with the Thoreau Society or hike, swim, skate, or ski—depending on the season. In addition to its connection with Thoreau, Walden Pond is special because its origin as a glacial kettle gives it excellent drainage. The water remains clean and clear throughout the summer and the thin, pebbled shores are crowded with sunbathers and swimmers.

Some **area reservations** for hiking and mountain biking include the following:

- **Blue Hills Reservation**, Milton, Canton, Quincy, Braintree, Randolph, and Boston, 617-698-1802, www.mass.gov/dcr; the mother of all local wild areas, it offers more than 7,000 acres of terrain. The hills and surrounding area have been managed for public use for over 100 years. In addition to forests, marshes, swamps, bogs, ponds, rivers, hills, and even some species of endangered wildlife, there are 16 historic sites on the land. Come here for camping, hiking, biking, fishing, swimming, horseback riding, golfing, rock climbing, skiing (cross-country and downhill), softball, and ice-skating. Climb to the top of the 635-foot Great Blue Hill, where you can see the entire metropolitan area, or hike the reservation's 125 miles worth of trails. If biking, remember to respect the "No Mountain Bicycling" signs that are posted in restricted areas. Open during daylight hours. Pets must be leashed. Some areas accessible via the Red Line (Ashmont and Mattapan T stations).
- **Breakheart Reservation**, Saugus, 781-233-0834, www.mass.gov/dcr; 640-acre hardwood forest with two freshwater lakes (Silver and Pearce), ponds, and seven rocky hills over 200 feet high. Visit Breakheart for fishing, hiking, bird watching, and swimming. No public transit access.
- **Elm Bank Reservation**, Wellesley, 617-333-7404, www.mass.gov/dcr; 182 acres of woods, fields, and old estate property surrounded by the Charles River on three sides. Come here for bird watching, fishing, boating, and hiking. No public transit access.
- **Middlesex Fells Reservation**, 781-727-1199, www.mass.gov/dcr; over 2,500 acres of rocky hills that run through Medford, Malden, Melrose, Stoneham, and Winchester. Popular for hiking, horseback riding, rock climbing, mountain biking, cross-country skiing, fishing, skating, swimming, picnics, and kites. Spot Pond, centrally located in the Middlesex Fells, allows for boating, sailing, kayaking, and canoeing (rentals are available). For mountain bikers, be aware that most trails are off limits; you can use all fire roads and specially designated trails. Dogs are allowed. Maps not sold at the reservation; you can buy one or order from the Friends of the Middlesex Fells, www.fells.org. Take the Orange Line to Wellington Station and then the #100 bus to the Roosevelt Circle Rotary.
- **Lynn Woods Reservation**, Lynn, www.flw.org; the second largest municipal park in the country, Lynn Woods offers 2,200 acres of wilderness, with 30 miles of trails for hiking, biking, running, horseback riding, and cross-country skiing. Three ponds in the reservation are used as Lynn's drinking water supply, so

no fishing, boating, or swimming is allowed. Dog-friendly, but they must be leashed. Not accessible by public transit.

- **Rumney Marsh Reservation**, Saugus and Revere, 617-727-5350, www.mass. gov/dcr; over 600 acres of salt marshes within the Saugus River and Pine River estuary. Visit for the natural and cultural history walks, fishing, hiking, boating, or bird watching. Take the Lynn/Salem bus to Route 107.
- **Weymouth Back River Reservation**, Hingham and Weymouth, 617-727-5290, www.mass.gov/dcr; visit here for walking trails and greenspace along the water at Stoddard's Neck and Abigail Adams Park. Take Hingham bus #220.
- **Wilson Mountain Reservation**, Dedham, 617-333-7404, www.mass.gov/dcr, is the largest remaining piece of open space in Dedham. It offers 213 acres for hiking and bird watching, and panoramic views of Boston and the Blue Hills. Not accessible via public transit.

For more nature preserves throughout the state, contact the **Trustees of Reservations** (www.thetrustees.org, 978-921-1944), an organization devoted to conserving historic and environmentally significant spaces in Massachusetts. They own and run property, waterfront, and open spaces throughout the state.

ISLAND PRESERVES

Some of Boston's most underutilized natural resources are the **Harbor Islands**. Visitors enjoy fishing, sea kayaking, guided walks, historic forts and ruins, and picnic areas on most of the islands. (Biking and in-line skating are not allowed.) Thirty-four islands lie within a large "C" shape of Boston Harbor. Only 11 islands are serviced via a ferry ride from Boston, including Bumpkin Island, Deer Island, George's Island, Grape Island, Great Brewster Island, Little Brewster Island, Lovells Island, Peddocks Island, Spectacle Island, Thompson Island, and World's End. A few others are open to visitors who reach them with their own boats. The islands are open from spring to fall, although their peak visiting time (and when you'll find the most transportation options) is on weekends from Memorial Day to Labor Day. Some special excursions and boat trips take place during the winter months, particularly those run by the **Friends of the Boston Harbor Islands** (781-740-4290, www.fbhi.org) and the DCR. Each island offers something entirely different. If you do plan on visiting any of them, bring fresh water and food because only one island (George's) offers concessions. For more information, visit www.bostonislands.com.

Getting to the islands requires some effort. Going to George's means just a 45-minute ferry ride from Long Wharf in Boston (daily), or from the Hingham Shipyard at Hewitt's Cove in Hingham (weekends), Pemberton Point in Hull, Squantum Point in Quincy (weekends), or Salem Ferry Landing in Salem (weekends). **Boston Harbor Cruises** (617-227-4321, www.bostonboats.com) provides the ferry service, which runs several times daily during the summer months. To get to any of the other islands from George's (with the exception of Little Brewster and Thompson) you must pick up the free inter-island water taxi. To get to Little Brewster Island, take the M/V Hurricane from Old Northern Avenue at Fan Pier, South Boston or Columbia Point at the JFK Library and Museum in Dorchester. These ferries depart twice daily (10 a.m. and 2 p.m.) on weekends from May to October. And finally, to get to Thompson Island, the Outward Bound ferry runs on Saturdays from June through August, departing at 11:30 a.m. from Northern Avenue at Fan Pier and at noon from EDIC Pier #10 off of Drydock Avenue in the Marine Industrial Park, both in South Boston. You can also take your own boat to George's, Bumpkin, Grape, Little Brewster, Lovells, and Peddocks islands, but you can dock only at George's; at the others only pick-up and drop-off are allowed.

Check with the following agencies for information about camping permits and reservations on the islands: the **DCR** manages Bumpkin, Gallops, George's, Grape, Great Brewster, Lovells, Peddocks and Spectacle islands. **Thompson Island Outward Bound Education Center** (617-328-3900, www.thompsonisland. org) runs Thompson Island. The **Massachusetts Water Resources Authority** (617-788-1170, www.mwra.com) has responsibility for Deer Island. World's End is run by the **Trustees of Reservations** (978-921-1944, www.thetrustees.org). The **Coast Guard** (www.uscg.mil/USCG.shtml) takes care of Little Brewster Island.

STATE PARKS AND FORESTS

STATE PARKS

The **Department of Conservation and Recreation (DCR)** runs state parks, popular for hiking, horseback riding, fishing, etc. In fact, although Massachusetts is one of the smaller states in the union, it has one of the most extensive parks systems. The western portion of the state is the most rural and is where most can be found. That said, there are still quite a few state parks within easy driving distance (about an hour or so) from Boston. If you plan on visiting a number of parks, a **Massachusetts ParksPass** allows for unlimited day-use parking access to state park facilities within the DCR that charge a parking fee. For information on purchasing a pass, and on the parks in general, including directions, locations, and what each offers, call 617-626-1250 or go to www.mass.gov/dcr.

STATE FORESTS

Many of the city and state parks and reservations are forested. Check with the DCR to see if a specific park near you includes forestland. In addition, the following state parks are designated specifically as forests. Go to www.mass.gov/dcr or call one of the following for more information:

- **Boxford State Forest**, Boxford, 978-686-3391
- **F. Gilbert Hills State Forest**, Foxboro, 508-543-5850
- **Georgetown-Rowley State Forest**, Georgetown, 978-887-5931
- **Harold Parker State Forest**, North Andover, 978-686-3391
- **Lowell-Dracut-Tyngsboro State Forest**, Lowell, 978-453-0592
- **Willowdale State Forest**, Ipswich, 978-887-5931

NATIONAL PARKS

National parks in the Boston area, overseen by the **National Park Service** (www.
nps.gov) are mostly historic rather than natural sites, with the possible exception of the Harbor Islands. Two of particular interest that also have some acreage
are the **Frederick Law Olmsted National Historic Site** (www.nps.gov/frla, 617-
566-1689), which includes his house and grounds in Brookline, or the **Minute
Man National Park** (www.nps.gov/mima, 978-369-6993), comprising 900 acres
of Revolutionary War history in Lexington, Concord, and Lincoln.

A two-hour drive from Boston, one of the most famous parks in the National
Park System, the **Appalachian Trail**, bisects the westernmost portion of Massachusetts on its way from Maine to Georgia. To learn more about the trail, or get
information on the parts of it within the state, visit www.nps.gov/appa.

WILDLIFE SANCTUARIES

Massachusetts is home to a bevy of wildlife refuges, many run by the **Massachusetts Audubon Society** (www.massaudubon.org, 800-AUDUBON). Opened
in 1896, it is the largest conservation group in all of New England, protecting
over 32,000 acres of land with 43 wildlife sanctuaries open to the public. Area
Audubon lands range from beaches and marshes to forests and mountains, and
present an array of green environs for hiking and learning about wildlife. The
society also offers educational programming. On conservancy lands visitors may
not bike, hunt, fish, trap, jog, bring pets, vehicles, firearms or alcohol—or remove
specimens.

Listed here are a few sanctuaries close to Boston:

- **Blue Hills Trailside Museum**, 1904 Canton Ave, Milton, 617-333-0690, www.
massaudubon.org/bluehills; interpretive center for the Blue Hills Reservation.
- **Boston Nature Center and Wildlife Sanctuary**, 500 Walk Hill St, Mattapan,
617-983-8500; two miles of trails and boardwalks past wetlands, woods, and
fields in the middle of the city.
- **Broadmoor Wildlife Sanctuary**, 280 Eliot St, Natick, 508-655-2296; nine miles
of trails through woodland, field, and wetland habitats.
- **Daniel Webster Wildlife Sanctuary**, off of Winslow Cemetery Rd in Marshfield; 481 acres of grass, woods, and wetlands. Excellent for bird watching.
- **Eastern Point Wildlife Sanctuary**, off Eastern Point Blvd in Gloucester; coastal

beach vistas, sea birds, and butterflies.

- **Habitat Education Center and Wildlife Sanctuary**, 10 Juniper Rd, Belmont, 617-489-5050; gardens, fields, meadows, woods, wetland containing a vernal pool, and two ponds on a former estate.
- **Ipswich River Wildlife Sanctuary**, 87 Perkins Row, Topsfield, 978-887-9264; Mass Audubon's largest sanctuary, with more than 10 miles of trails, canoeing, camping, glacial formations, and river wildlife.
- **Joppa Flats Wildlife Sanctuary**, 1 Plum Island Tpke, Newburyport, 978-462-9998; migratory birds, salt marshes, mudflats, rivers, bays, and coastal waters.
- **Marblehead Neck Wildlife Sanctuary**, Risley Rd, Marblehead; swamp, thickets, and woodlands on the coast. Birds are plentiful, especially warblers.
- **Moose Hill Wildlife Sanctuary**, 293 Moose Hill St, Sharon, 781-784-5691; Mass Audubon's oldest sanctuary, with nearly 2,000 acres of forest, grassland, swamp, and bog.
- **Nahant Thicket Wildlife Sanctuary**, Furbush Rd, Nahant; four-acre patch of red maple swamp. Very limited trail access.

The **Crane Wildlife Refuge,** operated for the past 30 years by the Trustees of Reservations (978-356-4351, www.thetrustees.org), is nearly 700 acres of protected area on the North Shore, near Ipswich's Crane Beach. The reservation includes a portion of Castle Neck River and the Essex River Estuary, the Great Marsh (salt), and several islands, including Long, Dilly, Pine, Patterson, Round, and Choate, the largest island. The reservation is open daily, year-round, for exploration. Deer hunting is permissible during hunting season. Dock a boat on Long Island for 3.5 miles of hiking and walking trails.

Further up the North Shore is the **Parker River National Wildlife Refuge** (www.parkerriver.org, 978-465-5753), located on Plum Island in Newburyport. This property far outstrips the Crane Refuge in size—over 4,600 acres of dunes, tidal pools, salt marsh, beach, and one drumlin—and is also one of the last remaining barrier beach-salt marshes in this portion of the country. You will find over 300 species of birds throughout the year, making it one of the most popular birding sites in America. Additionally, you can come here to hike, canoe, kayak, surf, fish, clam, and hunt waterfowl during appropriate seasons.

Another popular reserve for birders is the **Great Meadows National Wildlife Refuge**, just west of Boston along the Sudbury and Concord Rivers. It encompasses the towns of Sudbury, Lincoln, Concord, Wayland, Bedford, Carlisle, and Billerica. The 3,000 acres of freshwater wetlands attract many migratory birds—220 species have been spotted there over the past decade.

BEACHES

Bostonians do love to go to the beach. After long cold winters, the welcoming miles of sun, sand, and surf on the New England coastline are especially enticing. There are a few beaches in the city, but area residents traditionally head to picturesque stretches along the north and south shores of Massachusetts. Weekends are often spent at B&Bs or rental houses on Cape Cod, Nantucket, or Martha's Vineyard. Those who like to get even further away will head to coastal New Hampshire, Maine, Rhode Island, and Connecticut.

Resist the temptation to swim in the Charles, as it is recovering from years of pollution. As it improves you can expect Magazine Beach in Cambridgeport to become popular once again.

The DCR maintains 16 miles of regularly cleaned ocean beaches, most of which are accessible by public transportation. DCR beaches have lifeguard services from the end of June to Labor Day, but many are open (albeit not guarded) year round. Call 617-727-5114 or visit www.mass.gov/dcr for details.

Easily accessible Boston beaches include:

- **Carson Beach, Castle Island Beach, City Point Beach, Pleasure Bay Beach, and M Street Beach,** Day Blvd in South Boston, 617-727-5290; take the Red Line to Broadway or the City Point bus to the end of the line.
- **Constitution Beach,** take the Blue Line to Orient Heights in East Boston.
- **Lovells Island** (Boston Harbor Island) in Boston Harbor; take the Blue Line to Aquarium, then take the ferry to George's Island and catch a free water taxi to Lovells Island.
- **Malibu Beach** and **Savin Hill Beach,** in Dorchester off Morrissey Blvd; take the Red Line to Savin Hill.
- **Tenean Beach** in Dorchester on Tenean St off Morrissey Blvd; take the Red Line to Savin Hill, then #20 bus to the beach.

Call the DCR for additional freshwater and saltwater swimming spots outside of Boston. There are many **private** and **state-run beaches** in the greater Boston area, reachable by car and public transport. In fact, the majority of Massachusetts' coastline is privately owned. Of the beaches open to the public, some require payment for use. Here are a few to consider:

- **Duxbury:** Duxbury Beach
- **Gloucester:** Cressey's Beach, Half Moon Beach, Good Harbor Beach, Long Beach, Niles Beach, Pavillion Beach, and Wingaersheek Beach
- **Hull:** Nantasket Beach
- **Ipswich:** Crane Beach
- **Marblehead:** Gashouse Beach and Devereux Beach, Marblehead
- **Manchester-by-the-Sea:** Singing Beach, White Beach
- **Marshfield:** Brant Rock Beach, Fieldston Beach, Green Harbor Beach, Humarock Beach, Rexhame Beach, and Sunrise Beach
- **Newburyport:** Plum Island, 6.5 miles of sandy beach run by Parker Wildlife Refuge, 978-465-5753, www.parkerriver.org
- **Revere:** Revere Beach has an eponymous stop on the Blue Line
- **Rockport:** Back Beach, Cape Hedge Beach, Front Beach, Old Garden Beach, and Pebble Beach

- **Scituate**: Egypt Beach, Hatherly Beach
- **Quincy:** Wollaston Beach, accessible via the Red Line

GREATER BOSTON AREA BEACHES AND STATE PARKS

BEACHES

If you make a run for the border to New Hampshire, you can go to Salisbury Beach and Hampton Beach. **Salisbury Beach** (technically in Massachusetts, although generally you have to cross over into New Hampshire for a minute to get there) is popular. Go in the fall and winter for the chance to spy harbor seals hanging out in the sun on the jetty. **Hampton Beach** (www.hamptonbeach.org), over the border in New Hampshire, is a scene that should definitely be experienced by everyone at least once. Whereas most beaches in the area are relatively serene, with a hot dog stand at best, Hampton Beach is more like the region's answer to Coney Island, complete with a boardwalk and loads of cars cruising the strip. To get there, just take I-95 or Route 1 North until you see the signs.

The famous **Cape Cod** is too vast to profile here. Suffice it to say that the arm of Massachusetts that stretches 40 miles out into the ocean has about 100 beaches. The best thing to do would be to pick a town—say Falmouth, Hyannis, or Provincetown—and then pick a beach. Most people don't go to the Cape for just the day. For more information go to www.capecodonline.com.

If you want to head to **Martha's Vineyard** for a few days, you will have a plentiful choice of beaches. You can make it down as a day trip, just be prepared for a three-hour commute (car, T, bus, and ferry) each way. When you get there, you can rent a bike or a Jeep and head to your choice of over 30 beaches. There are wildlife preserves and state parks there, too. Of all the beaches, South Beach might be the most popular, but be careful—the undertow is fierce.

In terms of commute and atmosphere, **Nantucket** is similar to Martha's Vineyard. It's further out than the Vineyard and a little smaller, so there are only about a dozen beaches. All Massachusetts ferries to Nantucket leave from Hyannis.

For more information on **Cape Cod, Martha's Vineyard,** and **Nantucket** go to the **Quick Getaways** section of the book.

STATE PARKS

The following **state parks** in the greater Boston area have saltwater beaches or lakes. Go to www.mass.gov/dcr for more:

- **Boston Harbor Islands**, 781-727-5290; reachable by ferry.
- **Ellsville Harbor State Park**, Route 3A, Plymouth, 508-866-2580
- **Cochituate State Park**, Route 30, Natick, 508-653-9641
- **Harold Parker State Forest**, 1951 Turnpike St, Route 114, North Andover,

978-686-3391
- **Walden Pond**, 915 Walden St, Concord, 978-369-3254
- **Demarest Lloyd State Park**, Barney's Joy Rd, Dartmouth, 508-636-3298

ADDITIONAL RESOURCES

The tourism industry in Massachusetts—with the coast, the seasons, the culture, and the history—is too broad to give a listing of tour agencies. For a good introduction to exploring your new state, contact the **Massachusetts Office of Travel and Tourism** (www.massvacation.com, 617-973-8500).

SINCE BOSTON IS A FOUR-SEASON TOWN, WINTERS ARE COLD AND often snowy, springs are mild and rainy, summers are hot and sunny, and autumns are crisp and colorful. Depending on where you are coming from, you may need to add to your wardrobe to cope with the seasons. And, although Boston is subject to the occasional blizzard, it's not prone to the more destructive and severe weather/environmental disturbances like tornadoes, floods, or earthquakes.

The Atlantic Ocean is an important moderating factor in the region's climate. In general, the closer you are to the ocean, the more temperate the weather. This rule applies for both summer and winter. In the summer, ocean breezes can keep coastal temperatures up to 10 degrees cooler than in towns just a few miles inland. In colder months, the ocean's presence keeps the coast slightly milder, and snowfall accumulations can often be higher inland as a result. On the downside, offshore storms sometimes create ravaging waves that punish sea walls, erode beaches, and sometimes flood nearby homes. The Atlantic also contributes to Boston's summer humidity.

Springtime in Boston is lovely but fleeting. Comfortably warm and breezy days are usually squeezed in between the last bitter cold days of winter, which often linger through March, and the sticky hot days of summer. March is a fickle month, sometimes offering a few warm days only to be followed by a sudden and fierce spring snowstorm. But, as April and May roll in, the mercury rises more predictably into the 40s, 50s, and 60s, with the last frost occurring before mid-May. Of course, there is the requisite amount of spring showers.

In the **summer**, get ready for the three "H's"—hazy, hot, and humid. Although the National Oceanic Atmospheric Administration (NOAA) data place average temps in the 60s, 70s, and lower 80s, those averages seem to belie the fact that it gets hot in these parts, and even when it is only in the 70s, the humidity can make it feel much, much hotter. While May and early June are not always miserable, July and August are heat wave season. For days at a time, daily temperatures can soar high into the upper 80s and 90s made worse with the ever oppressive humidity. During these days, there is no escaping the heat, save for air-conditioned buildings and the occasional afternoon thunderstorm. Temperatures don't cool down much at night, which is something to consider when looking for a place to live. If it doesn't have air conditioning, be sure your prospective new home has some kind of cross ventilation. Summer brings people to the city *en masse*, be they locals or tourists. Bars, restaurants, parks, stadiums, and T trains are packed to the gills with people enjoying the warm weather. Many restaurants open their windows, and extend their dining areas to patios, which fill up quickly; outdoor bars along the waterfront can be positively hopping, even on the first warm night of the season. As is typical in most parts of the country, **allergy sufferers** will have problems in the spring and summer here, particularly in the greener suburbs. Even on city streets, you will often find your car coated in green pollen during the spring when the trees and flowers are first in bloom.

Boston experiences the quintessential New England **autumn**, with crisp days, gorgeous fall foliage, and returning college students. Temperatures drop dramatically between September and November, falling from the 70s to the 40s and tending to the colder side of that range. It's not unheard of for Boston to experience the effects of an offshore hurricane during the late summer and early fall. They tend to hit once every few years, but beyond a few downed trees and power lines they are rarely very destructive. Fall's arrival becomes apparent in the refreshingly cooler nights of late August, and by the end of September or early October, a hard frost will settle in overnight. In October, visitors come in droves for foliage tours, but locals have the benefit of watching the leaves turn their brilliant reds and yellows right outside of their windows. Of course, it is also fun to take a "leaf peeping" drive in the neighborhood, or perhaps swing up to Vermont, New Hampshire, or Maine for the weekend. As with the spring, fall weather can vary, bringing a few surprisingly warm days. (Eighty degrees on Halloween is not out of the question; then again, neither is a dusting of snow.) Such unseasonably warm weather in the late fall after the first killing frost is called **Indian summer**, and locals love it.

Come mid- to late-November, it's pretty much **winter**, which stays sometimes through March. The coldest months are December, January, and February, with average temperatures in the 20s and 30s. Recently, El Niño, and its counterpart La Niña, have been regularly affecting Boston's winter weather, giving the area either exceptionally warm (El Niño) or cold and snowy (La Niña) winters. Some winters, temperatures barely dip below the freezing mark; others bring seemingly endless weeks of single-digit temperatures. Having a white Christmas in Boston is possible but never predictable; the average annual **snowfall** is 41 inches and some of that can certainly hit in December. Unlike other residents of some eastern seaboard cities, Bostonians are not afraid to drive in the snow, and unless the storm is a doozy, school and work probably won't be cancelled during a snow event. The most fearsome winter storms in these parts are called Nor'easters, which bring lots of snow or even blizzards. Technically, a Nor'easter is a strong area of low pressure that moves in off the Atlantic and collides with cold arctic air from Canada, bringing heavy snow or rain (if it picks up enough moisture on its way in), oversized waves, and gusty northeasterly winds. Outside of these events, the good news is that temperatures rarely drop below zero here (although on windy days, the wind chill makes it feel much colder than thermometer readings), and there is a good bit of winter sunshine.

During winter it is wise to take some precautions. Proper outer gear is essential: warm coat, hat, scarf, and mittens or gloves. Snow boots are also a good idea. In your car you should keep a small shovel and a bag of sand or road salt in case you get stuck. A car mat placed under the tire has been known to work as well. Car owners will also want decent all-season or snow tires, windshield wiper fluid with antifreeze, and an ice scraper. Also, those needing to park on the street should pay attention to street crews. If you don't move your car before a storm, you may find that the snowplow has buried it while clearing the street, or worse, on main arteries, the city will tow during "snow emergencies" (look for postings on the street).

METRO BOSTON WEATHER STATISTICAL INFORMATION

Below are Boston's average temperatures, snowfalls, rainfalls, etc., according to the NOAA (www.noaa.gov):

Month	AVG. LOW	AVG. HIGH
January	22°F	36°F
February	23°F	38°F
March	31°F	46°F
April	40°F	56°F
May	50°F	67°F
June	59°F	76°F
July	65°F	82°F
August	64°F	80°F
September	57°F	73°F
October	47°F	63°F
November	38°F	52°F
December	27°F	40°F

- Prevailing wind: from the west
- Average wind velocity: between 10 and 13 mph
- Lowest recorded temperature: -18.4°F (February 1934)

- Highest recorded temperature: 104°F (July 1911)
- Average number of days per year over 90°F: 12
- Average number of days per year below freezing: 62.2
- Average number of days per year below 0°F: 1
- Normal annual precipitation: 43.76 inches

On average, Boston experiences clear skies 27% of the time, partly cloudy skies 28% of the time, and cloud cover 45% of the time. The clearest months are August through October. The cloudiest months are January and March. Boston isn't terribly foggy; on average, it gets about 23 days per year when visibility is less than a quarter mile. It usually only rains about three or four inches at a time here, but the largest significant rainfall ever recorded in one day was 8.4", back in 1955.

AIR POLLUTION

Boston is not known for its poor air quality. Even in downtown Boston on a hot, humid summer day, you'll probably be just fine. That said, you will hear television meteorologists discussing "bad air days" (ratings range from good to moderate to unhealthy to very unhealthy) throughout the summer, especially on the really hot and muggy days. This is because strong sunshine and high temperatures are key factors in the generation of "bad ozone," the predominant ingredient in smog, which is a powerful lung irritant. Days coined "unhealthy for sensitive groups" may be noticeable to the old, the young, and people with asthma or other respiratory diseases. On days where conditions are rated "very unhealthy," even those without respiratory problems might be affected. Symptoms include wheezing, coughing, sore throat, chest pain, asthma, shortness of breath, and susceptibility to respiratory infection.

The **"ozone season"** generally lasts from May through September, depending on the weather. The peak hours for ozone problems are in the afternoons and evenings; therefore, if you're concerned, try to stay inside during those hours. Boston sees its worst ozone episodes when a "Bermuda high"— a large, high-pressure weather system over the Atlantic Ocean that expands westward across the US—scoops up the air pollution along the eastern seaboard cities from Washington D.C. to New York City, and then sweeps it in a northeasterly direction.

During the ozone season, you can get the **daily ozone forecast** through the state web site, www.mass.gov, by clicking on "For Residents," then "Environment," and then "Air Quality." The EPA provides a chart to help you understand air quality ratings and what they mean for you—the higher the number of the Air Quality Index (AQI), the worse the air. To learn more about ozone, visit the Massachusetts Department of Environmental Protection's Ozone FAQ page on their web site: http://www.mass.gov/dep/air/index.htm.

Other air quality–related groups and resources include:

- **Project Clean Air**, www.projectcleanair.org, 661-833-5740
- **EPA's AirNow**, www.airnow.gov
- **Massachusetts Department of Environmental Protection**, www.mass.gov/dep, 617-292-5500

INSECTS

In the summer the significant insect concerns are mosquitoes and ticks. Aside from being plain pesky, mosquitoes are an issue because of **West Nile virus**, which causes an infection similar to encephalitis. Although the virus most commonly plagues birds and horses, it is possible for a person bitten by a mosquito carrying West Nile to become infected. According to the Massachusetts Department of Health (DPH), those that are bitten by an infected mosquito may exhibit symptoms such as fever, headache, body aches, and rashes. Those suffering a more severe case may also have a high fever, neck stiffness, stupor, disorientation, coma, tremors, convulsions, and paralysis, and approximately 10% of those with these more serious symptoms may die, particularly the elderly. The best prevention is to avoid going out for prolonged periods at night, particularly to woodsy or swampy areas, to wear bug spray, and to make sure you have screens on your windows. Each spring and summer the state evaluates the mosquito population and sprays where necessary. For more information on this issue, the DPH has a web page and phone line devoted to the West Nile virus: www.state.ma.us/dph, 866-MASS-WNV.

Deer ticks, which are known to carry **Lyme disease**, are also a big concern in New England, and unlike West Nile virus, it is considered endemic in the state of Massachusetts. In 2005, the state's confirmed Lyme disease incident rate per 100,000 was 36.3—a 46% increase from 2004. Although it likely won't kill you, its symptoms can be painful and lifelong. Lyme disease is an infection caused by a corkscrew-shaped bacterium that is passed through a tick bite. In the early stages, you may feel like you have a bad case of the flu; in later stages, it can severely affect your joints, nervous system, and heart. The good news is that tick bites are easily avoided and if you have been bitten there is treatment. The first sign that you might have Lyme disease is, of course, finding a small tick in your skin. Second, you may develop a classic target-like rash around the bite—usually occurring within three and thirty days. If you have found a tick or if you develop this classic rash, get yourself to the doctor quickly. Your physician will probably give you a blood test and then put you on antibiotics, which, if administered soon enough, can be an effective treatment. To prevent being bitten there are precautions you should take. Ticks tend to be found in the tall grasses and plants near dunes, woods, and ponds. Should you need to visit such an area, wear a long-sleeved shirt and long pants that are tucked into your socks. Light colors are preferable so that you can readily spot a tick. Also, spray yourself with insect repellent containing DEET (check the label for use on young children). Before heading home, be sure to check everyone, dogs too, for ticks. They sometimes burrow into your scalp, so look and feel closely. If you do find a tick, don't panic, but do pull it straight out (slowly and steadily) with a pair of thin-tipped tweezers. For more information on Lyme disease, check with the Massachusetts DPH at www.state.ma.us/dph or call them at 617-983-6800.

LTHOUGH BOSTON WAS FOUNDED BY PURITANS AND THEN RUN by wealthy Protestants, Boston's religious landscape underwent a sea change in the 19th and 20th centuries when the Irish Catholic population boomed and political leadership of the city and the state changed as a result. In this part of New England, Catholicism is still dominant, tying into the Italian, Irish, and Latino populations so prevalent here. Other religions, including Judaism, Islam, and Hinduism—as well as many other branches of Christianity—are also well represented, with numerous churches, temples, and mosques catering to a variety of religions throughout the metro region.

You may prefer having an acqaintaince or friend recommend a place of worship, but if you would rather do your own investigating, and the Yellow Pages seem outdated, we've listed a number of helpful online directories here with their corresponding faiths.

If you are intersted in becoming involved in interfaith projects, try visiting the **Greater Boston Interfaith Organization** at www.gbio.org.

Below is a sampling of different houses of faith that are in the Boston area. Certainly, it is not a comprehensive list.

BAHÁ'Í

Although Bahá'í houses of worship may differ from one another in architectural style, they are often stunning, and are recognizable by their nine sides and central dome, which symbolize "the diversity of the human race and its essential oneness." To read up on the Bahá'í religion, visit its main web site, www.bahai.org. To find out about the local Bahá'í community, go to www.bostonbahai.org.

- **Boston Bahá'í Center**, 595 Albany St, Boston, 617-695-3500
- **Bahá'í Faith Study**, 1 Fairfield St, Salem, 978-744-4587

BUDDHIST

Buddhism dates back over two millennia, and today over 350 million people across the globe consider themselves Buddhists. There are many different sub-traditions, including **Zen, Tibetan, Vajrayana (Tantric)**, and **Mahayana**.

For information on Buddhism check out www.buddhanet.net; for Boundless Way Zen (formerly known as the Zen community of Boston), go to www.zcboston.net.

CHRISTIAN

There is a wide range of Christian denominations; for a comprehensive list of churches check out http://netministries.org or www.forministry.com. You can also contact the **National Council of Churches** (212-870-2227, www.ncccusa.org), which publishes the *Yearbook of American & Canadian Churches*, a directory listing thousands of Christian churches. Order one or browse the directory links at www.electronicchurch.org.

AFRICAN METHODIST EPISCOPAL (AME)/EPISCOPAL ZION

If you'd like to find an AME or Episcopal Zion church in your neighborhood, you can consult AME's directory on the web, www.ame-church.com/directory. Not only does it provide a church locator, there is also a contact number for each.

Some local AME Churches include:

- **Bethel African Methodist Episcopal Church**, 215 Forest Hills St, Jamaica Plain, 617-524-7900, www.bethelame.org
- **St. Paul AME Church**, 37 & 85 Bishop Richard Allen Dr, Cambridge, 617-661-1110, www.st-paul-ame.org

ANGLICAN/EPISCOPAL

The Episcopal and Anglican churches are both descended from the Church of England. The Episcopal Church took root in America as early as 1607, with the first permanent English settlement in Jamestown, Virginia. There are plenty of Episcopal and Anglican churches in Boston, many are pretty, and a couple of them are even quite famous. There is the **Old North Church** (a.k.a. Christ Church, 193 Salem Street, 617-523-6676, www.oldnorth.com), that is to say, *the* Old North Church, where the lanterns were hung on the night of Paul Revere's famous ride in 1775. This beautiful historic building, which was built in the style of Christopher Wren in 1723, is smack dab in the middle of the North End and remains an active church. Also famous, **Trinity Church** (206 Clarendon Street, 617-536-0944, www.trinityboston.org) is one of Boston's most prominent landmarks. Built in the 1870s in the "Richardsonian Romanesque" style, Trinity Church is a hallmark of American architecture. It commands a prominent position in the middle of Copley Square, and attracts many visitors.

For general information about the **Episcopal Church of the US**, visit www. episcopalchurch.org; for the **Anglican Church** worldwide, go to http://anglicans online.org. At the local level, you can access information on the Anglican and Episcopal Diocese of Massachusetts at www.diomass.org, which offers a great deal of information on local spiritual life, including a detailed listing of churches in the region.

ASSEMBLY OF GOD

Assemblies of God are the largest Pentecostal denomination of the Protestant church in the US, and greater Boston is home to a dozen or so assembly churches. The Assembly of God official web site, http://ag.org/top, is informative and provides a complete directory of its churches nationwide.

A few Assembly of God churches in the Boston area are:

- **Boston Worship Center**, 9 Salutation St, Boston, 617-723-2226, http://boston worshipcenter.org
- **Christ the Rock Church**, 48 Pleasant St, Dorchester, 617-825-9425, www. christtherockboston.org
- **Grace Christian Center of the Assemblies of God**, 825 E 4th St, South Boston, 617-436-8005
- **North Shore Assembly of God**, 77 Kennedy Dr, Malden, 781-321-2121, www. northshoreag.org

BAPTIST

American, Free Will, and **Southern Baptists** all have congregations in Boston. To find out more about Southern Baptists go to www.sbc.net; for more on Free Will Baptists, go to www.nafwb.org; and for American Baptists, go to http://abc -usa.org, or, locally, www.tabcom.org.

Some Baptist churches in the Boston area include:

- **Concord Baptist Church**, 190 Warren Ave, Boston, 617-266-8062, www.cbc boston.org
- **First Baptist Church of Boston**, 110 Comm Ave, Boston, 617-267-3148, www. firstbaptistchurchofboston.org
- **Hill Memorial Baptist Church**, 279 N Harvard St, Brighton, 617-782-4524
- **Old Cambridge Baptist Church**, 1151 Mass Ave, Cambridge, 617-864-9275, www.oldcambridgebaptist.org

- **Twelfth Baptist Church**, 150-160 Warren St, Roxbury, 617-442-7855, www. tbcboston.org

CHRISTIAN SCIENCE

The Church of Christian Science, started by Mary Baker Eddy, has its world head-quarters in Boston; the **Mother Church**, as the complex is called, is nothing less than magnificent. Located in the middle of the Fenway, the Christian Science campus covers 14 acres of land, which is comprised of the church building, a re-flecting pool, a reading room, the Mary Baker Eddy Library for the Betterment of Humanity (a museum including the Hall of Ideas, colorful and stunning Mappa-rium, and Quest Gallery), and the offices of the *Christian Science Monitor* (www. csmonitor.com). While the entire complex is a draw for tourists, the church itself is a magnificent Romanesque building with a bell tower, stained glass windows, and a 13,290-pipe organ. To learn more about the library and visiting the sites, go to www.marybakereddylibrary.org. To learn more about the Mother Church and Christian Science in general, visit www.tfccs.com.

Area Christian Science churches include:

- **First Church of Christ, Scientist**, The Mother Church Headquarters and General Offices, 175 Huntington Ave, Boston, 617-450-2000, www.tfccs.com
- **Second Boston Church of Christ, Scientist**, 33 Elm Hill Ave, Roxbury, 617-442-8448
- **Cambridge First Church of Christ, Scientist**, 13 Waterhouse St (at Mass Ave), 617-354-2866
- **Newton First Church of Christ, Scientist**, 391 Walnut St, 617-332-6376
- **Quincy Church of Christ Scientist**, 20 Greenleaf St, 617-472-0055

CHURCH OF GOD

The worldwide Church of God web site, http://www.wcg.org, has information about the religion, and a listing of churches around the world.

Area Churches of God include:

- **Church of God of Prophecy**, 270-72 Warren St, Roxbury, 617-427-7766
- **Shawmut Community Church of God**, 600 Shawmut Ave, Boston, 617-445-3263
- **Church of God of Prophecy of Mattapan**, 118 Hollingsworth Rd, Milton, 617-698-6457

CHURCH OF THE NAZARENE

For information about the Church of the Nazarene and a church locator service, try the main web site for the Church of the Nazarene, www.nazarene.org.

Area churches include:

- **Cambridge Church of the Nazarene**, 234 Franklin St, Cambridge, 617-354-5065
- **Church of the Nazarene of Somerville**, 52 Russell Rd, Somerville, 617-628-1898
- **Church of the Nazarene**, 1450 Trapelo Rd, Waltham, 781-890-7629
- **Immanuel Church of the Nazarene**, 806 Blue Hill Ave, Boston, 617-825-1766
- **Second Church in Dorchester, Church of the Nazarene**, 600 Washington St, Dorchester, 617-825-2797

CONGREGATIONAL/UNITED CHURCH OF CHRIST

The Congregational Church, also known since the 1950s as the **United Church of Christ** (**UCC**), is a Protestant denomination loosely connected to the Puritans who settled Massachusetts. As a result of this tie to early American heritage, many of the Congregational churches around Boston are not only old, but look the part of a New England church: picturesque white steeples with front doors opening directly onto the sanctuary, and rows of wooden pews. Historically significant Boston UCC churches include **Park Street Church** (One Park Street, 617-523-3383, www.parkstreet.org) and **Old South Church UCC** (645 Boylston Street, 617-536-1970, www.oldsouth.org). Located atop Beacon Hill across from the State House, the Wren-inspired red brick Park Street Church was founded in 1809, and is one of the more commanding architectural sites in the city, particularly when it casts its soft lights over the Boston Common at night. Old South Church, built in 1875 of Roxbury puddingstone (the state rock), has a congregation that dates back to 1699, with famous parishioners including Samuel Adams, William Dawes, Benjamin Franklin, and Phyllis Wheatley. Parishioners met at two other sites, including the Old South Meetinghouse of Downtown Crossing, before building the Old South Church. In Harvard Square, the **First Church of Cambridge** (11 Garden Street, 617-547-2724, www.firstchurchcambridge.org), has been standing since 1872.

For more information on the local Congregational community, try the **Massachusetts Conference of the UCC** (www.macucc.org) or check with the **Congregational Library and Archives** (14 Beacon Street, 617-523-0470, www.14beacon.org).

CHURCH OF CHRIST

For information on the Church of Christ, and for a church directory, go to their main web site: http://church-of-christ.org.

Area Churches of Christ include the following:

- **Brookline Church of Christ**, 416 Washington St, Brookline, 617-277-2452
- **Mattapan Church of Christ**, 574 River St, Mattapan, 617-298-0151
- **Blue Hills Church of Christ**, 1505 Blue Hill Ave, Mattapan, 617-296-5882
- **Church of Christ in Roxbury**, 81 Walnut Ave, Roxbury, 617-442-5826

FRIENDS (QUAKER)

Members of the **Society of Friends**, a.k.a. **Quakers**, can trace their church's roots back to some of the first Europeans to settle in the Americas. Persecuted in England for their beliefs, and then again in Massachusetts by their fellow Puritans, some did manage to remain in Boston, but more fled to New Jersey, North Carolina, Virginia, Maryland, New York, Rhode Island, and Pennsylvania—the latter two of which were their strongest and best-known colonies. To learn more about the Friends church, visit www.quaker.org.

Local Friends Houses include:

- **Beacon Hill Friends House**, 6 Chestnut St, Boston, 617-227-9118, www.bhfh.org
- **Friends Meeting At Cambridge**, 5 Longfellow Park (Harvard Sq), 617-876-6883, www.brightworks.com/quaker

INTERDENOMINATIONAL/INDEPENDENT/NONDENOMI-NATIONAL

The following churches are a few that identify themselves as independent, or interdenominational, or nondenomimational:

- **Boston Chinese Bible Study Group**, www.bcbsg.org
- **Chinese Christian Church of New England**, 1835 Beacon St, Brookline, 617-232-8652, www.cccne.org
- **Community of Faith Christian Fellowship**, 410 Washington St, Brighton, 617-783-2833, www.cfcfboston.org
- **Emmanuel Gospel Center**, 2 San Juan, Boston, 617-262-4567, www.egc.org
- **Metropolitan Community Church** (MCC), office at 4258 Washington St #9 in Roslindale, 617-973-0404, www.mccboston.org; services are held in the Old West Church at 131 Cambridge St.

- **United Parish in Brookline**, 210 Harvard St, Brookline, 617-277-6860, www. unitedparishbrookline.org

JEHOVAH'S WITNESSES

For information about Jehovah's Witnesses or to find a kingdom hall, visit www. watchtower.org or www.jw-media.org.

CHURCH OF JESUS CHRIST OF LATTER-DAY SAINTS (MORMON)

Boston's Mormon population is particularly active in Belmont, where the Boston Temple is located (86 Frontage Road, 617-993-9993). For more information on the Church of Jesus Christ of Latter-day Saints, visit www.lds.org; for more about Boston's Mormon community, visit the Massachusetts Boston Mission site at www.mbmission.com.

LUTHERAN

Lutherans in the U.S. largely belong to the Evangelical Lutheran Church in America; go to www.elca.org for information and a listing of churches. The second largest conference of Lutherans in the country is the Missouri Synod; to find out more go to www.lcms.org for church listings, or investigate a few of the following.

Some local ELCA Churches include:

- **Christ Lutheran Church**, 597 Belmont St, Belmont, 617-484-5552, www.clcbel mont.org
- **Faith Lutheran Church**, 201 Granite St, Quincy, 617-770-0853
- **Resurrection Lutheran Church**, 94 Warren St, Roxbury, 617-427-2066, www. resurrectionroxbury.org
- **University Lutheran Church**, 66 Winthrop St, Cambridge, 617-876-3256, www.unilu.org
- **St. Paul Evangelical Lutheran Church**, 929 Concord Tpke, Arlington, 781-646-7773, www.stpaularlington.org

A few LCMS churches:

- **First Lutheran Church of Boston**, 299 Berkeley St, Boston, 617-536-8851, www.flc-boston.org
- **Trinity Lutheran Church**, 1195 Centre St, Roslindale, 617-327-8866
- **Wollaston Lutheran Church**, 550 Hancock St, Quincy, 617-773-5482, www. wlchurch.org

MENNONITE

One million Mennonites are spread throughout the world, with a little over 450,000 in the U.S. While Massachusetts isn't home to many Mennonites, Boston does house the **Mennonite Congregation of Boston** (155 Mass Ave., Cambridge, 617-868-7784, http://congregationofboston.ma.us.mennonite.net), which was founded in 1962 by those Mennonites who were in the area for academic reasons. Since 1966, the congregation has been dually affiliated with both the Eastern District and the Atlantic Coast Confrence, but is welcoming to all, regardless of background. Though Mennonites lack a sizable population here, they do a great deal of community work, operating the Ten Thousand Villages fair trade store in Central Square, participating in the Neighborhood Action Food Program, and offering bible study classes for children. For more information about the Mennonite Church of the USA, try www.mennoniteusa.org.

METHODIST (UNITED)

Listings of Boston-area Methodist churches can be found on the New England Conference of the Methodist Church web site, www.neumc.org.

Some area churches include:

- **Community United Methodist Church**, 519 Washington St, Brighton, 617-787-1868
- **Grace United Methodist Church**, 56 Magazine St, Cambridge, 617-864-1123, www.gbgm-umc.org/cambridgegrace
- **Greenwood Memorial United Methodist Church**, 378A Washington St, Dorchester, 617-288-8410, www.gbgm-umc.org/greenwoodmemorial
- **Old West Church**, 131 Cambridge St, Boston, 617-227-5088, www.oldwestchurch.org
- **St. Andrew's United Methodist Church**, 171 Amory St, Jamaica Plain, 617-522-1535

ORTHODOX (COPTIC, EASTERN, GREEK, ALBANIAN, RUSSIAN, ETC.)

For more information on the Orthodox Church in America, visit www.oca.org. For information on Greek Orthodoxy in particular, try the **Greek Orthodox Archdiocese of America** at www.goarch.org

Some area churches include:

- **Albanian Orthodox Church of St. John the Baptist**, 410 W Broadway, South Boston, 617-268-3564
- **Annunciation Cathedral**, Parker and Ruggles Sts, Boston, 617-731-6633, www.

annunciationcathedral.net
- **Holy Trinity Orthodox Cathedral**, 165 Park Dr, Boston, 617-262-9490, http://holytrinityorthodox.org
- **St. George Antiochian Orthodox Church**, 55 Emonsdale Rd, West Roxbury, 617-323-0323, www.stgeorgeofboston.org
- **St. George Cathedral Albanian Orthodox Church in America**, 523 E Broadway, South Boston, 617-268-1275, www.saintgeorgecathedral.com
- **Saint John the Baptist Hellenic Orthodox Church**, 15 Union Park St, Boston, 617-536-5692, www.saintjohnthebaptist.org

PENTECOSTAL/CHARISMATIC

For more information about the **Pentecostal/Charismatic Churches of North America** and to find a local church, go to www.pccna.org, or **see above** under **Assembly of God.**

For more about the **International Communion of the Charismatic Episcopal Church**, go to www.iccec.org.

PRESBYTERIAN (USA)

A Protestant Church with its roots in 17th-century England, it was the Scottish and Irish who brought Presbyterianism to the US in the late 1600s. The largest Presbyterian branch in the US is the **Presbyterian Church** (**USA**); find them on the web at www.pcusa.org.

Area Presbyterian churches include:

- **Church of the Covenant**, 67 Newbury St, Boston, 617-266-7480, www.churchofthecovenant.org
- **First Presbyterian Church in Brookline**, 32 Harvard St, Brookline, 617-232-7962, www.fpcbrookline.org
- **First United Presbyterian Church of Cambridge**, 1418 Cambridge St, Cambridge, 617-354-3151
- **First Presbyterian Church of Quincy**, 270 Franklin St, Quincy, 617-773-5575, www.firstpresbyquincy.org
- **New Covenant Presbyterian Church**, 1310 Centre St, Newton, 617-558-3223, www.ncpcboston.org

ROMAN CATHOLIC

Roman Catholicism is the predominant religion in Boston. Although the recent Catholic clergy sexual abuse scandal probably hit hardest in Massachusetts, with many parishes closing, the state is still home to a population of firm believers.

According to the Roman Catholic Archdiocese of Boston, there are more than two million Catholics in the greater Boston area, eight affiliated hospitals and medical centers, and six colleges and universities. If you are interested in Catholic schools for your children, there are 149 schools catering to K–12 children; go to www.abcso.org for a listing.

Your source of information for Catholic life is the **Roman Catholic Archdiocese of Boston** (2121 Comm Ave, Boston, 617-254-0100, www.rcab.org). For Catholic media outlets, there is **Boston Catholic Television** (BCTV, www.catholictv.org), America's oldest Roman Catholic newspaper, *The Pilot* (www.thebostonpilot.com), and **Boston Catholic Radio** (www.bostoncatholic.com).

A few area churches include:

- **Cathedral of the Holy Cross**, 1400 Washington St, Boston, 617-542-5682, www.angelfire.com/ma4/cathedral/home.html
- **St. Brigid Parish,** 841 E Broadway, South Boston, 617-268-2122, www.stbrigid parish.com
- **St. Clement Eucharistic Shrine**, 1105 Boylston St, Boston, 617-266-5999, www.stclementshrine.org
- **St. Columbkille Parish**, 321 Market St, Brighton, 617-782-5774
- **St. Joseph Parish**, 68 William Cardinal O'Connell Way, Boston, 617-523-4342, www.stjosephsboston.com
- **St. Paul Parish**, 29 Mount Auburn St, Cambridge, 617-491-8400, www.stpaul parish.org

SEVENTH DAY ADVENTIST

For information on Seventh Day Adventists, go to www.adventist.org, where you will also find a directory of churches worldwide.

Area Seventh Day Adventist churches include:

- **Boston Temple Seventh Day Adventist Church**, 105 Jersey St, Boston, 617-536-5022, www.bostontemple-sda.org
- **Cambridge Seventh Day Adventist Church**, 62 Dexter St, Medford, 781-391-2908
- **Jamaica Plain Spanish Seventh Day Adventist Church**, 40 Elm St, JP, 617-983-1076
- **Spanish Boston Temple Seventh Day Adventist Church**, 50 Stoughton St, Dorchester, 617-436-6802
- **Temple Salem of the Seventh Day Adventists**, 222 Woodrow Ave, Dorchester, 617-288-8845

UNITARIAN UNIVERSALIST ASSOCIATION (UUA)

The Unitarian Universalist Association (UUA) dates back to 1961, when the Universalism and Unitarianism movements officially merged. The **UUA's Headquarters** are at 25 Beacon Street. To contact the UUA, go to http://uua.org. Visit the **Mass Bay District of UU Churches** at http://www.mbduua.org.

Some Boston area congregations include:

- **Arlington Street Church**, 351 Boylston St, Boston, 617-536-7050, www.asc boston.org
- **First Church in Boston**, 66 Marlborough St, Boston, 617-267-6730, www.first churchboston.org
- **First Church in Jamaica Plain,** 6 Eliot St, JP, 617-524-1634, www.firstchurchjp. org
- **First Parish in Cambridge**, 3 Church St, Cambridge, 617-876-7772, www.first parishcambridge.org
- **First Parish Church in Dorchester**, 10 Parish St, Dorchester, 617-436-0527, www.firstparish.com

UNITY CHURCHES

For information about local Unity Churches, visit the Association of Unity Churches' web site: www.unity.org.

ETHICAL SOCIETIES

Ethical Society of Boston, P.O. Box 38-1934, Cambridge, MA 02238, 617-739-9050, www.bostonethical.org; not a conventional religious organization, ethical societies offer a meeting place and fellowship to members and visitors. Acknowledging that humans are both individualistic and social in nature, the society explores what it means to understand the inner workings of self and how to relate to each other in a respectful, ethical, and moralistic way. For more information go to www.ethicalsociety.org.

HINDU

Hinduism is as complex and multifaceted as the many gods it incorporates. Nearly 13% of the world's population is Hindu. Although most still live in India, there are roughly one million Hindus in the United States. Two Boston area temples are:

- **Sri Lakshmi Temple**, 117 Waverly St, Ashland, 508-881-5775, www.nehti.org
- **International Swaminarayan Temple**, 405 Andover St, Lowell, 978-934-9390

ISLAM

To tap into the local Islamic community try the **Islamic Society of Boston** (204 Prospect Street, Cambridge, 617-876-3546, www.isboston.org), or the **Islamic Center of New England** (470 South Street, Quincy, 617-479-8341, www.icne. net).

Other area Islamic centers and mosques include:

- **Boston Islamic Center**, 3381 Washington St, Jamaica Plain, 617-522-1881
- **Islamic Center of Boston**, 126 Boston Post Rd, Wayland, 508-358-5885, www. icbwayland.org
- **Masjid Al-Quran**, 35 Intervale St, Dorchester, 617-445-8070
- **Mosque for the Praising of Allah**, 724 Shawmut Ave, Roxbury, 617-442-2805, www.mosquepraiseallah.com

JEWISH

Boston has a sizable Jewish population; the heaviest concentrations are in Newton and Brookline, where they make up at least one third of the total population. Other areas include Marblehead, Swampscott, Peabody, Framingham, Needham, and Sharon. The local media outlet is the *Jewish Advocate*, which you can subscribe to online at www.thejewishadvocate.com or by calling 617-367-9100. For socializing, try the **Jewish Community Centers of Greater Boston**, 333 Nahanton Street, 617-558-6500, www.jccgb.org. And finally, for information on everything and anything Jewish in the Boston area, go to www.shalomboston. com. If you are a student, professor, or otherwise affiliated with one of Boston's many colleges and universities, you can likely attend your school's Hillels or Chabad houses. Here are a few local congregations:

CHASIDIC

- **Congregation B'nai Jacob of Boston and Newton**, 15 School St, Boston, 617-227-8200; 955 Beacon St, Newton, 617-965-0066, www.rebbe.org
- **Congregation Lubavitch**, 100 Woodcliff Rd, Chestnut Hill, 617-469-4000, www.congregationlubavitch.org
- **Lubavitcher Shul of Brighton**, 239 Chestnut Hill Ave, Brighton, 617-782-8340
- **Congregation Beth Pinchas/New England Chasidic Center**, 1710 Beacon St, Brookline, 617-734-5100

CONSERVATIVE

- **Congregation Kehillath Israel**, 384 Harvard St, Brookline, 617-277-9155, www.congki.org
- **Congregation Mishkan Tefila**, 300 Hammond Pond Pkwy, Chestnut Hill, 617-

332-7770, www.mishkantefila.org
- **Temple B'nai Moshe**, 1845 Comm Ave, Brighton, 617-254-3620, www.temple bnaimoshe.org
- **Temple Emeth**, South and Grove Sts, Chestnut Hill, 617-469-9400, www.temple emeth.org
- **Temple Reyim**, 1860 Washington St, Newton, 617-527-2410, www.reyim.org

ORTHODOX

- **Adams Street Shul**, 168 Adams St, Newton, 617-630-0226, www.adamsstreet. org
- **Congregation Beth-El Atereth Israel**, 561 Ward St, Newton Centre, 617-244-7233, www.bethnewton.org
- **Congregation Kadimah-Toras Moshe**, 113 Washington St, Brighton, 617-254-1333
- **Congregation Shaarei Tefillah**, 35 Morseland Ave, Newton Centre, 617-527-7637, www.shaarei.org
- **Young Israel of Brookline**, 62 Green St, Brookline, 617-734-0276, www. yibrookline.org

RECONSTRUCTIONIST

- **Shir Hadash Reconstructionist Havurah**, 1310 Centre St, Newton, 617-965-6862, www.jrf.org/shirhadash/
- **Congregation Dorshei Tzedek**, 60 Highland St, West Newton, 617-965-0330, www.dorsheitzedek.org

REFORM

- **Beth-El Temple Center**, 2 Concord Ave, Belmont, 617-484-6668, www.ma002. urj.net
- **Temple Israel**, 477 Longwood Ave, Boston, 617-566-3960, www.tisrael.org
- **Temple Ohabei Shalom**, 1187 Beacon St, Brookline, 617-277-6610, www.oha bei.org
- **Temple Shalom of Newton**, 175 Temple St, West Newton, 617-332-9550, www. templeshalom.org
- **Temple Sinai of Brookline**, 50 Sewell Ave, Brookline, 617-277-5888, www. sinaibrookline.org

NON-MOVEMENT AFFILIATED

- **Progressive Chavurah**, various locations, www.chav.net

- **Boston Synagogue**, 55 Martha Rd, Boston, 617-523-0453, www.boston synagogue.org
- **Congregation Eitz Chayim**, 136 Magazine St, Cambridge, 617-497-7626, www.eitz.org
- **Temple Beth Zion**, 1566 Beacon St, Brookline, 617-566-8171, www.tbzbrook line.org

NEW AGE

Information about the local **Subud** community can be found at **Subud Boston** (www.subudboston.org). To learn more about Subud in general, visit the official site of their world association at www.subud.org.

The other major New Age religion in these parts is **Wicca**. Although Wiccans do call themselves witches, this name is often misinterpreted—they do not engage in Satanism or devil worship, as many mistakenly believe, but rather focus on revering nature. Perhaps because of Salem's history, many Wiccans live in and around Boston, and Salem itself has quite a healthy population of Wiccans, sustained no doubt by the crossover with the tourism industry. There is even a self-appointed, official Witch of Salem—a woman named **Laurie Cabot**, who runs a shop called **The Cat, The Crow, and The Crown** (www.lauriecabot.com). For information on the local Wiccan scene, check out some of the New Age shops in Salem or try one of the following:

- **Goddess Womyn**, www.geocities.com/goddesswomyn13/
- **Society of Elder Faiths**, www.elderfaiths.org

SIKH

Although there are over 20 million Sikhs throughout the world, only 220,000 live in America. There is enough of a Sikh population in Boston for a gurdwara: **Gurdwara Guru Nanak Darbar** (226 Mystic Avenue, Medford, www.gurunanakdarbar. net). For more information on Sikhism, go to www.sikhs.org.

S ERVING AS A VOLUNTEER IN A NEW CITY CAN BE BENEFICIAL FOR both you and your new community. Charitable organizations and even area museums are often under-funded, and many rely heavily on volunteer labor. As a volunteer you will be providing your community with a valuable service—as well as tapping into a social circle with those who share your concerns.

THINGS TO REMEMBER

- Experience is not always required; most agencies are more than willing to train their volunteers.
- Choose a charity based on your interests and talents.
- National charities you may already be familiar and/or associated with probably have offices in the Boston area; look in the Yellow Pages for local chapters of the American Red Cross, American Cancer Society, Habitat for Humanity, Big Brothers/Big Sisters, Amnesty International, and others.
- For opportunities, check bulletin boards at your office, church, neighborhood stores, and school; check the Yellow Pages under "social and human services"; go to www.volunteerboston.org for an alphabetical and categorical listing of organizations; check your local newspaper or read on for more helpful information.

HOW YOU CAN HELP

HOMELESS AND HUNGRY

Like most cities, Boston has a homeless population; shelter and care for the city's homeless, especially during the cold winters, is a major concern. Volunteer jobs include monitoring and organizing shelters; providing legal help; ministering to psychiatric, medical, and social needs; raising money; manning phones; and caring for children in shelters. Many people solicit, organize, cook, and serve food to the destitute at sites throughout the city. Still others deliver meals to the homeless and homebound. During the summer, there are opportunities to plant and harvest vegetables to be donated to shelters.

CHILDREN

If you enjoy working with children, and/or are just a big kid yourself, you can tutor in and out of schools, be a Big Brother or Sister, teach music and sports in shelters or at local community centers, run activities in the parks, entertain children in hospitals, or accompany kids on weekend outings. Schools, libraries, community associations, hospitals, and other facilities providing activities and guidance for children are all worth exploring.

HOSPITALS

The need for volunteers in both city-run and private hospitals is manifold; from interpreters to laboratory personnel to admitting and nursing aides, many volunteers are required. If you just want to be helpful, you might assist in food delivery or work in the gift shop. Most city hospitals are large and busy, and many are in need of help.

THE DISABLED AND THE ELDERLY

You can read to the blind, or help teach the deaf. You can also make regular visits to the homebound elderly, bring hot meals to their homes, sit and keep them company, or teach everything from nutrition to arts and crafts in senior centers and nursing homes.

EXTREME CARE SITUATIONS

Helping with suicide prevention, Alzheimer's and AIDS patients, rape victims, and abused children is a special category demanding a high level of commitment—not to mention emotional reserves and, in many cases, special skills.

THE COMMUNITY

Work in your neighborhood. Block associations and community gardens are run strictly by volunteers. You can help out at the local school, nursing home, settlement house, or animal shelter.

THE CULTURE SCENE

There are museums all over the city in need of volunteers to lead tours or lend a hand in any number of ways. Libraries, theater groups, ballet companies, and even local film festivals have plenty of tasks that need to be done. Fundraising efforts also require many volunteers to stuff envelopes and/or make phone calls.

POLITICS

Get signatures, make phone calls, or work on a favorite politician's campaign. Boston is known for its strong (and sometimes revolutionary) opinions. For a nonpartisan group, check out the **Massachusetts League of Women Voters** (www.lwvma.org), who make it their mission to inform voters about public policy, elections, and candidates. Or just walk through Boston Common near Park Street or Harvard Square in Cambridge on almost any summer weekend, and talk to the hordes of protesters or signature collectors who are fighting for causes of all magnitudes and spectrums.

WHERE YOU CAN HELP

SPECIFIC NEED ORGANIZATIONS

Numerous organizations in Boston address various causes like homelessness, hunger, disease and disability. For example, there is the Food Project, a promoter of social change through agriculture; Rosie's Place, a sanctuary for poor and homeless women; Ethos Care, an advocate for the elderly; Home for Little Wanderers, a child and family service agency; Boston Living Center, a resource for those living with HIV/AIDS; Greater Boston Guild for the Blind, a provider of services for those with vision loss; Pine Street Inn, a resource for homeless men and women; and many others.

INSTITUTIONS

Hospitals, like Massachusetts General Hospital, Children's Hospital, Brigham and Women's, Beth Israel, and others, are always in need of volunteers. Go to the hospital's web site, or give them a call for more information. The Boston Museum of Science, Museum of Fine Arts, Franklin Park Zoo, Boston Historical Society, and more use volunteers regularly as well. And don't forget libraries, local schools, universities, animal shelters, theaters and other city institutions that are also mostly underfunded and rely on a veritable army of volunteers to survive.

THE RELIGIOUS CONNECTION

Individual churches and synagogues (in particular, those serving the homeless and the needy), and church federations such as the Greater Boston Jewish Coalition for Literacy, the Catholic Charitable Bureau of the Archdiocese of Boston, and the Combined Jewish Philanthropies of Greater Boston, use volunteers for a variety of activities. The **St. Vincent Pallotti Center**, a national organization, has a regional office in Brighton (2121 Comm Ave., 617-783-3924) where they teach college students about Christian service, assemble and distribute a directory of local part-time volunteer opportunities, and organize other special projects. Visit www.pallotticenter.org for more information.

THE COMMUNITY

Neighborhood associations are a great way to have a voice, whether it be to complain about a constantly littered sidewalk or to come up with a plan to help stop crime; of course, it is also a great way to meet your neighbors! A listing of the city's associations can be found on **www.abnboston.org**. If you're interested in **urban gardens**, you may want to check out **www.bostonnatural.org** to learn about volunteering at a community garden near you. Of course, local schools, parks, and shelters always need volunteers as well.

MULTI-SERVICE ORGANIZATIONS

Once again, don't forget such well-known groups as the Salvation Army, American Red Cross, March of Dimes, United Way, and Visiting Nurse Service; they can always use a helping, and caring, hand!

THE CORPORATE CONNECTION

Corporations encourage employee voluntarism through company-supported projects such as literacy programs, pro bono work, and management aid to non-profit groups. Check with your company personnel or public relations department to see if your firm is involved in any specific project. Many corporations have also set up programs with the United Way.

REFERRAL SERVICES

If you would like to donate your time but don't know where to start, try one of several umbrella organizations that find volunteers for affiliated agencies. At these referral services, staff members can help you determine the tasks you would be interested in doing, where to do them, and when.

- **Boston Cares**, 190 High St #4, Boston, 617-422-0910 ext. 200 for general inquiries, www.bostoncares.org; Boston Cares allows people the flexibility to volunteer when they can, without an ongoing commitment. Once you register through the Boston Cares web site and take a one-hour training course, you will receive weekly listings of current projects looking for volunteers. If something strikes your interest and you have the time to spare, sign up—it's that easy!
- **Boston Jaycees**, 1 Beacon St, Boston, 888-274-8682, www.bostonjaycees.org; as the city's junior chamber of commerce, the Boston Jaycees organizes volunteer and leadership opportunities for women and men between the ages of 21 and 40.
- **Chelsea Community Volunteer Center**, 300 Broadway, Chelsea, 617-889-6080, www.chelseacollab.org; organizes Chelsea residents and businesses to help them enhance their community through public service.
- **Harvard Public Service Network**, a Harvard organization that works to provide support and resources to the 40 public-service student groups on campus. If you are a Harvard student looking to be involved in social change, go to www.fas.harvard.edu/~pbh/psn for more information.
- **Leonard Carmichael Society**, 101 Lincoln Filene Center, Medford, 617-627-3643, http://ase.tufts.edu/lcs; if you are a Tufts student looking to do community service, this student-run organization offers 36 programs divided into five different interest groups. Check out their web site or monthly newsletter for information on the current semester opportunities.
- **People Making a Difference**, P.O. Box 120189, Boston, 617-282-7177, www.pmd.org; sign up online and PMD will e-mail you listings of volunteer projects in the Boston area—if you are interested, respond back before the deadline, and you will be sent an information packet in the mail. Most projects are accessible by public transportation, and if one is not, PMD will provide alternative transportation for you.
- **Single Volunteers Boston**, www.svboston.org; organization aiming to connect local singles with a common interest in voluntarism. One-time volunteer events range from cleaning up the banks of the Charles River to helping out at community gardens and festivals, and are followed by social mixers. Free to join; must be 21+.
- **Volunteer Solutions**, www.volunteersolutions.org; lists a great number of local organizations that are currently looking for volunteers.

GETTING AROUND

BOSTON'S CLOSE QUARTERS, LIMITED AND EXPENSIVE PARKING, AND good mass transit system all combine to make car ownership more of an option than a requirement for many residents. Indeed, about a third of the city commutes via public transportation, and more people walk to work here than in any other US city. Most Boston neighborhoods have everything you might need—grocery stores, laundromats, Dunkin Donuts—within walking distance, and MBTA service is more than adequate to most parts of the city (often even quicker than driving when you take traffic into account). Still, while owning a car can be a hassle—you will inevitably accumulate parking tickets, try as you might to avoid them—it is not an impossibility, even in downtown's crowded confines. Furthermore, outside of the city, and even in some Boston neighborhoods not well-served by the subway (West Roxbury and Roslindale, for instance), most residents find that car ownership borders on necessity. For those who don't want the fuss and muss of owning a car, but still like to have one readily available for mall runs or daytrip getaways, you can join **Zipcar** (www.zipcar.com, 866-4ZIPCAR), an hourly car rental subscription service. If you plan to live in Boston without a car, pick up a copy of *Car-Free Boston*, a publication by the Association for Public Transportation (617-482-0282, www.car-free.com), available at most bookstores.

BY CAR

Driving in Boston is confusing at best; it is agonizingly frustrating and panic-inducing at worst. Finding your way around the old, narrow, and seemingly random maze of streets is no picnic, and the impatience and aggressive driving habits of locals only add to the stress for newcomers. Footpaths laid the first trails for early roads here, and the area's hilly topography discouraged the development of a grid system for city streets. The best advice: buy a good map of the entire metro area (not just Boston) and be patient. It might seem daunting at first, but because the city is so small, you'll soon come to recognize the winding, one-way streets that only days ago were your archenemy. With the Big Dig finally completed, the once-legendary traffic on area expressways and major highways has lessened somewhat. However, during rush hours you'll likely turn to the city streets and local roads, no matter how narrow or crooked, seeking alternatives to the gridlock on the major arteries.

For the uninitiated, the most intimidating New England traffic institution is known as the "rotary," elsewhere called a "roundabout" or "traffic circle." These are often used in place of traffic lights, especially when more than two streets intersect. Vehicles already in the circle (look to your left) have the right of way, but it pays to be assertive; if you can jump in without getting in anyone's way, go for it.

A final caution: some Boston drivers can be impatient, aggressive, and expressive (read: honking, swearing, yelling, or cutting you off... many times simultaneously).

For information on the main urban streets and thoroughfares, reference the Street Address Locator in the **Introduction**. Some of the **major highways** in and around Boston are as follows:

- **I-93** is the main north-south expressway. Running south from Vermont, through New Hampshire, the Merrimack Valley, and suburbs north of Boston, it enters the city in Charlestown and crosses the **Zakim Bridge** before darting underneath the heart of the city for a 3.5-mile stretch (thanks to the Big Dig). Through the city and south of it, I-93 hosts portions of Route 1 and **Route 3**; in Quincy, Route 3 splits off to the southeast, toward Cape Cod. I-93 ends at its junction with I-95, southwest of the city in Canton.
- **Route 1** was the original US Highway serving the east coast from Maine to Florida. It approaches Boston from the north as an active three-lane highway lined with stores, restaurants, and malls, runs through Chelsea, and then crosses the **Tobin Bridge** ($3 toll inbound) into Charlestown. There it joins up with I-93, following it south through the city and onto a portion of I-95/128 before breaking off on its own again in Dedham.
- **Route 2** is simply Comm Ave until it crosses the Charles at the Boston University Bridge. Once on the other side of the river, it runs along Memorial Drive, the Fresh Pond Parkway, and the Alewife Brook Parkway before it evolves into a three-lane highway, heading northwest through Arlington, Belmont, Lexington, Concord, and beyond. Route 2 offers a scenic drive to Western Massachusetts.
- **I-90**, the Massachusetts Turnpike ("The Pike"), is the main east-west artery serving the Boston area. It begins at Logan Airport in East Boston and runs di-

rectly downtown via the Ted Williams Tunnel, where it intersects with I-93, and then heads west through the city and its western suburbs toward upstate New York and, ultimately, Seattle. **Note:** I-90 is a toll road from Boston to Springfield. You can use a Fast Lane Pass or E-ZPass to save time at the tollbooths; see below for details.

- **I-95**, which runs the length of the East Coast, approaches Boston from the south via Providence, Rhode Island. It then picks up local **Route 128** and wraps around the Boston metro area in a semi-circle, essentially forming a beltway 10–12 miles outside the city; this section of highway is *always* referred to locally as Route 128, not I-95. The two diverge in Peabody, with Route 128 continuing on to Gloucester and I-95 running north to the New Hampshire seacoast and Maine.

- **Route 9** begins as Huntington Avenue in Boston before heading west through Brookline, Newton, and the western suburbs as a divided two-lane highway lined with shopping malls, restaurants, and stores.

Are you confused yet? Don't despair. Learning your way around metro Boston by car is a challenge that will only be mastered by trial and error. You'll know you have fully assimilated when you're able to get across town during rush hour without getting trapped in traffic. Ex-Bostonians report boredom with cities that are laid out on a grid. After all, where's the challenge if a street doesn't double back on itself, changing names two or three times along the way?

If you'll be taking toll roads regularly, **Fast Lane** (www.masspike.com, 888-525-3278), sponsored by the Massachusetts Turnpike Authority, is an electronic toll collection program that allows you to pay your toll electronically—i.e., no scrounging for change, and no waiting for cars ahead of you. There are Fast Lane booths at every toll statewide, and a Fast Lane pass works interchangeably at E-ZPass lanes in other states like New York, New Hampshire, and Maine. A transponder costs $25.55, and you can transfer it from car to car.

CARPOOLING

Aside from cutting down on traffic, saving money on gas, and saving the environment, carpooling can save you time on your daily commute because some routes have carpool-only lanes during rush hour for vehicles with 2 or more people. If you'd like to start or join a carpool call **Caravan for Commuters, Inc.**, a private nonprofit organization, at 888-4-COMMUTE, or go to www.commute.com.

PARK & RIDES

MassHighway, the MassPike, and the MBTA sponsor Park & Ride lots at dozens of suburban locations, where commuters can park their cars along major highways—usually for free—and then carpool the rest of the trip. Almost all suburban commuter rail and subway stations have discounted parking lots as well. Visit www.ctps.org/bostonmpo/info/pnr/pr.htm for a map of all Park & Ride locations statewide.

CAR RENTAL

If you're living car-free in Boston, but need some wheels for a weekend getaway, the hub of car rental activity is obviously Logan Airport—there, you will find branches of all the major rental agencies. Most of them also operate satellite locations downtown, though they may charge slightly more for the convenience—in particular, **Enterprise** (www.enterprise.com), **Budget** (www.budget.com), **Dollar** (www.dollar.com), **Hertz** (www.hertz.com), **Alamo** (www.alamo.com), and **Avis** (www.avis.com) have neighborhood rental lots throughout Boston and Cambridge. Also check out ZipCar (see the chapter introduction) for a more long-term solution to renting a car in Boston.

TAXIS

You'll find taxi stands all over the city, particularly near the more tourist-oriented parts of town, and you can also hail one on major streets or call and schedule a pick-up. Some popular cab stands are those in front of Faneuil Hall by the greenhouse, in Cambridge's Harvard Square in front of the Coop, and in Brookline on Harvard Street right in Coolidge Corner. There isn't a stand in the North End, but tourists go there so often that you can count on finding a cab there easily, day or night. The same goes for Newbury Street and Boylston Street in the Back Bay. However, other areas that are a little further out of the way, like Charlestown, do not have many roving taxis, so call for a pick-up.

As far as hailing cabs goes, paying attention to the "For Hire" light on the tops of taxis is pointless. Whether they're lit up or not is completely irrelevant—cab drivers here just don't attend to them, so your basic strategy should be to hail away. Another wrinkle is that, due to exclusivity regulations, Boston cabs are not allowed to pick up fares in Cambridge—even after dropping off a passenger there—and vice versa. Drivers can be fined up to $500 for breaking this rule, so don't be offended when an empty taxi from a neighboring community seems to ignore you on its way out of the city.

If you have a problem with a driver or lose something in a cab, Boston taxicabs are regulated through the **Hackney Carriage Office, Boston Police Department** (154 Berkeley Street, Boston, 617-343-4475, www.cityofboston.gov/police/taxi.asp). In other areas, check with your city or town hall for regulations.

Here are a few local cab companies if you need to call for a pick-up. You can also check the Yellow Pages for a company that services your neighborhood.

- **Boston Cab**, 617-536-5010
- **Boston Town Taxi**, 617-536-5000
- **Brookline Town Taxi**, 617-232-2800

- **Cambridge Taxi**, 617-547-3000
- **City Cab of Boston**, 617-536-5100
- **Independent Taxi Operators Association**, 617-426-8700
- **Metro Cab**, 617-242-8000

BY BIKE

It is not unusual to see people biking to work in and around Boston, and it is a particularly popular means of transit among the huge student population. The most popular locale for bicycle commuting—students and worker bees alike—is in socially conscious and eco-friendly **Cambridge**, which provides **bike lanes** on most of its main streets.

For those who want to bike and ride, bikes are allowed on the Red, Orange, and Blue lines of the T during off-peak hours—weekdays from 10 a.m. to 2 p.m. and then after 7:30 p.m., and all day on weekends. Bikes are not permitted on any Green line trains, the Mattapan trolley, or at the Park Street and Government Center stations. They are only allowed at Downtown Crossing station if you are transferring. As for the commuter rail, you may bring your bike on any train any time outside of rush hour. Bikes are allowed on all MBTA boats and ferries at all times. And the crosstown buses have bike racks on their front available for use at all times, but ask the driver for help.

Safety when you're biking is a concern, particularly in brazen Boston. Be a defensive rider and wear protective gear, especially a helmet.

The local group **Caravan for Commuters** offers good information and specifics on why and how you should bike to work—go to www.commute.com for details. For more information on biking in the city, check the **Sports and Recreation** chapter, or try one of the following:

- **Massachusetts Bicycle Coalition**, www.massbike.org, 617-542-BIKE
- **Massachusetts Bicycle Plan Update**, www.massbikeplan.org; tracks progress of the state's Bicycle Plan improvements, and hosts maps of existing and planned bike paths statewide.
- **Cambridge Bicycle Program**, www.cambridgema.gov/cdd/et/bike/
- **League of American Bicyclists**, www.bikeleague.org

BY PUBLIC TRANSPORTATION

MBTA

Home to the first subway system in North America, Boston's public transportation network is efficient, relatively cheap, and far-reaching, if not exactly perfect. The **Massachusetts Bay Transportation Authority (MBTA)** operates the subway—simply called the "**T**"—as well as bus lines, commuter rail, and some commuter boats in the metro region. (Note: while the "T" most commonly refers to the subway system, it is also used to refer to the MBTA as a whole.)

When you begin taking the T, you have to remember just two things: inbound and outbound. Inbound always means going toward downtown Boston—no matter which direction that might be—and outbound always means going away from downtown Boston. What constitutes "downtown Boston" will vary depending on where you board the train—though typically it refers to Park Street, Government Center, or Downtown Crossing—so pay attention to the signs at any given station. One of the first things you should do is familiarize yourself with an MBTA map that shows all the T routes. Most of the large stations have free bus schedules and subway maps available. Contact the MBTA for questions and clarifications about schedules, fares, passes, etc., at 617-222-3200, or visit www.mbta.com.

The **four rapid transit train lines** that service the Boston area all intersect downtown, and you can transfer between them at no extra charge. The lines are known by their colors: blue, orange, red, and green. The Green Line—the oldest of the four, dating back to its first trip in 1897—runs almost entirely above ground, and its cars more resemble street trolleys than the modern subway cars of the Blue, Red, and Orange lines. The **Silver Line**, while considered part of the subway system (and priced likewise) by the MBTA, is actually a bus line with a dedicated express lane that helps it avoid some downtown traffic. Its main route runs down Washington Street from downtown to Dudley Square Station in Roxbury; it also connects the airport terminals and South Boston waterfront to South Station.

- The **Blue Line**, so named because it goes under the ocean, serves mainly the outlying areas in Revere and East Boston. Most importantly, the Blue Line goes to Logan Airport.
- The **Orange Line** is a long, north-south route beginning at the Malden/Melrose border and making stops in Everett, Somerville, and Charlestown before reaching North Station in Boston. Continuing south, it serves downtown, Chinatown, the South End, Roxbury, and Jamaica Plain before terminating at the border of Roslindale.
- The **Red Line**, named for the crimson of Harvard University (where it used to terminate), is the main route serving Cambridge and west Somerville. From Cambridge, it crosses the Charles and hits most of the big downtown stops—Park Street, Downtown Crossing, and South Station—before splitting into separate routes in South Boston. **Ashmont** trains continue on through Dorchester and link up with the Mattapan trolley, while **Braintree** trains run through Quincy.
- The **Green Line**, named for its many stops along the Emerald Necklace, actually has four different routes that begin to diverge at Copley: **B** trains meander down Comm Ave through Allston-Brighton to Boston College; **C** trains follow Beacon Street through Brookline to Cleveland Circle; **D** trains go the farthest

(and fastest) west, through Brookline and Newton to Riverside; and **E** trains run down Huntington Avenue, through Mission Hill to Heath Street.

The **cost** of riding the T increased in early 2007, when the MBTA abandoned its old token system in favor of plastic, rechargeable "CharlieCards" and paper "Charlie Tickets"—but it's still quite reasonable. With a CharlieCard, you can ride on any subway line for $1.70, with unlimited connections underground and free transfers to local buses. (If you use cash or a paper Charlie Ticket, there is a surcharge of 30 cents, bringing your ride to $2.) Note: at some outdoor T stations, where there are no turnstiles or gates (particularly at above-ground Green Line stops), you must board at the front of the train and swipe your pass or pay the driver. The T offers special **discounts** for seniors, youths, and passengers with disabilities. For fare specifics, contact the MBTA at 617-222-3200 or visit www.mbta. com.

A **Monthly LinkPass** costs $59 per month, and is valid for unlimited travel on all subway and local bus lines (excludes express buses). Passes are available for purchase online or at T sales offices located at Back Bay, Downtown Crossing, Harvard, North Station, and South Station; 1-day, 7-day, and student passes are also available.

Bikes and pets are permitted on the T, although there are some restrictions. Of course, service animals are allowed on all trains at all times. Non-service dogs are allowed on all trains during non–rush hour periods, although technically this is at the driver's discretion. Your dog must be leashed, and it may not annoy other passengers or take up a seat. Bikes are allowed on Red, Orange, and Blue line trains during non-peak hours (10 a.m. to 2 p.m. and after 7:30 p.m. on weekdays, and at any time on the weekends). They are never allowed, however, on the Green Line, nor may you bring them to the Park Street or Government Center stations. They are allowed at Downtown Crossing only if you are changing trains.

For questions about the T, visit www.mbta.com, or call:

- **MBTA Main Switchboard**, 617-222-5000
- **Travel Information Line**, 617-222-3200 or 800-392-6100; TTY 617-222-5146
- **Customer Relations** (i.e. complaints), 617-222-5215
- **Pass by Phone Orders**, 877-927-7277
- **Lost & Found**, 617-222-5000
- **Senior Citizens/Transportation Access Passes**, 617-222-5976, TTY 617-222-5854
- **The Ride**, 617-222-5123; TTY 617-222-5415
- **Lift Bus Info & Reservations**, 800-LIFT-BUS; TTY 617-222-5854
- **MBTA Police**, 617-222-1212 (emergency), 617-222-1000 (business)

BY BUS

The MBTA runs over 170 bus routes that canvas the entire metro region, including **Local**, **Inner Express**, and **Outer Express** routes. Most local buses offer "feeder service," meaning they link neighborhoods and suburbs to train stations, though some do operate as backbones of the transit system. Express buses typically make just a few stops locally before running directly into downtown. The price schedule is as follows:

- With a CharlieCard, local bus rides cost $1.25, including free transfer to other local bus lines and discounted transfer to the subway; Inner Express buses cost $2.80, and include free subway transfer; Outer Express buses cost $4.00, including free subway transfer.
- When paying the cash-on-board/Charlie Ticket surcharge, a local bus ride will cost you $1.50, Inner Express buses cost $3.50, and Outer Express buses cost $5.00; no subway transfers.

Monthly bus passes come in a few varieties: a Monthly Local Bus Pass costs $40 and includes unlimited travel on all local bus lines; an $89 Monthly Inner Express Pass offers unlimited use of all Inner Express and local buses, subway lines, and Inner Harbor Ferries; and the $129 Monthly Outer Express Pass covers unlimited travel on Outer and Inner Express and local buses, all subway lines, and Inner Harbor Ferries.

BY COMMUTER RAIL

The commuter rail system connects downtown Boston with its suburbs and satellite cities—in some cases up to 60 miles away—reaching as far as Newburyport to the north, Worcester to the west, and Providence, Rhode Island to the south. Its 13 lines, shown in purple on MBTA maps, are operated by the T, and all trains depart Boston from either North Station or South Station. (It's possible to connect to commuter rail trains at a few T stations as well, including Back Bay, Porter Square, Forest Hills, and others.) Fares are more expensive than the T, ranging from $1.70 to $7.75 for a single ride; if there is a ticket office at the station you board at, purchase a ticket there to avoid the cash-on-board surcharge of up to $2. There are also monthly passes available, most of which include free subway transfers; check www.mbta.com for rates. The last outbound trains usually depart around midnight. Most commuter rail stations have parking, usually only $2–3, but there are exceptions, especially as you near downtown. A new line serving Weymouth, Cohasset, and Scituate is currently under construction; also note that the Foxborough station is open only during events (concerts and Patriots games) at Gillette Stadium. Contact the MBTA (617-222-3200) for additional commuter rail information.

BY FERRY

If you live along or near the area's expansive coastline, ferry travel can provide a quick and efficient commuting alternative to heavy highway traffic. The MBTA operates year-round commuter ferries between downtown Boston and Charlestown, Hingham, Hull, Quincy, and Logan Airport. In the summer, seasonal ferries run to farther-off ports like Salem and even Provincetown. While commuting via ferry can get dicey during winter cold snaps—when service is sometimes suspended due to ice in the harbor—it thankfully doesn't get *that* cold here too often.

Below are the **MBTA's commuter ferry routes**. With the exception of the Long Wharf–Quincy–Hull ride, you can bring your bike on board at no charge. They all have ample weekday service; ferries out of Long Wharf run on weekends and holidays as well. Monthly passes are available; check www.mbta.com for rates and schedules.

- Long Wharf (near the Aquarium)–Charlestown Navy Yard
- Long Wharf–Fore River Shipyard, Quincy–Pemberton Point, Hull–Logan Airport
- Rowes Wharf (near South Station)–Hewitt's Cove, Hingham Shipyard

The MBTA's **Harbor Express** (617-222-6999, www.harborexpress.com) connects Hull and Quincy with **Logan Airport**; an adult ticket is $12 one way. **Massport** (617-428-2800, www.massport.com) operates an Airport Water Shuttle from Rowes Wharf seven days a week; tickets are sold on board and cost $10 one way or $17 round trip.

City Water Taxi (www.citywatertaxi.com, 617-422-0392) provides boat transport to destinations all over Boston Harbor, including Logan Airport, Long Wharf, Fan Pier (South Station), the Bank of America Pavilion, Lovejoy Wharf (North Station), and many waterfront hotels and restaurants. Water taxis cost $10 per person and run daily from 7 a.m. to 10 p.m., Monday–Saturday, and until 8 p.m. on Sundays. Limited stops in the winter.

Other regional ferry operators, including seasonal or summer-only routes, include:

- **Bay State Cruise Company**, 617-748-1428, www.baystatecruises.com; provides seasonal ferry service to Provincetown from the World Trade Center in Boston. Regular ferry (weekend only) costs $33 round trip; high-speed ferry costs $69 round trip.
- **Boston Harbor Cruises**, 617-227-4321, www.bostonharborcruises.com; runs a high-speed ferry from Boston's Long Wharf to Provincetown ($70 round trip) during the summer.
- **Capt. John Boats**, 508-747-2400 or 800-225-4000, www.provincetownferry.com; express ferry between Plymouth and Provincetown. $36 round trip for adults.

- **Hy-Line Cruises**, 508-778-2600 or 800-492-8082, www.hylinecruises.com; operates passenger ferries to Nantucket and Martha's Vineyard from Hyannis, and between the two islands. Adult rates range from $27 to $59; bicycles $12 extra.
- **Island Queen**, 508-548-4800, www.islandqueen.com, provides passenger-only ferry service between Falmouth and Martha's Vineyard. $15 adult round trip; bikes $6 extra.
- **Salem Ferry**, 978-741-0220, www.salemferry.com; 45-minute ride connects Salem's waterfront to Central Wharf in Boston. May–October, fares range from $6 to $22 round trip.
- **Steamship Authority**, 508-477-8600, www.steamshipauthority.com; runs ferries from Woods Hole in Falmouth to both Oak Bluffs and Vineyard Haven on Martha's Vineyard, from New Bedford to Martha's Vineyard, and from Hyannis to Nantucket. Fares vary; cars permitted.

AMTRAK

Trains are a favored mode of travel for Bostonians heading to New York City or even Washington, D.C. Most **Amtrak** trains depart South Station and stop at Back Bay Station, both of which are in the heart of downtown Boston. Compared to getting to Logan Airport, checking in an hour and a half early, and taking a cab upon arrival from JFK or LaGuardia, the train ride to New York—arriving at Grand Central Station in Midtown—is often a quicker door-to-door option than flying. Amtrak's **Acela Express** line, in particular, is a luxury high-speed train that zips along the Northeast Corridor, connecting Boston to Washington, D.C. by way of Providence, New York City, Philadelphia, Baltimore, and other cities. Acela Express trains travel at speeds up to 150 m.p.h., taking you to New York in three and a half hours, and to D.C. in under seven. Not only are the trains faster, they're nicer too—you can plug in your laptop, spread out at a conference table, or retreat to the quiet car. Of course, you pay for the faster service, but if you've got to make the trip and prefer not to fly, it's a comfortable way to go.

Standard Amtrak trains are also convenient for trips to Connecticut, Rhode Island, Philadelphia, Maryland, Maine, or Canada. You can board **Amtrak** trains at four metro Boston stations: **Back Bay** (145 Dartmouth Street), **South Station** (Atlantic Avenue and Summer Street), **North Station** (135 Causeway Street at Canal Street), or **Route 128** (50 University Avenue in Westwood). South Station is the big central terminus. Contact Amtrak (800-USA-RAIL, www.amtrak.com) for more information.

NATIONAL/REGIONAL BUS SERVICE

The national bus carrier **Greyhound** (800-231-2222, 617-526-1800, www.grey hound.com) services the Boston area, along with its local affiliate **Peter Pan Bus Lines** (800-343-9999, www.peterpanbus.com) and a number of smaller, **regional bus lines** (check the Yellow Pages under "Bus"). Travel is available to pretty much everywhere—there are also regular commuter buses that run daily from Maine, New Hampshire, Western Massachusetts, and Cape Cod. Most buses depart from the Bus Terminal at South Station (700 Atlantic Avenue), though some make stops elsewhere in the city on their way into and out of town.

Greyhound and Peter Pan run buses every hour from South Station to the Port Authority in **New York City**, and they are popular—not only because they are much cheaper than the train or plane, but because they are fast, usually getting to New York in about four hours. **Note**: some Greyhound and Peter Pan buses leave earlier than their scheduled times—yes earlier—seemingly without regard for whether they are full, or if there are passengers that might arrive at the last minute.

If you don't mind no-frills budget travel, the cheapest ride you'll find to the Big Apple is on a "Chinatown bus." Running from Boston's Chinatown neighborhood to the one in New York (and now D.C. as well), these buses gained widespread popularity among students and cost-conscious travelers over the past decade. Buses leave every hour (every half hour on holidays) and usually cost just $15 each way. **Fung Wah** (www.fungwahbus.com, 617-338-1163) is the oldest and best-known operator, though it has been in the news lately for safety violations; **Lucky Star** (www.luckystarbus.com, 617-426-8801) is their main competitor.

BY AIR

As the fish swims, **Logan International Airport** is only two miles from downtown Boston—though, on the day before Thanksgiving, it might as well be two hundred. Still, driving to Logan under normal circumstances has significantly improved in recent years. The opening of the Ted Williams Tunnel lessened the load somewhat on the Callahan and Sumner tunnels, and allowed eastbound Mass Pike traffic to continue uninterrupted directly to the airport. Logan itself is set up like a giant rotary, with departure traffic on one level and arrivals on another, making pick-up and drop-off runs fairly easy.

If you're seeking alternate means of getting to Logan there are plenty of options. For starters, the T's Blue Line goes to Airport Station; however, unlike the El at O'Hare or the Tube at Heathrow, it doesn't run directly to the terminals. Instead, there are free and frequent Massport shuttle buses from the T station to the various terminals—it will add a few minutes to your trip, so plan accordingly. The Silver Line runs a rapid transit bus service between the terminals and South

Station, where you can connect to the Red Line or commuter rail. See below for information on buses and shared shuttle vans to and from Logan.

Taxis to and from Boston run about $20–$30 (plus tolls and tip), and get more expensive farther outside the city; there are cab stands outside each terminal. Another option is a water taxi or ferry, including the **Harbor Express** (www.harborexpress.com, 617-222-6999), **Rowes Wharf Water Transport** (www.roweswharfwatertransport.com, 617-406-8584), and **City Water Taxi** (www.citywatertaxi.com, 617-422-0392). From the airport dock, a free Massport shuttle bus will take you to your terminal. Logan offers an inter-terminal accessible van for persons with disabilities; call 617-561-1769 with questions. For more information and tips on getting to and from the airport, visit www.massport.com/logan or call 800-23-LOGAN.

Logan is one of the 20 busiest airports in the country, and almost every major carrier operates flights in and out. **Teminal A** hosts Delta Airlines and its shuttles; **Terminal B** hosts American Airlines, America West, Air Canada, Alaskan Airlines, Spirit Airlines, and US Airways; and **Terminal C** serves United, JetBlue, Continental, Midwest, Cape Air, and Air Tran. **Teminal E** handles all international arrivals and departures, including a number of daily nonstop flights to Europe; international carriers include Aer Lingus, Air France, Alitalia, British Airways, Iberia, IcelandAir, KLM, Swiss, and Virgin Atlantic, among others.

One notable exception is **Southwest Airlines**, which flies instead to nearby **Manchester Airport** (603-624-6539, www.flymanchester.com) in New Hampshire and **T.F. Green Airport** in Providence, Rhode Island (888-268-7222/401-737-8222, www.tfgreen.com). Both are about an hour away, but offer easier—and much cheaper—parking than Logan, and can sometimes save you money on fares.

PARKING AT LOGAN

Since 9/11, parking in front of airport terminals is prohibited. You may quickly drop off or pick up a passenger, but otherwise you'll need to circle the airport loop or put your car in a lot. **Short-** and **long-term parking** for all terminals is available in the Central Parking Lot, with access to all terminals via a pedestrian bridge on level four. Rates are $2 for the first 30 minutes, $5 for the first hour, and increase incrementally to $22 per day; there is no weekly rate. In addition, Terminals B and E have their own lots with similar rates (up to $24/day); your car is subject to a security search before entering the Terminal B lot. For **long-term parking**, try the Economy Lot: $16/day, $96/week. A free 24-hour shuttle will bring you from this lot to any of the terminals. For all Logan Airport parking facilities, you must take your ticket with you, and pay inside at an Exit Express Parking Pay station before returning to your car. Cash and all major credit cards are accepted.

AIRPORT BUS SERVICE

Two MBTA bus routes, #448 and #459, run to Logan, along with the aforementioned Silver Line. Private bus companies, including Bonanza, Plymouth & Brockton Bus Lines, Concord Trailways, C&J Trailways, and Vermont Transit, also provide service to Logan (see the Yellow Pages under "Bus"). In addition, there are **shared shuttle vans**:

- **Ace American**, 800-517-2281; service to Boston hotels and Waltham/Newton, 9 a.m. to 1 a.m.
- **Easy Transportation**, www.easytransportationinc.com, 617-445-1107/617-869-7760; service to most Boston hotels every 20 minutes, other locations by reservation, 8 a.m. to 2 a.m.
- **Flight Line, Inc.**, www.flightlineinc.com, 800-245-2525/800-942-5044; shared and direct ride services from northern Massachusetts and southern New Hampshire. Also serves Manchester Airport.
- **JC Transportation**, www.jctransportationshuttle.com, 800-517-2281; shuttles pick up at terminals every 15 minutes, 7 a.m. to 2 a.m.
- **Knights Airport Limousine Service**, www.knightsairportlimo.com, 800-822-5456; door-to-door service to metro-west area; also services Manchester Airport and T.F. Green Airport in Providence.
- **Logan Express**, www.massport.com, 800-23-LOGAN; for park-and-ride-type service between Logan and Braintree, Framingham, Peabody, and Woburn.

FLIGHT DELAYS

You can find information on flight delays or track specific flights online through your airline's web site, or at www.massport.com/logan/.

CONSUMER COMPLAINTS—AIRLINES

To register a complaint against an airline, call or write the Department of Transportation: 202-366-2220, Aviation Consumer Protection Division, C-75 Room 4107, 400 7th Street SW, Washington, DC 20590.

BOSTON, A MAJOR TOURIST DESTINATION FOR PEOPLE FROM around the globe, a financial center, and host to dozens of colleges and universities, has an array of temporary lodgings. Options run the gamut from bare-bones hostels to provisional motels to ornate classic New England hotels.

For newcomers who need a temporary place to stay while looking for a permanent home, you may be able to take advantage of the transience of the area's student population. Although there is a glut of colleges and universities, most do not offer housing to non-students during the summer; however, many students live off campus and, as such, need to sublet their year-long leases during the summer months.

If you are going to stay at a hotel (as opposed to taking a short-term rental), keep in mind that room rates vary by the season. In summer, prices rise along with the temperatures, but there is also an increase in the fall during leaf-peeping time. Local conventions, graduations, and other events will also affect room availability and pricing.

The following list of places to stay is just a glimpse of the full bevy of lodgings available in Boston. For a more complete listing, look in the Yellow Pages, pick up an AAA travel guide (free to members), or check with the **Massachusetts Lodging Association**, www.masslodging.com, 617-720-1776.

Once you've found the hotel, motel, inn, or other option that suits your fancy, you've got to decide how you want to reserve your room. Do you want to call and reserve directly or go through a reservation service? If you contact the hotel directly, don't forget to ask about packages and weekend specials. Here are a few reservation services and online travel agents that can assist you with finding a place to stay:

- **Central Reservation Services**, www.reservation-services.com, 800-555-7555
- **Cheap Tickets**, www.cheaptickets.com

- **Direct Hotels Discount**, www.direct-hotels-discount.com/boston, 800-780-5733
- **Expedia**, www.expedia.com
- **Hotels.com**, www.hotels.com
- **Hotel Reservations Network**, www.hoteldiscount.com, 800-715-7666
- **Hotels Cheap**, http://boston.hotelscheap.org, 1-877-HOTELS-2
- **The-hotels.com**, www.boston.the-hotels.com, 800-297-0144
- **Hotwire**, www.hotwire.com
- **Info Hub Specialty Travel Guide**, www.infohub.com
- **LowestFare.com**, www.lowestfare.com
- **Orbitz**, www.orbitz.com
- **Quickbook**, www.quikbook.com, 800-789-9887
- **Tom Parsons' Best Fares**, www.bestfares.com
- **Travelocity**, www.travelocity.com
- **Travelweb**, www.travelweb.com
- **Travel Zoo**, www.travelzoo.com
- **TurboTrip.com**, www.turbotrip.com

Things to consider: when making reservations through any discount site, it is always wise to ask about their cancellation policy. It is also smart to inquire whether the rate quoted includes the hotel tax or not; hotels in Boston charge a 12.45% tax per day, while suburbs charge only the state tax of 5%.

LUXURY HOTELS

The following luxury accommodations begin around $250 and go up (and some *way* up) from there. Rates vary greatly based on availability and season.

- **Boston Harbor Hotel**, 70 Rowes Wharf, Boston, 800-752-7077, www.bhh.com; spa resort with gorgeous views of the harbor and the city.
- **Boston Park Plaza Hotel & Towers**, 64 Arlington St, Boston, 617-426-2000, www.bostonparkplaza.com; often you can find surprisingly good deals at this historic hotel located in the heart of the Back Bay.
- **Charles Hotel**, 1 Bennett St (Harvard Sq), Cambridge, 617-864-1200 or 800-882-1818, www.charleshotel.com
- **Doubletree Hotels & Guest Suites**, 800-222-TREE, www.doubletree.com; three in Boston, one in Cambridge, and one in Waltham.
- **Fairmont Copley Plaza**, 138 St. James Ave, Boston, 800-257-7544, www.fairmont.com
- **Fifteen Beacon**, 15 Beacon St, Boston, 617-670-1500, www.xvbeacon.com
- **Four Seasons Hotel**, 200 Boylston St, 617-338-4400, www.fourseasons.com/boston; prices range from $350 to $775 depending on the suite, view, and season. Ask about weekend specials.
- **Hilton**, 800-774-1500, www.hilton.com; one in the Back Bay, one in the finan-

cial district, and one at Logan Airport. The Logan Airport hotel and the financial district hotel sometimes dip below $200.

- **Jury's Boston Hotel**, 350 Stuart St, Boston, 617-266-7200, www.jurysdoyle. com; Irish hotel chain located in the former Boston Police Headquarters. Rates start at about $190 (off peak) and go up from there.
- **The Lenox Hotel**, 61 Exeter St at Boylston, Boston, 800-225-7676, www.lenox hotel.com; some weekend specials start as low as $199.
- **Nine Zero Hotel**, 90 Tremont St, Boston, 866-906-9090, www.ninezerohotel. com; they offer some decent packages and specials, plus if you drive a hybrid vehicle, you receive $20 off your stay.
- **Omni Parker House**, 60 School St, Boston, 617-227-8600, www.omnihotels. com, is America's longest continuously operating luxury hotel. The Omni Parker offers some amazing deals, including a Red Sox package for $289/night.
- **Royal Sonesta Hotel**, 40 Edwin Lane Blvd, Cambridge, 617-806-4200, www. sonesta.com/Boston; views of the Charles River and the Boston skyline.
- **Taj Boston**, 15 Arlington St, Boston, 617-536-5700, www.tajhotels.com

MIDDLE-RANGE HOTELS

The following hotels range between about $100 and $200 nightly. Many are national chains.

- **Best Western**, 800-780-7234, www.bestwestern.com; three in Boston, one in Cambridge, and 12 in the greater Boston area.
- **Embassy Suites Hotel Boston at Logan Airport**, 207 Porter St, Boston, 617-567-5000, www.embassysuites.com
- **Harborside Inn**, 185 State St, Boston, 617-723-7500, www.harborsideinnbos ton.com
- **Holiday Inn Select Government Center**, 5 Blossom St, Boston, 617-742-7630, www.holiday-inn.com
- **Hyatt Hotels & Resorts**, www.hyatt.com: Hyatt Harborside at Logan Airport, 101 Harborside Dr, 617-568-1234, Hyatt Regency, 575 Memorial Dr, Cambridge, 617-492-1234, and Hyatt Regency Boston, 1 Avenue de Lafayette, Boston, 617-912-1234
- **Inn at Harvard**, 1201 Mass Ave, Cambridge, 617-491-2222, www.theinnathar vard.com; if the Inn is booked, try its less expensive sister, **The Harvard Square Hotel**, 110 Mount Auburn St, Cambridge, 617-864-5200, www.harvardsquare hotel.com
- **Marriott Hotels/Residence Inns**, 888-236-2427, www.marriott.com; eight in Boston (including the Boston Tremont Hotel, a historic hotel), two in Cambridge, one in Brookline, and over 30 in the surrounding suburbs. During the off-peak season these hotels are mid-range, but in the summer their prices better represent those of a luxury hotel.

- **Radisson Hotel Boston**, 200 Stuart St, 617-482-1800, www.radisson.com; six in the greater Boston area. Depending on the date you book, the Radisson Hotel Boston straddles the line between mid-range and luxury hotel.
- **Seaport Hotel & World Trade Center**, 1 Seaport Lane, South Boston, 877-SEA-PORT, www.seaportboston.com
- **Sheraton Hotels & Resorts**, 888-625-5144, www.starwood.com/sheraton; one in Boston (Sheraton Boston), 39 Dalton St, 617-236-2000; one in Cambridge (Sheraton Commander), 16 Garden St, 617-547-4800; and seven in the suburbs.
- **Westin Hotels**, www.starwood.com/westin; Westin Copley Place, 10 Huntington Ave, 617-262-9600; Westin Boston Waterfront, 425 Summer St, 617-532-4600; Westin Waltham–Boston, 70 Third Ave, Waltham, 781-290-5600. The Westin Copley Place tends to be higher priced than the others.

INEXPENSIVE HOTELS

If budget matters more than ambiance, check one of the following; prices range between $60 and $150 per night:

- **Home Suites Inn**, 455 Totten Pond Rd, Waltham, 866-335-6175
- **Best Western Terrace Motor Lodge**, 1650 Comm Ave, Brighton, 617-566-6260; close to both Boston College and Boston University.
- **Choice Hotels**: Sleep Inn, Comfort Inn, Quality Inn, Clarion, Rodeway, MainStay, and Econo Lodge, 800-424-6423, www.choicehotels.com; all of these are located in the surrounding suburbs, except for the **Comfort Inn**, 900 Morrissey Blvd, Boston, 617-287-9200, which is located near the John F. Kennedy Library and Museum.
- **Constitution Inn**, 150 Second Ave, Charlestown Navy Yard, 617-241-8400, www.constitutioninn.com; reduced rates for military personnel and AAA members.
- **Days Inn**, www.daysinn.com, 1800 Soldiers Field Rd, Boston, 617-254-0200; 1234 Soldiers Field Rd, Boston, 617-254-1234; there are many more in the suburbs of Boston as well.
- **Hampton Inn**, 800-HAMPTON, www.hamptoninn.com; 811 Mass Ave, Boston, 617-445-6400; 191 Monsignor O'Brien Hwy, Cambridge, 617-494-5300; and there are eight more in the larger metro area as well.
- **Red Roof Inn**, 800-RED-ROOF, www.redroof.com; five in the greater Boston area.
- **Shawmut Inn**, 280 Friend St, Boston, 617-720-5544, www.shawmutinn.com; located only a short walk from Faneuil Hall, the North End, and Boston's Waterfront.

EXTENDED STAY HOTELS

If your stay will be longer than a week, you may prefer an extended stay option, where the rooms are more like small furnished apartments than traditional hotels—with kitchenettes, refrigerators, and onsite laundry. You can expect to pay as low as $65 and as high as $350 per night. Note: you're most likely to find these in the suburbs, rather than the city.

- **Extended Stay America**, 800-EXT-STAY, www.exstay.com; locations in Braintree, Burlington, Danvers, Marlborough, Peabody, Tewksbury, Waltham, Westborough, and Woburn. Prices are generally under $100 per night.
- **Homewood Suites**, 800-CALL-HOME, www.homewoodsuites.com; locations in Peabody and Billerica. Rates range between $100 and $150 per night.
- **Residence Inn by Marriott**, 800-331-3131, www.residenceinn.com; locations in Boston, Cambridge, and throughout the greater Boston area.

SHORT-TERM LEASES/CORPORATE HOUSING

A short-term lease or corporate apartment might be a good option, depending on your situation. Rates range from about $300 per week for a studio to $1,400 per week for a two-bedroom. There may be a discount if you commit to a month's stay.

- **AAA Corporate Rentals**, 120 Milk St, Boston, 617-357-6900, www.furnished apt.com; studios available. Throughout Boston, including Back Bay, Beacon Hill, North End, Financial District, South End, and the Waterfront.
- **Agency Suites**, 617-536-1302, www.463beacon.com; furnished apartments (studios, one- and two-bedrooms) in the Back Bay, Copley Square, and Kenmore, available to rent weekly or monthly. Prices start at $595 per week. Discounts available for US Government and Military affiliates.
- **Apartment Resources**, 94 Adams St, Waltham, 781-893-1130, www.apart mentresourcesboston.com; studio apartments in Waltham to rent per week or month.
- **Baron Associates**, 229 Berkeley St, Boston, 617-437-0337, www.baron.re.com; furnished rentals, including studios.
- **Commonwealth Court Guest House**, 284 Comm Ave, Boston, 800-424-1230, www.commonwealthcourt.com; located in a Back Bay brownstone.
- **The Copley House**, 239 W Newton St, Boston, 800-331-1318, www.copley house.com; studios and one-bedroom apartments in beautiful townhouses throughout the South End and Back Bay.
- **J. E. Furnished Apartments**, 617-479-4110, http://jefurnishedapartments. com; studios, one-bedroom, and two-bedroom units located in Quincy and Waltham to rent monthly.
- **Oakwood Corporate Housing**, 800-888-0808, www.oakwood.com
- **Short-Term Solutions**, 247 Newbury St, Boston, 617-247-1199, www.short -term.com; luxury short-term furnished apartments.

BED & BREAKFASTS

B&Bs are charming and homey. Of course, they're more popular in the country, but there are some in the city as well. Try checking out www.bedandbreakfast. com/massachusetts.html for a more comprehensive list. Here are a few:

- **Bed & Breakfast Agency of Boston**, 617-720-3540 and 800-248-9262, www. boston-bnbagency.com; furnished apartment suites with locations throughout the city.
- **Charles Street Inn**, 94 Charles St, Boston, 617-314-8900, www.charlesstreet inn.com
- **Encore Bed and Breakfast**, 116 W Newton St, Boston, 617-247-3426, www.en corebandb.com; located in Boston's South End in a 19th-century townhouse.
- **Gryphon House**, 9 Bay State Rd, Boston, 617-375-9003, www.innboston.com; located between the Back Bay and Kenmore Square in a turn-of-the-century brownstone.
- **John Jeffries House**, 14 David G. Mugar Way, Boston, 617-742-0313, www. johnjeffrieshouse.com; near Mass General Hospital at the foot of Beacon Hill, they offer rates ranging from $175 for a deluxe suite in the peak season to $105 for a studio in the off season.
- **La Cappella Suites**, 290 North St, Boston, 617-523-9020, www.lacappella suites.com; located in the North End.
- **Mary Prentiss Inn**, 6 Prentiss St, Cambridge, 617-661-2929, www.maryprentiss inn.com; Greek Revival–style inn situated close to Harvard Square.

HOSTELS/YMCAs

Hostels are *the* low-budget travel lodging of choice among students. They offer no frills—with communal bunk rooms, mandatory out-of-room times, curfew— but you can't beat the price; ditto for residence YMCAs and YWCAs. For more options, go to www.hostels.com, www.ymca.com or www.ywca.org. Here are a few options in the Boston area.

- **Abercrombie's Farrington Inn**, 23 Farrington Ave, Allston, 617-787-1860; prices start at $25 for a dorm room.
- **Boston Backpackers Youth Hostel**, 234 Friend St, Boston, 617-723-0800; located near North Station area. Rates start at $30 per night in a dormitory-style room.
- **Hostelling International Boston**, 12 Hemenway St, Boston, 617-536-9455, www.bostonhostel.org; if you are a member of Hostelling International, you can stay here for $28 to $45 a night for a bed in a dorm room or between $69 and $99 nightly for a private room. Without a membership card, your price goes up by $3. (See below for their summer-only accommodations.)
- **YMCA of Greater Boston**, 316 Huntington Ave, 617-536-7800; a single costs $45 per night without a bath. Men only from September to May.

- **YWCA Boston/Berkeley Residence**, 40 Berkeley St, Boston, 617-375-2524, www.ywcaboston.org; $56 per night for a single; $86 per night for a double; $99 per night for a triple. Breakfast is included.

SUMMER ONLY

In Boston, since many students live in off-campus housing, you can likely find a summer sublet. Check boston.craigslist.org/sub/ for sublet listings. Also, there is one summer-only youth hostel, open from June to August: **Hostelling International Boston at Fenway**, 575 Comm Ave, Boston, 617-267-8599, www.bostonhostel.org/fenway/.

ACCESSIBLE ACCOMODATIONS

Perhaps because of its compact size and good public transit system, Boston is a very disabled-friendly city. Hotels are required to provide handicap-accessible rooms, the sidewalks have ramps, and handicap- parking spaces are found even in the tightest parts of town, kept open by parking meter attendants armed with steep ticket fines.

A number of hotel chains in Boston have a particular reputation for offering services for people with disabilities: **Hilton Hotels** (800-774-1500, TTY 800-368-1133, www.hilton.com), **Hyatt Hotels** (800-532-1496, TTY, 800-228-9548, www.hyatt.com), **Sheraton Hotels** (800-325-3535, TTY, 800-325-1717, www.starwood.com/sheraton), and **Marriott Hotels** (800-228-92920, TTY 800-228-7014, www.marriott.com). Because accommodations can vary from community to community—and from hotel to hotel—you should call ahead and check with the particular hotel you're planning on staying at to discuss your specific needs and their provisions. Federal law requires a hotel to guarantee reservations for handicapped-accessible rooms, but only if it does so for regular rooms. And if you're concerned about your security, you can always ask the hotel to remove the handicap sign from the door, should there be one.

Other good resources with information about accessible accommodations include the **Massachusetts Office on Disability** (617-727-7440, TTY 800-322-2020, www.state.ma.us/mod); **Access Tours** (www.accesstours.org, 800-929-4811), which puts together packages for tours; and **Society for Accessible Travel & Hospitality** (212-447-7284, www.sath.org) offers advice and publishes a magazine for disabled travelers called *Open World*. For more information on services for people with disabilities, check the **Helpful Services** chapter of this book.

ONE OF THE BEST PERKS OF LIVING IN THE CITY IS THE OPPORTUNITY to get *out* of it once in awhile. Bostonians are privileged to have all of New England at their doorstep—its cultural and geographical variety offers retreats for any season. Summer beach days and camping trips give way to fall foliage drives, winter ski weekends, and springtime maple festivals—all within easy reach.

MASSACHUSETTS

- **Salem** is chock full of sights commemorating the Puritans who first settled there and, of course, the infamous witch trials of 1692. It's about 45 minutes north of the city by car, and the commuter rail can get you there in a half hour. Sights and museums include the Witch History Museum, the Salem Maritime National Historic Site (includes Custom and Derby houses), the House of Seven Gables (as in Nathaniel Hawthorne), the New England Pirate Museum, Pioneer Village, and Pickering Wharf. For more information and links to area attractions, visit www.salemweb.com or www.salem.org.

- Also on the north shore is **Cape Ann**, which includes the communities of Gloucester, Rockport, Essex, and Manchester-by-the-Sea. While a trip to Salem is all about history, a trip to Cape Ann is all about the Atlantic. You can drive there in less than an hour, or take the commuter rail to stops in Manchester, Gloucester, and Rockport. Besides the 18 beautiful beaches (Gloucester's Good Harbor and Wingaersheek Beaches, and Manchester's Singing Beach are probably the most popular), things to see include the Cape Ann Historical Museum, lighthouses dating back to 1789, whale watches, and Hammond Castle, a stone replica of a medieval castle. After a day at the beach, many visitors stop by Woodman's of Essex for their famous fried clams. Theater lovers head to the Gloucester Stage Company (founded by Israel Horowitz), and for local art, check out the artists' colony in Rockport or the Rocky Neck colony in

Gloucester. Visit www.capeannvacations.com or www.cape-ann.com for tourist information.

- American history buffs can head northwest of the city to **Lexington** (http://ci.lexington.ma.us or www.libertyride.us), and **Concord** (www.concordnet.org or www.concordma.com). The first battles of the American Revolution were fought in these two towns, and later some of the great New England writers and Transcendentalists made their homes here. Things to see include the Lexington Battle Green, Minuteman Statue, Buckman Tavern, Hancock-Clarke House, Munroe Tavern, National Heritage Museum, George Abbott Smith Museum, Minute Man National Historic Park, Old North Bridge, Ralph Waldo Emerson House, Walden Pond, Old Manse, Orchard House (Home of Louisa May Alcott and her family), Wayside, Thoreau Lyceum, Concord Museum, Fiske House, Hartwell Tavern, Paul Revere Capture Site, and Sleepy Hollow Cemetery.

- **Plymouth** is an easy 40-mile trip south of Boston, down I-93 to Route 3, or by commuter rail. Some things to see and do include visiting Plymouth Rock, the Mayflower II (recreation of the original), and Plimoth Plantation (living history village that recreates the original 1627 pilgrim settlement). Also popular are the Plymouth National Wax Museum, the Mayflower Society Museum, and historic houses like The Spooner House, Hedge House, Sparrow House, and Howland House. See www.visit-plymouth.com for further details.

- Curled like a weightlifter's flexed arm, **Cape Cod** ("the Cape") draws millions of tourists each summer from Boston and beyond—some for a long weekend, others for the entire season. With over 500 miles of unspoiled coastline, the Cape has long been a popular retreat for anyone with the time and money to spend there. Most points on the Cape are at least an hour and a half drive from Boston—Provincetown (or "P-town"), at the very tip, takes about 3 hours—and legendary traffic at the Sagamore and Bourne bridges on virtually every summer weekend will add to that time considerably. Many visitors stay at a B&B for a weekend, or rent a cottage for longer stays—with the high-speed ferry from Boston to Provincetown (2 hours), even a day trip is possible. Between water sports, golf, fresh seafood shacks, homemade ice cream and candy stores, picturesque lighthouses and landscapes, antique shopping on quaint Route 6A, the renowned Cape Cod Baseball League, and a pulsing arts and theater scene in predominantly gay P-town, summer brings something for everyone on the Cape. However, its beaches are still the biggest draw. Generally speaking, the farther out you get, the more pristine the coast; the Cape Cod National Seashore, between Chatham and Provincetown on the Outer Cape, is a protected expanse of dunes, ponds, cranberry bogs, and a 40-mile stretch of sandy beaches. For a full list of beaches, things to do, and places to stay, visit www.capecodchamber.org.

- Often mentioned along with Cape Cod are "the islands"—**Martha's Vineyard** and **Nantucket**, off the southern coast of the Cape. Both islands, with beaches and boats aplenty, rich maritime histories, and shingled saltbox houses covered with gray, sea-weathered wood, embody the picturesque epitome of seaside New England. Of the two, the Vineyard is closer, bigger, and considered more laid back, though both are fairly exclusive. (Another common perception, whether accurate or not, is that Democrats go to the Vineyard, and Republicans to Nantucket; if you remember, the Vineyard was a favorite vacation destination of President Clinton's.) Ranging from bustling harbor villages like Vineyard Haven and Edgartown, to the colorful gingerbread houses of Oak Bluffs, to quiet, remote areas like Aquinnah, the Vineyard is a diverse island. Nantucket, meanwhile, at one third the size of its neighbor, is more blue-blooded and strict in its charm. Once the whaling capital of the world, the town works hard to maintain its irresistible quaintness and natural beauty; building regulations are tightly enforced, making property values here some of the highest in the northeast. Both islands are accessible by ferry from the mainland. There are daily departures to the Vineyard from Woods Hole (car ferry), Falmouth, New Bedford, and Hyannis; the trip takes about 45 minutes. Ferries to Nantucket leave from Hyannis; the passenger-only fast ferry takes an hour, while the car ferry takes about 2 hours. Reservations are recommended in the summer, particularly if you're bringing a car. (You can also take a bike, or rent a Jeep once you get to either island.) For the seasick, time-pinched, or well-to-do, both islands have airports as well, with year-round and seasonal commercial flights. For more information on airline service, as well as ferry schedules, events, activities, and places to stay, check out www.mvy.com or www.mvol.com for Martha's Vineyard, and www.nantucket.net, www.nantucketchamber.org, or www.nantucketonline.com for Nantucket.

- Finally, if you're looking for a more rural, woodsy, quiet place to get away, think about the **Berkshires**. About two hours west of Boston by car (via the Mass Pike, or a little longer but a lot more scenic via Route 2), the Berkshires are a gentle range of low mountains through the western part of the state, near the New York border. Amid the hills and forests that dominate the region lie some of the state's proudest colleges—Williams, Smith, Amherst, the University of Massachusetts, and Mt. Holyoke. And although this part of the state is distinctly un-touristy, Berkshire activities center on the arts and the outdoors—skiing, hiking, boating, fishing, and camping. Other attractions are the Massachusetts Museum of Contemporary Art (Mass MoCA), Clark Art Institute, Williamstown Theatre Festival, Tanglewood (summer home of the Boston Symphony Orchestra), Shakespeare & Co. (summer Shakespeare theater), Jacob's Pillow Dance Festival, Berkshire Theater Festival, Norman Rockwell Museum, Hancock Shaker Village, Berkshire Museum, the Appalachian Trail, the Mohawk Trail, Mount Greylock, Williams College Museum of Art, Arrowhead (Herman Melville's home), Berkshire Botanical Garden, and Bash Bish Falls.

For more information on what to do close to home, try the **Greenspace and Beaches** chapter, as well as the **Massachusetts Office of Travel and Tourism** (617-973-8500 or 800-227-MASS, www.massvacation.com).

NEW HAMPSHIRE

Anyway you slice it—up I-95, I-93, or Route 3—southern New Hampshire is less than an hour away from Boston. Yet, while New Hampshire is geographically close, it can feel very different. By and large, where eastern Massachusetts is densely settled and urban, New Hampshire is sparse and rural; where Massachusetts is firmly liberal and Democratic, New Hampshire is more conservative and Republican; where Massachusetts has been called "Taxachusetts," New Hampshire is virtually tax-free…you get the idea. Whether you want to hit the ski slopes for the weekend, go antiquing in the country, or spend summers on a lake, New Hampshire is worth exploring.

- The **White Mountains**, just over 2 hours north of Boston on I-93, provide great year-round opportunities for outdoor adventure—hiking, skiing, and camping—and are more rugged than any you'll find in Massachusetts. Franconia Notch and Mounts Monadnock and Washington are local hiking favorites (beware of Mt. Washington's proclivity for harsh weather during the off-season). Ski resorts (and their frontier-chic towns like Lincoln and North Conway) pepper the entire region; check out www.skinh.com for tourist information.
- At the southeast tip of the state is **Hampton Beach** (www.hamptonbeach. org). With its loud strip of stores and boardwalk amusements, it seems the antithesis of the rest of New Hampshire. However, if you want that Coney Island feel, it is only about an hour by car from Boston.
- Farther north and inland is the Lakes Region, anchored by **Lake Winnipesaukee** (www.winnipesaukee.com), the largest body of water in New Hampshire at 182 miles around. While Weirs Beach plays host to some honky-tonk and boardwalk arcades—not to mention Motorcycle Week, which attracts a deluge of enthusiasts from all over the country each June—most of the area is more subdued and geared toward relaxation. Boating, swimming, sailing, fishing, golf, water parks, and hiking opportunities abound. Many Bostonians take advantage of this retreat's proximity (2 hours by car up I-93), and relative affordability compared to the Cape, to buy summer homes here.
- Elsewhere in New Hampshire you'll find storybook New England towns and cities, like Portsmouth, Concord, and Hanover. **Portsmouth** (www.portsmouthnh.com) is the hub of New Hampshire's abbreviated Atlantic seacoast, and sits just across the Piscataqua River from Maine. Along with neighboring Exeter, Portsmouth is a quaint and cute relic of colonial New England, and its brick sidewalks are lined with cozy coffeehouses, shops, and restaurants frequented by students from the nearby University of New Hampshire. At the center of the state (up I-93) is its capital, **Concord** (www.ci.concord.nh.us), home to most of New Hampshire's historical sites and museums. About two and a half hours northwest of Boston (up I-89 from Concord), at the border of Vermont, is postcard-pretty **Hanover** (www.hanovernh.org), better known as the home of Dartmouth College.

For more, contact the **New Hampshire Division of Travel and Tourism Development** (800-FUN-IN-NH, www.visitnh.gov).

VERMONT

While Massachusetts consistently leans left, and New Hampshire to the political right, Vermont does its own thing. One of only a few states that began as an independent republic, Vermont values civil liberties and individual freedoms—it was the first state to officially abolish slavery in its constitution, the first to sanction same-sex civil unions, and the very last to allow a Wal-Mart.

With a statewide population on par with that of Boston proper, Vermont is a rural, lovely composite of rolling hills and mountains, dairy farms, white clapboard inns, and country stores. Big industry has largely bypassed the state, and tourism remains its chief moneymaker. In winter, the **Green Mountains** flood with skiers from hundreds of miles around, and summer brings visitors back for horseback riding, mountain biking, alpine slides, and hiking. However, Vermont's breathtaking fall foliage (courtesy of its syrup-producing sugar maples) makes autumn high season—countryside B&Bs fill up well in advance.

While southern Vermont is a 2-hour drive from Boston, many parts are quite farther—its biggest city, **Burlington,** is about three and a half hours away. A delightful little city on Lake Champlain, Burlington's downtown buzzes with music, markets, and more, fueled by students from the University of Vermont, St. Michael's College, and other local schools.

A few other places to visit in Vermont include: **Bennington**, **Barre** (pronounced "Barry"), **Manchester** (big with shoppers and the après ski crowd), **Middlebury**, **Montpelier** (Vermont's capital, for the State House and Vermont Museum), **Waterbury** (for the Ben & Jerry's Ice Cream Factory), **Plymouth Notch**, **St. Johnsbury**, **Woodstock** (for the Vermont Raptor Center and a 165-foot chasm four miles east of town called Queechee Gorge), and the **Northeast Kingdom** (the northernmost part of the state). Check out the **Sports & Recreation** chapter or www.skivermont.com for skiing information; go to www.travel-vermont.com for general tourism resources.

MAINE

Once upon a time, Maine, the land of moose and lobster, was actually part of Massachusetts. Not until 1820 did it become a state in its own right. By far the largest New England state, it's bigger than all the rest combined, though its population doesn't keep up—due in no small part to the cold and inclement winter weather.

While northern Maine is sparsely populated—areas near the Canadian border are as close as you'll come to No Man's Land in New England—southern Maine's long, scenic coast, large Sebago Lake, densely wooded forests, and less crowded ski resorts offer plenty of vacation spots for Bostonians.

- Maine's capital is **Augusta**, but there is much more to see and do in the far bigger **Portland** (www.portlandmaine.com). A laid-back coastal town, with all the sea air, coffeeshops, and 19th-century red brick streets of a very small Seattle, Portland is about two hours from Boston via I-95.
- About 30 minutes north of Portland is **Freeport** (www.freeportusa.com), an aesthetically pleasing center of commercial chain store outlets, including the L.L. Bean flagship store, which is open 24 hours a day, 7 days a week, 365 days a year. Many families make an annual pilgrimage to Freeport to outfit everyone for the year. There are also factory outlets just over the New Hampshire border in **Kittery** (www.thekitteryoutlets.com).
- While Maine isn't as readily associated with ski vacations, and its mountains tend to be a farther drive than those in New Hampshire and Vermont, it also means less traffic to—and on—the slopes. The two most popular resorts are **Sunday River** and **Sugarloaf/USA**; check www.skimaine.com for more details.
- Other spots to check out include the beautiful, sprawling **Acadia National Park** near **Bar Harbor** (great for camping), **Sebago Lake, Kennebunkport, Old Orchard Beach** (boardwalk-style beach town), **York, Bangor, Bath**, and college towns like **Waterville** and **Lewiston**, to name a few. For more, call the **Maine Office of Tourism** (207-287-5711, www.visitmaine.com).

RHODE ISLAND

The smallest state in the country, Rhode Island—or "The Ocean State," as it's known—nonetheless has plenty to offer visitors within its humble borders.

- The state capital of **Providence** (www.providenceri.com) is about an hour south of Boston, via I-95 or the commuter rail. It's a small but active city; prominent institutions of higher education, like Brown University and the Rhode Island School of Design, ensure that the coffee shops and bars on Thayer Street are always busy. And if Boston's North End doesn't live up to your expectations, try the pasta and pastries in Federal Hill—the largest Italian neighborhood in New England. Other attractions include the RISD (pronounced "Riz-Dee") Museum of Art, the Tony award–winning Trinity Repertory Theater Company, WaterFire (when bonfires blaze atop the surfaces of downtown's rivers), Benefit Street, Providence Preservation Society, Old State House, Athenaeum, First Baptist Church, John Brown House, Haffenreffer Museum of Anthropology, Heritage Harbor Museum, and Roger Williams Park.
- In the days of the Rockefellers and Vanderbilts, **Newport** (www.gonewport. com) was the summer playground for the rich and richer. No expense was spared in the building of palatial summer homes. Today, summer brings Bostonians of every ilk to Newport (about 30 miles south of Providence by car, or an hour and a half from Boston). Some take advantage of the beach and waterfront bar scene (summer shares of rental houses are big with the post-

college crowd); others come for the historic sites or the 3.5-mile Cliff Walk that meanders along the mansions of the city's gilded age; still others flock to the annual **Newport Folk Festival**, where singers of no small reputation set up camp for a few days, and the **Newport Jazz Festival**, the "grandfather of all jazz festivals," whose three-day bill is filled, yearly, with genre legends and rising stars. Other things to see include Trinity Church, Touro Park, Touro Synagogue, Hunter House, Wanton-Lyman-Hazard House, the Museum of Newport History, the Doll Museum, the Tennis Hall of Fame, and the mansions: Hammersmith Farm (Jackie O's childhood summer home), Kingscote, the Elms, Chateau-sur-Mer, the Breakers, Rosecliff, Beechwood Mansion, Marble House, and Belcourt Castle.

- Finally, **Block Island** is like Nantucket's subtler, smaller, quieter little sister. It's a good place to go to catch some sun and sand along with peace and quiet. Ferry service will take you there in the summer from Point Judith, RI.

For more information, check out the official **Rhode Island tourism** site, www.visitrhodeisland.com.

CONNECTICUT

Instead of going to New Hampshire, Maine, or Rhode Island, some Bostonians are willing to drive a little further to Connecticut's long coastline; summer homes and cottages are popular in many of its small towns along the Atlantic. The northern half of the state—before you reach what are essentially suburbs of New York City—is quiet, rural countryside, similar to western Massachusetts, and dotted with quaint New England small towns and farms.

- These days, the biggest tourist draws are the casinos: **Foxwoods** (www.foxwoods.com) is run by Native Americans from the Mashantucket Pequot tribe, and **Mohegan Sun** (www.mohegansun.com) is run by Mohegans. Both are about an hour and a half drive from Boston down I-95 or I-395 (via the Mass Pike).
- Other places to visit in Connecticut include **New Haven** (for Yale University and its museums and theaters), **New London**, **Norwalk**, **Mystic** (seaport and aquarium), and **Hartford** (Harriet Beecher Stowe House, Mark Twain House, Wadsworth Athenaeum, and Old State House).

For more information on things to do and see in Connecticut, contact the **Connecticut Tourism Office** at 888-CTvisit, or go to www.CTvisit.com.

NATIONAL PARKS

In Massachusetts alone, there are 17 parks, sites, and trails run by the National Park Service, including the Appalachian Trail, which runs through part of every New England state except Rhode Island. Some national park areas, such as the Cape Cod National Seashore and the Boston Harbor Islands, are preserved natural environs. Others, like the Adams National Historic Park and the JFK National Historic Site, are historic in nature. In Maine there are St. Croix Island on the northern coast (207-288-3338), Roosevelt Campobello International Park in Lubec (506-752-2922), and the biggie, Acadia National Park in Bar Harbor (207-288-3338). New Hampshire has the Saint Gaudens National Historic Site in Cornish along the border with Vermont (603-675-2175), and in Vermont there is the Marsh-Billings-Rockefeller National Historic Park in Woodstock (802-457-3368). Connecticut offers the Quinebaug and Shetucket Rivers Valley in Putnam (860-963-7226), and Weir Farm in the southwest corner of the state (203-834-1896). In Rhode Island, the National Park Service runs three sites: Blackstone River Valley in northern Rhode Island (401-762-0250), Roger Williams National Memorial in Providence (401-521-7266), and Touro Synagogue in Newport (401-847-4794).

If you would like more information or would like to make camping reservations, contact the **National Park Service** at 800-365-2267, www.nps.gov.

NATIONAL FORESTS

If you enjoy camping in a National Forest, there are plenty of options. In the White Mountains of Maine, you can camp at the Basin Campground and Cold River, both 15 miles north of Fryeburg, or Hastings Campground off Route 113 just south of Gilead. Offerings in the White Mountains of New Hampshire include Barnes Field Campground and Dolly Copp Big Meadow, both just miles south of Gorham. Other options include the Campton Campground (exit 28 of I-93); Covered Bridge is six miles west of Conway; Osceola Vista Campground and Waterville Campground are both near Waterville Valley; Sugarloaf Campground is just east of Twin Mountain in the central part of the state; and White Ledge Campground is in Albany near Conway. In Vermont there is Winhall Brook at Ball Mountain Lake in Jamaica (802-824-4570), or Hapgood Pond just east of Manchester in the Green Mountains (802-824-6456). Indian Hollow at Knightville Dam in the Berkshires (413-667-3430) is the only National Forest in Massachusetts, and Connecticut's only one is West Thompson Lake in North Grosvenordale (860-923-2982). There are none in Rhode Island. For more information, contact the **National Forest Service** at 877-444-6777 or visit www.recreation.gov.

The Appalachian Mountain Club also runs a number of seasonal and year-round mountain lodges, cabins, backcountry shelters, and full-service camps in the Berkshires and White Mountains; call 617-523-0655 or visit www.outdoors. org for rates and locations.

A BOSTON YEAR

TO GET A HANDLE ON WHAT'S HAPPENING IN AND AROUND Boston, you'll want to check the ***Boston Globe's*** daily "Sidekick" or weekly "Calendar" section, ***The Phoenix***, ***The Weekly Dig***, or the ***Improper Bostonian***. Other options are the **Greater Boston Convention & Visitors Bureau** (888-SEE-BOSTON or www.bostonusa.com) and the **Mayor's Office of Arts, Tourism and Special Events** (617-635-3911 or www.cityofboston.gov/arts/). In the meantime, here are some annual events:

JANUARY

- **Chinese New Year**; festivities take place for three weeks (can go into February), held in Chinatown. Includes dragon dancing and fireworks. Call 888-733-2678 for information.
- **Boston Celtic Music Festival**; a 3-day, all-ages event celebrating local Celtic music and dance. Held at various venues in the Boston area; check www.yellowcarmusic.com/bcmfest/ for details.
- **Martin Luther King Jr**. **Birthday Celebration**; various events held on the third Monday in January.

FEBRUARY

- **Beanpot Hockey Tournament**; the hockey teams of Harvard, Northeastern, BU, and BC face off at the TD Banknorth Garden. This is a big deal and sells out early! Go to www.beanpothockey.com for tickets and information.
- **Black History Month**; events and lectures around town, as well as special tours and programs on the Black Heritage Trail.

- **Boston Wine Expo**; largest consumer wine event in the country, held at the Seaport World Trade Center. Call 877-946-3976 or visit www.wine-expos.com/boston/ for details.
- **New England Boat Show**; largest boat show in the Northeast, with over 600 sail and motorboats. Held at the Boston Convention and Exhibition Center; see www.naexpo.com/boatshow/.

MARCH

- **Evacuation Day**; celebrated only in Suffolk County on March 17th, commemorating the day in 1776 when the British redcoats ended their occupation of Boston.
- **New England Spring Flower Show**; five acres of landscaped gardens, flower arrangements, and horticultural displays at the Bayside Expo Center. Hosted by the Massachusetts Horticultural Society. For more information, visit www.masshort.org.
- **Reenactment of the Boston Massacre**; historical reenactors haul out their muskets and colonial garb and gather at the Old State House to act out the Boston Massacre. Run by the Bostonian Society; www.bostonhistory.org or 617-720-1713.
- **St. Patrick's Day Parade**; the weekend of St. Patrick's Day brings one of the largest parades in the country to South Boston. No dyeing the river green here, but you will see floats, bands, veterans, and of course, overflowing pubs. For more information, visit www.saintpatricksdayparade.com/boston/.

APRIL

- **Boston Marathon**; the world's oldest annual marathon and one of the biggest running events in the country, held on the third Monday in April—a local holiday known as Patriots' Day. Over a million spectators line the course all the way from Hopkinton to the finish line in the Back Bay. Visit www.bostonmarathon.org or call 617-236-1652 for more information.
- **Independent Film Festival of Boston**; growing indie film festival that spotlights a mix of features, documentaries, and shorts made outside of the Hollywood studio system. Held at the end of April; visit www.iffboston.org for schedule and tickets.
- **Lantern Hanging**; on the Sunday before April 19th, two lanterns are hung in the steeple of the Old North Church to commemorate Paul Revere's ride. Call 617-523-6676 for more information.
- **Patriots' Day Parade/Reenactment**; each Patriots' Day, Paul Revere rides again, and a full-scale reenactment takes place on Lexington Green.
- **Swan Boats** come out of winter storage at the Boston Public Garden, www.swanboats.com.

- **WBCN Rock n' Roll Rumble**; as prestigious as battle of the bands can get at this point. This event has pitted Boston's best bands against each other in nightclubs throughout the city since 1979.

MAY

- **Armenian Fair**; cultural foods and wares, held annually in Watertown. Call 617-923-0498.
- **Figawi Race**; sailboat race between Cape Cod and Nantucket over Memorial Day weekend; go to www.figawi.net.
- **Harpoon Brewstock** is an indoor/outdoor beer festival at the Harpoon Brewery in South Boston. Call 617-574-9551 or visit www.harpoonbrewery.com for more information.
- **Lilac Sunday**; the third Sunday in May, visit the 400+ varieties of lilacs in bloom at the Arnold Arboretum in Jamaica Plain. For more information, visit www.arboretum.harvard.edu.
- **Make Way for Ducklings Parade**; on Mother's Day, parents and kids dress up like the book characters and parade around Beacon Hill.
- **New England Celebrates Israel**; festival of Israeli music, dancing, sports, shopping, crafts, jewelry, and food. Call 617-457-8788 or visit www.celebrateisrael.org for details.
- **Spring Planting Moon**; three-day Native American pow-wow at the fairgrounds in Marshfield or (sometimes) Topsfield, marking the beginning of the planting season. Thrown by the Massachusetts Center for Native American Awareness, 617-884-4227 or www.mcnaa.org.
- **Somerville Open Studios**; over 300 artists open their doors to the public in this weekend-long event; see www.somervilleopenstudios.com for details.
- **South End Open Market** opens for summer. The Manhattan-style outdoor marketplace happens every Sunday through October, excluding holiday weekends.
- **Street Performers Festival** in Faneuil Hall Marketplace.
- **Wake Up the Earth Festival**; community festival held at the Southwest Corridor Park in Jamaica Plain, adjacent to the Stonybrook T stop. Go to www.spontaneouscelebrations.org for performance schedules and information.
- **Walk for Hunger**; each year over 40,000 people participate in the oldest continual pledge walk in the US, raising over $3 million while walking the scenic 20-mile route through the city. Visit www.projectbread.org for more info.

JUNE

- **African Festival**; food, music, dance, and wares from the African continent; held in Lowell. Visit www.africanfestivallowell.org for information.
- **AIDS Walk/Run**; on the Esplanade. Call 617-424-WALK or go to www.aac.org for more details.
- **Annual American Indian Pow-wow**; held in Canton, sponsored by the Order for the Preservation of Indian Culture. Features music, drumming, and food.
- **Bloomsday Celebration**; local James Joyce enthusiasts meet under the Old Elm Tree in the public garden to read from *Ulysses*; call 617-635-4505. Arts & Society (www.artsandsociety.org) holds a Bloomsday celebration on Martha's Vineyard, featuring Irish folk music, drama, and storytelling.
- **Boston International Film Festival**; visit www.bifilmfestival.com for schedule and information.
- **Bunker Hill Day**; third weekend in June, a reenactment of the Battle of Bunker Hill and a parade in Charlestown.
- **Cambridge River Festival**; mile-long arts festival along the Charles featuring music, food, family entertainment, and art installations. See www.cambridgeartscouncil.org.
- **Grecian Festivals** at St. Athanasius the Great in Arlington, 781-646-0705, Annunciation of the Virgin Mary in Woburn, 781-935-2424, Taxiarchae-Archangels Greek Orthodox Church in Watertown, 617-924-8182, and St. Constantine and Helen in Cambridge, 617-876-3601.
- **Jacob's Pillow Dance Festival**; summer-long dance festival held in western Massachusetts; see www.jacobspillow.org.
- **Jimmy Fund Scooper Bowl**; eat ice cream for charity—your entrance fee gets you all the ice cream you can eat and the proceeds go to the Jimmy Fund, to support research and care for children and adults at the Dana-Farber Cancer Institute. Held at City Hall Plaza; call 800-52-JIMMY or visit www.jimmyfund.org for more info.
- **Lesbian & Gay Pride Festival**; usually coincides with the AIDS walk, during the first week of June. Closes with a parade in the South End and a carnival; information available at 617-262-9405 or www.bostonpride.org.
- **Massachusetts Special Olympics Summer Games**; the largest statewide athletic competition for people with intellectual disabilities. Go to www.specialolympicsma.org for more information.
- **Nantucket Film Festival**; this growing entertainment industry event typically brings Hollywood brass to the island, screening independent, studio-produced, and foreign films with an emphasis on screenwriting and storytelling. Call 212-708-1278 or see www.nantucketfilmfestival.org for info.
- **Polish Festival**; traditional music, food, and mass, held in New Bedford. Call 508-992-9378 for information.
- **Saint Peter's Fiesta**; parades, prayers, midnight procession, fireworks, food,

rowing races, and more in Gloucester. Attracts an annual attendance of over 100,000; call 978-283-1601 or visit www.stpetersfiesta.org.

- **Sommerfest**; the Schul-Verein throws a German summer festival in the woods of Walpole, featuring beer, music, and wurst, Bavarian style. Call 508-660-2018 or go to www.germanclub.org for details.
- **Tanglewood Music Center**; summer home of the BSO in Lenox, MA; 888-266-1200, www.bso.org.
- **Two Sisters Pow-wow**; held in Lowell, with drummers, singers, dancing, storytelling, crafts, and food. Call 978-459-7214 for information.
- **Williamstown Theatre Festival**; beginning in June, this summer-long celebration of theatre in the Berkshires includes workshops, readings, and free performances. Call 413-597-3400 or visit www.wtfestival.org for schedule and information.

JULY

- **Bastille Day**; upscale block party hosted by the French Library and Cultural Center in the Back Bay, celebrated with French food, wine, music, and dancing. For information call 617-914-0400 or visit www.frenchlibrary.org.
- **Boston Pops Concert & Fireworks**; the city celebrates the Fourth of July on the Esplanade with a concert in the Hatch Shell by the Boston Pops, culminating in a fireworks display over the Charles River. Visit www.july4th.org for information.
- **Cambridge Summer Music Festival**; city's largest annual classical music festival; details at www.cambridgesummermusic.com.
- **Cape Verdean Independence Day Festival**; at City Hall Plaza, put on by the Cape Verdean Task Force, 617-442-6644.
- **Festival Betances** is a Puerto Rican celebration that attracts 10,000 people to the South End for a parade, music, dance, food, and local crafts.
- **Glasgow Lands Scottish Festival**; clan dinner, bagpipes, haggis, wool spinning, pony rides, duck herding, etc., held in Northampton; go to www.glasgowlands.org.
- **Harborfest**; seven-day long Fourth of July festival, including concerts and the **Chowderfest** at City Hall Plaza. Call 617-227-1528 or visit www.bostonharborfest.com.
- **Italia Unita Festival**; Italian food, music, dancing, and carnival in East Boston; see www.italiaunita.org.
- **Lantern Floating Festival**; traditional Buddhist memorial ceremony includes drumming, dance, and choral music. Visit www.foresthillstrust.org for details.
- **Lowell Folk Festival**; celebrates the music, dance, storytelling, food, and crafts of the ethnic immigrants who came to Lowell for factory work. Three days of free performances on six stages, held the fourth weekend of the month. Visit

www.lowellfolkfestival.org for more info.

- **North End Festivals**; the feast days of Catholic saints are celebrated in the North End with parades, food, music, games, and traditional ceremonies on many weekends throughout July and August. Saint Anthony's Feast, held in late August, is the largest Italian religious festival in New England; see www. stanthonysfeast.com.

- **Puerto Rican Festival**; held in Franklin Park, with a parade, bands, dancing and carnival rides; call 866-481-0695 or visit www.prfestma.org for details.

- **USS *Constitution***; the USS *Constitution* takes an annual spin around Boston Harbor on the Fourth of July, firing a 21-gun salute. Call 617-426-1812 or visit www.ussconstitutionmuseum.org.

AUGUST

- **August Moon Festivals**, in Chinatown and Quincy, celebrate the toppling of the Yuan Dynasty in A.D. 1368. Highlighted by traditional Asian food, including mooncakes with messages hidden inside.

- **Boston Antique & Classic Boat Festival**; show of vintage vessels and a blessing of the fleet. Held at Hawthorne Cove Marina in Salem Harbor, 617-666-8530, www.by-the-sea.com/bacbfestival/.

- **Boston Chinatown Festival**; food, wares, martial arts displays, and other entertainment.

- **Caribbean Carnival**, held the weekend before Labor Day at various venues. Celebrates Caribbean culture with traditional food, arts, crafts, parade, and dance; go to www.bostoncarnivalvillage.com.

- **Dominican Independence Celebration**; in Roxbury, with food, parades, floats, and dancing.

- **Feast of the Three Saints**; Italian *festa* in Lawrence celebrating saints Alfo, Filadelfo, and Cirino. Call 978-681-0944 or visit www.threesaintsinc.org.

- **Gloucester Waterfront Festival**; pancake breakfast, lobster bake, whale watches, music, nautical crafts, etc., during mid-August in Gloucester.

- **India Day**; traditional dancing, music, and food on the Esplanade. Call 617-626-4970 for info.

- **Irish Connections Festival** in Canton; one of the largest Irish cultural festivals on the East Coast, featuring three days of Irish music, step dancing, drama, sports, crafts, vendors, an author's tent, and children's events. Organized by the Irish Cultural Center: 888-GO-IRISH or www.irishculture.org.

- **Latin American Festival**; 35,000 come to enjoy food, drink, dancing, music, and goods from all over South America, held on Worcester Common in Worcester. Call 508-798-1900.

- **Provincetown Carnival Week**; GLBT Mardi Gras event held the third week of August; visit www.ptown.org/happenings/carnival for a schedule.

- **Restaurant Week**; over a hundred gourmet (and otherwise difficult-to-afford) restaurants in the area offer reduced-price three-course, prix fixe meals for lunch and dinner; Monday–Friday, reserve early. See www.restaurantweek boston.com for details.
- **Rhythm & Roots Festival**; three-day Cajun/Creole festival held annually in Charlestown, RI. Visit www.rhythmandroots.com or call 888-855-6940 for information.
- **Roxbury Film Festival**; showcasing films celebrating people of color; go to www.roxburyfilmfestival.org.
- **Southeast Asian Water Festival**; third Saturday in August at the Lowell Heritage State Park. Celebrates Cambodian, Laotian, and Vietnamese cultural events with foods and painted boat races; see www.lowellwaterfestival.org for details.
- **Taste of Boston**; gastronomical festival attracting over 100,000 attendees to benefit the Greater Boston Food Bank; call 617-779-3496.

SEPTEMBER

- **Art Newbury Street**; sidewalk art, food, and music with exhibitions by the local galleries. Held during the end of September.
- **Boston Blues Festival at the Hatch Shell**; visit www.bluestrust.com for details.
- **Boston Film Festival**; long-running local film festival held the second week in September; visit www.bostonfilmfestival.org or call 617-523-8388 for information and schedule.
- **Brazil Independence Festival**; over 3,000 people turn out for the food-filled salsa party on Magazine Beach in Cambridge.
- **Eastern European Festival**; polka, eat pirogi, and listen to accordion music with Latvians, Poles, Czechs, and Lithuanians in Deerfield. Call 413-774-7476 for more information.
- **Harwich Cranberry Festival**; kid-friendly festival with fireworks, family picnic on the beach, parade, county jamboree, and a cranberry bog in full bloom. Held in mid-September; call 508-430-2811 or go to www.harwichcranberry festival.org.
- **Italian Festival of Saints Cosmas and Damian**; night carnival, healing service, and mass in East Cambridge. Call 617-661-1164 or visit www.cosmas-and -damian.com.
- **King Richard's Faire**, the local Renaissance Festival opens each Labor Day and goes through October. Held in Carver, MA; for information call 508-866-5391 or see www.kingrichardsfaire.net.
- **Open Studios**; Boston artists invite the public into their workspaces for the largest Open Studios event in the country. Events occur on most weekends

from mid-September through early December, rotating by neighborhood; visit www.bostonopenstudios.org for more information.

OCTOBER

- **Boston Fashion Week**; area fashion designers put on fashion shows, parties, and panel discussions during the second week of the month; see www.bostonfashion.com.
- **Columbus Day**; parade and the day off, the second Monday in October.
- **Harvard Square Oktoberfest**; traditional Bavarian Oktoberfest with food, music, art, and beer in Harvard Square; go to www.harvardsquare.com/events/oktoberfest/.
- **Head of the Charles Regatta**; the world's largest two-day rowing event takes place on the Charles River on the 2nd weekend in October, and draws up to 300,000 people each year. Food vendors and live music stages line the river on the Cambridge side; visit www.hocr.org for full details.
- **Pumpkin Festival**; family-friendly event on Boston Common includes pumpkin carving and a record-holding Jack-O-Lantern lighting ceremony. See www.lifeisgood.com/festivals/pumpkin-festival for information.
- **Salem's Haunted Happenings**; the famously occult city of Salem celebrates Halloween for two weeks with a parade, haunted house tours, magic shows, and psychics' fair. Details at www.hauntedhappenings.org.
- **Spooky World**; Halloween theme park at Gillette Stadium: 978-838-0200, www.spookyworld.com.
- **Tufts 10K Race for Women**; popular annual charity running event. Call 888-767-RACE or go to www.tufts-health.com/tufts10k/.

NOVEMBER

- **Thanksgiving at Old Sturbridge Village**; recreation of early Thanksgivings in this colonial living history village; see www.osv.org.
- **Veterans Day parades and memorial services**; various locations throughout Boston.

DECEMBER

- **Bazaar Bizarre**; unique holiday craft fair offering one-of-a-kind handcrafted wares from local independent artists; see http://www.bazaarbizarre.org/boston.html for information.
- **Christmas Tree Lightings**; at the Prudential Center and at Boston Common on the first weekend in December.
- **Cultural Survival Bazaar**; fair trade holiday market featuring crafts, rugs,

clothing and countless other indigenous wares and cuisine; visit www.cs.org or call 617-441-5400 for information.

- **First Night**; Boston's New Year's Eve celebration includes performances throughout the city, ice sculptures, and a fireworks show. See www.firstnight. org for full details.

- **Holiday Art Sales**; student and professional art sales offer an inspired respite from mall shopping; at Mass Art (www.massart.edu), School of the Museum of Fine Arts (www.smfa.edu), and Fort Point Arts Community (www.fortpoint arts.org).

- **Reenactment of the Boston Tea Party**; on December 13th or the nearest Sunday, actors reenact the Boston Tea Party, beginning at the Old South Meeting House and then parading down to the waterfront.

F ROM EMERSON TO PLATH TO KEROUAC, MASSACHUSETTS HAS been home to more than its fair share of famous writers. Being an academic mecca of sorts, many writers have once, if even for a short time, lived or studied in Boston; in turn, its campuses and neighborhoods have been featured as the backdrop for numerous novels.

Below is an abbreviated list of the writings by native sons and daughters, books about Massachusetts's history, as well as architectural books, local guides, and children's titles.

You should be able to find most of these books in your local library or bookstore (see **Literary Life** in the **Cultural Life** chapter for a list of libraries and bookstores):

BOSTON—ARTS AND ARCHITECTURE

- *AIA Guide to Boston* by Susan and Michael Southworth (Globe Pequot Press)
- *Boston Boy: Growing up with Jazz and Other Rebellious Passions* by Nat Hentoff (Alfred A. Knopf); about Boston's jazz scene.
- *A Guide to Public Art in Greater Boston, from Newburyport to Plymouth* by Marty Carlock (Harvard Common Press)
- *The Fading Smile: Poets in Boston from Robert Lowell to Sylvia* Plath by Peter Davison (W.W. Norton & Company)
- *The Life of Emily Dickinson* by Richard B. Sewall (Harvard University Press)
- *Literary New England: A History and Guide* by William Corbett (Faber and Faber)
- *The Literary Trail of Greater Boston* by Susan Wilson and the Boston History Collaborative (Houghton Mifflin)
- *Lost Boston* by Jane Holtz Kay (Mariner Books); history of Boston through architecture, which is being lost to time.

CHILDREN'S PICTURE BOOKS

- *Journey Around Boston From A to Z* by Martha Zschock (Commonwealth Editions)
- *Lost!* By David McPhail (Little Brown); the story of a bear who finds himself lost in the big city (Boston).
- *Make Way for Ducklings* by Robert McCloskey (Viking Press); this children's classic takes place in Boston. Fans will be excited to see the duckling statues in the Public Garden and attend the parade on Mother's Day in Beacon Hill.
- *Sleds on Boston Common: A Story from the American Revolution* by Louise Borden (Margaret K. McElderry)
- *The Town That Got Out of Town* by Robert Priest (David R. Godine); when all the people of Boston leave town for Labor Day weekend, the city's buildings and infrastructure decide to go on a vacation of their own to visit their old friend Portland, Maine.
- *We're Off to Harvard Square* by Sage Stossel (Commonwealth Editions)

FICTION

- *A Man with a Squirrel* by Nicholas Kilmer (Henry Holt and Company); murder mystery that takes place in Beacon Hill.
- *Asa, As I Knew Him,* and *Far Afield* by Susanna Kaysen (Vintage Books)
- *Back Bay* by William Martin (Warner Books)
- *The Bell Jar* by Sylvia Plath (Perennial)
- *Blunt Darts* by Jeremiah Healy (Pocket); detective novel set in the area.
- *The Collected Works of Edgar Allan Poe—Volumes II and III: Tales and Sketches* by Edgar Allan Poe (Belknap Press of Harvard University Press); master of the macabre, Poe was born in Bay Village in 1806.
- *Heartbreak Hill: The Boston Marathon Thriller* by Tom Lonergan (Writers Club Press)
- *House of Sand and Fog, Bluesman, The Cage Keeper and Other Stories, We Don't Live Here Anymore,* and others by Andre Dubus III
- *Interpreter of Maladies* by Jhumpa Lahiri (Houghton Mifflin); short story collection about life and love in and around Cambridge. Winner of the Pulitzer Prize.
- *Johnny Tremain: A Novel for Old and Young* by Esther Forbes (Dell); about a young silversmith's growing up in Revolutionary War–era Boston.
- *The Lieutenant, In the Bedroom, Separate Flights, We Don't Live Here Anymore, Finding a Girl in America,* and other works by Andre Dubus (Vintage Books); this beloved writer lived on the North Shore until his passing in 1999.
- *Little Children* by Tom Perrotta (St. Martin's Griffin)
- *Little Women, Jo's Boys, Little Men,* and many others, including some lesser-known books for adults by Louisa May Alcott (Price Stern Sloan)

- *Mortal Friends* by James Carroll (Little Brown & Company)
- *Mystic River, A Drink Before the War,* and others by Dennis Lehane (Harper); Detective/thriller novels that take place in Boston's tougher neighborhoods. The film version of *Mystic River* won two Oscars.
- *On the Road, The Dharma Bums, The Subterraneans, Big Sur, Desolation Angels, Tristessa, Visions of Cody, Maggie Cassidy,* and more by Jack Kerouac (Penguin USA); a commemorative monument to Kerouac stands in his hometown of Lowell, north of Boston.
- *Prep: A Novel* by Curtis Sittenfeld (Random House)
- *Ragged Dick,* by Horatio Alger (Viking Press)
- *Rabbit, Run, Rabbit Redux, Rabbit is Rich, Rabbit at Rest,* and many more by Pulitzer Prize–winner and *New Yorker* contributor John Updike; Updike resides in small-town Massachusetts, where many of his novels are set.
- *The Scarlet Letter* and other works by Nathaniel Hawthorne (Library of America); born in Salem in 1800, most famous for bringing the story of Hester Prynne to life.
- *While I Was Gone* and *The Good Mother* are just two of the novels by local author Sue Miller (Harper & Row).
- *Zodiac* by Neal Stephenson (Bantam Spectra); eco-thriller set in and around Boston.

NONFICTION—BIOGRAPHY AND AUTOBIOGRAPHY

- *A Clearing in the Distance: Frederick Law Olmsted and America in the Nineteenth Century* by Witold Rybczynski (Touchstone Books)
- *A Death in Belmont* by Sebastian Junger (W.W. Norton); what begins as the account of a shocking murder in this quiet Boston suburb (where bestselling-author Junger grew up), opens into a fascinating study of two men who may have been the notorious Boston Strangler.
- *All Souls: A Family Story from Southie* by Michael Patrick MacDonald (Ballantine Books)
- *The Autobiography of Benjamin Franklin* (Touchstone)
- *The Autobiography of Malcolm X* (Penguin Books)
- *Dr. Seuss & Mr. Geisel: A Biography* by Judith Morgan (Random House)
- *Eminent Bostonians* by Thomas H. O'Connor (Harvard University Press)
- *The Fitzgeralds and the Kennedys: An American Saga* by Doris Kearns Goodwin (Simon & Schuster)
- *Girl, Interrupted* by Susanna Kaysen (Vintage)
- *John Adams* by David McCullough (Simon & Schuster)
- *Mrs. Jack: A Biography of Isabella Stewart Gardner* by Louise Hall Tharp (The Isabella Stewart Gardner Museum)
- *The Rascal King: The Life and Times of James Michael Curley,* 1874-1958 by Jack Beatty (Addison-Wesley); James Michael Curley was a famous Boston politi-

cian who served as mayor, governor, and congressional representative; he also served time in prison.

- *Saints and Strangers: Being the lives of the Pilgrim Fathers and their families, with their friends and foes; and an account of the posthumous wanderings... and the strange pilgrimages of Plymouth Rock* by George S. Willison (Parnassus Imprints)
- *The Secret Six: The True Tale of the Men Who Conspired with John Brown* by Edward J. Renehan (University of South Carolina Press)
- *We Can't Eat Prestige: The Women Who Organized Harvard* by John P. Hoerr (Temple University Press)

NONFICTION—REGIONAL POLITICS & HISTORY

- *All on Fire: William Lloyd Garrison and the Abolition of Slavery* by Henry Mayer (St. Martin's Griffin)
- *Black Mass: The True Story of the Unholy Alliance Between the FBI and the Irish Mob* by Dick Lehr and Gerard O'Neill (Perennial)
- *Blizzard of '78* by Michael Tougias (On Cape Publications)
- *Boston A to Z* by Thomas H. O'Connor (Harvard University Press)
- *The Boston Globe Historic Walks in Old Boston* (4th edition) by John Harris (Globe Pequot Press)
- *The Boston Irish: A Political History* by Thomas H. O'Connor (Back Bay Books)
- *The Boston Italians: A Story of Pride, Perseverance, and Paesani* by Stephen Puleo (Beacon Press); Puleo is also the author of *Dark Tide: The Great Molasses Flood of 1919.*
- *Boston: A Topographical History* by Walter Muir Whitehill and Lawrence Kennedy (Harvard University Press)
- *The Boston Massacre* by Hiller B. Zobel (W.W. Norton)
- *Boston: Photographic Tour* by Ted Landphair and Carol M. Highsmith (Random House)
- *Boston Rediscovered* by Ulrike Welsch and William O. Taylor (Commonwealth Editions)
- *The Boston Tea Party* by Benjamin Woods Labree (Northeastern University)
- *Boston Then and Now* by Elizabeth McNulty (Thunder Bay Press)
- *Cityscapes of Boston* by Robert Campbell and Peter Vanderwarker (Mariner Books)
- *Common Ground* by Anthony J. Lukas (Alfred A. Knopf); history of the 1960s busing crisis.
- *The Great Boston Trivia & Fact Book* by Merrill Kaitz (Cumberland House)
- *Indian New England Before the Mayflower* by Howard S. Russell (University Press of New England)
- *Inventing the Charles River* by Karl T. Haglund and Renata Von Tscharner (MIT Press)

- *The Last Hurrah* by Edwin O'Connor (Back Bay Books); about the Irish political machine.
- *Lexington and Concord: The Beginning of the War of the American Revolution* by Arthur B. Tourtellot (W.W. Norton)
- *Mapping Boston* by Alex Krieger, David Cobb, and Amy Turner (MIT Press); well-illustrated history of the city's geographical evolution.
- *The Other Bostonians: Poverty and Progress in the American Metropolis, 1880-1970* by Stephan Thernstrom (iUniverse.com)
- *Paul Revere's Ride* by David Hackett Fischer (Oxford University Press)
- *Petticoat Whalers: Whaling Wives at Sea, 1820-1920* by Joan Druett (University Press of New England)
- *Planning the City Upon a Hill: Boston Since 1630* by Lawrence W. Kennedy (University of Massachusetts Press)

FOOD

- *Boston Neighborhoods: A Food Lover's Walking, Eating, and Shopping Guide to Ethnic Enclaves in and Around Boston* by Lynda Morgenroth and Carleen Moira Powell (Globe Pequot Press)
- *Candyfreak: A Journey through the Chocolate Underbelly of America* by Steve Almond (Harvest Books); Almond is a local who is involved in the Boston literary scene.
- *The Cook's Guide to Boston Restaurants* by Rebecca Hayes (Boston Common Press)
- *Secret Boston: The Unique Guidebook to Boston's Hidden Sites, Sounds & Tastes* by Laura Purdom and Linda Rutenberg (ECW Press)
- *Zagat Survey: Boston Restaurants* (Zagat Survey, LLC)

LOCAL GUIDES AND QUICK GETAWAYS

- *Fodor's Around Boston with Kids: 68 Great Things to do Together*
- *Fun With the Family in Massachusetts: Hundreds of Ideas for Day Trips With the Kids* by Marcia Glassman-Jaffe (Globe Pequot Press)
- *The Lobster Kids' Guide to Exploring Boston* by Deirdre Wilson (Lobster Press)
- *Moon Handbooks: Massachusetts* by Jeff Perk (Avalon Travel Publishing)
- *New England Camping: The Complete Guide to More Than 82,000 Campsites for Tenters, Rovers, and Car Campers* by Carol Connare and Stephen Gorman (Foghorn Press)
- *Quick Escapes Boston: 25 Weekend Getaways from the Hub* by Sandy MacDonald (Globe Pequot Press)

SPORTS AND RECREATION

- *25 Mountain Bike Tours in Massachusetts: From Cape Cod to the Connecticut River*

(Second Edition) by Robert Morse, David DeVore, and Jane DeVore (Backcountry Press)
- *26 Miles to Boston: The Boston Marathon Experience from Hopkinton to Copley Square* by Michael Connelly (Parnassus Imprints)
- *Country Walks Near Boston* by Alan Fisher (Rambler Books)
- *The Curse of the Bambino* by Dan Shaughnessy (Penguin USA); history of the Red Sox losing streak.
- *Exploring In and Around Boston on Bike and Foot* by Lee Sinai and Joyce S. Sherr (Appalachian Mountain Club Books)
- *Fly-Fishing Boston: A Complete Saltwater Guide from Rhode Island to Maine* by Terry C. Tessein (Countryman Press)
- *Mountain Bike America: Greater Boston* by Jeff Cutler and Beachway Press (Globe Pequot Press)
- *Now I Can Die in Peace: How ESPN's Sports Guy Found Salvation, with a Little Help from Nomar, Pedro, Shawshank, and the 2004 Red Sox* by Bill Simmons (ESPN Books)

F OR THE MOST PART, INFORMATION HERE IS INCLUDED FOR THE CITY of Boston only. If you live in one of the surrounding communities, contact your town or city hall or visit your town or city web site (listed under your community's description in the **Neighborhoods** chapter) to look up the appropriate information.

ANIMALS

- **Angell Memorial Animal Hospital**, 617-522-7282, www.angell.org
- **Animal Bites**, call 911
- **Animal Rescue League of Boston**, 617-426-9170, www.arlboston.org
- **Boston Animal Control**, includes dog licensing and animal adoption, 617-635-5348, www.cityofboston.gov/animalcontrol/
- **City of Boston Animal Shelter and Adoption Center**, 617-635-1800
- **MSPCA Angell Animal Care and Adoption Center,** 617-522-5055, www.mspca.org/boston
- **MSPCA Angell Animal Medical Center**, 617-522-7400, www.mspca.org/boston
- **Quincy Animal Shelter**, 617-376-1349, www.quincyanimalshelter.org

    Note: Dog licenses can be obtained through your city or town clerk's office.

AUTOMOBILES

- **AAA Southern New England**, 800-JOIN-AAA (membership), 800-AAA-HELP (roadside service), www.aaa.com
- **Abandoned Vehicle Removal** (through BTD) includes impounded vehicles as well, 617-635-4500, www.cityofboston.gov/transportation/abandoned.asp

- **Boston Transportation Department** (BTD), 617-635-4680, www.ci.boston. ma.us/transportation/; contact for all tickets, towing, boot removal, etc.
- **BTD Tow Lot**, 617-635-3900
- **Massachusetts Consumer Affairs & Business Regulation, Auto**, 617-973-8787 (consumer hotline), www.mass.gov/consumer
- **Massachusetts Registry of Motor Vehicles**, 617-351-4500, 800-858-3926, www.mass.gov/rmv
- **National Highway Traffic Safety Administration (NHTSA) Auto Safety Hotline**, 888-327-4236, www.nhtsa.gov

BIRTH AND DEATH RECORDS

- **City of Boston, Registry Division**, 617-635-4175, www.cityofboston.gov/registry/
- **City of Cambridge, City Clerk**, 617-349-4260, www.ci.cambridge.ma.us/~CityClrk/
- **Massachusetts State Registry of Vital Records**, 617-740-2600, www.vitalrec.com/ma.html

CHAMBERS OF COMMERCE

- **Arlington Chamber of Commerce**, 781-643-4600, www.arlcc.org
- **Brookline Chamber of Commerce**, 617-739-1330, www.brooklinechamber.com
- **Chamber of Commerce of East Boston**, 617-569-5000, www.eastbostonchamber.com
- **Cambridge Chamber of Commerce**, 617-876-4100, www.cambridgechamber.org
- **Greater Boston Chamber of Commerce**, 617-227-4500, www.bostonchamber.com
- **Malden Chamber of Commerce**, 781-322-4500, www.maldenchamber.org
- **Medford Chamber of Commerce**, 781-396-1277, www.medfordchamberma.com
- **Newton/Needham Chamber of Commerce**, 617-244-5300, www.nnchamber.com
- **South Shore Chamber of Commerce**, 617-479-1111, www.southshorechamber.org
- **Somerville Chamber of Commerce**, 617-776-4100, www.somervillechamber.org
- **Waltham–West Suburban Chamber of Commerce**, 781-894-4700, www.walthamchamber.com
- **Watertown-Belmont Chamber of Commerce**, 617-926-1017, www.wbcc.org

For additional towns and cities, search on www.chamberofcommerce.com.

CONSUMER COMPLAINTS AND SERVICES

- **AARP**, 888-OUR-AARP, www.aarp.org
- **Attorney General's Consumer Hotline**, 617-727-2200 or 888-514-6277, www. ago.state.ma.us
- **Attorney General's Insurance Consumer Helpline**, 888-830-6277, www.ago. state.ma.us
- **Better Business Bureau**, 508-652-4800, www.bosbbb.org
- **Boston Bar Association**, 617-742-0615, www.bostonbar.org
- **Consumer Product Safety Commission**, 800-638-2772, TTY 800-638-8270, www.cpsc.gov
- **Division of Professional Licensure**, 617-727-3074, www.state.ma.us/reg/ home
- **Federal Trade Commission (FTC)**, 877-FTC-HELP, www.ftc.gov/ro/northeast. htm
- **Federal Citizen Information Center (FCIC)**, 888-878-3256, www.pueblo.gsa. gov
- **Help Me Hank** (WHDH-TV), www.whdh.com/features/main/helpmehank, email helpmehank@whdh.com
- **Massachusetts Bar Association**, 617-654-0400, TTY 617-338-0585, www. massbar.org
- **Massachusetts Board of Bar Overseers/Office of the Bar Counsel**, Attorney and Consumer Assistance Program, 617-728-8750, www.mass.gov/obcbbo
- **Massachusetts Division of Insurance**, 617-521-7794, TTY 617-521-7490, www.state.ma.us/doi/
- **Massachusetts Office of Consumer Affairs & Business Regulation**, 617-973-8787or 888-283-3757, www.mass.gov/consumer
- **MassPIRG (Massachusetts Public Interest Research Group)**, 617-292-4800, www.masspirg.org
- **Mayor's Office of Consumer Affairs and Licensing**, 617-635-3834, www. cityofboston.gov/consumeraffairs/
- **National Consumers League**, 202-835-3323, www.natlconsumersleague.org
- **WBZ Call for Action**, 617-787-7070, www.wbz1030.com

CRIME

- **Attorney General's Insurance Fraud Hotline**, 617-573-5330
- **Boston Area Rape Crisis Center**, 617-492-RAPE, www.barcc.org
- **Boston Guardian Angels**, 617-282-2500, www.guardianangels.org
- **Boston's Neighborhood Crime Watch**, 617-343-4345, www.bostoncrimewatch. com
- **Crime in Progress**, 911
- **Governor's Auto Theft Strike Force**, 800-HOT-AUTO

- **Massachusetts Office for Victim Assistance**, 617-727-5200, www.mass. gov/mova
- **Massachusetts Most Wanted**, 800-KAPTURE, www.massmostwanted.org
- **Massachusetts Neighborhood Crime Watch Commission**, 888-80-WATCH
- **Massachusetts State Police Terrorism Tip Line**, 888-USA-5458
- **SafeFutures** (Boston), 617-635-4920, www.cityofboston.gov/bcyf/safefutures. asp
- **Safe Neighborhood Initiative**, 617-727-2200 ext. 2308
- **Sex Offender Registry Board**, 978-740-6400, 800-93-MEGAN, www.mass. gov/sorb
- **Sexual Assault Prevention and Survivor Services**, 617-624-5457, www. mass.gov/dph/fch/sapss

CRISIS HOTLINES AND SUPPORT GROUPS

ADDICTIONS

- **Al-Anon/Alateen**, 888-4AL-ANON, www.al-anon.alateen.org
- **Alcoholics Anonymous**, 617-426-9444, www.alcoholics-anonymous.org
- **Alcohol Abuse and Addiction**, 800-851-3291, 24-hour hotline
- **Alcohol and Drug Free Hotline**, 877-785-8337
- **Alcoholism Information 24-Hour Hotline**, 800-252-6465
- **Cocaine Anonymous**, 800-347-8998, www.ca.org
- **Focus on Recovery Helpline** (alcohol/drugs), 800-234-0420
- **Gamblers Anonymous**, 617-338-6020, www.gamblersanonymous.org
- **MA Substance Abuse, Information, and Education Hotline**, 800-327-5050, http://www.helpline-online.com/index.aspx
- **National Treatment Referral Hotline,** 800-375-4577, www.nationalhotline. org
- **Smoker's Quitline**, 800-TRY-TO-STOP, www.trytostop.org

CHILD ABUSE & FAMILY VIOLENCE

- **Child-At-Risk Hotline**, 617-232-4882, 800-792-5200 (to report suspected child abuse in Mass.), www.jbcc.harvard.edu/programs/hotline.htm
- **Childhelp's National Child Abuse Hotline**, 800-4-A-CHILD, www.childhelp usa.org
- **Common Purpose** (batterers' group), 617-522-6500, www.commonpurpose. com
- **Emerge** (batterers' group), 617-547-9879, www.emergedv.com
- **Girls and Boys Town National Hotline**, 800-448-3000, TTY 800-448-1833, www.girlsandboystown.org
- **Massachusetts Society for the Prevention of Cruelty to Children**, 617-587-1500 (after hours hotline, 508-767-3005), www.mspcc.org

- **National Domestic Violence Hotline**, 800-799-SAFE, TTY 800-787-3224, www.ndvh.org
- **New Hope Domestic Violence & Rape Crisis Hotline**, 800-323-HOPE, www. new-hope.org
- **Parental Stress Line**, 800-632-8188, www.pcsonline.org/about/programs/ helplines.htm
- **Parents Helping Parents**, 800-882-1250, www.php.com
- **Safelink** (domestic violence hotline), 877-785-2020, TTY 877-521-2601, www. casamyrna.org/programs/safelink.html

RAPE

- **Boston Area Rape Crisis Center**, 617-492-RAPE or 800-580-5908 (non-crisis line, 617-492-8306), www.barcc.org
- **National Sexual Assault Hotline**, 800-656-HOPE, www.rainn.org
- **Llamanos y Hablemos (Spanish Rape Crisis Hotline)**, 800-223-5001 (Monday through Saturday 9-5), 800-870-5905 (24 Hour Hotline), www.llamanos. org/

SUICIDE

- **National Hopeline** (suicide hotline), 800-SUICIDE, http://hopeline.com/
- **National Suicide Prevention Lifeline**, 800-273-TALK, www.suicidepreven tionlifeline.org
- **Samaritans 24-Hour Suicide Helpline**, 617-247-0220, 508-875-4500, or 877-870-HOPE, www.samaritansofboston.org
- **Samariteens 24-Hour Suicide Helpline** (for teens), 800-252-TEEN, www. samaritansofboston.org

DISCRIMINATION

- **Americans with Disabilities Act (ADA) Information Hotline**, 800-514-0301, TTY 800-514-0383
- **Attorney General's Civil Rights Division**, 617-727-2200, www.ago.state. ma.us
- **Attorney General's Elder Hotline**, 888-AG-ELDER
- **Attorney General's Fair Labor Hotline**, 617-727-3465 (Boston), 508-990-9700 (New Bedford)
- **Boston Civil Rights Commission**, 617-635-2500, www.cityofboston. gov/civilrights
- **Boston Commission for Persons with Disabilities**, 617-635-2500, www. cityofboston.gov/civilrights/disability.asp
- **Boston Human Services Cabinet**, 617-635-1413, www.cityofboston.gov/ humanservices

- **Disabled Persons Protection Commission**, 617-727-6465 or 800-426-9009 (V/TTY), www.state.ma.us/dppc/
- **Massachusetts Commission Against Discrimination** (MCAD), 617-994-6000, www.state.ma.us/mcad/
- **Massachusetts Department of Housing and Community Development**, 617-573-1100, TTY 6170573-1140, www.state.ma.us/dhcd/
- **Massachusetts Department of Occupational Safety**, 617-626-6975, www.mass.gov/dos
- **US Department of Fair Housing & Equal Opportunity** (FHEO), 800-669-9777, TTY 800-927-9275, www.hud.gov/offices/fheo/
- **Women's Commission**, 617-635-3138, www.cityofboston.gov/women/

ELECTED OFFICIALS

BOSTON

- **Boston Assessor**, 617-635-3742, www.cityofboston.gov/assessing/
- **Boston City Clerk**, 617-635-4600, www.cityofboston.gov/cityclerk/
- **Boston City Council**, 617-635-3040, www.cityofboston.gov/citycouncil/
- **Boston City Hall**, 617-635-4000, www.cityofboston.gov
- **Boston Election Department**, 617-635-2400, www.cityofboston.gov/elections/
- **Boston Mayor's Office**, 617-635-4500, www.cityofboston.gov/mayor/

COUNTY

- **Middlesex County District Attorney's Office**, 617-379-6500, www.middlesexda.com
- **Norfolk County District Attorney's Office**, 617-472-2515, www.state.ma.us/da/norfolk
- **Suffolk County District Attorney's Office**, 617-522-4471, www.state.ma.us/da/suffolk

STATE

- **Attorney General's Office**, 617-727-2200, www.ago.state.ma.us
- **Governor's (and Lieutenant Governor's) Office**, 617-725-1100, www.mass.gov
- **President of the Senate**, 617-722-1500, www.state.ma.us/legis/member/t_m0.htm
- **Secretary of the Commonwealth's Office**, 617-727-7030 or 800-392-6090, www.sec.state.ma.us
- **Speaker of the House of Representative's Office**, 617-722-2500, www.state.

ma.us/legis/memmenuh.htm

- **State Auditor's Office**, 617-727-6200, www.state.ma.us/sao/
- **Treasurer and Receiver General's Office**, 617-367-3900, www.state.ma.us/treasury/
- **US House of Representatives**, 202-224-3121, TTY 202-225-1904, www.house.gov
- **US Senate**, 202-224-1388, www.senate.gov

For all information on wards and precincts in Massachusetts, and the elected officials in them, your source is the **Elections Division of the Secretary of the Commonwealth**, www.sec.state.ma.us/ele/eleidx.htm.

EMERGENCY

- **Fire, Police, or Medical Emergency**, 911
- **Boston EMS**, www.cityofboston.gov/ems/
- **Boston Fire Department**, 617-343-3550, www.cityofboston.gov/fire
- **Boston Police Department**, 617-343-4200, www.cityofboston.gov/police/
- **FEMA Disaster Assistance Information**, 877-336-2734, www.fema.gov
- **Massachusetts Emergency Management Agency (MEMA) Info Line**, 508-820-2000
- **No Heat Complaints**, 617-635-4500
- **Poison Control Hotline**, 800-222-1222, www.aapcc.org

ENTERTAINMENT

- **ArtsBoston** (includes **Bostix**), 617-262-8632, www.artsboston.org
- *Boston Globe* (Arts Section), www.boston.com
- *Boston Herald* (Arts Section), www.bostonherald.com
- *Boston Phoenix* (Arts & Entertainment paper), www.bostonphoenix.com
- **Citysearch**, www.boston.citysearch.com
- **DigitalCity**, www.digitalcity.com/boston
- **Live Nation**, www.livenation.com
- **Mayor's Office of Arts, Tourism, and Special Events** (Boston), 617-635-3911, www.cityofboston.gov/arts
- **New England Theater**, 411, www.netheater411.com
- **StageSource**, 617-720-6066, www.stagesource.org
- **TheaterMirror**, www.theatermirror.com
- **Ticketmaster**, 617-931-2000, www.ticketmaster.com
- **Weekly Dig**, 617-426-8942, www.weeklydig.com

FEDERAL OFFICES/CENTERS

- **Federal Citizen Information Center**, 888- 8 PUEBLO, www.pueblo.gsa.gov
- **Social Security Administration**, 800-772-1213, TTY 800-325-0778 (both 7 a.m. to 7 p.m., Monday–Friday), www.ssa.gov; click "contact us" to locate the nearest office.

HEALTH & MEDICAL CARE

- **AIDS Action Hotline**, 800-235-2331, TTD/TTY 617-437-1672, www.aac.org
- **Childhood Lead Poisoning Prevention Program & Lead Paint Hotline**, 800-532-9571 or 617-624-5757, www.state.ma.us/dph/clppp
- **Children's Medical Security Plan**, 888-665-9993
- **Commonwealth Connector**, 877-MA-ENROLL, www.mahealthconnector.org
- **Health Care for All Helpline**, 800-272-4232, www.hcfama.org
- **HIV/AIDS Bureau**, 617-624-5300, www.state.ma.us/dph/aids/hivaids.htm
- **Hospice Care**, 800-962-2973 or 781-255-7077, www.hospicefed.org
- **Massachusetts Bureau of Family and Community Health**, 617-624-6060, www.state.ma.us/dph/fch/index.htm
- **Massachusetts Commission for the Blind**, 617-727-5550, www.mass.gov/mcb
- **Massachusetts Dental Society** (dental referrals), 508-480-9797 or 800-342-8747, www.massdental.org
- **Massachusetts Department of Health**, 617-624-6000, TTY 617-624-6001, www.state.ma.us/dph
- **Massachusetts Department of Mental Health**, 617-626-8000, TTY 617-727-9842, www.state.ma.us/dmh
- **Massachusetts League of Community Health Centers**, 617-426-2225, massleague.org
- **Mayor's Health Line**, 800-847-0710
- **National Alliance for the Mentally Ill (NAMI)**, 800-950-6264, www.namiorg
- **Planned Parenthood League of Massachusetts**, 617-616-1660 or 800-258-4448, www.pplm.org
- **US Department of Health and Human Services**, 877-696-6775, www.hhs.gov

HOUSING

- **Building Problems/Inspectional Services**—Boston, 617-635-5300
- **Boston Department of Neighborhood Development**, 617-635-3880, www.cityofboston.gov/dnd/
- **Boston Fair Housing Commission**, 617-635-2500, www.cityofboston.gov/civilrights/housing.asp

- **Boston Housing Authority**, 617-988-4130, TTY 800-545-1833 ext. 420, www.bostonhousing.org
- **Boston Redevelopment Authority** (BRA), 617-722-4242, www.cityofboston.gov/bra/
- **Boston Rental Housing Resource Center**, 617-635-7368, www.cityofboston.gov/rentalhousing/
- **Citizens' Housing and Planning Association**, 617-742-0820 (voice and TTY), www.chapa.org
- **Fair Housing Information Clearinghouse**, 800-343-3442, www.hud.gov/progdesc/fhip.cfm
- **Housing Consumer Information Centers**, 800-224-5124, www.masshousinginfo.org
- **Massachusetts Commission Against Discrimination**, 617-994-6000, www.state.ma.us/mcad
- **Massachusetts Department of Housing and Community Development** (DHCD), 617-573-1100 or TTY 617-573-1140, www.state.ma.us/dhcd/
- **Massachusetts Housing Partnership Fund**, 617-330-9955 or 877-MHP-FUND, www.mhp.net
- **National Fair Housing Advocate**, www.fairhousing.com
- **Office of Consumer Affairs and Business Regulation**, 617-973-8787 or 888-283-3757, www.state.ma.us/consumer/
- **State Board of Building Regulations and Standards**, 617-727-3200, www.state.ma.us/bbrs
- **US Department of Housing and Urban Development** (HUD), discrimination complaints, 617-565-5308, www.hud.gov

LEGAL REFERRAL

- **Boston Bar Association**, 617-742-0615, www.bostonbar.org
- **Boston Public Defender's Office**, 617-482-6212, www.state.ma.us/cpcs/pdpage.htm
- **Cambridge Public Defender's Office**, 617-868-3300, www.state.ma.us/cpcs/pdpage.htm
- **Dedham Public Defender's Office**, 781-326-0632, www.state.ma.us/cpcs/pdpage.htm
- **Massachusetts ACLU**, 617-482-3170, www.aclu-mass.org
- **Massachusetts Board of Bar Overseers**, 617-728-8700, www.state.ma.us/obcbbo/
- **Massachusetts Bar Association**, 617-338-0500, www.massbar.org. Dial-A-Lawyer 617-338-0610.
- **National Consumer Law Center**, 617-542-8010; www.consumerlaw.org
- **Roxbury Public Defender's Office**, 617-445-5640, www.state.ma.us/cpcs/pdpage.htm

LIBRARIES (MAIN PUBLIC)

- **Arlington**, 781-316-3200, www.robbinslibrary.org
- **Belmont**, 617-489-2000, www.belmont.lib.ma.us
- **Boston**, 617-536-5400, www.bpl.org
- **Brookline**, 617-730-2370, www.brooklinelibrary.org
- **Cambridge**, 617-349-4030, www.cambridgema.gov/~CPL
- **Dedham**, 781-751-9284, www.dedhamlibrary.org
- **Malden**, 781-324-0218, www.maldenpubliclibrary.org
- **Medford**, 781-395-7950, www.medfordlibrary.org
- **Milton**, 617-698-5757, www.miltonlibrary.org
- **Needham**, 781-455-7559, www.town.needham.ma.us/Library/
- **Newton**, 617-796-1360, www.ci.newton.ma.us/Library
- **Quincy**, 617-376-1301, http://thomascranelibrary.org
- **Somerville**, 617-623-5000, www.somervillepubliclibrary.org
- **Waltham**, 781-314-3425, www.waltham.lib.ma.us
- **Watertown**, 617-972-6431, www.watertownlib.org

MARRIAGE LICENSES

City and town clerks issue marriage licenses in Massachusetts. Look for your city web site, mentioned in the resources following each neighborhood or city profile.

- **City of Boston, Registry Division**, 617-635-4179, www.cityofboston. gov/registry/

PARKING

- **Boston Office of the Parking Clerk—Resident Parking Permits**, 617-635-4680, **Abandoned/Impounded Vehicles**, 617-635-4500, **Parking Tickets**, 617-635-4410; www.cityofboston.gov/transportation/parkprogr.asp
- **Boston Transportation Department** (BTD), 617-635-4682, www.ci.boston. ma.us/transportation/. Contact for all tickets, towing, boot removal, etc.
- **BTD Tow Lot**, 617-635-3900

For information on parking rules, tickets, towing, and snow emergencies, as well as parking clerk information, see the **Getting Settled** chapter or visit your community's web site.

PARKS & RECREATION DEPARTMENTS

You can find information on the municipal and statewide parks and recreation departments in the **Sports and Recreation** chapter.

- **Boston Parks Department**, 617-635-PARK, www.cityofboston.gov/parks

POLICE

Check your neighborhood or city profile for the address and phone number of your local police department. Check out www.cityofboston.gov/police/district to find your Boston neighborhood police department.

- **Police Emergencies**, dial 911
- **Boston Police** (business), 617-343-4200, www.cityofboston.gov/police/
- **Harvard University Police**, 617-495-1212, www.hupd.harvard.edu;
- **Massachusetts Executive Office of Public Safety**, 617-727-7775, www.state.ma.us/eops/
- **MBTA Police** (emergency) 617-222-1212; (business) 617-222-1100, www.mbtapolice.com
- **MIT Police**, 617-253-1212, http://web.mit.edu/cp/www/
- **State Police**, 508-820-2300, www.state.ma.us/msp/
- **US Coast Guard**, 617-565-8656, www.uscg.mil
- **US Marshall**, 617-748-2500, www.usdoj.gov/marshals/

POST OFFICES (MAIN)

- **Boston: Fort Point Station**, 25 Dorchester Ave near South Station, 617-654-5302, open 24 hours.
- **US Postal Service**, 800-275-8777, www.usps.com

  For information on branch post offices, go to your community's description in the **Neighborhoods** chapter or check out the USPS locator at www.usps.com.

ROAD CONDITIONS/TRAFFIC INFORMATION

- **Boston DPW**, 617-635-4900, www.cityofboston.go/publicworks
- **MBTA**, 617-222-3200 or 800-392-6100, www.mbta.com
- **Massachusetts Highway Department**, 617-973-7800, www.state.ma.us/mhd
- **Massachusetts Turnpike Authority (MTA)**, 617-248-2800, www.masspike.com

- **National Highway Traffic Safety Commission**, www.nhtsa.dot.gov
- **SmarTraveler**, 617-374-1234, www.smartraveler.com
- **State of Massachusetts Highway Safety Bureau**, www.mass.gov/ghsb

SANITATION & GARBAGE

- **Arlington DPW**, 781-316-3108, www.town.arlington.ma.us/Public_Docu ments/ArlingtonMA_DPW
- **Belmont DPW**, 617-993-2680, www.town.belmont.ma.us/Public_Docu ments/BelmontMA_PublicWorks
- **Boston DPW**, 617-635-4900, www.cityofboston.gov/publicworks
- **Boston DPW, Recycling Hotline**, 617-635-4959
- **Boston DPW, Sanitation Division**, 617-635-7574
- **Bottle Bill Hotline**, 617-556-1054, www.bottlebill.org
- **Brookline DPW, Sanitation Division**, 617-730-2156, www.townofbrookline mass.com/Dpw/
- **Cambridge DPW**, 617-349-4800/ TDD 617-349-4805, www.cambridgema. gov/TheWorks/
- **Dedham DPW**, 781-751-9350, http://www.dedham-ma.gov/
- **Malden DPW**, 781-397-7160, www.ci.malden.ma.us/government/
- **Massachusetts Bureau of Waste Prevention**, Department of Environmental Protection, 617-292-5500, www.state.ma.us/dep/bwp/
- **Massachusetts DEP – Hazardous Waste Hotline**, 800-343-3420 or 617-292-5898
- **Massachusetts DEP – Used Oil Hotline**, 617-556-1052
- **Medford DPW**, 781-393-2421, www.medford.org/Pages/MedfordMA_DPW
- **Milton DPW**, 617-898-4868, www.townofmilton.org/Public_Documents/ MiltonMA_DPW
- **Needham DPW**, Recycling Transfer Station, 781-455-7534, www.town.need ham.ma.us/DPW
- **Newton DPW – Solid Waste and Recycling**, 617-796-1000, TDD 617-796-1089, www.ci.newton.ma.us/DPW/recycling
- **Quincy DPW**, 617-376-1953, www.ci.quincy.ma.us
- **Somerville DPW**, 617-666-3311, www.ci.somerville.ma.us/departments.cfm
- **Waltham DPW**, 781-314-3855, 781-314-3390 (recycling), www.city.waltham. ma.us/pubworks/
- **WasteCap of Massachusetts**, 781-679-2176, www.wastecap.org
- **Watertown DPW**, 617-972-6420, www.ci.watertown.ma.us/index. asp?nid=63

SCHOOLS

- **Boston Public Schools**, 617-635-9000, www.bostonpublicschools.org

- **BPS Superintendent's Office**, 617-635-9050, www.bostonpublicschools.org
- **Massachusetts Department of Education**, 781-338-3000, TTY 781-439-2370, www.doe.mass.edu
- **Massachusetts DOE Parent Information Line**, 800-297-0002, www.doe.mass.edu
- **Massachusetts Parent Information and Resource Center**, 617-236-7210, www.pplace.org
- **MCAS Parent Information Hotline**, 866-MCAS220

For additional information, check the resources in the **Childcare and Education** chapter.

SENIORS

- **AARP**, 800-OUR-AARP, www.aarp.org
- **American Bar Association Commission on Law and Aging**, 202-662-8690, www.abanet.org/aging/
- **Boston Elderly Commission**, 617-635-4366, www.cityofboston.gov/elderly/
- **Elder Abuse Hotline**, 800-922-2275 (V/TDD)
- **Massachusetts Attorney General's Elder Hotline**, 888-AG-ELDER, www.ago.state.ma.us
- **Massachusetts Executive Office on Elder Affairs**, 617-727-7750, www.mass.gov/eldershomepage
- **National Academy of Elder Law Attorneys**, 520-881-4005, www.naela.org
- **National Council on the Aging**, 202-479-1200, TTY 202-479-6674, www.ncoa.org
- **National Senior Citizens Law Center**, 202-289-6976; www.nsclc.org
- **Prescription Advantage**, 800-243-4636, TTY 877-610-0241
- **Resource for Aging, Inc.**, 800-AGE-INFO, www.ageinfo.com
- **Social Security and Medicare Eligibility Information**, 800-772-1213, www.ssa.gov
- **U.S. Administration on Aging**, 800-677-1116

SHIPPING SERVICES

- **Boston Craters & Freighters**, 800-736-3335, www.cratersandfreighters.com
- **DHL Express**, 800-CALL-DHL (800-225-5345), www.dhl-usa.com
- **FedEx**, 800-GO-FEDEX (800-463-3339), www.fedex.com/us/
- **UPS**, 800-PICK-UPS (800-742-5877), www.ups.com
- **US Postal Service Express Mail**, 800-ASK-USPS (800-275-8777), www.usps.com

SPORTS

- **Boston Bruins**, 617-624-BEAR, www.bostonbruins.com
- **Boston Celtics**, 617-523-3030, www.nba.com/celtics
- **Boston College Eagles**, 617-552-GOBC, http://bceagles.cstv.com/
- **Boston Red Sox**, 877-REDSOX9, www.redsox.com
- **Boston University Terriers**, 617-353-GOBU, www.bu.edu/athletics
- **Harvard University Crimson**, 877-GOHARVARD, www.athletics.harvard.edu
- **MIT Engineers**, 617-253-1000, http://mitathletics.cstv.com/
- **New England Patriots**, 800-543-1776, www.patriots.com
- **New England Revolutions**, 800-543-1776, www.revolutionssoccer.net
- **Northeastern University Huskies**, 617-373-GONU, www.gonu.com
- **Tufts University Jumbos**, 617-627-3232, http://ase.tufts.edu/athletics/
- **Umass/Boston Beacons**, 617-287-7800, www.athletics.umb.edu

STREET AND SIDEWALK MAINTENANCE & SAFETY

- **Abandoned Bicycles**, 617-635-7560
- **Boston DPW**, 617-635-4900, www.cityofboston.go/publicworks
- **City Bike Rack Problems**, 617-635-4004
- **Missing Traffic Signs**, 617-635-4283
- **Other Road User Complaints** (bikers, motorists, taxis, etc), htp://www.cityof boston.gov/transportation/bikeinfo.asp
- **Potholes**, 617-635-7555
- **Problem Catch Basin Grates**, 617-989-7000
- **Sidewalk Repair Requests**, 617-635-4950
- **Unchanging Traffic Lights** (they don't turn green), 617-635-4688

TAXES

FEDERAL

- **Internal Revenue Service Teletax Information Line**, 800-829-4477, www.irs.gov

STATE

- **Massachusetts Department of Revenue**, 617-887-MDOR or 800-392-6089, TTY 617-887-6140, www.dor.state.ma.us
- **Telefile**, 617-660-2001

BOSTON

- **Assessing**, 617-635-4264, www.cityofboston.gov/assessing/
- **Excise Tax Information**, www.cityofboston.gov/excise/
- **Taxpayer Referral and Assistance Center**, 617-635-4287, www.cityofboston.gov/trac/

TIME

- **Time**, 844-2525 (any area code)
- **U.S. Naval Observatory Atomic Clock**, 202-762-1401

TOURISM AND TRAVEL

- **Greater Boston Convention and Visitors Bureau**, 888-SEE-BOSTON or 617-536-4100, www.bostonusa.com
- **International Association for Medical Assistance to Travelers**, 716-754-4883
- **Massachusetts Office of Travel and Tourism**, 617-973-8500 or 800-227-MASS, www.massvacation.com
- **National Park Service**, www.nps.gov
- **Secretary of State's Citizens Information Service**, www.sec.state.ma.us/cis/cisidx.htm

TRANSPORTATION

AIRPORTS

- **Logan Airport**, 617-567-5400 or 800-23-LOGAN, www.massport.com /logan
- **Hanscom Field**, 781-869-8000, www.massport.com/hansc
- **Worcester Regional Airport**, 888-FLY-WORC, www.massport.com/worce/
- **Manchester-Boston Regional Airport** (NH), 603-624-6539, www.flymanchester.com
- **T.F. Green Airport** (Providence), 888-268-7222 or 401-737-8222, www.pvdairport.com

BUS SERVICE

- **Greyhound**, 800-231-2222 or 617-526-1800, www.greyhound.com
- **Lucky Star Transportation**, 617-426-8801, www.luckystarbus.com
- **Peter Pan Bus Lines**, 800-343-9999 or 413-781-3320, www.peterpanbus.com

  Regional bus lines can be found in the Yellow Pages under "Buses."

FERRIES

- **Bay State Cruise Company**, 617-748-1428, http://boston-ptown.com/
- **Boston Harbor Cruises**, 617-227-4321, www.bostonharborcruises.com
- **Capt. John Boats**, 508-747-2400 or 800-242-2469, www.provincetownferry.com
- **City Water Taxi**, 617-422-0392, www.citywatertaxi.com
- **Harbor Express**, 617-222-6999, www.harborexpress.com
- **Hy-Line Cruises**, 508-778-2600 or 800-492-8082, www.hy-linecruises.com
- **Island Queen**, 508-548-4800, www.islandqueen.com
- **MBTA** (route and schedule info), 617-722-3200, www.mbta.com
- **Rowes Wharf Water Transport**, 617-406-8584, www.roweswharfwatertransport.com
- **Steamship Authority**, 508-477-8600, www.steamshipauthority.com

SUBWAY/THE "T"

- **MBTA** (route and schedule info), 617-222-3200, www.mbta.com

TAXIS

- **All Area Taxi**, 617-536-2000
- **Boston Cab**, 617-536-5010
- **City Cab of Boston**, 617-536-5100
- **Independent Taxi Operators Association**, 617-282-4000
- **Metro Cab**, 617-242-8000

     For a larger listing, look under "Taxi" in the yellow pages.

TRAINS

- **Amtrak**, 800-872-7245, www.amtrak.com
- **Cape Cod Central Railroad**, 888-797-RAIL or 508-771-3800, www.capetrain.com
- **Commuter Rail** (route and schedule information), 617-222-3200, www.mbta.com

UTILITIES

- **Attorney General's Utilities Hotline**, 888-514-6277, www.ago.state.ma.us

ENERGY/HEAT/WATER/ELECTRIC

- **Boston Water and Sewer Commission**, 617-989-7000, www.bwsc.org
- **Ecological Innovations Oil Buying Network**, 617-349-6247, 800-649-7473
- **EPA's Safe Drinking Water Hotline**, 800-426-4791

- **KeySpan Energy Delivery**, 800-732-3400, www.keyspanenergy.com
- **Massachusetts Department of Public Utilities**, 800-392-6066, or 617-305-3500, www.state.ma.us/dpu
- **Mass Energy Consumers Alliance** (formally Boston Oil Consumers Alliance), 617-524-3950, www.massenergy.com
- **Massachusetts Water Resources Authority**, 617-242-6000, www.mwra.com
- **National Grid** (formally Mass Electric), 800-322-3233, www.nationalgrid.us.com
- **NSTAR Electric**, 800-592-2000, www.nstaronline.com
- **NSTAR Gas**, 800-592-2000, www.nstaronline.com

TELECOMMUNICATIONS/CABLE

- **AT&T**, 800-222-0300, www.att.com
- **AT&T Wireless**, www.wireless.att.com
- **Comcast**, 800-COMCAST, www.comcast.com
- **DirecTV**, 800-237-5988, www.directv.com
- **Dish Network**, 800-732-6401, www.dishnetwork.com
- **Do Not Call Registry**, 888-382-1222, www.donotcall.gov
- **GTC Telecom**, 800-486-4030, www.gtctelecom.com
- **IDT**, 800-CALL-IDT, www.idt.com
- **Massachusetts Department of Telecommunications and Cable**, 800-392-6066 or 617-305-3531, TTY 800-323-3298, www.state.ma.us/dtc
- **MCI-WorldCom**, 800-444-3333, www.mci.com
- **Qwest Communications**, 800-899-7780, www.qwest.com
- **RCN**, 800-RING-RCN, www.rcn.com
- **Skype**, www.skype.com
- **Sprint**, 800-877-7746, www.sprint.com
- **T-Mobile**, 800-TMOBILE, www.t-mobile.com
- **Verizon**, 800-870-9999, www.verizon.com
- **Vonage**, 1-VONAGE-HELP, www.vonage.com

WEATHER

- **Boston Emergency Storm Center**, 617-635-3050, www.cityofboston.gov/storm/
- **Local Weather Service**, 617-936-1234
- **National Weather Service**, 508-828-2672, www.nws.noaa.gov
- **The Weather Channel**, www.weather.com

ZIP CODE INFORMATION

- **USPS Zip Codes Request**, 800-275-8877, www.usps.com

Jon Gorey and **Gina Favata** were married in 2007 on one of Boston's Harbor Islands. Gina holds an M.A. in Writing and Publishing from Emerson College, and Jon is a singer/songwriter, best known for his 2004 anthem, "The Scarlet Letter"—which may or may not have helped the Red Sox win their first World Series in 86 years. In between wayward bouts of international wanderlust, the two have made homes in Allston, the Back Bay, Brighton, Cambridge, Quincy, and Somerville…and are now looking at you, Jamaica Plain!

READER RESPONSE

We would appreciate your comments regarding this 4th edition of the *Newcomer's Handbook® for Moving to and Living in Boston: Including Cambridge, Brookline, and Somerville.* If you've found any mistakes or omissions or if you would just like to express your opinion about the guide, please let us know. We will consider any suggestions for possible inclusion in our next edition, and if we use your comments, we'll send you a free copy of our next edition. Please e-mail us at reader-response@firstbooks.com, or mail or fax this response form to:

Reader Response Department
First Books
6750 SW Franklin, Suite A
Portland, OR 97223-2542
Fax: 503.968.6779

Comments: _____

_____

_____

_____

_____

_____

_____

_____

_____

Name: _____

Address: _____

_____

_____

Telephone: (___) _____

Email: _____

6750 SW Franklin, Suite A
Portland, OR 97223-2542
USA
P: 503.968.6777
www.firstbooks.com

RELOCATION TITLES

Utilizing an innovative grid and "static" reusable adhesive sticker format, *Furniture Placement and Room Planning Guide...Moving Made Easy* provides a functional and practical solution to all your space planning and furniture placement needs.

MOVING WITH KIDS?

Look into *The Moving Book: A Kids' Survival Guide*.

Divided into three sections (before, during, and after the move), it's a handbook, a journal, and a scrapbook all in one. Includes address book, colorful change-of-address cards, and a useful section for parents.

Children's Book of the Month Club "Featured Selection"; American Bookseller's "Pick of the List"; Winner of the Family Channel's "Seal of Quality" Award

And for your younger children, ease their transition with our brand-new title just for them, *Max's Moving Adventure: A Coloring Book for Kids on the Move*. A complete story book featuring activities as well as pictures that children can color; designed to help children cope with the stresses of small or large moves.

GOT PETS?

The Pet Moving Handbook: Maximize Your Pet's Well-Being and Maintain Your Sanity by Carrie Straub answers all your pet-moving questions and directs you to additional resources that can help smooth the move for both you and your pets.

"Floats to the top, cream of the crop. Awesome book; I'm going to keep one on the special shelf here." – Hal Abrams, Animal Radio

NEWCOMER'S HANDBOOKS®

Regularly revised and updated, these popular guides are now available for Atlanta, Boston, Chicago, London, Los Angeles, Minneapolis–St. Paul, New York City, Portland, San Francisco Bay Area, Seattle, and Washington DC.

"Invaluable ...highly recommended" – Library Journal

If you're coming from another country, don't miss the *Newcomer's Handbook® for Moving to and Living in the USA* by Mike Livingston, termed "a fascinating book for newcomers and residents alike" by the *Chicago Tribune*.

Introducing NEWCOMER'S HANDBOOKS® NEIGHBORHOOD GUIDES!

This new series provides detailed information about city neighborhoods and suburban communities, helping you find just the right place to live. The first volume is for Dallas-Fort Worth, Houston, and Austin. More locations to come!

6750 SW Franklin Street
Portland, Oregon 97223-2542
Phone 503.968.6777 • Fax 503.968.6779
FIRST BOOKS www.firstbooks.com